The Spanish Ulcer

The Spanish Ulcer

A History of the Peninsular War

David Gates

DA CAPO PRESS

A CIP record for this book is available from the Library of Congress.

ISBN 0-306-81083-2
Reprinted by arrangement with the author
First Da Capo Press edition 2001

Published by Da Capo Press
A Member of the Perseus Books Group
http://www.perseusbooksgroup.com

Da Capo Press books are available at special discounts for bulk purchases in the U.S. by corporations, institutions, and other organizations. For more information, please contact the Special Markets Department at the Perseus Books Group, 11 Cambridge Center, Cambridge, MA 02142, or call (617) 252-5298.

1 2 3 4 5 6 7 8 9 10—05 04 03 02 01

CONTENTS

PART SIX: NEMESIS BY DEGREES

Sketch from *The Dickson Mss*, London, 1905

PREFACE

This book is an attempt to fill what I have long regarded as a glaring and peculiar gap in the literature on the Napoleonic Wars. It is now fifty years since Sir Charles Oman produced the last volume in his monumental *History of the Peninsular War*. In that time, several excellent small-scale studies have appeared which deal with strictly limited topics within the subject – mostly on sieges and the campaigns of Wellington. However, publications which cover the war as a whole have been remarkably disappointing.

As an avid student of the Napoleonic era for the past fifteen years, I have searched in vain for a study of reasonable dimensions which provides an in-depth description of events throughout the Peninsula, without being too exhaustive. The existing histories would seem to fall into two categories: works which treat the subject so superficially as to be virtually useless, and narratives of such colossal proportions that they are somewhat over-detailed, almost unreadable and extremely expensive.

The first category embraces virtually all of the more recent studies. Usually accompanied by an irritatingly jingoistic – or blatantly unimpartial – style, a common failing is to concentrate almost exclusively on the campaigns of Wellington and his immediate opponents. The conflict waged against the French by secondary British generals and the actual Iberian armies and nations, although crucially important, is either totally disregarded or is dismissed in a few brief comments. This betrays a failure to grasp the very core of the military and political problems confronting the French. It can – and often does – even call into question the title of the book: a work which only tells selected parts of the story cannot accurately be described as a history of the war, particularly when omissions frequently include the bulk of the five years of major campaigns that occurred in the Peninsula's southern and eastern reaches. Just because relatively few British troops and commanders were involved in them, they are not to be dismissed as insignificant – either in isolation, or in their broader, strategic functions.

At the other end of the scale, one has the magnificent narratives written by the likes of Napier, Foy, Gomez de Arteche and Oman. These works are indisputable masterpieces – both in terms of historical research and endurance writing. However, for the present-day reader, these histories have several significant drawbacks.

In the first instance, some of these authors actually took part in the conflict and, at times, allowed their own feelings and prejudices to play too great a role in their presentation of the 'facts'. Secondly, all of these studies are now getting rather dated. Napier's, for example, originates from 1828 and Sir Charles Oman – whose work is the most recent – published the first of his seven volumes over eighty years ago. Consequently, to the modern reader, the styles might seem rather 'heavy', if not long-winded, and there is, of course, no reference to the considerable amount of material that has been discovered over the past five decades. By combining the sources lodged in the very libraries that Oman and Arteche utilised with more recent findings – such as the papers of George Hennell and John Aitchison – I have been able to rectify this latter problem; producing a work which is more up to date in terms of modern scholarship and knowledge. Thirdly, the authors concerned were writing in an age very different from our own and this had a tremendous bearing on their work – particularly the size of their compositions and their presentation. In the past, studies running to several large volumes were quite acceptable; they were not excessively costly to produce, nor were people short of time to examine them. Nowadays, however, reading habits have changed considerably and more rigorous standards of scholarship apply. Fourthly, many of these works are now very difficult if not impossible to obtain – at least for home study – and if one wishes to purchase a set of, say, Napier, an extremely high retail price is to be expected. This puts them well out of the reach of the average book buyer, and even few institutions are prepared to allocate such relatively large sums from their limited resources to the purchase of such specialist collections.

Thus, these huge, multi-volume studies – excellent though they are in many ways – are somewhat inappropriate to the present-day student of the Peninsular War. Something a little less weighty is required, but without going to the other extreme. I have, therefore, attempted to produce a reasonably detailed study in a single large volume, supplemented with maps and statistical data. Whilst sufficiently exhaustive to serve as a work of reference for most readers, it should, at the same time, be concise enough to be quite readable and, I hope, prove enjoyable. Of course, to compress the subject matter into one such book has been a difficult undertaking. One could, for example, devote an entire volume to the analysis of the sieges of Saragossa – as has, indeed, been done by others – or to the effects on Iberian society and politics that the war was to have. But this is primarily intended to be a history of the military operations, and whilst I have made reference to the major economic, political and social factors that influenced their conduct I have not sought to examine these issues in detail. The modern studies of these dimensions of the conflict by such writers as Artola and Lovett will be found to be quite exhaustive.

It only remains for me to express my gratitude to the many people who have assisted me in the production of this book. Firstly, one should acknowledge the debt owed to such past historians as Sir Charles Oman, Gomez de Arteche and Maximilien Foy without some of whose basic research a study of this kind would take a lifetime to complete. I also wish to thank Professors Christopher Bartlett, Michael Howard and Peter Parish for their encouragement and advice; Miss Norma Aubertin-Potter and Miss Alyx Bennett of the Codrington Library, Oxford, who, with good humour, tolerated my incessant requests for manuscripts and innumerable books; Mr. C. M. Woolgar, archivist of the Wellington Papers, Southampton University; the staffs of: the Public Records Office, Kew; the British Library, London; the National Library of Scotland, Edinburgh; the *Archives de Guerre*, Vincennes; the *Bibliothèque Nationale*, Paris; the *Biblioteca de Palacio*, Madrid; the *Biblioteca Nacional*, Madrid; and the *Arquivo Historico Militar*, Lisbon. I am also indebted to those people who guided me over various battlefields and helped me in preparing the maps, and to Mr. Adam Sisman and the publishers who made the book possible. Last, but not least, are the many good friends – notably Lorrie, Richard, Gill and Claudia – whose encouragement kept me going at times when my spirit began to flag. I can only regret not having produced a work more worthy of all their support.

D.E.G. Oxford, 1984.

The
Spanish
Ulcer

PART ONE

Introduction

Overleaf: The *Dos de Mayo*, 1808 (*Photo:* Fotomas)

Chapter I

THE ORIGINS OF THE PENINSULAR WAR

By July 1807, with his spectacular series of victories over Austria, Prussia and Russia, Napoleon had secured a position of apparent total dominance in Central Europe. The Peace of Tilsit and its accompanying alliance with the Tsar marked the end of hostilities in that region, leaving the French emperor free to turn his attention to his relations with Spain which had been causing him mounting concern.

Napoleon's interference in the Iberian Peninsula has been seen as straightforward evidence of his greed and ambition. However, whilst there is some truth in this theory, it is an oversimplification. Besides any aspirations based solely on the more dubious parts of his nature, the emperor believed there to be sound strategic and economic reasons for intervening in Spain and Portugal. It was essentially these considerations – coupled with his unscrupulousness, and his failure to grasp the political and military complexities involved – that led Napoleon to embark on a venture that ultimately proved to be a major cause of his downfall.

Prior to 1805, Napoleon had been bent on combining the fleets of Europe to challenge Britain's naval supremacy and had seen Spain and her powerful battleships as a valuable ally. However, the Trafalgar disaster, followed by the elimination of the Danish fleet at Copenhagen, completely undermined his calculations and left his whole maritime policy in shreds. Judging British naval power to be in a virtually unchallengeable position, Napoleon was left with little option but to seek some other means of compelling his most implacable enemy to make peace. His intensification of the Continental System – a boycott of British exports – sought to achieve this by bringing the 'nation of shopkeepers' to their knees through economic strangulation, rather than by direct, military confrontation.[1] A series of Imperial decrees steadily extended the trade barrier throughout Europe: Austria and Russia closed their ports, whilst Denmark – justifiably outraged at the Copenhagen raid – actually declared war.

Britain responded by imposing a counter blockade of Europe, aimed at controlling French trade.[2] Backed up by patient, unglamorous work by the Royal Navy, a series of Orders in Council forbade neutral vessels to trade with Napoleon's empire, except on terms regulated by Britain. Whilst this restriction caused mounting friction – and, ultimately, war with the United States – it enabled Britain to inflict great economic hardship on her continental neighbours; fuelling anti-French sentiments. Not only was Europe eager to buy British metal and cloth goods, it was also desperate for colonial produce such as coffee, sugar and spices in which Britain now enjoyed a complete monopoly. Smuggling erupted on an enormous scale, and even some of Napoleon's own officials made sizeable fortunes dealing in black market goods and 'licences' for local contrabandists.[3]

Nevertheless, the loss of so many trade outlets caused appreciable distress in industrial Britain and a total disaster was only averted chiefly because the System was not applied long or consistently enough to take full effect. Throughout the years after Tilsit, gaps were to appear in Napoleon's blockade through which British goods could pour: Sweden continued to trade until 1810 when she was forced into line and then Russia opened her ports in 1812.[4]

In 1808, however, with most of Europe supporting the System, the only significant gap Napoleon had left to close was the Iberian Peninsula: Portugal was not involved in the embargo and Spain was only a half-hearted, technical participant. As long as such countries on the European mainland continued to import Britain's produce, the blockade as an instrument of policy was doomed to fail. Thus, to impose the System, Napoleon was forced to intervene militarily in the Peninsula in 1808, and against Russia in 1812 – both ventures ending in catastrophe for France.

After Tilsit, the emperor's desire to crush Britain grew into an obsession. His reaction to the Copenhagen raid was a torrent of threats: 'It will be necessary to close all the ports of Europe to them . . . , to drive all the English ambassadors from the Continent and even to have all their private individuals arrested'.[5] He concocted staggering plans to thrust French and Russian troops into Spain and the Balkans, through Gibraltar and Constantinople into Africa, and finally to India – wiping out Britain's commercial interests and strategic bases. Nothing much came of this grandiose scheme of course, but the invasion of Spain can well be regarded as Napoleon's first step down what he planned to be a very long road of conquest.

Despite the shattering of Napoleon's maritime policy at Trafalgar, relations between Spain and France remained good until, on the eve of the Battle of Jena in 1806, Godoy – First Minister of King Charles

IV – issued a proclamation rallying Spain against a foe who, although unnamed, was clearly France. Napoleon, his armies fully engaged against Prussia, was thoroughly alarmed at the prospect of Spanish intervention and a possible attack on French territory – a fear that was to haunt him throughout the wars of 1806 and 1807.[6] Although Godoy was quick to retract the proclamation after Napoleon's victory at Jena, his assurances of loyalty fell on deaf ears. Disillusioned and embittered, Napoleon had lost all real faith in his ally and, from early 1807, steadily increased his forces along the Pyrenees.[7]

Although the alliance was outwardly maintained, Godoy's treachery had placed the two countries on a collision course. Napoleon was so incensed by his behaviour that, as soon as the Tilsit pact was signed, he considered declaring war on Spain and began to conspire against her.[8] Eventually, however, judging Portugal to be a more pressing problem, the emperor decided to leave his perfidious neighbour alone – at least for the time being. There was, after all, no rush to deal with the fickle Godoy and, furthermore, Spain might prove useful in any future conflict with Portugal or, indeed, *vice versa*. Nevertheless, to demonstrate his loyalty to France, Godoy was required to provide a. large contingent of his best troops for Napoleon's Baltic garrisons.[9]

Throughout the summer of 1807, France and Spain pressurised Portugal to align with the rest of Europe against Britain. However, an old friend of London and mindful that any conflict could lead to Britain seizing her South American colonies, Portugal was reluctant to toe the Imperial line. In an effort to placate both sides, John – Portugal's Prince Regent – attempted to steer a middle course, but only succeeded in annoying all concerned. 'If Portugal does not do as I wish', Napoleon ranted at Lisbon's representative in late September,

> the House of Braganza will not be reigning . . . in two months! I will no longer tolerate an English ambassador in Europe. I will declare war on any Power that receives one after two months from this time! I have 300,000 Russians at my disposal, and with that powerful ally I can do everything. The English declare that they will no longer respect neutrals on the sea; I will no longer recognise them on land![10]

Faced with such intransigence, Prince John hastily implemented several ostensibly anti-British measures, but Godoy and Napoleon remained unimpressed. Diplomatic relations steadily deteriorated, with France and Spain making detailed war-plans.

Napoleon now indulged in various intrigues with the gullible Godoy. It was agreed – by the secret Treaty of Fontainebleau – that Portugal would be partitioned by Spain and France, with Godoy himself receiving a large principality. Godoy, however, had still greater ambitions. The favourite of the queen, he had risen from the ranks of her guards to a position of ministerial omnipotence. Despised by the court aristocrats led by Prince Ferdinand – the king's son and heir – the upstart 'Sausage Maker' as he was known had designs on the throne himself.[11] A complex series of plots and counter-schemes (the 'Affair of the Escurial'), ensued and culminated in the prince being imprisoned by his father for treason. Ferdinand was later pardoned but, utterly discredited, left the unscrupulous Godoy as apparent successor to King Charles.

Meanwhile, on the pretext of compelling Portugal to join the Continental System, Napoleon had begun moving men across Spain on 18 October. The leading corps, 25,000 troops commanded by General Junot, was proceeding to Lisbon when the Affair at the Spanish court gathered momentum. Fearing a sudden crisis, Napoleon urged Junot to thrust down the Tagus Valley to Lisbon. The general duly complied, but the Tagus was not the ideal communication route that it appeared on the emperor's map and the French troops, buffeted by the gruelling autumn weather, found the terrain difficult, barren and inhospitable. Fortunately for Junot's battered columns, however, the Portuguese offered absolutely no resistance and on 30 November, with only 1,500 men about him, Junot entered Lisbon – having covered 300 miles in only fourteen days.

The failure to oppose Junot's exhausted troops epitomised the utter capitulation of the Portuguese authorities: 'The invasion', noted one observer, 'was an armed parade, not a war.'[12] Throughout November, Prince John had sought to compromise with Napoleon and Spain, and had even declared war on Britain. Such diplomatic ruses, however, did not appease his opponents. With Junot already in Portugal and 25,000 Spanish troops moving towards the frontier, Godoy and Napoleon – fearful of some British conspiracy to buy time – advocated immediate partition. Abandoning all hope, John, escorted by a Royal Navy squadron, fled to Brazil. Hours later, French soldiers entered Lisbon.

The civil authorities seemingly collaborating with the invaders, the Portuguese people took matters into their own hands and a serious riot erupted in Lisbon on 13 December. By then, however, Junot had gathered his straggling columns together and easily quelled the rising. Ordering the dissolution of the tiny Portuguese Army, he then began a programme of exactions which the infuriated population, lacking weapons and leaders, were powerless to resist.[13]

A sinister calm fell over Portugal and Napoleon began preparing his next move. The apparent ease with which Junot had seized the country lulled the emperor into a false sense of conquest. The Portuguese question seemed closed and the time had come to deal with Godoy. The evident consternation at Charles' court convinced Napoleon that Spain would fall as easily as Portugal had; a short, sharp military coup and the country would tumble into his hands. 'If I thought it would cost me 80,000 men I would not attempt it, but it will cost me no more than 12,000', he confidently predicted. Such a victory, he reasoned, would give him a valuable source of troops and money, and close the last European door to British trade. Then, the benefits of the Imperial enlightenment would be extended to the new territories. Meritocracy and the *Code Napoléon* would sweep away the old, corrupt order – just as they had done in Germany and elsewhere.[14]

However, by thinking in these terms, the emperor severely under-estimated both the military problems involved in a conquest of the Peninsula and the inherent conservatism of the Spanish. Despite its faults, Spain's social structure enjoyed the support of the over-whelming majority of the population. The Catholic Church was immensely powerful and regarded Napoleon with deep suspicion, particularly after 1807 when relations between Rome and Paris deteriorated sharply. The sense of national honour was also more intense than the emperor realised – until it was too late – and his plan for extending the *Code* beyond the Pyrenees proved nothing more than an anathema to the bulk of the Iberian people. As he was later to confess: 'I thought the system easier to change than it has proved in that country, with its corrupt minister, its feeble king and its shameless, dissolute queen.'[15]

Not only did Napoleon seriously underestimate the difficulties involved in seizing Spain, he was also excessively optimistic in calculating some of the benefits he hoped to gain from the country. The value of the Bourbon war-machine was questionable – the Army was regarded as a joke in military circles and the Navy had never recovered from Trafalgar. Above all, however, the emperor's esti-mations of the financial benefits attached to a conquest were exces-sively high. Doubtlessly fascinated by Spain's history of Imperial splendour, Napoleon was convinced that the country was enor-mously wealthy when, in fact, she was virtually bankrupt. More-over, he entertained hopes of utilising the markets of Spain's South American colonies.[16] But such plans were bound to fail in the face of British sea-power and, furthermore, the dependencies themselves were already seeking to end their ties with their motherland – a process Napoleon's invasion only served to accelerate.

Thus, it would seem that in the case of Spain the emperor's sense of opportunism got the better of him. By staking all on military intervention, Napoleon the diplomat was setting Napoleon the soldier an impossible task. Indeed, from 1807 onwards, one sees a marked decline in the skill with which France's foreign affairs were handled; a phenomenon that stemmed from two principal factors. Firstly, Napoleon himself began to show symptoms of megalomania – with all that implied for his handling of policy – and, secondly, shortly after Tilsit, he lost the services of his most able diplomat, Count Talleyrand. Although something of a disreputable character, Talleyrand, as an international statesman, dominated the early-Napoleonic era with a skill that has rarely been equalled. After Tilsit, however, he became increasingly alarmed at Napoleon's growing capacity for self-delusion. Already concerned by rising German nationalism and France's deteriorating relations with Rome, Talleyrand's anxiety reached new heights over the Franco-Russian entente – an agreement he strongly opposed.[17] The emperor's latest scheme – to tangle with a nationalistic, Catholic Power like Spain – was, in Talleyrand's opinion, a cardinal error which could bring down the whole empire. Refusing to have anything to do with the matter, the count tendered his resignation and the vital position of Foreign Minister was passed to Champagny – an obscure official who, in terms of ability, proved a mere shadow of his predecessor.

Without the restraining hand of Talleyrand, the emperor turned all his energies to the destruction of the Spanish state. Indulging in diplomacy of the most unscrupulous kind, he discarded the Treaty of Fontainebleau and steadily strengthened his army in Spain – Moncey, Dupont and Duhesme led some 70,000 more men over the Pyrenees, while further units collected in southern France. Godoy, meanwhile, continued attempts to negotiate with Napoleon who simply fobbed him off; disappearing on a tour of Italy and rejecting a suggestion that Ferdinand should marry an Imperial nominee. Dismissing this proposal was perhaps a serious error. Controlling the Peninsula through a Bourbon puppet would probably have proved far more successful policy than that of attempting to impose French rule through military might. This was, however, but an early instance of Napoleon's deteriorating diplomatic skill. Having lost much of his grasp of the finer points of international statesmanship, he was to increasingly resort to seeking military solutions to all his problems – a trend that was to contribute significantly to his downfall.

Outmanoeuvred diplomatically and militarily, Godoy could do little but watch as the French moved into an ever greater area of Spain. Finally, convinced that the Spanish would not miss their feeble rulers, Napoleon struck. On 16 February, by deceit or overt hostility, French soldiers seized control of numerous strategic installations – notably the frontier fortresses and Barcelona – allowing fresh masses of Imperial troops to pour across the Pyrenees with complete impunity.[18]

Godoy responded by recalling the Spanish forces aiding Junot and advising the Royal family to leave Madrid for the Americas. The populace, however, blamed him for the situation and the announcement of the Royal family's departure provoked a major riot. Order was only restored when Prince Ferdinand proclaimed that the unpopular minister had been dismissed and, after narrowly escaping being lynched, Godoy was taken into protective custody. This, however, was interpreted as further defence of the 'Sausage Maker' by the king. Fresh disorder erupted and only ended when Charles agreed to abdicate in favour of Ferdinand. An unholy alliance between a mob and aristocrats had ended the *ancien régime*.[19]

It was against this background that Marshal Murat, the Commander-in-Chief of the French forces in Spain, arrived at Madrid with 20,000 troops. He refused to recognise Ferdinand as the rightful monarch and, manoeuvring with considerable adroitness, Napoleon now lured Ferdinand to Bayonne to 'discuss the matter'. Once on French soil, Napoleon advised him that an Imperial prince would take over the Spanish throne.

Predictably, Ferdinand rejected Bonaparte's demand that he should abdicate. Accordingly, the emperor produced his 'master card': Charles, the ex-queen, and Godoy were summoned, who proclaimed Napoleon as their saviour and insisted that Ferdinand had usurped the throne by obtaining his father's abdication under duress. Still bitter over the Affair, Charles – egged on by Napoleon – was fully convinced of Ferdinand's evil intentions and, after berating his son for his treason and threatening him with execution, secured Ferdinand's abdication before surrendering his own rights to Napoleon. By 10 May 1808, the Spanish throne – on paper at least – belonged to the French emperor.

Had he ruled through a Bourbon puppet, Napoleon's long-term strategy in the Peninsula may well have succeeded but, as usual, he handed his latest acquisition to one of his relations and his brother Joseph was proclaimed king. This was a fundamental error. The Spaniards might not have liked their rulers, but they regarded them as preferable to some imposed, foreign dictator. Napoleon could establish Joseph on the throne, but he could not give him popular support.

Meanwhile the situation in Madrid had deteriorated rapidly, as Murat – a simple, unsophisticated soldier – squabbled with the

Regency *Junta* established by Ferdinand to govern in his absence. Tension steadily mounted and, on 2 May, as the remainder of the Spanish Royal family left for Bayonne, the citizens turned on isolated French soldiers.[20]

Brutally suppressed by Murat with appalling bloodshed, the *Dos de Mayo* Rising triggered a national revolt. Napoleon – encouraged by the apparent success of his military coup and the capitulation of the Spanish authorities – had not reckoned on the reaction of the population at large. Calling up 18,000 men, the Asturias declared war on France on 25 May and were quickly followed by the other provinces. The Peninsular War had begun.

Chapter II

THE IBERIAN THEATRE

I The Armies

THE SPANISH ARMY

Spain's forces had barely been influenced by the military innovations of the Revolutionary and Napoleonic Wars, and in 1808 the somewhat outdated Royal Army comprised the following units:

Household Troops:
Two regiments of Foot Guards, each with three battalions of 1,000 men. Two cavalry regiments of five squadrons. A squadron totalled 120 men.

Line Infantry:
Thirty-five regiments of three battalions. Each battalion consisted of four companies, including one of grenadiers, and numbered over 700 men. In keeping with Eighteenth Century practice, the Army also contained foreign regiments: one Neapolitan, three Irish and six Swiss formations, all with three battalions, except for the Swiss which had only two.

Light Infantry:
Twelve battalions, each of six companies of 200 men.

Cavalry:
Twenty-four regiments, each of five squadrons. Twelve regiments were designated as 'heavy' cavalry, six regiments were hussars and the rest were light dragoons. On paper a unit totalled 800 sabres but, in practice, this figure was rarely achieved due to a chronic lack of suitable horses. In May 1808, for example, there were just 15,000 riders with only 9,000 mounts.

Artillery and Engineers:
Four field regiments of ten batteries; each battery numbered around 120 men. Only six of the forty units were horse artillery. There were

also 2,000 gunners in fortresses, divided into twenty-one batteries, and 1,000 sappers and engineers.

Militia:

Forty-three battalions, each of 600 men. There were also four provincial grenadier regiments; each of 1,600 men, divided into two battalions.[21]

THE PORTUGUESE ARMY

In September 1809, the following units were in existence:

Line Infantry:

Twenty-four regiments, each comprising two battalions of seven companies. A battalion had a theoretical establishment of 770 bayonets, plus senior staff, musicians etc; giving a regimental total of 1,550. Field strength, however, usually averaged 1,300 troops.

Light Infantry:

Six battalions of *cacadores*, each comprising seven companies of 110 men, including a company of *atiradores* (marksmen). These regiments were trained as light infantry, clothed in brown and armed with rifles. In 1811, the number of formations was doubled by the conversion of the Lusitania Legion and the creation of three new units.

Loyal Lusitania Legion:

Raised by Sir Robert Wilson, this unit comprised three battalions of ten companies each; a company having 100 rank and file. There was also a battery of artillery and a few cavalry troopers. The Legion was disbanded in 1811 and the infantry battalions became the 7th, 8th and 9th *Cacadores*.

Cavalry:

Twelve regiments of medium cavalry, each of four squadrons. A regiment had a theoretical establishment of 600 men. However, this figure was rarely fulfilled, and a strength of around 500 sabres was typical.

Artillery and Engineers:

There is no evidence to suggest that Portugal had any horse artillery units. This arm does not seem to have been popular with the Iberians – the Spanish only had forty horse guns out of a total of 250 field pieces. However, including numerous fortress batteries and the like,

Portugal had around 5,000 gunners, divided into four regiments of ten companies each, plus an engineer corps of a few dozen men.

Militia:
These troops played a particularly important role in the campaigns between 1810 and 1812. The country was segregated into forty-eight conscription districts, each providing one regiment of two battalions. A battalion had twelve companies. The theoretical strength of a regiment was 1,500 of all ranks, but this was rarely achieved. Whole units were seldom called out; the two battalions taking it in turns to serve for up to six months at a time. The conscription districts were grouped into three military divisions, each of sixteen regiments: one division covered the north of the country, one the centre and one the south.

Besides these highly organised reservist units, the Portuguese *levée en masse* furnished a vast body of *Ordenanza* for internal defence. Armed with whatever weaponry was available – usually pikes – and given rudimentary training, these part-time civil guards were identical to the *somatenes* raised by some Spanish provinces. Mostly peasants officered by *bourgeoisie*, they were not, as one French general remarked 'capable of maintaining themselves on a battlefield.' But in fortified lines and as skirmishers they could be quite useful, and left 'the major part of the English and Portuguese forces unencumbered.' In May 1810, the *Ordenanza* totalled 329,000 men.[22]

THE BRITISH ARMY

At the time of the Napoleonic Wars, Britain's regular Army consisted of over one hundred infantry and more than twenty cavalry regiments. The following units were involved in the Peninsular conflict at some time:

Line Infantry and Foot Guards:
A British heavy infantry battalion officially consisted of ten companies of around 100 men each; one company being grenadiers and another light infantry. Occasionally, more than one battalion from a particular regiment would be located in a given theatre of war, but this was fairly unusual. Altogether, fifty-one regiments of the line saw service in the Peninsula between 1808 and 1814, along with the three Guards regiments that were then in existence.

Light Infantry:
Permanently established formations of these troops were a relatively

new development in the British Army, but by 1814 there were six light regiments in being: the 52nd, 43rd, 51st, 68th, 85th, and 71st, all armed with short muskets. There were also a few units of riflemen, notably the 95th Regiment and the 5/60th. Rifles, though more accurate than muskets, were slower to load, harder to procure and difficult to maintain in good order. Consequently, they were few in numbers and had rather limited tactical applications; being primarily used for long range sniping.

Cavalry:
The British employed a sizeable force of mounted troops: the Lifeguards and Horseguards all saw service, as did three regiments of dragoon guards and three of dragoons. Four hussar and eight light dragoon regiments were also used. All of these units fielded between one and four squadrons of about 100 men each.

Artillery and Engineers:
Eleven brigades (batteries) of foot artillery were employed in the Peninsula and several batteries of horse artillery. A battery usually consisted of six pieces. There was also a small corps of engineers and sappers.

The King's German Legion and other Auxiliaries:
The King's German Legion was raised in 1803 from Hanoverian refugees. It consisted of five cavalry regiments (two of which were initially heavy, but were converted to light dragoons), several line and two light battalions, plus horse and foot artillery.

The two other foreign units that consistently served with Wellington's forces were the Brunswick *Oëls Jäger* and the *Chasseurs Britanniques*. The former was a small regiment of German riflemen that, usually broken down into individual companies and attached to the army's various divisions, performed skirmishing duties. The latter, a unit of French *émigrés*, also acted as skirmishers, but their principal pastimes seem to have been desertion and indiscipline.[23]

THE IMPERIAL FRENCH ARMY

There was a tremendous variety in the quality of soldiers that Napoleon committed to the Peninsula at various stages of the war. The first French Army to march into Spain in 1808, for example, was predominantly composed of inexperienced conscripts: Bessières' corps, for instance, contained just 2,000 reasonably seasoned men, whilst the cavalry was particularly weak; out of 12,000 troopers, a mere 1,250 had had any real previous experience. Junot's 'Army of Portugal' was little better either: out of 30,000, only 17,000 men even approached veteran status.

On the other hand, the army Napoleon himself led into Spain in the autumn largely consisted of experienced troops. However, one should never forget that France had been at war for many years and this continual drain on her forces could only lead to a deterioration in the overall quality of her soldiery. Bloodbaths like Eylau, in 1807, wiped out much of the cream of the French Army and by the time the Peninsular War was in full swing many of the troops that had won Austerlitz and Jena were dead.

Given this constant attrition, it is remarkable that the French Army remained such a potent force for so long, but a steady deterioration was inevitable and perceptible: for the Austrian war of 1809, Napoleon was obliged to call on fresh masses of conscripts and, after the *débâcle* of 1812, he was forced to withdraw units from Spain to give his eastern forces a nucleus of reasonably seasoned troops. Nevertheless, even in the closing stages of the Peninsular conflict the French proved formidable opponents, especially at Sorauren and Toulouse.

Line Infantry:
A line regiment could have from one to five battalions on service, each of six companies. Every battalion had one grenadier, one *voltigeur* and four fusilier companies, each with a theoretical strength of 140 bayonets. As far as can be ascertained, sixty-four line regiments participated in the Peninsular War.

Light Infantry:
These units were organised on the same basis as a line regiment: with one grenadier, one *voltigeur* and four centre companies (called *carabinier, voltigeurs* and *chasseurs* respectively).

Cavalry:
The difficult terrain encountered in the Peninsula greatly deterred the French from employing heavy cavalry. Consequently, apart from a tiny handful of provisional *cuirassiers* and a small regiment in Suchet's theatre, the heaviest mounted troops consistently used were dragoons, of which sixteen regiments saw service.

In addition, eleven regiments of *chasseurs à cheval*, seven hussar regiments and several lancer units all deployed contingents in the Peninsula at some stage of the war. Regiments usually fielded between one and four squadrons of around 100 men each.

Artillery:

Students of Napoleon's Central European campaigns will be struck by the relatively small numbers of cannon employed in Spain. This is largely explained by the terrain and a chronic shortage of horses. Cannon needed teams to pull them and the bigger the gun, the larger the team. Moreover, the famed big guns of the French artillery were unsuited to the atrocious roads and mountainous topography of the Peninsula. Consequently, siege guns excluded, the largest cannon tended to be mere eight-pounders, and the majority were fours and sixes. Foot batteries usually had eight pieces, horse artillery units had six.

Imperial Troops:

In addition to actual French units, Napoleon deployed a very large number of Imperial troops in the Peninsula. Poland, Switzerland, Italy, Hanover, Baden, Westphalia and Nassau joined with smaller states in providing thousands of soldiers of all arms for the conflict. Moreover, some French commanders took to enlisting disaffected Spaniards in special *Juramentado* regiments. Marshal Soult had some success in this field in Andalusia, and King Joseph tried desperately hard to establish his own Spanish divisions to end his military dependence on Napoleon. However, *Juramentados* were generally very unreliable and prone to desert at the first sign of trouble.

National Guards:

Particularly towards the end of the war, when France was fighting to defend her own borders, several units of National Guards appeared on the western front. These reservists were organised into cohorts (the equivalent of battalions in the regular army), and several cohorts formed a legion. Although brave and determined, these amateur soldiers were poorly equipped and lacked experienced officers. Nevertheless, they did their best against the Anglo-Portuguese veterans and played a credible part in the battles on the Pyrenees.[24]

II Battlefield Tactics and Weaponry

The largest battlefield unit of the wars was the army corps, but only the French used such formations in the Peninsula. A corps would consist of two or more divisions, which subdivided into brigades. These, in turn, were composed of several regiments, each with one or more battalions consisting of several companies.

In 1812, the French abolished the corps structure of their forces in Spain and, from then onwards, the largest tactical unit was the division. A typical French or Spanish division would have 4,000 infantry, plus a battery of artillery. Wellington's, however, usually had a couple of British brigades, with several battalions of Portuguese attached, giving a total of approximately 6,000 infantry, plus artillery.

A Napoleonic infantry regiment consisted of between one and five battalions, though most had two in any particular theatre. Each battalion subdivided into several companies of around 100 men each. One company was usually designated light infantry and another was composed of grenadiers. The latter troops were the biggest and most experienced in the battalion, while the light company provided more-agile, seasoned soldiers for skirmish and outpost duties. The bulk of the unit consisted of 'fusilier' or 'centre' companies, which were made up of men ranging in experience from veterans to new recruits.

A cavalry regiment would consist of several squadrons of around 100 troopers each. Regiments combined to form cavalry brigades and divisions, which usually had batteries of horse artillery in attendance. The cavalry corps – seen in Napoleon's other theatres – was almost unheard of in the Peninsula; such massed horse formations being irrelevant to the type of warfare encountered.

Mounted troops were further classified as 'light', 'medium' or 'heavy' cavalry, depending on their function. Light cavalry – hussars, *chasseurs* and lancers – were essentially intended for reconnaissance, screening and pursuit, but also fulfilled a role on the battlefield. Medium cavalry were invariably dragoons and were capable of shock action against enemy soldiers who had been weakened by infantry and artillery attacks. Dragoons were, in theory, trained foot troops as well as horsemen, but only the French units seem to have had any real skill as infantrymen. Genuine heavy cavalry were rarely seen in the Imperial armies in the Peninsula; the famous *cuirassiers* and *carabiniers* staying on the Eastern European front. However, the British employed several regiments which, although unarmoured, were deemed 'heavy' cavalry and the French utilised large numbers of heavy dragoons in numerous spectacular actions, such as Ocaña.

The standard weapon of Napoleonic period infantry was the muzzleloading, smooth-bore, flintlock musket. They were around 42 inches long, weighed between ten and fifteen pounds, and were fitted with a detachable bayonet of up to 16 inches in length. They fired a lead ball, which weighed about an ounce. The loading procedure for these guns was a complicated undertaking, performed in up to twenty consecutive movements. The soldier would take a ball cartridge from the pouch on his hip and tear off the top with his teeth. A little of the powder of the cartridge was then poured into the flashpan of the musket and the remainder driven to the bottom of the barrel with a ramrod. The soldier would then spit the bullet – retained in his teeth with the top of the cartridge – into the barrel on top of the charge and ram that down firmly, too. When the musketeer squeezed the trigger, a flint ignited the powder in the flashpan which, in turn, detonated the main charge under the bullet. Damp powder, worn flints and blocked touch-holes caused numerous misfires and, in the excitement of battle, it was common for ramrods to be lost; often having been inadvertently left in the barrel when the trigger was pulled.

The lack of rifling in the barrel and the irregular shape of the ball rendered the musket highly inaccurate. It actually had the capability to propel a bullet for up to 1,000 yards, but the effective range was really less than 100 yards and, even then, the chances of hitting a specifically selected target were minimal. Thus, to achieve any sort of worthwhile result, it was necessary to group as many guns together as possible and fire them simultaneously to create a hail of bullets in the general direction of the target. By the law of averages, at least some of the shot would take effect.[25]

The formations used on the battlefield were, therefore, designed to enable every man to use his firearm effectively. The most efficient way of doing this was to deploy the troops in close-order lines. It was found that formations of up to three men deep were viable: thicker lines prevented the fourth and subsequent ranks from seeing the enemy, let alone shooting at them. Furthermore, while any rear ranks were virtually useless to their own side, they presented their opponents with an excellent target.

With these factors in mind, heavy infantry were usually deployed in three-deep lines, but this could be adjusted to suit prevailing conditions. For example, in difficult terrain – where cavalry could not act and so solidity became less important – foot troops could safely deploy in just two ranks. This system also enabled a battalion to cover a larger front, but then it was rather thin if engaged in *mêlée*. Moreover, in a musketry exchange, the two-deep line was prone to suffer from 'shrinkage' due to lack of reserves; gaps would appear and the files would have to move inwards to maintain a cohesive front. On the other hand, the three-deep line tended to be more stable; the men in the rear rank stepping forward to replace casualties in the front.

A major departure from the principle of deploying troops so that they could all use their weapons was the utilisation of columns. In terms of manoeuvrability, such formations were greatly superior to lines. A compact, narrow column could keep its alignment far better than a thin wall of men stretching for hundreds of yards. Moreover, to deploy into line or square from column was a relatively easy task, whereas a line could only redeploy with difficulty and appreciable danger. Mixtures of lines and columns could be particularly effective and the 'mixed order' was one of Napoleon's favourite devices. Such formations combined the fire-power of the line with the flexibility and attacking potential of the column, giving the commanding officer the best of both worlds.

However, the mixed order was rarely employed in the Peninsula; the French commanders preferring to use simple columns. Of course, when confronted with a line, the column – really intended for shock action – proved hopelessly inferior in terms of fire-power. In the latter formation only a few dozen men – often out of thousands – could actually fire, whereas all the troops in the line could see the target. Given such inequality between the opposing forces, it is little wonder that the column was invariably shot to pieces by the line.

Indeed, the defeat of French columns by British lines was a prominent feature of the War and some discussion of it is essential. A column was really intended only for shock action and was never designed to assail unshaken lines of enemy infantry. As Napoleon himself observed: 'Columns do not break through lines, unless they are supported by a superior artillery fire'.[26] Accordingly, a preliminary artillery bombardment and a constant fusillade from skirmishers would be used to weaken the line both materially and psychologically, and *only then* would columns be sent into the attack. By that time, however, the defence would be on the verge of collapse and the mere sight of the serried, charging columns was invariably enough to precipitate a rout. Even if the line did attempt to stand, it would be in such disorder that disciplined, effective musketry would prove impossible and the column would sweep through it. By use of such tactics, French armies had smashed through defensive lines all over Europe for years. Indeed, at Jena, in 1806, they utterly routed an army whose pre-eminence in linear tactics was renowned.

In the Peninsula, however, Wellington and his colleagues were to evolve a tactical system that effectively neutralised the standard French mode of attack. Firstly, as the French General Thomas Bugeaud recollected, 'The English generally occupied well chosen defensive positions having a certain command, and they showed only a part of their forces.'[27] Not only did this drastically restrict the possibilities the attacking French had for aimed artillery fire, it also often prevented them establishing the size of the opposing force and the extent of its position. Thus, at Bussaco, Reynier – thinking it was their flank – attacked the Allies' centre and at Salamanca Marmont was to make a similar error.

INFANTRY BATTALION FORMATIONS

Each company would (usually) be deployed in three ranks. The position of the *élite* companies varied. They are shown here at the front of the column, but the grenadiers were often placed at the rear as a reserve. The light troops, of course, were frequently deployed in a skirmish screen.

COLUMN:

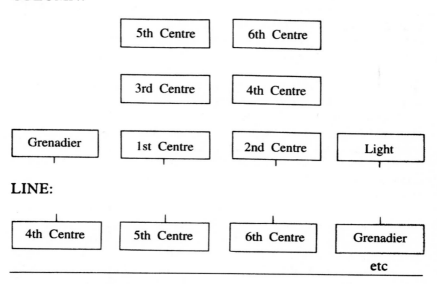

LINE:

Secondly, to prevent the French *voltigeurs* exploring the British position and carrying out their essential fusillade, a screen of skirmishers would be positioned some distance in front of the main Allied line. The light companies from the various British battalions in the Allied force would be joined by hundreds of Portuguese *cacadores*, along with detachments from the 95th Regiment and the Fifth Battalion of the 60th. This would produce a screen of such density that the *voltigeurs* could barely penetrate it. Indeed, Wellington's protective sheath of light infantry was often of such dimensions that French officers took it to be his front line and frequently claimed in their reports to have breached it before being repulsed by his 'second' line.[28]

The French 'softening up' forces having been dealt with, it only remained for the Allies to repulse the attacking columns that eventually came forward. 'In great haste, without studying the position, without taking time to discover whether there were means to make a flank attack, we marched straight on', recalled Bugeaud, 'taking the bull by the horns.' As the French columns advanced, they would come under increasingly heavy fire: artillery positioned along the crest of the enemy ridge would bombard them, whilst the riflemen and, as the range decreased, musketeers of the Allied skirmisher screen riddled them with sniper fire before retiring to unmask the supporting heavy infantry.[29]

Having discovered a perfectly intact line in front of them, the French commanders then had the unenviable task of either redeploying their troops under fire or trying to barge a way through. Most chose the latter option, but neither had much to recommend it. Columns were no match for lines in a musketry duel and, as Bugeaud witnessed, charges risked being shot into the ground:

The men became excited, called out to one another, and increased the speed of their march; the column became a little confused. The English remained quite silent with ordered arms, and from their steadiness appeared to be a long red wall ... Very soon we got nearer, crying *"Vive l'Empereur! En avant! A la baïonnette!"* Shakos were raised on the muzzles of muskets, the march became a run, the ranks fell into confusion, the agitation became tumult; shots were fired as we advanced. The English line remained silent, still and unmoved, with ordered arms, even when we were no more than 300 yards distant, and it appeared to ignore the storm that was about to break. The contrast was striking; in our innermost thoughts, we all felt that the enemy was taking a long time in firing, and that this fire, held for so long, would be very unpleasant when it came. Our ardour cooled. The moral power of a steadiness which nothing can shake ... overcame our minds. At this moment of painful expectation, the English wall shouldered arms; an indescribable feeling would fix many of our men to the spot; they began an uncertain fire. The enemy's steady, concentrated volleys swept our ranks; decimated, we turned round seeking to recover our equilibrium; then three formidable cheers broke the silence of our opponents; at the third they were on us, pushing our disorganised flight.[30]

There may have been relatively little the French could do about Wellington screening his lines from artillery fire, but there was no real excuse for letting their light troops be overwhelmed with such disastrous consequences. Light infantry were usually plentiful and in any case the French were remarkably good at improvisation: the Revolutionary Wars had been won largely through the use of skirmisher swarms and during the wars of the empire there were plenty of examples of entire divisions being deployed as *tirailleurs*. Thus, both the capability and the precedent were there.

Nevertheless, in the Peninsula, French commanders rarely used more than the *voltigeur* companies of line regiments for skirmishing. Indeed, even the light infantry battalions were invariably deployed in close order formations. Thus, a typical Imperial division of eight battalions would field around 800 skirmishers – far fewer than the total attached to an average British division.[31] However, besides the unnecessary numerical weakness of their skirmisher screens, Imperial commanders habitually committed other tactical errors. The sophisticated interplay and coordination of lines, columns and *tirailleurs* that had characterised the victory-studded performance of the French infantry since the late 1790s was rarely seen in Peninsular battles. This trend, it has been argued, was due to the steady deterioration in the quality of the French troops, which compelled their commanders to use primitive tactical formations.[32] However, to survive on a Napoleonic battlefield, soldiers *had* to be able to perform – in the heat of action, across all manner of terrain – the type of complex evolutions one can see executed by our current day Foot Guards at the Trooping of the Colour, and most Napoleonic period French infantry were perfectly capable of fighting in a whole variety of formations. The three-deep line, for example, was standard, drill-book material and was used to great effect by Ferey's division at Salamanca – some four years after the beginning of the war. Similarly, at Albuera in 1811, the V Corps, supported by skirmisher swarms, attacked in *l'ordre mixte* and so very nearly broke the Allied line.

However, such tactical flexibility was rarely seen. All too often French infantry were hurled at unshaken lines in simple, dense, narrow columns with insufficient skirmisher, artillery and cavalry support. Despite repeated thrashings, perceptive, intelligent commanders like Soult persisted in this clumsy practice, although many junior French officers were justly critical of it.[33] But the history of warfare is dotted with similar phenomena: in the American Civil and Franco-Prussian Wars, generals repeatedly launched closely-packed infantry and sabre-wielding cavalry against troops armed with weapons that were far more accurate and fired more rapidly than anything dreamt of in Napoleon's time. Again, in the First World War, troops were to be sent against entrenched machine-guns and rapid-fire artillery in similar formations to those used in battles fought over 100 years before in the Iberian Peninsula.

Besides the line and the column, the other basic infantry formation was the square. This could be formed by any unit of foot soldiers – ranging from clumps of skirmishers to whole divisions – but usually consisted of one or two battalions. The rank and file would form the walls of a hollow rectangle and the officers, colours *etc*, would stand in the centre. The formation was intended for defence against cavalry attacks (which were invariably delivered in columns or lines) and, against unsupported horsemen, was virtually impenetrable. The front rank of the square would kneel to present an impenetrable hedge of bayonets, from behind which subsequent ranks would fire volleys at the attackers. Unless the cavalry had infantry or artillery support, the square was almost certain to repel any assault and the history of the Peninsular War is dotted with incidents where cavalry, usually British, hurled themselves at such formations with fatal results.

For example, on 9 July 1810, the day that Ciudad Rodrigo surrendered to Massena's army, General Robert Craufurd's command encountered a French foraging party of two hundred infantry a little to the west of the beleagured fortress. The British general promptly sent his six cavalry squadrons into the attack against what appeared to be easy prey, only to receive a painful lesson in tactics. At the advance of the hostile cavalry, the French, under a Captain Gouache, formed square and, with admirable coolness, waited until their would-be assailants were within ten paces before delivering a series of lethal volleys. After losing many men to no avail, Craufurd abandoned the attack and retreated, while Gouache's little band marched on to rejoin the main French forces. The captain was later decorated and promoted; Craufurd received a stinging rebuke from Wellington.

The lesson is clear: steady infantry deployed in square had little to fear from cavalry alone and were likely to emerge triumphant from any engagement. Only on very rare occasions – such as at Garcia Hernandez, in 1812 – were squares broken by unsupported horsemen, and here the infantry seem to have been both extremely unlucky and in poor spirits.

But if the infantry were assailed before they could deploy into squares, the advantage rested with the cavalry; particularly if they attacked from the rear or flank. Lines were especially vulnerable to cavalry assault, as the battle of Medellin demonstrates and, at Albuera, Colborne's British brigade was virtually exterminated when caught deployed in such a formation by enemy horsemen. Infantry columns, being more compact and solid, stood a marginally better chance, but the only truly safe formation was the square and, whenever seriously threatened by cavalry, Napoleonic foot troops would invariably seek to form one. However, this reaction could often be used against them. Cavalry had only to give the impression that they were about to charge and the infantry would deploy. The enemy could then attack the square with infantry and

INFANTRY SQUARES

A BATTALION SQUARE:

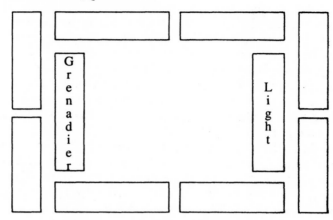

A TYPE OF REGIMENTAL SQUARE:

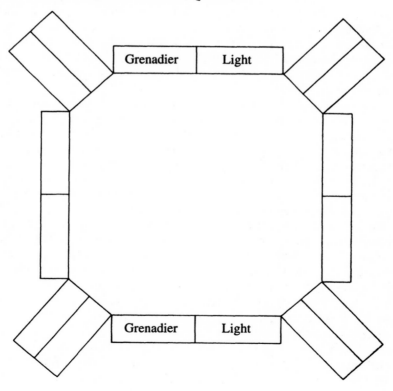

cannon, sending in their cavalry merely to complete the destruction.

Finally, a few words about artillery. Napoleonic cannon was divided into two types: horse and foot. In the case of the former, the gunners rode alongside their pieces, whereas the crews of foot batteries had to walk. Horse artillery was, therefore, considerably more mobile than foot artillery and was usually used to give cavalry close support.

A typical battery had six pieces; usually several cannons with one or two howitzers. The projectile trajectory of a cannon was virtually horizontal, while that of a howitzer could range up to a high arch. Guns were classified by the weight of the shot that they fired; howitzers by the width of the barrel's bore.

Napoleonic ordnance was basically a larger version of the smooth-bore musket and was loaded in much the same way. There was no recoil absorption mechanism and, after firing, the cannon had to be manhandled back into position. Projectiles consisted of round shot (which was a solid metal ball), grapeshot and canister. The latter two were essentially anti-personnel devices, usually consisting of metal balls packed in tins (canister), or in bags (grapeshot). If metal shot was not available, horseshoe-nails, glass, pebbles, and the like could be used to fill the containers. Howitzers could also fire fused-shells – hollow metal balls packed with explosives, with a projecting fuse. The fuse was ignited by the explosion of the propelling charge in the howitzer barrel and would be designed to burn for the time taken for the shell to arrive over the target. It would then explode the shell and rain fragments in all directions. But this required great skill and judgement on the part of the gunners, and most fused shells landed on the ground before exploding. Shells were also good incendiaries and were often used as such.

The weaponry of the Napoleonic era might seem crude when compared with the laser-guided 'hardware' common in present-day armies. However, they were absolutely lethal when used correctly. The one-ounce musket balls fired by standard small-arms could inflict appalling injuries and, at close range, were capable of passing through three men in a row. A round shot did not just kill a man or a horse, it smashed the target to pieces, penetrating up to as many as twenty ranks of infantry.[34] For closer work, the bayonets of the foot troops and the sabres and lances of the cavalry were horribly efficient.

A simple comparison between the Battle of Borodino and the first Battle of the Somme (1916), illustrates the lethality of Napoleonic weapons. In the case of the latter – so often cited as the ultimate in battlefield carnage – 60,000 British casualties were sustained on 1 July. This was a terrible toll, inflicted by the sophisticated military

CAVALRY FORMATIONS

The classic mode of assault for a cavalry regiment was by successive squadrons; each squadron formed in two lines, with the troopers riding boot to boot. Thus, a regiment of four squadrons would attack in eight lines, one behind the other. Each line would have a frontage of between forty and fifty men. However, on suitable terrain and with sufficient space, a regiment might charge with all its squadrons in line abreast. In this case the frontage would be of the order of two hundred sabres.

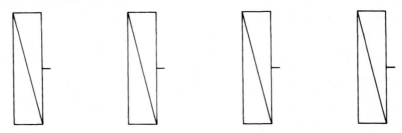

A REGIMENT OF FOUR SQUADRONS DEPLOYED IN COLONNE SERRÉE. (The intervals between the squadrons would be at least twelve metres.)

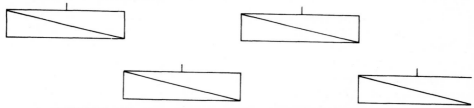

A REGIMENT OF FOUR SQUADRONS DEPLOYED EN ÉCHELON.

---

products of the 20th Century. However, at Borodino – fought over 100 years earlier – in one day's bloody fighting some 70,000 French and Russian troops were killed or wounded.[35]

III Sea-Power

The struggle for maritime supremacy between France and Britain played a leading role in the origins of the Peninsular War, and the latter power's eventual naval dominance was to have a decisive effect on the outcome of the Iberian conflict. Without the Royal Navy, Britain's fight in the Peninsula could never have been waged and certainly not with the success that was eventually achieved. As well as ferrying troops to and from the war zone, the fleet transported virtually all the gold, equipment, food and munitions used by the Allied armies and guerillas. Without this service, it is difficult to see how any large-scale, organised resistance could have been offered to the French; the indigenous resources of the Peninsula were not even adequate to sustain so much as a few small, Iberian divisions.

Moreover, whereas the lack of any naval support of their own confined the French to moving via the appalling Peninsular roads, the Allied forces could frequently transport men and *matériel* by sea; a method that was invariably safer, cheaper and quicker. This provided them with enormous advantages in the fields of logistics and strategy. The very fact that the theatre was bounded on three sides by water made it relatively easy for an army in difficulties – such as Moore's, in 1809 – to rendezvous with a fleet and be spirited away from under the enemy's nose. The troops could then be disembarked in some distant quarter; either in a friendly port to recuperate, or behind enemy lines to wreak fresh havoc. Supplies, too, could often easily be landed wherever they were needed, and several beleagured positions such as Cadiz and Gibraltar – and, indeed, the Lines of Torres Vedras – were exclusively rearmed and revictualled by sea.

With the remnants of their own fleet blockaded in Central European ports, the French had no force to counter effectively these maritime operations. Eternally threatened with landings on the sea-shore, their army had to detach thousands of badly needed troops to patrol beaches, garrison ports and man coastal batteries. In 1810, for example, two Allied squadrons – based on Ferrol and Corunna – tied down some 20,000 Imperial troops along the Biscay coast. A further 20,000 soldiers were needed to invest the naval base at Cadiz, and several thousand more spent their time fruitlessly chasing Allied detachments that constantly embarked and disembarked along the Andalusian coast. Very few of these men ever saw an enemy ship or soldier, but they had to be deployed to counter the possible threat of attack.

Furthermore, these sea-shore guards frequently became targets in themselves. Required to patrol enormous lengths of coastline, they were invariably thin on the ground and easy prey for amphibious forces composed of thousands of men. Many small detachments were annihilated before assistance could arrive (by which time the raiders had usually departed), and, in 1811, Marshal Victor's whole army corps sustained a serious defeat when attacked at Barrosa by a fleet-borne force numbering 12,000 men.

Even when they were not acting in support of ground forces, the Allied navies could strike at any target within cannon range of the sea. Prowling up and down the Iberian coasts, they sank enemy shipping, bombarded French columns on the coastal highways and shelled forces besieging friendly, shore-line installations. By these means, the maritime units of Britain, supported by some Spanish and Portuguese squadrons, made a thorough nuisance of themselves and rendered the enemy's operations infinitely more difficult and often impossible.

This total naval dominance lasted until mid-1812, when another force interfered, albeit indirectly, on the side of the French. Ever since the incident between the 'Leopard' and the 'Chesapeake' in 1807, relations between London and Washington had been steadily deteriorating. The British system of impressment was totally alien to the American doctrine of 'freedom of the seas' and fresh maritime clashes, in 1811, strained matters to breaking point. Finally, on 19 June 1812, the United States declared war on Britain and the Royal Navy was obliged to devote a hundred vessels – including eleven ships-of-the-line – to a blockade of the American coast. Even the mighty British navy sagged under the burden of sealing off two continents simultaneously and the French joined their new-found allies in taking advantage of their overstretched opponents. Imperial naval vessels, backed by a powerful force of privateers and American ships, instigated a relentless campaign against British vessels and, by summer 1814, about 800 merchantmen had been sunk, damaged or captured, many of them in home waters. With ships like USS 'Argus' rampaging up and down the English Channel, Wellington's formerly smooth supply system was appreciably disrupted. Fortunately for the Allied cause, however, 1812 proved to be the turning year in the Peninsular conflict and Wellington – now firmly established on the continent – was not too desperately incommoded. Nevertheless, until its end in December 1814, the American War did severely complicate matters in the European theatre and, above all, illustrated Wellington's reliance on the Royal Navy.[36]

IV   Logistical Difficulties

A matter of great importance in the shaping of the war was the question of logistics. The theatre of operations constituted one of the most barren and underdeveloped areas in Europe. Approximately eighty per cent of Spain and Portugal was incapable of supporting an army for any length of time, and certain districts – notably Estremadura and the borderlands between the two countries – were practically deserts.[37] In such an unfavourable environment the feeding and general supplying of armed forces proved a major problem, and the degree to which the two sides ultimately coped with the difficulties largely explains the outcome of the war.

Without regular convoys of merchantships, there is no conceivable way that Wellington could ever have supported his vast forces. Not only did he have to feed and equip the considerable British contingent, he also made over enormous quantities of *matériel* to his Spanish and Portuguese allies. Indeed, the importance of the fleet in keeping the Allies in provisions and munitions cannot be stressed too strongly – although the solitary example of the Lines of Torres Vedras will serve to illustrate the point quite adequately. Had the Royal Navy not proved capable of maintaining both the colossal military garrison and virtually all of Lisbon's civilian population, this vast series of fortifications would have become an untenable death-trap in a matter of days. The very foundations of Wellington's defence of Portugal would have vanished and the whole question of a continued British presence would have fallen into doubt. That, during 1811, the Allied army did not share the fate of that of Massena, was almost entirely the responsibility of the navy.

The fleet constituted only the first link in Wellington's logistical chain, of course. Once the supplies were landed, they had to be moved to the army's theatre of operations. Thus, a network of transport systems and depots was essential. Perfecting this vast machinery took some time and, particularly in the early years of the war, it broke down with annoying regularity. There were few navigable rivers available for use and the Peninsular roads were generally atrocious, especially in periods of bad weather. Moreover, conveyances and animals to pull them were always in short supply and, as late as 1813, we find Sir Augustus Frazer complaining that, in the British army, 'Nine hundred mules are wanting in the Artillery Department alone, and I believe 3,000 or 4,000 in that of the Commissariat'.[38] However, despite such difficulties, fortune was predominantly on the side of the Allies as far as logistics were concerned and a brief study of their opponents' problems quickly reveals why.

Although past masters at living off the land, the French were also obliged to supplement the Peninsula's scanty resources with vast convoys from outside. These usually originated in France and, with the absence of any fleet, had to be moved via the appalling Iberian roads. However, in addition to the problems they shared with the Allies, the French found their supply network constantly disrupted by guerilla bands and the rebellious population. *If* enough vehicles could be procured to form a convoy and *if* a large enough escort could be spared to guard it, it still took an inordinate period of time to move any distance. Consequently, the operations of the Imperial armies at the front were repeatedly undermined or delayed by shortages of such basic equipment as munitions, rations, horses, money, clothing and weapons.

Unable to rely on their forces being adequately supplied by convoy, French commanders had to resort to extracting provisions locally – much to the annoyance of the indigenous population. Although the Imperial troops were exceedingly good at this, it did have severe limitations and introduced peculiar complications to the conduct of military operations. 'The Emperor seems to ignore the food question' complained Marshal Marmont in February 1812.

> This is the important problem; and if it could be ended . . . , his orders could be executed with punctuality and precision. . . . the English army is always concentrated and can always be moved, because it has an adequate supply of money and transport. Seven or eight thousand pack mules bring up its daily food . . . His Majesty may judge from this fact the comparison between their means and our's – we have not four days' food in any of our magazines, we have no transport, we cannot draw requisitions from the most wretched village without sending thither a foraging party 200 strong; to live from day to day, we have to scatter detachments to vast distances, and always to be on the move . . .[39]

Again, on 2 March, Marmont complained to Napoleon that

> Lord Wellington is quite aware that I have no magazines, and is acquainted with the immensely difficult character of the country, and its complete lack of food resources . . . He knows that my army is not in a position to cross the Coa, even if nobody opposes me, and that if we did so we should have to turn back at the end of four days, unable to carry on the campaign, and with our horses all starved to death.[40]

Thus, not only did the disorder in the French logistical system affect the feeding and supplying of the troops, it also served to restrict and hamper their commanders in the formation and execution of strategy. To live, the Imperial armies had to disperse and, once they had scattered, they were easy prey for concentrated Allied forces. As Wellington observed: 'The more ground the French hold down, the weaker will they be at any given point.' In time, Napoleon's Peninsular generals came to realise that large armies simply starved and small armies were defeated.

However, when obliged to live off the land the Imperial troops demonstrated a quite remarkable ability to do so and in this sense were vastly superior to their opponents. Staggered by the resilience of the French army in the desert-like conditions of Portugal, Wellington wrote to Lord Liverpool on 21 December 1810, that

> It is certainly astonishing that the enemy have been able to remain in this country so long; and it is an extraordinary instance of what a French army can do. It is positively a fact that they brought no provisions with them, and they have not received even a letter since they entered Portugal. With all our money and having in our favour the good inclinations of the country, I assure you that I could not maintain one division in the district in which they have maintained not less than 60,000 men and 20,000 animals for more than two months.[41]

This generous tribute from their arch-enemy is a clear testimony to the resourcefulness and endurance of the French troops, and the Imperial armies were to consistently give impressive displays of such qualities. In contrast, the Allies, particularly the British, seem to have been peculiarly inept at surviving without plenty of supplies. Even in times of minor food shortages, indiscipline erupted on a vast scale. The British divisions went to pieces in the lean days after Talavera for example – despite the fact that at least some rations were still being issued – and, as late as the Waterloo campaign of 1815, we find Wellington commenting to his Prussian colleagues that 'I cannot separate from my tents and supplies. My troops must be well kept and well supplied in camp, if order and discipline are to be maintained.'[42]

Thus, in their ability to extract provisions from the scanty resources of the country, the French had no equals. Nevertheless, the Peninsula was just too barren to supply adequately the enormous Imperial forces and the insuperable obstacles the French faced in the field of logistics were to have a most decisive effect on the outcome of the war.

V   The Spanish Nation in Arms

The war that was waged by the Spanish – as distinct from the other Allied Powers – can be divided roughly into three levels of activity. Firstly, there was the 'traditional' war conducted by the Spanish regular Army and its supporting militia formations. It has been the practice of many historians to pour scorn on just about everything these forces did and a good deal of this criticism is justified.[43] However, the fact remains that without the Spanish Army it is doubtful that the Allies would have won the war. Whilst it is true that their soldiers and generals performed excessively badly on a large number of occasions, it is also the case that Spanish units behaved outstandingly well on others: Baylen, Tamames and Alcaniz are all examples of clear-cut Peninsular victories by indigenous armies and, at San Marcial, in 1813, a major Imperial offensive was brought to a complete standstill by the determined Spanish troops that lay in its path. Indeed, by the later months of the war, the Spanish were providing some units of extremely good quality and the troops of General Freire, for example, behaved with conspicuous gallantry in the bloody fighting for Toulouse.

Ironically, the point most often neglected about the Spanish Army was its greatest contribution to the Allied cause. At the outset of the Peninsular conflict there were well over 100,000 men on the service's rolls and by 1812, despite innumerable calamities, there were still 160,000 regular troops in being. This vast army was larger than the Portuguese and British divisions *combined*. Admittedly, many of the soldiers had neither the training nor equipment for open combat, but they did prove most valuable in such operations as blockades and sieges; releasing thousands of better troops for the more demanding undertakings elsewhere. Without this support, it is difficult to see how the depleted Anglo-Portuguese field army would have been able to take the offensive and, consequently, victories such as Salamanca would have become impossible.

Furthermore, irrespective of the quality of their men, the Spanish armies constituted a threat that the French quite simply could not ignore. Any sizeable concentration of enemy soldiers had to be engaged, or at least contained, by a sufficiently strong force of Imperial troops; otherwise they were free to go on the rampage with impunity. Consequently, a colossal percentage of the French army was rendered unavailable for operations against Wellington because innumerable Spanish contingents kept materialising all over the country. In 1810, for example, when Massena invaded Portugal, the Imperial forces in the Peninsula totalled a massive 325,000 men, but only about a quarter of these could be spared for the offensive – the rest were required to contain the Spanish insurgents and regulars. This was the greatest single contribution that the Spaniards were to make and, without it, Wellington could not have maintained himself on the continent for long – let alone emerge triumphant from the conflict.

Besides having to cope with the Spanish regular Army, the French were constantly under attack from organised gangs of guerillas. Supplied by the British, these bands could number anything from a few dozen to several thousand men, and constituted some of the most vicious and resourceful opponents that the occupation forces had to deal with. Led by such men as Sanchez and the Minas, they lurked in the remote and inaccessible corners of the Peninsular mountains; descending at every opportunity to prosecute the traditional warfare of the partisan: disrupting enemy communications and supplies, attacking couriers and Iberian collaborators, and mounting 'hit and run' raids against weak or isolated Imperial detachments.[44] As Clausewitz observed in *On War*, the scattered resistance of guerilla bands will not lend itself to major actions, but an insurrection – within the framework of a war conducted by regular armies – can be most effective. Indeed, the nature of the Peninsular conflict satisfies all five of the conditions Clausewitz cited for successful partisan warfare: the war must be fought in the country's interior; it must not be decided by a single blow; the theatre of operations must be reasonably large; the terrain must be rough and inaccessible; and the national character must be suited to that manner of warfare.[45]

In addition these roving bands were a priceless source of information for Allied generals. Because of the guerillas' activities, Wellington remarked, 'The French armies have no communications and one army has no knowledge of the position or of the circumstances in which the others are placed, whereas I have knowledge of all that passes on all sides.'[46] Indeed, so severely harassed were the French lines of communication that scores of vital messages failed to get through. In early 1812, for example, hardly any of the correspondence between King Joseph and Marshal Marmont reached its destination, with the result that, amongst other things, the marshal was quite unaware that Joseph's 'Army of the Centre' was *en route* to join him and, consequently, went ahead and fought the Battle of Salamanca with 14,000 men less than he might have had. Likewise, on a number of occasions, Wellington owed his salvation to the intelligence role of the guerillas. Immediately after Talavera, for instance, he confidently marched off to attack what he believed to be only 10,000 French troops with a force 18,000-strong. In fact, the Imperial 'detachment' consisted of three entire army corps and numbered well over 50,000 men. Had Wellington not received a timely warning of his miscalculation from the guerillas, it is extremely probable that in the ensuing battle both he and the British army would have ceased to be active factors in the scenarios of the Peninsular War. As it was, he was able to retreat in time.

Thirdly, there was the general resistance to Joseph's imposed rule that largely stemmed from the Iberian popular classes. This has been described as 'a continuation of the quasi-constitutionalist movement against Godoy's "dictatorship".'[47] Certainly, as the majority of Spaniards who collaborated with the French – *Afrancesados* – came from the upper classes, popular resistance to the invaders had the overtones of a social conflict. It was, noted one French general, 'A war of the poor against the rich'.[48]

The *Afrancesados* fell into three groups: those who saw cooperation with the French as a potentially more fruitful policy than confrontation; those who hoped that Joseph's rule would lead to invigorating reforms; and those who, fearing the popular nature of the resistance, sided with Joseph's new order against the forces of revolution.[49] To the popular classes, however, all *Afrancesados* were traitors and cooperation with the French was out of the question. Led by local soldiers, notables, gentry and clerics, thousands of armed peasants would assist in the defence of the larger cities, notably Saragossa.[50] This, of course, put the civilian population very much 'in the firing line'. Inevitably, atrocity gave rise to counter-atrocity and, in six years of war, thousands of people who officially were non-combatants were butchered.[51]

King Joseph tried desperately to win over his recalcitrant subjects, but apart from gaining a few *Afrancesados*, who were prime targets for the guerillas and partisan assassination squads, he failed. 'Spanish public opinion was inexorable', one member of his government recalled;

> it rejected everything coming from us – even benefits. Thus, the King and his counsellors spent themselves in fruitless labours. Nothing answered their expectations and the void in the treasury – the worst danger – showed no sign of diminution. On the contrary, the financial distress increased every day and the unpleasant means which we were compelled to employ in order to supply the never-ceasing needs of the army, completely alienated the nation from us.[52]

Thus, the Spanish 'nation in arms' presented the French with a host of virtually insuperable, political and military problems. They may have lacked the polished professionalism of the British Light Division but, in the long run, they probably inflicted considerably more damage on the French forces than all of Wellington's pitched battles combined. The sieges of Gerona alone cost the Imperial armies over 20,000 casualties and, exclusively from sickness and guerilla raids, the French forces in the Peninsula lost approximately 100 men per day for over four years: a total of some 164,000 casualties. It is, therefore, easy to see how the war in Spain bled the French army white and, whilst the Anglo-Portuguese forces delivered the hammer-blows, it was the civilian populations, particularly the Spanish, that bore the brunt of the suffering.[53]

VI   Command and Control

The Peninsular conflict – and Napoleonic Wars in general – took place in an era when communications were far less developed than they are today. There was no such thing as a radio or a telephone, and orders and other information had to be transmitted almost exclusively by means of hand-written dispatches, usually carried by mounted messengers.

Such a medium was obviously prone to setbacks at the best of times. Firstly, the message had to be *physically* taken from the writer to the recipient – a task which, especially in the Peninsula, could be exceedingly difficult – and should the dispatch fall into the wrong hands the information it contained could prove very useful to the opposition. Even if a French courier, for example, managed to avoid hostile peasants and marauding guerillas, then poor roads, a lame mount, long distances and bad weather conditions could also lead to fatal delays in the transmission of orders. Furthermore, the intended recipient of the missive could well be located at the heart of an engagement of some kind, and this could expose the bearer to all sorts of hazards and complications. Commanding generals conducting battles had to manipulate their formations by the cumbersome means of written directions which had to be conveyed to the relevant unit commander by an aide. The difficulties involved in such an undertaking should not be underestimated. The unfortunate soldier, clutching a scribbled note and dodging shot and shell, was expected to gallop into the midst of the fighting and, from amongst the thousands of embattled men about him, find a particular officer who, as far as anyone knew, might be dead or lying in some distant field hospital.

If, however, we assume that the courier safely negotiated the dangers on his route and finally got the orders through to the appropriate officer before they went out of date, then illegible writing, spelling errors, ambiguous wording and similar distortive features could render the dispatch virtually useless, or completely alter its meaning. The notorious charge of the Light Brigade at Balaclava, in 1854, is a prime illustration of the sort of calamity that such 'friction' – as Clausewitz called it – can cause and similarly attributable events can be found in every military conflict; the Peninsular War being no exception.

Certain other problems in the field of command and control also made matters extraordinarily difficult, particularly for the French. The first of these was the way Napoleon delegated responsibility to his lieutenants in the Peninsula. Over the course of the war, he made repeated alterations to the division of authority amongst his subordinates in an effort to balance a number of considerations. Reluctant, for political reasons, to confer too much power on any one individual, the emperor experimented with a series of military districts, each under the supreme authority of a particular army officer. This only heightened the intense, personal rivalries that already existed between some of the marshals and the net result was a chronic breakdown in the co-ordination of their respective efforts.[54] Furthermore, while several of the military governors were extremely able, many of the marshals and generals employed in the Peninsula were unsuited to and inexperienced in the independent command of large armies and, without Napoleon close at hand to guide them, put in performances ranging from mediocre to bad.

In the midst of this confused hierarchy lay King Joseph and his advisers. Although officially head of state, the monarch enjoyed little real power and, during the period from spring 1810 to winter 1811, he was reduced to nothing more than one of eight military governors. Caught between his Imperial brother – who regularly accused him of making war 'like a postal inspector' – and the feuding marshals, Joseph was in a deplorable dilemma. On the one hand, he was held responsible by Napoleon for all that went on in the Peninsula while, on the other, he had little authority for most of the time and could barely control the wayward military governors. The hapless monarch found this state of affairs quite unbearable and, on a number of occasions, threatened to abdicate – only to be bullied back into line by his dominating brother.

All of this did little to smooth the conduct of military operations and, after years of divided rule had contributed to the collapse of the French position in Spain, the emperor finally relented and, in March 1812, made Joseph his supreme representative in the Peninsula. However, by this time the king had completely lost touch with affairs in the various regions and, having enjoyed a period of virtually unrestricted power, the military governors were more than reluctant to submit themselves to the rulings of Joseph.[55] Despite his Imperial mandate, the king soon discovered that nothing had changed; whenever he attempted to coerce his 'subordinates' they merely appealed directly to Napoleon himself. Trapped in a position of responsibility, yet without any corresponding authority, the unhappy Joseph tottered on until the summer of 1813 when, in the wake of the Vitoria disaster, the emperor finally relieved his brother of the crown he had never really wanted.

The tendency of the military governors to 'cut out the middle man', King Joseph, and make direct approaches to Napoleon himself frequently led to the direst consequences, as the emperor – relying exclusively for his information on written dispatches which, when he received them, were often weeks old – attempted to control a war being fought hundreds of miles from Paris. Often, the unfortunate king would not even be advised of the strategic arrangements that his brother and a particular general had concocted together, and many of Joseph's plans were consequently smothered in infancy by the surreptitious intervention of Napoleon. Although the emperor candidly confessed that 'I am too far away, and the position of the enemy changes too often for me to be able to give advice ...',[56] he could not resist the temptation to dabble – both directly and indirectly – in the handling of the Peninsular conflict. Indeed, his failure to appoint – and uphold – one individual to a position of supreme command in Spain inevitably meant that he himself would be called upon to arbitrate between the various parties and generally provide the overall guidance that was lacking.

This, however, was but one dimension of the story. Not only was Napoleon's information from the Peninsula often weeks old when he received it but, just as frequently, the military governors, anxious to please their demanding master, sent reports which were misleading to say the least. In the dispatches of even relatively honest officers, like Marshal Suchet, one can find countless examples of exaggeration and other such distortions. Often the emperor would see through the 'white-wash', but usually he had no means of verifying whether what he read was true or false. The following extract, from a letter to his Minister of War about Talavera, adequately illustrates Napoleon's predicament:

> Inform Marshal Jourdan that I am extremely displeased with the inaccuracies and falsehoods contained in his reports of the 26th, 27th, 28th and 29th of July, and that this is not the first time in which the government has been so trifled with. He said on the 28th, that he had seized the field of Talavera, while subsequent reports show that we were repulsed ... Tell him that this infidelity towards the government is a regular crime, and that this crime might have had fatal results, as the news that the English had been beaten was about to influence my determinations ... He may say what he likes in the *Madrid Journal*, but he has no right to disguise the truth from the government.[57]

Thus, with little reliable information coming his way and given his own unwillingness to return to the Peninsula after early 1809, the emperor's attempts to control the war through the medium of written instructions – a formidable task at the best of times – proved to be an undertaking which even the greatest soldier since Alexander the Great could not fulfil particularly well. The technology of the day was simply incapable of providing him and his staff with the sort of split-second communications that would have made the undertaking anywhere near viable. One has only to look at the current example of the Russian attempts to subdue Afghanistan to realise that armies – with facilities and innovations beyond anything that Napoleon and his contemporaries could ever have dreamt of – are still strained by the type of warfare that he encountered in the Peninsula. For their part, the Allied governments vested almost total responsibility for the conduct of military operations in Wellington who, consequently, was able to manipulate all the forces at his disposal more efficiently than his opponents and to take great advantage of the inherent weaknesses of the French position – including the lamentable flaws in their command structure.[58]

Thus, the French attempts to conquer the Peninsula were constantly undermined by a series of ineluctable military and political problems. Having gained a superficial, military triumph over the greater part of the Iberian kingdoms, Napoleon found himself confronted with the age-old puzzle of trying to win popular support for an imposed government. In this vital field, he was singularly unsuccessful and what had originally begun as an opportunist gamble – which was expected to cost 'no more than 12,000 men' – rapidly deteriorated into a gruelling war of attrition that was to drag on for six long years. This exerted a colossal drain on the empire's resources and, in addition to leading to numerous calamities in the Peninsula itself, the 'Spanish Ulcer' was to have devastating repercussions for Napoleon's position in Europe as a whole. That the emperor would have been wise to cut his losses and withdraw from Spain altogether cannot really be doubted. Such a move was, however, completely unpalatable to Napoleon: his prestige and pride were too bound up with the fate of the venture, and he could hardly open negotiations with the 'rebel' Spanish government.

Thus, denied any real hope of a diplomatic solution, the faithful French army slogged away at their thankless task, desperately trying to secure the elusive, decisive victory. Constantly ravaged by battles, guerillas, the climate, starvation and disease, thousands of men were to be lost from its ranks whilst, overwhelmed by the inherent difficulties involved in the war, one after another of Napoleon's leading subordinates had their military reputations tarnished or destroyed. Having succeeded only in exposing his empire to a costly second front, Napoleon was to rue the day he sent his troops into the Peninsula: as the magnitude of his error emerged, it became evident that he had placed himself on a course to disaster.

Royal Horse Artillery coming into Action (Royal Library, Windsor. Reproduced by Gracious Permission of Her Majesty The Queen. Copyright reserved)

British Foot Artillery (Royal Library, Windsor. Reproduced by Gracious Permission of Her Majesty The Queen. Copyright reserved)

A Spanish Hussar (From *Memoires du Colonel Delagrave*, Paris)

Spanish Line Infantry men (From *Memoires du Colonel Delagrave*, Paris)

Spanish Grenadiers (From *Memoires du Colonel Delagrave*, Paris)

An officer of the 'Alcantra' Portuguese Dragoons (From *Memoires du Colonel Delagrave*, Paris)

Troops and camp followers on the march. (National Army Museum, London)

Soldiers and their wives on the march. Drawing by Rowlandson (National Army Museum, London)

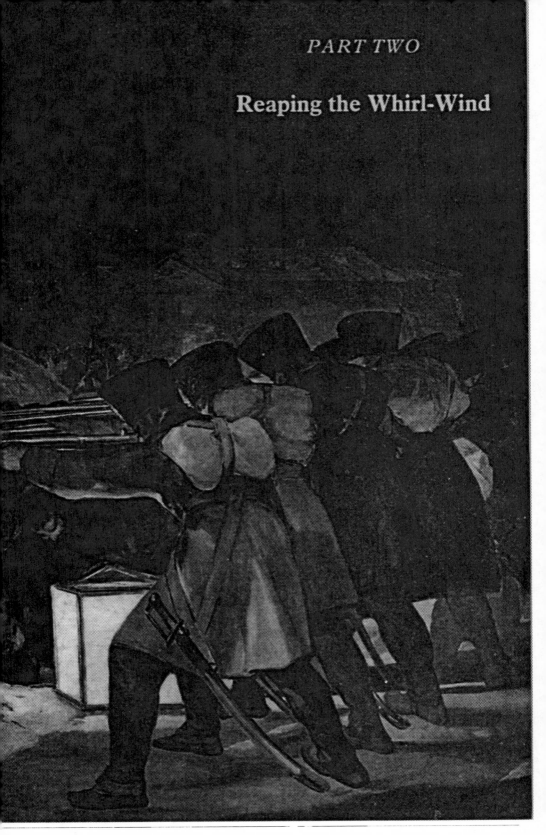

PART TWO

Reaping the Whirl-Wind

Overleaf: The *Tres de Mayo* by Goya (*Photo:* Museo del Prado)

THE PENINSULA – REGIONAL DIVISIONS

Chapter III

THE SPANISH IN REVOLT

I The 'Unhappy Business of Baylen'

By mid-May, 1808, the whole of Spain was up in arms against the French. Separate *Juntas* led the revolt from Murcia, Aragon, the Asturias, Seville, Catalonia and Galicia. Whilst the military capabilities of these areas varied enormously, the main Spanish forces were concentrated in the north-west and south-west. The French, on the other hand, had a mass of troops about Madrid (with lines of communication snaking back to Bayonne); Junot – cut off in Portugal – and various detachments in Catalonia. Thus, generally they occupied the centre of the country, while the *Juntas'* forces held the periphery. Everywhere, however, the people turned on the invaders, attacking isolated contingents, murdering couriers, disrupting supplies and so on. The Imperial forces gradually found that they controlled only those parts of the Peninsula they could keep under their bayonets, and that messengers and supply convoys needed strong escorts if they were to reach their destination.

However, inadequate information and slow communications, plus the successful quelling of the *Dos de Mayo* Rising had convinced the emperor's viceroy, Murat, that opposition to the French occupation was limited to a few isolated outbreaks of disorder which could easily be suppressed by flying columns. Until well into June, he continued to send relatively optimistic reports to France and so, from the outset, Napoleon was badly misinformed about the true nature of the conflict.

To deal with the supposedly isolated trouble spots, the emperor drew up a plan which Murat put into operation during the last week of May. A large reserve was to be kept at Madrid, while General Dupont was to move on Cordova and Seville. Marshal Moncey, supported by a column from Duhesme's command in Catalonia, would put down the insurrections at Valencia and Cartagena, while Marshal Bessières maintained the lines of communication in the north, and detached forces to crush the rebels in Santander and Saragossa.

In accordance with these instructions, Dupont marched on Andujar with 13,000 troops, arriving there on 5 June. Becoming increasingly aware of the general nature of the rising, he pushed on towards Cordova where masses of peasants were arming under Don Pedro de Echavarri. In addition to 12,000 such volunteers, the Spanish commander had some 1,400 regular troops with eight guns and, realising the defence of Cordova was a political necessity, he put his doubts aside and drew his whole force up to confront Dupont at the Alcolia Bridge, on the River Guadalquivir.

Here, in the first real engagement of the war, the Spanish sustained a severe defeat. Although they were mostly green conscripts, Dupont's men were crack troops in comparison to their raw, disorganised opponents. The whole of Don Pedro's force was routed in a matter of minutes and fled past Cordova without attempting to defend it further. A few random shots at Dupont's vanguard gave the Imperial general an excuse to reject the town's capitulation and he promptly ordered his men to storm the walls.

What followed was a disgrace and such scenes were to be repeated many times in the coming years. The French looted Cordova with little regard for life or property: the town was sacked, women were raped and dozens of civilians were killed. In revenge, insurgent bands massacred French stragglers and outposts. Already, the war was taking on a particularly brutal nature, with both sides committing appalling atrocities.

Dupont soon found himself totally isolated in a region seething with rebellion. Beset by doubts, with his couriers literally butchered and with no sign of reinforcements, he abandoned Cordova and retreated eastwards. However, instead of retiring to the relative safety of the mountain defiles, he lingered on the plains around Andujar, determined to fulfil his mission. But, alarmed by the advance of General Castaños' army of 34,000 Spaniards, he sent out powerful columns to make contact with any aid Murat might have dispatched.

Reinforcements were, indeed, in the offing and, on 27 June, General Vedel arrived at La Carolina with 6,000 infantry and 600 cavalry. However, Dupont failed to put this extra strength to good use, either in an offensive or defensive style. Instead of deploying Vedel in the mountain passes to secure his communications and line of retreat, or gathering all his forces for an immediate strike at Castaños on the plains, he summoned the new units to Baylen and continued to remain, inactive, with his main force at Andujar. Worse still, when General Gobert was sent by Madrid to reopen and secure

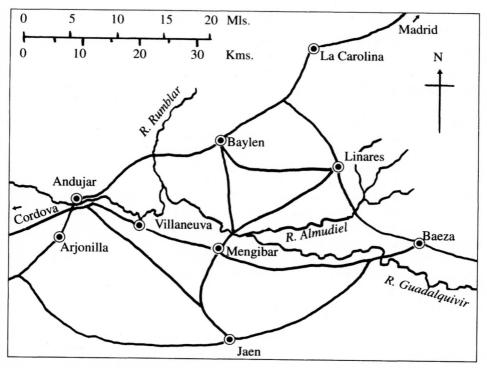

THE BAYLEN CAMPAIGN:
THEATRE OF OPERATIONS

contact with Dupont, the latter ordered him to bring his division to join in the pointless operations about Andujar. Thus, by 7 July, the French commander had over 20,000 men sitting idle, while his adversary, puzzled by the enemy's inactivity, finalised preparations for an assault across the Guadalquivir.

To implement his offensive, General Castaños divided his forces into three columns. The first, 12,000 men under the Spanish commander himself, was to march on Andujar; the second, commanded by Coupigny, was 8,000 strong and directed on Villa Neuva; the third, some 10,000 troops led by General Reding, had orders to seize Mengibar. Believing the French to have 14,000 men at Andujar, Castaños planned to pin these down with a feint frontal attack, while the other two Spanish columns swung in from the east and assailed their rear. The Imperial units that lay in the path of Reding and Coupigny were thought to be small flank-guards, and were not expected to prove much of an obstacle to the *attaque débordante*.

The Spanish opened their offensive against Dupont's extended line on 14 July, and drove the French pickets from the river at Mengibar. However, instead of concentrating to destroy the widely separated enemy columns, the Imperial commander, strengthened in his defensive attitude by news that Moncey had been checked at Valencia, contented himself with some minor adjustments to his dispositions and merely reinforced Vedel at Baylen with elements of Gobert's units which had been left at La Carolina.

The next day saw Castaños pushing home his assaults in earnest, only to discover that he had greatly miscalculated Dupont's strength. Likewise, Reding found himself confronted by Vedel's entire division instead of a weak flank-guard, and quickly curtailed the action. Dupont, however, was so shaken by the vigour of Castaños' attack, that he called on Vedel for reinforcements. In view of Reding's feeble assault, that general underestimated the size of the hostile force before Mengibar and, leaving only two battalions there, marched throughout the night to the aid of his commander. Arriving at Andujar on the afternoon of 16 July, he discovered that Castaños had simply repeated his demonstration of the day before and that Coupigny had, again, merely toyed with the defence at Villa Neuva.

But the news from Mengibar was disastrous. Reding, utilising all his 10,000 men, had scattered the skeleton force left in the settlement and had successfully crossed the Guadalquivir. General Gobert had tried to stem the rout by rushing forward the handful of available reinforcements but, by evening, he was mortally wounded and his stricken command was retreating on Baylen. The French left flank had been turned.

Once again, despite his superior numbers, artillery and cavalry, Dupont hesitated to take the initiative. Instead of falling on Castaños and rolling up the extended Spanish army from west to east, he divided his forces once more: he would try to retain Andujar, while Vedel was to take his weary men back to rally the defeated left wing and contain Reding.

On arrival at Baylen, however, a horrified Vedel discovered that Gobert's successor, Dufour, had evacuated the town and had marched on La Carolina, where a Spanish column was apparently threatening the passes and, thus, the army's communications with Madrid. Assuming that the hostile force was that of Reding, Vedel dispatched warnings to his commander-in-chief and hurried his exhausted men forward to join Dufour.

This northward march, executed without any attempt to verify the enemy's true dispositions and movements, placed Dupont's entire army at risk and, indeed, was to prove a fatal blunder. The column threatening La Carolina was not Reding's at all; it was composed of several hundred raw levies, detached to menace the French left as best they could. Reding was, in fact, still about Mengibar, where he had regrouped following his victory over Gobert. Thus, having united with Dufour at noon on 18 July, Vedel was disgruntled to find no real threat to the passes and, shortly after, orders arrived for him to return to Andujar. He duly turned his footsore columns about and began retracing his steps to join Dupont.

By this time the Spanish were also astir. Reding and his men, joined by Coupigny's column, had resumed the advance at noon on 17 July. Convinced that the bulk of the enemy army still lay about Andujar, Castaños reverted to his original plan. Reding was directed on Baylen and, by evening, having encountered no resistance, had occupied it in strength – ready to move his entire command against Dupont's rear at first light.[59] Dismissing any hostile units to the north-east as mere dregs from the earlier actions, he failed to realise that Vedel was approaching with 11,000 troops. However, before dawn the next day, fighting broke out to the west of Baylen. The French commander-in-chief, alarmed by the gap between himself and Vedel, had finally retreated from Andujar and his vanguard had blundered into Reding's outposts.

In response to Dupont's unexpected move, Reding hastily drew up 14,000 men and twenty guns in a fairly strong position along the hills to the west of Baylen. As a further precaution, he also deployed several units to guard the road from La Carolina. Meanwhile, Dupont's vanguard commander, Chabert, underestimating the strength of the force before him, opened fire with his solitary battery and sent his 3,000 men into the attack. Swept by converging fire and hopelessly outnumbered, his troops were easily halted by the Spaniards and, after a bitter struggle, repulsed with considerable loss.

Dupont now arrived and took control himself. Fearing that Castaños might fall on his rearguard at any moment, he proceeded to send his troops forward in piecemeal assaults, as soon as they came on to the field. His troops, having marched all night along the hilly, sinuous road, were both exhausted and strung out, and to commit them to battle in dribs and drabs was foolhardy in the extreme. Despite gallant efforts by his provisional dragoons and *cuirassiers*, the Spanish managed to beat off two more attacks and, by 12.30, with Castaños bearing down on his rear, Dupont was in dire straits. Grouping his exhausted conscripts around his last formed battalion, he led them in a final bid to break Reding's line. Again, the assault made considerable progress and parts of the Spanish force were soon on the verge of dissolution. However, the French had no reserves to exploit the breakthrough and, after another heated contest, they

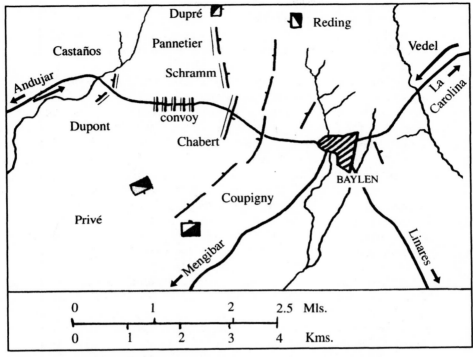

THE BATTLE OF BAYLEN
19 July 1808 (closing stages)

CASTAÑOS' ARMY:

1st Division (Reding)
Infantry (11 reg's)	=	8,450
Cavalry (6 reg's)	=	900
Artillery etc.	=	370
Total:	=	9,720

2nd Division (Coupigny)
Infantry (10 reg's)	=	7,230
Cavalry (2 reg's)	=	520
Artillery etc.	=	200
Total:	=	7,950

3rd Division (Jones)
Infantry (9 reg's)	=	4,700
Cavalry (4 reg's)	=	700
Artillery etc.	=	200
Total:	=	5,600

4th Division (La Peña)
Infantry (8 reg's)	=	5,560
Cavalry (1 regt)	=	540
Artillery etc.	=	200
Total:	=	6,500

GRAND TOTAL = 29,770 men with 25 guns.

DUPONT'S ARMY:

Division Barbou
(Chabert) 4th Reserve Legion	=	2,300
4th Swiss Regt.	=	500
Guard Marines	=	500
(Schramm) 2 Swiss reg's	=	1,300
(Pannetier) 3rd Reserve Legion	=	1,600
Garde de Paris	=	1,000
Artillery etc.	=	300
Total:	=	7,500

Cavalry
(Dupré)		
1st Prov. Chasseurs	=	510
2nd Prov. Chasseurs	=	580
(Privé)		
1st Prov. Dragoons	=	720
2nd Prov. Dragoons	=	640
2nd Prov. Cuirassiers	=	300
Total:	=	2,750

GRAND TOTAL = 10,250 men with 18 guns.

were again driven back down the slope. With his whole force demoralised and physically exhausted, Dupont was lost. The sound of Castaños' vanguard attacking his baggage column signalled the end and, with his Swiss troops deserting to the enemy *en masse*, the French commander sued for terms.

Meanwhile, Vedel had been sluggishly marching on Baylen from the east, when he found his path barred by one of Reding's brigades. Attacking this force he drove it back, but called off his troops when he heard of the cease-fire and waited for further instructions. After long negotiations, Dupont agreed to surrender the remaining 8,200 men of his own command and ordered Vedel to lay down his arms, too. Vedel promptly capitulated and even commanded his outposts at La Carolina and beyond to join in the shameful surrender.

Thus, nearly 20,000 Imperial troops passed into captivity, many of whom could have escaped with ease. Under the terms of the capitulation, the whole force should have been shipped back to France, but only Dupont and his generals were returned. Fewer than half of the rank and file ever saw their homes again.[60]

Napoleon, of course, was absolutely infuriated by the reverse. 'There has never been anything so stupid, so foolish or so cowardly since the world began,' he complained. 'It is perfectly clear from Dupont's own report that everything was the result of the most inconceivable incapacity on his part.'[61] Irrespective of the causes, however, the defeat of Dupont at Baylen was of great significance. The news spread across the Peninsula and, indeed, throughout Europe; forming a large crack in the edifice of French invincibility and rallying fresh opposition to Napoleon's tyranny.[62]

II Moncey in Valencia

While Dupont was marching on Cordova, Marshal Moncey had left Madrid with some 9,000 men to deal with the insurrectionists in Valencia. Hoping that the Spanish would expect him to use the main road through Almanza, he took the relatively difficult route over the hills, through Cuenca, to take them by surprise.

In this, he was completely successful. Sweeping through the feeble Spanish detachments guarding the River Cabriel and the Cabrillas defile, he avoided the main enemy forces that were searching for him on the Almanza highway and arrived at the city of Valencia on 26 June. The inhabitants of that place had not been idle. Improvised earthworks and fortifications had been constructed all over the city, and irrigation channels had been used to flood many of the surrounding fields, rendering them impassable. With the Guadalviar covering their northern flank, the defence could concentrate on the few areas where an assault was practicable. Accordingly, the approaches to these points were covered by large batteries of heavy calibre guns and some 20,000 men – mostly armed peasants – were deployed along the threatened sectors.

His terms for capitulation rejected, Moncey drove the enemy's outposts into Valencia and, on 28 June, attempted to storm the perimeter. Doubtlessly, after his easy victories in the hills, the marshal expected the defence to evaporate before a determined assault and he was surprised by the staunch opposition his enthusiastic conscripts met. From behind their walls and barricades, the Valencians poured a hail of shot and shell into the exposed Imperial troops, driving them off with serious losses. Moncey's cannon could do little either; being silenced or forced back by the heavier and more numerous Spanish pieces.

After losing over 1,000 men in two attacks, the French commander had to acknowledge defeat. His 8,000 conscripts, with no siege guns, were simply inadequate to the task before them. Storming Valencia was clearly out of the question and there was no sign of the supporting column Duhesme was supposed to have dispatched from Catalonia. Furthermore, the surrounding country was up in arms and was also known to contain a sizeable enemy field army. Realising that nothing was to be gained by lingering in his current position, Moncey wisely decided to write off Valencia and retired on Madrid via the Almanza road, hoping for a decisive clash with the Spanish regular divisions on the way.[63]

However, such a manoeuvre was totally unforeseen by the marshal's adversaries and, as he thrust to the south-west, he encountered only trifling resistance. The Spanish general, Cervellon, convinced that the French would retreat by the way they had come and determined not to be caught unawares again, had moved his army to the Cabrillas defile to bar the enemy's path. Thus, more by accident than design, the major clash that both belligerents had anticipated failed to occur and, brushing aside the few peasant bands that attempted to stop him, Moncey returned to New Castile and opened up communications with Madrid.

Nevertheless, the French marshal had not entirely abandoned his hopes of a decisive engagement with Cervellon and he loitered on the plains around San Clemente in case the enemy's army should materialise. However, after several days of fruitless waiting, Moncey's scheme was curtailed by fresh orders from Madrid and, in mid-July, he reluctantly completed his withdrawal, bringing the Valencian expedition to a close.

Thus, by the second week of July, the forces of Dupont and

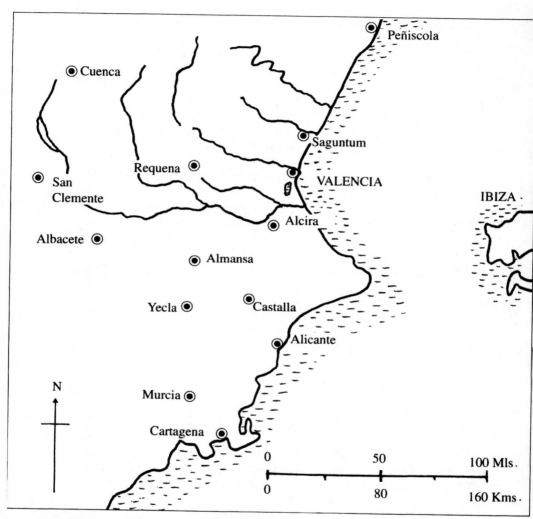

Cuenca

Peñiscola

San Clemente

Requena

Saguntum

VALENCIA

IBIZA

Albacete

Alcira

Almansa

Yecla

Castalla

Alicante

N

Murcia

Cartagena

| 0 | 50 | 100 Mls. |
| 0 | 80 | 160 Kms. |

MONCEY IN VALENCIA:
THE GENERAL THEATRE OF OPERATIONS

Moncey had completely failed to pacify Andalusia and Valencia. The latter commander had suffered a bloody rebuff and his colleague's expedition had ended in disaster. The struggle in Catalonia, however, was only just beginning.[64]

III The Struggle for Catalonia, May 1808–Spring 1809

Madrid's conception of the rebellion in Catalonia was, again, one of isolated outbreaks of revolt. Such an impression was totally incorrect. As elsewhere, the whole population was up in arms and the French strategy of sending flying columns to major towns was to prove as ineffective here as it had in other regions.

The Imperial commander entrusted with the conquest of Catalonia was General Duhesme, who had some 5,500 Italian and 7,000 French troops at his disposal. His orders were to hold Barcelona, crush the rebels in Lerida and Manresa, and to send a column to help Moncey quell Valencia. Had Duhesme been faced with the sort of factional disorder that Madrid envisaged such a scheme might have been reasonably practical. However, given the actual state of affairs, the general and his 12,000 soldiers were woefully inadequate for such a daunting task. Nevertheless, eager to obey his instructions, Duhesme set his doubts aside and tried to implement the various projects: General Chabran was dispatched with 3,000 men to aid Moncey, while General Schwartz took a similar number to secure Manresa and Lerida.

Unfortunately for Duhesme, the realities of the situation soon prevailed over his good intentions. Leaving Barcelona on 4 June, Schwartz found the countryside seething with hostile levies (*somatenes*) and was brought to a complete halt at the Bruch Pass. Gripped by panic, the general hastily retreated, calling on Duhesme for reinforcements. Thoroughly alarmed by this development, the French commander-in-chief recalled Chabran to strengthen Schwartz's column and a fresh attempt was made to force the defile. Still, however, the Imperial troops could make no headway and, after some probing attacks had been repulsed, retired on Barcelona once more.

Increasingly aware of the general nature of the rising, Duhesme now began to fear for his communications with France. Taking 6,000 men, he set off up the coastal highway, dispersing a colossal swarm of *somatenes* blocking his path at Mataro. However, like the waves of an ocean broken by a ship, the levies returned in the wake of the French columns and, by the time Duhesme reached Gerona, all contact had been lost with his base.

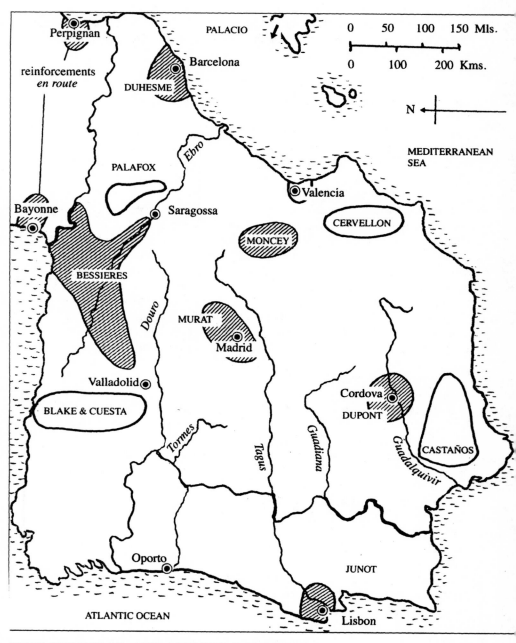

THE GENERAL STRATEGIC SITUATION,
Mid-June 1808

After unsuccessfully summoning the fortress to surrender, the Imperial general launched his troops at Gerona's defences. Lacking heavy artillery support, they were beaten off just as Moncey's men had been at Valencia. With insufficient forces to invest the city and the country rising all about him, Duhesme, leaving Chabran's brigade to hold Mataro, sullenly retraced his steps to Barcelona. However, within days he was on the move again. Increasingly frustrated, he struck at a mass of Spanish irregulars along the Llobregat river and scattered them into the hills. Likewise, Chabran ventured out in search of a battle, but failed to secure one and, harassed by the *somatenes* at every turn, retired to Mataro. Totally baffled as to how to deal with such volatile opponents, the Imperial forces now reverted completely to the defensive and anxiously awaited the arrival of reinforcements.

Help was, indeed, on the way, but of a rather limited kind. Napoleon – gradually beginning to realise the difficulties facing Duhesme – had dispatched General Reille to support him. Reille's division was a poor quality, extemporised formation that was scattered throughout southern France. Consequently, it was as late as 5 July before the general had assembled a mere quarter of his projected 8,000 troops. Nevertheless, impressed by the urgent need to aid the scanty forces in Catalonia, he left a nucleus of soldiers at Perpignan for his converging units to group around and marched to relieve the beleagured garrison of Figueras.

Having successfully concluded this operation without too much difficulty, Reille, now joined by the rest of his division, was free to turn his attention to the Spanish-held fortress of Rosas. However, the disgruntled general soon found its powerful garrison – skilfully supported by a British naval squadron – to be very determined and he rapidly abandoned all hopes of seizing the place. Deciding it could be safely ignored, at least for the time being, he turned southwards and the last days of July saw him approaching the enemy stronghold of Gerona.

Duhesme, too, was astir. On hearing of Reille's advance, he had left Barcelona with the bulk of his forces and had moved to join him. Meeting stiff resistance from the *somatenes*, his columns suffered appreciable losses before uniting with Reille's vanguard near Gerona on 24 July. Now, with plenty of siege guns at his disposal and mindful of the check he had sustained in June, Duhesme rejected storm tactics and settled down to investing the fortress. Although recently reinforced by 1,300 regulars from the Balearic Islands, the stronghold should have proved relatively easy to capture. However, operations proceeded at an inordinately slow pace and the French never completely surrounded the city, enabling the Spanish to move in men and *matériel* at will. It was as late as 12 August before the besiegers' batteries were sufficiently close to inflict real damage on the defences and, by that time, some alarming developments were taking place elsewhere in the province.

The moment Duhesme had moved the bulk of his forces out of Barcelona, hordes of *somatenes*, quickly joined by General Del Palacio and his 5,000 regular troops from the Balearic Islands, blockaded the city.[65] Meanwhile, a second contingent of regulars, commanded by the Conde de Caldagues, had marched to join the *somatenes* harassing the French about Gerona, where the first rumours of Baylen caused a sharp deterioration in the morale of the Imperial forces and gave that of their opponents a significant boost.

Apparently unmoved by these complications and convinced that Gerona was about to fall, Duhesme ignored Barcelona's frantic pleas for assistance and continued with his dilatory siege. However, his complacency soon led to disastrous consequences. Completely unhindered in his advance by the enemy, Caldagues arrived at the beleagured city during the second week of August and attacked Reille's troops from the rear while the garrison staged a sortie against his front. Assailed from two sides, Reille's soldiers were only saved by the skill of their commanding officer, who managed to extricate them without serious loss. Nevertheless, the morale of the Imperial forces was now so low that the troops rejected all calls to retake the captured earthworks and Duhesme was left with no alternative but to abandon the siege. Accordingly, during the night of 16 August, the French destroyed their remaining siege guns and stores, and set out for their respective bases; Reille marching back to Figueras, while Duhesme returned to Barcelona.

However, the Spanish had no intention of allowing their enemies to escape quite so lightly. Although Reille retired with comparative ease, the Catalans made every effort to prevent Duhesme relieving Barcelona. Continually harassed by the *somatenes*, the French general soon found that the coastal road had been mined and barricaded, and that prowling British warships shelled his ponderous columns at every opportunity. Increasingly desperate, he eventually destroyed all his guns, ammunition and baggage, and fled across the hills to Barcelona. Cutting a path through the blockading forces, he reached the city on 20 August with his divisions reduced to a starving, demoralised mob and incapable of further offensive operations.

The defeat at Gerona proved to be a turning point in Napoleon's conception of the situation in Catalonia. For some time, he had been preparing to reinforce Duhesme, and Reille's division had been intended as a first instalment. However, the rapid deterioration in

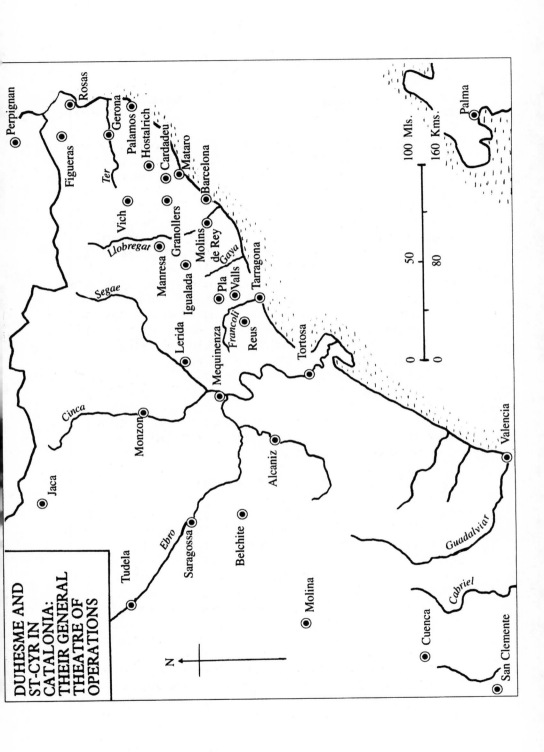

DUHESME AND
ST-CYR IN
CATALONIA:
THEIR GENERAL
THEATRE OF
OPERATIONS

N

Perpignan

Rosas

Figueras

Gerona

Ter

Palamos

Hostalrich

Cardadeu

Mataro

Barcelona

Vich

Granollers

Llobregat

Molins
de Rey

Manresa

Gaya

Igualada

Pla

Valls

Tarragona

Segae

Francoli

Reus

Lerida

Mequinenza

Tortosa

Cinca

Monzon

Alcaniz

Jaca

Valencia

Guadalviar

Ebro

Saragossa

Belchite

Tudela

Cabriel

Molina

Cuenca

San Clemente

Palma

100 Mls.

160 Kms.

50

80

0

0

the state of affairs convinced the emperor that many more troops and a more talented commanding officer were required to redress the balance. Accordingly, in late October, he dispatched General St-Cyr with a large force to the support of Reille's formations and, on 7 November, the new general opened his campaign by investing Rosas.

The fortress was manned by some 3,000 troops of varying quality, backed up by several Royal Navy vessels. At the sight of the advancing enemy columns, the garrison had evacuated the civilian population and prepared for a long struggle. However, once the French had their heavy guns in position, the fortunes of the defenders rapidly declined. Despite gallant efforts by the garrison, the besiegers made steady progress and a breach soon appeared in the fortress walls. On 26 November, Italian troops from St-Cyr's army stormed forward and established a foothold in the town from which they could not be dislodged. Although a second thrust by the Italians was contained, the defenders quickly began to lose hope and, with the siege batteries ripping the defences apart, the garrison launched a desperate sortie in an effort to take the French trenches. Repulsed with heavy losses, the Spaniards poured back into the fortress in utter disorder and, shortly after, capitulated. As the British flotilla hastened out of the bay, St-Cyr's troops occupied the battered stronghold, gathering in a rich booty of stores, guns and ammunition.

With Rosas under French control and the threat to his rear thus removed, St-Cyr was now free to press on to the relief of Barcelona. Leaving Reille with a strong division to guard the communications with France, he duly set out with 17,000 troops and by the second week of December had arrived at the fortress of Gerona.

This formidable stronghold completely commanded the highway to the south and thus posed a serious threat to St-Cyr's advance. However, the French general could ill afford to besiege the city if Duhesme was to be relieved in time. Accordingly, having failed to entice the garrison outside where he could deal them a decisive blow, St-Cyr sent his cannon and baggage back to Reille, and bypassed the fortress via mountain tracks. By the time the Spanish had discovered what had happened and were able to dispatch a column in pursuit, the French army had executed a brilliant forced march and, driving the local *somatenes* before them, were already emerging from the hills at Cardadeu.

The officer in overall command of the blockade of Barcelona, General Vives, had some 24,000 troops at his disposal, and was prosecuting the investment at a leisurely pace when he heard of the fall of Rosas and St-Cyr's subsequent advance. Although disturbed by these tidings the Spanish general was convinced that the enemy's army would be halted at Gerona, and it was 11 December before news arrived that the French had slipped past the fortress and were moving swiftly southward. Nevertheless, Vives seems to have remained complacent. Instead of moving the bulk of his ample forces against St-Cyr, he dispatched no more than General Reding's division to hold Cardadeu and stayed with the rest of his army before Barcelona. However, rapidly having second thoughts about this ill-considered move, he assembled another weak brigade and marched to Reding's assistance.

With this relatively paltry addition to the force near Cardadeu, Vives had no more than 8,500 infantry, 600 cavalry and seven guns to confront St-Cyr, when the French general attacked him on 16 December. The Spanish brigades were drawn up on a steep, wooded ridge in the Besos Valley and St-Cyr had some initial difficulty in determining their strength. Nevertheless, aware that there were other enemy units at hand – notably the Geronese column at his back – the French commander resolved to plough his way through Vives' corps before it could be reinforced. Confident that his troops could 'bulldoze' their way through any fire that their inexperienced opponents might deliver, he detached a division to guard his rear and formed most of his remaining 13,000 men into a solitary, gigantic column. The plan of attack was simple: the hostile line was to be ruptured at one crucial point, by a single sledge-hammer blow.

Although St-Cyr's tactics might appear crude, there was a good deal of sense behind them. The Spanish formations contained a high proportion of raw recruits and were dangerously susceptible to such blunt, psychological pressure. Moreover, the French divisions – lightly equipped for their rapid and difficult march – lacked significant ammunition stocks and were totally devoid of artillery, making a quick victory highly desirable. When the strategic situation is also taken into consideration, there can be little doubt that the French commander advocated the correct policy and, indeed, the initial fortunes of the assault were to illustrate this. In direct disobedience to his orders, the officer at the head of the column, General Pino, sought to deploy his battalions and attack on a broad front. His troops were repulsed, and it was only when a furious St-Cyr took personal control and reformed the impressive, narrow column that the Spanish line melted away and the French broke through. The Imperial cavalry swept in to complete the rout and Vives' troops fled in terror, sustaining over 2,500 casualties and losing most of their cannon. The French losses neared 600 men, mostly incurred in Pino's abortive assault.[66]

St-Cyr wasted no time in resuming his march to Barcelona. At his

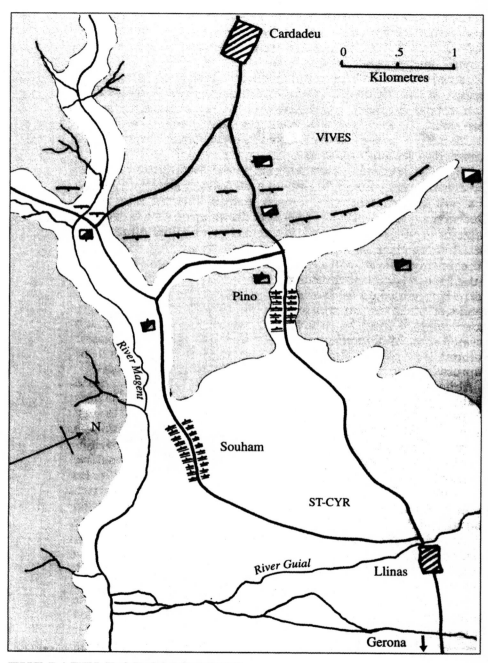

THE BATTLE OF CARDADEU,
16 December 1808

approach, the Spanish blockading forces fled across the Llobregat river and, on 17 December, the French relief column entered the city in triumph. However, having replaced Duhesme as Commander-in-Chief, St-Cyr did not dally in the fortress for long. As soon as he had replenished and strengthened the garrison, he took the bulk of his corps and set out in pursuit of Reding and Caldagues, who had concentrated some 15,000 men along the Llobregat near Molins de Rey.

Arriving before the enemy's position on 21 December, the French general located a number of places where his army could ford the river. With 18,000 men at his disposal, he decided to launch a diversionary attack with Chabran's division on the bridge at Molins de Rey, while the majority of his troops slipped over the shallows and turned the Spanish right wing. The plan worked well enough and Reding, hopelessly outmanoeuvred, was soon in retreat. However, Chabran failed to turn his feint into a full assault when his adversaries began to falter. Consequently, the Spanish army managed to escape complete destruction, although the French did capture all twenty-five of their artillery pieces, much of their stores and ammunition, and took 1,200 prisoners including General Caldagues.

There followed a period of recuperation and reorganisation for both armies. St-Cyr rightly judged himself too weak to tackle the mighty fortress at Tarragona, and busied himself collecting food-stuffs and equipment for his divisions. Reding, having superseded the inept Vives, was also fully occupied reconstructing his defeated and demoralised forces: he received reinforcements in the form of 6,000 regulars from the south and the Balearic Islands, and by February 1809 had a well-equipped and enthusiastic corps ready to take the field.

The Spanish commander immediately went onto the offensive. Leaving a strong garrison at Tarragona, he sought to move around St-Cyr's right wing, by dispatching General Castro's division to Igualada, on the Lerida highway. This manoeuvre extended Reding's army across forty miles of difficult terrain and St-Cyr quickly seized the opportunity to concentrate against just one of the widely-separated enemy columns. Marching with all speed from his central position, he fell on Castro with three divisions while a fragment of his army, under Souham, contained Reding's main force in the Gaya Valley.

The opening shots of the new campaign were fired on 17 February, as Chabot and Castro clashed near the little settlement of Capellades. At first, the weak French formation was driven back, but help soon arrived in the shape of the battalions of Pino and Chabran and, after a stiff fight, Castro's units recoiled in disorder. Nevertheless, the

Spanish general attempted to stand at the village of Puebla de Claramunt and a second struggle was in the offing when he heard that another French detachment, under General Mazzuchelli, had swept round his flank and was in full march for Igualada. Threatened with encirclement and anxious for the safety of his depots, Castro promptly retreated and only narrowly beat Mazzuchelli to Igualada. However, relentlessly pursued by the converging French columns, the Spanish army fell into ever greater confusion as it poured through the town and, despite Castro's efforts, many men and his divisional stores were captured by the enemy.

There followed a rather confused series of marches and counter-marches. St-Cyr had planned to transfer the bulk of his corps to Souham's wing and had already reached Villardona when he heard that Reding was moving to succour Castro. Alarmed for his new-found depot at Igualada, the Imperial commander was about to retrace his steps when fresh intelligence revealed that Reding – concerned that the French might penetrate between him and Tarragona – was nearing the Gaya Valley once again. With a clear chance of a decisive battle at hand, St-Cyr cancelled all earlier orders and resolved to intercept the enemy on his march: Souham was directed to sever the road at Valls, while Pino occupied the town of Pla, some nine miles to the north.

But, unfortunately for the French, Reding was in such a desperate hurry that he marched all through the night of 24 February and, at 6.00 the next morning, his vanguard arrived at Valls, catching Souham unawares. Despite their stubborn resistance, the heavily-outnumbered Imperial troops were gradually edged off the highway and Reding began filtering his forces across the River Francoli. However, the Spanish troops were tiring rapidly and the lethargic withdrawal was still under way when St-Cyr galloped onto the scene at the head of a cavalry brigade.

Convinced that he was about to be assailed in strength, Reding, rather than continuing his retirement, deployed his whole force, baggage and all, ready to fight a full-scale battle. Puzzled but delighted by his adversary's behaviour, St-Cyr readily accepted the challenge and rushed up every available unit. As the hours ticked by, he anxiously eyed the enemy positions, expecting the hostile masses to retreat. The Spanish, however, remained quietly on the Sierra Alta and by 4.30 St-Cyr had enough troops forward to launch an assault.

Reding had eight guns and over 11,000 men in a strong position overlooking the shallow Francoli and the 13,000 French beyond. Towards 5.00 pm, with cavalry between the infantry brigades, the Imperial formations crossed the river and began to ascend the

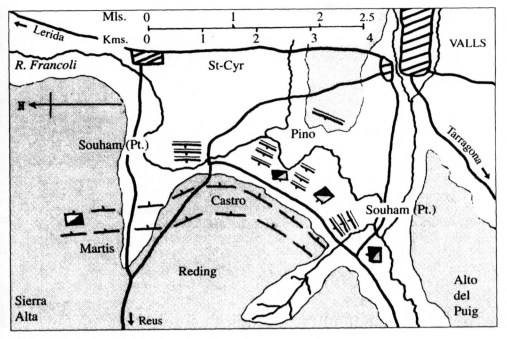

THE BATTLE OF VALLS, 25 February 1809

REDING'S ARMY:
Castro's Division:

Swiss Regt.	=	500
Granada Regt.	=	1,860
Santa Fé Regt.	=	2,300
Antequera Regt.	=	1,100
Total:	=	5,760

Martis' Division:

Walloon Guards	=	430
Castile Grens.	=	1,300
Baza Regt.	=	800
Soria Regt.	=	1,000
2nd Savoia Regt.	=	800
Palma Militia	=	350
Total:	=	4,680

Cavalry etc:

2 hussar reg's	=	700
8 guns	=	100
Total:	=	800

GRAND TOTAL = 11,240.

ST-CYR'S ARMY:
Souham's Division:

1st Léger		
42nd Line		
Misc.		
Total:	=	5,500

Pino's Italian Division:

1st Léger		
2nd Léger		
4th Line		
6th Line		
7th Line		
Total:	=	6,500

Cavalry etc:

Napoleon Dragoons		
Italian Chasseurs		
24th Dragoons		
Total:	=	1,200
12 guns	=	150
Total:	=	1,350

GRAND TOTAL = 13,350.

enemy's ridge. The defenders rapidly opened a heavy and well-directed fire, but the French – deployed in massive columns for maximum psychological effect – ignored their mounting casualties and, with cries of '*Vive l'empereur!*', pressed eagerly onward to close with the enemy. However, the long-awaited clash did not come. Increasingly overawed by the terrifying array of advancing bayonets, the Spanish battalions began to waver and retire. Finally, when the French were still many yards distant, the defenders' line shuddered, broke and poured back in headlong rout, sweeping away Reding's reserves as they did so.

The battle was lost before it had really begun, but the Spanish commander refused to acknowledge defeat. Placing himself and his staff at the head of a cavalry regiment, Reding led them forward in a desperate charge at the French 24th Dragoons. This gallant but rash attack was rapidly crushed by the Imperial troopers and only succeeded in adding to the Spaniards' humiliation: Reding himself was mortally wounded and nearly all the other senior officers were killed, disabled or captured. The rest of the stricken army fled towards Tarragona, but 1,500 men had been killed or wounded in the action and a similar number taken prisoner. All of Reding's guns, baggage and stores were also captured.

Having dealt the enemy a crushing blow, St-Cyr rested his weary men and attended to his 900 casualties before pushing onwards to Tarragona. However, lacking siege artillery and aware of an epidemic in the fortress, the French commander rejected vigorous offensive action and merely blockaded the city: cutting the roads at Valls and Reus.[67]

Thus, Tarragona, isolated from the interior, became a disease-ridden refuge for Reding's beaten men, while Gerona remained as a threat to the invaders' communications. Despite several major victories, the French generals had failed to subdue Catalonia and they now cried out to the emperor for more troops to finish the task. Thousands more men of both sides were to perish in this province before the struggle was over.[68]

Chapter IV

THE INTRACTABLE NORTH

I   Collapse at Cabezon

In Napoleon's grand scheme of May 1808, Marshal Bessières, Duke of Istria, was allotted the task of quelling the northern provinces. Bessières had 25,000 troops at his disposal, and he quickly moved against the insurrectionists in the Ebro Valley and Old Castile; one of his columns quashing resistance at Logrono, on 2 June. Meanwhile, General Merle led another detachment from Burgos to Santander and, after suppressing the rising as far as Reynosa, turned to deal with the potentially more dangerous rebellion at Valladolid.

Here, General Cuesta had gathered about 5,000 Spanish troops under the rather grand title of 'The Army of Castile'. Actually, this force had only four pieces of ordnance and, apart from 300 veteran cavalrymen, consisted entirely of inexperienced, inadequately trained volunteers. Nevertheless, the aged Spanish officer was determined to take the offensive and he moved east to cut the Burgos-Madrid road.

The first clash occurred at the bridge of Cabezon, where the Valladolid-Burgos highway crosses the River Pisuerga. Merle's detachment had united with another French force under the dashing Antoine Lasalle, who assumed overall command. Having concentrated some 9,000 men, Lasalle was preparing to advance against Cuesta when, much to his surprise and delight, the Spanish general rashly brought his forces over the river and offered battle. Prudence dictated that Cuesta should have remained on the far bank or, indeed, have destroyed the crossing altogether. However, he and his enthusiastic men were impatient to engage the invaders, irrespective of the circumstances under which they would have to fight. And they were dire: the only line of retreat lay across a solitary, narrow bridge, and Cuesta's 5,000 inexperienced men were no match for a disciplined force of professional soldiers nearly double their number.

On the morning of 12 June, Lasalle led his cavalry into the attack

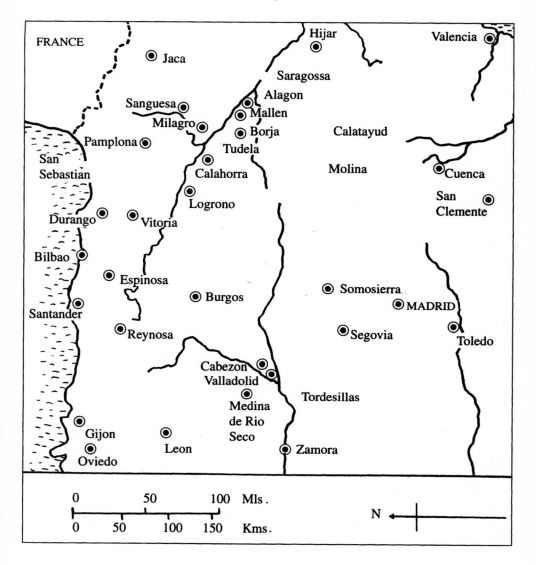

CENTRAL AND NORTH-EASTERN SPAIN

and, in a matter of moments, the long-awaited engagement was over. Predictably, the raw Spanish recruits were swept aside by the *beau sabreur* and his determined troopers. Unit upon unit was systematically broken, scattered and slaughtered. Pursued by the enemy horsemen, the pitiful remnants of the 'Army of Castile' streamed back across the Pisuerga river and along the highway to Valladolid. With his whole command ripped to tatters, Cuesta could offer no further resistance and, as Lasalle entered the city in triumph, the Spanish continued their flight to the west.

For a total casualty list of less than fifty men, Lasalle and Merle had completely routed their opponents and had secured one of the most important towns in northern Spain. Judging his own forces to be sufficient to retain the city, Lasalle sent his colleague to resume his anti-insurgent activities on the Biscay coast. Exhibiting considerable skill and moving with remarkable speed, Merle crushed the militia and armed peasants who attempted to bar his path and, sweeping through the defiles beyond Reynosa, eventually marched into Santander on 23 June. Within a month of opening their campaign, the French had established a position of apparent dominance over much of the north of the Peninsula. Stunned and demoralised by their recent defeats, a considerable time passed before the Spanish were ready to renew the conflict.

II The First Siege of Saragossa

Meanwhile, there had been some significant developments in Aragon. At Saragossa, the able Joseph Palafox was busy constructing an army around the few regular Spanish units in the area. By dint of almost superhuman efforts, he collected 7,500 new recruits, organised a munitions factory, enlisted numerous half-pay and retired officers, and imposed a general levy of horses for his cavalry and draught teams. However, he lacked seasoned soldiers, having no more than a weak volunteer battalion, a few sappers and gunners, and the 300 troopers of the 'King's' Dragoons – only a third of whom had horses. Furthermore, while there were plenty of cannons in Saragossa, the Spanish general could only provide trained crews for a handful of them.

Against this makeshift force, Bessières had dispatched General Lefebvre-Desnouettes with two batteries, 1,000 horse and 5,000 infantry. The first combat took place at Tudela, on 8 June, where Lefebvre scattered 2,000 levies and 3,000 armed peasants who had bravely barred his path to Saragossa. Retreating to Mallen, their commander, General Lazan, offered battle once more, only to be routed with terrible losses. In a final bid to keep the enemy at bay, Palafox himself moved north and put 6,000 men into line at Alagon. However, with only 150 cavalry, four cannons and 500 regular infantry to support them, his inexperienced conscripts were swiftly overwhelmed. Wounded and unhorsed, the Spanish general fled to

Saragossa with the bulk of his routed army. His adversary, meanwhile, continued his advance; arriving at the city on 15 June.

The situation confronting Lefebvre was not dissimilar to that which Moncey had faced at Valencia. Saragossa also stood on a plain, protected by a river to the north. Another river covered the east side, leaving only the south and west faces open to assault. The whole city was composed of closely-packed, sturdy buildings which lent themselves to defence, and was surrounded by an old wall, some twelve feet high. The garrison consisted of the forces retrieved from Alagon, plus around 5,000 armed peasants: about 11,000 men in all.

After his easy victories in the field, Lefebvre – like Moncey – assumed that a determined attack would easily overthrow any resistance. Accordingly, he directed his French infantry against the western walls of the city, while his Polish troops rushed the Santa Engracia Gate. In the meantime, his two batteries of ordnance opened fire on the numerous Spanish earthworks and a spirited artillery exchange was soon under way.

As the Polish cavalry swept through the Santa Engracia ingress, the French foot soldiers stormed into the buildings of Saragossa's western quarter. After a confused and bloody struggle which lasted several minutes, the Imperial infantry were finally ousted by their tenacious opponents and, retiring to a safe distance, regrouped to mount a fresh attack. The Polish horse, meanwhile, had recklessly charged into the heart of the city, suffering heavily from the small-arms fire that poured from every window. Their supporting infantry had fallen behind them and were inextricably locked in a murderous contest with the defenders of Santa Engracia. Unable to make any impact on the crowded, solid buildings, the Poles, too, had to retire and eventually joined their French colleagues in reforming outside the walls.

Unmoved by this sanguinary setback, the Imperial general again launched his men into the attack. This time, the French infantry breached the city's outer defences and broke through both of the western gates. On their right, the reorganised Polish regiments also returned to the fray but, encountering obstinate resistance, could barely penetrate beyond Santa Engracia. With every house bristling with muskets, and the narrow lanes barricaded and swept by Spanish cannons, the attackers made little headway and, after twenty minutes of furious fighting, were forced to retreat once more.

Unable to make any genuine progress, or, indeed, to retrieve his cannon under the withering enemy fire, the French general sullenly retired his battered units and awaited reinforcements. A fresh Polish regiment arrived on 21 June and other Imperial troops were close behind them. Nevertheless, Lefebvre's situation was rapidly

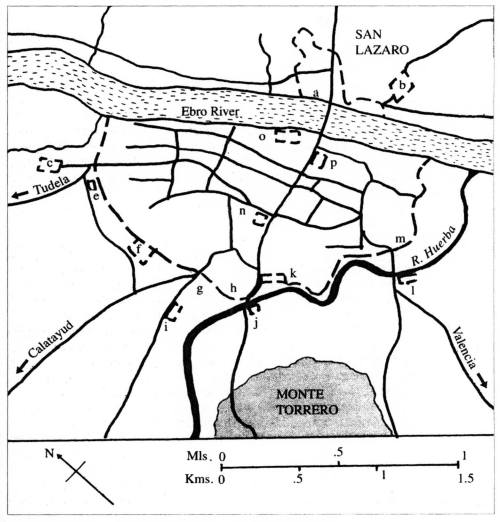

THE CITY OF SARAGOSSA AT THE TIME OF
THE PENINSULAR WAR

KEY

– –	=	City walls & principal buildings.	h	=	Santa Engracia Gate.
			i	=	Capuchin Convent.
a	=	San Lazaro Convent.	j	=	Pillar Fort.
b	=	Jesus Convent.	k	=	Santa Engracia.
c	=	Aljafferia.	l	=	San Josef Convent.
d	=	Portillo Gate.	m	=	Quemada Gate.
e	=	Augustinian Convent.	n	=	San Francisco Convent.
f	=	Trinitarian Convent.	o	=	Pilar Church.
g	=	Carmen Gate.	p	=	Cathedral.

deteriorating. Faced with the resolute Saragossans, he had lost around 700 men to no avail and now he learnt that a 4,000-strong relief column was moving towards the city, placing his communications in jeopardy.

The French general rose to the challenge. Taking the bold decision to maintain the siege with only half of his men, he led the remaining 3,000 in a pre-emptive strike at the advancing Spanish detachment. While the Saragossans were kept busy by feint attacks, Lefebvre slipped away and, surprising the enemy column, routed it with terrible casualties. Barely a quarter of the shattered relief force eventually trickled into the beleagured city, and even this tiny handful had to use circuitous routes and the relatively unguarded, northern suburbs as their means of entry. Meanwhile, the flow of Imperial reinforcements continued: General Verdier arrived with 3,500 men, followed by siege cannon and other units.

Replacing Lefebvre, Verdier got down to the task in hand. As an opening move, he evicted the 500 Spaniards defending the dominating hill of Monte Torrero and established his siege batteries along it. At midnight on 30 June, no less than forty-six pieces of heavy ordnance opened fire on Saragossa and, after twelve hours of continual bombardment, Verdier's infantry renewed the assault.

However, despite the tremendous havoc wrought by the besiegers' artillery, the defenders were as determined as ever. After a prolonged and bitter struggle all the French attacks were repulsed, with a total loss of around 500 casualties. Increasingly desperate, Verdier now resorted to all-out siege tactics. But with only 13,000 troops at his disposal he was unable to seal the city off entirely, and the Spanish maintained a flow of men and supplies with little difficulty.

Persevering, the Imperial commander pushed his batteries and trenches forward. Outlying buildings were taken despite fanatical resistance and, on 4 August, Verdier began a systematic bombardment of the city walls; silencing the enemy cannon and tearing several yawning gaps in the defences. Three assault columns now rushed the breaches; driving the Spanish back with horrifying losses, but steadily losing their own momentum. After fighting of the utmost ferocity – in which the French took about half of the city – the Saragossans counter-attacked at dusk, flinging their masses against the sturdy buildings occupied by Verdier's men. Units became trapped in isolated houses and little quarter was shown by either side. No less than 2,000 Frenchmen fell and the Spanish casualty toll was even higher. However, despite their immense losses, Palafox's men remained indomitable and by nightfall Verdier had lost all but a few disjointed sectors of the city.

As the fighting lapsed into a desultory fusillade across the corpse-strewn alleys and ruins, the French commander became increasingly disconsolate over the state of affairs both before him and elsewhere. News of the Baylen calamity arrived, and the inability of his hard-pressed forces to seal off the city, coupled with the advance of yet another Spanish relief column, convinced Verdier that the siege was lost. Using up his vast ammunition stocks in a remorseless bombardment, he finally ordered withdrawal on 13 August and, destroying anything he could not take with him, set out to rejoin his superiors.

Thus concluded the first siege of Saragossa. In the murderous struggle for control of the city, the Imperial army had sustained no less than 3,500 casualties, and the fact that all their efforts were in vain constituted a major blow to their prestige and martial reputation. However, the Spaniards' victory was bought at enormous cost. Amongst the military alone, fewer than half of Palafox's original 7,500 levies survived the ordeal, while the regular units and the innumerable small detachments that slipped through the French cordon from time to time also suffered appalling casualties. Needless to say, there were hundreds of civilian dead and wounded, too.

Palafox had rejected Verdier's demand for his surrender with the comment that this was 'War to the knife'. Apart from its sanguinary nature, however, Saragossa epitomised the nationalism that was sweeping across the Peninsula; it underlined that the French were at war not only with an army, but with the entire Spanish population.[69]

III   Medina De Rio Seco

While the battle for Saragossa was still raging, Cuesta had collected the remnants of his broken 'Army of Castile' at Benavente. To the 350 cavalrymen and three infantry battalions he was able to gather, he added three battalions of levies, but failed to provide a solitary cannon for his entire force. Nevertheless, the proud old man expected great things of his dispirited soldiers and still favoured open battle with the French, despite Cabezon. He called on the *Juntas* in Galicia and the Asturias to send him forces for a fresh advance on Valladolid, whose recapture, he argued, would pose a serious threat to the enemy's communications with Madrid and would incite mass risings throughout northern Spain.

The Asturias sensibly refused to have much to do with Cuesta and his dubious schemes and, to keep him quiet, they sent him a token force of two weak battalions of recruits. The Galicians, on the other hand, directed their considerable army, under General Blake, to join in the Valladolid venture. They had some 25,000 men under arms with more in training and, although Blake favoured waiting for the French to come and attack him in the hills, his superiors decreed otherwise and, reluctantly, he marched to join Cuesta.

Cuesta insisted on taking supreme command of the two Spanish forces and, whilst Blake managed to persuade his colleague to leave a division in reserve, his warnings that, with only thirty cannon and 1,000 horse, they were too weak to confront the French in the open fell on deaf ears. Adamant that Valladolid would be the objective, Cuesta set the army in motion on the morning of 12 July.

Warned of the Spaniards' advance Marshal Bessières hastily assembled a field army to challenge this latest threat. His divisions were widely scattered, and he had to maintain many garrisons as well as the siege at Saragossa. Nevertheless, by calling up every available unit in the close vicinity of his headquarters, the Duke of Istria concentrated a force of no less than 14,000 troops, 1,200 of whom were cavalry. The soldiers ranged in quality and experience from Imperial Guardsmen to conscript and provisional formations but, supported by forty pieces of ordnance, they were a formidable contingent nonetheless and marched with remarkable celerity to try conclusions with Cuesta.

The two armies clashed near Medina de Rio Seco in the early hours of 14 July. Cuesta and Blake fielded 21,000 infantry, 600 cavalry and twenty guns – drawing them up in a bad position, with insecure flanks and a poor line of withdrawal in the event of a retreat. Cuesta's appalling tactical dispositions aggravated the situation: his forces were split into two portions, with a vast gap between them. General Blake commanded the foremost section, while his superior lingered with the second contingent, many yards to the rear. This glaring hole in his opponent's line immediately drew Bessières' attention and he resolved to strike through it; pinning down Cuesta's units while he enveloped and crushed the Galicians. Accordingly, he told off the single division of General Mouton to contain the enemy's northern wing, while the bulk of the Imperial army, supervised by the marshal himself, executed the main assault.

Supported by a heavy barrage from a twenty piece battery on the Monclin Mound, Bessières' left began a cautious attack on Blake's position; Merle's troops steadily edging westwards to outflank and envelop the Galician line. The Spanish general responded as best he could, keeping up a lively fire with his few artillery pieces and repeatedly extending his forces further to the right in a desperate effort to keep the enemy at bay. Whilst all this manoeuvring was still going on, Mouton had commenced his pinning attacks against Cuesta's distant battalions and soon the Spanish commander-in-chief was completely embroiled in the petty skirmishing to his front,

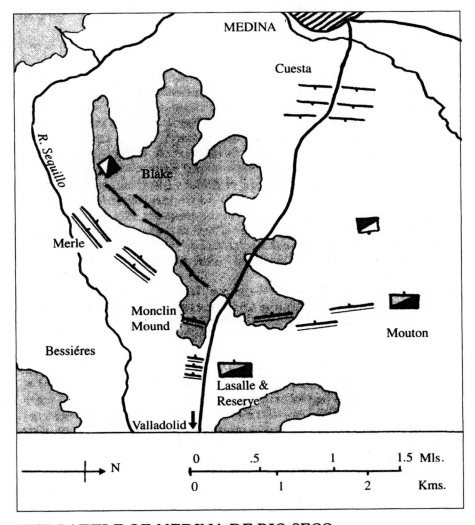

THE BATTLE OF MEDINA DE RIO SECO,
14 July 1808

SPANISH FORCES:
21,000 infantry
   600 cavalry
   300 artillery etc
─────
21,900 men & 20 guns.

FRENCH FORCES:
12,200 infantry
 1,200 cavalry
   600 artillery etc
─────
14,000 men & 40 guns.

leaving the hard-pressed brigades of Blake isolated and unsupported.

Bessières' plan was working perfectly and he wasted no time in implementing the next phase. From their position in reserve on the Valladolid highway, the massed squadrons of Lasalle's light cavalry galloped forward and swept into the yawning gap that separated the two halves of the Spanish army. Simultaneously, Merle's infantry began to press home their frontal assaults and the gunners on the Monclin Mound redoubled their efforts; every salvo ploughing bloody furrows in the hostile formations. Assailed by horsemen on their open left flank and with enemy infantry overrunning their supporting artillery, the bulk of Blake's command suddenly broke ranks and fled westwards in the most frightful disorder. Pursued by the triumphant Imperial cavalry, the wing was saved from complete destruction solely by the heroic efforts of a Navarrese battalion who, despite appalling casualties, covered the retreat of their broken comrades and held off the enemy until the panic-stricken masses had crossed the Sequillo river.

Having dealt Blake's divisions a decisive blow, the French now turned on Cuesta. Forming a new line and bringing up his remaining reserves, Bessières advanced to complete his victory before the Spaniard could retire across the Sequillo. However, although that was doubtlessly his best available course of action, Cuesta had no intention of retreating. Deploying his leading battalions into columns, the Spanish general sent his men forward to assail the enemy's right and centre. Although some grenadiers did gain a momentary success over the middle of Bessières' line, the outcome of this uphill assault against a numerically stronger force of elated troops was hardly in any doubt. Overlapped on each flank, the Spanish were caught in a withering crossfire, plunged into disarray and routed. Ordering two battalions to cover the retreat, their commander fled to Medina. His own wing had suffered relatively lightly, but Blake's formations had lost over 3,000 men and all their artillery. Bessières' casualties, on the other hand, totalled 500 at the most.

The Duke of Istria, however, quickly halted the pursuit. His troops had been marching and fighting from 2.00 am until midafternoon, and he was reluctant to go too far beyond the Sequillo. This was, perhaps, a serious error. A vigorous follow-up must have culminated in a Spanish defeat of catastrophic proportions. Nevertheless, the French had effectively eliminated the threat of a large-scale attack on the communications between Bayonne and Madrid and, his route secured, the 'Intrusive' King Joseph was able to travel to the latter place in relative safety. However, his triumphant stay was short-lived. News of the Baylen disaster and disquieting reports from Portugal led to the invaders abandoning the capital on 1 August. Within a few days, all the troops they could extricate were retiring to adopt a defensive stance along the line of the Ebro river. The initial illusions of conquest were utterly shattered and several years of bitter warfare lay ahead.[70]

Chapter V

BRITAIN INTERVENES

I Junot in Portugal

Following the May risings in Spain, General Junot's shaky position
in Portugal began to deteriorate further. The Spanish troops that had
joined him in invading the country either deserted or had to be
imprisoned to prevent them doing so, and although a general
Portuguese rebellion had been avoided so far this was only because of
the lack of means for one: the civil authorities were collaborating
with the French, the military had been disbanded, and the people
needed weapons and leaders before they could resist the invaders.
Apart from the dubious support of the Portuguese civil administration, the Duke of Abrantes, isolated from the Imperial forces in
Spain, had only one source of potential aid: namely Admiral Siniavin's Russian naval squadron. But, though technically a French ally,
Siniavin was decidedly cool and, although he offered to fight any
British fleet that materialised, he refused to provide men for even the
most mundane land operations. Thus, Junot found himself with only
26,000 French soldiers to hold down a country of 30,000 square
miles which threatened to burst into revolt at any moment.

Inevitably, this loose grip on the country could only grow weaker,
and when, on Godoy's orders, General Belesta withdrew his Spanish
forces from northern Portugal, rebellion broke out across the region:
a 'Supreme *Junta* of the Kingdom' was formed under the Bishop of
Oporto; the militia was re-established and mobilised; regular units
were reconstructed and masses of enthusiastic peasants flocked to
join a new national army.[71] Most significantly, the *Junta* appealed to
Great Britain and Galicia for aid.[72]

The British had sustained some serious reverses in sending small
expeditionary forces to assist various risings against France and her
allies – notably in Holland in 1799 and at Buenos Aires eight years
later. The only feasible means Britain had of striking at Napoleon's
empire was with her navy and, as in later wars, faced the problem of

trying to oppose what was essentially a land-based power, largely immune to naval attack. Napoleon's venture into the Peninsula, however, gave Britain the opportunity to commence a war on the continent that would exert a continual drain on French resources and create the possibility of a two-front scenario. It was an attractive proposition for British generals and politicians who had rejected such policies in the past and were reluctant to go beyond limited aid. The national nature of the Peninsular rising and the stalemate in the maritime conflict secured the necessary change in their attitudes, and both Opposition and Government united in granting assistance to the Iberians: troops, equipment and money were sent to aid the rebels[73] whilst, as an opening gesture, the Royal Navy dispatched a fleet to rendezvous with General La Romana's 'hostage' corps at Gothenburg. The operation was an outstanding success and, soon, these 15,000 Spanish troops were on their way back to their motherland to join the struggle.

Meanwhile, the Portuguese rebellion had spread to the southern provinces. French columns detached to assist Dupont and Bessières in Spain had to be recalled and, with British units threatening to land at any moment, Junot began to concentrate his scattered forces. At the end of June, he garrisoned the fortresses of Almeida, Elvas and Peniche, fortified Setubal and concentrated the bulk of his army at Lisbon. Ominously, some isolated units had difficulty in extricating themselves from their former positions as the country rose around them. But the lack of weapons prevented the Portuguese from putting many organised regiments into the field and, although General Loison's forces in the north were severely harassed, the majority of Junot's army regrouped without serious loss.

Having massed 25,000 troops about Lisbon, Junot detached 7,000 men to quell the insurgents west of the Guadiana river. This column, commanded by General Loison, arrived at Evora on 29 July and routed a force of 3,000 men. After sacking the town, Loison went on to defeat the peasants defending Elvas and was about to take Badajoz when he was recalled to the capital. Sir Arthur Wellesley had landed at Mondego Bay with a British expeditionary force and the Duke of Abrantes was hastily preparing for battle.

After Trafalgar, Britain's unchallengable naval might and his series of wars in Central Europe had compelled Napoleon to abandon any plans to invade England, and as the danger of invasion receded the British found themselves in a stronger position to help the Iberians than they had been for some years. The Spanish revolt had curtailed any renewal of action in Argentina – releasing 9,000 men – and Castlereagh's army reforms provided for 40,000 militia to be promoted to regular status every year; their places being taken by volunteers.[74] More units were withdrawn from the Baltic and the Mediterranean, providing a further 15,000 troops. Thus, 40,000 men could be spared for service in the Peninsula. However, there were severe shortages of mounted troops and no organised supply system, and although Wellesley tackled the latter problem with some success he made little impression on the cavalry shortage, fielding only 400 troopers alongside 18,000 infantry.

On landing at Mondego Bay, Wellesley heard the welcome news of Dupont's capitulation at Baylen and, later, General Spencer arrived with units drawn from the Mediterranean. Everything seemed to be going reasonably well. However, logistical problems soon marred this state of affairs and several days had to be spent in trying to organise a commissariat for the army. Eventually, a somewhat inadequate train of wagons and carts was patched together, but horses and draught animals remained in short supply and, indeed, sufficient teams for only three of the five artillery batteries could be provided. The remaining cannons, along with 200 precious cavalry troopers who had no mounts, had to be left at Mondego. Nevertheless, Wellesley resolved to take the offensive immediately and, on 9 August, the Allied forces of one Portuguese and six British brigades set out down the coastal highway towards Lisbon.

Wellesley soon encountered General Delaborde's French division which was slowly withdrawing towards Lisbon, seeking to buy time for Junot to complete his concentration. Administering a sharp rebuff to the pursuing British rifles near Brilos, Delaborde retired in good order to Rolica, where he deployed his division and offered battle on 17 August.

Originally, Delaborde's command had consisted of less than 6,000 troops with five cannon, but by the time he reached his chosen battle position this figure must have diminished. Several units, including a whole battalion of Swiss troops, had been deployed as garrisons, and he had suffered casualties from sickness and skirmishes. Against the 4,000 men he is estimated to have fielded at Rolica, Wellesley could bring 13,000 British and 2,000 Portuguese, backed by eighteen guns.

Hoping to outflank and envelop the enemy's position, Wellesley advanced his forces in a broad arc with the wings pushed forward. However, at the last moment, the hostile line suddenly executed a planned withdrawal, avoiding the British snare. Falling back with great skill, the French took up a new position a mile behind the first one, compelling Wellesley to attempt his pincer movement yet again. Unfortunately for the British general, however, his centre failed to await the development of the outflanking manoeuvres and surged into the attack. Delaborde greeted them with great professionalism,

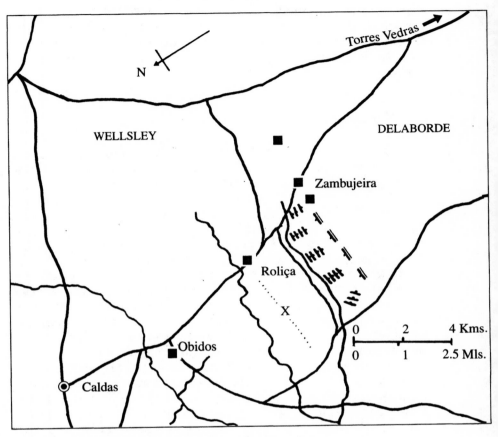

THE ACTION AT ROLICA, 17 August 1808.

X = Delaborde's initial position.

employing the same concealment tactics Wellesley himself was to use so successfully in the coming years. For two hours, Hill and Nightingale's brigades struggled to get forward, but could make little progress. Time and again, they bravely fought their way to the crest of Delaborde's ridge, only to be attacked whilst deploying and swept back down the slope.

However, Sir Arthur's numbers eventually began to tell and, as the flank attacks started to close in, Delaborde decided it was time to leave. Again, he executed a perfect withdrawal – his cavalry and alternate infantry battalions brushing off the disordered enemy skirmishers – but, on reaching the pass behind Zambujeira, he found it too cramped to hastily evacuate all his command and lost three cannon and some prisoners to the Allies. Nevertheless, he had not done badly. Not only had he accomplished his aim of buying time for Junot to concentrate, he had also occupied and defied a corps of four times his strength for an entire day and had inflicted 500 casualties.

II Vimiero and the Cintra Convention

Abandoning the pursuit of Delaborde, Wellesley moved on Vimiero, uniting with some 4,000 British troops who had just landed. Meanwhile, an increasingly despondent Junot continued to regroup. With the recall of Loison, the Alemtejo insurgents had risen again and were threatening the Tagus estuary. A fresh column had to be dispatched to crush them, whilst the Duke of Abrantes, fearful for the safety of Lisbon, deployed a further 7,000 men – one third of his army – to guard the city. Failing to realise that Lisbon's fate ultimately rested on the outcome of his approaching battle with the British, he allowed this geographical feature to dominate his strategy and neglected to gather every available resource for a decisive engagement. Not only was this bad in itself but, as the city's garrison was drawn from several field units, the policy also severely disrupted the organisation of the forces destined to fight at Vimiero.

On the evening of 15 August, Junot marched all his available units on Villafranca. Confusion as to the enemy's location caused some countermarching but, by the Eighteenth, Junot had learnt that Delaborde was at Montechique and Wellesley was near Vimiero. Although Delaborde was some way off and his own command was rather strung out, Junot resolved to attack as soon as he had reorganised his army. Keeping his cavalry in a single body, he divided the infantry into two divisions and formed a reserve of grenadiers by merging the various regimental companies into battalions. Adding 700 gunners and train troops with twenty-three cannons, he disposed of around 14,000 men – 4,000 less than Wellesley.

At dawn on 21 August, Junot's divisions finally arrived in front of the Allied army. Wellesley's defensive position was immensely strong, but lacked a suitable escape route should he have to retreat. Retrograde movements, however, were far from the British general's mind. Prior to Junot's arrival, he had himself been preparing to advance, and readily offered battle.

The Allied corps was deployed along a chain of hills which ran from south-west to north-east. Vimiero lay in the right centre, in the Maceira Valley, with steep, rugged gradients to the south. The

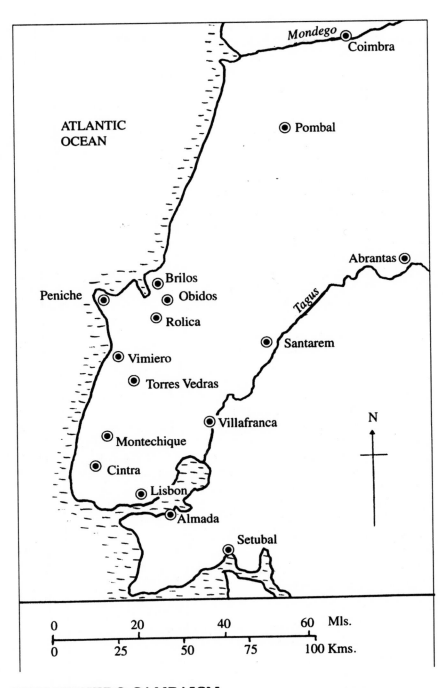

THE VIMIERO CAMPAIGN:
THEATRE OF OPERATIONS

slopes to the north of the settlement were more gentle, but a ravine running along the eastern edge of the mountain chain presented a severe obstacle to the French as far north as Ventosa. Just to the south of Vimiero itself lay an isolated hill which Wellesley regarded as the key to his line and, indeed, was to be the site of some extremely heavy fighting.

The British general, expecting Junot to attack the right wing, had concentrated the bulk of his men there. After a hasty reconnaissance, however, Junot rejected the idea of an assault up such daunting slopes and resolved to make his main effort against the isolated mound near Vimiero, whilst other units turned Wellesley's left. Accordingly, Brennier's brigade of 3,000 men and the 600 troopers of the 5th Provisional Dragoons were sent north to outflank the British position. Meanwhile, the remainder of the French army massed before Vimiero.

From his elevated command post, Wellesley soon fathomed the enemy's intentions and shifted his brigades accordingly; weakening his right to strengthen the left and centre. Junot, in turn, noticed the British manoeuvres and, fearing that Brennier would be overwhelmed, detached Solignac's brigade to his support. This left only two brigades, the grenadier reserve and 1,400 horsemen to assault Vimiero itself – less than 8,000 troops in all. Neglecting to wait until his flanking movement had begun to take effect, Junot lunged at the enemy's centre immediately with the four-and-a-half battalions of Thomières and Charlot's brigades. Advancing in three-deep lines, but with one battalion behind another, the French infantry came steadily onwards, their *voltigeurs* preceding the columns. Directly before them, guarding the isolated mound near the village, were the British brigades of Fane and Anstruther, screened by the terrain and with a dense mass of light troops protecting their front. The French officers could see little of their adversaries' position and the *voltigeurs*, heavily outnumbered, made slow progress. However, despite the stiff resistance of the British light companies and a well-directed fire from twelve guns, the Imperial formations rolled inexorably forward. Collecting at a hedge part way up the hill, they charged and drove the hostile skirmishers back, obliging Anstruther to detach several more companies to extricate his riflemen.

This had only just been accomplished when Thomières' attack fell on Fane's units; the two leading battalions striking the somewhat extended 50th Foot and inclining to their right as they did so. Seizing the opportunity, the right-hand companies of the 50th swung forward, firing into the enemy's exposed left flank. Attempting to direct retaliatory fire at this new threat and simultaneously maintain their forward momentum, the French battalions degenerated into a

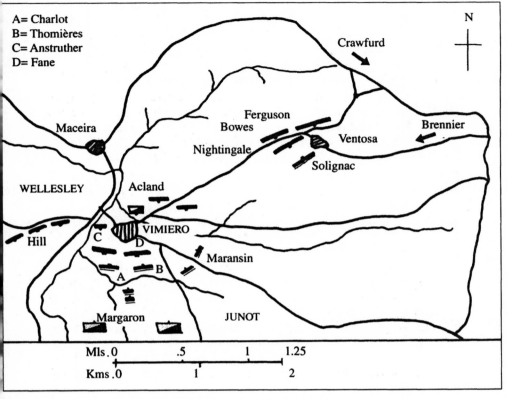

BATTLE OF VIMIERO, 21 August 1808

FRENCH ARMY

Division Loison:
Brigade Charlot (2 batts)
Brigade Solignac (3 batts)
Total = 4,140 men.

Division Delaborde:
Brigade Brennier (4 batts)
Brigade Thomières (2+ batts)
Total = 5,720 men.

Grenadiers (4 batts)
Total = 1,350 men.

Cavalry (4+ Regs)
Total = 2,000 men.

Artillery etc.
Total = 700 men

GRAND TOTAL = 13,910

BRITISH ARMY

Hill's Brigade (3 batts)	= 2,658
Ferguson's (3 batts)	= 2,450
Nightingale's (2 batts)	= 1,520
Bowes' (2 batts)	= 1,813
Crawfurd's (2 batts)	= 1,830
Fane's (3 batts)	= 2,000
Anstruther's (4 batts)	= 2,700
Acland (3 batts)	= 1,330
Trant (Portuguese)	= 1,750
Cavalry (Port.)	= 250
Cavalry (Brit.)	= 250
Artillery etc.	= 230
GRAND TOTAL	= 18,781

confused mass. Finally, when their supporting artillery panicked and drove their teams back through their own infantry, the whole body collapsed and fled back down the slope in terrible disorder.

In their attack on Anstruther's units, Charlot's men enjoyed little success either. Indeed, the whole affair was over in a matter of minutes. Whilst they were held at bay by a series of crashing salvoes from the 97th Foot, the 52nd Foot slipped round their left flank and poured in a devastating volley. Assailed from two sides, the French rapidly broke and retreated, abandoning their artillery to the enemy.

The first attack having been repulsed with serious loss, Junot drew on his grenadier reserve; sending two battalions forward. They promptly came under a devastating fire from at least three enemy battalions and twelve guns, and officers and men fell by the score. Hopelessly outnumbered and with their formation shot to pieces, the gallant grenadiers stubbornly pushed forward for some distance. But it soon became clear that the attack was doomed to fail, and after twenty bloody minutes they recoiled in confusion.

Junot, however, had not yet finished. Although the last two assaults had failed miserably, he now sent his two remaining battalions of grenadiers forward in a futile attack on Vimiero itself. Anstruther, threatened by this move, sent the 43rd Foot to engage the left of the French column while, simultaneously, General Acland brought down four companies and two guns from the northern ridge to assail the enemy's right. After a bitter struggle, including a good deal of bayonet fighting, the grenadiers were evicted from the village and joined the rest of their forces in retiring. Seeing the enemy faltering, Colonel Taylor led out the 500 Allied cavalry to pursue the broken, hostile infantry. However, quickly intercepted by Margaron's troopers, his whole force was utterly routed. Taylor himself was killed and a large percentage of his men also failed to return. After this sanguinary check, Wellesley's units were reluctant to press their advantage any further and the French were able to complete their withdrawal, covered by their powerful cavalry.

As the last moments of the battle about Vimiero were being played out, Junot's flanking movement was just coming into operation. General Brennier had marched further and further north, seeking a passage over the ravine which guarded the British ridge. In the meantime, Solignac had found such a crossing point and had started west, emerging near Ventosa. Unaware that the main engagement was already lost and that his own operations were now meaningless if not dangerous, the French general dutifully began his flank attack. Advancing blindly against the concealed troops of Bowes, Ferguson and Nightingale, he had little chance. His three battalions suddenly found themselves confronted by seven British, who were supported by a further two brigades. Shot down by the converging fire of the enemy regiments, the French broke ranks and fled, abandoning their three cannons. Solignac, badly wounded, could do little to stem the rout.

As the British were chasing his colleague's shattered units, Brennier's forces finally emerged from the ravine. His four battalions charged and scattered the 71st and 82nd Regiments, and even recaptured Solignac's guns. However, the Imperial general could not hope to maintain himself in the midst of several enemy brigades for long and eventually the French retreated into the ravine, covered by their cavalry. Brennier himself was wounded and taken, and his troops, expecting to be pursued, abandoned the cumbersome artillery to their foes.

Actually, the British were not in pursuit. After only two-and-a-half hours the battle was over and the French were everywhere in retreat. Certainly, a vigorous follow-up would have caused more severe damage, for Junot had only ten guns still in action, plus his cavalry, and two battalions belatedly summoned from Lisbon. Why the British did not advance was puzzling to men on both sides, but they were not to know that a change of command had occurred at the Allied headquarters.

Sir Harry Burrard had arrived to take over the expeditionary force. Although he had landed earlier, he had been content to leave the conduct of the battle to Wellesley. However, once the engagement was won he refused to let the army go onto the offensive, insisting that Junot had a hidden reserve and that his cavalry was too powerful. He also made some valid points regarding the appalling logistical situation and the lamentable condition of the Allied cavalry and artillery. Rightly or wrongly, he refused to go on and the battle ground to a halt. For a total loss of 720 men, Wellesley's forces had inflicted nearly 2,000 casualties on their opponents and had captured thirteen guns. Even without a pursuit, it was a victory they could be proud of.

A despairing Junot retired, unmolested, gathering the fragments of his broken divisions. It was now obvious that he could not hope to keep a French presence in Portugal, for he faced an all-out rebellion by the population, supported by a substantial, victorious British army. He could get no assistance whatsoever out of Admiral Siniavin, and with Spain in revolt there was no hope of reinforcements from across the border.

Accordingly, Junot sought terms from the allies. Anxious to secure Portugal without further ado, the British negotiators conceded virtually all the French demands in return for Junot's total withdrawal from the country. Thus, under the so-called Convention of Cintra, the 'Army of Portugal' was shipped back to France by the Royal Navy – much to the annoyance of Wellesley and the Portuguese.

The French evacuation began on 13 September and within seven weeks all their forces had left the country. They carried off large quantities of loot to which they laid claim, however dubiously, under the Convention, often stretching the agreement to its limits. Of course, such behaviour only served to antagonise the Portuguese further and there were some ugly scenes on the quayside as the French departed.

Out of a total force of 30,250 Imperial troops sent to Portugal, 25,747 were evacuated: between 2,000 and 3,000 having been killed and the rest (mostly Swiss and Germans) having deserted.[75] Thus, Junot succeeded in returning over 25,000 fully armed men to Napoleon – a remarkably high figure under the circumstances. However, he had not seen the last of Portugal. Within a couple of years he was back, trying conclusions once again with the victor of Vimiero.[76]

Chapter VI

THE FRENCH RESURGENT

I Back to the Ebro

We have now seen how the first French attempt to conquer Spain had ended in virtually total failure: a remorseless struggle was under way in Catalonia; Dupont had been annihilated in Andalusia; Moncey had been repulsed at Valencia and, whilst Bessières had gained some considerable victories, Saragossa had not fallen, nor had the north been pacified. The Battle of Baylen, however, proved the crushing blow to the invaders' schemes and, when the rumours of the disaster were confirmed, the French relinquished their shaky grip on the interior and, on 1 August, began to withdraw to the line of the Ebro. Still more bad news followed. With Junot's defeat at Vimiero on the Twenty-first and the signing of the Cintra Convention, Portugal went the way of Spain and, by mid summer 1808, it seemed that the Imperial forces had only narrowly escaped being swept from the entire Peninsula.

Napoleon was both amazed and infuriated by this series of reverses – not to mention the damage they did to his prestige in Europe. Already, Austria – encouraged by Baylen and burning to avenge the defeats and humiliations of former years – was making threatening noises and another war in Central Europe seemed likely. Anxious to conclude the conquest of the Peninsula at the earliest opportunity, the emperor drew up elaborate instructions for Joseph to implement. However, he soon discovered that by the time such missives arrived the situation had changed so much as to render them completely obsolete. Deciding that only he, at the head of a vast army, could redeem the position, Napoleon directed 130,000 troops to leave Germany for Spain immediately and, having devised various contingency plans for use in the event of a war with Austria, reaffirmed his alliance with Russia and left for the Peninsula, reaching Bayonne on 3 November.

Meanwhile, events in Spain had moved at a leisurely pace. King

Joseph and his dispirited army waited on the Ebro for the expected enemy onslaught, but it failed to materialise. The French, most of the Spanish leaders felt, were now a spent force and the tedious task of hustling them back over the Pyrenees was one that could wait until more important matters had been dealt with. Only General Castaños had the wisdom to see that the invader was far from defeated but, disregarding his calls for mobilisation and re-armament, his colleagues persisted in their complacent state of mind and turned their attention to the conduct of internal power struggles.

Consequently, it was a full thirteen days after the French evacuated the city before the Spanish army's vanguards finally marched into Madrid, and then more time was wasted in lengthy altercations over the future constitution of the state and whether a Commander-in-Chief should be appointed to co-ordinate the military forces of the various provinces. After days of heated debate, which highlighted the intense rivalries and prejudices that existed between the *Juntas*, it was agreed that a supreme, Central *Junta* would be established at Seville. The important question of the nomination of a Commander-in-Chief, however, was not resolved and, when hostilities were resumed, the armies of the various regions continued the struggle in their independent, rather haphazard manner.[77] This lamentable state of affairs persisted until the autumn of 1812 when, despite the opposition of several Iberian generals, Wellington was finally appointed to the post.

II   Imperial Intervention

It was the end of August before sufficient Spanish forces had lumbered forward to exert much pressure on the French at all. Even then, the operation undertaken – an attack on Milagro, with a view to an advance along the Ebro – was performed in such a feeble manner that the French easily beat it off and concluded that it had been meant as nothing more than a diversion. Three weeks passed before there was any fresh activity and, this time, it was at Reynosa, the other end of King Joseph's line, where General Blake had mustered 32,000 Galicians and Asturians.

Ignoring calls to cooperate with the *Juntas'* other forces, Blake advanced on 10 September with the intention of taking Bilbao, rousing Biscay and enveloping the French right wing. Ten days later, his vanguard captured the city, and Joseph's Chief-of-Staff, Jourdan, responded by ordering more troops to the upper Ebro where they united with the first of Napoleon's reinforcements from Germany.

THE GENERAL STRATEGIC SITUATION AT
THE START OF NAPOLEON'S OFFENSIVE

Leading 10,000 men in a counter-stroke, Marshal Ney dislodged the Galician vanguard from Bilbao and drove them back. However, unwilling to risk a battle with Blake's entire army, he left 3,000 troops in the town and returned to the Ebro; taking up a position opposite General Pignatelli's 10,000 Spaniards at Logrono. Further along the river, at Lodosa and Calahorra, were two more Iberian divisions, totalling 15,000 men, with a further 7,000 troops under General Llamas at Tudela. This whole force of around 30,000 bayonets and 3,000 sabres formed Castaños' 'Army of the Centre'. To the east, about Sanguessa, General O'Neille threatened the Imperial left with two divisions of the 'Army of Aragon'.

The opposing formations now studied each other for days. The French were busy reorganising their units and consolidating their compact position while awaiting the emperor and the reinforcements from Germany. The Spaniards, meanwhile, instead of trying to strike quickly before Napoleon and his vast forces arrived, wasted time formulating staggering schemes for a Baylen-like encirclement of Joseph's entire army. No sooner had they begun the preliminary manoeuvres for this outrageous plan than Ney launched a surprise, limited attack on Pignatelli, whilst Moncey struck at the Spanish about Lodosa. Pignatelli's green recruits routed without firing a shot, and Moncey annihilated two battalions of enemy infantry as his forces overran Lodosa and captured its bridge. Having been dealt a serious blow, Castaños abandoned his encirclement scheme and regrouped toward Tudela, distributing Pignatelli's demoralised troops among his other divisions.

Meanwhile, Blake had retaken the offensive in Biscay. Faced by overwhelming numbers, General Merlin evacuated Bilbao on 11 October and retired to Durango where he was reinforced and offered battle. The Spanish commander now detached nearly 11,000 troops to guard against any French descent from around Vitoria and, after procrastinating until late October, resumed his advance. However, Blake discovered that Merlin's sparse force had been replaced by three whole divisions under Marshal Lefebvre and that Marshal Victor's corps was also marching up to threaten his right flank. The two French commanders were under strict orders from Napoleon not to take offensive action until he gave the signal,[78] but Lefebvre could not resist having a crack at his adversaries. Attacking suddenly, he thrust Blake back but, unable to catch his opponent's main body, sullenly retired to Bilbao – unwittingly releasing the 8,000-strong Spanish right wing he was unaware he had trapped in the mountain passes. As they dashed for the safety of their principal force, Blake launched a counter-attack to cover their withdrawal and, in the ensuing fighting, the tail of Lefebvre's retiring corps was

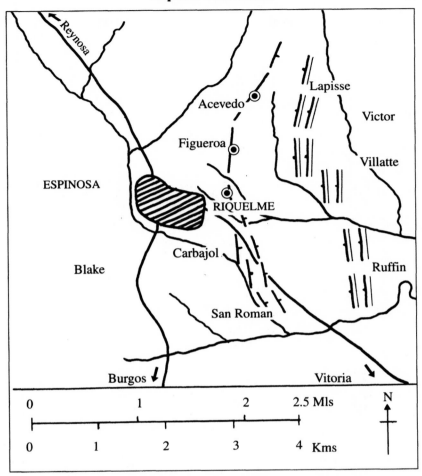

THE BATTLE OF ESPINOSA, 11 November 1808

roughly handled by the converging hostile columns. Infuriated, the Duke of Danzig hurried his divisions back to rescue his rearguard and, joining with Victor, set out in pursuit of the retreating Galician army.

When the Spanish commander finally halted, at Espinosa, to confront the pursuing marshals, his forces had been whittled down to less than 23,000 men with six cannon. On 10 November, Victor's vanguard probed the strong enemy position, but was beaten off after a gruelling, two-hour fight. Reinforced by the arrival of more of his corps, the Duke of Bellune tried again in the late afternoon, but was repulsed once more. However, the next day, instead of assailing the

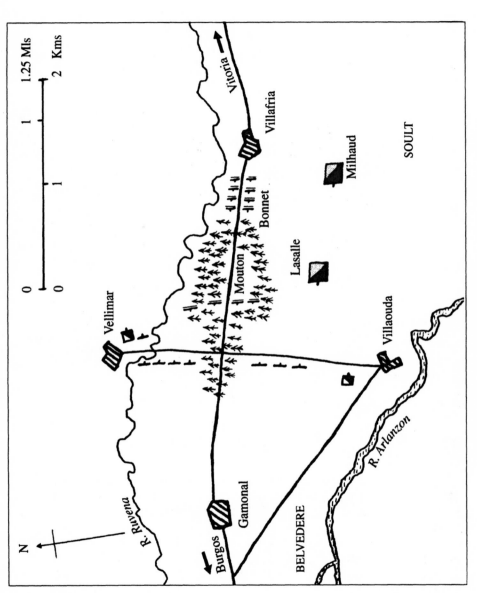

THE BATTLE OF GAMONAL, 10 November 1808

enemy's centre and right as before, he turned their left and then launched a frontal assault. The result was decisive. Blake's left flank crumpled before the onset, and Victor's cheering troops rolled up and routed the whole Galician line. When the Spanish general finally rallied the fugitives at Reynosa, he had but 12,000 exhausted men with no artillery. The French had sustained about 1,000 casualties, mostly on 10 November.

In the meantime, Napoleon had amassed sufficient forces to open his grand counter-offensive. After weeks of patiently waiting behind the Ebro, the Imperial hounds were unleashed and they surged forward in search of their quarry. On 10 November, Marshal Soult, who had superseded Bessières as commander of the II Corps, marched for Burgos at the head of the French army. This central column was to threaten Madrid, while other units peeled off to the right and left to envelop Blake's Galicians in the north and Castaños' 'Army of the Centre'.

Soult soon encountered Belvedere's Spanish divisions, drawn up across the highway at Gamonal, and, using a large wood for cover, moved forward 5,000 cavalry and two infantry brigades. Taken completely by surprise, Belvedere's right and centre were engulfed by the enemy horse before they could form square. Five of the Iberian battalions were trampled down immediately and the rest were swept from the field. General Lasalle then wheeled his troopers into the rear of the Spanish left wing, while Mouton's infantry charged their front. Assailed by the converging Imperial units, that formation, too, was utterly broken and fled down the road in the wildest confusion. In this short but sanguinary episode, Belvedere's army was effectively destroyed; losing over 2,500 dead and wounded, 1,000 prisoners, twelve standards and all its ordnance. Soult's casualties totalled a few dozen men.

With Burgos secure, Napoleon began the vast strategical manoeuvre he had planned. As his cavalry fanned out over the plains of Old Castile, Soult set out for Reynosa to cut Blake's retreat and Ney was dispatched to encircle the 'Army of the Centre'. Seeing the enemy pincers closing around him, Blake jettisoned his few remaining pieces of equipment and plunged into the mountains, exhorting and cajoling his famished men over the rugged terrain. He eventually reached Leon with a 'half-starved and straggling mob, without officers and all mixed in utter confusion'. The *Junta*, however, was not impressed and promptly replaced him with General La Romana.

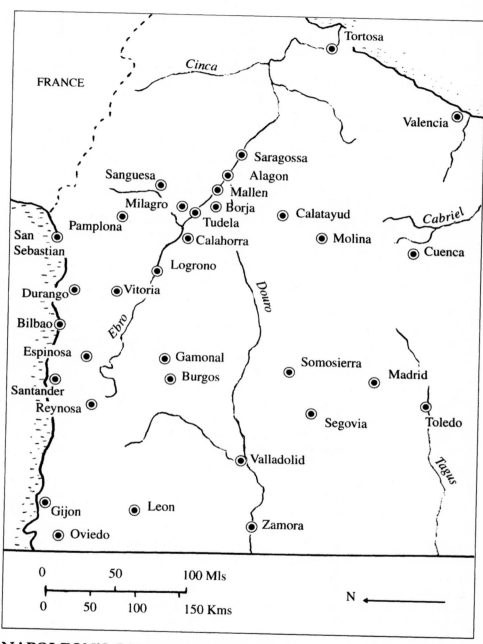

NAPOLEON'S COUNTER-OFFENSIVE:
THEATRE OF OPERATIONS

III Tudela

As the operations in the north drew to a satisfactory conclusion, Napoleon, moving with his customary flexibility, turned his attention to the destruction of the 'Army of the Centre'. Leaving Soult to pacify Biscay and complete the rout of Blake's fleeing divisions, he summoned Victor's corps to Burgos, where 20,000 Imperial troops were already poised to advance on Madrid. Then, anxious to strike before Castaños could react to the changing strategic situation, the emperor immediately ordered the III Corps across the Ebro to pin the 'Army of the Centre' to its current position. Simultaneously, Marshal Ney's units continued advancing eastwards and by 23 November were descending on Castaños' rear.[79]

Separated from Blake by dozens of miles – and, now, by thousands of Imperial soldiers – Castaños was unaware that his army was in dire peril. Following the French attack on Lodosa and the subsequent dismemberment of Pignatelli's division, the Spanish commander had withdrawn to Tudela to adopt a defensive stance. However, on 5 November, the Supreme *Junta* overruled his objections and directed him to resume the offensive immediately. Any hope of formulating an effective strategy was rapidly lost as *Junta* political 'observers' repeatedly interfered with the plans of their military colleagues: one scheme after another was commenced and then abandoned. Thus, the 'Army of the Centre', already thinned by dysentery and exposure, exhausted itself in pointless marches.

Suddenly, on 21 November, the arguments at Castaños' headquarters ended with the news that the French III Corps was astir and that another Imperial force (Ney's) was marching against the army's rear. Moving to evade the closing trap, the Spanish commander retired to a defensive position which stretched for over six miles from Tudela towards the settlement of Cascante. Judging his 26,000 men to be an insufficient force to hold the line, Castaños called on the Aragonese for support. After lengthy bickering, Palafox belatedly ordered General O'Neille's two divisions to join the right of the 'Army of the Centre'. O'Neille, however, executed his march too slowly and, on 23 November, when the French appeared before the Tudela position, only Castaños' own troops were in their battle stations and much of the front was completely undefended.

Marshal Lannes, who had overall command of the Imperial forces, found himself confronted by a clearly unfinished line of battle. His cavalry reported Spanish troops at Cascante and Tudela, but the intervening countryside was unoccupied by enemy soldiers. Resolving to contain the Iberians' left wing while striking at their right, the French commander divided his army into two portions: the first,

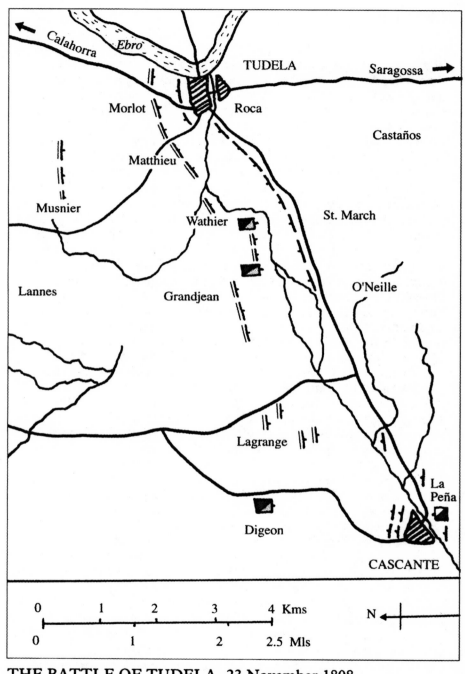

0	1	2	3	4 Kms
0		1		2	2.5 Mls

N ←

THE BATTLE OF TUDELA, 23 November 1808

consisting of the entire III Corps, marched along the highway to Tudela; the other, comprising two cavalry brigades and Lagrange's division of the IV Corps, moved against Cascante. Neither of the Imperial columns encountered any resistance, for, although Castaños disposed of some 3,000 cavalry, he had neglected to post a single picket to observe the French or warn of their advance.[80]

Thus, as Wathier's cavalry arrived within yards of Castaños' position, the Spanish commander was still busy hurrying O'Neille's divisions across the Ebro in an effort to close the yawning gap between La Peña's troops at Cascante and the forces about Tudela. Suddenly, the battle erupted. Without pickets to alert them to the enemy's advance, the Spaniards were taken by surprise and a fierce struggle ensued for control of the heights above the town. In the preliminary skirmishing, the attackers confirmed the existence of the huge gap separating the two wings of the Spanish army and Lannes was duly informed. Frantically, Castaños sought to fill this void; ordering La Peña to move across and urging Grimarest to bring up his distant division. However, the former general simply ignored his commander's directives, whilst the latter, out of sight of the field, moved far too slowly to be of any assistance.

Making full use of the knowledge he had gained, Lannes sent in a second attack that proved decisive. Morlot's division stormed the heights before them and proceeded to drive the broken opposition through Tudela and down the Saragossa road. Simultaneously, O'Neille's troops were assailed frontally and on their wide-open left flank. Falling into ever greater disorder, the hastily assembled Spanish line was finally ruptured by a cavalry charge at its centre; the French troopers wheeling to take the shattered battalions in the rear. Unable to withstand this onslaught, the whole wing quickly collapsed and fled; leaving 4,000 casualties and twenty-six guns littering the Tudela plain.

Meanwhile, having ignored his chief's frantic pleas, La Peña had frittered his time away in petty bickering with the few enemy troops before him. When Lagrange's infantry division arrived to support the cavalry spearhead, the French still only mustered some 9,000 men in this sector of the field – to which La Peña and Grimarest could easily oppose 20,000 troops. However, the Spanish commanders contented themselves with watching the discomfiture of the rest of Castaños' army and, after losing 200 men in their desultory skirmishing with the enemy's light troops, beat a hasty retreat in the direction of Borja, bringing the battle to an ignominious end.

Fortunately for the 'Army of the Centre', Ney failed to come up to seal their fate from behind. Marching 120 miles in six days over appalling roads, he arrived just too late to intercept the Spaniards' retreat. Nevertheless, Tudela was a significant French victory and, together with Espinosa in the north, brought Napoleon's great double envelopment to a successful climax.[81]

IV Napoleon at Madrid

The emperor, at the head of 45,000 men, resumed his march to Madrid on 22 November. Comforted by the success of the manoeuvres in the north and east, he pushed on to the Somosierra Pass, which he found defended by some 9,000 troops, hastily gathered together by General San Juan. The Spanish corps was an extemporised formation, consisting of units of the 'Army of the Centre' left by Castaños in the capital, and a hotchpotch of odd battalions, volunteers and levies. Nevertheless, strongly entrenched at the head of the pass, they constituted a formidable barrier to the French advance and the task of dislodging them was obviously going to be a tedious affair.

Toiling up the lateral slopes of the valley to turn the flanks of the hostile formation, Ruffin's division had only just commenced this operation when the emperor, irritated by the delay, turned to his escort squadron – eighty-seven Polish horsemen – and ordered them to take the position for him with a frontal attack. This they unquestioningly attempted to do, but, charging up the narrow highway in column, they were swept by the fire of sixteen cannon and practically wiped out. As the remnants of this heroic little band limped back down the hill, Ruffin's infantry finally came into action and, seeing the enemy line begin to waver, Napoleon immediately sent forward Montbrun with 1,000 more cavalry. Crumbling before this properly co-ordinated assault, the Spanish managed only a few wild shots before abandoning their cannon and taking to their heels; leaving the pass to their victorious adversaries.[82]

The last obstacle in their path having been removed, the French continued their drive on Madrid and, arriving at the city on 1 December, found a hastily improvised defence being mounted by a few hundred regulars and hordes of armed peasants – all entertaining hopes of emulating the heroes of Saragossa. However, the lack of physical defences and the overwhelming might of the Imperial forces soon convinced the capital's dignitaries that serious resistance was impossible.[83] Once a French division had established a foothold in the city suburbs and a vast battery had appeared on the dominating position of the Retiro Heights, the *Junta* quickly sued for terms.

The remnants of the Spanish field armies were quite incapable of preventing the fall of Madrid, although certain units did endeavour to try. General San Juan's two divisions made a feeble advance from Sergovia on 2 December, but, on hearing of the capitulation, mutinied and fled without having encountered a solitary enemy soldier. Their rout continued for sixty miles, during which time they abandoned their equipment and lynched their commander, supposedly for treason.[84] La Peña, retiring west after his disgraceful behaviour at Tudela, also tried to intervene but, hotly pursued by Ney, was intercepted by the I Corps and driven off towards Cuenca. Thus, the capital remained firmly in the emperor's grasp.

Once master of Madrid, Napoleon proceeded to violate many articles of the capitulation and busied himself with social and political reforms. Several liberal and valuable measures were introduced, but were resented as the imposed decrees of a conqueror. His laws dealing with the Church were singularly unpopular – being seen as attacks on religion itself, in a country that was staunchly Catholic – whilst the reinstatement of King Joseph and the imposition of an oath of allegiance on his unwilling subjects only antagonised the Spaniards further.[85]

Of course, Napoleon was also preparing to complete his conquest of the Peninsula. By mid-December, 40,000 Imperial troops had collected at Madrid and more were on the way – notably Junot's VIII Corps, who had recently arrived from France following their repatriation by the Portuguese. While Soult, with 17,000 men, was to quash the remaining pockets of resistance in Old Castile and Leon, Marshals Lefebvre and Victor were to ready themselves to move against Lisbon and Seville respectively. For the time being though their divisions were to be rested, and they duly went into camps to the south and east of the capital.[86]

However, Napoleon's calculations were about to be rudely disrupted. After spending weeks mustering a large army at Lisbon, the British were again astir and were destined to change the whole face of the coming campaign with a dramatic advance into the heart of the Peninsula.

Chapter VII

THE BRITISH CAMPAIGN IN SPAIN
1808–9

I The March to the Douro

After Sir Harry Burrard and his immediate successor, Sir Hew Dalrymple, had hastily concluded the controversial Cintra Convention with the French, the British government, horrified by the public outrage it caused, recalled the officers involved to face a court of enquiry.[87] With Burrard, Dalrymple and Wellesley all away, the command of the army in the Peninsula passed to Lieutenant General Sir John Moore, who had arrived at the end of August 1808 from the Baltic.

Moore took up his post on 6 October, and orders shortly arrived for him to advance into Leon with 20,000 men and assist the Spanish in any way he thought prudent. A second British column, 12,000 troops under General Sir David Baird, was also to take part in the campaign; landing at Corunna in order to rendezvous with Moore near Valladolid. Accordingly, leaving 10,000 men to garrison Lisbon and other strategic points in Portugal, Sir John set out for Salamanca in the middle of October.[88]

However, the transport and logistical problems that bedevilled all armies in the Peninsula soon plunged the British commander's calculations into confusion. Moore and his staff were remarkably ignorant of the geography of the country they were to cross, and little useful information could be extracted from the Portuguese. Mistakenly believing the direct road to Salamanca through Coimbra unsuitable for heavy traffic, Sir John dispatched all his artillery, train and cavalry on a circuitous 400 mile journey through Badajoz, Talavera and Escurial. They were not to arrive in Salamanca until 3 December, three weeks after the infantry.

Meanwhile, Baird, too, was having appalling difficulties getting his contingent to the rendezvous point. Having made a belated landing at Corunna on 26 October, he was horrified to discover that the Spanish authorities were unable to offer even the crudest logistical support for the offensive he was about to undertake. Thus, more precious time was wasted as the British general, greatly irritated by the indifference and ineptness of his Iberian allies, dispatched commissariat officers to comb the surrounding countryside for mules, oxen and carts. By dint of their efforts, a minimum number of transport vehicles and draught animals were eventually cobbled together and the army was, at last, able to begin its advance. Nevertheless, the execrable Galician roads – worsened by the deteriorating weather conditions – rapidly reduced Baird's progress to a crawl and, by 22 November, his toiling columns had penetrated no further than Astorga.

Moore was, meanwhile, having second thoughts about the campaign. Ever since Sir John had arrived at Salamanca, the tidings of Napoleon's grand offensive had been percolating through and, by the end of November, the British commander had heard of the rout of Blake at Espinosa, the annihilation of Belvedere's 'Army of Estremadura' and the destruction of Castaños at Tudela.[89] With the French expected at Madrid within the week and the Spanish field forces apparently irremediably shattered, it seemed that the situation was already hopeless and that for the British to advance further into the Peninsula would be tantamount to committing suicide. Painfully aware that he had custody of his country's only disposable army, Moore was unwilling to take any excessive risks and, rejecting the entreaties of the Supreme *Junta*, reluctantly ordered a withdrawal to Portugal.

Nevertheless, no sooner had Sir John's army set out for Lisbon than fresh dispatches from the east caused him to undergo a change of heart. Firstly, 5 December saw the arrival of encouraging news from Madrid. Apparently, the population of the capital had been infected with the spirit of Saragossa and were offering determined resistance to Napoleon's besieging army. The same day, a letter arrived from La Romana at Leon, in which the Spanish general assured his British ally that he had rallied Blake's defeated divisions and was ready to take the field with 23,000 reliable men.[90] On the basis of these pieces of information, Moore, now with cavalry and artillery at his disposal, resolved to strike a blow at the French communications with Burgos and thus oblige the enemy to relinquish their grip on Madrid. A captured dispatch – revealing the isolation of Soult's scattered II Corps – convinced Sir John of the feasibility of the scheme[91] and, in mid-December, he set out to implement it; marching north with 21,000 bayonets, sixty-six guns and 2,500 sabres.

The proposed manoeuvre was a potentially lethal undertaking, but Moore was aware that, occasionally, war called for a spot of calculated gambling. However, much of the information on which his strategy was based was incorrect: Madrid had surrendered to Napoleon on 4 December and, secondly, the emperor's army in the Peninsula – understood by Moore to be barely 80,000 strong – was nearer three times that figure. Although by 11 December he had received the gloomy tidings of the fall of the capital and odd snippets of information regarding Napoleon's strength also came his way, Moore was never fully alerted to the sheer size of the Imperial forces before him and, thus, the innate dangers of his plan were greater than even he realised.

The news of Madrid's surrender rendered the original objective of Moore's strategy obsolete. Nevertheless, judging that an attack on the French communications could still seriously disrupt Napoleon's offensive – by drawing the emperor's attention away from Andalusia and Portugal – the British general decided to maintain his advance against Soult. Accordingly, the redcoats crossed the Douro at Zamora and Toro and, on 20 December, finally united with Baird's detachment.

The next day, the British opened their attack on Soult's unsuspecting units with a raid on his foremost picket. Surprising a group of Imperial cavalry at Sahagun, General Paget's horsemen caught the enemy in the act of forming up and, in a trice, virtually annihilated two squadrons. However, while Moore allowed his men a forty-eight hour rest, fugitives from the broken French picket fled to their main body. Warned of the imminent danger to his scattered formations, Soult wasted no time in sending to the emperor for reinforcements and ordering the immediate concentration of his corps.

Actually, Napoleon was already hurrying northwards. He had been aware of the presence of Moore's army at Salamanca for some time, and had been able to make a good deal of capital in the propaganda sphere out of the manner in which the 'perfidious islanders' seemingly stood and watched whilst their Spanish allies were being slaughtered. However, by 19 December, the emperor had been warned that Sir John's formations were astir and, apparently, moving towards Valladolid. Instantly realising what Moore had in mind, 'Le Petit Caporal' saw a golden opportunity to swing into the British general's rear, while Soult contained him frontally. With any luck, the hostile divisions would be completely encircled and, with one crushing blow, Britain's precious Peninsular army would be destroyed.

Roused into action by this exciting possibility, the emperor dictated reams of orders to his headquarters' staff. The expeditions to Lisbon and Seville were to be temporarily shelved, and every unit

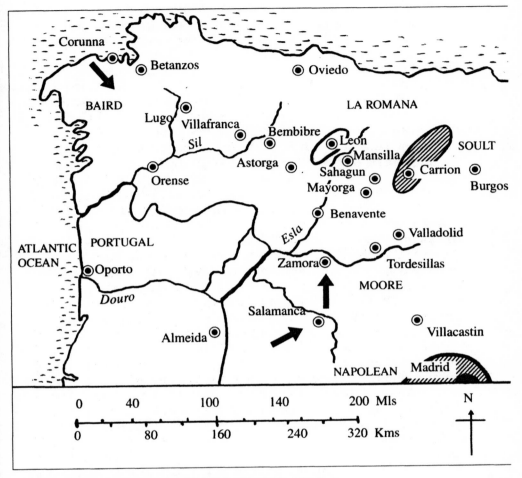

MOORE'S CAMPAIGN IN SPAIN, 1808–9:
THE THEATRE & INITIAL DISPOSITIONS

not needed at Madrid was to be committed to the destruction of the
insolent British intruders.[92] Within hours, Ney's VI Corps was
spearheading the advance of some 80,000 Imperial troops towards
the Guadarrama Pass and by the evening of 23 December, having
forced his way over the mountains in appalling weather, Napoleon
was leading his frozen divisions through Villacastin. Thinking that
Moore's communications stretched back from Valladolid through
Tordesillas, the emperor now believed himself to be in a commanding strategic position; thousands of his troops being poised to fall on

the British rear at first light.[93] Although Moore's march to the Douro had clearly lured Napoleon away from the south of the Peninsula, it remained to be seen if the British general could avoid the rapidly closing French pincers.

But the emperor's calculations were based on inaccurate information. Moore's army was actually a good deal further north than the Douro Valley and, on the afternoon of 23 December, was completing its preparations for the attack on the regrouping French II Corps. The British general had resolved to open his assault at dawn on 24 December. However, only hours before the scheduled attack, disquieting reports that Napoleon was rushing north began to arrive at the British camp. Realising that the 'bubble had burst', Moore turned his advancing columns around and, leaving his cavalry to screen his withdrawal, went into headlong retreat for Corunna.

Slowly but surely, the true nature of the situation became more evident to Napoleon and, wheeling his divisions onto a north-westerly course, he hurried his men forward to cut his adversary's line of retreat across the River Esla. Meanwhile, Soult – realising that he was confronted by no more than a few cavalry – joined the emperor in the so-called 'race for Benavente'. By this time, however, the first British column, under Baird, was already crossing the Esla at Valencia de Don Juan and Moore himself was within a few miles of Benavente. Although the French cavalry maintained a remorseless pursuit of the retiring redcoats, they proved unable to stop the enemy reaching the safety of the latter place and arrived just in time to see the last of Moore's units filtering across the river. Spurring after them, Lefebvre-Desnoettes led part of the Guard cavalry across the Esla and, after some success over the British pickets, was outflanked by the 10th Hussars and vigorously attacked. Outnumbered, breathless and disordered, the *chasseurs* were swept back over the river, losing seventy prisoners including Lefebvre-Desnoettes himself.

After this episode, the pace of the hunt slackened somewhat and Moore slipped away quite easily, although there were signs of growing indiscipline in his formations. However, General La Romana – who had advanced to aid his ally – lost half his force of 3,000 men in a disastrous engagement at Mansilla on 30 December, and was compelled to relinquish Leon and 2,000 wounded to Soult the following day. In the last hours of 1808, he joined the British at Astorga, where the Spanish column was described as having 'More the appearance of a large body of peasants, driven from their homes, famished and in want of everything, than a regular army.'[94] Amid scenes of terrible suffering, the retreat of the Allied forces continued.

Sensing that Moore had escaped destruction and that this wild-goose chase was leading the Imperial forces far into the Galician mountains, Napoleon left the conduct of the pursuit to Soult and, taking the bulk of the army, returned to Madrid. However, news of political intrigues at Paris and that Austria was mobilising sufficiently alarmed the emperor to make him hand control of his Peninsular affairs to King Joseph. Within a month, '*Le Tondu*' was safely back in the Tuileries, preparing for a fresh confrontation with the Hapsburgs.

Soult, meanwhile, dutifully maintained the pressure on the retreating Anglo-Spanish forces in Galicia; his 25,000 infantry and 6,000 horsemen hounding them across increasingly difficult terrain, in deplorable weather. Everywhere, the Imperial cavalry encountered evidence of the enemy's mounting demoralisation: the road was littered with abandoned wagons and other equipment; and scores of stragglers, sick and wounded were captured at every turn. At Bembibre, the French dragoons rounded up hundreds of drunken British troops and, at Villafranca, Moore's deserters were found to have looted their own army's depots. While the British divisions were bent on reaching Corunna where the Royal Navy was to evacuate them, La Romana's command had no such haven to run to. Accordingly, as they neared the Sil river, the Allied armies separated; the Spaniards heading for Orense. Although primarily interested in destroying Moore's redcoats, the Duke of Dalmatia was not prepared to let La Romana slip away unmolested: Franceschi's troopers duly fell on his rearguard at the Foncebadon Pass, hacked down scores of their fleeing opponents, and took another 1,500 prisoner.

Over the next few days, most of Moore's army degenerated into a rabble as mounting demoralisation, cold and hunger took their toll. The continual forced marching killed off even the toughest veterans, whilst *matériel* – ranging from wagons to the military chest – was abandoned. All that stood between the frost-bitten, tattered redcoats and the 'Duke of Damnation' – as they had dubbed him – was Paget's rearguard, whose comparative order amongst the confused masses about them was conspicuous. These brave regiments fought a series of stubborn defensive actions to buy time for the broken army to withdraw in safety; checking the pursuing French at Cacabellos, Lugo and Betanzos. Thanks to them, Moore's corps reached Corunna late on 11 January.

Like those in Dunkirk in May 1940, the British forces in Corunna were in dire peril; trapped, with their backs to the sea and with little of their discipline left intact. However, much of Soult's army was still strung out over the Cantabrian Mountains and the prospect of assailing such a strong position – defended by British soldiers, who were renowned for their tenacity – was hardly attractive to the marshal. Notwithstanding these considerations, he did feel obliged to make some effort to incommode his opponent and began to collect his scattered divisions for an assault. However, the appearance of the long-expected British transport fleet and the evident destruction of Moore's stores – notably the detonation of 4,000 barrels of gunpowder which, even from three miles away, shattered every window in Corunna – convinced Soult that his adversary's escape was imminent and, realising that he could delay no longer, he resolved to attack on 16 January. The sight of the Imperial army taking up positions for an engagement came as no surprise to Moore, and he earmarked some 15,000 infantry and twelve guns to cover the embarkation.

II Corunna

The corner-stone of Moore's selected battle position was the Monte Moro, just outside Corunna. Although it was overlooked to the south by the ridges of the Palavea and Penasquedo Heights, and was bounded on its northern side by an area of open ground, it was a formidable line nonetheless and Sir John was confident that he could hold it in the coming engagement.

The first clash occurred on 15 January when, as a preliminary move, Soult drove the British outposts from the Palavea and Penasquedo plateaus, and began to cannonade the main enemy position. An attempted counter-attack by the 5th Foot was repulsed with considerable loss and the French formations continued deploying, unmolested, across the rugged terrain. The significance of the relative weakness of Sir John's right flank was not lost on the Duke of Dalmatia, nor, indeed, on the British themselves. 'The right had a bad position; yet, if we lost it our ruin was inevitable',[95] noted one Highlander. Accordingly, the French marshal planned to turn his opponents at this their weak spot, whilst containing their centre and left wing. By noon on 16 January, the Imperial forces were in position and, at 2.00 pm, Soult's principal battery opened fire on Elvina.

Supported by a heavy artillery bombardment, Mermet's division surged forward and fell on Bentinck's brigade in the British right-centre. Moore's light troops were quickly evicted from Elvina and the French promptly opened a two-pronged assault; eight battalions advancing up the slopes beyond the village, whilst others wheeled to assail Bentinck's right. Detaching one regiment to face this threat to his flank, Bentinck, under Sir John's supervision, led the 50th and

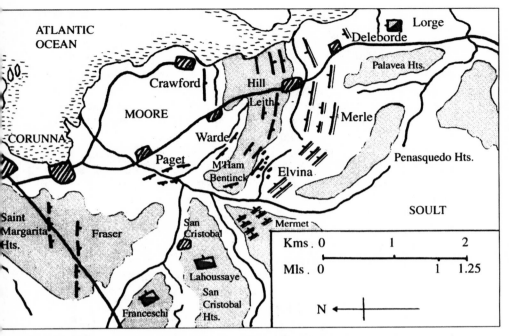

THE BATTLE OF CORUNNA, 16 January 1809

SOULT'S ARMY:

Div. Merle
2nd Light (3 batts)
4th Light (4 batts)
15th Line (3 batts)
36th Line (3 batts)
TOTAL = 6,200 men

Div. Lahoussaye
4 dragoon regts.
= 1,600 men

Artillery
500 men with 36 cannon.

Div. Delaborde
17th Light (3 batts)
76th Line (4 batts)
86th Line (3 batts)
4th Swiss (1 batt)
TOTAL = 5,500 men

Div. Lorge
4 dragoon regts.
= 1,600 men

Div. Mermet
31st Light (4 batts)
47th Line (4 batts)
122nd Line (4 batts)
2nd Swiss (2 batts)
3rd Swiss (1 batt)
TOTAL = 7,500

Div. Franceschi
3 light & 1 dragoon regts.
= 1,300 men

GRAND TOTAL = 24,200

MOORE'S ARMY:

1st Div. Baird
1st Foot Gds. (Warde) = 2,000
1, 26, 81 Ft. (Manningham) = 1,600
4, 42, 50 Ft. (Bentinck) = 1,500

3rd Div. Fraser
6, 9, 23, 43,
38, 79, 82 Ft. = 2,600

Artillery
200 men with 12 cannon.

2nd Div. Hope
36, 71, 92 Ft. (Crawford) = 2,000
51, 59, 76 Ft. (Leith) = 1,600
2, 5, 4, 32 Ft. (Hill) = 2,000

Reserve Div. Paget
20, 52, 95,
28, 91 Ft. = 1,500

GRAND TOTAL = 15,000

42nd forward and waded into the enemy above Elvina. A brilliant charge drove Soult's men from the settlement, but they reformed and turned on the pursuing 50th, routing them and inflicting grievous casualties. Nevertheless, Moore refused to be ruffled and, calmly rallying the fugitives, brought up two Guard battalions to sustain the hard-pressed 42nd. After a further period of bitter confrontation, the French finally recoiled into the village and thus, albeit with some difficulty, the ridge to the north of the settlement remained under British control.

In spite of this reverse, the French persevered; keeping up a galling fusillade from inside the village, while their artillery fire played havoc with the enemy's line. Moore himself fell – mortally wounded by a round shot – and for some time the struggle continued to be desperate. However, throwing in units of Warde's and Manningham's brigades, the redcoats eventually began to make progress. Thrusting into the streets of Elvina, they were constantly joined by still more reinforcements and, after an interval of furious bickering, Mermet and Merle finally relinquished their grasp on the settlement.

Meanwhile, towards San Cristobal, Lahoussaye's cavalry and elements of Mermet's division had moved forward to contain the British units about Corunna. Making slow progress over the difficult terrain, they were eventually confronted by Paget's formations; who proceeded to hold them at bay with musketry salvoes. Likewise, on Lahoussaye's left, Franceschi's troopers found Corunna itself protected by Fraser's brigades, and were also halted and driven back. The action along this part of the front gradually deteriorated into a petty fusillade and, as the lengthening shadows told of the approaching night and Soult's principal attack force went into retreat, the French containing columns also retired.

With the repulse of the Duke of Dalmatia's main thrust and the withdrawal of his pinning attacks, the battle slithered to a halt. 800 British and perhaps 1,400 French had fallen. Sir John Moore died within minutes of the end of the fighting and a magnanimous Marshal Soult later erected a memorial to mark the grave of one of Britain's greatest soldiers. On Moore's death, General Hope assumed control of the expeditionary force and successfully concluded the evacuation of Corunna. Eventually some 26,000 battered men were safely returned to England; many of them too sick to take up arms ever again.[96]

Despite the victory at Corunna and the fact that Moore's bold venture had – as hoped – utterly disrupted Napoleon's plans for the conquest of the Peninsula, the whole affair was dismissed as a catastrophe. Over 7,000 men had been lost on the expedition and Britain's only field army had been jeopardised. As Canning had once warned Moore: 'You will recollect that the army which has been appropriated by His Majesty to the defence of Spain and Portugal is not merely a considerable part of the dispensable force of this country. It is, in fact, the British army.'[97] That army now lay in ruins.

With the apparent failure of the expedition, the triumph of Vimiero faded and, once more, doubts were expressed as to the wisdom of the 'interventionist' policy. That Moore's campaign had irretrievably shattered Napoleon's reconquest of Portugal was overlooked and it was to be some time before the full implications of this were appreciated. That Wellesley could return to Lisbon and operate fresh armies from a free Portugal was Moore's achievement. Without it, Britain's involvement in the Peninsula needs must have been sharply curtailed.

Chapter VIII

VICTOR ON THE GUADIANA

With the indigenous field armies heavily defeated and the British driven from the country, the winter of 1808 seemed full of promise for the Imperial forces in Spain. The projected invasion of Portugal – delayed by Moore's interference – could now go ahead while news of St-Cyr's victory at Molins de Rey and Lannes' progress against Saragossa strengthened existing hopes of bringing the conflict to its final conclusion. However, the interminable guerilla warfare continued to occupy vast numbers of French soldiers and the ever resilient Spaniards were soon raising new divisions to fling into the fray. Napoleon's impression that his Peninsular venture was nearing its end was far from correct.[98]

I The Uclés Campaign

In the weeks following its disastrous defeat at Tudela, the remnants of the 'Army of the Centre' had retreated to Cuenca where it had been reinforced and reorganised. On Christmas Day 1808, commanded by the Duke of Infantado, it began an advance on Madrid; the garrison of the capital having been severely depleted by Napoleon's columns leaving in pursuit of Moore. King Joseph thus found himself in a parlous position which was made considerably worse by Lefebvre taking his corps on an unordered drive towards Avila.[99] Only some 9,000 Imperial troops were immediately available to protect the city, whereas Infantado disposed of over 20,000 men.

Fortunately for the king, however, the Spanish commander proceeded at a leisurely pace and, after evicting a French dragoon brigade from Tarancon, brought his advance to a halt. Making full use of this lull, Joseph hurried reinforcements into the capital and quelled some minor risings that had been instigated by Infantado's expected arrival. By 8 January, 20,000 more troops were available and the king promptly dispatched Victor, with 16,000 men, to confront the 'Army of the Centre'.

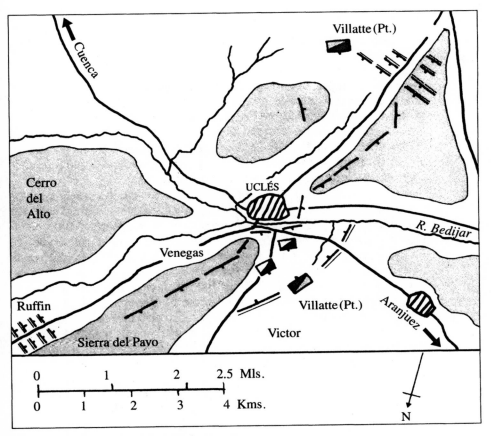

THE BATTLE OF UCLÉS, 13 January 1809

VENEGAS' FORCES:
Infantry: 22 small battalions	=	9,500
Cavalry: 9 small regiments	=	2,000
Artillery: 4 guns	=	480
Total:	=	11,980

VICTOR'S FORCES:
Division Ruffin: 9 battalions	=	5,000
Division Villatte: 12 battalions	=	7,000
Total infantry:	=	12,000
Division Latour-Maubourg: 6 dragoon regiments	=	2,500
Corps cavalry (Beaumont): 2 light regiments	=	1,300
Total cavalry:	=	3,800
Artillery etc: 32 guns	=	500

On 13 January, the marshal encountered Infantado's vanguard –
9,500 infantry, 2,000 cavalry and four guns – arrayed along the hills
to either side of the village of Uclés. The Spanish, under General
Venegas, were hopelessly over extended: apart from a solitary
battalion left in reserve, the whole corps was drawn out in a single
line. The Duke of Bellune promptly resolved to envelop his adversary's right wing and ordered Ruffin's division eastwards to swing
round the enemy's flank. In the meantime, the battalions of General
Villatte, supported by the bulk of the Imperial cavalry, advanced to
try conclusions with the Spanish left and centre.

Villatte's assault was a complete success and his first brigade,
having routed the entire enemy left wing, was soon pounding on the
very walls of Uclés. A despairing Venegas was forced to draw units
from his right to try to stem this progress and Victor responded by
vigorously engaging the now-weakened forces north of the town.
This onset proved decisive; the whole Spanish army fleeing eastwards – straight into the arms of Ruffin. Needless to say, this fresh
onslaught completed the discomfiture of Venegas' recoiling army
and, in the massacre that followed, the Spanish lost all their artillery,
twenty standards, 6,000 prisoners, and over 1,000 killed or
wounded. Victor sustained barely 200 casualties. Advised of the
calamity, Infantado and his main column fled into Murcia, hotly
pursued by the French cavalry who relieved them of their remaining
cannon and took numerous captives. After only one serious action,
the duke's new 'Army of the Centre' was more than half destroyed.

Victor, leaving a strong cavalry screen in La Mancha, now moved
west to take part in operations against Portugal. However, General
Cartaojal, having rallied and reinforced Infantado's depleted regiments, soon resumed the Spanish efforts to move into New Castile
and threaten Madrid. An attack on Digeon's dragoons at Mora, in
mid-February, heralded the coming storm and General Sebastiani
immediately moved his French infantry forward to support the
retiring horsemen.

Alarmed by this sudden increase in the enemy's strength, the
Spanish probing columns retreated, losing a skirmish at Consuegra.
Beset by doubts, Cartaojal dallied about Manzanares and, before
resuming the advance, complied with an order from the *Junta* to
send 5,000 men to Estremadura. After roughly handling a French
picket near Toledo, he was chased by Sebastiani with 13,000 troops
and driven beyond the Guadiana at Ciudad Real. Determined to end
the game of 'cat and mouse', the infuriated French general seized the
Peralvillo Bridge in the face of bitter opposition and flung his army
across the river on 26 March.

Denied the protection of this natural obstacle, Cartaojal led his

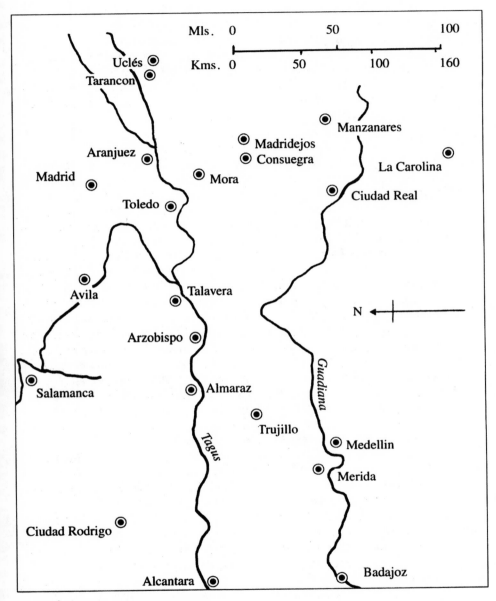

Mls. 0   50   100

Kms. 0   50   100   160

Uclés

Tarancon

Manzanares

Madridejos

Consuegra

Aranjuez

La Carolina

Madrid

Mora

Ciudad Real

Toledo

Avila

Talavera

N ←

Arzobispo

Almaraz

Guadiana

Salamanca

Trujillo

Medellin

Tagus

Merida

Ciudad Rodrigo

Badajoz

Alcantara

UCLÉS AND MEDELLIN:
THE THEATRE OF OPERATIONS

infantry in a headlong retreat. However, his few cavalry proved hopelessly incapable of protecting the withdrawing divisions from the pursuing French, whose squadrons quickly overthrew the enemy horsemen and ploughed into the retreating foot soldiers – inflicting 2,000 casualties, and taking five cannon and three standards. Torrential rain put an end to the chase, but the dregs of the 'Army of the Centre' reached La Carolina before Cartaojal was able to restore order. The *Junta* promptly replaced him with General Venegas.[100]

II   Medellin

While the opposing armies in New Castile were shadowing each other, Cuesta – quite unperturbed by his disastrous defeat at Medina the previous July – was busy organising forces in Estremadura. Taking three newly constituted divisions, he eventually moved up the Tagus and destroyed the great bridge near Almaraz before deploying his 15,000 men along the high ground behind the river. Impotent in the face of such strength and the difficult terrain, Lasalle's Imperial cavalry marked time, awaiting Marshal Victor with two infantry divisions and six dragoon regiments. They duly arrived from Uclés – bringing the French army up to 5,000 horse, 17,000 foot and sixty guns[101] – but Victor judged his corps to be far too weak to overthrow Cuesta and invade Portugal as Napoleon's latest plan prescribed. However, a determined King Joseph dismissed the marshal's objections and directed him to proceed as ordered. Accordingly, on 15 March, the grumbling marshal led his men across the Tagus through Talavera and Arzobispo; Leval's German division promptly colliding with Cuesta's right wing at the Ibor Gorge.

Unwilling to be manoeuvred out of his location, Cuesta had detached a division of 5,000 men with six cannon to hold the gorge. Deployed in an excellent defensive position, they offered determined resistance and inflicted some 500 casualties on Leval before abandoning their artillery and fleeing. However, with his flank turned, Cuesta's situation became untenable. He regrouped his divisions towards Trujillo and marched southwards to unite with the 5,000 troops *en route* from Cartaojal's command. The Spanish general then turned his army about and took the offensive, moving against Victor's camp at Medellin.

The morning of 28 March saw Cuesta advancing with some 20,000 infantry, 3,000 cavalry and thirty pieces of ordnance. Against him, Victor could bring 13,000 bayonets, 4,500 sabres and fifty cannon. Ignoring the advantages the terrain offered for a defensive action, Cuesta formed his units into a line of attack some four miles long and only four men deep. This was, of course, an extremely dangerous formation to adopt, for, if it should be assailed by cavalry, one solitary break could spell disaster for the entire corps. However, the Spanish general had formulated yet another of his grandiose schemes and, this time, planned to envelop the more compact enemy forces and destroy them with converging fire.

For his part, the French marshal had deployed his army with the bulk of the cavalry on the wings. Unable to strike at the enemy's flanks because of the Guadiana and Hortiga rivers, the Imperial horse waited for an opportunity to rush the thin, hostile lines frontally and, when he thought he glimpsed an opening, Latour-Maubourg did just that. Of course, charging formed infantry in the front was a potentially deadly undertaking and, on this occasion, it failed. As they bore down on Henestrosa's division, the French squadrons were met by a hail of musketry and canister, and promptly recoiled – exposing two supporting German battalions as they did so. Along with the hastily reformed cavalry troopers, these units were pressed into retreat. Seeing his right wing falling back, the Duke of Bellune had no option but to bid his left retire as well.

For two hours, the French conducted a skilful, fighting withdrawal until they finally halted in a defensive arc, a little to the south of Medellin.[102] Elated by their earlier success, the battalions of Del Parque and Henestrosa came on with extraordinary resolution. Nevertheless, as they came under a murderous fire from a ten-piece battery in the midst of the enemy's line, they swerved to each side of the ordnance; falling on the infantry to the left and right of the artillery, and becoming involved in a ferocious *mêlée* which ebbed and flowed around the guns. Grasping his opportunity, Latour-Maubourg galvanised his squadrons into action once more and wheeled them into the open Spanish flank. Realising that his infantry would be destroyed unless he intervened, Cuesta tried desperately to intercept the Imperial cavalry with his own horsemen. However, his troopers – mostly veterans who had recently returned from the Baltic – bluntly refused to advance and, carrying Cuesta away with them as they fled, raced from the field in disorder.

The French infantry – deployed in square to protect them against possible cavalry attack – had been in serious danger from Del Parque's advance, but Latour-Maubourg's troopers now galloped in to crush the threat. The long thin lines of Spanish foot soldiers were an easy target for the dragoons and, in a trice, half a dozen battalions were hacked down or routed. Soon, Cuesta's entire left wing had ceased to exist and, leaving their victims lying in gruesome, bloody heaps, the frenzied Imperial cavalry squadrons dashed off in search of new prey.

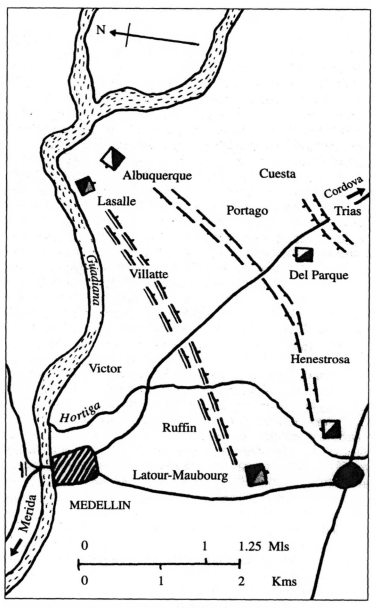

THE BATTLE OF MEDELLIN, 28 March 1809

At the sight of his colleague's success in the west, Lasalle, bored with standing idle, also roused his squadrons into action and suddenly counter-attacked. His *chasseurs* easily overthrew the Spanish lancers before them and then, followed by the Imperial infantry, bore down on Albuquerque's isolated division. Simultaneously, Latour-Maubourg – returning with one of his brigades from the pursuit of Cuesta's routed horsemen – assailed it from the rear. It would be difficult to imagine a more adverse set of conditions for foot troops to be caught in and, indeed, attacked in the front by infantry, and on their flanks and rear by cavalry, Albuquerque's helpless soldiers were exterminated where they stood.[103]

The whole Spanish army now fled south across the plain in hopeless disorder and the French cavalry raced after them, inflicting appalling casualties. Lasalle claimed that the 'disgusting Spaniards' lost 14,000 men at Medellin. Certainly, by the time a thunder-storm brought an end to the carnage, at least 8,000 Spanish lay dead, with another 2,000 taken prisoner.[104] Victor's soldiers also carried off nine standards and twenty guns. Estimates of the French losses range between 300 and 2,000 men, although 1,000 would seem to be more credible.[105]

While Cuesta retired to lick his wounds, Victor marched on Merida where he halted and resumed his requests to King Joseph for more resources. Pleading that his corps could barely hold Estremadura, he demanded the return of 9,000 of his men that Madrid had detached under General Lapisse. Without these soldiers, he claimed, he could not possibly undertake any invasion of Portugal. Nevertheless, Joseph refused to return Lapisse's column to Victor's sphere of operations and, consequently, the marshal was unable to execute the march on Lisbon that the emperor's strategy called for. Thus, a whole army was missing from the projected offensive into Portugal; a factor that was to compromise the venture from the outset.

Chapter IX

THE RETURN TO SARAGOSSA

Following his victory at Tudela in November, Marshal Lannes had pushed on to Saragossa, while Ney pursued the remnants of Castaños' shattered army towards Cuenca. Ney was then recalled by Napoleon to take part in the campaign against Moore, and Lannes, pleading illness, relinquished his command to Moncey and returned to France. After the engagements and marches of recent weeks, the new commander found he had no more than 15,000 troops with which to deal with Saragossa and, judging this force to be inadequate, he withdrew to Alagon to join with Marshal Mortier's V Corps before returning to beleaguer the city.

After their successful resistance of the 1808 siege, the Saragossans had become complacent and had persistently delayed preparing the city for any resumption of hostilities. However, at the news of the rout of the 'Army of the Centre', General Palafox realised that an Imperial column might arrive at any moment. Galvanised into action, the Aragonese embarked on an ambitious rearmament programme: scores of labourers were drafted into the city to work on the neglected fortifications and to assemble the stores necessary for a long siege, while Palafox gathered the remains of O'Neille's broken divisions and set about constructing dozens of new units. By the time the French appeared, he had 34,000 regular troops, supported by 10,000 armed peasants, all deployed within impressive fortifications[106] and backed by 160 cannon. Against them, Moncey could bring 38,000 infantry, 3,000 sappers and gunners, 3,500 cavalry and 144 pieces of ordnance. The stage was set for a Herculean struggle.

At eight o'clock on the morning of 20 December, the French assailed the dominating heights of the Monte Torrero, the hill from which their artillery had wrought such destruction in the first siege. The Spanish had intended to cover it with defences in an effort to prevent any repetition of that but, when Moncey arrived, only one redoubt had been constructed on its slopes. After an hour-long

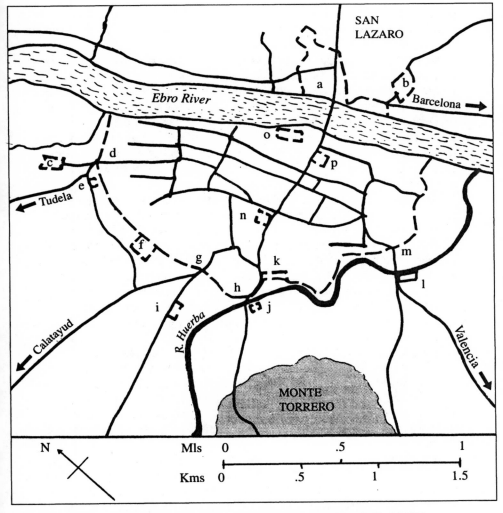

THE CITY OF SARAGOSSA AT THE TIME OF THE PENINSULAR WAR

KEY

-- = City walls and principal buildings
a = San Lazaro Convent
b = Jesus Convent
c = Aljafferia
d = Portillo Gate
e = Augustinian Convent
f = Trinitarian Convent
g = Carmen Gate
h = Santa Engracia Gate
i = Capuchin Convent
j = Pillar Fort
k = Santa Engracia
l = San Josef Convent
m = Quemada Gate
n = San Francisco Convent
o = Pilar Church
p = Cathedral

bombardment, the divisions of Morlot and Grandjean drove the 6,000 men defending this outpost into the city, capturing seven cannon and a standard as they did so.

However, a second French attack – on the deceptively weak-looking defences of San Lorenzo – was not so successful. Here, General Gazan, somewhat confused over the exact meaning of his orders, sent six battalions forward and, after a degree of initial progress, encountered formidable fortifications around the Convent of Jesus. The French commander, fearful of being overwhelmed by the more numerous Spaniards, retired and went over to the defensive, protecting his exposed flanks by flooding fields with water from the Ebro.

His terms for surrender well and truly rejected, Moncey began the siege in earnest on 23 December and soon had several parallels under construction. His replacement by Junot and the recall of Mortier and 10,000 troops slowed the pace of the operation somewhat but, by 10 January, French batteries had begun shelling the outlying Pillar Fort and the Convent of San Josef. The latter building quickly crumbled under the bombardment and dozens of the garrison were killed or wounded. So heavy were the losses, that Palafox was obliged to send in three fresh battalions and finally launched a desperate sortie in an effort to silence the pernicious enemy ordnance. The attempt failed and, the following day, Grandjean's infantry evicted the remnants of the defenders, taking fifty prisoners in the process. The Pillar Fort quickly followed suit; being stormed and captured by the 1st Regiment of the Vistula Legion, who only lost three men in the action. The pitiful remnants of its Spanish garrison fled across the Huerba to the safety of Saragossa, only stopping to destroy the bridge behind them.

In spite of heavy enemy artillery fire, the Imperial sappers worked on and soon had four batteries deployed against the south-east sector of Saragossa's defences, with a further five facing those fortifications about Santa Engracia. At ranges of less than 200 yards, these guns tore great gaps in the walls, and Palafox realised that storming-parties and street fighting would soon be upon him. With fever rampant in the city, his position seemed to be deteriorating rapidly and he now concentrated on preparing the inner defences for the inevitable French assault.

By 27 January the breaches were large enough for storming parties and, at noon that day, an attack force swarmed out of the trenches and assailed the battered walls. Although one column was beaten off, three others made appreciable inroads into the defences – the 1st Vistula Regiment even took the Capuchin Convent, behind Santa Engracia. Marshal Lannes, who had returned to take command, now began the task of penetrating the jungle of alleyways and sturdy houses before him. Rejecting the storm tactics used in the first siege, he planned to move slowly and methodically through the city, sapping and mining each block to avoid the terrible losses that Verdier had incurred. He was right to do so. Whenever the orders were ignored and simple storming tactics utilised, casualties were out of all proportion to any gains, and the French soon settled down to the established procedure.[107]

Amid scenes suggestive of a later battle at a place called Stalingrad, the defenders maintained fanatical resistance despite fearsome losses. Heroic struggles for individual buildings took place, notably the San Augustin Convent where, at one point, the French held the altar end of the chapel and exchanged shots for hours on end with Spaniards entrenched in the nave and belfry. The slaughter continued unabated and, by 4 February, Palafox's garrison was in a lamentable state with 10,000 dead and a further 14,000 sick or wounded. Typhus was rife and on top of the military's losses were hundreds of civilian casualties. The gaps in the besiegers' ranks, too, were far from insignificant: 'We must halt and wait for reinforcements', complained Belmas, an engineer, 'or we shall all perish and be buried in these cursed ruins before we can rout out the last of these fanatics from their last stronghold.'[108]

Busy constructing parallels and batteries before San Lorenzo, General Gazan was ordered to resume the offensive at the beginning of February and, on the Eighth, he finally captured the formidable Jesus Convent. Elsewhere, too, Lannes continued to make progress, particularly around Santa Engracia. In one incident alone, a mine destroyed the San Francisco Convent – killing 400 Aragonese troops and demolishing Palafox's main equipment workshop.[109] On 18 February – after fifty-two siege guns had ripped eight major breaches in the defences – the French assaulted and overran San Lazaro. Their retreat over the Ebro cut, the garrison was virtually annihilated, losing over 1,500 prisoners. Throughout the afternoon, the besiegers continued to effect ever deeper inroads and, finally, on 20 February, Saragossa succumbed to the inevitable and concluded a pact of capitulation.

Lannes had captured a smoking ruin in which 54,000 people had perished. The survivors of the military garrison numbered a pathetic 8,000 men – of whom 1,500, including Palafox, were sick. Lannes had lost 4,000 killed in action, with another 6,000 men cut down by fever. Thousands of non-combatants had also fallen and about a third of the city had been completely ruined.

Although ultimately defeated, the defenders of Saragossa had once more covered themselves with glory and had given the invader a demonstration of fanatical, national resistance. It was a demonstration the French army was never to forget and, at Gerona and elsewhere, it was to inspire Spaniards to maintain replica struggles that have few parallels in the history of war.[110]

Interior view of the ruined church of the General Hospital after the first siege of Saragossa
(Fotomas)

View of Gerona (From *Los Guerilleros de 1808* by E. Rodriguez-Solis, Madrid, 1887)

Augustina, 'Maid of Saragossa', became a symbol for the heroic resistance against the French after her prominent participation in the defence of Saragossa in 1808–9 (Fotomas)

Fighting in the Church of San Augustino, Saragossa (Museo de Zaragossa)

General Jose Palafox (From *Los Guerilleros de 1808* by E. Rodriguez-Solis, Madrid, 1887)

D. Mariano Alvarez (From *Los Guerilleros de 1808* by E. Rodriguez-Solis, Madrid, 1887)

Soult's forces pursue the British over the snow-covered mountains of Galicia.
Drawing by Sir Robert Ker Porter (Fotomas)

Corunna harbour at the time of the explosion of Moore's powder store, 1809.
Drawing by Sir Robert Ker Porter (Fotomas)

PART THREE

Guerre À Outrance

Overleaf: An episode in the second siege of Saragossa (*Photo:* Giraudon)

Perpignan
Gerona
Cardadeu
Barcelona
Molins de Rey
ST-CYR
Tarragona
REDING

MEDITERRANEAN
SEA

0   50   100   150 Mls
0   100   200 Kms

N

Ebro
LANNES   Saragossa
PALAFOX

Valencia

Bayonne

Douro

Cuenca
INFANTADO
Uclés

Vitoria

Burgos

Madrid   VICTOR & JOSEPH
LEFEBVRE   Toledo

Avila
Arzobispo
Almaraz

Guadalquivir

Astorga
NEY

Guadiana

Medellin
CUESTA

Tagus

SOULT

ROMANA
Orense

Almeida

Elvas
CRADOCK

Corunna
MOORE

Oporto

ATLANTIC
OCEAN

Lisbon

THE GENERAL STRATEGIC SITUATION,
Early-January 1809

Chapter X

SOULT'S INVASION OF PORTUGAL, SPRING 1809

I Soult's Road to Oporto

After the Battle of Corunna and the British evacuation of Spain, Soult had turned his attention to the invasion of Portugal. In the grand strategy he drew up in late 1808, Napoleon had envisaged a three-pronged offensive into that country consisting of Soult's corps from the north, Lapisse's 9,000 men from the east and Victor's forces from the south. On paper, Soult had 40,000 men at his disposal, but after the rigorous campaign in Galicia thousands of his troops were sick and he could only muster some 20,000 men. Although he experienced great difficulty in equipping all of these and a chronic shortage of horses and transport vehicles compounded his problems, the Duke of Dalmatia persevered. As an opening move he took the Spanish naval base at Ferrol on 26 January, capturing eight battleships, three frigates and several thousand prisoners. Of more immediate value, however, were the enormous equipment stockpiles, including 20,000 British muskets. This windfall enabled Soult to make good some of his army's material deficiencies and to proceed with the projected invasion of Portugal.

Nevertheless, his position remained difficult. Large numbers of sick greatly thinned the French ranks, as did the need for detachments to suppress the local insurgents. Further – and perhaps more significantly – Soult had as little idea of the condition and whereabouts of the forces of Victor and Lapisse as they had of his. Indeed, effective co-ordination of their respective armies was out of the question over such distances, in a hostile country and in an atmosphere of such ignorance.

Turning over the occupation of Galicia to Ney's corps, Soult's forces moved off on 30 January, the cavalry of Lahoussaye and Franceschi spearheading the advance. The Spanish fortresses of Vigo and Tuy capitulated without resistance, and the French were soon at Campo Saucos on the Portuguese frontier. Here, however, the rain-swollen Minho proved impassable and Soult was obliged to head upriver towards Orense.[111]

His new route lay over difficult mountain tracks and his columns were constantly harassed by guerillas in the narrow gorges. Easily blocked, these soon proved impassable for all but the lightest traffic, and Soult was eventually compelled to detach all his heavy ordnance and wagons. Escorted by an entire division under General Lamartinière, they returned to Tuy. The main force, meanwhile, struggled on to Orense.[112]

Once there, Soult spent some days regrouping and resting his weary units. Shrugging off disquieting reports from Ney regarding the insurrection in Galicia, he scattered the local insurgent bands and moved south on 4 March; his vanguard promptly encountering the tattered remnants of General La Romana's army. Since their abortive effort to assist Moore's redcoats in the Corunna campaign, the Spanish general's battered divisions had been recuperating and were quite unaware of Soult's proximity. La Romana beat a hasty retreat and, although his rearguard was overtaken and cut to pieces and his supply train was lost, succeeded in slipping the bulk of his command away to the east.[113] Furious that La Romana's corps had eluded annihilation once more, Soult resumed his trek southward and, on 9 March, crossed into Portugal.

The only force immediately available to oppose him was the ragged command of General Silveira. Fewer than half his 10,000 men had received anything other than elementary training and, realising that no help could be expected from La Romana, the Portuguese general wisely sought to withdraw before the advancing foe. However, one Portuguese column was overtaken and routed by General Foy and, disobeying Silveira's orders, 4,000 more troops insisted on attempting to defend Chaves. Quickly encircled by overwhelming numbers of the enemy, they capitulated without firing a shot. With half of his corps destroyed, Silveira fled eastwards, shadowed by a French dragoon brigade.[114]

Soult resumed his drive on Oporto but, a few miles outside Braga, found a mass of 25,000 irregulars barring his path and duly concentrated his forces for a major engagement. It was to prove a brief but bloody affair. The Portuguese volunteers posed no real threat to the French in an open battle. Virtually devoid of training, discipline, organisation and effective weaponry, they compounded these awesome disadvantages by lynching their commander – General Freire – when he imprudently advocated the realistic but unpatriotic policy of withdrawal.[115] His reluctant successor, Eben, shared Freire's misgivings but declined to voice them and only hours after

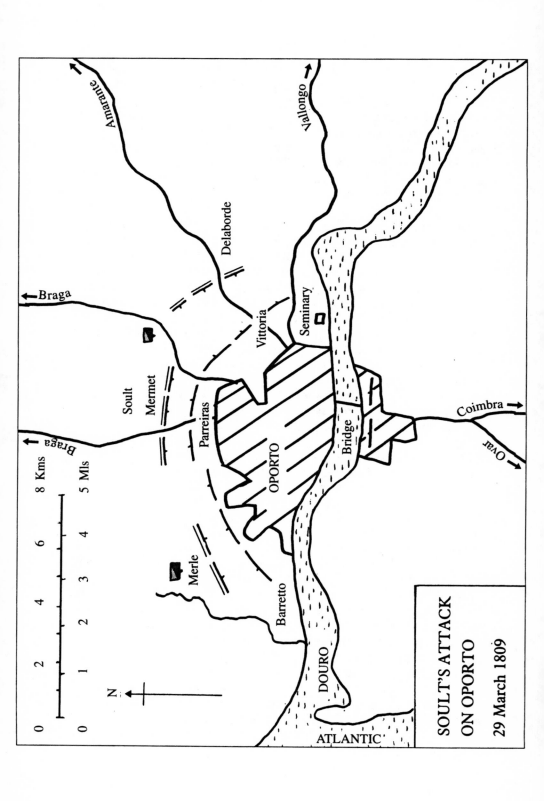

SOULT'S ATTACK
ON OPORTO
29 March 1809

OPORTO

Braga
Braga
Soult
Mermet
Parreiras
Merle
Barretto
Vittoria
Seminary
Bridge
DOURO
ATLANTIC
Delaborde
Amarante
Vallongo
Coimbra
Ovar

N

0 2 4 6 8 Kms
0 1 2 3 4 5 Mls

his appointment the engagement started. The French broke through almost immediately and, sweeping their opponents aside with horrendous losses, marched on to Oporto. The insurgents, however, returned to wreak havoc with harassment tactics and within days of the departure of Soult's main body his communications were under attack. Tuy and Vigo were encircled and, indeed, assisted by a British naval squadron, the guerillas secured the surrender of the latter on 28 March.

The day before Vigo fell, Soult reached Oporto. The suburbs north of the Douro were protected by a large belt of hastily constructed redoubts, garrisoned by 30,000 men with 200 artillery pieces. Against these, Soult could only bring some 16,000 troops – 3,000 of whom were cavalry and largely useless against such earthworks. Accordingly, the marshal rejected simple frontal attacks in favour of a more subtle plan to dislodge the opposition and drive them into the Douro. A series of probing attacks induced them to transfer units from their centre to strengthen their wings and then, on 29 March, an entire division was launched against each flank. The poorly trained defenders could only maintain a sporadic, inaccurate fire, and Merle and Delaborde's soldiers soon made enormous inroads. As the Portuguese commander responded by drawing more regiments from the centre to bolster the crumbling wings, Mermet's division suddenly swarmed forward from their concealed positions to assail the weakened centre of the hostile line. In minutes the redoubts here had fallen and Oporto's defences were split asunder.[116]

Seeing their centre hopelessly ruptured, the defenders broke into flight. Slipping away to the east, General Vittoria's wing eluded Delaborde's troops with slight losses, but the Portuguese centre and left were less fortunate. Pursued by Merle's command, the latter corps found their retreat barred by the Douro estuary and, herded into the shallows, either drowned or were captured or sabred by the French cavalry. The centre met with a still more ghastly fate. Driven through Oporto, the stream of fugitives, swollen by scores of civilians, descended on the one bridge that spanned the Douro. But, lest the French might follow the crowd across the water, a Portuguese officer raised the central drawbridge, trapping the fugitives between the river and Soult's forces.

The consequences were tragic. Pushed by the panic-stricken masses behind them, rank upon rank of people fell from the quayside and drowned, while dozens more were killed in the crossfire between the French and the Portuguese batteries beyond the river. It took Soult's troops some thirty minutes to clear the hysterical crowd away, by which time 4,000 people had perished. Nor were the

French prevented from crossing the Douro. Using pieces of timber to bridge the gap, Mermet's infantry fought their way onto the south bank and by noon the whole of Oporto was under Soult's control.[117]

It was a major victory. For fewer than 500 casualties Soult had secured Portugal's second city with its valuable dockyards and arsenals intact. Moreover, the Portuguese had sustained appalling losses; some 200 guns had been taken, and between 6,000 and 20,000 men had been slain, wounded or captured.

Nevertheless, Soult's position remained precarious. The population was more hostile than ever and the partisan war ceaselessly sapped the strength of his field army. His communications with Ney had been severed, and his last report from Galicia was now a month old and far from comforting. He had no tidings of Victor or Lapisse, and was unaware that Victor's offensive had fizzled out with a battle at Medellin the previous day.

Desperate for news, Soult despatched a division under Heudelet to relieve the beleaguered northern garrisons and to make contact with Ney. Simultaneously, a second division, under Loison, was sent east to drive off Silveira (who had resumed the offensive) and to find Lapisse. 3,000 more troops were deployed to maintain contact with these flying columns. With half his army now engaged in merely trying to maintain his gains, a further advance was out of the question and Soult, having thrown Franceschi's cavalry and Mermet's infantry forward in a screen, remained at Oporto awaiting developments.

II   The Expeditions of Heudelet and Loison

Brushing the insurgents aside, Heudelet made his way to the dilapidated fortress of Valenza on the River Minho. The scanty garrison quickly surrendered and communications were opened with Lamartinière's command beyond the river in Tuy. That stronghold had been seriously pressed, and Lamartinière reported the fall of Vigo and the subsequent loss of contact with Ney's VI Corps. Equally concerned by the severance of his links with the 'Army of Portugal', Ney had sent Maucune's brigade south for news of Soult and on 12 April it arrived at Tuy.

Maucune was dismayed by the news of Soult's predicament and had equally gloomy tidings regarding the VI Corps: the Galician insurgents had surrounded Villafranca, cutting Ney's communications with Madrid, and the general situation deteriorated further each day. A despondent Maucune retraced his steps, while Heudelet and Lamartinière, deciding their position was untenable, evacuated the Minho Valley and retired on Braga.[118]

Meanwhile, to the east, Silveira and Loison were trying conclusions in the Tamega basin. While Soult was tackling General Freire's motley force outside Braga in March, Silveira had rallied his corps and taken the offensive. Marching on Chaves with 10,000 troops, he had overwhelmed its little garrison and had thrust downriver to Amarante.

When Loison arrived to confront him early in April, he found the Portuguese strongly entrenched behind the Tamega: their artillery dominated the solitary crossing and Silveira had also taken the precaution of mining the bridge so as to be able to destroy it at the first sign of trouble. After an unsuccessful attempt to force a passage, Loison – nervous, lacking in initiative and unsuited to independent command – appealed for reinforcements. Soult, however, was still busy allotting more troops for the sector when Silveira, encouraged by his earlier successes, suddenly counter-attacked. Although beaten back he thoroughly alarmed Loison who, despite being given as many as 9,000 of Soult's 21,000 troops, still failed to make any headway against the enemy's position.

Indeed it was 2 May before an opportunity finally arose to break the deadlock. Screened by fog, a handful of engineers crept across the bridge and sabotaged the fuses on the mines. An entire brigade then stormed over the crossing and fell on Silveira's startled army. Leaving all their cannon and five standards in the enemy's hands, the panic-stricken Portuguese made for Lamego. Loison's buoyant troops, meanwhile, occupied Silveira's redoubts.[119]

But this victory only marginally diminished Soult's problems. The situation in upper Portugal was worse than ever, and now disquieting rumours arrived that fresh British divisions had landed at Lisbon and were moving north. The marshal had no idea how true these reports were and he still had no information regarding Lapisse or Victor. Altogether, Soult's situation remained bleak and he was not the only French commander having difficulties: Ney, too, was struggling, and it is to his operations in Galicia and the Asturias that we will now turn.[120]

Chapter XI

A CRISIS IN THE NORTH-WEST

I   The War in Galicia and the Asturias Expedition

When Soult had moved against Portugal in February, he had left
Marshal Ney to deal with the growing rebellion in Galicia. Ney's VI
Corps totalled some 17,000 effectives at this time and was far too
weak to contain a rugged province of 10,000 square miles, infested
by 30,000 insurgents. Indeed, Soult himself was later to estimate the
forces required for a conquest of Galicia at at least 45,000 troops –
nearly three times Ney's available strength. Napoleon, failing to
grasp the nature of the revolt in Spain, issued orders to the Duke of
Elchingen similar to those he had given to commanders elsewhere in
the Peninsula. There was the usual talk of 'flying columns', 'making
examples', 'utilising the Spanish authorities' and so on. By such
policies, he assumed, the VI Corps would be easily capable of
holding Galicia and, indeed, should be free to release units for service
in other theatres.

However, such calculations were quite unrealistic. Ney tried
frantically to crush the opposition, without success. He virtually
gave up attempting to pacify the southern reaches of Galicia, and left
the garrisons in Tuy and Vigo to fend for themselves. He had to
deploy entire brigades to keep a grip on Santiago and Lugo, and a
division was required to hold the Corunna-Ferrol area.[121] A further
two brigades were absorbed in pacifying the Mondonedo district.
Again, the drain of garrisoning their conquests was weakening the
Imperial field forces and rendering them largely incapable of offensive action.

Furthermore, the insurgents were not the only foes Ney had to
contend with. The British navy, too, was active along the coast,
while inland the armies of La Romana and the Asturias were on the
prowl. With the fall of Vigo and Soult's evacuation of Tuy the
situation became even more serious and, when the insurrectionists
succeeded in surrounding Villafranca, the Duke of Elchingen

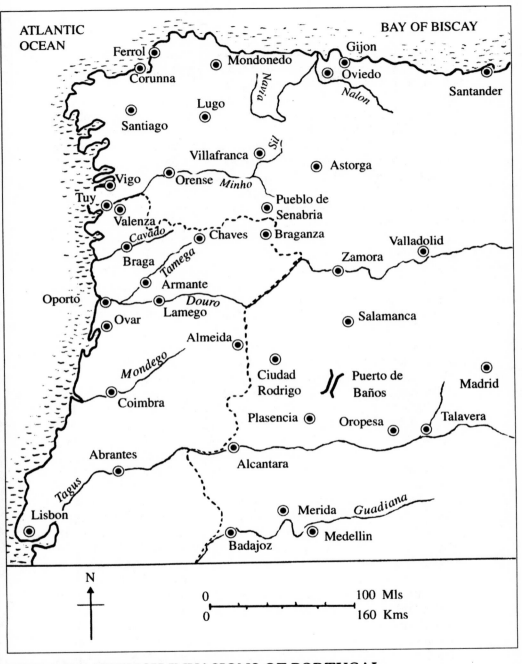

THE (1809) FRENCH INVASIONS OF PORTUGAL
AND THE ASTURIAS: THEATRE OF OPERATIONS

found himself severed from the interior and his superiors in Madrid.[122]

It was primarily this interruption in communications that jolted King Joseph into sending a column to Ney's assistance, but, as units had to be summoned from as far afield as Aragon to assemble this modest force of 7,000,[123] it was May before it reached Ney at Lugo. And his joy at seeing it soon evaporated; for the corps' commander, General Kellermann, then explained that Madrid desired him to take part in a concerted attack on the Asturias: Kellermann was to retrace his steps and strike into the south of the principality, while General Bonnet, at Santander, and Ney attacked from the east and west respectively. Accordingly Ney apprehensively mustered the bulk of his corps at Lugo, while Kellermann marched for the southern frontiers of the Asturias.

At this time, that region was perhaps the most independently minded of all the Spanish provinces. It had made little effort to assist General Blake in his Biscay campaign of the previous autumn and had declined to give his successor, La Romana, any aid in the grim days following the Espinosa disaster. Indeed, the Asturian *Junta* watched the fall of Old Castile and Galicia with apparent indifference. Showing scant regard for any broader strategical or political objectives, they devoted themselves to protecting their own frontiers and retained their 20,000 troops in a purely defensive stance.

Such regional jealousies could only assist the French, and General La Romana had little time for them. Following his sanguinary brush with Soult's vanguard on 5 March, that stalwart of earlier fights had left the more depleted units of his corps at Puebla de Senabria and had descended on Villafranca with 6,000 men. Capturing the solitary French battalion there,[124] he had detached General Mahy with the bulk of his force to the Navia Valley while he himself headed for Oviedo.

The events following his arrival augured ill for the stability of future Spanish governments. When the Asturian *Junta* again declined to grant him any aid, La Romana simply had his escort battalion disperse the assembly and secured his demands by threats;[125] an early instance of the Spanish military's tendency to interfere in politics. As one horrified observer wrote: 'Can one deny, that Spain is governed by soldiers? How can I help seeing that this is the kind of government that threatens my grandchildren?'[126]

La Romana's efforts to move the ill-gotten *matériel* to Mahy's encampment were, however, rudely interrupted by the French offensive. Marching by tortuous mountain paths, Ney's VI Corps appeared in the Navia Valley on 14 May and, sending Mahy scuttling westwards, advanced on Oviedo. Summoning General Ballesteros'

Asturians from the east of the province, La Romana combined his escort with a few other troops and set out to hold the bridges over the River Nalon. The French, however, easily pushed him aside and Oviedo fell on 19 May, followed by Gijon the next day.

Meanwhile, Kellermann and Bonnet had struck from the south and east. As the former's 7,000 troops crushed 3,000 Asturians at Pajares, the latter moved with 5,000 men against Ballesteros who, on hearing the tidings from Pajares and Oviedo, retired to the mountains. Unable to find him, Bonnet linked up with Ney and Kellermann in the interior.[127]

Thus, much of the Asturian army avoided obliteration, and the French were left looking nervously over their shoulders at their exiguous garrisons in Galicia and Biscay. Finally, on 22 May Ney abandoned the campaign and rushed back to the west, while Bonnet, alarmed by the news that Ballesteros was marching on Santander, retraced his steps there. Finding the town had already fallen, he united with the displaced garrison and mounted an energetic counter-attack which swiftly dislodged Ballesteros' troops. Sustaining 3,000 casualties, they were scattered in all directions, Ballesteros himself escaping by sea.[128]

II Wilson Bluffs Lapisse

Whilst the French offensive against the Asturias was taking place, events in Portugal moved towards a climax with the resumption by the British of active operations. The officer left to command the British forces in Portugal during Moore's venture into Spain was General Sir John Cradock. He consistently evinced little desire to do anything except withdraw[129] and, on hearing of Moore's flight to Corunna and the subsequent advance of Napoleon and Lapisse, began to concentrate his units as a prelude to evacuating the Peninsula.

Other British officers, however, disagreed with this alarmist and defeatist policy. General William Beresford, who since February had been entrusted with the reconstruction of the Portuguese Army, shrugged off Cradock's gloomy predictions and continued with his allotted task.[130] Nor was General Rowland Hill prepared to toss aside the fruits of Vimiero without a struggle and, when Soult's corps appeared in the north, successfully urged the hesitant Cradock to make at least a token advance against the marshal.[131]

But of all the opponents of evacuation, Sir Robert Wilson was the most outspoken and determined. He had followed Moore to the Spanish frontier with his brigade of Lusitania Legion and, when

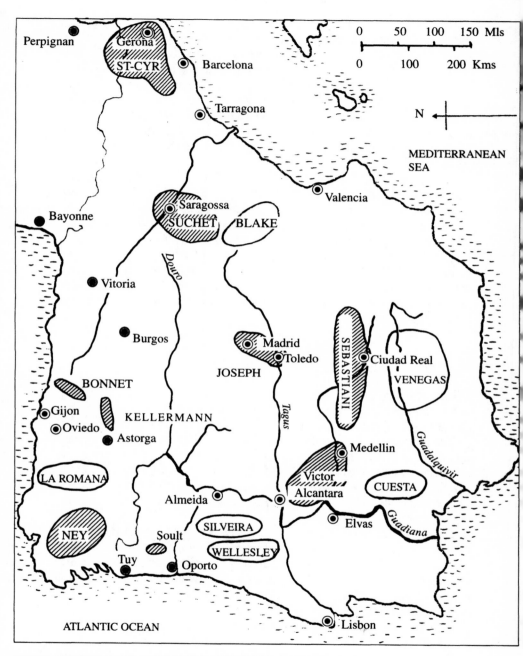

THE GENERAL STRATEGIC SITUATION,
Mid-May 1809

news of Moore's retreat arrived and Cradock ordered general withdrawal, he had staunchly refused to comply. Realising that nothing save his 1,200 men stood between Portugal and the oncoming corps of Lapisse, Wilson deployed half his brigade in the fortress of Almeida and dispersed the rest in a long, flimsy screen across the enemy's path. He then harried the opposition with such remorseless energy that the dazed Lapisse, convinced he was confronted by at least 12,000 troops, switched completely to the defensive.

Thus, like Soult's corps stalled on the Douro, the second prong of the French offensive was effectively contained. But Wilson, a 'very slippery fellow',[132] was not content. He struck at Lapisse's communications with Marshal Victor by throwing a detachment into the Puerto de Baños, the main pass linking Leon with Estremadura. This crisis prompted Victor to intervene. For lack of resources his own offensive in the south had also ground to a standstill, and he now called on King Joseph to return Lapisse's column – officially part of the I Corps – to his sphere of operations. Eventually, the king agreed and, in early April, Lapisse was ordered to rejoin the Duke of Bellune, via Alcantara. Luring Wilson's supposed large army away from the passes with elaborate feints against Ciudad Rodrigo, Lapisse hastened southwards, sacked Alcantara and ultimately united with Victor at Merida.[133]

III Wellesley's Advance to Oporto

Exonerated by the enquiry into the conclusion of the Cintra Convention, Sir Arthur Wellesley resumed command of the British forces in Portugal on 22 April. With him came the first of many reinforcements, raising Cradock's army to over 23,000[134] men and demonstrating a renewed British commitment to confronting Napoleon in the Peninsula.

This followed lengthy cabinet discussions on the viability of maintaining a British presence in Portugal in the face of French military might. Following the Corunna evacuation, pressure had been exerted on the government to withdraw Cradock's forces, too. Cradock himself advocated this policy and he was not alone: other senior military personnel, many statesmen and large numbers of the general public favoured ending Britain's intervention in the Peninsula. A memorandum compiled by General Sir John Moore also served to strengthen this view: 'I can say generally', Moore had written in November 1808,

that the frontier of Portugal is not defensible against a superior force. It is an open frontier, all equally rugged, but all equally to be penetrated. If the French succeed in Spain it will be vain to attempt to resist them in Portugal. ... The British must in that event, I conceive, immediately take steps to evacuate the country.[135]

However when consulted by Lord Castlereagh, the Secretary for War, Wellesley produced a radically different estimation: 'I have always been of the opinion that Portugal might be defended,' he wrote, 'whatever might be the result of the contest in Spain ...' Wellesley argued that, even if Spain should fall, the French would need a field army at least 100,000 strong to subdue Portugal and, given the extent of their existing commitments in the Peninsula and throughout Europe, he saw no prospect of them finding such a force, particularly as Austria's mobilisation was virtually complete and her long-expected offensive into southern Germany was imminent. Urging the consolidation of Britain's foothold in Portugal while Napoleon's attention was focused elsewhere, he called for 'very extensive pecuniary assistance and political support' for the regency government established in Lisbon after Cintra: '. . . The Portuguese military establishments, upon the footing of 40,000 militia and 30,000 regular troops, ought to be revived; ... in addition, His Majesty ought to employ an army in Portugal ...' This British force, he believed, should 'not be less than 30,000 men, of which number 4,000 or 5,000 should be cavalry, and there should be a large body of artillery.' Such an army, he reasoned, should both safeguard Portugal from invasion and 'as long as the contest should continue in Spain ... would be highly useful to the Spaniards, and might eventually decide the contest.'[136]

Opting for this optimistic analysis, Castlereagh boldly supported Wellesley's proposals and persuaded the cabinet to adopt them. Within days, plans based on his recommendations for perpetuating the struggle had been laid and Wellesley was directed to return to Portugal.

He found the French offensive had stopped dead in its tracks: Soult had halted at Oporto, Victor was quiescent near Merida and Lapisse had been turned aside by Wilson. Wellesley quickly perceived the explanation for all this: the invaders had failed to balance the need to concentrate their forces for effective offensive action against the necessity to disperse them to secure supplies and garrison their acquisitions. Now, from his central position, it would be relatively easy for Wellesley to pin down one of the scattered enemy forces while launching a decisive blow against another. Deciding that his first victim would be Soult,[137] he set about preparing his units. He had some 30,000 British troops and, thanks to Beresford, around

16,000 Portuguese. It was agreed that the main force, 18,500 men with 24 cannon, would advance directly on Oporto, while Beresford led a 6,000 strong column towards Lamego to combine with Silveira's army and outflank the enemy.[138] Meanwhile, Wellesley positioned General Mackenzie with 12,000 troops about Abrantes, 'either to impede or delay Victor's progress, in case he should come in while I am absent.'[139] On 2 May Wellesley joined the main force at Coimbra.

Completely in the dark as to what was going on to the south – and, indeed, in most other directions – Soult had little warning of the gathering storm. Wellesley advanced undetected, encouraged by reports that the enemy army was divided: many units were preoccupied on the Tamega; others were dispersed between the Minho and Oporto. The planned union of Beresford's column with Silveira also held out exciting strategic prospects: Soult's position on the Douro would be turned; his communications with the east would be cut and his isolation from Victor completed; and his subordinate, Loison, might be overwhelmed and defeated.

The victory that general secured at Amarante, however, proved a telling blow for Wellesley's hopes and swung the strategic balance markedly in Soult's favour. With the news that Silveira's corps was temporarily inoperative loomed the danger that Loison might now prove too strong for Beresford's turning column. Nor was this the only setback the Allied preparations received. At much the same time, Soult was alerted to Wellesley's proximity by a French traitor, Argenton, the leader of a tiny group of disaffected officers in the 'Army of Portugal'.

Argenton had been in regular contact with the Allies[140] and now rashly revealed their plans to Soult himself, calling on the marshal to renounce Napoleon. Doubtlessly, Nicolas Jean de Dieu Soult was an excessively vain and ambitious man. He had spent much of his sojourn at Oporto indulging in political intrigues aimed at securing himself the Portuguese throne and was later to 'play the viceroy' with gusto in Andalusia. Nevertheless, he was a loyal soldier of the emperor, and promptly had Argenton and his fellow conspirators arrested for treason. That done, he quickly prepared his forces to withstand Wellesley's impending counter-offensive: Franceschi's screen beyond the Douro was alerted; Loison was directed to secure the army's line of retreat through Braganza; and all other detachments north of the Douro were instructed to combine at Amarante without delay.

The early hours of 10 May saw Wellesley's main column thrusting up the Oporto highway. To the west, General Hill's two brigades – seeking to turn the enemy's right flank and prevent their withdrawal to Oporto – sailed across Lake Ovar and landed near the town of that name. However, marching by night through unfamiliar countryside proved more difficult than the British staff had anticipated, and the columns became intermixed and suffered delays. Although Wellesley's cavalry screen blundered into Franceschi's pickets at around 5 am, without the infantry – still well to the rear – they could make no progress and, after a petty skirmish, Franceschi fell back on Mermet's division. Hurrying forward his infantry, Wellesley endeavoured to mount a double envelopment of the hostile line. But, apart from the 31st *Léger* who became involved in a running fight with some cavalry and lost 150 men, the French again slipped away with minimal casualties.[141] Hill, bogged down in the swampy countryside to the west, also proved unable to intercept Franceschi's retreat and the French column gained Oporto without further loss or interference; crossing the Douro and destroying the bridge behind them.[142]

With Franceschi's screen retrieved and Wellesley left stranded beyond the Douro, Soult felt more secure than he had for some time and proposed a leisurely retirement eastwards through Amarante. But in so reasoning he made two major miscalculations. By dismissing Wellesley's column as being neutralised he underestimated the martial abilities of its commander. Moreover, the success of Soult's plan rested on the volatile Loison, into whose dubious care the route to the east had been entrusted. This, as we shall see, was to have fatal consequences.

IV   Loison's Withdrawal from Amarante

Since his victory at Amarante on 2 May, Loison had barely stirred. Reports of hostile troop movements about Lamego, however, induced him to probe to the south-east and his vanguard soon made contact with the Allied corps under Beresford who, linking up with Sir Robert Wilson's brigade *en route*, had united with Silveira's regrouping army and had thus amassed over 11,000 bayonets and sabres. Daunted by the enemy's strength and position, Loison hastily retreated, and by 12 May had regained Amarante.

But his flight did not stop there. Gripped by panic once again, the fickle general – without informing Soult or pausing to evaluate the strategic repercussions[143] – abandoned this nigh impregnable position and retreated towards Braga. The crossing over the Tamega which Silveira had effortlessly held for four weeks thus fell into Beresford's hands, and the Allied pincers began to close on the unsuspecting French along the Douro.

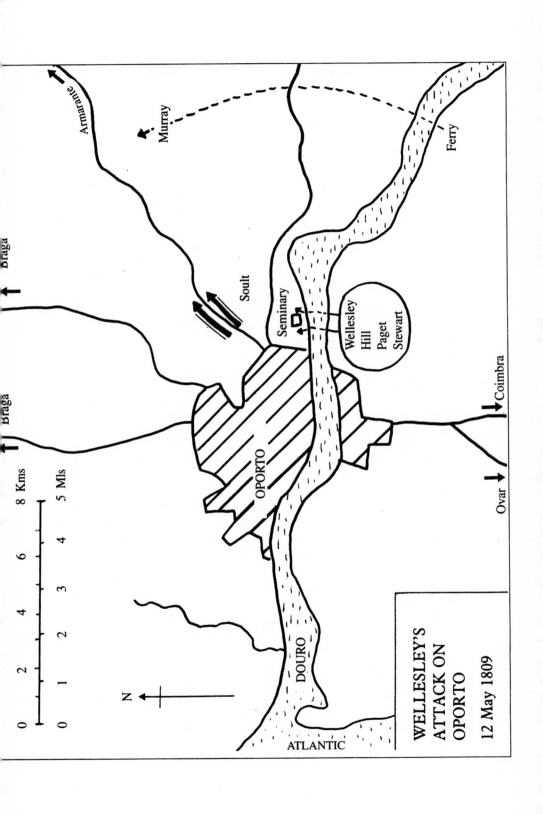

WELLESLEY'S
ATTACK ON
OPORTO

12 May 1809

V   The Action at Oporto and Soult's Retreat from Portugal

Lulled into complacency by his seemingly unassailable position behind the Douro, Soult had not meanwhile taken sufficient precautions to ensure that Wellesley could not cross to the northern bank. Although the flat, lower reaches of the river and the central quays of Oporto's harbour were liberally posted with sentries, the eastern suburbs and the difficult terrain further inland were devoid of French troops. This was a glaring omission which Wellesley, gathering his own and Hill's detachment on the south bank, was quick to notice. On 12 May – as Loison evacuated Amarante – a handful of Allied soldiers crossed the river and, undetected, severed four large barges from their moorings. Crowding into these boats, men of the 3rd Foot then crossed to the vast, unguarded Bishop's Seminary and established a foothold on the northern bank.[144]

Minutes ticked by and still the French remained quiescent. Wellesley, meantime, had eighteen guns wheeled into a dominating position on the south bank and the barges returned for more infantry. Suddenly, furious fighting erupted as General Foy – alerted to the landing – rushed his brigade into Oporto's eastern suburbs and attacked the seminary.

By now, however, the British were too heavily entrenched to be easily dislodged. Advancing over open ground against 1,000 troops ensconced behind high, thick walls, Foy's soldiers were mowed down by the score. Salvoes from Wellesley's battery added to the carnage and, by silencing the few cannon dragged forward to bombard the seminary and the barges plying across the river, swiftly brought Foy's attack to a standstill.

Soult, meanwhile, roused by his staff, had dashed out to rally his startled army. Determined to oust the defenders of the seminary, he called up all the sentries from the waterfront and pitched them into the fight.[145] This, however, only sealed his downfall; for dozens of Portuguese civilians rushed to the quays and manned the scores of boats brought to the north bank to keep them out of Allied hands. Sailed to the far shore, these craft returned crammed with British soldiers. Soon, most of Wellesley's units were across and, attacked from all sides, the French went into headlong retreat to the east.

As Soult's broken corps fled along the Amarante road, a new menace suddenly loomed on their flank. A little column of British troops, two battalions and two squadrons under General John Murray, had repaired a scuttled ferry and had crossed the Douro east of Oporto. Daunted by their numbers, Murray himself declined to take any action against the disorganised foe, but General Charles Stewart, galloping up from Oporto, insisted on leading one of the squadrons in a charge. The 14th Light Dragoons promptly fell on Soult's rearguard and, although sustaining heavy casualties themselves, took 300 prisoners.[146]

By evening, Soult had shaken off his pursuers and had reached Baltar, some ten miles beyond Oporto. That night he received a belated dispatch from Loison, advising him that Amarante had been evacuated and that the road to the east was blocked by Beresford. The Marshal was horrified. The spectre of Baylen loomed before him as he suddenly realised that he was trapped between 30,000 converging enemy troops. There was only one way out. Destroying everything that could not be carried, he plunged into the mountains to the north and, by way of winding hill paths, emerged in the Avé Valley on 13 May. Uniting with Loison and the garrisons from the Minho, he headed for Tuy. But, as an ensign in Wellesley's pursuing columns recalled,

> On getting to Guimaraes he heard a strong division of our army was at Braga. This obliged him to change his route and he now directed his retreat on Chaves, but finding Marshal Beresford, who had marched that way, on his front he again altered his route – fled across the mountains . . . and thus escaped into Galicia with [his] men, dispirited and disarmed, without ammunition, artillery and indeed every sort of store.[147]

On 19 May, as Ney's VI Corps paraded through Oviedo in triumph, Soult's footsore and famished divisions finally reached Orense, having lost 4,000 men and virtually all their equipment.[148] The French had once again been driven from Portugal, and Wellesley, his objective fulfilled, turned his army south in search of fresh prey.

VI   Concluding Events in Galicia and the Asturias, 1809

It only remains for us to bring the episodes of the war in Galicia and the Asturias that we have touched on to their respective conclusions.

We left Marshal Ney hurrying back to Galicia after the attempt to occupy the Asturias. The Galician patriots had taken full advantage of the marshal's absence, and the already hard-pressed French garrisons found themselves in ever deeper difficulties. General Mahy – after his flight from the Navia Valley – led his 6,000 men in an attack on Lugo, and the garrison was only saved by the fortuitous arrival of Soult's corps as they continued their retreat from Orense. Meanwhile, the 2,000 men left to recuperate by La Romana at

Puebla had merged with 8,000 irregulars to form the 'Division of the Minho' and attacked Maucune's command near Santiago. Maucune – losing one sixth of his 3,000 troops – was ousted from the town and only spared further casualties by the arrival of Ney meanwhile, who drove the enemy off. Returning from the Asturias in Ney's wake, La Romana reassumed command of the forces with Mahy and skilfully slipped past Soult's columns to Orense, where he established contact with the 'Minho Division'.

Thus, Ney's VI Corps and Soult's II Corps were united in northern Galicia. Between them, the marshals had 33,000 effectives, though Soult's divisions were desperately short of equipment. Ney handed over what *matériel* he could spare and the weakest units were evacuated to Villafranca. The two commanders then turned to the question of to what task they should apply their new-found strength.

As was often to be the case in the Peninsula, however, the marshals did not find co-operation easy. Ney was primarily interested in conquering Galicia – a task for which he needed Soult's assistance – whereas Soult, sick of the hostile Portuguese and Galicians, was more anxious about the threat Wellesley could pose if he should turn into Spain. Eventually, the Duke of Dalmatia fobbed his colleague off by agreeing to give the VI Corps support from the east while it marched southward; the aim of this nebulous scheme being to catch the insurgents in a pincer movement and thus bring them to battle or push them into the Atlantic.

It was a plan of doubtful merit. It is inconceivable that the Galicians would have allowed themselves to be crushed by the converging French forces – they were bound to slip away through some gap. Soult, however, had no real intention of implementing the agreed strategy and, covering his withdrawal with a screen of false promises, set out for Zamora. The VI Corps, meanwhile, concentrated and marched south.

Predictably, Ney's offensive rapidly ran out of steam. Brought to a halt before an impregnable position held by the enemy, he lingered in southern Galicia until 9 June, hoping for some sign of Soult's expected flanking manoeuvre. Finally, having discovered that the Duke of Dalmatia had reneged on his agreement and was actually well into the plains of Leon, the infuriated marshal evacuated Galicia and withdrew to Astorga.

But the chain of French withdrawals had not yet ended. Left alone in the Asturias, General Kellermann also found himself in dire straits. His division – an extemporised formation composed of odd units requisitioned from other hard-pressed regional commanders – was dangerously overstretched and the situation deteriorated further with the recall of Colonel Robert's two regiments (3,000 bayonets) to

Aragon. This, coupled with the evacuation of Galicia and the subsequent release of La Romana's corps for operations in the Asturias, compelled Kellermann to relinquish the principality and retire on Leon. Thus, by mid-June, most of north-west Spain had thrown off the French yoke.

Chapter XII

A TALE OF TWO CITIES

I The Struggle for Aragon, 1809

At much the same time that events in the north-west were reaching their climax, the war in Aragon was also gathering pace. The fall of Saragossa – the great symbol of the resistance movement – on 20 February had boosted the sagging morale of the French and had provided the Imperial propaganda machine with a major triumph to boast about. Strategically, too, the city's fall proved a crushing blow for the Spanish armies. Every available unit had been committed to the battle and had ultimately been destroyed or captured. While the French had two *corps d'armée*, under Junot and Mortier, at their disposal, Aragon and the adjacent districts were left virtually stripped of Spanish troops. Indeed, apart from the 4,000 strong division of General Lazan, only a few guerillas remained.

The Imperial generals promptly set about overrunning the province. Mortier took the northern half; Junot's III Corps drove Lazan off towards Tortosa and conquered the south. Although weary and dispirited after their struggle for Saragossa, the French found the Aragonese stunned and demoralised by the fall of their capital. Little resistance was encountered, particularly in the plains of the Ebro Valley, and Mortier even secured the surrender of the remote Pyrenean fortress of Jaca, opening a fresh communication route with France.[149]

Although the fortress of Mequinenza refused to yield, the French continued to make considerable progress. Having easily overrun the central valley, Junot dispatched Grandjean's division into the southern *sierras*, capturing Alcaniz and even penetrating into Valencia to take Morella. The Spanish, however, began to rally. A cavalry regiment sent by Mortier to seek news of St-Cyr's dispositions in Catalonia found its return barred by hordes of militia and had to remain attached to the VII Corps. Another Imperial column was chased from Molina by growing masses of insurgents, and

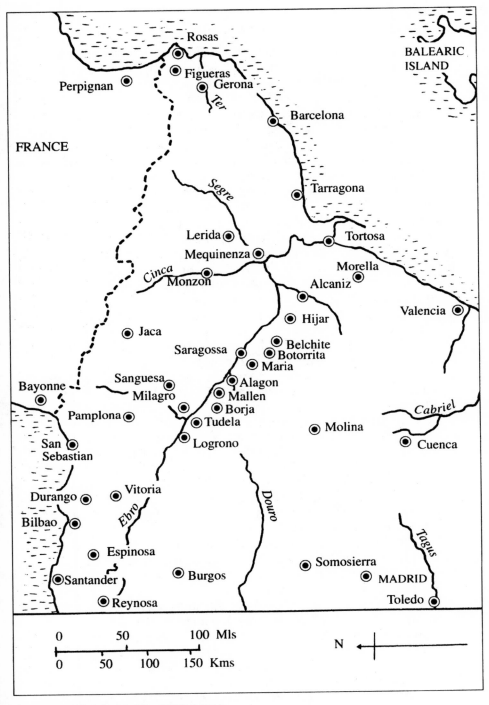

SARAGOSSA AND GERONA:
THE THEATRE OF OPERATIONS

Grandjean's 5,000 men – faced by increasing partisan resistance and the advance of a large Valencian division – were obliged to quit Morella, Alcaniz and many of their other gains.

Worse was to come, for early April saw a drastic alteration to the strategic balance in Aragon. Fearing that he might need Mortier's corps for the war against Austria, Napoleon directed it to Logrono where it would be close at hand if required. Thus, overnight, the French occupation forces fell by fifty per cent and Junot found his commitments doubled. Furthermore, the III Corps was not particularly strong: grave losses had been incurred in the battle for Saragossa, most of Morlot's division were escorting prisoners to France and two other regiments had been loaned to Kellermann for the Asturian expedition. This left Junot with 15,000 troops – in a province of 15,000 square miles. Nor was the general enthusiastic about his command; for the emperor had also decreed that he was to be superseded by Suchet, a division commander in the V Corps.

Events elsewhere were to further complicate the issue. The growing crisis in the north-west led to the V Corps being moved forward to support Ney, Soult and Kellermann. Consequently, Suchet was at Valladolid when he received his new commission and had to trek back to Saragossa under heavy escort. Several weeks elapsed before the arrival of the new commander, during which the Aragonese took full advantage of the frailty of the occupation forces and dealt them two telling blows.

Early in May, a Colonel Perena led a mass of militia in a successful attack on the small French garrison at Monzon. Determined to retake the town, General Habert threw a thousand *élite* infantry and some *cuirassiers* across the Cinca, but the river flooded suddenly and cut this column off. Habert then moved upstream to Monzon itself to try to force a crossing, but Perena was too strongly entrenched. Surrounded by hordes of militia, the stranded French detachment wandered around the eastern bank until, their ammunition exhausted, they were forced to surrender. Only the cavalry escaped by swimming the swollen river. Encouraged, the whole locality rose against Habert and he beat a hasty retreat – relinquishing all north-east Aragon to the insurgents.

More bad tidings followed. After Espinosa General Blake had been offered command of an army recruited in the *Coronilla* (the ancient kingdom of Aragon, and its dependencies of Valencia and Catalonia). Mustering Lazan's division and the Valencian division of General Roca, Blake led this new 'Army of the Right' against Laval's brigade near Alcaniz and drove him into the plains. Thus, by mid-May, the French were being pushed back towards Saragossa and their grip on Aragon was becoming dangerously weak.

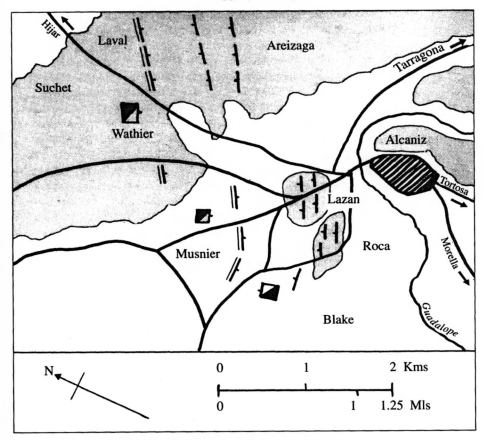

THE BATTLE OF ALCANIZ, 23 May 1809

When Suchet finally joined his new command on 19 May – the day Soult's army stumbled into Orense and Ney took Oviedo – he found the III corps decimated, ill-equipped and demoralised. But he had little option but to take the offensive and reverse the trend of recent weeks, for Blake was now threatening Saragossa, whose defence was an absolute imperative.

Having done everything in his power to improve the morale and material condition of his army,[150] Suchet set out to confront the enemy. Taking Musnier's reserve division and bidding Habert follow him, he joined Laval at Hijar on 23 May, thus concentrating fourteen battalions and five squadrons with eighteen guns – approximately 8,000 troops altogether. Before him, along a chain of three heights to the east of Alcaniz, were ranged Blake's 9,000 men: the southern and central hills were occupied by Roca's Valencians; the northern eminence by Aragonese units. All of Blake's nineteen cannon were in the centre, masking Alcaniz.

After the repulse of a cautious attack by Laval's Brigade on the Aragonese positions, Musnier formed the three battalions of the 114th and the two battalions of the 1st Vistula Regiment into one vast column of 2,600 men and assailed the Spanish centre. Pounded by grapeshot from the nineteen enemy guns and fired on from their right by Roca's Valencians, the attacking units halted well short of the hostile line, disintegrated and fled. Wounded in the foot, Suchet reformed his broken units and, covered by his reserve, retired on Hijar. Contented with this small success, Blake declined to pursue and halted to assimilate a fresh column of Valencians into his army – raising it to 25,000 men. Suchet was only too relieved to get away without further fighting: defeat in his *début* action had further weakened the morale of his troops and, by the time they reached Hijar, panic had reduced them to a disorganised mass.

Encouraged by his victory and the growth of his army, Blake now moved against Saragossa, advancing through the hills to Belchite. Suchet, realising the magnitude of the threat, pleaded with Madrid for reinforcements, but was merely promised the return of Colonel Robert's two regiments from the Asturias – and weeks would pass before they could arrive. By 13 June, Blake was in the Huerba Valley, only twenty miles from Saragossa. He had 20,000 effectives, divided into three divisions under Lazan, Roca and Areizaga. For the final advance, this last formation was sent down the right bank of the river to Botorrita, the other two continuing down the left bank to Maria. Suchet, realising that the enemy had to be challenged, marched out to meet them and, on 14 June, his vanguard collided with Blake's and drove it in.

The stage was set for an epic struggle. Suchet realised that defeat would probably lead to the fall of Saragossa and the evacuation of Aragon – which alone would compromise the whole French strategic position in Spain. However, if one remembers that, at this time, the expeditions of Soult, Ney and Kellermann had also faltered, one can see that defeat in Aragon might easily have led to King Joseph having to evacuate the whole Peninsula. It is as well that Suchet was unaware of the overall significance of his battle; for, to this newly-appointed commander, the prospect of losing the hard-won pearl of Saragossa was daunting enough.

Both sides spent the rest of 14 May in taking up their positions. Leaving the 2,000 men of Laval's brigade to protect Saragossa from any assault by Areizaga's column, Suchet drew up his remaining 9,000 troops opposite Blake's principal force at Maria. The next day,

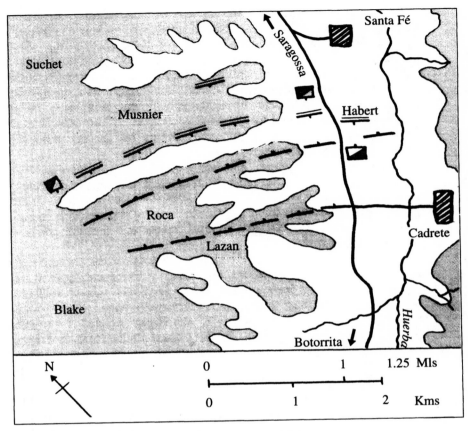

THE BATTLE OF MARIA, 15 June 1809

having learnt that Robert's 3,000 men were likely to arrive at any moment, he resolved to delay any action until the afternoon and refused to be drawn by a Spanish probing attack on his left. About noon, Blake launched a heavy attack against Musnier's division on the French right, clearly intending to envelop it. Engaged frontally by the 114th Regiment and assailed on the flank by Polish lancers, the attacking columns ground to a halt and, decimated by a heavy fusillade from the French *voltigeurs*, recoiled to their starting positions. Suchet, encouraged by this success and by the news that Robert would arrive at 4 pm, promptly counter-attacked and directed the whole of Musnier's command against Roca's reforming battalions. In the ensuing scrimmage, neither side gained any tangible advantage and the fighting came to an abrupt end when a deluge of hail swept across the field.

By the time the storm had cleared, Robert's column had arrived behind the French left. Comforted by this accession of strength, Suchet now pushed forward this hitherto unengaged wing, which advanced across the low ground near the Huerba and fell on Blake's right. Wathier's cavalry quickly routed the opposing Spanish troopers and then wheeled into the exposed flank of their supporting infantry who, simultaneously attacked from the front by Habert's foot troops, were swept away or hacked down. In minutes, Blake's flank had been turned and his army driven off the one road that linked him with Areizaga's command.

Blake refused to panic. He led forward the second *échelon* of Lazan's division and succeeded in mitigating the effects of Suchet's breakthrough. Although his army lost 5,000 men and was driven back, it maintained its unity and finally retreated southwards in good order, crossing the Huerba beyond Maria and linking up with Areizaga's division.

Suchet, surprised by the resilience of his opponent, organised a concentric attack by his own and Laval's command against the regrouping foe. On 16 May he marched for Blake's camp at Botorrita. But his exhausted soldiers proved incapable of anything except a leisurely advance and the 'Army of the Right' evaded the closing pincers with little difficulty. Blake retired to Belchite and again offered battle. By this time, however, defeat and retreat were taking their toll in the Iberian ranks: 3,000 men had deserted, the remainder were weary and despondent, and they had lost sixteen of their twenty-five guns at Maria. Although the position at Belchite was strong, it could not compensate Blake for the losses sustained by his army.

The morning of 18 June saw the short-lived action at Belchite. Blake's 12,000 men and seven cannon were deployed before the town and on the hills to each side. With 13,000 men at his disposal, Suchet elected to ignore the enemy's centre and struck at their more open left wing; Musnier's division forcing the defenders from their position and back into Belchite. Meanwhile, Habert unleashed an assault on the Spanish right. But at the very moment that his battalions engaged the enemy, a stray shell landed in Blake's ammunition stores. The ensuing, tremendous explosion convinced the Spaniards that they were being attacked in the rear and their whole line retreated in chaos.[151]

Abandoning their cannon, the 9,000 fugitives of the 'Army of the Right' fled towards Morella and Tortosa. Leaving Musnier's division to observe them, Suchet established several strong garrisons and returned to Saragossa.[152] The concentration of the III Corps to engage Blake had necessitated the evacuation of most of Aragon and, while retaking the central valley of the Ebro proved relatively easy, the conquest of the mountains to the north and south presented a more thorny problem. This terrain was ideally suited to the operation of the small, insurgent armies led by such men as Perena, Renovales, Gayan and Sarasa. It was virtually impossible to eliminate such determined, resourceful and elusive foes, but, by the end of the year, Musnier and Laval had scored some notable victories in the southern and northern *sierras* respectively; administering some sharp blows to the guerillas, destroying their bases and supplies, and establishing fortified outposts from which columns could operate against them. The guerillas learnt to avoid battle wherever possible – except on their terms – and pursued the traditional partisan war of hitting isolated detachments, murdering stragglers, and disrupting communications and supplies.

II Alvarez's Masterpiece: The Third Siege of Gerona

Whilst Suchet was battling with Blake for supremacy in Aragon, another epic chapter in the history of the war was being written beyond the mountains in Catalonia. Following his victory at Valls on 25 February – five days after Saragossa fell – General St-Cyr had rejected moving against Tarragona and had elected to tackle Gerona. That fortress, having defied two sieges, still threatened his communications through the province and, like Saragossa, had come to symbolise the enduring national resistance movement. For French strategy and morale it was imperative that Gerona should fall, and April saw the Imperial forces preparing for a fresh siege with engineers, sappers, heavy ordnance and supplies being assembled by Generals Reille and Verdier.

By May, all was ready. With the bulk of the Spanish regular forces marching with Blake against Suchet, only Coupigny and 6,000 troops remained around Tarragona. Convinced that this force was no threat, St-Cyr left Duhesme with a strong garrison at Barcelona and struck northwards with most of his corps, placing his divisions in a cordon to cover the impending siege. Simultaneously, Verdier moved up with his independent command of 10,000 men and, reinforced by a weak division from St-Cyr's army, invested Gerona on 24 May – the day after Suchet's repulse at Alcaniz.

The antiquated fortress was garrisoned by some 6,000 troops, supplemented by the usual masses of armed peasantry. The Catalan commander, Mariano Alvarez, a competent and determined officer,[153] had bent every effort to build up the city's defences with earthworks and barricades.[154] But after several days of careful

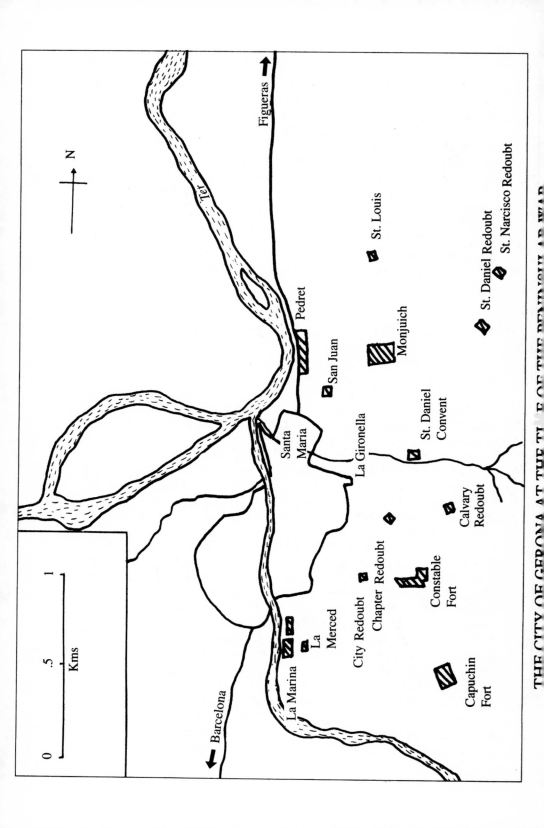

THE CITY OF GERONA AT THE TIME OF THE PENINSULAR WAR

reflection – doubtlessly influenced by his bitter experience at the first siege of Saragossa – Verdier had formulated a plan for the reduction of the fortress. He had insufficient troops to surround Gerona, but was convinced that if he could take the dominating Castle of Monjuich the Spaniards would quickly surrender. Accordingly, on 6 June work began on a series of trenches and batteries across the Monjuich plateau.

In the next ten days the besiegers battered the outlying redoubts of San Louis, San Narciso and San Daniel, occupied the suburb of Pedret and began a merciless bombardment of Santa Maria. However, to Verdier's astonishment, Alvarez retaliated with a spirited counter-attack at dawn on 17 June. Wresting control of Pedret from their startled opponents, the Spaniards destroyed all the siege works in the suburb before being evicted by Verdier's reserves.

This setback delayed the French advance but, by 20 June, the redoubts of San Louis and San Narciso had been taken, and San Daniel rendered so untenable that the Spaniards evacuated it. The besiegers were now able to close in on Castle Monjuich. Unable to excavate trenches in the bare rock of the plateau, the French hauled up thousands of sandbags to erect an enormous battery only 400 yards from the fort. This was dubbed the *'Batterie Impériale'* and, from 3 July, pounded Fort Monjuich with its twenty heavy cannon which proved deadly at such short range. Despite a galling fire from the Catalans in the Calvary Redoubt and the Constable outpost to the south, the French gunners kept up their bombardment and, soon, a yawning 25 yard gap had appeared in the stronghold's north-eastern corner.

On 7 July, Verdier ordered forward the first storming-parties. Advancing in two columns, 4,000 grenadiers and *voltigeurs* hurried across the plateau. The smaller formation headed for the northern wall of Monjuich, while the larger struck at the enormous breach in the north-east bastion. The bulk of the Spanish artillery having been silenced by the *batterie*, the assailants had only to endure the fire of a few light pieces. Consequently, they reached the walls with relatively little loss, only to be met by a tremendous discharge of musketry which swept away whole ranks. The besiegers persevered, but on struggling into the breach found it littered with *chevaux-de-frise* and sealed at the rear. Unable to get forward, the Italians leading the column were annihilated by the small-arms fire that rained down from every building, and soon the whole formation had melted away.

After his experience at Saragossa, one might have expected Verdier to call off his infantry to let his artillery further weaken the opposition before attempting another attack. Instead, the general ordered the column forward again, only to have it repulsed as before.

Although he had now sustained 1,000 casualties for no tangible advantage, Verdier persisted and a third, equally unsuccessful, attack was launched. Simultaneously, the smaller column assailing the northern wall finally broke before the defenders' musketry and, as the wrecks of his assaults staggered back across the plateau, Verdier conceded defeat.

This costly failure had serious repercussions for French morale. Desertion further reduced Verdier's sickly army and, with his troops utterly dejected, the general could do little except maintain his bombardment and push his siege works forward. In this, however, he enjoyed considerable success and, by 4 August, his trenches were penetrating the ditches at the foot of Monjuich's walls. Realising that the end was at hand, the defenders launched a desperate sortie on 9 August, seeking to destroy the French batteries. Although they did considerable damage before being driven off, Alvarez's men bought only a few hours' respite and, on 10 August, finally evacuated the outpost, demolishing its remaining fortifications as they left. Verdier quickly occupied the smouldering ruins, firmly convinced that the surrender of Gerona would soon follow.

But Alvarez remained defiant and the French commander was obliged to apply still more pressure: batteries and trenches were constructed along the northern front of the town – between La Gironella and Santa Maria – and another bombardment was begun. By the end of August four breaches had been ripped in the defences and much of the Santa Maria quarter had been levelled by the systematic shelling. Casualties steadily mounted among the defenders and their food stocks became perilously low, yet still they refused to submit.

Urged by Alvarez's frantic pleas for aid, the Supreme *Junta* at Seville ordered an immediate attempt to relieve Gerona, and General Blake – recently returned from his defeat in Aragon – was directed to march from Tarragona at once. Blake was unenthusiastic. His subordinate, Coupigny, had tried to feed reinforcements into Gerona in July, but his main column had been virtually annihilated by one of St-Cyr's covering divisions; only twelve men out of 1,500 reaching the beleaguered city.[155] Disheartened by this and the collapse of other projects for Gerona's relief, Blake also despaired at the state of his 'Army of the Right'. After the catastrophe at Belchite on 18 June, the bulk of his troops were, at least temporarily, a spent force. Furthermore, new levies to fill his depleted ranks were unobtainable: Aragon now lay at Suchet's mercy and could not spare a man; the Valencians were reluctant to contribute any more troops to operations outside their own province and the Catalans had hurled every available soldier into defending Gerona. Thus, to fill the ranks of his demoralised army Blake had to utilise whatever local recruits could be found. He eventually scraped together twenty-four infantry battalions, two artillery companies and four troops of cavalry: barely 14,000 soldiers, mostly of dubious quality.

Having learnt from bitter experience that open battles with the French were to be avoided, Blake sought to slip past St-Cyr's covering army without a serious engagement. But St-Cyr was determined to bring on such a clash and, as soon as he learnt that Blake was astir, began to concentrate his divisions. Convinced that the destruction of the enemy field army would precipitate the surrender of Gerona, Verdier left a skeleton force before the city and marched to join in St-Cyr's pre-emptive strike.

However, the French scheme for a decisive battle rapidly disintegrated. While the cautious Blake occupied their main force with noisy demonstrations, Garcia Conde descended on Gerona with 4,000 men and a huge column of supplies. Arriving on 1 September, Conde surprised a weak outpost of Italians and utterly routed them. Then, having handed over the supplies and half his men to Alvarez, he rejoined Blake who had lured St-Cyr far afield before bolting to safety. Alerted by the routed Italians, a furious Verdier countermarched with 6,000 men to find that, as well as being resupplied and reinforced, the Geronese had made good use of the respite granted them by his absence: new defences had been erected; the debris had been cleared from the base of the breaches and fresh sorties had again destroyed his foremost earthworks.

Having spent several days repairing and completing his lines of investment, Verdier resumed the siege on 11 September. His cannon were soon pounding the city again and the damaged forward trenches were being re-excavated when the Spaniards launched yet another foray against the earthworks. This raid enjoyed appreciable success and set the besiegers' preparations back by four days. But by 19 September Verdier felt sufficient progress had been made to risk an assault.

Assisted by a feint attack by St-Cyr against the city's western walls, Verdier launched four columns against the breaches between La Gironella and Santa Maria. Braving a tremendous musketry fire, they flung themselves on the defenders with varying degrees of success. The column on the right was made up of Italians, who scaled the breach only to find a four yard deep trench immediately behind it. Although they held their position for some time, the relentless fire from neighbouring buildings eventually proved too much and they retreated in confusion. On their left, French and German battalions struggled to effect an entry at the other breaches and, despite the terrible fire, succeeded in pushing across the walls into the buildings beyond – only to be driven out by a vicious counter-attack. Unde-terred, they rallied and advanced once more, penetrating into the buildings and falling on the defenders with their bayonets. A bloody contest raged in the ruins for fifteen minutes before Alvarez's reserves finally ousted the attackers.

This repulse had worse effects on the besiegers' morale than had the failure against Fort Monjuich, on 7 July. The three divisions making up Verdier's army had, by now, been reduced from 14,000 to only 4,000 effectives. Scores had perished; still more had deserted or fallen sick. The lengthy cannonades had drained the ammunition reserves, the remaining troops were weary and demoralised, and Alvarez was far from beaten. The latest reverse proved too much: Generals Morio and Lecchi left for France, and a disgruntled Verdier simply abandoned his army and followed suit. Deserted by his colleagues, St-Cyr assumed control of the siege force as well as his own and, rejecting further offensive action, resolved to starve Alvarez into submission. Accordingly, he deployed his 16,000 troops in a tight cordon around Gerona and waited.

This new strategem had encouraging results. Alvarez was desper-ately short of rations, and the situation in Gerona after four months of siege was appalling. Conde's mule train had only brought in eight days' supplies and Alvarez found himself unable to provide so much as a subsistence diet for the 15,000 mouths in the city. Desperate, he appealed once more to the *Junta* and Blake for aid.

Their reply – an order for a fresh effort to relieve Gerona – was greeted apprehensively by Blake who considered himself lucky to have fared so well with the Conde expedition and doubted that the wily St-Cyr would be so easily fooled a second time. However, he dutifully told off 6,000 troops to escort a vast supply column. Trusting in surprise, he hoped to penetrate St-Cyr's cordon at one point – and might have succeeded, had the rest of the enemy screen been distracted. Blake, however, neglected to arrange any such diversion and, when O'Donnell's relief column attacked St-Cyr's outposts, the French commander simply directed his other forces against the enemy's flank and rear. Cutting O'Donnell off from the convoy and his rearguard, St-Cyr captured the entire mule train and inflicted serious losses on its escort. O'Donnell and the vanguard took refuge beneath the walls of Gerona; the rest of his division, having suffered 2,000 casualties, fled southwards to Blake's main body at Hostalrich.[156]

This success brought St-Cyr's command of the VII Corps to a triumphant conclusion. Recalled by Napoleon, he left for Perpignan where he arranged for fresh supplies and 4,000 convalescents to be forwarded to Gerona, the siege of which was now entrusted to

Marshal Augereau. That officer was not eager for his new position and sought to avoid its responsibilities for as long as possible. It was 12 October before he assumed command of the equally unenthusiastic troops, who were further shaken on the foggy night of the Thirteenth October when O'Donnell's brigade broke through their lines and escaped beyond the Ter.

In view of his force's appalling morale and numerical weakness, Augereau pursued much the same policy as his predecessor. Apart from a few feint attacks on weaker parts of the wall, the marshal contented himself with a constant, if slow, bombardment of the city. After Verdier's poundings, the Geronese were unlikely to be cowed by such weak fire. Indeed, they celebrated the feast of San Narciso with a traditional street procession – unperturbed by the falling shells![157] But their situation was grim. Their food stocks were virtually exhausted and the toll in sick, wounded and dead was continually climbing.[158] Disease was rife and, as autumn descended, infections like typhus and pneumonia combined with exposure to cut down the garrison in droves. The siege moved into its seventh month, demoralisation began to pervade the defenders' ranks and, for the first time, there was talk of surrender.

Finally, early in November, Augereau managed to deal a decisive blow. Blake, having gathered his scattered forces, made yet another attempt to relieve Gerona; pushing forward to probe the French positions and assembling a new supply convoy at Hostalrich. Augereau responded by trying to force a decisive battle, but Blake again refused to oblige and, after days of fruitless marching and countermarching, the marshal resorted to a different strategem. Realising that both the motive behind Blake's curious manoeuvres and Gerona's fate rested on the food convoy reported at Hostalrich, he dispatched General Pino with three brigades to attack the depot. Pinning down its scanty garrison, Pino captured and burnt the stores at trifling cost to himself, thus ending Blake's hopes of succouring Gerona and prolonging the siege.[159]

With this faint hope extinguished, morale fell further amongst Alvarez's wretched garrison. On 19 November, several senior officers deserted and told Augereau of their dire situation. Heartened, he brought up fresh stores of ammunition and recommenced full siege operations; his gunners soon tearing yet another breach in the wall. Of still greater significance, however, was the progress made by the besieging infantry. 2 December saw an assault by Pino's Italians on the suburb of La Marina and, four days later, they stormed the City Redoubt in a daring night attack. This key fortification guarded the communications between the city and its outlying defences, and the ailing Alvarez was obliged to throw every available man and gun into an effort to retake it. For several hours the Italians were subjected to remorseless attacks by the desperate Spaniards, but the position remained firmly in Pino's hands and he pressed still further forward as the Geronese recoiled.

Retreat turned into rout as Alvarez's men were driven at bayonet point from one position after another. By late afternoon on 7 December not only the City Redoubt but also the Chapter and Calvary fortifications had fallen. Completely cut off from Gerona, with no independent supply depots, it could only be a matter of days before the remaining outlying strongholds surrendered. Tired, sick and despondent, Alvarez resigned, and the morale of the Geronese finally broke. A pact of surrender was concluded and, on 11 December, 3,000 walking scarecrows dragged themselves from the ruined city and laid down their weapons. In addition to the 5,000 deaths the garrison had suffered, half the town's 13,000 civilians had perished, and thousands more joined the 1,200 soldiers wounded in the fray. The French losses were no less horrific; being around 14,000 men, for which Augereau found himself in possession of a smoking ruin, so disease-ridden that he hardly dared to occupy it.[160]

Thus, the French succeeded in taking Gerona at the third attempt. However, it had taken them seven months and 14,000 casualties to crush this symbol of the national resistance, and the story of the heroic defence of the city became an inspiration to all who resisted Napoleon's legions. Gerona even came to rival Saragossa as the embodiment of Spanish patriotism. To the French, the capture of the city represented a major triumph, but to the Catalans and the rest of the indigenous population of the Peninsula went a moral victory which further strengthened their resolve to drive out the invaders.

Chapter XIII

THE TALAVERA CAMPAIGN

I   The Preliminary Movements

When, in April 1809, he first devised his strategy for resisting the latest French invasion of Portugal, Wellesley had written to Castlereagh: 'I should prefer an attack on Victor, in concert with Cuesta, if Soult were not in possession of a fertile province of this kingdom, and the favourite town of Oporto, of which it is most desirable to deprive him.'[161] Having flung Soult back into Spain, the British commander was now free to join Cuesta's forces and implement this original preference.

Leaving Silveira's army and the Portuguese militia to watch the Galician frontier, Wellesley marched to unite with Mackenzie's corps of observation. That force had already clashed with Victor, for, on 14 May – two days after Soult was dislodged from Oporto – the marshal had pounced on Mayne's brigade of Lusitania Legion and militia at the important bridging point of Alcantara. Ousted from the town, the Portuguese had clung tenaciously to some earthworks on the Tagus' northern bank, but withered away before the remorseless fire of Victor's artillery. Finally, as the French infantry advanced to clinch the victory, Mayne attempted to destroy the bridge with a mine. But the sturdy Roman structure defied demolition, Victor's troops crossed and Mayne's battered corps recoiled.

On retiring to Merida, however, Victor discovered that Cuesta's army had recovered from its thrashing at Medellin on 28 March and was operative again. Seriously alarmed, he pleaded with Madrid for reinforcements. The high command, however, was currently swamped with demands on its meagre resources; for news had just arrived of Suchet's repulse at Alcaniz and Soult's retreat from Portugal. Moreover, Wellesley was now likely to strike into Old Castile, where only a solitary division of Mortier's corps was available to confront him. Everywhere the Imperial forces were being forced onto the defensive and, indeed, the I Corps was eventually

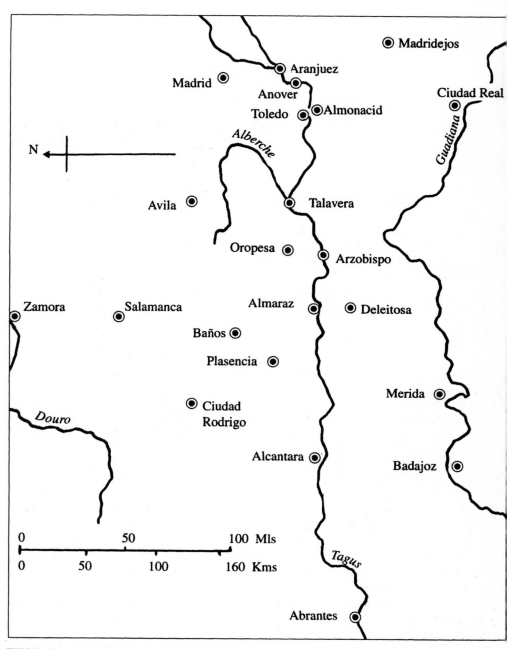

N

Madridejos

Aranjuez

Madrid

Anover

Toledo Almonacid

Ciudad Real

Guadiana

Alberche

Avila

Talavera

Oropesa

Arzobispo

Zamora Salamanca Almaraz Deleitosa

Baños

Plasencia

Merida

Douro

Ciudad
Rodrigo

Alcantara

Badajoz

| 0 | 50 | 100 Mls |
| 0 | 50 | 100 | 160 Kms |

Tagus

Abrantes

THE TALAVERA CAMPAIGN:
THEATRE OF OPERATIONS

ordered to withdraw behind the Tagus to assist in the expected operations against the British. Accordingly, during June, Victor took up a defensive stance between Talavera and Almaraz while, further east, General Sebastiani pulled his IV Corps back from Ciudad Real to Madridejos.

Meanwhile, the Allies were formulating a strategy for their attack on Victor. Cuesta obstinately argued for one of those elaborate encircling manoeuvres which, since Baylen, had dominated Spanish strategic thinking. Wellesley, however, preferred something simpler: his forces were tired after the long marches of recent weeks and reinforcements to fill their depleted ranks were slow in arriving; provisions and the money to buy them were in short supply and, generally, his army's logistical system remained primitive. A lengthy, complex offensive was to be avoided if possible.

The strategic question had still not been resolved when, on 28 June, the British army left Abrantes to rendezvous with Cuesta. Wellesley disposed of some 20,000 men and thirty cannon, divided into four divisions under Hill, Mackenzie, Sherbrooke and Campbell. A further 8,000 troops garrisoned Lisbon or were *en route* to the field army. While Robert Wilson's 1,500 Portuguese formed a flank guard for Wellesley's advance, Beresford was left with the bulk of the Portuguese Army to secure the frontier between Silveira's corps and the forces on the Tagus. Cuesta, meanwhile, had mustered some 34,000 infantry, 7,000 cavalry and thirty guns, with which he was advancing on Almaraz.[162]

Unable to communicate effectively in the insurgent-ridden country, the French had no idea what was afoot. Lost in the fog of war, Joseph was ignorant of developments only miles from his capital. In early July he was still unsure whether Wellesley was poised to invade Galicia or Castile, or if he was regrouping at Lisbon. To compound his difficulties, Sebastiani's retirement in line with Victor had tempted General Venegas and his Spanish 'Army of La Mancha' to advance out of their mountain refuge and threaten Madridejos. Although Venegas had no more than 20,000 men, Sebastiani estimated the enemy at over 40,000 and Joseph – drawing troops from Victor's sphere and his own reserve – rushed to his aid, sending Venegas scurrying back to the hills. The king, however, had to abandon the chase when an ominous message arrived from Victor: 10,000 Allied troops had crossed the Tagus at Almaraz. Thoroughly alarmed, Joseph took his reserve and, leaving Sebastiani on the Guadiana, hurried westwards.[163]

Finding his position between Talavera and Almaraz devoid of supplies, Victor had, meantime, been obliged to stage a further retreat. Burning the bridge at Almaraz, he retired to Talavera on 26

June and took up a fresh position behind the Alberche. Cuesta, using pontoons, crossed the Tagus with his vanguard the next day, before halting to wait for Wellesley who was still many miles to the west.

On 11 July, the British commander arrived to formulate a plan of campaign. The Allies knew that Victor lay ahead with 22,000 men and that King Joseph was likely to join him with another 12,000. This gave the French a force of 34,000 troops at Talavera, with an estimated 10,000 more (actually 20,000) under Sebastiani at Madridejos. It was decided that Venegas and his 26,000 men could contain Sebastiani,[164] but there was some concern that Soult or, more likely, Mortier might descend from the north-west if the Allies threatened Madrid. Mortier was thought – incorrectly – to be at Avila and, thanks to some dispatches taken from General Franceschi (who was captured by guerillas while on reconnaissance), the Allies knew that Soult was at Zamora. Convinced that Soult could not field his battered corps for some time, Wellesley felt that 10,000 Spaniards should be told off to guard against any move by Mortier. Cuesta, however, disagreed and consequently only a handful of troops – mostly Wilson's command – were detached to protect the northern flank of the planned advance on Madrid.[165]

Certain that Venegas could tie down Sebastiani's forces by a spirited drive on the capital, Wellesley and Cuesta believed that they would only have to deal with the 34,000 French at Talavera, against whom they could bring an overwhelming 56,000 troops. To try to doubly ensure success, Venegas was ordered to move on Madrid via Aranjuez and thus draw Sebastiani some seventy miles to the east of Victor – well out of supporting range. Furthermore, the 'Army of La Mancha' was given a strict timetable to comply with so that Wellesley and Cuesta would be certain of its relative position as the campaign developed.

After spending some time in trying to acquire food supplies – which in barren central Spain was proving as big a task for him as it was for Victor – Wellesley began the advance to the Alberche on 18 July. He had around 21,000 men when he reached Oropesa, where he united with Cuesta's forces of 27,000 infantry and 6,000 cavalry. Around noon on 22 July, the Spanish vanguard came up against Latour-Maubourg's dragoons before Talavera, but could make no progress until Anson's British cavalry arrived and threatened the French right flank. Retiring beyond Talavera, the dragoons were joined by a small detachment of infantry, retreating from the town. The Spanish horse made a few half-hearted charges but were easily driven off and, followed at a respectful distance, Latour-Maubourg continued his withdrawal, crossing the Alberche to join Victor's whole corps.

Wellesley was anxious to attack the next morning and, indeed, prepared for an assault over the Alberche. Cuesta, however, was reluctant to comply. It was 24 July before he could be persuaded to advance and, by that time, Victor – having evaluated the enemy's strength – had retreated. When dawn illuminated what had been the position of the I Corps, there was not a French soldier in sight. Victor had stolen a march of ten miles over his opponents and they had missed their chance to attack him before he could combine with Joseph. Wellesley was justifiably furious and refused to advance any further. Apart from any other considerations, his army's logistical system was proving woefully inadequate and the troops were down to half-rations. Proud, old Cuesta, however, insisted that he would pursue the enemy alone and promptly marched for Toledo.

The Allies' calculations were also going awry in other ways. Venegas had failed to pressurise the IV Corps sufficiently, with the result that Sebastiani – advised of the situation to the west – abandoned Madridejos and, leaving a small garrison in Toledo, marched his entire corps to support Victor. Likewise, King Joseph left a skeleton garrison to hold Madrid and rushed out to the I Corps with every available man of his Reserve. Thus, when Cuesta arrived near Toledo on 25 July, he found himself confronted by almost all the French army in New Castile – nearly 50,000 troops.

Unknown to the Allies, a still greater menace was lurking to their rear. By an Imperial decree dated 12 June, Soult had been given command of the VI, V and II Corps. He was to unite them and sweep Wellesley into the sea. The Allies were somewhat in the dark as to the true situation in north-west Spain, and were unaware that Ney had retreated from Galicia and that Kellermann had retired from the Asturias. Because of these withdrawals, Soult easily united the three corps and thus massed over 50,000 troops. Advised of the situation in New Castile, the marshal led his whole army in a sweep to the south; planning to emerge at Plasencia behind Wellesley and Cuesta.

Unaware of this impending blow, the Allies continued with their plans. Cuesta, having realised the size of the enemy forces before him, suddenly lost his offensive ardour and went into headlong retreat. The French, jubilant at finding the Spanish army separated from Wellesley, raced after him. Falling on his rearguard, Merlin and Latour-Maubourg's cavalry attacked with such ferocity that its annihilation seemed certain. Without their infantry, however, the Imperial horsemen were unable to exploit their advantage and, although in great disorder, the Spanish army regained the Alberche.

II   The Battle of Talavera

Wellesley, meanwhile, had thrown two divisions onto the eastern bank to cover Cuesta's crossing of the river, after which these formations began to retire; Mackenzie's division bringing up the rear. However, unknown to the British, the first French infantry had now arrived and, slipping over a ford to the north, Lapisse's division had occupied the woods lining the river bank. Discovering Mackenzie's brigades, Lapisse then deployed his battalions and launched them into the attack.

Mackenzie's pickets – badly placed and more interested in Victor's cavalry over on the eastern bank – failed to see the French infantry until it was too late and, driving forward with tremendous *élan*, Lapisse's troops soon routed the 88th, 31st and 87th. Wellesley, galloping down from his main position, found that the enemy onset had shattered Mackenzie's left and centre, but had not, as yet, touched his right wing regiment – the 45th. Using this as a bulkhead, he rallied the 31st, while the other routed battalions regrouped behind some rifle companies who were also attempting to stand. Gradually, the startled division extricated itself and retreated over the plain to Wellesley's main force. The jubilant French sent them on their way with a few rounds from their horse artillery, but the British cavalry prevented any serious pursuit being mounted. Nevertheless, Mackenzie lost nearly 450 men in the action; Lapisse very few.

Crossing the Alberche in force, Victor's troops deployed and began a mild bombardment. The artillery exchanges did little harm to either side, but when some French cavalry rode towards part of the front held by Cuesta's troops four battalions let off a tremendous volley and, with yells of 'Treason!', fled from the field apparently terrified by the sound of their own firing.[166] Although most of the fugitives were eventually hustled back into line, many deserted their colours, carrying away some of the British baggage guard and spreading panic in the army's rear. Wellesley could only look on in disbelief, as did the enemy cavalry who had started the rumpus. The volley had not even touched them – they were too far out of range.

The position the Allies had chosen to defend extended for three miles to the north of Talavera. Roughly following the Portina Brook, it ran along a cultivated plain before climbing over more open terrain to the Cerro de Medellin. This was a long piece of upland, presenting a steep scarp slope to the French in the east and gentle dip slopes to the west and south. Beyond lay a lateral valley, 800 yards across, flanked to the north by the mountains of the Sierra de Segurilla.

Sir Arthur and Cuesta had agreed that the British contingent

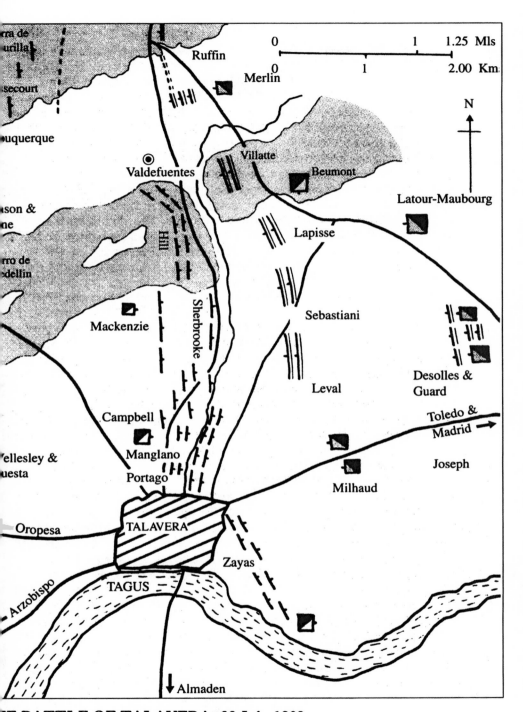

THE BATTLE OF TALAVERA, 28 July 1809

would occupy the northern sector and the Spaniards the area around Talavera itself. Accordingly, General Hill's division drew up on the reverse slope of the *cerro*, with Sherbrooke and Mackenzie's troops on their right, forming the middle of Wellesley's line. The whole of the British cavalry deployed behind the centre, while Campbell's Fourth Division formed the right wing. To the south of Campbell's five battalions lay the 32,000 men of Cuesta's army, strongly entrenched around Talavera. The Allies mustered 52,000 men against King Joseph's 46,000.

After the artillery exchange, an uneasy calm had descended. The British were convinced that there would be no further fighting that day and, having posted their pickets, settled down for the night. Victor, however, had other ideas. Realising the importance of the dominating height of the *cerro*, he resolved to take it with a night attack and thus endanger the whole enemy position before the battle proper began. Accordingly, Ruffin's division advanced to implement this risky venture, of which King Joseph had not even been informed.

Coming up against the Portina, two of the three French regiments got into difficulties. The left hand column, the 96th, finding that the stream here ran through a deep chasm, barely managed to cross it and fell so far behind as to take virtually no part in the attack. The right hand column, the 24th Regiment, got lost in the dark and strayed into the lateral valley to the north. Thus, only the central column, the 9th *Léger*, actually scaled the slopes of the *cerro* and established contact with the British.

Its two leading battalions crept up the hill and surprised Lowe's brigade of the King's German Legion. In seconds the legionnaires were routed and, suffering serious losses, fled southwards. General Hill rode forward to discover what was happening and, mistaking the French infantry for British, was among the enemy before he realised his error and turned about. Lucky to be alive, Hill now led forward Stewart's brigade who caught the enemy in the act of reforming and drove them pell-mell down the hill.[167] Suddenly, feeling its way through the dark, the third battalion of the 9th *Léger* appeared to the left of the British line. Unable to deploy, it was broken by a volley and joined the disorderly retreat, bringing Victor's attack to a gory conclusion.

By daybreak on 28 July, the entire army of King Joseph was arrayed on the plains before the Allied position, most of it in front of the British sector. Influenced more by Victor's enthusiasm than anything else, Joseph had reluctantly consented to a fresh attack on the *cerro* and, at 5 am, a single French cannon fired to announce its commencement. Immediately, over fifty other guns sent a hail of shot into Wellesley's position. Hill's troops on the *cerro* retired to the safety of the reverse slopes where they were reasonably sheltered. Sherbrooke's division, however, deployed on the level plain, were completely exposed to the deadly fire.

After some time, Ruffin's division – on the extreme right of Joseph's army – descended into the smoke-filled valley and began to climb the slopes of the *cerro*. Soon, the skirmishers of Hill's regiments retreated into their lines as the French, arrayed in three regimental columns, emerged from the gloom and advanced towards the crest of the hill. Simultaneously, Hill marched his division to the skyline where its sudden appearance caused the Imperial columns to hesitate. Before they could recover their composure, the British line poured a murderous volley into their ranks from only forty yards.

Although there were 5,000 troops in Ruffin's division, their deep, columnar formations rendered most of them incapable of using their muskets, whereas every one of Hill's 4,000 men could fire. Repeatedly raked by volleys, the attacking columns ground to a halt and fell into confusion. Meanwhile, Sherbrooke – puzzled by the inactivity of the French immediately before him – seized his opportunity and directed one of his battalions to assail the left flank of Ruffin's formation. Simultaneously engaged on two sides, the columns wavered and, when Hill ordered the charge, broke and fled, leaving 1,300 dead and wounded littering the slopes.

With the repulse of Victor's second attempt to take the hill, the battle came to a temporary halt. The two sides agreed to a short armistice while they evacuated their wounded, and many of the French sat down to breakfast while debating the next move. Jourdan, Joseph's Chief-of-Staff, pointed to Victor's failure to make any headway and advised that the army should stay on the defensive until Soult could arrive in the enemy's rear. Although the king was inclined to agree, he was increasingly swayed by the ranting Victor, who insisted that the British would break before an all-out attack and that if such an attack was not mounted they would all have the emperor to answer to.[168]

The vacillating monarch finally had his hand forced by the arrival of two dispatches. The first was from Soult: he was marching southwards, but had been delayed by difficulties in replacing his lost cannon, and might not be at Plasencia until 5 August. The second letter was from the governor of Toledo, warning Joseph that Venegas was getting dangerously close to Madrid. His capital threatened, the king concluded that he had no choice but to agree to Victor's demands. With Soult too far off to be of assistance, the available army was too weak both to contain Wellesley and Cuesta and drive Venegas away. A decisive victory at Talavera was essential to release forces for the defence of Madrid.

Accordingly, a plan of attack was drawn up. Victor's corps was to assail the *cerro* again, but this time the frontal assault would coincide with a flank attack launched from the lateral valley to the north. Prudently deciding to ignore the formidable position of Cuesta's troops. Joseph told off a cavalry division to contain them, while all of Sebastiani's infantry were to drive against the British centre. Leval's Germans were to assail the British right; the bulk of the cavalry, a line brigade and the Royal Guard constituted the reserve.

At about 2 pm, the French renewed the attack. Eighty guns began a preliminary bombardment to which Wellesley could reply with only thirty-six pieces. After half an hour, the cannon along the left wing and centre of the Imperial army began to fall silent as the infantry advanced. The first unit to close with the enemy was Leval's German division on the extreme left of Joseph's army. Struggling through the wooded terrain, Leval lost sight of the other divisions and, fearful of falling behind, urged his battalions to hurry forward. Quickening their pace, his troops were actually the first to make contact with the enemy; driving the pickets of Campbell's division out of the olive groves and across the clearing beyond. Minutes later, Leval's rather disordered formations encountered Campbell's front line of three regiments, a redoubt containing ten guns, and elements of Cuesta's left wing. Greeted with a storm of grape-shot and musketry, Leval's men halted and stood at a distance, firing volleys. Their central battalions torn to shreds by the battery in the redoubt, they began to recoil, and when Campbell ordered the charge Leval's centre and right retreated into the thickets with the British in pursuit.

Having spiked the guns of a captured battery, Campbell withdrew from the groves to his main position, leaving the enemy to regroup. The left wing elements of Leval's command, fearful of being cut off, rejoined their retreating comrades and, thus, this section of Wellesley's line was left clear of enemy troops.

Further north the situation was somewhat different. Here, Sherbrooke's eight battalions were under attack from Sebastiani and Lapisse. After the murderous French artillery bombardment, a mass of skirmishers, followed by serried battalion columns, advanced to complete the destruction of Wellesley's centre. Waiting until the enemy were within fifty yards, the British line fired one devastating volley and charged.

Struck by the fire of 4,000 muskets, the leading French formations suffered appalling casualties and fled. However, when the elated British brigades pursued their opponents across the Portina, they found the French rallying behind their second line and in minutes the hunters had become the hunted. Attacked from all sides, they were driven back across the brook in chaos and suffered terrible casualties, the Guards alone losing over 600 men. Hard on their heels came the triumphant French, pressing forward into the gap in Wellesley's line. With Sherbrooke's division shattered, only the meagre British reserves stood between Sebastiani and victory.

Flinging every available man into the fight, Wellesley rallied the remnants of Sherbrooke's brigades as Mackenzie led forward his three battalions. Sebastiani's men came on with tremendous *élan* and soon a terrible exchange of musketry was under way with whole companies mowing each other down at point-blank range. To the left of Mackenzie's defence, the situation was even more critical: Brigadier Langwerth had been killed and half his troops wiped out, the other two brigades – those of Low and Cameron – had each lost a third of their strength, and all three were streaming back across the Portina in wild disorder. With no reserves left, Wellesley pulled a strong battalion down from the *cerro* and with these troops and a battery of six-pounders, succeeded in buying time for the three routed brigades to rally.

Like Sebastiani's men, Lapisse's division attacked with determination and the fire-fight was soon raging along the whole front of Wellesley's centre. With incredible tenacity, the two sides massacred each other with close range musketry for about twenty minutes until Sebastiani – assailed on his left flank by Cotton's cavalry – sullenly retired. Lapisse's men, their general dead, joined this retreat and slowly the fighting in the centre came to an end, both sides having lost over 1,700 men.

Further south, Leval – having rallied his broken Germans on his reserves – had again assailed Campbell's position. His depleted units waded through the olive groves and fell on the defenders' lines, but could make little impression. Once more, the heavy Allied musketry and artillery fire brought the attackers to a standstill and sent them streaming back in retreat, harried by Spanish cavalry.

Meanwhile, the French turning movement to the north of the *cerro* was begining to develop. From his elevated position, however, Wellesley had long seen it coming and had reinforced his left accordingly: Anson and Fane's British cavalry and Bassecourt's Spanish infantry division had already been moved into the lateral valley, and were now joined by Albuquerque's horsemen. By the late afternoon some 10,000 Allied bayonets and sabres were ready to confront any threat in this quarter.

Against these forces Victor had deployed Ruffin's tattered division and Cassagne's brigade from Villatte's command. To their left, the rest of Villatte's division was poised to attack the *cerro* from the front – once the flank attack had developed – and, meantime, maintained a heavy and accurate cannonade of Hill's units. Advancing cautiously, Ruffin deployed and came up level with the northern tip of the *cerro*. Annoyed by artillery fire from the Allied batteries, his men had reached the farm of Valdefuentes when he noticed a movement amongst the enemy cavalry: Wellesley, having seen the action in the centre satisfactorily concluded, had arrived to supervise the operations and had ordered Anson to attack.

At the sight of the confident advance of the enemy horsemen, the French formed square to receive them. The British troopers sped over the plain towards Villatte's formations, but when they were 150 yards away disaster suddenly struck. Hidden by the long grass, a dried-up watercourse – some three yards wide and two yards deep – lay in their path. Too late to pull up, the front line of galloping horsemen plunged over the precipice, quickly followed by the second rank. The effect was appalling. In seconds, the 23rd Light Dragoons were reduced to a tangled, bloody heap of dying men and horses. A few avoided the shambles and picked their way across, but the regiment was effectively destroyed.

To the left of the 23rd, the 1st Light Dragoons of the King's German Legion also encountered the watercourse, although here it was broader and shallower and inflicted less damage. Anson must have seen that to continue was futile, but he made no attempt to extricate the remains of his command and, with the remnants of his reckless brigade, struggled on over the trench. The charge was suicidal. After riding to within a few paces of the fire-fringed squares formed by the 24th Line and the 27th *Léger*, the K.G.L. dragoons routed towards their own lines, followed by most of the 23rd. The rest, however, galloped between Villatte's formations and assailed Merlin's supporting cavalry. Brilliantly led, his *chasseurs* surrounded and virtually annihilated the reckless British troopers: only a handful escaped.

Anson's cavalry destroyed, the initiative again lay with Ruffin. By now, however, he had learnt of the defeat of the main attack and, abandoning the planned assault on the *cerro*, retired. Joseph debated hurling his 5,000-strong reserve at Wellesley's battered line, but, tangible success seeming improbable and fearful that Cuesta might launch a counter-attack, he rejected further offensive action; bringing the battle to an end. As a gruesome finale, grass fires – kindled by the artillery shells – swept across the *cerro*, with obvious implications for the wounded lying there. The bulk of the Imperial army hurried eastwards to intercept Venegas' march on Madrid and, by dawn, only Victor's corps, left to observe the Allies, remained on the Alberche.

Wellesley and Cuesta had emerged triumphant, but Talavera was a Pyrrhic victory. The British alone sustained nearly 5,500 casualties, including two generals killed, and many units had been terribly mauled. Cuesta seems to have lost 1,200 men between his retreat from Toledo and the end of the battle, so Allied casualties totalled 6,700 in two days. French losses were somewhat greater: around 7,270, including Lapisse. They also lost many field officers – notably in Sebastiani's division, where every colonel was wounded.

But, by fighting, the French had gained themselves a crucial respite. Awesome difficulties would have to be surmounted before Cuesta and Wellesley could resume the offensive. The latter's army in particular had suffered severely and, despite the arrival of Craufurd's Light Brigade – who had executed a remarkable march from Lisbon in a vain effort to reach Talavera before the battle[169] – the Allies' forces had dwindled. Furthermore, Wellesley's 4,000 wounded had swamped his scanty medical facilities and, because of the breakdown of his logistical arrangements, his divisions – their rations cut by two thirds – were withering away with starvation. There were no vehicles or horses to evacuate the invalids or to bring supplies from Plasencia.[170] Nor was Cuesta in any position to help, the state of his corps being little better.[171]

Thus, as late as 1 August, Wellesley had to confess to Castlereagh that 'The extreme fatigue of the troops, the want of provisions, and the number of wounded to be taken care of have prevented me from moving from my position.'[172] His impetus was exhausted, and until his army was 'rested and refreshed' he could not renew the offensive. Nevertheless, he remained optimistic. Confident that the French were too feeble to contain both the Allied forces at Talavera and Venegas' 'Army of La Mancha', he predicted that either Joseph or Victor, or both, would eventually be overwhelmed and forced to retreat, leaving Madrid to the Allies.

III   The Flight Beyond the Tagus

The strategical situation, however, was not as promising as Cuesta and Wellesley believed. Not only had their own advance ground to a halt, but, as we shall see, Venegas had completely mishandled his operations. Furthermore, although repeatedly warned of Soult's southward march, Wellesley consistently underestimated his strength, putting it at under 15,000 troops.[173] In fact, Soult had over 50,000 men and was already sweeping through the mountain passes towards the Tagus Valley, routing the scanty forces left by the Allies to prevent such a move.

Nevertheless, Soult's advance against his communications eventually prodded Wellesley into action. Victor – alarmed by the unexpected appearance of Robert Wilson's little flank column further north – panicked and bolted towards Madrid, leaving the Allies unobserved on the Alberche.[174] When news arrived that Soult was nearing the mountain passes, Wellesley, convinced of the weakness of his force, persuaded Cuesta to reinforce the guards with another division. However, on the very day that Bassecourt set out, Soult swept into Plasencia, seizing Wellesley's depots and cutting his communications. Wellesley resolved to challenge him forthwith. Leaving his wounded and Cuesta's troops at Talavera, he confidently marched off with 18,000 effectives, arriving at Oropesa on 3 August.

The British were, of course, courting disaster. Soult had three *corps d'armée* and was furiously thrusting east to seize the crossings over the Tagus. With Ney's VI Corps bearing down on them, the remnants of the Spanish pass guards fled across the pontoon bridge at Almaraz and dismantled it. Simultaneously Bassecourt, seeing the situation irretrievably lost, hastened back towards Oropesa. Meanwhile, Mortier's V Corps, leading Soult's army, headed for the bridge at Arzobispo and on the night of 3 August clashed with Wellesley's cavalry screen.

A remarkable coincidence now occurred which revealed the strategic perceptions of each of the commanding generals to his opposite number: Mortier's cavalry intercepted a dispatch from Wellesley to General Erskine at Lisbon, stating his intentions and the view that Soult had, at most, 12,000 men; while Cuesta received a letter – captured by guerillas – in which Soult revealed to King Joseph that he would be in the Allies' rear with upwards of 30,000 troops.[175] Cuesta immediately forwarded this to Wellesley and put his own army into retreat for Oropesa. Barely able to provide transport for his own wounded, he left the 4,000 injured British to fend for themselves. Some 1,500 were too ill to move and were left to the French; the rest attempted to walk to Oropesa. However, 500 perished along the road and many others were invalided for life by the exertion.

Reactions to the captured information can be imagined. Soult was exuberant; for he now knew Wellesley's position, strength and plans. Wellesley, on the other hand, was ashen as the realities of his situation dawned upon him: if he remained at Oropesa or continued westwards, he and his irreplaceable army would be obliterated – a disaster that would terminate Britain's intervention in the Peninsula and topple Portland's ministry. Thus, as soon as Cuesta arrived, Wellesley prescribed an immediate withdrawal across the Tagus through Arzobispo. But Cuesta, favouring a pitched battle with Soult, refused to budge and eventually the British retreated alone. As the French massed before him, however, Cuesta's confidence evaporated and, after a sharp skirmish, he sheepishly hastened after his ally.

The Imperial forces now closed in for the kill. As Wilson's little column – forsaken by the main Allied body – was chased westwards from the Alberche by detachments from the local French garrisons, Victor's I Corps returned to Talavera, ready to descend on the flank of the Allied divisions debouching through Arzobispo. Soult, meanwhile, pursued Cuesta and soon encountered his rearguard – Bassecourt's division, supported by sixteen cannon and twenty squadrons of cavalry – entrenched in a seemingly impregnable position at the south end of the bridge over the Tagus. Soult, however, was not easily deterred and, locating a small ford a little along the river, launched a surprise attack at noon on 8 August.

It was as daring as Wellesley's assault at Oporto. Complacent in their formidable position, the Spaniards were patently unprepared: most of them were eating, drinking or sunbathing when Soult's cavalry suddenly splashed across the ford and attacked their flank. Lahoussaye's dragoons made short work of the few Spanish actually in position and were swiftly reinforced by some infantry who bravely stormed the bridge. Too late to prevent the French from consolidating their foothold, the bulk of Bassecourt's command now appeared. A desperate cavalry charge failed to save the situation and, as the Spanish horsemen fell in droves before Lahoussaye's troopers, the infantry took to their heels. Ruthlessly harried by the Imperial cavalry, Cuesta's stricken rearguard fled into the mountains, leaving 1,400 casualties and fourteen of the seventeen guns taken from the French at Talavera.[176]

But by the time Soult had secured the bridge, Wellesley's retreat was well under way and Cuesta's main body was not far behind. The road to Deleitosa was steep and difficult; whole infantry companies were needed to help drag the wagons and guns forward, and progress was painfully slow. Losses from hunger were worse than ever, accelerated by the demands of the rugged path.[177] Concerned lest Soult should ford the Tagus at Almaraz too, Wellesley rushed forward Craufurd's Light Brigade to support a Spanish contingent already there. Their presence and the lack of a ford or bridge prevented Marshal Ney from crossing the river with his VI Corps and he moved off to rejoin Soult.

Soult though had rejected the idea of any further advance into the Estremadurian mountains. Realising that Cuesta and Wellesley had escaped serious defeat, he was preparing plans for a fresh offensive into Portugal. However, King Joseph ordered Ney to return to Leon to support Kellermann's scanty forces, and refused permission for

Soult to march west.[178] Such a move, he argued, would leave Victor exposed to any new attack by Cuesta and Wellesley, which might lead to the fall of Madrid.[179] Unwilling to court such a disaster, the king insisted that Soult remain on the defensive, deploying his remaining two corps between Plasencia and Talavera. This both secured the Tagus Valley against any new incursions by Wellesley and released Victor's corps for operations against Venegas, who was now King Joseph's prime target.

IV   Venegas and the Long Road to Almonacid

We left Joseph hastening east after his defeat at Talavera in a bid to keep the 'Army of La Mancha' from Madrid. Actually, the situation was not as desperate as he imagined. Venegas – after permitting Sebastiani's IV Corps to slip away from Madridejos on 24 July – had continued his lethargic performance and had halted on the Tagus. Although his patrols bickered with the French garrison at Toledo, he evinced no desire to advance and, to his opponents' surprise and relief, remained quiescent at Aranjuez while Joseph concentrated his Reserve, Milhaud's dragoons and Sebastiani's corps between Toledo and the capital, ready to bar the Madrid-Aranjuez highway or support Victor on the Alberche as circumstances dictated.

This deadlock continued for several days, during which the retreat of Wellesley and Cuesta and the subsequent release of Victor's forces deprived Venegas of the initiative. Judging the time ripe for a counter-offensive, Joseph summoned the I Corps and moved south on 5 August. Deeming the enemy position too formidable to risk a frontal assault, he elected to manoeuvre; directing Sebastiani through Toledo and Milhaud across the little ford at Anover. The diminutive Spanish units observing these places were scattered and, by 9 August, Joseph had a sizeable force on the south bank with the rest of his divisions not far behind. However, Venegas seems to have anticipated the manoeuvre: he had already shifted one of his divisions west and was following with the other four. Ignoring a warning from Cuesta that the whole Allied strategy had collapsed and wilfully disobeying an order to retreat, Venegas, suddenly filled with energy and estimating the forces of Milhaud and Sebastiani at no more than 16,000 troops, resolved to attack immediately.[180]

At dawn on 11 August, the 'Army of La Mancha' took up position along the hills on each side of the small town of Almonacid. Venegas deployed his troops in a similar style to that which he had used – with disastrous consequences – at Uclés: his infantry drawn out in a long, thin line, only one brigade in reserve and the bulk of his artillery in

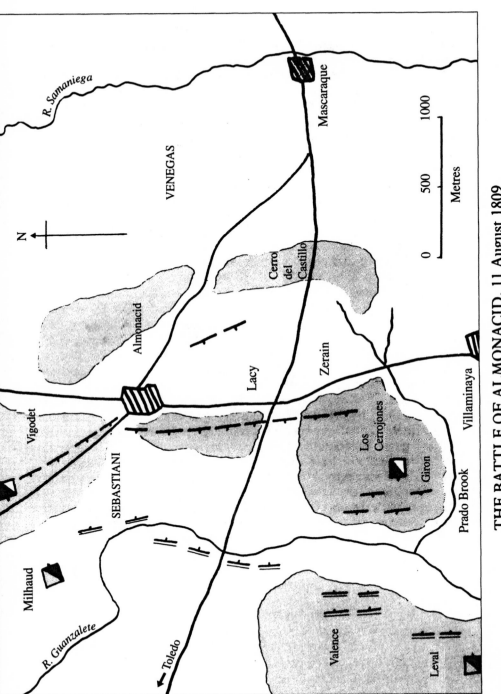

THE BATTLE OF ALMONACID, 11 August 1809

the centre. His cavalry, some 2,800 sabres, protected his flanks. He had about 24,000 men in line, with forty guns; Sebastiani had but 14,000 troops immediately available.

Nevertheless, the French seized the initiative. Before Venegas could open his attack Sebastiani lunged forward. Pinning down the enemy centre and right with his own division and Milhaud's troopers, he sent his other two divisions against their left on the key eminence of Los Cerrojones. Enveloped by Leval's formations and assaulted frontally by Valence's Poles, General Giron's first brigade gradually collapsed and was driven from the hill. Belatedly, Venegas moved his sole reserve – Giron's second brigade – to bolster his crumbling left, but the lost ground could not be retrieved. With the wing being pushed back relentlessly, the Spaniard struggled to maintain his centre, against which Sebastiani now led forward his own division to administer the *coup de grâce*.

Attacked in the flank and front, Zerain and Lacy's battalions were rapidly put to flight, and the French wrested control of Almonacid. At this point, the whole Spanish army withdrew to a second position along the Cerro del Castillo, from where they made a fervent attempt to restore their order and to continue the struggle. For a few moments it seemed as though they might rally, but the roar of cannons and the blaring of bugles announced the arrival of the leading elements of King Joseph's Reserve. With help flooding in, the IV Corps surged forward once more, Venegas' left and centre again collapsed and the 'Army of La Mancha' was thrust into full retreat.[181]

Although Vigodet's division fought a gallant rearguard action which saved the army from complete destruction, Venegas lost his baggage, over half his cannon, 2,000 prisoners and 3,500 in dead and wounded. The French sustained 2,400 casualties.[182] Coming within days of the retreat from the Alberche and Bassecourt's defeat at Arzobispo, the calamity completed the rout of the Allies' offensive and, with the onset of the hot season, the weary regular armies took a welcome rest. The insurgent war, however, continued unabated.

Chapter XIV

THE *JUNTA'S* AUTUMN OFFENSIVE, 1809

I The Allies' Catalogue of Gloom

The retreat of Wellesley and Cuesta to Almaraz marked the beginning of a series of Allied reverses that dragged on through the remainder of 1809. At the news of Wellesley's retrograde movement and the disasters that had overtaken Bassecourt and Venegas, British euphoria over the victory at Talavera evaporated and, by the time his command reached Almaraz, Sir Arthur – soon to be Viscount Wellington – was reduced to writing that 'With an army which a fortnight ago beat double their numbers, I should now hesitate to meet a French corps of half their strength.'[183]

The campaign had, indeed, utterly exhausted his forces. The importance of sound logistics in the barren Peninsula had been painfully underlined, while the collapse of the strategic arrangements made by Wellington with the Spanish had weakened his soldiers' confidence in his judgement: '. . . The great miseries which our troops have suffered', wrote one officer,

> are in no small degree to be attributed to a presumption of infallibility, which . . . Wellington appears to have entertained for his own plans . . . There is now but one opinion of the late campaign – the army in the Peninsula are unanimous and the nation appears to be of their opinion. In arranging . . . his operations with the Spaniards . . . Wellington appears entirely to have forgot the . . . inactive disposition of the people with whom he had to cooperate, nor does he appear to have bestowed much consideration on the nature of the country through which he had to march and the . . . *extreme deficiency* of medical stores showed he entertained no apprehension of a reverse – in short, ere he had quitted Abrantes . . . , he had already in imagination triumphed in Madrid.[184]

Furthermore, Cuesta's tantrums and the gross inefficiency of the Spanish war machine had bitterly disillusioned Wellington. 'In the distribution of their forces,' he complained of the Central *Junta*, 'they do not consider ... military operations so much as political intrigue and the attainment of petty, political objects.'[185] Henceforth, he insisted, cooperation with them would be kept at a diplomatic arm's length until

> The evils of which I think that I have reason to complain are remedied: till I see magazines established for the supply of the troops and a regular system adopted for keeping them filled; [and] till I see an army on whose exertions I can depend, commanded by officers capable and willing to carry into execution the operations ... planned by mutual agreement ...[186]

Clearly, there were problems enough in the Peninsula. But the news from elsewhere was gloomier still. The Austrian offensive into southern Germany – launched on 9 April – had raised the hopes of all those opposed to Napoleon. The Archduke Charles had crossed the frontier without a formal declaration of war and had surprised the scattered enemy corps. For some time the position of the French seemed critical, but Napoleon himself arrived and with seven days of brilliant marches, manoeuvres and battles shattered the Austrians. Vienna fell on 13 May and, a week later, the French crossed the Danube at Aspern-Essling. Despite the bloody check he received there the emperor went on to redeem the situation with his customary flexibility, and finally broke his opponents at Wagram on 6 July. Within a week, Austria had sued for peace.

The tidings of the Treaty of Znaim reached Wellington as he retreated from Talavera and he realised that massive French reinforcements – and possibly Napoleon himself – would soon be *en route* to Spain. More bad news followed. Encouraged by Aspern-Essling and alarmed by French naval preparations in the Scheldt estuary, Britain landed 40,000 troops at Walcheren in August. However, like most of Britain's attacks on the fringes of Napoleon's Imperial tapestry, the expedition failed miserably and 30,000 sick and exhausted men were all that could be salvaged.

For the second time in months a British army had returned from the continent in ruins, and once again the policy of interventionism was subjected to enormous criticism; the Whigs in particular, disillusioned with coalitions and expeditions, urging the country to make peace with France – a proposal that enjoyed little support from those who remembered the abortive Treaty of Amiens.[187] Seriously ill, Portland eventually resigned and a new Tory ministry under Spencer

Perceval took office. But faith in the idea that British arms would ultimately triumph had been gravely weakened and Canning was reduced to asking Wellington whether

A British army of 30,000 men acting in co-operation with the Spanish armies, could be reasonably expected either to effect the deliverance of the whole Peninsula, or to make head against the augmented force which Bonaparte might now be enabled to direct against that country?[188]

Wellington's reply – given in two dispatches of 14 November – was that

The enemy ought to make the possession of Portugal their first object, . . . when their reinforcements shall arrive in Spain. . . . I conceive that till Spain shall have been conquered, . . . the enemy will find it difficult, if not impossible, to obtain possession of Portugal, if His Majesty should continue to employ an army in the defence of this country, and if the improvements in the Portuguese military service are carried to the extent of which they are capable. . . . The enemy have neither the means nor the intention of attacking Portugal at present. . . . When they shall receive their reinforcements, they can be successfully resisted.[189]

Wellington concluded that 'I do not think they will succeed with an army of 70,000 or even of 80,000 men', and was confident that even against a force 100,000 strong it would be possible to keep Lisbon free by a series of concentric fortifications, supplied and supported by the Royal Navy. As long as Lisbon remained in his hands, Britain would have her continental foothold and the French position in the Peninsula would remain precarious.

Impressed by these arguments, the cabinet resolved to continue the struggle and Wellington prepared to resist the French offensive that he had prophesised. 'We must make our arrangements for the defence of Portugal,' he wrote on 20 November, 'according to the plan we settled . . .'[190] His surmise proved correct: Napoleon had concluded that dislodging the British from Portugal was now of paramount importance: 'The only danger . . . is the English army,' he insisted; 'the rest can never hold the field against us.'[191] The tattered British divisions withdrew to Badajoz and more plentiful supplies, while Wellington issued instructions for the building of the Lines of Torres Vedras – the formidable, concentric defences envisaged about Lisbon[192] which, a year later, were to prevent the French from sweeping him into the sea.

II The *Junta*'s Armies and Arrangements

Meanwhile, like their British counterparts, the Spanish politicians were facing a crisis. Tottering under a growing storm of criticism over its handling of the war, the Central *Junta* found its influence rapidly dwindling. Devised as a purely interim government, it was faced by a mounting clamour for its replacement by the National *Cortes* – a feudal body, dating from the era of Charles V. With provinces such as Valencia and Estremadura turning openly recalcitrant, the *Junta* was forced to make concessions and plans to summon the *Cortes* were agreed.[193]

However, if the *Junta* was out of touch with public opinion, the *Cortes* was little better. Established on almost medieval lines, that body was totally obsolete, most members being returned by towns with little modern significance. In short, it suffered from many of the anomalies found in the British Parliament before 1832 – but on a scale which was far worse – and would need overhauling before it could be representative of Spain and her people. Furthermore, with half the country under French occupation, enormous practical problems hampered the electing of the *Cortes*.[194] Thus, its first meeting was repeatedly postponed, while committees established by the *Junta* squabbled over the new government's composition.[195]

Against this background, the *Junta* sought desperately to save itself from destruction. Convinced that a glorious military victory would silence their critics and stem the tide of constitutional reform, they drew up plans for a fresh attempt to liberate Madrid. Although Wellington was unwilling and unable to contribute a single soldier,[196] the *Junta* still had sizeable Spanish forces at their disposal and, undeterred by the costly failure of the June offensive, resolved to gamble these in an autumn campaign.

Their strategy was not unlike that used by the Allies in the Talavera campaign. Again, two main armies would simultaneously thrust at Madrid from different directions, forcing the French to divide their forces. To complicate matters still further for the Imperial generals, a third corps would threaten the Talavera district, pinning down the large numbers of French troops there and thus preventing King Joseph utilising them in the defence of the capital. If all went according to plan, the Spanish high command was confident that the French forces about Madrid would then be overwhelmed on one, if not both, of the attacking fronts.

During the late summer of 1809, the *Junta* instructed General Del Parque in the north-east to supersede La Romana, and to assemble a major army from the units of Galicia and the Asturias which, untroubled by the French since Ney and Kellermann evacuated

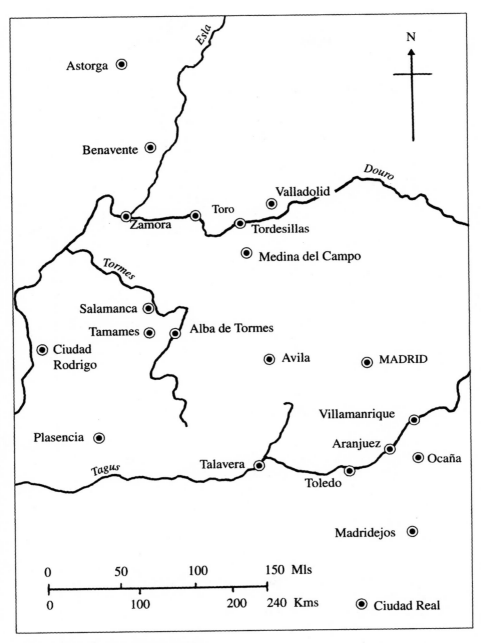

THE OCAÑA CAMPAIGN:
THEATRE OF OPERATIONS

them, were able to muster over 40,000 regular troops for field service. New recruits and 1,000 cavalry detached from the Tagus Valley raised Del Parque's strength until, by late September, he had nearly 30,000 men concentrated at Ciudad Rodrigo, with 20,000 others *en route*.

200 miles away, General Areizaga set about the creation of the other major force by disbanding Cuesta's old command and moving the bulk of it eastwards. With the remnants of Venegas' troops and new recruits, Areizaga gathered an impressive and well-equipped army of over 50,000 men, including 6,000 cavalry. This new 'Army of La Mancha' constituted one of the best forces ever assembled by the Spanish in the entire war and gave the *Junta* high hopes of securing the crushing victory they sought.[197]

The third body of Spanish troops involved in the campaign was the containing force deployed in the Talavera district. Led by the Duke of Albuquerque, it was primarily composed of those elements of Cuesta's old army that had not joined Areizaga. It never contained many reliable units – Areizaga having removed the better regiments for his own command – and was further weakened when the *Junta* directed Albuquerque to furnish a garrison for Badajoz and a large detachment of cavalry for Del Parque's corps. Indeed, by September, the duke had been mulcted of nearly half his original force and could barely field 10,000 men against the three French *corps d'armée* in the vicinity of Talavera.

III   The Battle of Tamames

Having garrisoned Ciudad Rodrigo and left a powerful detachment to guard his communications with Galicia, Del Parque set the 'Army of the Left' in motion at the end of September. Moving by a circuitous route through the hills, he advanced on Salamanca, headquarters of Ney's VI Corps – the only major French force in the province. Ney's divisions were in poor condition. They had not been reinforced since they entered Galicia in February and, since the collapse of that abortive expedition, they had been involved in Soult's drive to the Tagus. Furthermore, as Ney returned north his troops had barged into Sir Robert Wilson's little column on its way back from Talavera to Portugal. A stiff action ensued and, although Wilson was routed and fled towards Castello Branco, the VI Corps suffered appreciable losses.

When news of Del Parque's advance percolated through to Salamanca, Ney was away on leave and the corps was in the not too capable hands of General Marchand. He dashed out to engage the

'Army of the Left' and, on 18 October, found Del Parque in a formidable position along the hills behind the village of Tamames with 20,000 infantry in line, supported by eighteen cannons and 1,500 cavalry. Although Marchand had only 14,000 troops and 14 guns, he elected to attack. Maucune's brigade of six battalions, supported by 600 horsemen, was ordered to turn Del Parque's left which lay on the relatively gentle slopes to the west. A second column, under Marcognet, prepared to storm the Spanish centre at the first sign of a breakthrough, while the 25th *Léger* scattered across the steep slopes at the eastern end of the hostile line and kept Losada's division in play.

Initially, all went well for the French. Pivoting on Tamames, Maucune's infantry struck at General La Carrera's division. Despite stiff resistance, the Imperial troops were soon pressing the Spanish left wing back and, in an effort to stem the advance, Carrera's cavalry trotted forward to threaten their flank, to which Maucune responded by throwing his right-hand regiment – the 69th – into squares. The Spanish horse galloped forward but were coolly received by the infantry and, after being broken by a single volley, retreated in confusion.

Meanwhile Maucune's cavalry had also gone onto the offensive: charging through the centre of Carrera's line, scattering the Spanish foot troops and capturing their artillery. This calamity signalled the start of a wholesale retreat by Del Parque's left wing and Carrera's division could only be rallied when Belvedere's battalions hastened to their support. Advancing up ever steeper slopes, the French could make no progress against this dense, new line and Maucune's attack slithered to a halt.

By then, however, Marcognet – encouraged by his colleague's initial success – had moved his six battalions against the Spanish centre as planned. Struggling up the steep slopes, his formations encountered heavy fire from twelve guns and were finally stopped by a series of devastating musketry salvoes. For several minutes the French troops stood in their exposed position, confusion growing rife as their officers tried to deploy them. Finally, as Del Parque ordered the charge, Marcognet's column disintegrated and fled back down the hill, pursued by the jubilant Spaniards.

Marchand rushed up his reserve brigade, but the engagement was lost. As Del Parque's cheering men returned to the safety of their ridge, Maucune abandoned his flank attack and the whole French corps retired into the valley, leaving 1,400 dead and wounded.

With only 700 casualties, Del Parque could claim a clear victory[198] – the first won by the Spanish field armies since Alcaniz. Flushed with success, he left Marchand fleeing north-east and headed for

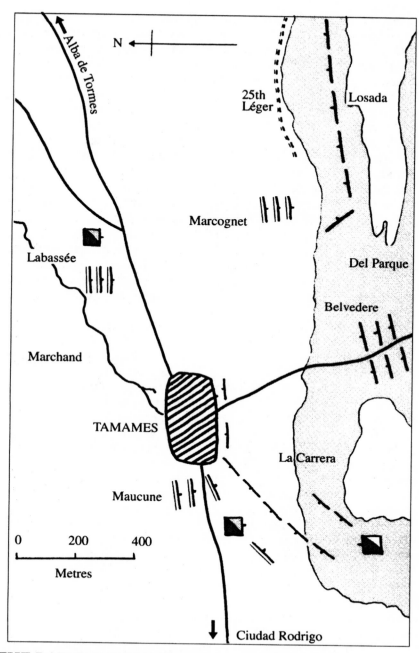

THE BATTLE OF TAMAMES, 18 October 1809

Ledesma in the Tormes Valley. Here, he absorbed Ballesteros' division of Asturians – who had marched south to join him – and thus concentrated nearly 30,000 troops. Full of confidence, he now advanced on Salamanca – hastily evacuated by Marchand – and entered it in triumph on 25 October.

Marchand's defeat led to a flurry of reinforcements rushing to the aid of the VI Corps. First to arrive was a column under General Kellermann, the commander of the garrisons in northern Leon. His disposable forces totalled no more than a dragoon division and seven assorted infantry battalions, but, leaving four of the latter to hold Benavente and Valladolid, he had marched with every available man – some 1,500 bayonets and 3,000 sabres.[199]

Arriving at Marchand's headquarters at Toro, Kellermann assumed command of the combined French forces. By retiring on the Douro rather than towards Avila, Marchand had permitted Del Parque to sever communications between the VI Corps and Madrid. Determined to reopen them, Kellermann swung east, crossed the Douro at Tordesillas, absorbed a brigade of reinforcements under Godinot and then marched on Salamanca.

Challenged by this advance, Del Parque opted to retire. But, instead of retracing his steps towards Ciudad Rodrigo, the wily Spaniard left Salamanca on 5 November and turned southwards. Kellermann dared not follow; for all of north Leon and Old Castile had risen in his absence. He reinstalled the strengthened VI Corps at Salamanca and rushed back to relieve his beleaguered garrisons beyond the Douro.

IV The Battle of Ocaña

Forty-eight hours before Del Parque evacuated Salamanca, Areizaga began his offensive. Covering eighty miles in only five days, he suddenly appeared to the south of Ocaña with 48,000 well-equipped infantry, 6,000 cavalry and sixty cannon. Hopelessly outnumbered, Milhaud's French dragoon regiments executed a fighting withdrawal, while King Joseph frantically searched for more troops to confront this unexpected threat to his capital. The significance of Del Parque's curious manoeuvres now became apparent. Having drawn off Joseph's reserves, the 'Army of the Left' had melted into the *sierras*, leaving Areizaga to deal a decisive blow against Madrid. The real danger lay to the south – not to the north-west.

Unimpressed by the noisy demonstrations Albuquerque's little army was making beyond the river, Joseph shifted his corps along the Tagus until no Imperial troops lay further west than Talavera.

This released most of Victor's and Mortier's divisions for the defence of Madrid, and while the latter marched for Toledo the I Corps – already there – threatened to descend on Areizaga's flank and rear.[200]

Surprised by Albuquerque's evident failure to contain Victor, Areizaga was loath to advance further. For three days he hesitated; giving the French a desperately needed respite in which to finish their preparations. Only late on 11 November – having lost any advantage he might once have had – did he resume his march on the capital, promptly colliding with Milhaud's dragoons and Sebastiani's Polish division at Ocaña.

There followed a confused skirmish between the cavalry of Areizaga's vanguard and the heavily outnumbered Imperial units. Milhaud's troopers skilfully lured the hostile horsemen into attacking Sebastiani's infantry squares. Without infantry support, the Spaniards could make no headway and, after losing 200 men in fruitless assaults, sullenly retired. Prudently deciding not to try conclusions with the main body of the 'Army of La Mancha', Milhaud and Sebastiani withdrew under cover of darkness, joining with Leval's German division at Aranjuez.[201]

12 November saw a radical change in Areizaga's deployments. Alarmed by the sabre-rattling of Victor at Toledo, he judged his flank and communications with La Mancha to be threatened; so, while Freire's cavalry probed towards Aranjuez, the rest of the army swung eastwards and began crossing the Tagus at the ford of Villamanrique – some twenty-five miles above the French position. King Joseph, meanwhile, continued with his concentration: by nightfall, he had Victor's corps at Aranjuez, and Mortier's at Toledo. Detachments from the VI Corps and Kellermann's command were *en route*, and a division of light cavalry had been dispatched to cover the roads leading east from Madrid.[202]

Although Areizaga constructed pontoon bridges to supplement the ford at Villamanrique bad weather and flooding slowed his passage to a crawl, and as late as 15 November most of the army had yet to cross. That same day, however, the Spanish cavalry screen encountered French patrols east of Madrid and reported that Victor's I Corps was approaching. At this, Areizaga ordered a complete withdrawal and soon had his entire force back on the Tagus' south bank – much to the chagrin of the French. But by now the strategic position of the 'Army of La Mancha' was becoming critical. With Victor close behind him and other Imperial units debouching through Aranjuez, Areizaga struck west for the highway at Ocaña.

The morning of 18 November saw the two hostile armies converging on that place. A major engagement was inevitable and it opened with the largest cavalry *mêlée* of the war, involving nearly 8,000 troopers. As the French cavalry vanguard – under Milhaud and Paris – approached Ocaña, they encountered General Freire's massed Spanish horsemen. Paris' light division charged the first hostile line and cut it to pieces, only to falter before the bulk of Freire's regiments. But help was at hand: with his customary expertise, Milhaud led his dragoons in a furious charge at Freire's formation. They ploughed a bloody path into the midst of the hostile column and a vicious *mêlée* was soon raging.

Despite their numbers, the Spanish could not resist the onslaught and they quickly fled, leaving behind 400 casualties. The French spurred after them, but halted at the approach of Areizaga's main body; its leading units were already in Ocaña, with long columns snaking back across the plains to the east. Lest his prey might retreat and elude him once more, King Joseph declined to wait for the distant I Corps and, by dawn on 19 November, had 34,000 troops supported by forty cannon drawn up before Ocaña, ready for battle. To the south – deployed on either side of the town – lay the 51,000 men of the 'Army of La Mancha'. But for a gully protecting the left wing of Areizaga's line and a few olive groves, the plateau was featureless. It was perfect terrain for cavalry.

Deterred by the gully, Soult – who had superseded Jourdan as the king's Chief-of-Staff – advised Joseph to ignore the enemy's left and to concentrate against their centre and right. The king agreed; deciding to strike at Areizaga's front and then, when the Spanish reserves were committed, to fall on his eastern flank. Accordingly, Senarmont – who had handled the artillery so brilliantly at Friedland[203] – gathered thirty pieces opposite Ocaña to contain the Spanish left. Behind this vast battery and to its right deployed two infantry brigades and the king's Reserve. Werlé's Poles and Leval's Germans, supported by Girard's division, marched against the Spanish right wing, while the massed French cavalry – screened by olive plantations – swung out to envelop their flank.

As the French artillery roared into action, the divisions of Leval and Werlé engaged the troops of Lacy and Castejon. Despite heavy fire from the enemy batteries the Imperial battalions edged their opponents back, and were making considerable headway when the Spaniards suddenly counter-attacked. The Germans and Poles recoiled, and Girard was forced to commit his division to stabilise the situation. Meanwhile, Milhaud's 3,500 cavalry had suddenly emerged from the groves at the eastern extremity of the Spanish position. This flank was protected by Freire's cavalry corps, who repeated their performance of the previous day and were driven from the field in disorder. While a few of Milhaud's horsemen pursued

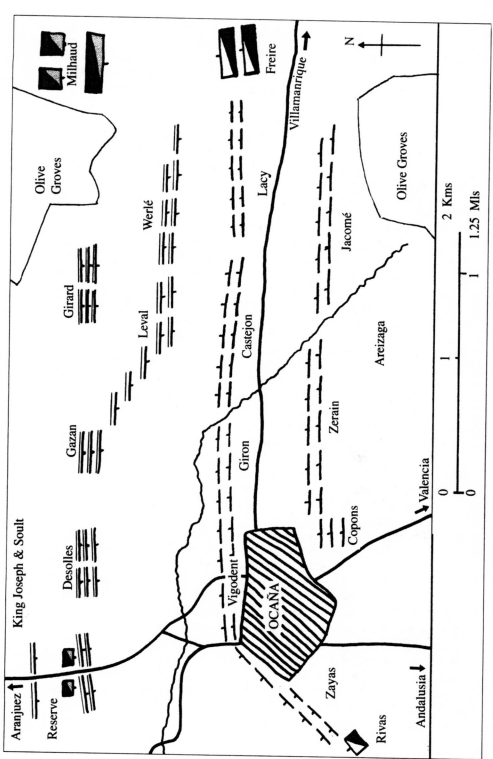

THE BATTLE OF OCAÑA, 19 November 1809

them, most of the French cavalry wheeled into the exposed flank of Lacy's infantry and swept westwards.

Milhaud's onslaught proved catastrophic for the 'Army of La Mancha'. Grappling with the hostile infantry to their front, the Spanish foot soldiers suddenly found themselves assailed by cavalry from the flank and rear. Unable to form square, entire divisions were successively rolled up, routed and slaughtered. Thousands of men perished; still more were captured. The second line of Areizaga's infantry went the same way. Although they had not yet been committed to the fight against Girard's battalions, they were attacked in the flank by Milhaud before they could deploy. Their right-hand formation – Jacomé's division – threw down their weapons as one man and surrendered, exposing the rest of the line to the French charges. Assailed on their flank by the enemy and battered by crowds of fugitives from the front, the second *échelon* of Spanish divisions quickly crumbled and broke into flight.

As the king's reserves descended on the enemy's centre to complete the rout, Areizaga fled. General Zayas abandoned his position behind the gully and rushed to the support of the rest of the army. He found the divisions of Copons and Vigodet retreating in some semblance of order, but the other formations had been hopelessly routed. With conspicuous gallantry, Zayas deployed his division and fought to keep the pursuing French at bay, but it was a futile operation and, five miles from the battlefield, his battered little force finally dissolved into the torrent of fugitives. Just as Zayas was being overwhelmed, Victor arrived with his cavalry and, having already exterminated Areizaga's rearguard and captured his baggage along the Villamanrique road, now joined with Joseph's squadrons in the pursuit of the shattered 'Army of La Mancha'.[204]

Fanning out over the New Castile plains, they pressed the routed Spanish with unrelenting energy and inflicted appalling casualties. By the time Joseph finally called a halt, his troops had captured over 14,000 prisoners, fifty cannon and thirty standards. They sustained 2,000 casualties – nearly all infantry in the divisions of Leval, Werlé and Girard. The number of Spanish dead and injured is virtually impossible to state with any certainty, but when Areizaga eventually rallied the fugitives only 24,000 men were found to be present – the divisions of Lacy, Zerain and Jacomé *combined* mustering only 3,500 bayonets. 12,000 troops remained unaccounted for, most of whom had probably fallen under the French sabres.[205]

V Kellermann's Triumph at Alba

A few days before the rout at Ocaña, Del Parque's 'Army of the Left' – encouraged by Kellermann's return to northern Leon and the withdrawal of other Imperial units to support Joseph – ventured from their mountain refuge and resumed operations against the VI Corps. Hopelessly outnumbered, Marchand again left Salamanca to the enemy and fell back to the Douro, uniting with Kellermann's *colonne mobile* – which had hastened to his assistance – at Medina del Campo. After fighting a cursory engagement there, however, Del Parque learnt of the Ocaña *débâcle* and, realising that Joseph's forces were now free to concentrate against him, went into immediate retreat for the sanctuary of the *sierras*. So rapid was his unexpected dash to the rear that Kellermann's cavalry had difficulty in maintaining contact. Nevertheless, on 28 November, they found him encamped at Alba de Tormes, with three of his five divisions still on the river's eastern bank. Kellermann realised that the whole enemy army might escape beyond the Tormes at any moment. On the other hand, he had nothing but his cavalry with which to attack, his infantry being many miles to the rear. Noticing the dangerously short distance between the Spanish pickets and their main position, he decided to risk a surprise assault to pin the enemy down until his infantry could arrive.

At the sound of the French bugles, the resting Spaniards struggled to form a defensive line. Anglona's cavalry rode forward to support their startled pickets and the three infantry divisions hastily deployed, but all was in vain. With Lorcet's *chasseurs* and hussars leading the way, four waves of French cavalry swept down. In moments Del Parque's cavalry had been destroyed and the French troopers were cutting down his infantry. Leaving 3,000 in dead, wounded and prisoners, half the Spanish foot soldiers fled towards the bridge of Alba and safety. The remainder managed to form square.

The French commander, however, refused to throw away his advantage by engaging them. Instead, for nearly three hours, he launched repeated feints that glued the Spanish to their positions and prevented them escaping to the far bank. Unable to move reinforcements across the crowded bridge, Del Parque watched helplessly from the western bank while, in the distance, the leading units of the French infantry loomed ominously into view.

But the full potential of Kellermann's victory was not to be exploited. The Spanish squares realised their fate was sealed unless they made a dash for the bridge and, in growing darkness, executed a disorderly retreat. Although they lost many more men, the bulk rejoined Del Parque. Nevertheless, for losses totalling 300, Kellermann had inflicted casualties of over ten times that number, capturing nine cannon, a large quantity of baggage and five standards into the bargain. His infantry arrived minutes too late to clinch an even greater victory, but the leading battalions evicted Del Parque's rearguard from Alba and seized the bridge over the Tormes.[206] Severely shaken, the Spanish commander ordered an immediate retreat rather than risk another clash with the victorious French. But it soon became clear that the battle had had a disastrous effect on his army's morale: during the night, the three divisions involved disintegrated and fled in all directions. It took Del Parque until the end of December to restore cohesion to his army and, even then, only 26,000 of the 29,000 men that had marched from Alba were back with the colours. Forced to winter in the barren *sierras* between Ciudad Rodrigo and Plasencia, the 'Army of the Left' was further diminished by malnutrition, cold and disease, and by the end of January totalled no more than 17,000 sickly troops.

Thus, the autumn campaign ended in gory defeat for the Spanish armies and sealed the fate of the Central *Junta*. Throughout, Areizaga and his political masters had underestimated the inherent complexities of their military strategy. Neglecting to furnish Albuquerque with adequate forces for his essential mission was a crucial error, which compromised the whole venture from the outset. Indeed, coordinating offensives launched from two widely separated points had generally proved more difficult than anticipated and the French – using their famed mobility to the full and enjoying the advantages of operating on interior lines – had been able to field sufficient forces on each front to secure success.

Although the *Junta* tried to stifle its critics by inflating Tamames and other minor successes of the campaign, there was no disguising that the operation had been a military catastrophe. Andalusia now lay wide open to French attack and even Wellington had been given cause to question his optimistic prognosis of 14 November: 'Circumstances have certainly altered materially since that letter was written,' he confessed,

> but . . . have they altered in such a manner as to induce me to think that with 30,000 men, which . . . I shall have in the course of a few weeks (together with the Portuguese army, which . . . is better than I ever expected . . . and wants only to be equipped as it ought), I shall not be able to save Portugal, or, at all events, to sell the country dearly?
> I think that if the Spanish armies had not been lost, . . . very large reinforcements indeed would have been necessary to enable

the French even to attack us. As it is, have we now no chance? Ought we to withdraw from the Peninsula, and give up the whole . . . to the conqueror? Will 10,000 men more, which will distress our means, supposing that Great Britain can afford to supply them, compensate for the loss of these Spanish armies, and put us in the situation in which my dispatch of the 14th November supposed we ought and should stand?

I think that if the Portuguese do their duty, I shall have enough to maintain it; if they do not, nothing that Great Britain can afford can save the country . . .[207]

Fortunately for Wellington, however, there was not to be an immediate French invasion of Portugal; though, as Jourdan – Joseph's Chief-of-Staff – observed, circumstances dictated that such a move would have been the best course of action: 'The English army', he wrote,

now being the only organised force in a state to face the Imperial troops, and its presence in the Peninsula being the thing that sustained the Spanish government and gave confidence to the Spanish people, . . . we ought to have set ourselves to destroy that army, rather than to have disseminated our troops in garrisoning the whole surface of Spain.[208]

Joseph, however, was bent on this latter course and, in January 1810, finalised plans for an invasion of Andalusia. Wellington, busy preparing the Lines of Torres Vedras, was thus given a crucial, ten-month respite.

VI   The French Invasion of Andalusia

The days immediately following Ocaña saw the Andalusians striving to get their defences in order and King Joseph consolidating his position. His immediate problem was to reinforce Kellermann, who was battling with Del Parque around Salamanca. Leaving Milhaud to mop up the fugitives from Areizaga's broken army, he ordered several columns to the assistance of the VI Corps and returned with the bulk of his forces to Madrid.[209] Days later, he received the welcome tidings of Kellermann's victory at Alba, and shortly afterwards the vanguard of Napoleon's reinforcements from Germany entered Spain. In the weeks ahead, some 90,000 fresh soldiers poured over the Pyrenees, sweeping Navarre and Old Castile clear of insurgents, and relieving Joseph's beleaguered garrisons. This influx of new troops – coupled with the victory at Alba – released thousands of men for field operations and permitted the king to make detailed plans for invading Andalusia.

An attack on that province had a good deal to recommend it. It was the largest, most populous and wealthiest in the country, and contained the capital of the 'rebel' government, Seville, with colossal arsenals and military stores. To Joseph – deeply troubled by financial difficulties – Seville alone would be a priceless acquisition. His regime was collapsing under the burden of maintaining the war and his Imperial brother's correspondence offered little hope. 'The new levies and immense armaments that I am making for Spain, continue to ruin me,' the emperor complained in November. Two months later, he commanded a secretary to

> Write to Laforest at Madrid, telling him to present notes on the impossibility of meeting the enormous expenses of Spain; that I have already sent three hundred million francs there; that the despatch of such considerable sums of money exhausts France [and that] ... the war with Austria cost me a great deal of money.[210]

By February, Napoleon had informed Joseph that, henceforth, only 80,000 francs a month would be allotted to Madrid and that every resource of occupied Spain was to be applied to maintaining the army.[211]

Joseph could see other advantages attached to a conquest of Andalusia. The Spanish authorities were known to be making every effort to prepare the province to resist an invasion. A torrent of decrees from the *Junta* had introduced conscription *en masse*, ordered the requisition of horses, money and plate, and begun the construction of fortifications in the passes of the Sierra Morena. Any delay on the king's part and the opportunity for an easy conquest would be lost. A sudden blow might annihilate the remnants of Areizaga's army and, perhaps, secure the capture of the *Junta*, along with Seville's military stores. The arguments for immediate action seemed overwhelming.

However, whilst there were clear advantages to be gained from a seizure of Andalusia, Joseph rather overlooked past experience in implementing the project. Even if the province did have much to offer in terms of money and political prestige, the drawbacks attached to a long-term occupation were enormous. Firstly, the French had found throughout the Peninsula that conquest was not enough: they had had to maintain garrisons to keep the district subjugated and this consumed vast numbers of troops – rendering

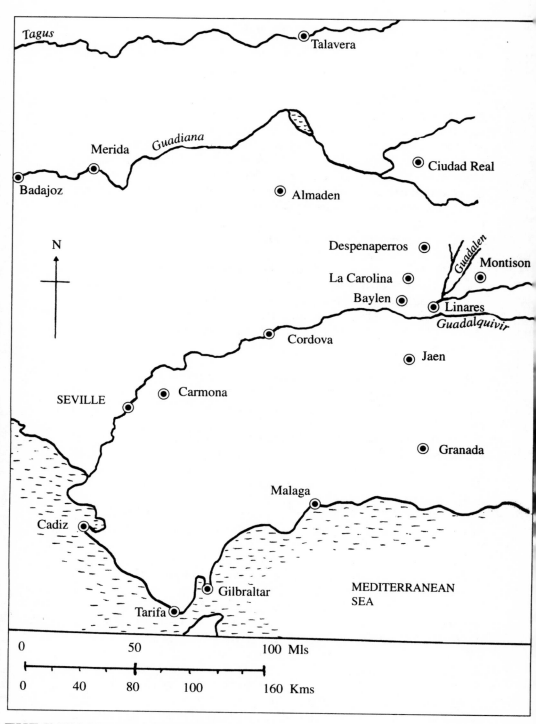

**THE INVASION OF ANDALUSIA:
THEATRE OF OPERATIONS**

further offensive operations difficult or impossible. Secondly, the maintenance of such an occupying force invariably proved expensive and eroded any initial financial benefit. In these respects Andalusia was to prove no different to any other region, and Joseph soon found that he had merely committed another 70,000 troops to the grinding war of attrition.

When the blow finally fell, the Andalusians were patently unprepared. Although the response to the *Junta*'s decrees had been good, there had been too little time to achieve anything of value. Only Albuquerque's 8,000 men and the rallied dregs of Areizaga's divisions – backed by a few thousand raw conscripts and some unfinished earthworks – stood between the French and Andalusia. Furthermore, the *Junta*'s tiny army had to cover a front of enormous dimensions: their left wing – consisting of Albuquerque's little force – lay about Merida, observing the French II Corps at Talavera. Eighty miles to the east the battered divisions of Copons and Zerain – some 4,500 men – held the passes around Almaden. Another sixty miles east of them lay Areizaga's main body – 19,000 men – stretching for nine leagues from La Carolina to Montison. Thus, there were some 32,000 Spanish troops spread over 167 miles, trying to contain French forces totalling over 80,000 men.

However, the difficulties of moving a large army through barren mountains in mid-winter limited the strategy the French could adopt. Eventually, Joseph elected to divide his forces into two columns. The first – Victor's 22,000 men – would thrust at Cordova and, once this manoeuvre was under way, the king and 40,000 more troops would sweep into the passes at La Carolina. With luck, Areizaga would be driven down the Guadalquivir into Victor's arms and his army would be destroyed. In the meantime, to pin Albuquerque down and to confuse the enemy, Reynier's II Corps mounted noisy demonstrations around Talavera.

Gathering reliable intelligence from a mountainous, 170-mile front posed grave difficulties for the Spanish high command. When Victor ousted Zerain from Almaden on 12 January, Areizaga was uncertain whether the attack was a feint or the beginning of Joseph's offensive, and the appearance of Mortier's V Corps near La Carolina and a probing attack by Sebastiani on Montison only deepened his confusion.

Six days after Zerain's defeat, however, Joseph initiated the attack on the passes at La Carolina and, too late, all became clear to Areizaga. Deploying whole regiments in skirmish order, Mortier led them up lateral valleys and across the hilltops to descend in the enemy's rear. He proved unstoppable and Areizaga's left wing was soon in flight. Simultaneously, General Girard dislodged Lacy and

Zayas' troops from Despeñaperros and drove them towards La Carolina. Intercepted by Mortier, they abandoned their artillery and, suffering frightful losses, scurried over the mountains to the south.

Meanwhile, Sebastiani had been trying conclusions with the extreme right of the Spanish army. After a vicious struggle, Vigodet's 6,000 troops were ousted from their position near Montison and fled down the Guadalen. Areizaga's reserve division – that of Arquillo – then appeared but, seeing the battle lost, sought to escape by retreating on Linares. By now, however, Mortier had seized that town and the horrified Spanish general found himself trapped between converging enemy forces. The situation was a virtual replica of Dupont's at Baylen – but with the roles reversed – and, only twenty-two miles from the site of that ignominious defeat, Mortier had the ironic satisfaction of receiving Arquillo's surrender.

While Joseph united with Victor and marched on Seville, Sebastiani chased the dregs of Areizaga's army across the Guadalquivir and, on 23 January, dispersed them in a brief fight outside Jaen. Cordova fell the next day but, on 28 January, some prisoners taken by Victor's cavalry alerted Joseph to the arrival of a Spanish army from the north-west. Apparently, the *Junta* had summoned both Del Parque and Albuquerque to protect Seville. The former was too distant to arrive in time, but Albuquerque, having reinforced the garrison of Badajoz, had moved to join Areizaga.

Assimilating the remains of Zerain's division into his column, Albuquerque halted at Carmora where some speedy intelligence work revealed the extent of Areizaga's defeat. Rightly judging Seville to be lost – it fell on 1 February – he marched for the island stronghold of Cadiz which, by some mishap, the French had neglected to seize. Joseph belatedly ordered the I Corps after him, but, arriving too late to prevent both Albuquerque and the *Junta* taking refuge in the impregnable fortress,[212] Victor could only blockade the place. Cadiz was to become a major problem for the forces occupying Andalusia and Joseph came to regret having overlooked it.[213]

Within days, the mighty field force that the king had moved into the province dwindled away: Sebastiani occupied Granada and probed into Murcia; Victor invested Cadiz; and elements of Mortier's V Corps moved towards the Guadiana. Meanwhile, La Romana – leading Del Parque's old army – belatedly arrived from the north and, joining with a detachment from Wellington's forces, sealed off the Portuguese frontier about Badajoz. Over extended by their existing commitments, the victorious French ground to a halt and by March 1810 their offensive power was spent. The task of maintaining their gains had, however, just begun.[214]

The River Douro at Oporto. Note the Pontoon bridge (National Army Museum, London)

The passage of the Tagus by Wellesley's forces on their way to Talavera (Fotomas)

Baggage-train following the army at Sierra de Estrella (Fotomas)

The retreat of the French from Arroya dos Molinos, 1811 (The Mansell Collection)

Wellington and Lord Raglan at Sorauren. Painting by T. J. Barker (Courtauld Institute of Art. Reproduced by Permission of The Duke of Wellington, Stratfield Saye, near Reading, Berks.)

British troops in bivouac at Villa Velha (BBC Hulton Picture Library)

Skirmish on the retreat to Busacco (The Mansell Collection)

The 23rd Light Dragoons plunge into a dried-up watercourse during the battle of Talavera
(The Mansell Collection)

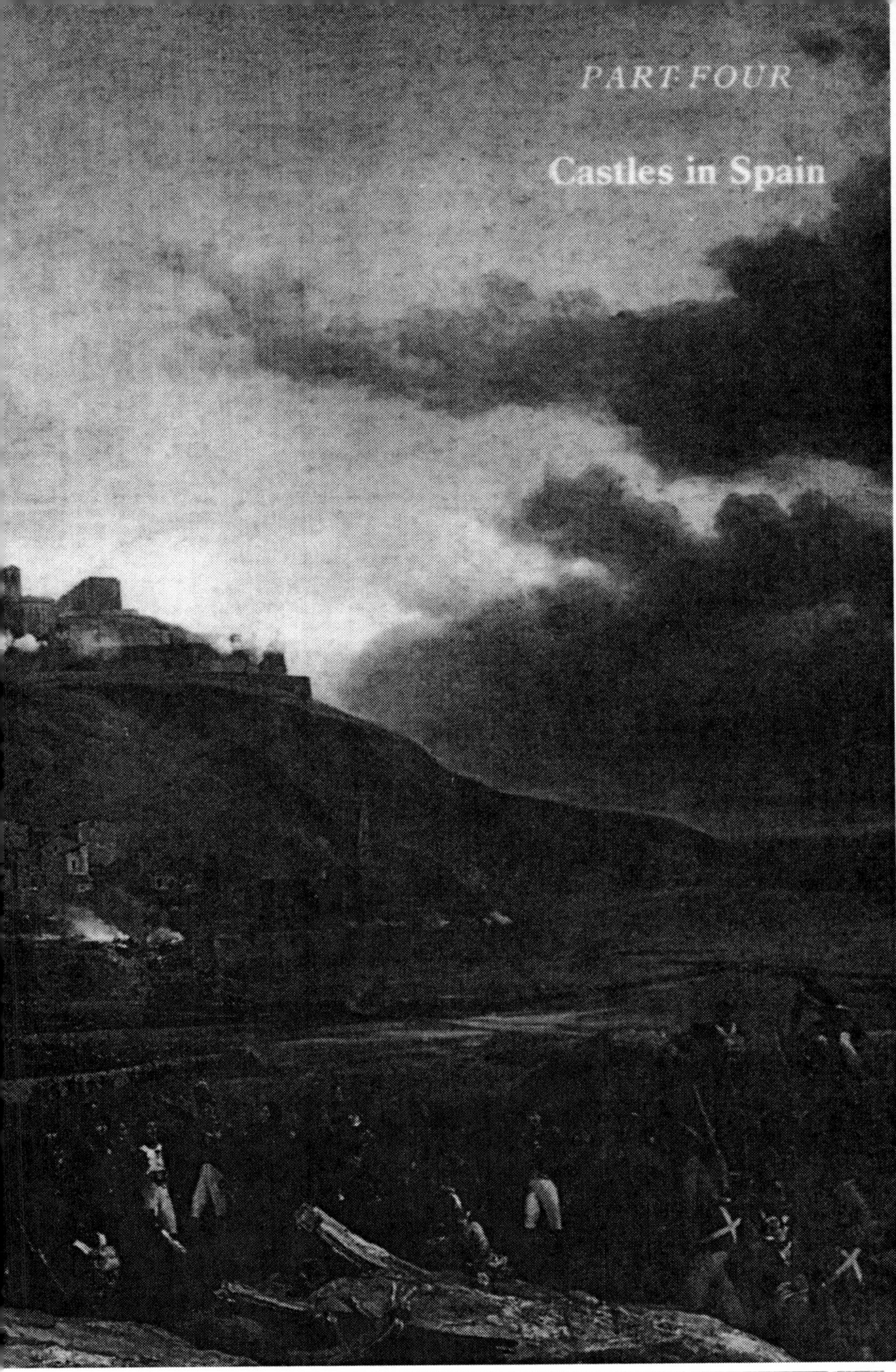

PART FOUR

Castles in Spain

Overleaf: Suchet's troops besiege Lerida (*Photo:* Giraudon)

Chapter XV

MASSENA'S INVASION OF PORTUGAL, 1810–11

I Plans and Preparations

The opening weeks of 1810 saw Napoleon increasingly anxious over the constant draining of his empire's resources by the 'Spanish Ulcer'. Like Jourdan, he had concluded that Spain's continued resistance was due to Wellington's presence in Portugal and, determined to crush this interloper once and for all, resolved to lead the Imperial forces in a fresh offensive against Lisbon.[215]

The likelihood and significance of such a campaign was not lost on Wellington. 'As long as we shall remain in a state of activity in Portugal,' he wrote in April,

> the contest must continue in Spain.... The French are most desirous that we should withdraw from the country, but know that they must employ a very large force indeed in the operations that will render it necessary for us to go away; and I doubt whether they can bring that force to bear on Portugal without abandoning other objects, and exposing their whole fabric in Spain to great risk. If they should be able to invade, and should not succeed in obliging us to evacuate the country, they will be in a very dangerous situation; and the longer we can oppose them, and delay their success, the more likely are they to suffer materially in Spain.[216]

The emperor's intention of personally supervising this decisive offensive was disrupted by the complicated issue of his divorce and remarriage. Desperate for an heir and eager to consolidate his new-found alliance with Austria, he became involved in the marriage negotiations. By mid-April, he had abandoned all thoughts of going to the Peninsula himself, and Marshal Massena, Duke of Rivoli and Prince of Essling, was appointed to command the 'Army of Portugal'.

Massena, though a magnificent general[217] who had recently

acquired more laurels in the triumphant Danube campaign, was old beyond his fifty-two years and evinced little enthusiasm for his new command. Furthermore, he was to have endless problems with his subordinates: Junot, mindful of his own failure in Portugal, resented him and wished him ill; Reynier disliked him and Ney, never an easy officer to control, became utterly recalcitrant.[218] From the beginning, the headquarters of the 'Army of Portugal' was a mass of bitter factions over which Massena struggled to impose his will[219] – a state of affairs hardly conducive to the efficient running of military operations.

After the humiliating reverses suffered by Junot and Soult, Napoleon was determined that, this time, Portugal would be overrun and the British driven from the continent. Massena was ordered to proceed 'methodically' and a vast army was put at his disposal: the flow of reinforcements into Spain was maintained, releasing the II, VI and VIII Corps for the offensive.[220] This provided 70,000 men to which, it was planned, the newly formed IX Corps would be added as soon as it could be moved up from Biscay. Kellermann and the 20,000 troops in Leon were also to support the marshal by guarding his communications and securing his northern flank; the fortresses of Astorga, Cuidad Rodrigo and Almeida were earmarked for capture; and a pre-emptive strike against the Asturias was organised.[221]

Meanwhile, the Allies prepared a staggering barrier of defences with which to foil the invasion. The basis of their campaign was a defensive strategy with three principal elements. Firstly, a vast belt of 'scorched earth' was secretly created between western Portugal and the Spanish frontier. This region was notoriously barren and underdeveloped, and to devastate it in times of war was an established Portuguese practice used with great effect against Spanish invading armies in 1640 and 1704. Every bridge, mill, ferry and boat was destroyed, foodstuffs and vehicles were removed or burnt and the entire population – humans and livestock – was evacuated. So confident were the Allies of the efficacy of this strategem that they regarded it as the corner-stone of their defences. Indeed, Wellington and his colleagues were hopeful that the French would be routed by simple starvation – the need to risk a major engagement with them being minimal.

To aggravate the terrible difficulties Massena would encounter in this desolate region, Wellington dotted the area with military detachments and strongholds. The fortresses of Almeida, Abrantes, Peniche and Elvas were strengthened, and earthworks were erected at strategic points throughout the country. Roads likely to be used by the French were ploughed up and barricaded, while those earmarked for the movement of Allied troops were improved. To man the

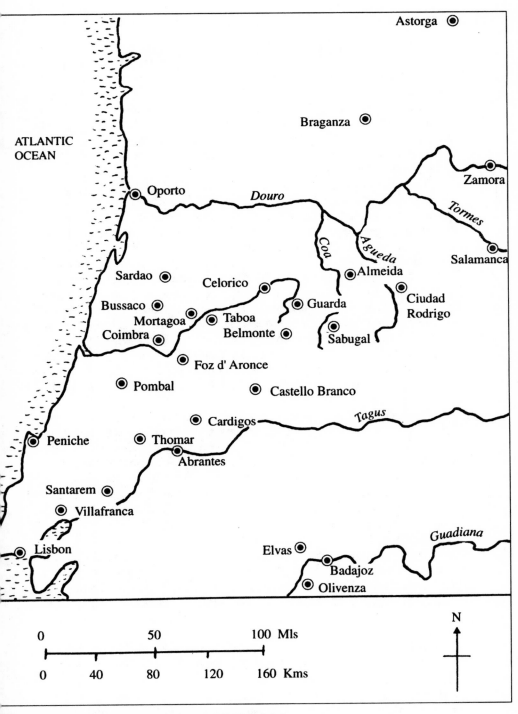

ATLANTIC
OCEAN

Astorga ◉

Braganza ◉

Douro

Oporto

Zamora ◉

Tormes

Coa

Agueda

Salamanca

Sardao ◉

Celorico

Almeida

Ciudad
Rodrigo

Bussaco ◉

Mortagoa

Taboa

Guarda

Coimbra ◉

Belmonte ◉

Sabugal

Foz d' Aronce

Pombal ◉

Castello Branco ◉

Cardigos

Tagus

Peniche ◉

Thomar

Abrantes

Santarem ◉

Villafranca ◉

Lisbon ◉

Elvas ◉

Guadiana

Badajoz

Olivenza

0	50	100 Mls

0	40	80	120	160 Kms

N

MASSENA'S INVASION OF PORTUGAL:
THEATRE OF OPERATIONS

installations and patrol the battle theatre, forty-eight Portuguese
militia regiments were utilised. Twenty were placed in garrisons, the
remainder formed into legions and allocated spheres of operation:
General Trant commanded seven regiments in the Douro and
Mondego Valleys; General Miller disposed of eight in the Oporto
district; six regiments formed the legion of General Silveira at
Braganza; while General Miranda had four regiments about
Thomar. The remaining three units, under General Le Cor, were
based on Castello Branco.

The sole purpose of these legions was to hamper French operations and to pass intelligence to the Allied command. They were to
play a crucial part in the coming campaign: Massena could barely
move without it being reported to Wellington; his communications
were repeatedly cut; his detachments and stragglers were ambushed.
Occasionally, the militia would engage exiguous units in open battle,
but usually they kept to guerilla warfare, intercepting couriers and
containing the movements of French reconnaissance and foraging
parties. Unable to range freely, the Imperial troops could neither
discover what lay ahead, nor feed themselves in the relatively tiny
areas of land they were effectively confined to. Thus defences – such
as the 'scorched earth' policy and the Lines of Torres Vedras – came
as an almost total surprise to Massena, and his inability to feed his
army was to prove the decisive factor of the campaign, just as the
Allies had hoped.

The second main element in their defences consisted of the
creation of a vast army, equal to anything Massena was likely to
assemble. Besides the 45,000 militia, Beresford's tireless work with
the Portuguese Army had yielded 45,000 regular troops. Founded on
British officer *cadres* and trained with British regulations, the
twenty-four line regiments, nine light battalions and twelve cavalry
regiments, although inexperienced, more than doubled Wellington's
field force. As the year progressed, he received fresh troops from
home, allowing the completion of the Fifth Division and the creation
of a sixth – giving him approximately 44,000 British soldiers. To
these were added La Romana's 8,000 Spaniards, some irregulars,
and various artillery and train troops. By October 1810 Wellington
had a field force of around 70,000 regulars, backed by a similar
number of reservists and militia, while Massena's whole army
numbered less than 70,000 men.

The third ingredient was a colossal barrier of fortifications and
natural obstacles stretching from the Atlantic, near Peniche, to the
Tagus estuary. Should the French penetrate so far towards Lisbon,
the Allies planned to retire within these defences and await their
opponent's inevitable starvation and retreat. Wellington had issued

instructions for the construction of the Lines as early as October 1809 and, by the time Massena began his invasion, they were almost complete. Over £100,000 had been spent on them and their existence was cloaked in secrecy – Massena was to penetrate beyond Pombal before gaining any inkling that there were fortifications of some kind ahead.

As the Lines were never seriously attacked, an extensive description of them is unnecessary. However, a few of the basic details may be of interest. This wall of barricades, redoubts, revetments and other fortifications stretched along the twenty-nine miles of mountains that link the Atlantic with the Tagus estuary. Constructed by militia and forced labour supervised by engineers, it contained a total frontage of some fifty-three miles of man-made defences, supplementing a formidable array of topographical obstacles. Wherever nature's barriers left a loophole, the Allied engineers obliterated it: large areas were flooded, ravines blocked, all trace of cover removed and thousands of yards of steep escarpment converted to sheer cliffs by blasting. Semaphore systems linked every command post and an elaborate road network allowed for the easy passage of reinforcements to any threatened sector. Supplied by the Royal Navy and with unassailable flanks, this Maginot Line of the Napoleonic era was impregnable by the standards of the day.[222]

II First Blood: The Asturias and Astorga

In the closing days of January 1810, as King Joseph's forces were completing their conquest of Andalusia, General Bonnet opened the preliminary offensive against the Asturias. His 7,000 men initially encountered only token resistance; Del Parque's disastrous autumn campaign having stripped Galicia and the Asturias of nearly all their forces. Oviedo fell on 31 January, but the French general's success was short-lived: the enemy counter-attacked and, for two months, a confused struggle dragged on – the regional capital changing hands three times before Bonnet emerged triumphant. However, holding down the conquered territory absorbed all his field force and his offensive capability soon evaporated. The Spanish, meanwhile, having evaded any serious defeat, regrouped to the west, where fresh recruits swelled their ranks to some 18,000 men. The continuing guerilla war was another threat: an estimated 20,000 insurrectionists were active between the Portuguese frontier and the Pyrenees. They tied down virtually all the French detachments in northern Spain and many reinforcements actually intended for Massena's army were siphoned off *en route* by hard-pressed garrison commanders.

Moreover, Allied naval flotillas, operating from Corunna and Ferrol, made repeated raids along the north coast, landing troop contingents – often 2,000 men – which struck at inland targets before being whisked away. Assailed from every quarter, it was all that Kellermann and Bonnet could do to maintain their current situation – let alone take on fresh commitments and support Massena. Throughout the year, the incessant pressure applied to the French communications and occupied territories proved an enormous vacuum into which scores of Imperial troops were sucked – effectively paralysing any efforts to assist the 'Army of Portugal'.

Although such problems augured ill for the offensive, preparations continued. While Bonnet was grappling with the Asturians, General Loison took elements of the VI Corps to secure the stronghold of Astorga. Finding it well fortified, Loison, unable to procure any heavy ordnance, settled down to await Junot's VIII Corps and a siege train, but when Junot arrived, he had no heavy guns and the French had to be content with the construction of trenches. With no heavy artillery of their own the garrison, too, were at a loose end. For weeks the stalemate continued, interrupted only by clashes between the besiegers and small, Galician relief columns that occasionally probed towards the place. Eventually, Junot – having requisitioned every big gun for miles around – extemporised a siege train and, by 21 April, a sizeable rupture had been made in the fortress walls. Elements of the 47th Regiment and the Irish Legion established a foothold in the town, and the garrison promptly capitulated: 2,500 Spanish soldiers surrendered, and 200 dead and wounded were found in the defences. The French casualties totalled 600.[223]

III   Ciudad Rodrigo

The next objective was the fourteenth-century castle of Ciudad Rodrigo on the River Agueda. Dominating the highway to Almeida and Coimbra, it was of vital strategic importance and Massena proposed to make it his base for the coming campaign.

The castle commandant, Herrasti, was an old but talented officer. He disposed of some 5,500 Spanish troops – mostly militia – to which he hoped Wellington, whose main force lay just to the west, would give assistance. But Wellington proved unwilling to compromise his entire strategy for defending Portugal by risking his irreplaceable army in a pitched battle on the plains of Leon. 'There is', he explained, 'a great deal of difference (particularly in the blood to be spilt) between fighting in a position which I choose, or in one in

which the enemy choose ... '[224] Ciudad Rodrigo was left to its fate
– a decision which soured Anglo-Spanish relations for months.

Such disagreements, however, were just one consequence of the
essentially defensive strategy that Wellington was to cling to until
1812. Refusing to risk battle except on his terms, he slowly built up
his forces, ready to take the offensive when years of attritional
warfare should have worn the French down. But such a policy was an
awesome burden for the Allies. As we have seen, the war and the
ministers directing it were repeatedly attacked by sections of the
British public who faced an ever mounting price in blood and gold.
The Portuguese, too, were steadily bankrupted by the conflict, and
Wellington's 'scorched earth' stratagem – whilst inflicting dreadful
losses on the French – also claimed the lives of perhaps 50,000
Portuguese peasants in 1810. Such suffering did little for civilian
morale; nor did the haunting fear that any retreat by Wellington was
the beginning of a general British withdrawal from the Peninsula
which would inevitably leave Portugal to the mercies of the French.
Lastly, there were those numerous 'croakers' in Wellington's army
who could never understand why even successful engagements were
usually rewarded by gruelling retreats through inhospitable countryside. As Wellington observed:

> Besides ... prejudice, founded on Sir John Moore's opinion,[225]
> there is ... general prejudice against any military operation in the
> Peninsula. ... But I have looked to the great result of our
> maintaining our position ... and have not allowed myself to be
> diverted from it by the wishes of the allies, and ... some of our
> own army, that I should interfere more actively ... or by the
> opinion of others, that we ought to quit the country ... [226]

Having spent a month assembling supplies and siege material,
Marshal Ney invested Ciudad Rodrigo on 30 May. The next day, as
his cavalry pushed Craufurd's Light Division out of contact with the
fortress, he began constructing bridges over the Agueda, crossed the
river and, on 15 June, established his first parallel.

Despite heavy fire from the citadel and minor sorties by the
garrison, the preparations went well and, on 25 June, forty-six heavy
cannon began bombarding the fortress. The Spanish replied with
every gun they had and one French battery was silenced, others
damaged and two magazines destroyed. Nevertheless, the besiegers
persevered and, that same night, the outlying Convent of Santa Cruz
– which had beaten off one attack – finally succumbed. The artillery
contest continued for four days, both sides suffering heavily.
However, the French steadily established supremacy and a large

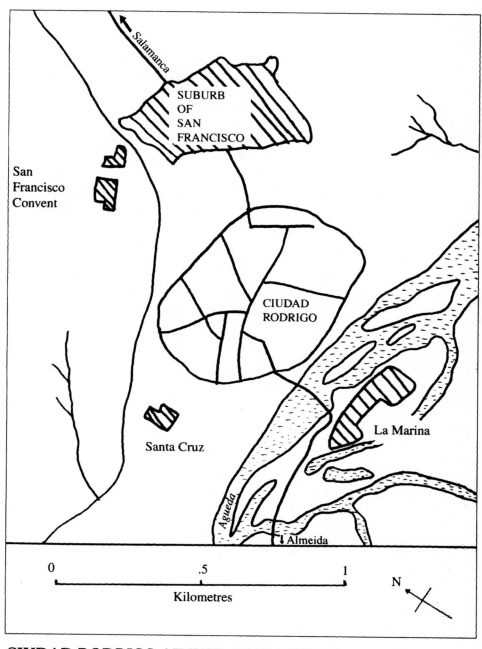

Salamanca

SUBURB
OF
SAN
FRANCISCO

San
Francisco
Convent

CIUDAD
RODRIGO

Santa Cruz

La Marina

Agueda

↓Almeida

0   .5   1

Kilometres

N

**CIUDAD RODRIGO AT THE TIME OF THE
PENINSULAR WAR**

breach appeared in the north wall. His surrender terms rejected, Ney pushed his ordnance still further forward and stormed the outlying suburb of San Francisco. After a stiff fight Herrasti's men retreated into Ciudad Rodrigo proper and the French, deploying heavy mortars in the suburban lanes, poured a hail of shells into the city. 28,000 rounds later, the breach had widened to forty yards, the town was a pile of debris, twenty-five per cent of the garrison were *hors de combat* and their food was virtually exhausted. Furthermore, limited advances by Junot's corps had driven back Craufurd another nine miles, completing the isolation of the fortress and extinguishing any remaining hopes of relief.[227]

Ney continued the bombardment until he was certain that Ciudad Rodrigo could not resist an attack and, on 9 July, personally led forward three battalions to storm the gaping breach. But the attack was never delivered: as the French troops advanced, Herrasti sued for terms. Impressed by his gallant resistance, Ney granted the garrison the full honours of war and, the next day, 4,000 Spaniards marched out and laid down their arms. The French had lost just 180 dead and 1,000 wounded.[228]

Ciudad Rodrigo subdued, Massena replenished his supplies and, on 23 July, ordered the VI Corps to move against Almeida – the last fortress barring the invasion route. Craufurd's Light Division fell back before Ney and, by evening, occupied a line stretching from the River Coa to a windmill in front of the fortress. Dawn revealed to Ney that the Allies' only line of retreat lay down a narrow, tortuous lane to a solitary bridge. Realising their rapid withdrawal would be impossible should he attack, he resolved to sweep them into the river.

Hoping to give the leading French formation a bloody reception, Craufurd elected to stand. However, he had grossly underestimated both Ney's generalmanship and the size of his forces. Craufurd's left wing – some riflemen, two Portuguese light battalions and the 43rd Foot – found itself confronted by the bulk of Loison's division and was soon in difficulties. Sagging under this onslaught, the startled line was then threatened from another quarter as the French 3rd Hussars swept down on their left flank. Although the gunners of Almeida managed to get a few wild shots off at the galloping horsemen, little could be done to stop them: they virtually exterminated the riflemen and then fell on the 43rd. Some dry stone walls impeded the cavalry's progress but, attacked in front by infantry and threatened on their flank by horsemen, the 43rd rushed to the rear – one group pushing over a wall to escape.

Their left routed, Craufurd's entire command, led by the cavalry and guns, went into precipitant retreat for the bridge. One vehicle,

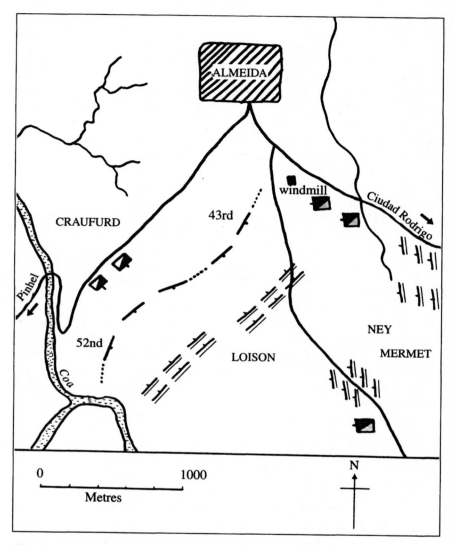

THE ACTION ON THE RIVER COA, 24 July 1810

however, failed to negotiate the lane's hairpin bends and crashed; impeding the fugitives' escape and aggravating their panic. They eventually gained the west bank, having lost over 300 men, but then it was realised that part of the 52nd had been cut off. Major McLeod of the 43rd

called on the troops to follow, and . . . rode towards the enemy . . . .

A mob of soldiers rushed after him ... as if the whole army had
been at their backs; the enemy's skirmishers ... stopped short,
and before they could recover from their surprise, the fifty-second
had passed the river ... [229]

Ney, however, convinced that the enemy's morale was irretrievably broken, attempted to cross the bridge to complete his victory.
But, by this time, Craufurd's division had rallied and, as one officer
commented, 'A few hundred French grenadiers, advancing to the
tune "Vive l'Empereur!" ... and so forth, were not likely to succeed
in scaring away three British and two Portuguese regiments, supported by artillery.'[230] The attackers were, indeed, repulsed with
heavy casualties and Ney sullenly retired to invest Almeida. Nevertheless, what Wellington later termed 'the foolish affairs in which
Craufurd involved his outposts',[231] had nearly ended in disaster.

IV   Almeida

Initially, Wellington hoped that Almeida would occupy the enemy
for many weeks: it was sturdier and better equipped than Ciudad
Rodrigo, and had a garrison of 4,500 Portuguese troops under the
able command of a British colonel – Cox. With over a hundred heavy
guns and vast stocks of food and ammunition, Cox was confident that
he could resist for weeks, if not months.

From the outset, however, Wellington's calculations seemed to be
going awry. Having invested the fortress, the VI Corps remained
quiescent. They were actually awaiting the arrival of Junot and the
siege train from Astorga, but to Wellington it appeared that something more sinister was afoot. 'I do not believe the enemy intend to
attack Almeida,' he wrote on 27 July. 'I have not heard of any
preparations for that purpose; and I suspect they are collecting a
large force to make a dash at me.'[232] Accordingly, he withdrew his
army down the Mondego to a more respectful distance from the
beleaguered fortress, leaving Cole's Fourth Division at Guarda with
a cavalry screen to protect the front.

But the 'dash' did not come. On 15 August the VI Corps was
joined by the long-awaited siege train – supplemented by cannon
taken at Ciudad Rodrigo. Assembling fifty-three heavy pieces, Ney
began a heavy bombardment and blasted a large rupture in the
south-east wall. The Portuguese resistance was ineffectual but
gallant and they maintained a steady reply to the French salvoes. For
a time, it seemed as though Wellington's hopes of a long siege might
be realised. But then disaster struck. At around 7 pm on 26 August,

the besiegers witnessed one of the most terrible spectacles of the Napoleonic Wars. A volcano-like explosion suddenly occurred in the midst of the fortress, instantly reducing much of it to debris. The luckless Portuguese had issued a leaking gunpowder barrel to one of their batteries which, on the way to the redoubt, had spilt its contents in a solid trail, stretching all the way back to the main magazine. An exploding French shell ignited this makeshift fuse which, in turn, detonated the tons of black powder in the storehouse. As well as destroying nearly all the garrison's munitions, the blast virtually exterminated the gun-crews and infantry lining the walls. Some 700 people perished – mostly soldiers – and the centre of the town was gutted.

Without powder and gunners, the garrison was loath to continue resistance. Cox urged them to fight on and sent Wellington urgent pleas for aid, but the explosion had utterly demoralised the Portuguese. On 27 August, Cox bowed to mounting pressure and appealed to Massena for terms. Subsequently, 4,000 men marched into captivity and Almeida passed under French control.[233] Massena's casualties were under 400 men – mostly wounded – whom he replaced by inducing Portuguese prisoners to take oaths and enlist in his army – a policy that later backfired as they all deserted at the earliest opportunity. Nevertheless, with the last fortress barring his path in his grasp, the invasion of Portugal could now begin.

V   Column and Line at Bussaco

The line of advance selected by Massena was through some of the most difficult country in Europe. The modifications Wellington had made aside, the area was barren and inhospitable at the best of times and, with no local resources, a vast and efficient logistical network was imperative. Incredible ignorance prevailed at the French head-quarters as to the topography ahead. Their maps were at least thirty years old and failed to show even major roads. Furthermore, although the emperor had given Massena several Portuguese guides, these proved worse than useless; having virtually no knowledge of the theatre's geography. Against this background, it is with little wonder that, on 18 September, we find Wellington commenting that, 'There are many bad roads in Portugal, but the enemy has taken decidedly the worst in the whole kingdom.'[234]

Indeed, from the outset, Wellington was confident that Massena would fail. In a letter to his brother on 20 August – before the invasion even began – he summarised what was to prove the fate of the French expedition:

Notwithstanding that they have so large a force ... it is not sufficient for their object, which will become every day more difficult. The people of Portugal are doing what the Spaniards ought to have done. They are removing their properties out of the enemy's way and taking arms·in their own defence. The country is made a desert and behind almost every ... wall the French will meet an enemy. To this add that they have the British and Portuguese armies in their front, ready to take advantage of any fault or weakness.[235]

On 2 September, the French advanced towards Celorico. In response Wellington – expecting a major assault at any moment – evacuated Guarda and withdrew his divisions still further down the Mondego. But despite his frantic efforts, Massena had failed to make good the deficiencies in his forces: there were not enough transport vehicles, and draught animals were in such short supply that a third of the army's cannon had had to be left in depots. Attempts to rectify these problems met with little success; for Kellermann's hard-pressed units could barely protect the marshal's communications, and convoys, if they arrived at all, were slow in coming. Massena paused to search for more troops to increase the size of both his field army and the formations protecting his rear. Soon, Reynier's II Corps arrived from the Tagus Valley and raised the 'Army of Portugal' to an impressive 65,000 men – excluding 3,500 in Ciudad Rodrigo and Almeida. However, of d'Erlon's IX Corps – currently being dragged into anti-guerilla operations in Biscay – there was no sign. With autumn approaching Massena could delay no longer and, on 15 September, reopened his offensive. As the French VI and VIII Corps thrust down the Mondego, the British cavalry screen steadily retired. It was not until 17 September – when the enemy began to cross to the north bank at Fornos – that Wellington had a clear idea of Massena's intended route and, satisfied that a small column that had penetrated to Taboa was only a diversion, he shifted his own divisions to the north of the Mondego and established them at Bussaco. 'We are in an excellent position,' he noted,

indeed one which cannot be easily attacked in front; and if they wait another day or two, they will be unable to turn it on the only vulnerable point. I shall do everything in my power to stop the enemy here. If I cannot ... I shall still try ... at Coimbra.[236]

Meanwhile, Massena was grappling with the appalling man-made and natural obstacles that barred his advance: the roads had to be constantly widened with picks and shovels to allow cannon and vehicles to pass and, toiling up the steep, sinuous lanes, his troops rapidly became exhausted and scattered – reducing their pace to a crawl and increasing their vulnerability to the raids of Trant's militia. Arriving at Vizeu, Massena wrote: 'It is impossible to find worse roads than these. . . . All our marches are across a desert; not a soul to be seen anywhere; everything is abandoned.'[237] Nevertheless, he persevered and, on 25 September, Reynier's vanguard encountered the Light Division near Mortagoa and drove them back to Wellington's chosen battle position.

The next day was spent preparing for battle. The French arrived in a steady stream and, by 27 September, Massena had most of his army up. The Allies had deployed 52,000 men with sixty guns along the towering, nine-mile ridge which stretched from the mountains of the Sierra de Alcoba to the Mondego. This 'damned long hill', as one British officer described it, was extremely steep and covered with heather. Other than the highway to Coimbra, only a few tracks crossed it, while a solitary lane ran along the rear slope where the Allied army was positioned. Its northern tip was crowned by the Bussaco Convent, shrouded in woods and barely visible to the French forces.

After a reconnaissance, Massena devised a plan of attack. The slopes were so steep and high that the French artillery and cavalry were deemed useless, and the execution of the assault fell almost exclusively to the infantry. Unable to see much of the hostile line in its battle-stations along the reverse slope, Massena underestimated its strength and extent. Mistakenly taking the Allied centre for their right wing, he decided that Reynier's corps would ascend the easiest part of the gradient (above San Antonio), break the opposing formation and then roll up Wellington's line towards the convent. Once Ney saw the II Corps crest the ridge, he was to pin the enemy down and complete their discomfiture by launching two divisions at their left-centre.

The scheme, however, was not popular with Massena's generals. Unassailable except with infantry – and, perhaps, with artillery firing at maximum range and trajectory – the ridge could be easily held by any army. Defended by tenacious British troops under a skilled operator like Wellington, such a position was virtually impregnable; a point adequately demonstrated to Junot at Vimiero. As Napoleon later remarked: 'Why the devil did Massena thrust himself into that muddle at Bussaco? Even in a plain country, columns do not break through lines unless they are supported by a superior artillery fire.'[238]

Reynier – who had fought the British in Italy[239] – also had his doubts but, at dawn on the twenty-seventh, he began the attack

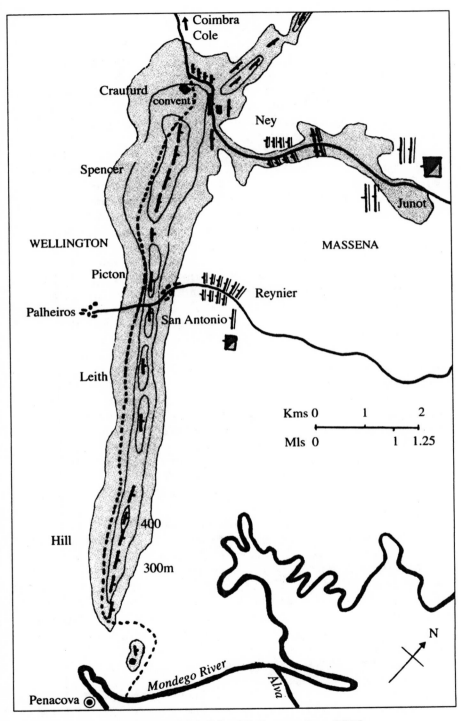

THE BATTLE OF BUSSACO, 27 September 1810

against what was believed to be Wellington's right wing. With a skirmish screen leading the way, the divisions of Merle and Heudelet – deployed in dense, narrow columns – climbed the steep slopes. Masked by the forward slope the Allied troops were also cloaked in mist. Consequently, Reynier could see little of his intended target. Tripping through the heather, the French battalions panted up the escarpment, driving in the enemy skirmishers. The undergrowth and thick fog rapidly spoilt their alignments, and the formations steadily strayed off course. Finally, Heudelet's leading regiment – the 31st Light – emerged from the mists on the track leading to San Antonio and attacked Chaplemond's Portuguese brigade. Raked by a volley from the 21st, the regiment struggled to deploy, but, as the British 74th and an Allied battery also opened fire, the French column ground to a halt, suffering terrible losses.

Meanwhile, Merle's division had emerged to the left of Chaplemond's troops. There were no Allied units along this part of the escarpment, and General Picton had to shift the 88th to the right and summon the 45th and 8th Portuguese from behind Chaplemond's line. The head of the breathless French column had gained the crest before these forces arrived and the British general wasted no time in attacking before the enemy could deploy. Rallying the fleeing Allied skirmishers, he united them with the 8th Portuguese and directed them at Merle's left flank. Opening fire from only fifty yards, this force halted the French column, which was simultaneously charged on its right flank by the 88th and 45th. Pounded by a battery rushed to support the extemporised defence, the French leading regiment – the 36th – rapidly disintegrated and fled towards San Antonio, carrying away the two unengaged regiments of Merle's division. Pursued by the Allies, they sustained great losses before regaining their lines, where a few salvoes from Massena's artillery sent Picton's men scrambling back up the hillside.

His assault collapsing, Reynier threw in his last reserve – General Foy's two regiments. Although disheartened by the sight of Merle's crumbling column, the 17th *Léger* and 70th Line duly ascended the slope and headed for a point between the two existing attacks; arriving on the right of the 31st *Léger*, who were still locked in their unequal combat with Chaplemond's brigade. However, the Allied reserves were also astir. Unmolested, the southern end of Wellington's line had dispatched Leith's division to support the centre. Hurrying along the ridge via the parallel road, Leith dropped off three regiments to reinforce Chaplemond and pushed on to assist against Foy.

He arrived not a moment too soon. Coming up against the 8th Portuguese and 45th minutes after they had repulsed Merle, Foy had ploughed into them and driven them back. A counter-attack by the 9th Portuguese and a militia battalion melted away and Foy's seven battalions were soon cresting the ridge. Pitching his leading brigade into the fight, Leith deployed the 9th Foot to enfilade the enemy's advance, while the 38th engaged the head of their formation. Their general wounded, the depleted and breathless French retreated before the converging attacks; bringing the fighting along this sector to a gory conclusion.

Meanwhile, in accordance with his orders, Ney had begun his attack. Loison's twelve battalions moved through the woods towards Sula, and dislodged Pack and Craufurd's skirmishers. Then, bombarded by twelve guns and galled by the fire of over 2,000 light troops, they advanced up ever steeper slopes towards the crest, where the 1,800 bayonets of the 43rd and 52nd Foot were hidden in a sunken road. When it seemed to Loison's division that nothing more than cannon opposed them, these troops suddenly rose and delivered a volley at only ten paces. The leading ranks of the enemy formation ceased to exist as over 1,000 officers and men crashed to the ground. Stunned by this onslaught, the French inflicted just five casualties before tumbling down the escarpment in wild confusion.

With eleven of Loison's battalions overthrown, the Allies only had to deal with his last, which had drifted away from the main body and emerged facing Coleman's regiments. Hopelessly outnumbered and disconcerted by the rout of its sister battalions, it was easily worsted by the 19th Portuguese and driven off to Sula. Here, it joined the rest of the battered division in bickering with Craufurd's skirmishers, Loison being unable and unwilling to risk another serious assault.

It remains only for me to narrate the attack by Ney's other division – that of Marchand. Whilst Loison was being thrashed by Craufurd, Marchand's units had advanced up the more gentle slopes in front of Spencer's division, towards the convent. A stiff fight soon erupted in the woods to the south of Sula as Marchand's men encountered a thick line of Allied light troops. Pushing these back, the disordered French emerged from the trees to blasts of musketry from Pack's brigade and slowly ebbed back down the escarpment. An attempt by Maucune's regiments to thrust up the lane from Sula also faltered before the fire of three batteries and, with the complete repulse of the II Corps and Loison, Ney abandoned the attack and retired.

Thus ended the Battle of Bussaco. The Allies had sustained some 1,250 casualties; the French 4,500, including more than 250 officers – an indication that the rank and file had been despondent from the outset and had had to be urged on by their leaders with excessive self-sacrifice. Indeed, the Imperial troops had laboured against awesome odds. As Napoleon had commented after Talavera: 'As long as they will attack good troops, like the English, in good positions, without making sure they can be carried, my men will be led to death to no purpose.'[240] There is no better example of such needless sacrifice than Bussaco, and few in Massena's 'Army of Portugal' were ever to forget it.[241]

VI   The Lines of Torres Vedras

After this gory repulse, Massena belatedly sent his cavalry in search of a way round Wellington's position. One was found near Sardao and, scattering Trant's militia, the French army gained the Oporto-Lisbon highway and turned southwards. Wellington, meanwhile, having checked the enemy and given his Portuguese units a triumphant baptism of fire, retreated on Coimbra.

Here, however, his orderly withdrawal deteriorated into a confused scramble as the city's 32,000 inhabitants fled before Massena's advance. Hustling the Allied rearguard over the Mondego, the famished Imperial troops entered the city on 1 October and, despite Wellington's precautions, managed to liberate several days' rations. But Massena remained ill at ease. To his veteran general's mind there was something sinister about Wellington's inconsistent conduct: a staunch defensive battle, followed by the relinquishing of miles of territory. Speculating that Wellington's destination was another Bussaco-like position, Massena resolved to force him to fight at the earliest opportunity.

Leaving a few companies to protect them, Massena billeted his 4,000 invalids at Coimbra and hurried after the Allies. Drenched by the first autumn rains, Montbrun's cavalry finally fell in with the enemy south of Pombal and, overthrowing Anson's horsemen, took numerous prisoners who revealed that Wellington's destination was 'the Lines' and gave Massena his first indication that some manner of defences had been constructed about Lisbon. Increasingly concerned, he urged his weary men onward and, on 11 October, Montbrun's troopers reached Villafranca; becoming the first French soldiers to lay eyes on the Lines of Torres Vedras.

Dumbfounded, Massena looked for a loophole in this staggering barrier, but in vain. On 14 October he conducted a personal reconnaissance and found 'Steeply scarped mountains and deep ravines . . . crowned with all that could be accomplished in the way of field fortifications garnished with artillery'.[242] With his food and ammunition supplies exhausted, his communications severed and no sign of d'Erlon's IX Corps, he now learnt that Trant had captured the hospitals at Coimbra. The situation was hopeless.

At a brief meeting of his despondent staff, an overwhelming majority agreed with Massena's evaluation and the following was penned to the emperor:

> The Marshal Prince of Essling has come to the conclusion that he would compromise the army of His Majesty if he were to attack in force lines so formidable, defended by 30,000 English and 30,000 Portuguese, aided by 50,000 armed peasants.[243]

Protected by a large escort, General Foy took this melancholy document and immediately set out for Paris.

Massena, however, was not a marshal for nothing. Determined to continue the campaign, he evacuated his cavalry, train and 11,000 sick to Santarem where he established a new base. Wellington, meanwhile, was confident that the French were finished. Late in October he wrote to Lord Liverpool that

> All the accounts which I have received of the distresses of the enemy for want of provisions, would lead to a belief that their army could not remain long in the position in which it is placed, and it is astonishing that they have been able to remain here for so long.[244]

Nevertheless, it was 14 November before Massena began his withdrawal. Carefully screening every move and lining his abandoned positions with straw dummies in uniforms,[245] he slipped away unnoticed. Twenty-four hours later, the Allies discovered his departure and set out in search of him. But the deteriorating weather soon convinced Wellington that nothing further could be achieved that year, and both armies retired into winter quarters.

VII Retreat

Hoping that Wellington might attack and bring about a decisive battle, Massena remained entrenched at Santarem. But the Allied commander, adhering to his policy, impatiently waited for the French to be starved into withdrawal. On 21 December he wrote to Liverpool:

> It is certainly astonishing that the enemy have been able to remain in this country so long; and it is an extraordinary instance of what a French army can do. It is positively a fact that they brought no provisions with them, and they have not received even a letter since they entered Portugal. With all our money, and having in our

favour the good inclinations of the country, I assure you that I could not maintain one division in the district in which they have maintained not less than 60,000 men and 20,000 animals for more than two months.[246]

This remarkable tribute was testimony to the determination and courage of the French army. However, bravery could not satisfy hungry mouths and Massena's situation became daily more miserable. A supply column under General Gardanne had left Ciudad Rodrigo in search of him on 20 November but, after struggling as far as Cardigos, had turned back in the face of appalling weather and constant militia attacks.[247] On 26 December the long awaited IX Corps appeared, having carved a path from Almeida, dropping off detachments here and there. But with no battle to fight d'Erlon's famished men merely aggravated the supply shortage and served little useful purpose.

In early February Foy, escorted by 1,800 troops, returned from Paris with the emperor's instructions. The document, already six weeks old, promised aid from Mortier in Andalusia and Joseph in central Spain. Encouraged, Massena clung to his position for another fortnight but, with no sign of the relief columns, he finally abandoned hope and, on 19 February, called a staff meeting. His officers were unanimous that retreat was inevitable, but there was some disagreement as to their route. It was suggested that the Tagus should be crossed and a path cut through to Andalusia, but this was rejected as too risky – Wellington would doubtless contest the evacuation and Beresford was known to be on the far bank with over 10,000 Allied troops. Massena resolved to retire by the way he had come and, in late February, began the evacuation of his invalids, and the few guns and vehicles he still had draught teams for.

By 4 March all of Massena's forces were in retreat, but two days passed before Wellington realised what was happening and could get his scattered divisions on the move. Occupying the burnt-out shell of Santarem, he hastened after Massena's army – now down to 44,000 effectives – with 46,000 well-equipped troops, all of whom had been adequately fed and rested throughout the winter. Nevertheless, he was still unwilling to risk a serious clash. 'The whole country affords advantageous positions to a retreating army', he complained, 'of which the enemy ... knows how to avail himself.'[248] Skilfully resisting at every turn, the French rearguard – led by Ney, soon to be dubbed '*le plus brave des braves*' by Napoleon – had to be manoeuvred out of one position after another as the 'Army of Portugal', finding Coimbra occupied by Trant, swung north-east through Foz d'Aronce.

Finally, on 22 March, after an incredible forced march over immensely difficult terrain, Massena's footsore columns staggered into Celerico and opened up communications with Almeida. After driving the enemy for 130 miles, Wellington's divisions, too, were exhausted. They had witnessed innumerable scenes of appalling atrocities committed by both sides[249] and, having left their logistical support far to the rear, were disintegrating with starvation and indiscipline. A halt was essential; Wellington duly called one.

VIII   Steps to the South and Defeat at Sabugal

Likewise, the French staff assumed that their forces would now be allowed to rest and recuperate. But Massena, anxious to redeem his reputation, announced to his flabbergasted officers that the army would immediately march for the Tagus Valley to launch a new offensive into Portugal. To Ney in particular, this was absurd. Supported by Reynier and Junot, he claimed that Massena's pride was getting the better of his sense of realism. The army was depleted, weary and lacking even basic equipment and the terrain to the south, with which Ney was familiar, was the most barren in all Spain. Massena, however, was implacable. He gave the VI Corps a direct order to march and when Ney refused to comply he was relieved of the command he had held for seven years. Cowed by this ruthless treatment, Reynier and Junot reluctantly obeyed and, on 23 March, the despondent French divisions roused themselves into motion once again.

Nevertheless, everyone in the army, save Massena, agreed that Ney's objections were based on fact, and when Reynier's II Corps ground to a halt as early as 27 March, both he and Junot reported that further advance was impossible. Massena reluctantly capitulated and issued orders for a countermarch: Junot promptly retired from Belmonte and the II Corps left Sabugal. But to his dismay, Massena now discovered that Wellington, having reinforced, rested and fed his remaining men, had been astir for some time and had arrived at Guarda on 29 March. The unexpected appearance of the enemy on the flank of their march sent the French hastening towards the Coa river. Here – having narrowly avoided a dangerous situation – the 'Army of Portugal' deployed along the eastern bank, taking up a lengthy position stretching north from Sabugal.

Wellington, however, was not far behind. Leaving 8,000 men to distract the bulk of Massena's army, he moved forward 30,000 troops for a surprise attack on the southern tip of the French line. Arriving before Sabugal on a foggy 3 April the British commander

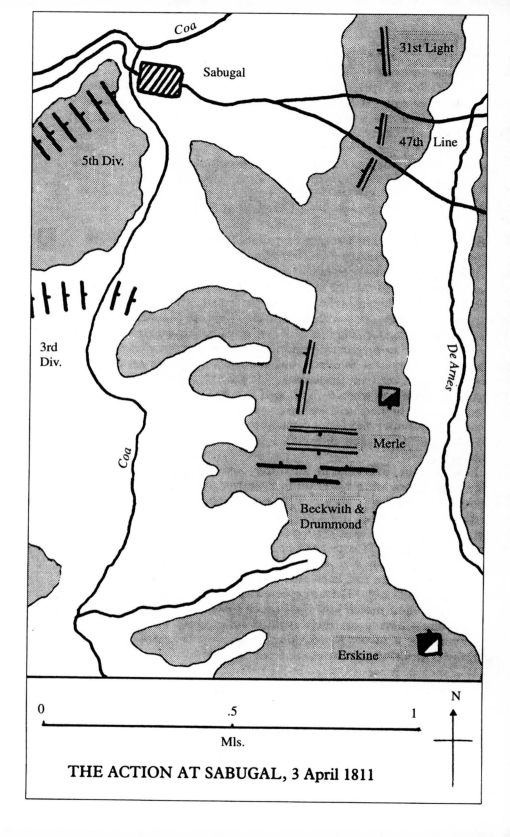

THE ACTION AT SABUGAL, 3 April 1811

dispatched the Light Division and two cavalry brigades to turn the enemy's left flank, while four other divisions staged a frontal assault. The flanking column soon lost its bearings in the mist and, instead of turning the French position, emerged in the very midst of Reynier's corps, taking them completely by surprise. Outnumbered and hopelessly scattered, they were easily driven back by the advancing Light Division, but returned to the fray with the arrival of their reserves. A bitter struggle raged across the enclosures for several minutes, before the British gained the upper hand and the French began to recoil. The fog then cleared and Reynier received his first glimpse of the mass of Allied troops poised to join in the attack from the west. Realising that to continue the fight could only lead to his ruin, he ordered his corps into retreat and, shaking off his attackers, struck northward for Massena's main body. Hampered by heavy rain, the pursuing Allies soon lost track of him and, content with their victory, occupied Sabugal.[250]

His left flank turned, Massena was obliged to abandon the Coa and retreat on Ciudad Rodrigo. His army was in an appalling state, having lost all but thirty-six of its vehicles and sixty per cent of its horses. The men were tired out and the cavalry was so weak that infantry had to be used for tasks usually performed by the mounted arm. Disenchanted with their commander and disheartened by their defeats and endless retreats, the troops longed only for an end to the campaign.

Finally, increasing the garrison of Ciudad Rodrigo to 3,000 men, Massena pulled his shattered divisions back across the border and brought them to rest at Salamanca on 11 April. His campaign in Portugal had cost him 25,000 men: 8,000 prisoners, 2,000 killed in action, and the rest victims of disease and starvation. Wellington's army was in a bad condition, too, but the attempt to drive the British into the sea had failed miserably and Portugal remained even more securely in Allied hands.[251] Napoleon was only impressed by results and Massena, having failed to provide them, was earmarked for replacement by Marshal Marmont. Nevertheless, the Prince of Essling's Peninsular campaigns were not quite at an end; for, as we shall see in Chapter XVII, he was to have one more clash with Wellington before Marmont arrived.

Chapter XVI

THE HARASSED VICEROY:
SOULT IN ANDALUSIA, 1810–11

I Soult's Predicament

While Wellington and Massena were battling for supremacy in Portugal, the war elsewhere continued unabated. Andalusia – now one of the military districts created by Napoleon in February 1810 – fell under the supreme jurisdiction of Marshal Soult who carried out his duties in the manner of a viceroy. He had three entire corps – the I, IV and V – at his disposal, over 70,000 troops, but even these were insufficient for his numerous commitments and he was obliged to entice Spaniards to serve in *Juramentado* regiments.

Despite such measures, the military situation remained difficult. Soult had the usual problems involved in holding down the insurrectionists and, furthermore, had to contend with several more organised threats to his position. East of Granada lurked the 12,000 remaining men of Areizaga's old army who, under General Freire, occupied the formidable fortress of Cartagena and executed raids against Sebastiani's IV Corps. To the north-west La Romana's 13,000 troops bickered with Mortier's divisions and, once Reynier's II Corps had left the region to join Massena's army, were able to mount ever greater incursions into Andalusia.

However, the largest drain on Soult's resources was Cadiz. After Albuquerque had thrown a contingent into it, in early-1810, the island stronghold had remained firmly in Allied hands and all of Victor's I Corps had been drawn into investing it. Supplied by sea, the garrison had been steadily augmented until, by May, it numbered 26,000 men. Although the French sealed the port off with impressive earthworks and 300 pieces of ordnance, denied any naval support they could do little else. Situated at the tip of a five-mile long peninsula which protruded from the island of Leon, Cadiz lay some three miles from the nearest French gun – double the range of even the largest pieces. Furthermore, Leon was separated from the

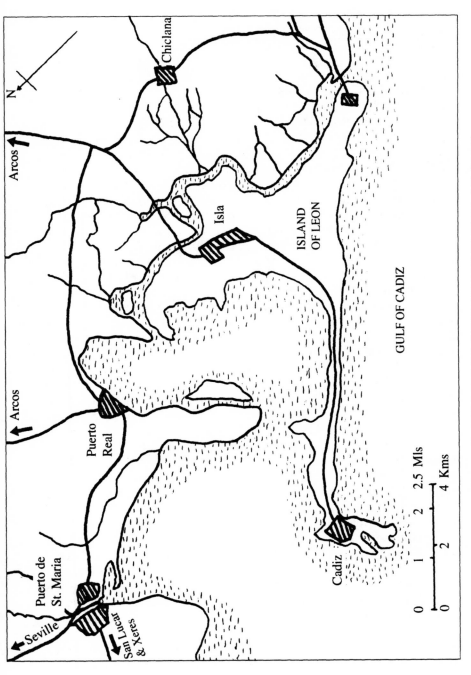

CADIZ AT THE TIME OF THE PENINSULAR WAR

mainland by 350 yards of water which were swept by heavy batteries and patrolled by gunboats.

This inexpugnable series of natural and man-made defences deterred the French from making any attempt to storm the island. However, as well as absorbing huge numbers of Imperial troops in futile siege operations, Cadiz – along with Gibraltar and Tarifa – also served as a base for Allied amphibious attacks. Centred on these ports, a large Anglo-Spanish fleet made repeated descents on Spain's southern coasts: blockading cities such as Barcelona, raiding French installations and supplying friendly forces with food and equipment. With no French warships to combat it, this flotilla ranged quite freely and, by landing troops, enabled the Allies to strike at inland targets far behind enemy lines. The huge garrison of Cadiz could safely detach many thousands of men for such operations and, as we shall see, the French were repeatedly harassed by armies that were embarked and disembarked by fleet. With his rear and communications constantly attacked, Soult found even short-term offensive operations difficult to sustain and spent much of his time vainly pursuing these elusive raiders.

As we have seen, towards the end of July 1810 Reynier's II Corps left its position on the Tagus to join Massena's army for the invasion of Portugal. Its departure left the Spanish forces in north-west Andalusia unmolested and, by 8 August, a column under La Romana had slipped through Gazan's scattered battalions and had penetrated to within eighty miles of Seville. Seriously alarmed, Soult dispatched Marshal Mortier with Girard's division to muster the local units and confront the intruder. A short, sharp clash ensued near Llerena and La Romana's 11,000 men recoiled. On approaching Badajoz, however, Mortier learnt of an amphibious landing by General Lacy near Huelva, and was obliged to send Gazan's division to drive him back to his ships. This Gazan did but, deprived of his services, Mortier proved unable to contain La Romana and by September the Spaniard was again in the ascendancy. The return of Gazan's footsore battalions tilted the balance back in Mortier's favour and the middle of the month saw La Romana again in retreat. Defeated outside Badajoz, he fell back in disorder but was saved from destruction by yet another attack on the enemy's rear. This time, Sebastiani's command had come under pressure from Freire's forces along the Murcian frontier. A frustrated Mortier had to abandon the chase and dash east to succour the IV Corps, only to find that Freire had withdrawn at his approach.

There followed a period of relative calm in which the Imperial troops took a well-earned rest. But their respite was not long: in October came tidings that Lord Blayney had landed with an Anglo-

Spanish army and was threatening Malaga. An anxious Sebastiani assembled 3,000 men and hastened to the aid of the tiny garrison. But he arrived to find that the enemy had been drawn into a bitter struggle for the outlying stronghold of Fuengirola – where a solitary company of determined Poles had held them off for two days – and, attacking the allies' rear, routed them; capturing Blayney and 300 others, and driving the remainder back to their ships.

But this reverse did not deter the Allies and fresh applications of pressure were soon prescribed for the weaker areas of Soult's defences. Their next check was, however, rather more serious. In November, General Blake – appointed to command the troops in Cadiz and along the Murcian border – instigated a new offensive to drive Sebastiani from Granada and, advancing at the head of Freire's small army, inadvertently barged into Milhaud's cavalry near Baza. Catching the Spanish leading division in columns of march, the veteran French commander made short work of his opponent, inflicting 1,500 casualties and taking six cannon. Blake fled back across the frontier into Murcia, where his defeat and the onset of winter dissuaded him from attempting further operations that year.

II Badajoz and the Gebora

A temporary, uneasy calm descended on the eastern reaches of Soult's territories – and the harassed marshal turned to the state of affairs on his western borders. Ever since the emperor had received Foy's report on the army's predicament in Portugal, he had been urging Soult to send assistance to Massena.[252] Although he could not spare the resources and knew that there were 30,000 Allied troops and six major fortresses between himself and Lisbon,[253] Soult felt obliged to do something and, judging that a blow against Badajoz would serve both his own and Massena's interests, he resolved to besiege it.

Having assembled 13,500 infantry, 4,000 cavalry and 2,000 train troops, he marched for the Guadiana but, after detaching Gazan's division to repel the latest incursion by La Romana, his column was so weakened that he declined to tackle his original objective and moved against Olivenza instead, arriving on 11 January 1811. The little fortress had never been repaired after a Spanish-Portuguese conflict in 1801 and was in a deplorable condition. The Spanish commandant, Herck, offered only token resistance and, after ten days, his 4,000 troops surrendered.[254] Soult – urged on by fresh orders from Napoleon – then moved apprehensively against Badajoz.

He opened the siege on 27 January, but it had hardly begun when

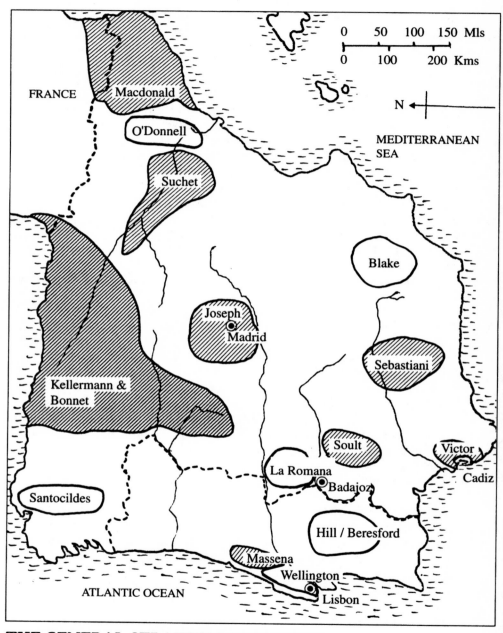

FRANCE

MEDITERRANEAN
SEA

Macdonald

O'Donnell

Suchet

Blake

Joseph
Madrid

Sebastiani

Kellermann &
Bonnet

Soult

Victor

Cadiz

Santocildes

La Romana
Badajoz

Hill / Beresford

Massena

Wellington

Lisbon

ATLANTIC OCEAN

0   50   100   150 Mls

0   100   200 Kms

N

THE GENERAL STRATEGIC SITUATION,
October 1810–March 1811

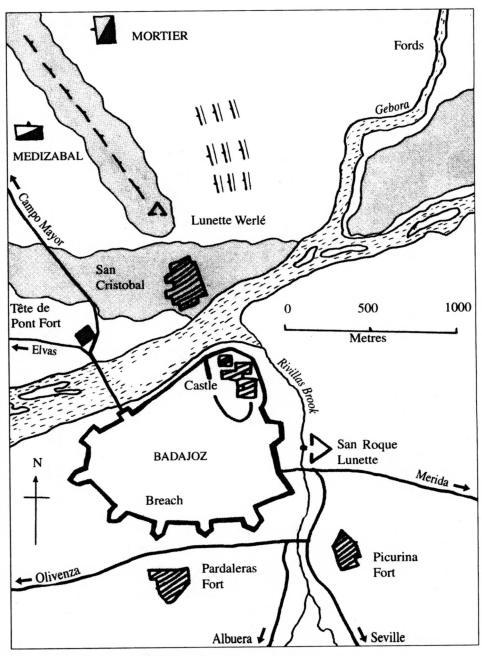

MORTIER

Fords

Gebora

MEDIZABAL

Campo Mayor

Lunette Werlé

San
Cristobal

Tête de
Pont Fort

← Elvas

Rivillas Brook

Castle

San Roque
Lunette

N

BADAJOZ

Merida →

Breach

← Olivenza

Pardaleras
Fort

Picurina
Fort

Albuera ↓

Seville ↓

0   500   1000

Metres

SOULT'S SIEGE OF BADAJOZ AND THE
BATTLE OF THE GEBORA

he was alerted to the advance of a Spanish army. The column was actually La Romana's 15,000 men, but he had died of a heart condition only days before and had been superseded by General Mendizabal. His forces still too weak to completely invest Badajoz, Soult was unable to prevent Mendizabal from reinforcing the garrison and, the following day, the French trenches were subjected to a determined sortie which was only driven off after bitter fighting. Having increased the fortress defenders to 7,000 men, Mendizabal placed his remaining 12,000 troops on the Heights of San Cristobal beyond the Guadiana. He then remained inactive for several days, convinced that the proximity of his army, plus Badajoz's own defences, would compel Soult to abandon the siege. However, the marshal, now rejoined by Gazan, acknowledging that Mendizabal's field force was indeed a major threat, resolved instead to destroy it.

Unnoticed by the complacent Spanish, Soult detached Mortier with 2,500 cavalry, 4,500 infantry and twelve guns. The French column slipped across the Guadiana on 19 February and, sending their cavalry on a long sweep around the enemy's open flank, fell on the unsuspecting foe. Mendizabal's troops were encamped on an excellent defensive position by the River Gebora, but, patently unprepared for action, they broke at the first exchange of fire and fled to the rear. They had not gone far when they encountered the French cavalry, who had already dealt with their Spanish counterparts and were striking east. Expecting the hostile troopers to attack, Mendizabal immediately threw his soldiers into two enormous divisional squares, only to see the enemy horsemen halt and mark time. After a few minutes, the pursuing Imperial infantry arrived and, joining their mounted comrades, waded into the hapless Spanish formations which were torn to pieces, 1,000 men being cut down and 4,000 taken captive. The remainder made off towards Badajoz or Portugal, leaving seventeen cannons and six colours in the hands of the victors. For only 400 casualties, Mortier had fulfilled his mission and, within hours, rejoined Soult.[255]

The Imperial forces could now concentrate on Badajoz. The fortress was strong and the governor, Menacho, was inspired and determined, but Soult's troops made rapid progress. The death of Menacho – killed whilst supervising one of his numerous sorties – disheartened the defence and, on 7 March, the French erected a battery of twenty-four pounders only fifty yards from the south wall. A twenty-yard gap soon appeared and on 10 March, General Imaz – Menacho's successor – capitulated.[256]

This timid surrender contrasted starkly with the resistance mounted at Gerona and Saragossa: Badajoz's garrison still numbered 8,000 effectives, had a month's ammunition and food, and was expecting a relief column, under Beresford, before long. The city's fall crowned a campaign in which, with only 20,000 men, Soult had seized two fortresses, taken 16,000 prisoners and virtually annihilated the Spanish army in Estremadura. Above all he was relieved at the operation's speedy conclusion; for three pieces of disturbing information had reached him on 8 March and his presence was urgently required elsewhere. The first was that Massena had evacuated Santarem and had retreated northwards, rendering Soult's diversion, impressive though it was, largely meaningless. The second was that Ballesteros' division of La Romana's army had again descended from the mountains near Huelva, had defeated General Remond and was moving against Seville. The third – and most alarming – was that an Anglo-Spanish force had landed at Algeciras and was threatening Victor's investment of Cadiz. Indeed, on 12 March, Soult learnt that the I Corps had been severely mauled in a battle at Barrosa. Once again, the situation to their rear obliged the French to abandon their offensive and, leaving Mortier at Badajoz with 11,000 troops, Soult hastened back to confront Ballesteros and succour Victor.

III Barrosa

We left the I Corps stoically blockading Cadiz, where they had been stationed since February 1810. Victor's position was, however, deteriorating. He had but 19,000 men and many of those were useless for open combat, being sappers and crews for siege guns. Furthermore, while he could make no progress against the fortress, he could not withdraw either; for its garrison now numbered 20,000 Iberians and 4,500 British – enough troops to overrun all of southern Andalusia or, indeed, to deal the isolated I Corps a major blow.

Such an attack was not long in coming. Safe in their impregnable position, the garrison of Cadiz assembled a large strike-force and ferried them to Algeciras where they united with a detachment from Gibraltar. Commanded by Generals Graham and La Peña, this column – totalling 5,000 British and 8,000 Spaniards – executed a difficult march through terrible weather and surprised an outpost of the I Corps on 2 March 1811. Simultaneously, the garrison of Cadiz – still 13,000 strong – implemented a vigorous foray against the lines and, although repelled, added to Victor's apprehension. Leaving his train troops and 2,000 infantry in the trenches, he marched east with 10,000 men. Deploying Villatte's command across the Cadiz road near Barrosa, he placed his other two divisions – those of Ruffin and Leval – to the north of the highway, on the flank of the advancing

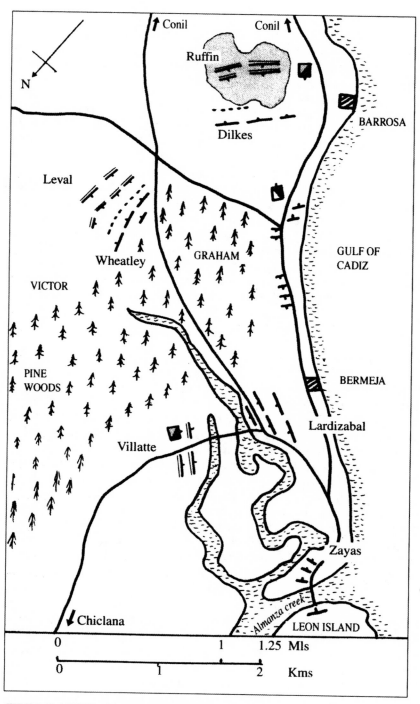

THE BATTLE OF BARROSA, 5 March 1811

Anglo-Spanish column. On 5 March – the day after Massena abandoned Santarem – La Peña's vanguard encountered Villatte's troops
and, supported by another sortie from Cadiz, drove them off the
road. Assimilating some local irregulars, the Allied army then
lumbered forward to threaten the lines of investment; the Spaniards
using the coastal highway, Graham's British taking a smaller, parallel track through the pine woods to the north.

Although disappointed that Villatte had failed to contain the
enemy for long, Victor was far from pessimistic. With the Allied
columns stretched across his front, he had two divisions poised to
deliver a surprise flank attack which promised to hustle them into the
sea. Ruffin's formation suddenly descended on the rear of the
Anglo-Spanish army and plunged it into panic. Leval, his advance
screened by the woods, directed his battalions at the centre.

Shortly after Ruffin opened his assault, Graham – denied a view of
events by the forest around him – heard the news of the French
onset. Deciding that his only hope was an immediate counter-attack,
he deployed Wheatley's brigade to confront Leval and sent Dilkes'
battalions against Ruffin. However, realising that to get them off the
woodland track and into suitable battle stations would take time,
Graham dispatched a column of light troops against each enemy
division to delay their advance for as long as possible: Browne's 500
'Flankers' set out for Ruffin; 700 other light infantry, under Barnard
and Bushe, marched against Leval.

Emerging from the woods, this latter contingent flung themselves
at the advancing foe, and a bitter fight was soon raging. The 400 men
of the 95th and the 300 Portuguese skirmishers took a terrible
mauling, but only after Bushe was killed and Barnard wounded did
they recoil. By this time, however, Wheatley had formed his battalions and, supported by the fire of ten guns, he routed the leading
French regiment, the 8th, inflicting grievous casualties and capturing the eagle. This disheartened the rest of Leval's formation, and
soon the entire division was pulling back.

Meanwhile, towards Barrosa, Browne's little column had engaged
Ruffin's command. Advancing up the heights, it was greeted by a
blistering volley and half the unit fell in seconds. The 'Flankers',
however, refused to yield and returned the enemy's fire with sporadic shots, buying precious moments for Dilkes' brigade to deploy in.
Indeed, moving up on Browne's right, the panting Guards and 67th
arrived just in time to save the situation.

Encouraged by his adversaries' battered condition, Ruffin had
directed the 24th Regiment and two grenadier battalions to sweep
the remaining 'Flankers' aside, but the French columns found their
opponents more resilient than expected. Instead of melting away

before the levelled bayonets, they joined Dilkes' men in delivering a series of volleys that halted the attack. The French struggled to deploy to return the salvoes, but all was in vain. As usual, the line's fire-power proved superior to that of the column and, although 350 British fell, their adversaries sustained 870 casualties.

The repulse of this attack heralded the end of the engagement. Ruffin's division recoiled and, leaving two guns and a hundred prisoners, joined Leval's men in headlong retreat. A resolute Victor managed to reform the fugitives behind his reserves, but the advance of some Allied cavalry plunged the French into fresh panic and the marshal fell back on Chiclana, abandoning another two cannon. For Allied casualties of 1,740, the French had sustained losses of 2,400 men, four guns and a standard. Graham had snatched triumph from the jaws of defeat, but recriminations split the Allied commanders and the British contingent withdrew onto Leon. An embittered La Peña followed shortly after, leaving a rather puzzled Victor free to invest Cadiz once more.[257]

IV   Beresford at Badajoz: The First Allied Siege

We left Soult returning from Badajoz on 13 March, in a desperate effort to save Seville from Ballesteros and succour Victor. His mere approach was enough to secure the first objective: Ballesteros, having penetrated to within a few miles of the provincial capital, retreated to his mountain refuge, hotly pursued by General Maransin's division. Nevertheless, Soult's respite was not long. Having ascertained that Victor was in no immediate danger, he was summoned back to Estremadura by Mortier, who had come under attack from a large Allied army.

When Soult had departed for Seville, Mortier had thrown a sizeable detachment into Badajoz and had crossed the frontier into Portugal. After securing the surrender of the scanty garrison of Campo Mayor, he dispatched a contingent under Latour-Maubourg to invest Albuquerque. On arriving before the fortress, these few hundred horsemen emulated Lasalle's celebrated capture of Stettin in 1806;[258] browbeating the powerful Spanish garrison into meekly accepting an impudent demand for their surrender. However, Mortier's celebrations were abruptly concluded by the appearance of Beresford's Allied army. When Massena had halted before the Lines of Torres Vedras, Wellington had taken the precaution of ferrying troops across the Tagus to deter the 'Army of Portugal' from passing to the south bank and uniting with Soult. As we have seen, this measure proved entirely successful and, when Massena subsequently retired towards Coimbra, these forces, under Hill, were left free and were eventually ordered to relieve Badajoz.

Beresford – who had replaced the ailing Hill – set his divisions in motion in early March. He had not gone far, however, when he was advised of the shameful surrender of the fortress and the subsequent advance of the French to Campo Mayor. Fresh orders from Wellington directed him to attack the enemy immediately, calling on Mendizabal for any assistance his shattered corps might provide.[259] Gathering every available man, he arrived at Campo Mayor on 25 March, taking the French completely by surprise.

The town was occupied by one infantry and three cavalry regiments under Latour-Maubourg, who was busy destroying the defences prior to withdrawing on Badajoz. He had already removed all the artillery and was demolishing the walls when Beresford's columns were spotted and the alarm raised. Although the Allies had over 18,000 troops at their disposal, the veteran French officer remained calm and, forming up his little command, hurried them off towards Badajoz. Seeing his prey eluding him, Beresford launched his 1,500 cavalry after them, but three miles had passed before the troopers came level with the head of the retiring column and obliged it to deploy.

The hostile cavalrymen having left their supporting infantry far behind, Latour-Maubourg was not too concerned. His infantry quickly formed square and his horsemen deployed beside them, while his few cannon fired canister into the advancing enemy formations. The Allied cavalry, under General Long, swept forward and a *mêlée* erupted between the 26th Dragoons and the British 13th Light Dragoons. After several minutes the outnumbered Imperial regiment retreated, pursued by the 13th who lost all control and, ignoring a French artillery convoy, chased the fugitives to the very gates of Badajoz. Here, retribution was at hand: Mortier galloped out of the fortress with his reserve and routed the exhausted light dragoons before dashing off to rescue Latour-Maubourg.

He, however, was more than holding his own. Having driven off the 26th Dragoons, Long had hurled a Portuguese regiment against the 2nd Hussars but, unsettled by a volley as they passed the French infantry, they broke on impact and fifty went down before the unit could be extricated. Long – having lost control of both the action and himself – now ordered his heavy cavalry brigade to attack the hostile squares, but the suicidal charge was halted by the timely arrival of Beresford and Latour-Maubourg completed his withdrawal without further ado.[260]

Beresford's forces now succumbed to the logistical problems that all armies faced in barren Estremadura. Shoes and food were in desperately short supply, and it was not until 3 April that enough pontoons had been scraped together to allow them to commence crossing the Guadiana.[261] However, barely had this operation begun than an abrupt flood swept away Beresford's extemporised bridge and trapped his vanguard on the eastern bank, exposing them to the full might of the French army for three days. Fortunately for the stranded contingent, however, the enemy was too busy to mount a major attack: Mortier had been recalled to Paris and superseded by Latour-Maubourg, and the defences of Badajoz were not yet fully repaired. Nevertheless, their cavalry occasionally raided the Allies' vedettes and, in one daring night attack alone, exterminated a whole picket of the 13th Light Dragoons at no cost to themselves.

The bridge repaired, the Allied army completed their crossing and approached Badajoz. Reluctant to face such overwhelming numbers in open battle, Latour-Maubourg left 3,000 men in the fortress and a weak battalion in Olivenza and retired to the Andalusian border. Here, observed by a screen of light troops under Colborne, he anxiously awaited Soult with reinforcements from Seville.

Beresford, meanwhile, had moved slowly forward. 9 April saw him at Olivenza, but he took three days to overwhelm the tiny garrison and seize the decrepit fortress. He was then free to beleaguer Badajoz,[262] but he encountered more delays as his staff struggled to procure a battering train. With great difficulty, twenty-three heavy cannon – many 200 years old – were dragged forward from Elvas, but few gunners and engineers could be found and the condition of the siege corps remained lamentably poor.[263] Wellington, having driven Massena from Portugal, now arrived on a flying visit and took personal control, preparing compendious orders for the siege and the resistance of any French relief column that should appear. About this time, Ballesteros – having evaded General Maransin's column – brought his division also to support Beresford, and the arrival of Alten's brigade of KGL light troops from Lisbon further swelled the Allied army's ranks. Including the 2,500 Spanish under Castaños (who had replaced Mendizabal) the force now numbered over 27,000 men and invested Badajoz on 6 May.

The French, too, were mustering their available strength. Having failed to overtake Ballesteros, Maransin united with Latour-Maubourg, concentrating 10,000 men on the Andalusian border. Soult, having wrung 15,000 troops from the battered I and IV Corps, joined them and, by 13 May, had 21,000 infantry, 4,000 cavalry and forty-eight cannon marching on Badajoz.

Meanwhile, the siege had begun in earnest. Wellington had returned to the north on 25 April and matters were back in the hands of Beresford. Although he did his utmost to comply with his lavish

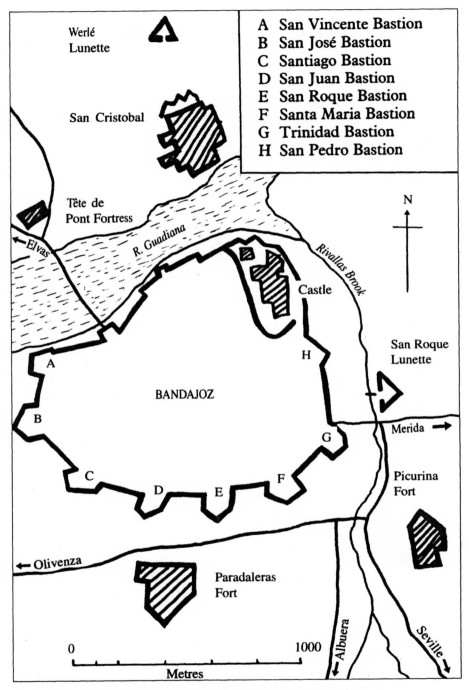

A	San Vincente Bastion
B	San José Bastion
C	Santiago Bastion
D	San Juan Bastion
E	San Roque Bastion
F	Santa Maria Bastion
G	Trinidad Bastion
H	San Pedro Bastion

Werlé Lunette

San Cristobal

Tête de Pont Fortress

← Elvas

R. Guadiana

Rivallas Brook

Castle

N

San Roque Lunette

BANDAJOZ

Merida →

Picurina Fort

← Olivenza

Paradaleras Fort

0   1000

Metres

← Albuera

Seville →

THE FORTRESS OF BADAJOZ DURING THE PENINSULAR WAR

directions, enormous problems were encountered and the besiegers made slow progress. It had been determined to take the dominating position of San Cristobal, but the surrounding ground was found to be very stony and the excavation of trenches proved impossible. The British began dragging gabions across the plateau to construct a battery. The work parties, however, were sitting targets for the French snipers and gunners, and a third of Beresford's engineers were picked off in one day alone. Moreover, the garrison executed a sortie on 10 May and destroyed much of the completed work before being driven off. Even then they got the better of the besiegers; pursuing the raiders too far, the British came under heavy fire from San Cristobal and lost over 400 men.

Demoralised, the Allies struggled to finish their redoubt. On 11 May they finally got some cannon into action, but the French gunners quickly silenced them and wiped out half of Beresford's remaining engineers in the process. The following day the besiegers tried again, only to see their replacement artillery dismounted in similar, peremptory style and much of the earthwork damaged. Beresford was on the verge of desperation when alarming news arrived from Colborne: Soult was advancing at the head of a large army and could be expected at Badajoz within the week. In accordance with Wellington's written instructions,[264] Beresford immediately wound down the siege operations: the remaining guns were withdrawn to Elvas and what *matériel* the overstretched transport corps could not extricate quickly was burnt. The army, meanwhile, began taking up position at Albuera, ready to confront Soult.

V Albuera

15 May saw Beresford amassing his divisions. By now, he had no less than 35,000 men with 50 guns; for, in another impressive amphibious operation, General Blake had landed with 8,000 Spanish troops from Cadiz and had marched up the Guadiana to join him. The Allied army was deployed in a strong defensive position across the undulating, treeless fields south of Albuera. Believing that the enemy would thrust up the highway to Badajoz, Beresford saw the village as the key to the battle and positioned his corps accordingly. The left wing - Hamilton's Portuguese division and most of the Portuguese cavalry – lay to the north of the Badajoz road. The centre – founded on Albuera itself – comprised the divisions of Cole and Stewart, supported by Alten's light brigade and over 1,000 horse. The southern section was made up of the four Spanish infantry divisions – some 12,000 men – backed by another mass of Allied

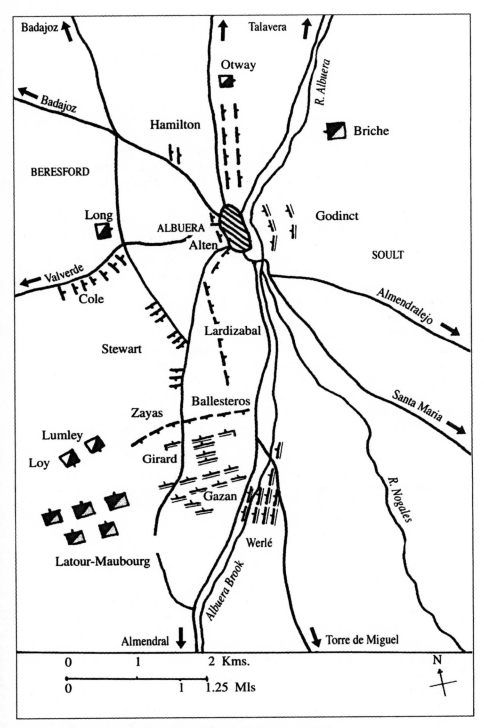

Badajoz

Talavera

Otway

R. Albuera

Badajoz

Hamilton

Briche

BERESFORD

Long

Godinct

ALBUERA

Alten

SOULT

Valverde

Cole

Almendralejo

Lardizabal

Stewart

Ballesteros

Santa Maria

Zayas

Lumley

Girard

Loy

R. Nogales

Gazan

Werlé

Latour-Maubourg

Albuera Brook

Almendral

Torre de Miguel

0   1   2 Kms.

0   1   1.25 Mls

N

THE BATTLE OF ALBUERA, 16 May 1811
(Situation at the start)

cavalry and several batteries of artillery. Mostly deployed on the reverse slopes of hills, Beresford's forces were largely out of the enemy's sight.

The Allied concentration was virtually complete when Soult's vanguard arrived and drove Colborne's screen back across the Albuera Brook. The marshal knew that Blake had landed from Cadiz and was anxious to strike at Beresford before the two hostile forces could unite. This had already taken place, but Soult – denied a view of most of Beresford's army and thus unable to calculate its size – felt certain that he had arrived in time to prevent the junction of his adversaries and formulated a strategy to keep things that way. Believing Blake to be marching up from the south, he resolved to turn Beresford's right flank, thus interposing himself between the two Allied forces. With any luck, Beresford would be defeated, and the relief of Badajoz secured. Then, over a field strewn with Allied dead, the French army would sweep southwards to deal with Blake.

Early on 16 May, the Imperial forces began to implement this imaginative scheme. 10,000 infantry, under Werlé and Godinot, supported by three cavalry brigades, launched a vigorous demonstration against Beresford's centre. As this was just what the Allied general had anticipated, he took the bait without hesitation, throwing in his reserves to assist Alten. Meanwhile, screened by some woods, Soult swung the divisions of Girard and Gazan southwards and suddenly emerged on Blake's right flank, his cavalry scattering Loy's Spanish horsemen and plunging their supporting infantry into panic.

An astounded Beresford galloped southwards and improvised a new line of defence, drawing part of Blake's men back at an angle to the main position and shifting the whole army to the right. With horsemen guarding their flanks, the French V Corps came on – one division behind the other – in a gigantic 'mixed order' formation. Girard's command led, but Gazan's was so close behind that the entire force soon coalesced into one vast body of 8,000 marching soldiers. Two of the French cavalry brigades deployed before Alten also wheeled to the south, galloped behind the V Corps and formed up on their left. Likewise, Werlé's 6,000 infantry swerved away from the Allies' centre and fell in behind Gazan's division. By means of these brilliantly executed manoeuvres, Soult succeeded in concentrating his whole army – save one infantry and one cavalry brigade – against Beresford's refused right wing.

Caught off balance, the Allies responded as best they could. The Second and Fourth Divisions, along with the cavalry reserves, hurried to the endangered sector and began to deploy behind Zayas' startled Spanish troops. By this time, however, Girard had moved within musket range of Blake's line and his skirmishers were riddling it with fire. After a few minutes, the *voltigeurs* skilfully peeled off to the flanks of Girard's formation as it advanced to finish the matter.

A tremendous musketry exchange erupted and men were falling fast when Stewart's Second Division appeared on the scene. Colborne's brigade was first to arrive and, seeing the deep French formation, Stewart could not resist sending him forward in an effort to outflank the column and rake it with lateral fire. At first, all went well. Colborne got his four battalions into line and wheeled them against Girard's left flank. Shaken by a devastating volley from only twenty yards, the outer files of the French division turned to face this new threat and, soon, whole companies were being swept away as the antagonists poured musketry into each other at ever diminishing ranges. The Allies steadily gained the upper hand and, attacked from two sides, Girard's units began to crumble.

However, Latour-Maubourg's cavalry was close at hand. Covered by gunsmoke and a lucky rain squall, the 1st Vistula Lancers and the 2nd Hussars suddenly swept into the open flank of Colborne's horrified troops. In minutes, the affair was over. Involved with the French infantry and caught before they could redeploy, the British battalions were rolled up and slaughtered. Five colours were taken, as was their supporting artillery battery and, of the 1,648 men in the three leading battalions, 1,248 were killed, wounded or taken. Only the 31st Foot managed to form square and avoid destruction.

While some of the French cavalry dragged away Colborne's battery, the bulk of them swerved past the 31st, scattered Beresford and his staff and attacked Zayas' troops in the rear. Much to their credit, the Spaniards endeavoured to beat off this onslaught while simultaneously maintaining their fire at Girard's column. Caught in the midst of this desperate scrimmage, the Allied commander and his entourage were only saved by the timely arrival of the 29th Foot who, rather unwisely, began firing on the dispersed lancers; most of the shot passing the horsemen harmlessly by and striking the rear ranks of Zayas' formation instead. Nevertheless, the pertinacious Spaniards stood their ground and almost certainly saved Beresford from disaster. With Colborne's battalions wrecked, the reserves not yet up and the whole wing falling into disorder, a charge by Latour-Maubourg's massed cavalry, supported by Girard and Gazan, could hardly have failed to inflict appalling losses. However, Zayas held his position and the French horse eventually made off towards their own lines. Two British dragoon squadrons who tried to pursue them were overthrown, losing their commanding officers and several men.

Throughout the rout of Colborne's brigade and the subsequent upheaval in the Allied rear, Girard had maintained his assault. His formations had suffered terrible casualties in the grinding battle of attrition with Zayas, and Colborne's short-lived counter-attack had also done considerable harm. By now, the leading battalions of the V Corps were in a deplorable state and Girard summoned Gazan's division to replace them. But Gazan's battalions were still struggling through the dregs of Girard's units, when the brigades of Hoghton and Abercrombie arrived to relieve Zayas. The ensuing musketry exchange even outdid the earlier contest for unadulterated butchery: in minutes, two thirds of Hoghton's 1,500 men and 2,000 French had fallen, and the casualties on both sides were lying in heaps, several bodies high.

Soult, in the meantime, had come to realise the true nature of the situation before him. It was now clear that Blake and Beresford had already united, and that they disposed of over 30,000 men. He cancelled his previous plan and went onto the defensive: Latour-Maubourg was refused permission to charge, and Werlé's infantry were retained in reserve.

Beresford, meanwhile, was still struggling to save his right wing. Abercrombie's three battalions were deployed to the left of Hoghton's shattered brigade and took some pressure off it, but the French continued to attack. Although desperate for more troops, the Allied commander dared not move Cole's division from containing Latour-Maubourg's horsemen and was obliged to summon Hamilton's Portuguese from the north of the field. However, by this time, some of these battalions had been sucked into the fighting around Albuera, where Godinot was locked in a struggle with Alten's KGL brigade, and it would be forty-five minutes before they could arrive. With defeat staring him in the face, Beresford frantically directed 3,000 Spaniards to relieve the defenders of Albuera so as to release the KGL. Alten complied, but Godinot was attacking so determinedly and the Spanish were so tardy in arriving that the village was lost to the French, creating yet another threat to Beresford's precarious position. Hoping that the Spaniards and elements of Hamilton's division would retake the settlement – or at least contain Godinot – the tired Legionnaires hastily regrouped and marched south to join the right wing.

Thus, the situation was critical when General Cole initiated a counter-attack which finally drove the French back. His division had been standing inactive before the enemy cavalry for some time when, without orders from Beresford, he moved forward to threaten Gazan's flank. Such a manoeuvre – across open plains, in the face of 3,500 hostile horsemen – was highly dangerous, and Cole attempted to reduce the risk of cavalry attack by deploying his forces into line with a deep column protecting the open wing. All the available cavalry advanced to guard his flank and rear but, nevertheless, the Fourth Division risked following in the footsteps of Colborne's ill-fated brigade.

At the sight of Cole's 5,000 bayonets, Soult realised that he would have to commit Werlé if Gazan and Girard were to be saved. Accordingly, he urged Latour-Maubourg to attack the Allied right and moved Werlé's troops forward obliquely to cover V Corps' left flank. The Imperial horsemen bore down on Harvey's column of Portuguese, which guarded Cole's open flank, but were received with a hail of musketry and brought to a halt. Unable to arrest the advance of the Fourth Division, Latour-Maubourg sullenly backed off as Werlé's 5,600 men marched forward to challenge Cole's line.

Although Werlé enjoyed a numerical superiority of around two to one, he, like Girard, had deployed his troops into extremely uneconomical formations. Advancing in three deep but narrow columns, his nine battalions could only bring some 360 muskets to bear, whereas every man in Myer's British brigade – some 2,000 – could use his flintlock. As Werlé's regiments emerged from the smoke, each of the three British Fusilier battalions – 1/7th, 2/7th and 23rd – confronted one of the hostile formations and a tremendous fire-fight ensued. Twenty minutes later the French broke and ran, leaving 1,800 dead and wounded lying in heaps on the blood-soaked plain. The battered Fusiliers, their brigadier and over 1,000 men having fallen, pursued their foe as best they could, but were soon brought to a halt by blasts of canister from Soult's artillery. Nevertheless, the rout of Werlé's assault proved to be the decisive moment of the battle. As the troops on their left gave way, Gazan's exhausted units also recoiled and Godinot abandoned his attack on Albuera. Within minutes, the entire French army was retreating eastwards.

Soult formed his cavalry, cannon and small infantry reserve into a formidable line on the far bank of the Albuera stream, but Beresford declined to continue the action and a fresh rain-storm finally brought the battle to a conclusion. The casualties on both sides were horrific: well over 4,000 British troops had fallen, plus 1,400 Spaniards and nearly 400 Portuguese. The French V Corps alone suffered losses of nearly fifty per cent and the Imperial casualties totalled 7,000.[265] After such butchery, neither side had the means or the will for further offensive action: Beresford withdrew his infantry to reinvest Badajoz, while his cavalry, under Lumley, shadowed Soult's retirement on Llerena. On arriving there, however, the marshal – anxious to establish the size and intentions of the forces that were following him – dispatched Latour–Maubourg's cavalry towards Usagre. But as his leading regiments were crossing the Matachel they were ambushed. Unable to deploy, or retreat across the crowded bridge, the head of the column was scattered, sustaining 350 casualties.

Lumley, however, fearful of receiving a dose of his own tactical medicine, declined to cross the river and the opposing forces duly settled into camps on their respective sides of the Matachel.[266] But this state of uneasy calm was not to persist for long. In the north Wellington had fought another battle with Massena and, as we shall see, some of the repercussions of that engagement were to have major consequences for the war in Estremadura.

Chapter XVII

THE WAR IN THE WEST AND SOUTH, 1810–11

I 'If Boney Had Been There': The Battle of Fuentes de Oñoro

Even before Massena was ousted from Portugal, the situation in the north of the Peninsula had been causing Napoleon concern. Incensed by the rivalry between the military governors and their failure to quell the insurgents, he resolved to place all the troops in the northern provinces under one command. Accordingly, in January 1811 he formed the 'Army of the North', placing the 70,000 men between Navarre and Salamanca under Marshal Bessières, Duke of Istria.

Predictably, Bessières enjoyed no more success than had his predecessors. Much of the area in his charge was mountainous and ideal for the activities of guerillas. Moreover, he simply lacked sufficient troops to meet all the commitments he was expected to fulfil. His 70,000 men were incapable of simultaneously holding down the entire territory, keeping Allied fleets from descending on the coast, supporting the 'Army of Portugal' and containing the 16,000-strong Spanish regular forces in the north-west. Thus, his difficulties were already tremendous when Massena's shattered army was ousted from its position along the Coa and finally staggered back into Spain.

Massena's divisions were in an atrocious condition and would evidently be out of action for weeks. In the meantime Wellington was free to prowl along the borders of Leon and, indeed, encircled Ciudad Rodrigo. However, with no siege cannon and his own army suffering from malnutrition, he soon abandoned the project and, while his forces regrouped and improved their logistics, undertook his flying visit to Beresford at Badajoz. By 29 April, he was back in the north, alerted to a sudden forward move by Massena.

After the series of crushing reverses sustained by that marshal,

Wellington expected him to be too dispirited to undertake any demanding project for some time. Massena, however, refused to acknowledge defeat and, although he knew he was to be replaced by Marmont, resolved to relieve Almeida and Ciudad Rodrigo. Following his arrival at Salamanca on 12 April, he worked feverishly to restore his army to a reasonable condition: the supplies and equipment that had accumulated in the city were issued and a complete overhaul of his divisions was begun. Some 42,000 infantry were eventually assembled, but horses and draught animals remained scarce: the five cavalry brigades could only field 3,000 sabres, while teams could be furnished for no more than thirty cannon.

To make good these deficiencies, Massena appealed to the 'Army of the North' for assistance. Napoleon later maintained that Bessières could have spared 10,000 men without serious difficulty, but, apart from a few horse teams and a battery of artillery, he dispatched no more than Lepic and Wathier's cavalry brigades – some 1,600 sabres. Although disappointed, Massena assimilated them and, concentrating the II, VI, VIII and IX Corps, assembled 42,000 foot, 4,500 horse and thirty-eight pieces of ordnance at Ciudad Rodrigo on 1 May. The next day he opened his offensive, advancing to relieve Almeida.

Rumours of his preparations had been percolating through to the Allies for some weeks and Wellington had organised his divisions for a fresh conflict. Anxious to thwart the relief of Almeida, he had selected a strong defensive position at Fuentes de Oñoro where a chain of heights overlooked the gorge of the River Dos Casas. His formations had suffered appreciable losses from starvation in the desolate terrain but, in addition to the units blockading Almeida, he still managed to muster some 35,000 bayonets, nearly 2,000 sabres and forty-eight cannon; two-thirds of the force being British.

With his customary skill, the Allied commander deployed his corps along the five miles of hills between Fuentes de Oñoro and Fort Concepcion. The right wing consisted of a strong force in Fuentes de Oñoro itself, with the First, Third, Light and newly formed Seventh Divisions in support. Ashworth's Portuguese brigade and most of Wellington's cavalry were also placed here. Further north – where the gorge of the river was exceedingly steep and plunged to a depth of 150 feet – Wellington felt a serious enemy attack was unlikely, so he stationed only the Fifth and Sixth Divisions there. In keeping with their usual practice as many troops as possible were hidden from the enemy's view, and only Wellington's cannon and skirmishers were visible when Massena's army arrived on the afternoon of 3 May.

After a detailed reconnaissance, the marshal rejected serious action against the northern sector of the Allied line and resolved to

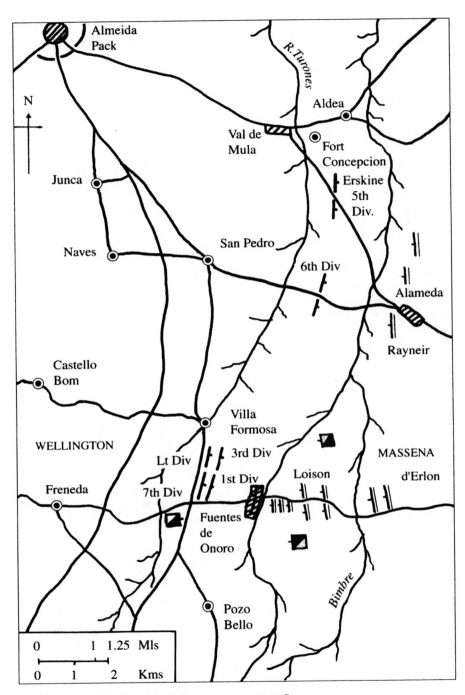

THE BATTLE OF FUENTES DE OÑORO,
3 and 4 May 1811

take Fuentes de Oñoro. The rambling village was visible on the lower slopes and it was clear that a major effort would be needed to secure it. Not only was there a sizeable garrison – 1,800 light troops and a line battalion, under Colonel Williams – but the sturdy buildings and numerous enclosures would lend themselves to defence. As a preliminary move, however, Massena sought to tie up the Allies' reserves in some indecisive fighting far from the intended point of attack and, accordingly, had part of Reynier's corps stage an impressive demonstration against Erskine's Fifth Division. It worked: Wellington was suitably alarmed and marched the Light Division across to bolster the left wing.

The task of securing Fuentes de Oñoro fell to Ferey's division of the VI Corps and, in due course, its five leading battalions, braving a heavy fire, charged across the Dos Casas – at this point narrow and shallow – and stormed into the tangle of gardens and buildings. After a few minutes, the assailants had turned the defenders out of several houses in the lower reaches of the town and, alarmed by the enemy's progress, Williams staged a counter-attack. A bloody struggle followed in which the French were driven back. But Ferey committed his second brigade, re-established his grip on the eastern sector of the village and penetrated to the church on the crest of the Allied position.

With Williams severely wounded and the French making steady progress, Wellington sent in three battalions from the First Division to support the faltering garrison. These spearheaded a second counter-attack, which ousted Ferey from most of his gains and drove his rapidly tiring men back across the stream. At this, however, Massena committed four of Marchand's battalions and they swiftly regained the lower reaches of the village. The struggle swayed to and fro amongst the lanes and houses, but neither side could make further headway and, with the onset of night, the fighting deteriorated into a desultory fusillade. French casualties totalled 650; the Allies' approached 260.

The next day, mindful of Bussaco, Massena had his cavalry explore the enemy line. It was discovered that Wellington's right flank was relatively open, and protected by only a few squadrons of horsemen and a solitary battalion in the village of Pozo Bello. The marshal formulated a new plan: while Reynier launched a fresh demonstration against Erskine, 20,000 troops would swing round Wellington's right flank and envelop it. Once this manoeuvre was coming to fruition, Ferey, backed by the IX Corps, would again storm Fuentes and punch a hole in the angle of the refused Allied line, completing the discomfiture of the beleaguered wing. Under cover of darkness, the Imperial units shifted position: two divisions

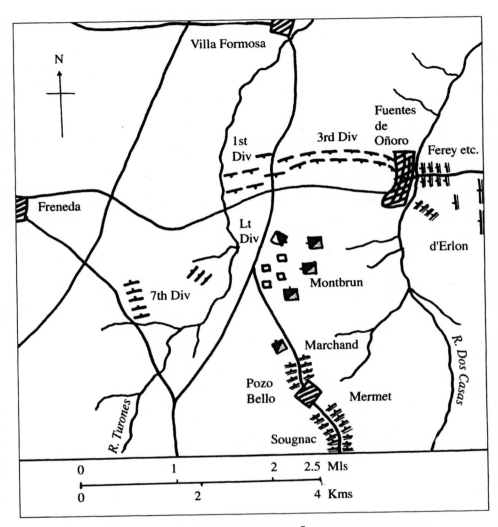

N

Villa Formosa

Freneda

1st Div

Lt Div

7th Div

3rd Div

Fuentes de Oñoro

Ferey etc.

d'Erlon

Montbrun

Marchand

Pozo Bello

Mermet

Sougnac

R. Turones

R. Dos Casas

0	1	2	2.5 Mls

0	2	4 Kms

THE BATTLE OF FUENTES DE OÑORO, 5 May 1811

from the VI Corps and one from the VIII Corps joined the bulk of the cavalry to mount the *attaque débordante*, while the remaining forces prepared to pin down Wellington's left and centre.

The Allied commander had anticipated that Massena might try an outflanking manoeuvre, but its size was to take him by surprise. During the night of 4 May, Wellington reinforced his right wing with the weak Seventh Division, and brought Craufurd and parts of the Fuentes garrison back to the central reserve. Nevertheless, the

Allied line was ill prepared for the storm that was about to break, and only the tenacity and skill of the British troops was to save them from a serious defeat.

At dawn on 5 May, Montbrun opened the French assault by unleashing his troopers on the enemy horse about Pozo Bello, while Marchand's division stormed the village itself and quickly ousted the Allied infantry there. The 85th Foot and 2nd *Cacadores* staggered out onto the plateau in disorder and were promptly assailed by swarms of cavalry. Although saved from complete destruction by the brave charge of some German hussars, the two regiments sustained terrible casualties and only narrowly succeeded in regaining the rest of Houston's Seventh Division.

But the crisis was only beginning. Urging his squadrons forward, Montbrun now threatened to cut off and exterminate Houston's fleeing battalions. Wellington was forced to send Craufurd's division to extricate them and, using the rest of his reserves, to hastily form a new line at a right angle to the main position. However, it was primarily because of the Allied cavalry that the Seventh Division escaped annihilation. Shrugging off heavy losses, they mounted repeated charges to keep Montbrun's cavalry and horse artillery at bay. Their sacrifice enabled Houston's shaken battalions to unite with Craufurd's men who, deployed in square, slowly withdrew across the plateau, followed at a respectful distance by Montbrun.

By now, however, the initiative had slipped from the Frenchman's grasp. Having left his infantry support far to the rear, Montbrun was unwilling to tackle Craufurd's steady squares, although he did his utmost to impede their retreat. The artillery of both sides could barely get forward because of the danger from the enemy's cavalry and, indeed, an attempt by Ramsay's Royal Horse Artillery troop to intervene led to one of the most celebrated incidents of the war. Finding part of his battery surrounded by hostile horsemen, this impudent officer limbered up his cannon and, to the chagrin of the French, galloped out of their very midst, scattering friend and foe in all directions. But not all of Wellington's units were as fortunate. Prowling across the plain in search of alternative prey, the French cavalry encountered a line of skirmishers detached by the First Division. Attacking this force in the flank, the 13th *Chasseurs* practically destroyed the three companies of Guards, inflicting over 100 casualties for little loss to themselves. This, however, was the last success for Montbrun's men. Faced with a solid wall of hostile infantry and supported by thirty-six cannon, they could make no further progress and, after a couple of minor charges, fell back to join their own foot troops.

His flanking force in position, Massena waited for the attack by

Ferey and d'Erlon to develop. In due course, Ferey's division stormed across the Dos Casas and fell on the defenders of Fuentes. Although greeted by a murderous fire from behind innumerable walls and barricades, the French drove forward with tremendous *élan*, and the 71st and 79th recoiled with heavy casualties. Nevertheless, the committing of another British battalion (2/24th Foot) tipped the scales and Ferey's depleted units began to give ground. At this, however, d'Erlon threw in three grenadier battalions, who quickly re-established the French position and drove the garrison as far back as the church on the crest of Wellington's ridge.

The critical moment had arrived and d'Erlon hurried forward several more units to clinch the victory. Wellington poured in a mass of light troops to reinforce the defenders and deployed Mackinnon's brigade of the Third Division in the rear of the settlement, but the French steadily gained the upper hand. In a last effort to secure the village, Mackinnon was ordered into the fray and, leaving the 45th Foot as a last reserve, led his other two battalions in columns of attack through the narrow lanes. The 88th promptly collided with the 9th *Léger* and a vicious bayonet fight ensued. After a desperate *mêlée*, the French recoiled and, joined by the rest of the Allied units, the 88th drove their opponents back to the Dos Casas.

The battle had been long and arduous and Wellington was later to admit: 'If Boney had been there we should have been beaten!'[267] However, having failed to secure Fuentes, Massena declined to execute a serious assault from his position on Wellington's flank. His artillery maintained a bombardment until two o'clock but, hopelessly outnumbered, suffered heavily from the return fire. Down in Fuentes, where 2,000 men had fallen in a few hours, neither side was prepared to attempt anything more and the fighting subsided into a petty musketry exchange across the corpse-strewn alleys. French losses totalled 2,200 men, while those of the Allies approached 1,500.[268]

Wellington prepared for another day's conflict, and set his men to building redoubts and trenches. But Massena had resolved to retire on Ciudad Rodrigo and abandon his plan to relieve Almeida. The Portuguese fortress was more of a liability than an asset – given the strategic situation – and the only thing of value was its garrison. Deciding that that could be saved, the marshal offered a reward of 6,000 Francs to any soldier who would carry a dispatch to the governor. Three men volunteered, one of whom completed the mission.

Having fired a signal gun to acknowledge receipt of his orders, General Brennier prepared to evacuate and demolish Almeida. While Massena retired eastwards, the garrison laid mines and secretly destroyed their stores and artillery. Around midnight on 10 May, Brennier placed himself at the head of his command and cut a path through the startled enemy pickets. Moments later, a series of explosions tore Almeida apart and roused Wellington's sleeping army. But although the Allies chased him relentlessly, Brennier avoided serious loss[269] and, gaining the French lines with most of his 1,300 men, marched in to a hero's welcome. Here, he discovered that the 'Army of Portugal' was under new management: Massena had finally been relieved of command by Marshal Marmont, Duke of Ragusa.

The new commander-in-chief was an able strategist and very efficient administrator. He was also outstandingly courageous, although his confidence tended to desert him at crucial moments. The first two months following his appointment were spent in a comprehensive reorganisation of his battered forces: the army corps structure was dismantled and six independent divisions formed; many senior officers – such as Junot, Marchand and Mermet – were replaced; the remnants of the weakest units were sent home to recruit; the devastated cavalry was dispatched to Bayonne to procure fresh horses; and the accumulated stores at Salamanca and Valladolid were issued. Furthermore, on Imperial orders, d'Erlon's IX Corps – a makeshift formation, comprising the fourth battalions of regiments in Soult's army – was broken up and the component parts forwarded to their mother units in Andalusia. By dint of these exertions the 'Army of Portugal' was rested, fed, paid and clothed for the first time in months.

Nevertheless, Wellington thought that it would be many weeks before the enemy could take the field again. Judging the northern front to be safe for the time being, he resolved to join Beresford in besieging Badajoz. Accordingly, in mid-May, he took the Third and Seventh Divisions and set out for Estremadura, leaving General Sir Brent Spencer with 28,000 men to watch Marmont and, in the unlikely event of an attack, to defend the Beira frontier.[270] Similarly, General Santocildes, commander of the Spanish forces in Galicia, was urged to mount an offensive to help pin down the French forces in the north until Badajoz had fallen.

II Wellington at Badajoz – The Second Allied Siege

Wellington arrived at Elvas on 19 May, where he received Beresford's report on the battle of Albuera. Its despondent tone and emphasis on the appalling British losses was too much for him: 'This won't do – write me down a victory',[271] he insisted. One of his aides

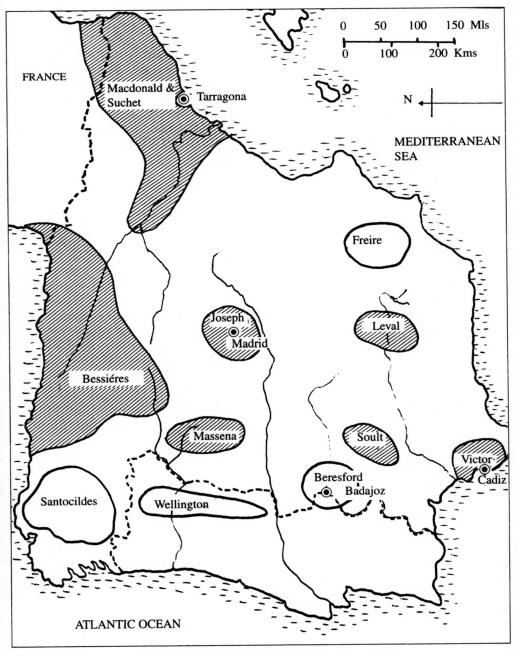

THE GENERAL STRATEGIC SITUATION, May 1811

rewrote the dispatch and only then was it forwarded to London. Wellington, meanwhile, pushed on to Badajoz, where he arrived the next day and took control of the siege preparations.

As an opening move, he returned the inept Beresford to his post at the head of the Portuguese military administration. General Hill, recently returned from England, replaced him and was entrusted with the forces allotted to contain Soult – the Second and Fourth Divisions, the Spanish formations and the bulk of the cavalry. This left the Third and Seventh Divisions and some Portuguese to invest Badajoz, and Wellington added more units from the northern front. By 29 May, sufficient forces were in position and the second siege of Badajoz was begun.[272]

The garrison consisted of no more than 3,000 troops under the command of General Phillipon who, having beaten off one siege, was determined to hang on at all costs and implemented every ruse his fertile mind could think of to keep the Allies at bay. Although outnumbered by five to one, he was to prove a most formidable adversary and, in his endeavour to take Badajoz, Wellington was to fare no better than Beresford had.

Fearful that Soult might retake the offensive, the Allies were desperate to secure Phillipon's fortress at the earliest opportunity. Wellington's plan was essentially the same as Beresford's – to breach the most formidable parts of the city's defences to bring about a quick victory. However, he soon encountered the same difficulties that had thwarted his predecessor. Although he had more siege guns, he had problems in finding sufficient crewmen, and trained engineers were still in short supply. Nevertheless, he persevered and, on the night of 30 May, parallels were begun opposite San Cristobal and the castle on the south bank of the Guadiana.

His sappers found the stony ground before San Cristobal even harder to dig than had Beresford's, for the ingenious Phillipon had cleared away what few inches of top-soil had existed. Denied any natural cover, the Allied engineers had to drag wool-packs and sandbags forward to protect their shallow excavations. But such crude barricades provided poor shelter from artillery fire and the work-parties sustained heavy losses with little progress being made. As late as 3 June, only a small battery had been constructed on this part of the front and that was quickly damaged by accurate shelling.

The parallel opposite the castle was, however, a little more successful. Here, the ground was more workable, but the trench – 800 yards from the target – was too distant. By 3 June, twenty guns were in position and a bombardment was begun. But the cannons – mostly antiquated pieces from Elvas – were not up to the task and, after a few hours' firing, their carriages were shaken to pieces and the

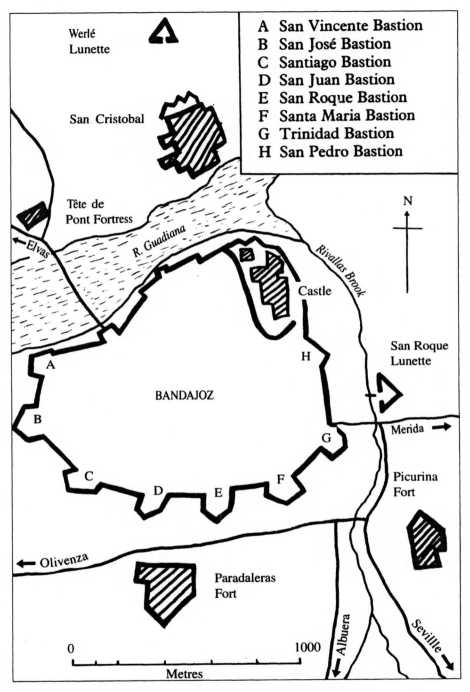

Werlé
Lunette

San Cristobal

Tête de
Pont Fortress

← Elvas

R. Guadiana

Rivallas Brook

Castle

N

San Roque
Lunette

A

B

BANDAJOZ

H

G

Merida →

C

D

E

F

Picurina
Fort

← Olivenza

Paradaleras
Fort

Albuera

Sevillle →

A	San Vincente Bastion
B	San José Bastion
C	Santiago Bastion
D	San Juan Bastion
E	San Roque Bastion
F	Santa Maria Bastion
G	Trinidad Bastion
H	San Pedro Bastion

0   1000

Metres

THE FORTRESS OF BADAJOZ DURING THE PENINSULAR WAR

barrels warped with the heat.[273] After three days of shelling, only modest damage was visible along the Castle and San Cristobal defences, and much of that was quickly repaired by the diligent French.

Desperate for success, Wellington elected to attack. At midnight on 6 June, a small force drawn from Houston's Seventh Division hurled itself at the damaged areas of San Cristobal, but soon discovered that the ditch at the foot of the wall had been cleared and the breach blocked by barricades and *chevaux de frise*. Unable to get forward, the storming-party was pelted with grenades and rocks, and blasted with artillery and musketry salvoes. The resourceful Phillipon had improved the fire-power of his meagre infantry forces by giving each man three loaded muskets and, in seconds, half the stormers were killed or wounded; the rest turned and fled.

After this bloody repulse, Wellington resorted to more bombardment, but by now the cannons from Elvas were so warped that they posed a greater threat to their own side than to Badajoz, and the only appreciable damage done was at San Cristobal where several iron naval guns were in action. But the French wasted no time in clearing away the debris and constructing defences behind the breaches. When Wellington risked a fresh assault, at 9 pm on 9 June, they were ready for him. 600 men from Houston's division advanced against the walls where just two companies of French infantry were deployed, but Phillipon had again equipped his troops with several fire-arms each, plus a vast stock of grenades and other projectiles. Engulfed in an avalanche of bullets and rocks, Houston's detachment sustained twenty-five per cent casualties for no tangible gain and were utterly routed.

The defenders cleared the breach once more and allowed Wellington to retrieve his wounded. By now, however, it was clear to the Allies that the siege was destined to fail. They had not breached the city's defences and the French field armies were already moving to Phillipon's assistance.[274] Marmont – alarmed by Albuera and the prospect of losing Badajoz – had agreed to come to Soult's aid and, having reconstructed his battered divisions with remarkable celerity, had set out on 14 May.[275] D'Erlon's corps had also arrived in the south and his 9,000 troops were likely to reinforce Soult at any moment. An Imperial field force of up to 60,000 men could be expected at Badajoz within the next few days and Wellington decided that no more time could be wasted: the army must retire or be destroyed. On 10 June the siege was lifted,[276] and the cannon and other equipment withdrawn across the Guadiana to Elvas. All of Wellington's forces followed save Blake's 10,000 Spaniards, who were dispatched to threaten Seville and thus draw away at least some

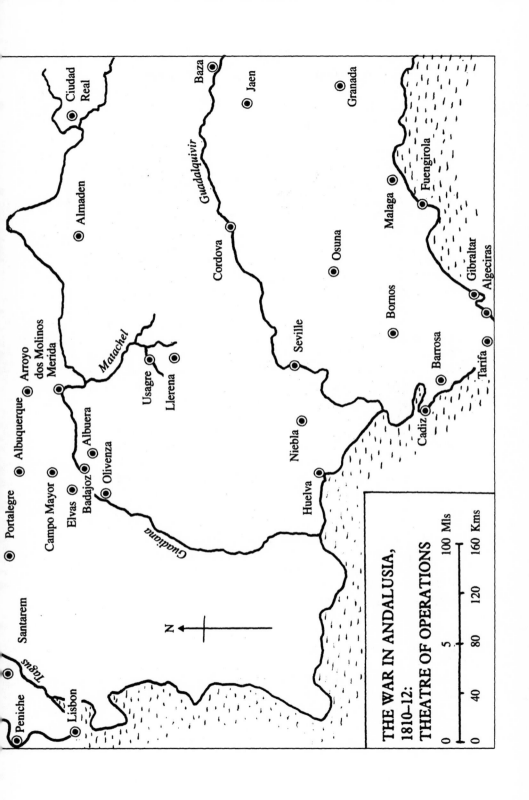

THE WAR IN ANDALUSIA,
1810–12:
THEATRE OF OPERATIONS

0	5				100 Mls
0	40	80	120	160 Kms	

of the advancing French. On 17 June, Wellington joined Spencer at Elvas – the latter general having shadowed Marmont in his march south – and, the following day, the three components of the French relief force united at Merida.

Soult and Marmont immediately struck west for Badajoz. After reinforcing and resupplying Phillipon's garrison, they set out in search of Wellington and, on 22 June, their cavalry patrols probed across the Guadiana. In the stiff skirmishing that followed,[277] Latour-Maubourg's troopers penetrated the Allied cavalry screen at several points and subsequently reported that Wellington had at least 50,000 men entrenched between Campo Mayor and Elvas. After past experience, the French commanders were reluctant to attack Wellington in his chosen position and while they debated the next move events elsewhere robbed them of the initiative. Already, Soult was receiving alarming reports of insurrection breaking out in his absence and, on 24 June, the news that Freire had resumed incursions into Granada and that Blake was threatening Seville obliged him to march east with the bulk of his forces. Deserted by their colleague, Marmont and d'Erlon rejected further offensive action and spent many days in replenishing Phillipon's stocks of food and ammunition. This done, Marmont then retired to the Tagus Valley, from where he could support the 'Army of the South' and where supplies were relatively more abundant.

An uneasy calm descended on the border of Estremadura. While Phillipon repaired Badajoz, Marmont and d'Erlon waited for Wellington to retake the offensive. He, however, grateful for the lull, rested and reorganised his forces: the arrival of a mass of cavalry reinforcements from Lisbon enabled him to double the number of mounted brigades to six, and two separate Anglo-Portuguese armies were formed. The first, under Wellington himself, was intended for use on the northern front and consisted of 41,000 infantry and 5,000 cavalry. The second, commanded by Hill, was to remain in the south and numbered some 9,000 bayonets and 4,000 sabres. By August 1811, these two formations were ready for action and Wellington promptly headed north for Ciudad Rodrigo with his seven divisions.

III A Crisis in Granada

We left Marshal Soult marching east on 24 June, in an effort to save Seville from Blake's latest offensive. Hearing that the Spanish general was investing Niebla, he moved to relieve it and, on 2 July, forced Blake to lift the siege and retreat. However, Blake promptly headed for the coast and, embarking on an Allied fleet, escaped from under the very noses of the pursuing French and regained Cadiz without serious loss. Thwarted again by enemy naval power, Soult turned his columns about and moved to the relief of the IV Corps in Granada.

Following their defeat at Baza in November 1810, Freire's Murcians had remained quiescent along the frontier. However, the onset of the Albuera campaign in May had forced Soult to withdraw many troops for action against Beresford, and Freire found himself faced by a much depleted IV Corps. Advancing at the head of 12,000 infantry and 1,500 cavalry, the Spanish general was reinforced from Cadiz and, by mid-July, had the French in Granada on the run. General Leval – who had superseded Sebastiani – struggled desperately to retain his grasp on the kingdom, but the enemy were just too powerful and the French were gradually edged back.

Urged into action by his frantic subordinate, Soult made an unexpected appearance with 12,000 troops on 9 August and, joining with Leval, counter-attacked and recovered much of the lost ground. Despite his initial advantage, Freire had conducted his offensive with a remarkable lack of energy and, once the French began to rally, he lost his nerve and went into precipitant retreat. Anxious to eliminate this nuisance once and for all, Soult raced after him and shattered his rearguard, inflicting 1,500 casualties. This heralded the almost total disintegration of Freire's army and it was hustled over the mountains back into Murcia, thousands of men being taken or killed and the rest scattered.[278]

IV Tiresome Tarifa

Having dealt Freire a crushing blow and repacified Granada, Soult now set out to try conclusions with Ballesteros who had landed at Algeciras from Cadiz and who, with his innumerable raids, had proved a constant thorn in the marshal's side. Soult was determined to annihilate him. However, when threatened Ballesteros merely retired to one of his bases – Tarifa and Gibraltar – under whose cannon he was safe. Unable to destroy this elusive foe in open battle, Soult decided that the only solution was to deny him use of his depots. Gibraltar was virtually impregnable, but an attack on Tarifa seemed a viable proposition.

Besides being a blow against Ballesteros, an assault on the port had much else to recommend it. Firstly, like Gibraltar and Cadiz, it was a major base for the Allied fleet that wrought such havoc along the south coast. Its capture would deny them this facility and would also enable Soult to communicate with the Moors in Tangier who would be a valuable source of horses and supplies. Furthermore, the Allies had deployed a growing number of ground forces at Tarifa. From October 1811 4,000 Anglo-Spanish troops were based here and, joining with Ballesteros' command, they took part in raids as far away as Cadiz. If Granada and eastern Andalusia were ever to be subdued Tarifa would have to be taken and so, in early December, Soult dispatched General Leval to besiege it.

Divided into three columns, Leval's 15,000 men set out on 8 December. The approach roads were atrocious and, hampered by Ballesteros and the local guerillas, the task force made painfully slow progress. Appalling weather conditions compounded their difficulties and it took nearly twelve days to cover only thirty miles. Furthermore, the area being especially barren the French were obliged to bring all their provisions with them, and most of these were consumed on the long march before the siege was even begun.[279] Finally, on 20 December the columns arrived before the fortress and drove the Allied skirmishers inside. Despite a couple of sorties by the garrison and the odd salvo from the flotilla, the French established their base camps and were soon bringing up their siege guns.

Tarifa was an ancient stronghold, built to resist arrows rather than cannon-shot. Although it contained 4,000 British and Spanish troops, it lacked heavy artillery and was unlikely to withstand a full siege. As the southern, western and eastern walls were visible from the sea, the French engineers rejected action against them so as to avoid the fire of the flotilla. Thus, circumstances dictated that the town be breached on its northern front and it was here that the besiegers constructed their batteries. The first was begun on the night of 23 December and, barely hampered by the ineffective enemy artillery, the French made rapid progress. Three days later a torrential storm sent the Allied fleet scurrying for shelter and flooded Leval's trenches, but, although the sodden earth was more difficult to excavate, the work-parties persevered and, on 29 December, the battery opened fire.

Although the walls were nearly ten feet thick, Tarifa's decaying masonry was no match for cannon-shot: the first round punched a hole right through the wall and penetrated into the buildings beyond. By mid-afternoon, most of the Allied guns had been silenced and a large gap had been ripped in the defences. The British garrison commander, Colonel Skerrett, urged evacuation, but the rest of the staff, led by the Spanish general, Copons, argued that the fortress was still defensible. General Campbell at Gibraltar ordered Skerrett to hold his position and, indeed, had the fleet withdrawn from Tarifa to prevent him evacuating his troops.

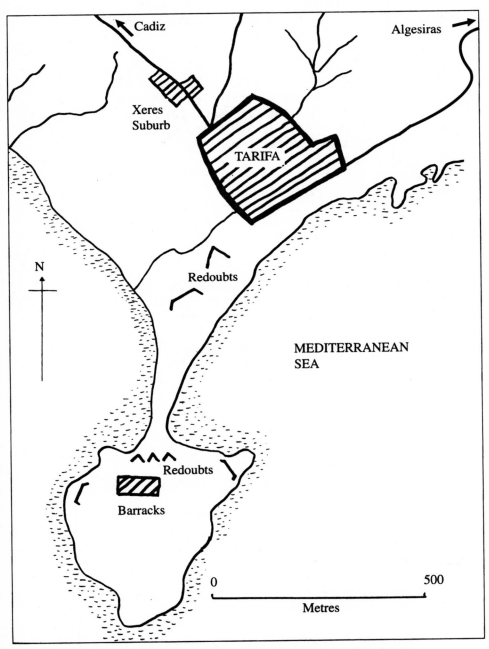

TARIFA AT THE TIME OF THE PENINSULAR WAR

The next day, Copons rejected a summons for the garrison's surrender and Leval intensified the bombardment. The breach soon widened to over twenty yards and, judging the walls to be untenable, the Allies concentrated on the preparation of internal defences. However, another downpour delayed any French assault, and caused tremendous flooding both in the town and out. When the attack finally came, the saturated condition of the ground ruined it: of the 2,200 men that waded through the mud to assail the walls, only a few dozen reached the rupture. Swept by the defenders' musketry, they retreated to their trenches, leaving 200 casualties littering the intervening quagmire.

The rain began afresh and the shivering French troops searched vainly for shelter. Leval's position was hopeless: his soldiers were soaked and demoralised; his excavations were inundated with water; his communications were flooded out; his ammunition was damp and, therefore, useless; his food supplies were virtually exhausted; and disease was cutting down both men and horses. There was nothing left to do but withdraw.

On 4 January 1812, the French lifted the siege. The mud proved a major obstacle and none of the cannon could be extricated. Destroying these and what remained of his other equipment, Leval led his despondent troops back over the mountains. 500 casualties had been incurred in the short operation and most of his corps had been affected by ill health. In all the project had proved a disaster for French morale and prestige, and had served only to weaken, rather than strengthen, Soult's grip on southern Spain.[280]

V   Diversions and Detachments

While Soult and his subordinates were grappling with their various adversaries in Granada, the Allied forces in Estremadura made two attempts to distract the marshal and relieve the pressure on Freire, Ballesteros and Tarifa.

When Marmont retired to the Tagus and Wellington marched for Ciudad Rodrigo, d'Erlon's 16,000 men and Hill's corps were left observing one another about Badajoz. This tranquil state continued until as late as 28 October, when Hill suddenly attacked an isolated brigade of General Girard's division at Arroyo dos Molinos. Joining a Spanish column, Hill pounced on his unsuspecting victim with over 11,000 troops. Outnumbered by more than five to two, Girard's units were swiftly hustled out of the settlement and, losing 1,300 men, scattered across the surrounding hills. Having thoroughly alarmed Soult, Hill retraced his steps to Portalegre and resumed his placid stance.[281]

After four more weeks of inactivity, however, he ventured east again in a bid to draw Soult away from Tarifa. This time his quarry was part of Dombrowski's division at Merida. But as Hill advanced, his cavalry screen blundered into a French foraging party who, forming square, repelled their assailants with heavy casualties and escaped to alert Dombrowski. He promptly retired to join d'Erlon's main force, leaving the frustrated Allies far behind. Nevertheless, the diversion had alarmed Soult and Hill again retired.[282]

Indeed, Soult's position was deteriorating rapidly: over the previous few months his forces had suffered several grave reverses, Badajoz had been threatened twice, and his opponents were becoming increasingly powerful and adventurous. Moreover, his army, already overstretched, was dwindling in size. Several pitched battles and the usual attrition had depleted many regiments, and Soult was soon to be deprived of several more altogether. In January 1812 Napoleon ordered him to stage a diversion against Murcia in support of Suchet who, as we shall see, was overrunning Valencia. He obliged with a raid on the provincial capital, but this tied up several cavalry units for some weeks. Similarly, the emperor's preparations for war with Russia also affected him for, along with other Peninsular commanders, he was called on to donate troops for the '*Grande Armée*' assembling in Central Europe. His 6,000 Poles were withdrawn and other units were earmarked for recall. By February, Soult was having difficulties mustering a field force of only 15,000 men; a development which augured ill for the future.

VI Stubborn Santocildes: The Spanish Offensive in Leon, Summer 1811

It only remains for us to examine events in the north and west during and after Wellington's abortive attempt to take Badajoz in June 1811.

As we have seen, when he set out for the Guadiana Wellington had urged General Santocildes to mount an offensive against the French forces in Leon. This, it was hoped, would prevent Bessières and Marmont from interfering in the operations against Badajoz, or from pressing Spencer's forces on the Beira frontier during Wellington's absence. But Marmont restored the fighting efficiency of his ragged divisions far faster than anticipated, and as early as 14 May set out, shadowed by Spencer, to join Soult and d'Erlon on the Guadiana.

Although he was expecting reinforcements from France, this left Bessières with only four infantry divisions, two cavalry brigades and a few detachments – about 60,000 men – to hold down and defend all the territory between Astorga and Biscay – some 40,000 square miles. We have already noted the immense difficulties he was experiencing prior to Marmont's departure, and with this development his situation inevitably deteriorated: Bonnet's division had to be pulled back from the Asturias, and on 18 June – the day Soult and Marmont united at Merida, and a week after Wellington abandoned his siege of Badajoz – Santocildes opened his offensive by advancing on Astorga with 20,000 infantry and 600 cavalry. Most were untried conscripts, but they were stiffened by a few seasoned units from Del Parque's old 'Army of the Left' which, when the bulk of that corps had marched for Seville in December 1809, had remained in the north. At their approach, Astorga's exiguous garrison withdrew and united with the majority of Bonnet's forces at Leon. Bonnet, however, was not prepared to let Santocildes go completely unchallenged and, supported by a column from Benavente, a detachment under General Valletaux was sent to probe the Spanish positions.

The ensuing affair proved to be a minor disaster for the French. Approaching the hostile line from two widely separated points, their columns failed to co-ordinate their actions. The Benavente detachment, deciding that the Spanish were too numerous and too strongly entrenched, set off back to their base unaware that Valletaux was plunging on to attack. His 1,000 troops duly hurled themselves against 8,000 Spaniards ensconced in strong defensive positions behind the Orbigo river. The assault was beaten off with terrible losses; Valletaux and many men being killed, and scores more wounded or captured. As the shattered battalions retreated to Leon, Santocildes followed them with commendable thoroughness and Bonnet was soon in such peril that both General Serras, at Benavente, and Bessières himself had to come to his assistance. The wily Santocildes, however, had no intention of fighting except on his terms and, at the approach of Bessières' footsore columns, retraced his steps to the Galician mountains.

Unwilling to pursue the Spaniard any further and with insurrection breaking out in the army's rear, the marshal abandoned the chase and hurried eastwards, leaving Serras and Bonnet to fend for themselves. But as the French forces before him dwindled, Santocildes returned to the offensive and the 'Army of the North' – now under the command of General Dorsenne, who had superseded Bessières – was again obliged to rush reinforcements to the western sector. The game of 'cat and mouse' continued until well into August and it was only when Dorsenne received his long-awaited troops from France that Santocildes' army was effectively contained. By that time, however, the Spanish had achieved their objectives; for, having abandoned the siege of Badajoz and reorganised his army,

Wellington had returned and his divisions were ready to assume the leading role once more.[283]

VII   A Lucky Escape

As we have seen, after relieving Badajoz and driving Wellington back to Elvas, Marmont had left d'Erlon to observe Hill and had withdrawn his own divisions to the Tagus Valley. From here, he could shift them to the support of Dorsenne or Soult as required and, to secure his way over the Tagus, he constructed two blockhouses – Fort Ragusa and Fort Napoleon – to defend the vital bridge at Almaraz, the most westerly crossing in French hands. He was then able to finish rebuilding the 'Army of Portugal' and was nearly ready to take the field again when he heard that Wellington was threatening Ciudad Rodrigo.

After reorganising his forces at Elvas in July, the British commander had marched north with seven divisions. He had resolved to leave the southern theatre alone for some time for, as Albuera and the second attempt to take Badajoz had demonstrated, when Soult was pressed he was prepared to evacuate large areas of Andalusia and bring overwhelming forces to his western frontier. On the other hand, when left unmolested, he had enough problems keeping control of his viceroyalty and could be relied on to ignore any attack on the over-stretched French forces in the north. Thus, Wellington decided that the next blow should be struck at the enemy in Leon and the fortress of Ciudad Rodrigo was selected as the objective. A train of heavy siege cannon recently arrived from Britain was put on barges at Oporto and sailed up the Douro to Lamego. But as they then had to make the difficult overland trip to the front, some considerable time elapsed before siege operations proper could begin.

Wellington, meanwhile, had invested Ciudad Rodrigo on 11 August and was awaiting the enemy's response. Dorsenne was still preoccupied with Santocildes and Marmont, far away on the Tagus, could not be expected to come forward for some days. However, neither of the French commanders was in any hurry to relieve the fortress, for they regarded Wellington's move as a damp squib: the stronghold had ample provisions to resist a long blockade, and they were also aware that the Allies lacked an effective battering train; rendering them incapable of seriously incommoding the garrison.[284] Only when intelligence reports warned that Wellington was bringing up siege cannon did they march to succour the fortress, concentrating nine divisions at Salamanca on 23 September.

Faced with this 58,000-strong army, Wellington seems to have lost his nerve. He declined to confront his adversaries in the plains about Ciudad Rodrigo and, leaving the Third and Light Divisions to maintain a cordon about the fortress, withdrew his main force to the hills west of the city. His confidence then swung to the opposite extreme. As Marmont's masses cautiously advanced, he refused to believe that the French intended anything but the revictualling of Ciudad Rodrigo and left his army in a dangerously scattered condition.

Marmont did, indeed, plan to resupply the fortress. But he was also keen to ascertain whether Wellington intended merely to blockade Ciudad Rodrigo, or whether he sought to besiege it properly. If the latter, the army would have to remain in the vicinity to prevent him from doing so.[285] Accordingly, on 25 September, the Imperial cavalry executed a series of sweeping reconnaissances in an effort to locate any siege train or depots and to establish the exact location of the Allied forces. General Wathier's light cavalry encountered the Sixth and First Divisions around Carpio and, after a trifling skirmish, reported their findings to Marmont.[286] Montbrun, meanwhile, led his troopers towards El Boden and found himself in the scattered encampments of Picton's Third Division.

The French cavalry general was staggered. There was no sign of any Allied reserves, and Picton's regiments were clearly dispersed all over the district and quite unprepared for action. This information was promptly passed back to Marmont, but he requested more details before sending forward his infantry.[287] This momentary respite gave Picton the opportunity to extricate his battalions from their parlous situation. Nevertheless, there was some bitter fighting as they struggled to close up. Without infantry support and on terrain unsuited to cavalry, the determined French horsemen galloped forward and assailed the Third Division, provoking repeated clashes along the summit of the ridge at El Boden. In one celebrated incident, a cavalry charge overran the Allied batteries along the crest of the hill, but the horsemen were so disordered and breathless after ascending the rugged slopes that a counter-charge by, of all things, infantry in line drove them from the plateau and resecured the guns.

By such efforts Picton's troops were saved from annihilation by the enemy cavalry, but as Marmont's infantry appeared on the horizon it became clear that the Third Division must retreat or be destroyed. Orders from Wellington directed Picton to pull back to Fuenteguinaldo and his units now streamed south-west in considerable disorder. The French cavalry followed, but, apparently deterred by the coolness of their opponents, made no real effort to halt the retreat and contented themselves with shelling the retiring

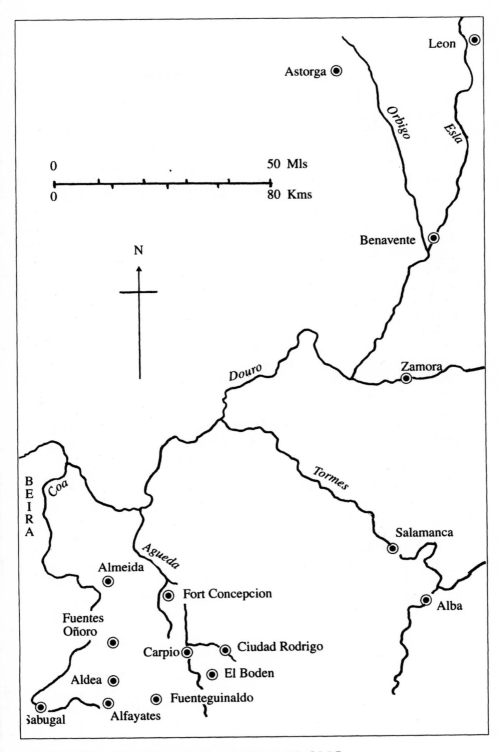

THE THEATRE OF OPERATIONS ALONG
THE BEIRA FRONTIER

columns with their horse artillery.[288] Eventually, the weary, powder-stained Third Division reached its destination, giving Wellington some 15,000 men. Against these, Marmont was advancing with over 20,000 troops, followed by 30,000 more.

26 September saw the French staff divided on their next course of action. With a superiority of three to one, Marmont and Dorsenne could have attacked and defeated Wellington without too much difficulty, but his apparent determination to fight gave them an uncomfortable feeling that matters were not as favourable as they seemed. After Bussaco and similar calamities, the Imperial armies had come to respect the 'Sepoy General' and, for fear of being led into a trap, were reluctant to press him in a position he had elected to defend. This time, as it happened, they had him at a disadvantage and a major triumph was within their grasp. However, Marmont's confidence seems to have deserted him on this occasion, for the only battle fought was one of wits – and that ended in a clear-cut victory for Wellington.

Having successfully bluffed his adversaries into inaction all day, the British general wasted little time in extricating his force. Under cover of darkness the army slipped away and, by morning, was converging on Alfayates. Following his hesitant behaviour on 26 September, Marmont, too, had gone into retreat and, for a while, the opposing armies were drawing away from one another. However, the Duke of Ragusa suddenly regained his earlier resolution: advised of Wellington's retreat, he took two divisions and two cavalry brigades and set out in hot pursuit. But this was a classic case of too little, too late. By the time he had regained contact with the Allied army, it had taken up a formidable defensive position beyond Aldea da Ponte. Apart from a brief skirmish there was no clash and, after a curt reconnaissance,[289] Marmont set off back to Ciudad Rodrigo.

This marked the end of Wellington's autumn campaign. As the weather deteriorated he put his forces into winter quarters and concentrated on the repair of Almeida's battered defences. The French, too, returned to their respective bases: Marmont withdrew to Almaraz, and Dorsenne reoccupied the Asturias and strengthened his garrisons in the east. An uneasy calm settled on the Portuguese frontier – but this very lack of activity led to one of the most significant developments of the war. Grossly underestimating the strength of the Anglo-Portuguese army and lulled into a false sense of security by the placid state of affairs in the west, the emperor called on Marmont to lend Suchet 12,000 troops for operations in Valencia. He reluctantly complied,[290] but, in doing so, set the scene for a decisive move by Wellington. With no less than 63,000 men at his disposal, the Allied commander knew that Marmont would now be too weak to contain him and the siege of Ciudad Rodrigo could go ahead. 'The movements of Marmont's army . . . to aid Suchet . . .', he wrote, 'have induced us to make preparations for the siege of Ciudad Rodrigo.'[291] That siege was to prove the beginning of the end for the French armies' grip on Spain.

Chapter XVIII

DEFIANT CATALONIA, DECEMBER
1809–10

I   The Aftermath of Gerona

Throughout Massena's invasion of Portugal and the subsequent fighting in the west, south and north of the Peninsula, the war in Catalonia had continued, largely unaffected by events in these other theatres. Although, in December 1809, Gerona had finally succumbed to Marshal Augereau's VII Corps after a siege lasting seven months, most of the province remained untamed. Barcelona and other occupied towns were invariably encircled by insurgents, while General Henry O'Donnell's 8,000 regular troops – the ramshackle remains of Blake's army which had tried so often to relieve Gerona – retained Tarragona and compounded Augereau's difficulties with attacks on his communications and detachments.

The French marshal was determined to end this state of affairs and, in January 1810, as King Joseph's forces poured into Andalusia, set out to try conclusions with O'Donnell. Leaving Verdier's old siege corps to recuperate, he advanced from Gerona with Souham and Pino's 12,000 men, the latter detaching a brigade to seal off Hostalrich (which had long served as a base for enemy operations), while Souham thrust down the Ter Valley to Vich. On arriving at Granollers, however, Augereau was aghast to find that O'Donnell had surprised a column that had ventured out of Barcelona. Two thirds of its 1,500 men had been killed, wounded or taken. Infuriated by this latest reverse, the marshal hurried southward and, on 24 January – a week before Joseph took Seville – arrived at Barcelona.

Dismissing the inept Duhesme as governor, Augereau set to replenishing the city's supplies. After weeks of insurgent blockade, they were perilously low and, as the exhausted, local resources could not support both the civilian inhabitants and the troops, a vast convoy of imports had to be organised. As such a train would present the insurrectionists and O'Donnell with a prime target, Pino's division was dispatched to escort it from Gerona. On his arrival there, however, he took some well-earned leave and General Severoli assumed command. Escorted by 8,000 troops under General Rouyer, the convoy duly arrived from France and, protected by three entire brigades, made its way south. Nevertheless, ploughing a path through the insurgents still proved slow and hazardous and March had nearly ended before the train finally reached Barcelona.

That O'Donnell did not launch an all-out assault on the straggling convoy was due to his preoccupation elsewhere. Mobilising the local militia to supplement his own troops, he had attacked General Souham at Vich on 20 February with 11,000 men. Outnumbered by more than two to one, the French soon found themselves fighting for survival. A bitter struggle ebbed and flowed around the town for most of the day, but a charge by the Imperial cavalry swept away O'Donnell's final assault and the Spanish retreated in disorder, leaving 1,900 casualties. French losses were nearly 700, and Souham, badly wounded, relinquished his command to General Augereau, the marshal's brother.

After this bloody episode, Augereau summoned his brother's battalions to Barcelona, concentrating his division with those of Rouyer and Severoli. However, the commander of the VII Corps had little intention of directing this vast field force himself; Catalonia was now a military district and he was too busy playing the viceroy to bother with such trivia as conducting campaigns. Mundane matters like that were, henceforth, to be handled by his sibling. Nevertheless, the marshal did deign to give his troops an objective and, contrary to Imperial orders to take Lerida, set them in motion for Tarragona late in March. Immediately, however, O'Donnell returned to the attack. Descending on the enemy's communications at Villafranca, he wiped out six companies of infantry before dashing back into the hills. A second successful raid, against an isolated unit at Manresa, caused over 1,000 French casualties and brought the Spaniard within striking range of Barcelona. This development provoked Augereau into hastily recalling his brother, and O'Donnell, having thus saved Tarragona from attack, retired to the mountains once more.

The indolent Augereau now abandoned his aggressive stance altogether and, in April, withdrew most of his army to Gerona. From the outset his performance had lacked spirit and Napoleon, increasingly disenchanted, now ordered his supersession by Marshal Macdonald, Duke of Tarentum.[292] He, however, could not arrive until June and, in the meantime, the VII Corps remained under Augereau's unenthusiastic direction. In that period the only notable achievement of his 40,000 men was the securing of Hostalrich: the garrison, faced with starvation, cut their way out on 12 May and thus left the stronghold to Severoli's troops.[293]

II   Sieges, Sieges

Meanwhile, Suchet continued to make progress in Aragon. Having temporarily suppressed the guerillas, he had set out in January 1810 for the Segre Valley; intending to tackle Mequinenza and Lerida, and establish contact with the VII Corps. His plans, however, were quickly disrupted. As King Joseph's forces swept across Andalusia and Granada, Suchet was ordered to stage a supporting diversion. After his experience at Seville, the king was convinced that the Spanish were totally demoralised and that the city of Valencia could be seized with little difficulty; the III Corps need only advance to secure it. Though unimpressed by this dubious argument, Suchet, obliged to obey, carved his way through the principality and arrived at the capital on 6 March.

His worst fears were promptly realised. Far from being submissive, the citizens, backed by 10,000 troops, were building up Valencia's defences in anticipation of an assault. Without siege artillery Suchet found himself in much the same position Marshal Moncey had in 1808 and, after four days of fruitless blockade, returned to Aragon. Another bout of anti-guerilla operations ensued and, having driven off these resilient foes and re-established communications between his garrisons once more, Suchet again set out for Lerida, arriving on 15 April.

This ancient settlement was encompassed by crumbling, old walls and had a citadel at its centre. Defended by 8,000 men under General Conde, it was just too big for Suchet's 13,000 troops to surround and he was still making preliminary preparations for the investment when he was alerted to the advance of a Spanish relief column.

Further investigation revealed that the hostile corps was O'Donnell's. When Augereau had withdrawn to Gerona in April, the Catalan field force had been left unmolested and, hearing of Suchet's movements, had marched for Lerida, General Ibarrola's division leading the way. They had to be challenged and, on 22 April, Suchet took Musnier's division and set off to intercept the enemy column. However, after hours of fruitless searching, the disgruntled Imperial general retraced his steps and was some three miles short of Lerida when he camped for the night. O'Donnell, having evaded the French patrols, had also halted near the besieged fortress and, the next day, his leading units fell on the weak formation of General Harispe to the east of the city.

Although appreciably outnumbered, Harispe refused to panic. Summoning Musnier's troops to his aid, he formed up his few battalions and hurled them at Ibarrola's division. Stunned by this staunch resistance, the Spanish were already wavering when Musnier approached. Ibarrola's disconsolate formations went into headlong retreat, but Musnier's men overtook them and a second conflict erupted near the village of Margaleff. The action was short-lived. Sweeping into the Spanish flank, the 13th *Cuirassiers* rolled up the hostile line and destroyed it piecemeal, inflicting terrible casualties. However, as this carnage drew to a close, O'Donnell arrived at the head of his second division. Seeing the battle lost, he attempted to withdraw but, after another frantic chase, his rearguard was virtually annihilated by the French cavalry. In the day's fighting, the Catalans appear to have lost 3,000 prisoners, and over 500 killed and injured out of 8,000 men; three guns and four standards were also taken. Suchet's casualties did not exceed 120.

Despite the rout of O'Donnell, General Conde continued to defy the French demands for Lerida's surrender. In view of this intransigence, Suchet stepped up his siege preparations and, by 7 May, had a battery of heavy guns in action. The old walls rapidly crumbled and, on 13 May, the besiegers stormed the breaches and wrested control of the town, the garrison retreating into the citadel. Determined to bring the operation to a speedy conclusion, the ruthless Suchet now ordered his troops to drive the civilian population into Conde's stronghold. Once the citadel was packed with both military personnel and innocent citizens, the French general battered it with howitzer fire. Sickened by the carnage amongst combatants and non-combatants alike, Conde surrendered the next day and 7,000 Spanish troops marched out into captivity. French losses in the siege and its related operations totalled no more than 1,000.

Suchet was now free to turn against the only remaining Spanish stronghold in the borderlands of Catalonia, Mequinenza. Situated on a towering cliff overlooking the confluence of the Segre and Ebro – the highest navigable point on the latter river – this small but formidable fortress was also an inland port and promised to be of value in any future operations on the Ebro delta. Suchet invested it on 15 May and, to get his siege guns within range, constructed a zigzag road, several miles long, up to the plateau where the castle stood. Dismayed by this ingenious invasion of their eyrie, the garrison – 1,000 men under Colonel Carbon – offered little resistance and, without waiting for an assault, capitulated on 18 June.[294]

III Tortosa

This victory released Suchet's field army for fresh operations and orders soon arrived from Paris for him to take Tortosa. That city guarded the one main highway that linked Catalonia with Valencia, and its bridge constituted the only crossing over the Ebro still in Spanish hands. It was of great strategic importance and, to facilitate its capture, Marshal Macdonald – now in command of the VII Corps – was to launch an offensive towards Tarragona to pin down O'Donnell's battered army.[295]

However, the French commanders soon found their respective projects hampered by a number of tiresome complications. While Suchet had been reducing Lerida and Mequinenza, the insurgents in Aragon had made appreciable progress against his diminutive garrisons. He was obliged to send flying columns to repacify the province and it was some time before he had all his units under his hand once more. Marshal Macdonald, like his predecessor, encountered great difficulty in supplying his forces: Catalonia had had to import vast quantities of food even in peace time and the outbreak of war and the disruption of the normal supply channels had exacerbated the problem. The supplies brought in by Augereau's great convoy had long been exhausted by Barcelona's garrison, and it was only after he had restocked the city's storehouses with food from France that Macdonald was free to move on Tarragona. Until the VII Corps could support him, Suchet declined to advance against Tortosa lest he should be troubled by O'Donnell. Thus, the offensive was delayed until August.

Since the disastrous action at Margaleff, O'Donnell had busied himself with the rebuilding of his shattered corps and, by August, had collected some 22,000 men – many being reluctant militia pressed into regular service. As the French had anticipated, Macdonald's preparations for a drive towards Tarragona lured the bulk of O'Donnell's divisions to the east and Suchet reached Tortosa relatively unopposed. However, his 12,000 men had no sooner arrived than another Spanish field army appeared. This was the Valencian corps of General Caro, and numbered some 10,000 bayonets and sabres. It seemed a serious threat, but Suchet, encouraged by the timid behaviour of his adversary, suddenly turned on him with a flying column and so terrified the inept Caro that he fled back into Valencia and resigned his command.[296] After this potentially dangerous episode, however, Suchet declined to besiege Tortosa until he should have the active support of Macdonald. Busying himself collecting *matériel*, he impatiently awaited his arrival from the east.

Macdonald was, indeed, finally astir. Leaving 30,000 troops to garrison Catalonia, he had marched to the assistance of Suchet with 16,000 men. O'Donnell did not challenge him and, by the end of August, the two French armies had united near Tortosa. It was agreed that Suchet's units, supported by the 2,500 troops of Pignatelli's brigade, would besiege the city, while the majority of Macdonald's forces would form a protective screen to ward off any attacks by relief columns. The divisions took up their respective posts and Suchet continued to bring stores down the Ebro from Mequinenza by boat. Progress, however, was painfully slow: insurgents harassed the convoys, and parts of Aragon repeatedly burst into rebellion, obliging Suchet to detach innumerable *colonnes mobiles*.

Meanwhile, deciding the French were too powerful around Tortosa, O'Donnell attempted to lure Macdonald away by molesting his vulnerable garrisons in northern Catalonia. Executing a brilliant forced march, he avoided the enemy's patrols and concentrated 6,000 troops to the east of Gerona. Supported by an amphibious force, he then pounced on General Schwartz's brigade, inflicting 1,200 casualties on his scattered detachments. Then, before the French could react, he vanished, leaving the whole district in pandemonium.[297]

Although this raid occurred on 14 September – the day before Massena invaded Portugal – it was October before news got through the insurgent ridden countryside to Macdonald. While deeply alarmed, he rightly judged that to return to Gerona would be pointless and, much to O'Donnell's disappointment, remained near Tortosa. After a series of petty attacks on VII Corps' screen had also failed to loosen the French grip on the city, O'Donnell was contemplating a second major raid when another logistical crisis finally compelled Macdonald to return to the north: partisan activity had halted his food convoys and Barcelona was again on the brink of starvation.

This was a threat Macdonald could not ignore and, in early November, he withdrew his divisions to Gerona. Here he found a large food convoy, reinforcements from France, and the veteran generals Souham and Pino who had returned from leave. After assimilating the new units and reorganising his depleted garrisons, Macdonald cleared the road to Barcelona and replenished its stores. On 10 December he rejoined Suchet, who had finally got his siege equipment forward and was ready to beleaguer Tortosa.

With an impressive series of concentric defences, manned by 7,000 troops, it was going to be difficult to capture. Suchet and his engineers decided that the best line of approach would be against the south wall, where the ground was soft and digging would be easier.

The siege began on 19 December. Firstly, to distract the garrison, a diversionary attack was mounted against the outlying Fort Orleans.

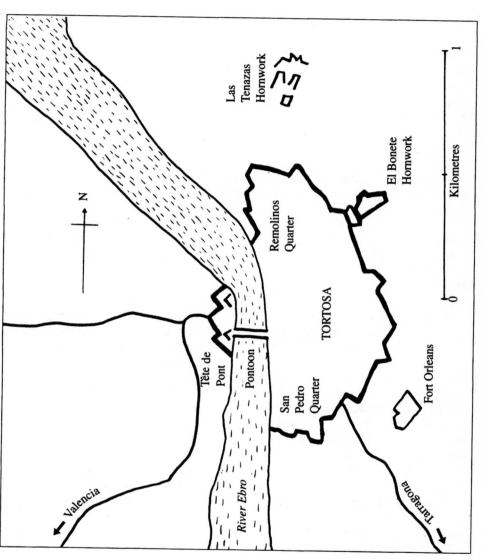

THE FORTRESS OF TORTOSA AT THE TIME OF
THE PENINSULAR WAR

Then, under cover of darkness, 2,000 men crawled forward to begin the first parallel in front of the southern suburb of San Pedro. It was not until dawn revealed their excavations that Lilli – Tortosa's aged and ailing commandant – realised what was happening. By then, however, a deep trench some 500 yards long had been constructed within 150 yards of the wall and, although it instantly became the target for a foray and heavy shelling by the Spanish, it rendered Lilli's position precarious from the outset. By 25 December the excavations were at the base of the wall and Lilli was obliged to fling his men into a series of desperate sorties. Three were repelled, but the fourth broke into the trenches and did appreciable damage before being driven off. Nevertheless, the garrison's respite was short: on 29 December the first French siege guns roared into action.

Deployed at such close range, Suchet's cannon inflicted terrible damage. Four batteries in the main trenches, supported by two on the far bank of the Ebro, pounded the walls of San Pedro to rubble, while others devastated the ramparts of Fort Orleans. A hail of mortar shells was poured into Tortosa's southern quarter to prevent the construction of internal defences and, within hours, most of the buildings here were in ruins or ablaze. Try as they might, Lilli's gunners could not return this pernicious fire and, by evening, every Spanish cannon in Fort Orleans and San Pedro had been silenced. Moreover, the pontoon bridge over the Ebro had been severely damaged and, under cover of darkness, the garrison of the *tête de pont* fled into the city proper.

By 1 January 1811, the French vice was tightening on Tortosa's battered defenders. Suchet had erected a battery of twenty-four pounders only twenty yards from San Pedro and his engineers had placed a mine beneath the suburb walls. Suitably cowed, Lilli asked for terms, only to reject them when offered. On 2 January, the French artillery again opened fire and were soon ripping enormous chunks of masonry out of the city's southern defences. As the inevitable assault columns assembled, the vacillating governor again sued for terms. This time, however, Suchet demanded unconditional surrender and threatened to show no quarter if he had to send in his infantry. Lilli promptly capitulated and 4,000 Spanish troops marched out to lay down their arms. Another 3,000 had been killed or wounded, or had deserted. French casualties totalled 400.[298]

Pleased with the cheap and rapid reduction of Tortosa, Suchet left Habert's division to occupy the city and returned to Saragossa with his captives. Macdonald, meanwhile, executed a sweep towards Valls, where elements of O'Donnell's army had been reported. However, just beyond that place, the marshal's vanguard – an Italian brigade, under Eugenio – fell in with the enemy and got into difficulties as the Catalans committed unit after unit to the fight. Their commanding officer mortally wounded, the Italians streamed back towards Valls and were only saved from destruction by the arrival of another brigade of Macdonald's army. Nevertheless, the vanguard had suffered over 600 casualties, compared with a Spanish loss of only 160. Appreciably disturbed, Macdonald closed up his straggling divisions and retired on Lerida to await Suchet's return.

This minor check to the French arms served to strengthen Napoleon's growing dissatisfaction with Macdonald and, in March, the emperor relegated him to minor operations. From now on he was to concern himself only with the pacification of northern Catalonia, and the bulk of his field force – some 17,000 men – was to be transferred to Suchet, who was given responsibility for the territories to the west of the Llobregat river and promised his marshal's baton if he should secure Tarragona. After spending several weeks in reorganising his augmented army, Suchet left a powerful force to hold down Aragon and moved south-east with three strong divisions. However, on 21 April he received a report that 4,500 Catalans had seized Figueras and that Macdonald was in grave difficulties. Apparently, a large force of Spanish irregulars had crept into the fortress by night and had caught the scanty garrison asleep. The guerillas had then set to defending the castle against French counter-strokes and O'Donnell's army, now under the command of General Campoverde, had marched to their assistance.

Though shaken by these tidings, Suchet refused to be deflected from his march on Tarragona. He had a direct order from the emperor and, besides, it would take him weeks to arrive at Figueras. Macdonald should appeal to Paris for reinforcements if he needed them and a French threat to Tarragona might oblige Campoverde to move south anyway. As it happened, Suchet's calculations were correct. The emperor did, indeed, send fresh troops to Macdonald while Campoverde, having lost a small action near Figueras, retreated to protect Tarragona. But Suchet beat him to it: his vanguard arrived on 3 May – the day Massena and Wellington first clashed at Fuentes de Oñoro – and by 8 May he had his entire force up.

IV   Tarragona

Tarragona was a large port protected by formidable defences and a garrison of over 6,500 troops under General Contreras. Nestling against the Mediterranean, its south side was inaccessible and

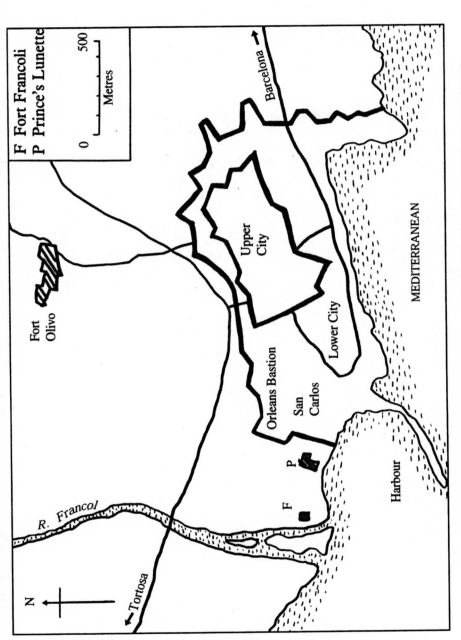

THE FORTRESS OF TARRAGONA DURING THE PENINSULAR WAR

approach to its northern and eastern walls was made difficult by mountainous terrain. Only the western quarter was open to assault and, fortunately for the French, the ground here was level and soft. However, Codrington's Anglo-Spanish naval squadron was lurking off the harbour, threatening to bombard any hostile entrenchments constructed on this side. As this could compromise the whole operation, Suchet had no option but to drive the ships away at the earliest possible moment. Accordingly, under the cover of darkness, his engineers erected a small fortress in which they installed a battery of twenty-four pounder cannons. Despite an incessant barrage from the fleet the work was soon finished and, on 13 May, Suchet's battery opened fire, forcing Codrington to retreat.

With his right flank secured, the French general was now free to deal with Tarragona itself, but the Allied naval forces continued to be a nuisance. Although they could no longer effectively bombard the earthworks, they passed in and out of the harbour with impunity and brought in several thousand Spanish troops to bolster the city's defences. In view of this and the reported advance of a relief column under General Sarsfield, Suchet wasted no time. Having driven Codrington back, he turned to deal with the outlying position of Fort Olivo which threatened to enfilade his trenches from the north. His troops made steady progress in its reduction, despite a sortie by the garrison in Tarragona itself, and he soon felt sufficiently sure of his position to commence the first parallel against the city's western walls. By 16 May – the day Beresford and Soult fought the Battle of Albuera – this was well advanced.

This development caused Tarragona's defenders increasing alarm and, on 18 May, a sortie was staged in an effort to retard the French advance. A stiff fight swayed across the earthworks for several minutes, after which the Spanish were driven back with heavy losses. The damage done to the parallel was of little significance, and the French soon repaired it and began to dig forward again. The garrison now sought to get in contact with Sarsfield's relief force and, on 20 May, another foray was mounted to cut through the besiegers' lines. As before, however, the Spaniards were quickly beaten back into Tarragona and, determined to prevent any repetition of the event, Suchet dispatched a small contingent to drive Sarsfield away. This was done with ease and, as this threat to his operations receded, the Imperial general redoubled his efforts to seize the city.

To begin with, he dramatically increased the activity before Fort Olivo. Up till now the besiegers had contented themselves with light attacks, but the next few days saw the construction of heavy batteries to breach the stronghold's defences. By 29 May serious damage had been inflicted and Suchet resolved to storm the outpost that night.

While a swarm of snipers opened fire to distract the garrison, two columns hurried forward to assail the walls. The first headed for the main breach in the north-east corner; the second passed round the building to scale the low wall that protected the south side. However, the latter unit of French infantry ran headlong into a column of Spanish troops who were on their way from the main fortress to reinforce Olivo. A confused *mêlée* erupted in which the two parties, hopelessly intermixed, lapped over the small rear wall and into the outpost. The main Spanish garrison – some 3,000 men – were leaping into this scuffle when Suchet's other column swept through the rupture in the north wall. Attacked from two sides, the Spaniards were overwhelmed: 1,400 were hacked down and the rest fled. French casualties totalled a little over 300.

The loss of Fort Olivo was a major blow to Contreras and, the following day, an attempt was made to retake it. Suchet, however, had anticipated such a move, and had spent the night in repairing and strengthening the fort's defences. When the assault came it was beaten off with heavy losses, despite the gallantry of the Spanish troops. After this sanguinary check, Contreras resorted to shelling the position with artillery. But this hardly perturbed the French who had taken the fort solely to secure the flank of their principal excavations, and they now advanced these at a furious rate.

Seriously disturbed, Contreras now sent General Campoverde to muster a relief army. He sailed on 31 May with several hundred men and landed further along the coast where he united with Sarsfield's command. On 16 June General Miranda also arrived from Valencia with a further 4,000 troops and, thus, Campoverde concentrated an army 11,000 strong. However, reluctant to face Suchet in an open battle, he moved against his lines of communication in an effort to draw him away from Tarragona.

Meanwhile, the Imperial army had continued to make headway: by 7 June the Spanish had been forced to abandon Fort Francoli and Suchet had wasted little time in occupying it. Despite an incessant bombardment from the Allied land batteries and the ships in the harbour, the French consolidated their new position by installing heavy cannons on Francoli's ramparts. Firing from only 100 yards, these badly damaged both the Orleans Bastion and the Prince's Lunette and, on the night of 16 June, the latter was carried with the bayonet and the garrison exterminated. As the French installed guns of their own in the captured lunette and proceeded to blow a hole in the south-west corner of the city, the garrison's morale plummeted. With no sign of the relief army, Contreras was still deliberating his next move when Suchet suddenly attacked. At 7 pm on 21 June, covered by a general bombardment and a diversionary assault on the north wall, five columns of infantry dashed forward and penetrated the breaches in the Orleans Bastion and San Carlos. Stunned by the sheer celerity of the onslaught, the Spanish managed only a few wild shots before fleeing in disorder and, in minutes, the French had overrun the whole of the lower city area, including the harbour.

While Contreras' depleted battalions cowered behind the decaying seventeenth-century walls of the upper city, the Spanish relief corps finally came within striking range. After days of petty, ineffectual attacks on the enemy's communications, Campoverde had advanced with his whole force to challenge the French grip on Tarragona and a full-scale clash seemed imminent. However, Suchet – none too concerned by the prospect of such an action – left a small force to maintain the investment and marched to crush the intruder. At the last moment, Campoverde's confidence failed him and the Spanish army went into headlong retreat; leaving Tarragona to her fate.

On Suchet's return to the fortress, the siege operations were intensified: by 28 June he had twenty-two heavy guns within 120 yards of the upper city walls and Contreras' last line of defence was crumbling. To add to the discomfort of the garrison, Colonel Skerrett – of Tarifa fame – arrived with 1,000 British troops from Cadiz; only to withdraw immediately, judging Tarragona to be lost.[299]

Finally, on 28 June, at 5 pm, three columns surged forward to attack the gaping breaches in the upper city's walls. A few men were shot down by the defenders' sporadic fire but the majority penetrated into the streets beyond and the first line of Spanish troops broke and fled. General Habert now led the Imperial infantry against the enemy's reserves and a sharp, bloody scrimmage ensued. For a moment it seemed as though the French tide might be stemmed, but as another column of the besieging army broke in on the north wall the defence collapsed and scattered. Contreras gallantly led his last formed unit into the attack, but in vain. Within minutes he was a prisoner, and the broken garrison was pouring in disorder out of the southern gate. The French troops near the harbour rushed to block this egress and most of the fleeing Spaniards were captured, killed, or herded back into the city. A handful escaped to the east, while a few more swam to the safety of the Allied ships, but Contreras' command was effectively destroyed and the great stronghold of Tarragona finally fell under French control.

As the last pockets of resistance were being mopped up and some of the more unruly Imperial soldiers turned to looting, Suchet assessed the extent of his victory. When all Contreras' reinforcements are taken into account, it would appear that he lost 15,000 men in the battle for the city; 7,000 being killed. The French sustained 1,000 dead, plus another 3,000 sick or wounded. With one blow Suchet had deprived the Catalans of their great base and sea port, had wiped out more than half of their regular army and had administered their morale a shattering blow. Moreover, Tarragona was but the latest in his long series of victories and, as his emperor had promised him, it secured him his marshal's baton.[300]

V The Price of Failure

On 29 June, an exhausted, solitary figure staggered into Campoverde's headquarters at Vendrils. It was General Velasco – one of the few to escape the Tarragona *débâcle*. His news of the city's fall utterly demoralised the Catalan field army and Campoverde's handling of the campaign became the subject of intense criticism. However, the arguing was abruptly concluded by the tidings that Suchet was again astir and marching to try conclusions with the hostile army. Prescribing an immediate retreat to the interior, Campoverde abandoned his depot at Villaneuva and, hours later, the French entered the town; capturing several ships and hundreds of wounded, and forestalling an attempted landing by Colonel Skerrett. But having narrowly escaped destruction at Suchet's hands, the inept Campoverde now fell victim to his own subordinates: General Miranda had his division shipped back to Valencia; other senior officers called for Campoverde's resignation and the evacuation of Catalonia; while the rank and file deserted in droves. Finally, in an effort to prevent the whole army disintegrating, General Lacy was sent by Cadiz to supersede the hated commander, and he led the remaining 3,000 troops into the hills to recuperate.

Suchet, meanwhile, had arrived at Figueras which, as we have seen, had been seized by the Spanish on 3 April – the same day that Wellington ousted Massena from Portugal with his attack on Sabugal. Macdonald was methodically starving the garrison into submission and, assured that he needed no assistance, Suchet set out for Lerida; driving the insurgents into the hills and leaving strong garrisons to keep the Barcelona highway open. This operation successfully concluded, Suchet – now officially a marshal – rested his troops and consolidated his position before embarking on his next project: the invasion of Valencia.

The garrison of Figueras had, meanwhile, found itself totally isolated by Macdonald's blockade. The battle for Tarragona having absorbed every local unit, no relief column could be expected and the defenders had little option but to cling to the fortress until their meagre supplies were exhausted. By mid-July they were starving and were obliged to release their prisoners to save food.[301] Still they refused to capitulate, and even resorted to eating dogs and rats. But this situation could not persist for long and, on 16 August, the garrison attempted to cut its way through the besiegers' lines. They failed; many were killed and the rest driven back into the stronghold. Three days later, the survivors surrendered.[302] Macdonald took 3,000 prisoners and found that 1,500 more of the garrison had perished during the siege. French losses were nearly as bad; for disease had spread through their camps. Though outstandingly heroic, the project had backfired for the Catalans: it failed to distract Suchet from Tarragona and, while it tied down many Imperial troops for weeks, it also bottled up every major Spanish unit in upper Catalonia when they could have been better employed in their usual 'hit and run' raids. Retaking Figueras was Macdonald's last significant operation: in September he was recalled to France.[303] Replaced by General Decaen, he joined the growing list of Napoleon's marshals whose military reputations had been tarnished, or ruined, by the 'Spanish Ulcer'.

Chapter XIX

POLITICAL, ECONOMIC AND MILITARY UNDERCURRENTS, c 1810–12

Although this is essentially a history of the military operations of the Peninsular War, some of the internal political, economic and social developments that influenced the conflict merit some examination.

Firstly, the financial burdens of the belligerents were enormous and Portugal, poor and underdeveloped to start with, was probably the hardest hit – despite annual British subsidies of £2,000,000. The French invasion of 1810–11 in particular led to an enormous drop in revenue at a time when expenditure was going through a phase of unparalleled expansion, and the side-effects of Wellington's scorched-earth stratagem aggravated the problem dramatically. With their agriculture laid waste, the Portuguese were obliged to import enormous quantities of costly foreign foodstuffs in an effort to avoid wholesale famine. Furthermore, the disruption, or annihilation, of a major portion of their few industries meant that little was available for export. Consequently, foreign currency reserves plunged and the balance of trade went out of control.

Against this background the Portuguese struggled to maintain the greatest war effort in their history. The population at this time was approximately 2,500,000, and more than four per cent were eventually drafted into the armed forces. By January 1812, for example, there were some 59,000 regular troops, supported by 52,000 militia and reservists. The government also had innumerable fortifications and defensive works to maintain, along with a small fleet. However, the Army was the major drain on resources: even seventy-five per cent of the total defence spending proved inadequate to meet its requirements. Shortages of munitions, food and clothing were common, and it was eventually discovered that the service's expenditure was virtually double its income.[304] To make up this shortfall the treasury issued paper money to supplement the specie in circulation. But this measure proved more of an economic liability than an asset and its net effect was to add inflation – at an annual rate exceeding thirty per cent – to the Regency's difficulties.

The British government, too, had its problems: not the least of which was finding and justifying the enormous subsidies paid to Portugal. In the years 1808–10 alone the monetary cost of maintaining the war was £13,500,000. 'This discussion about money,' Wellington wrote to a friend in January 1810,

> ... the distress ... we have felt ever since I arrived here, and ... the increasing demands upon the funds ... at our disposal, must tend to convince you that Great Britain has undertaken a larger concern in Portugal than she has the means of executing.[305]

Indeed, within a year Wellington was being warned by Lord Liverpool that it was

> The unanimous opinion of ... the government ... that it is absolutely impossible to continue our exertion upon the present scale in the Peninsula for any considerable length of time.[306]

However, finding the revenue was only part of the problem; for, as banknotes were regarded as worthless in the Peninsula, every transaction had to be conducted in specie and such vast amounts of gold and silver were difficult to procure. The British even took to issuing dividend bonds to conserve their coin stocks, but the specie question continued to be a daunting problem and had a significant effect on the conduct of military operations. 'The people of Portugal and Spain', Wellington advised Liverpool in January 1810, 'are tired out by requisitions not paid for, of the British, Spanish, Portuguese and French armies; and nothing can now be procured without ready money.'[307] Indeed, great quantities of cash were required simply for the army to move and Wellington frequently complained about the effect insufficient finance was having on his prosecution of the war. 'I do not care how many men ... the government send here,' he wrote in March 1810, 'provided they ... supply us with proportionate means to feed and pay them.'[308] But two years later he had to warn Liverpool that

> We owe not less than five million Dollars. The Portuguese troops and establishments are likewise in the greatest distress, and it is my opinion, as well as that of Marshal Beresford, that we must disband part of that army unless I can increase the monthly payments of the subsidy. ... It is not improbable that we may not be able to take advantage of the enemy's comparative weakness in this campaign for sheer want of money.[309]

In fairness to the cabinet, Wellington received all the specie they could lay their hands on, but even this proved insufficient and, in June 1812, he again wrote to the Prime Minister that 'The troops are four months in arrears of pay; the Staff of the army six months; and the muleteers nearly twelve months; and we are in debt for every article of supply, of every description.'[310] The problem persisted and, indeed, as the war rolled into France the Allies – anxious to pay for all their requisitions and so avoid a popular backlash – found their need for hard currency only increased.

Finance, however, was not the only difficulty facing Perceval. The casualty lists from the Peninsular conflict were steadily growing and the government faced considerable criticism over its policy. When it was announced in February 1810 that a further 14,000 British troops were to be committed, Whigs and Tories alike protested fiercely and a proposal to reduce Wellington's army to 35,000 men was only defeated after a bitter debate.[311]

Indeed, the next two years continued to be troubled times for the government – on both the domestic and foreign fronts. In October 1810 King George III finally succumbed to mental illness and, the following February, the Prince of Wales – well known for his Whig attitudes – was declared Regent. Between the time of the monarch's breakdown and the transfer of authority to the prince, Perceval's government hung in the balance. But the regent kept the ministers he had inherited and, tottering on through bad harvests and Luddite riots, Perceval's administration finally reached the fateful year of 1812. Then, as Napoleon prepared to march on Moscow, the ministry sustained a series of terrible blows: Wellesley, the Foreign Secretary, resigned,[312] Perceval was assassinated and the United States of America declared war on Britain.

Although the two missing ministers were more than adequately replaced – by Lords Castlereagh and Liverpool respectively – the American war stretched Britain's hard-pressed resources still further. Certainly, London was fortunate that these hostilities did not erupt earlier and lead to more drastic repercussions for the conduct of the Peninsular War. As it was, the naval conflict had an appreciable impact on Wellington's precarious logistical arrangements, and the war generally consumed resources that could barely be spared from the European theatre. Indeed, it was not until the end of 1813 that the American war ended, by which time the Peninsular conflict was virtually over. But for two years Britain had struggled to maintain a war on two fronts, and in America at least had sustained some serious reverses.[313]

The Spanish administration, too, had a host of problems to solve. As we have seen, after the fall of Seville in February 1810 the

Supreme *Junta* had fled to Cadiz to await their replacement by the National *Cortes*. But it was an extraordinarily complex task to hold elections in an occupied country and then get the representatives to a beleaguered island off the south coast. Consequently, it was as late as 24 September before the *Cortes* went into session and then only half the elected members were present. Furthermore, the assembly was bitterly divided on ideological grounds. It was elected on a proportional basis and thus established on democratic foundations. However, this was something of an anomaly in early nineteenth-century Spain. The nation was generally conservative by nature and many people had declined to vote in what were already less than perfect elections. This helped give rise to an assembly which was artificially rich in liberals and, as the Peninsular War drew to a conclusion, these idealists found themselves locked in a spiralling power struggle that sought to decide the country's post-war order.

While the conservatives saw the *Cortes* and its executive – the Council of Regency – as existing solely to prosecute the war in the name of the absent King Ferdinand, the liberals saw it as the only organised group capable of resisting a return to the 'ministerial despotism' of Godoy's time. Like the British reformers of 1832 they sought to develop and secure representation for a modern, bourgeois society and, accordingly, increased the influence of the middle classes by means of a property-based franchise. The traditional power centres of Spanish society – the Church and the monarchy – were weakened: the latter by the passing of a constitution in 1812; the former by far-reaching legislation introduced the following year.[314]

But such radicalism ultimately proved unpopular for two main reasons. Firstly, many *Afrancesados* supported King Joseph and the French precisely because they wanted such reforms – already introduced by Napoleon elsewhere – to be implemented in Spain. It was, therefore, easy for the conservatives to link liberalism with Bonapartism and thus portray it as anti-Spanish. Secondly, the radicals were seen as cultured, educated, town-dwelling bureaucrats who had little in common with the mass of Spanish society. As one historian concluded: 'The conservative, largely rural reaction against the radicalism of an *élite* provided the groundswell for the return to absolutism in 1814.'[315]

Factionalism was not the only problem facing the *Cortes*. The formal war against the French was an immense undertaking and Spain's vast armies had to be led, supplied and paid for. There was, furthermore, a growing revolt in Spain's South American colonies. Unwilling to grant them independence, the *Cortes* had to send reinforcements to America when every soldier was needed at home. The colonial war had a twofold significance in Spain's rapidly deteriorating financial position: while it increased expenditure, it also interrupted the flow of silver and gold from the mines of Latin America which formed the principal source of revenue for maintaining the war against France. Thus, the *Cortes* had little choice but to take a firm line with the recalcitrant dependencies.

Another development was the increasing tendency of the Spanish Army to interfere in political affairs. We have already noted how General La Romana dispersed the Oviedo *Junta* in 1809, and throughout the war there were similar incidents. Indeed, in 1813 the *Cortes* embarked on a politically motivated reshuffle of all their general officers – provoking a severe altercation with Wellington who had been made Commander-in-Chief. The issue was related to the political polarization of Spanish society; the Army was predominantly conservative at this time and when Ferdinand returned to Spain the military supported his bid for a return to unfettered despotism. In a coup in May 1814, the liberal movement was driven underground and its leaders killed or imprisoned. But that proved only the beginning of modern Spain's tragic history of internal division. Over the next few years even parts of the Army became disaffected under autocratic misrule, and in 1820 joined with the outlawed liberals in a gory revolt to restore the 1812 constitution. Such bitter factionalism continued into the twentieth century and culminated in a horrendous civil war. Indeed, to this day Spain is racked by dangerous political polarization.[316]

Finally, we should look at the power struggle within the French military hierarchy which was to have an increasing impact on their conduct of the war after 1809.

As we saw in Chapter II, during February 1810 Napoleon supplanted King Joseph in his role as supreme commander by a number of independent military governors who were answerable directly to him rather than to Madrid.[317] After tolerating this for a year, Joseph's patience was at an end and a flurry of acrimonious correspondence between him and his brother culminated in the king offering to abdicate. This rather shook Napoleon and, anxious to avoid any scandal, he tempted Joseph back into line with a series of token gestures: Jourdan was reinstated as the king's chief-of-staff; all senior officers were required to send him regular reports and the annual subsidy to his treasury was increased. Although this maintained Joseph in a position where his power was still more apparent than real, it staved off the threatened abdication and kept the reluctant king reasonably content for another year.

However, at the end of that time the emperor was obliged to return his brother to absolute authority, but not because of pressure from Joseph. As relations between France and Russia deteriorated and the

Tsar took to openly flouting the Continental System, Napoleon prepared to invade Russia. In view of his impending remoteness from the seat of government at Paris, the emperor finally resolved to put all his forces in Spain under the ultimate authority of the king. In March 1812, orders were sent to all the marshals and commanding generals in the Peninsula, directing that from now on they were to obey the commands of Madrid. Thus, at the stroke of a pen, Joseph was returned to a position of supreme, martial responsibility and the military governors who had ruled for so long were relegated to a secondary role.

In practice, however, this well intentioned move had only limited effects. As Jourdan noted in his memoirs:

> The king had been allowed to have no direct relations with the generals-in-chief for two years. He had no exact knowledge of the military situation in each of their spheres of command, nor was he better informed as to the strength, organisation and distribution of the troops under their orders.[318]

Attempts to extract this information from the jealous military governors failed and the marshals continued to appeal directly to the emperor over the king's head. The unfortunate monarch's first orders to both the 'Army of the South' and the 'Army of Portugal' were completely disregarded and, as far as dealings with Suchet were concerned, Jourdan recorded that 'His relations with the King consist of a polite exchange of views, not in the giving and taking of orders. His Majesty's control over this army is purely illusory.'[319]

Against this background of organised chaos, Jourdan compiled a memorandum on the situation in Spain, identifying two major problems: that the army was, in effect, an army of occupation; and that the weaknesses of the logistical system prevented it from being otherwise. He concluded that,

> Two measures were indispensable: first, to render the army mobile by providing it with ample transport and by establishing large magazines on all lines of communication – without which all permanent concentration of large forces, and all continuous operations were impossible. Second, to abandon the deplorable system of occupying as much territory as possible – of which the real object was twofold: firstly, to enable the armies to live off the country; secondly, to appear in the eyes of Europe to dominate the whole of Spain.[320]

Jourdan's memorandum cut to the heart of the matter. Due to a lack of transport and magazines, and the necessity to maintain innumerable garrisons, Imperial forces of over 230,000 men were virtually incapable of sustained offensive operations. Wellington, on the other hand, could mass some 60,000 troops against either the 'Army of the South' or the 'Army of Portugal' and defeat it before the other had even been alerted to the danger. In an effort to reduce this threat, Jourdan proposed the formation of a large central reserve. As the emperor could spare no more troops and there were none surplus to requirements in the Peninsula itself, he advocated the evacuation of Andalusia so as to release 70,000 men for the support of Marmont. But, abandoning all of southern Spain was a step that Napoleon was not prepared to sanction, and an Imperial dispatch dated 9 May rejected Jourdan's scheme and called for the maintenance of the *status quo*. The despairing Chief-of-Staff recorded that

> If only instead of 'hold all you have, and conquer the rest bit by bit', we had been told that we might evacuate some provinces and concentrate the troops, there would have been much good in the instructions. The King might have dared to abandon the South in order to keep down the North, if he had not received this dispatch.[321]

Jourdan's prediction, however, was soon fulfilled. After years of wearing the French down and consolidating his position in Portugal, Wellington was finally ready to take the offensive. The early days of 1812 were to see him embark on a brilliant seizure of Ciudad Rodrigo, followed by the capture of Badajoz and the infliction of a crushing defeat on Marmont. Faced with this series of calamities, the French found that they must abandon Andalusia after all and, although Soult's 70,000 troops later ousted the Allies from Madrid, by that time the tide had definitely turned and the Allies were in the ascendancy.

The French storm Tarrago[na]
(From *Los Guerilleros de 18[...]*
by E. Rodriguez-Solis,
Madrid, 1887)

The attack on the main
breach at Ciudad Rodrigo
the British Third Division
Note the blazing fuses on t[he]
shells (The Mansell
Collection)

The 88th storm Badajoz Castle (National Army Museum, London)

Busacco: The attack by Reynier's corps (BBC Hulton Picture Library)

Salamanca: The charge of Le Marchant's cavalry (The Mansell Collection)

Salamanca (BBC Hulton Picture Library)

The Guerilla leader Juan Martin (From *Los Guerilleros de 1808* by E. Rodriguez-Solis, Madrid, 1887)

General Julian Sanchez (From *Los Guerilleros de 1808* by E. Rodriguez-Solis, Madrid, 1887)

General Eroles (From *Los Guerilleros de 1808* by E. Rodriguez-Solis, Madrid, 1887)

PART FIVE

The Turning of the Tide

Overleaf: Wellington enters Madrid, 1812 (*Photo:* BBC Hulton Picture Library)

Chapter XX

SUCHET INVADES VALENCIA

I Saguntum

Following his capture of Tarragona in June 1811, Marshal Suchet proposed to invade Valencia. Reinforced from France, his forces had risen to 70,000 troops by September and, as we have seen, during the next month Napoleon ordered 12,000 more – under Montbrun – to join him from Marmont's 'Army of Portugal' on the Beira frontier.

But Suchet's need to maintain numerous garrisons proved a tremendous drain on these resources. Generals Decaen and Musnier had to be given 23,000 men each to hold down their respective charges of Catalonia and Aragon and, thus, the marshal's field army had dwindled to little more than 20,000 troops when he advanced from Tortosa on 15 September.

However, the Spanish forces available to meet this threat were not strong. After their recent appalling drubbings the Catalans could offer no help and, as we have seen, Freire's Murcians had just been crushed by Soult in Granada. The Valencians own units numbered some 36,000 soldiers, but too many were inexperienced recruits who, lacking even basic equipment and training, were unlikely to pose much of a danger to Suchet's seasoned veterans. Indeed, the only reliable formations available to General Blake – who had arrived from Cadiz to command the Valencian army – were the two small divisions of Zayas and Lardizabal which had fought under him at Albuera. With such a weak army Blake was reluctant to take the offensive, and so he concentrated on strengthening Valencia's decrepit fortifications.

The first fighting took place on 19 September. Thrusting down the coastal highway, Suchet's army encountered small Spanish garrisons at Oropesa and Peñiscola but, refusing to be side-tracked, blockaded the outposts and pushed on to secure the bridge at Villareal. They poured over the Mijares and on 23 September – two days before Wellington and Marmont's forces clashed at El Boden – arrived before the ancient fortress of Saguntum. Blake had begun reconstructing the ruined castle walls and a contingent of his troops was ensconced in the stronghold. Hoping to catch them unaware, Suchet launched a sudden night attack on 27 September, but his columns were spotted and, sustaining heavy losses, recoiled in disorder.

Irritated by this sanguinary check and unwilling to leave the powerful stronghold dominating his communications, Suchet summoned his siege artillery and set about investing the fortress. Anxious to keep the enemy busy in operations along the Palancia river, Blake responded by dispatching two divisions to menace his adversary's flanks, but Suchet drove them off with little difficulty and continued his preparations unmolested. His siege guns lumbered forward from Tortosa and, stopping at Oropesa, pounded the garrison into submission before resuming the march south. They finally arrived at Saguntum on 16 October, and after forty-eight hours of heavy bombardment, an impatient Suchet decided that the time was ripe for an assault and promptly unleashed his foot troops in a second bid to storm the walls.

But the artillery preparation had not been as effective as the marshal had hoped and, unable to penetrate the imperfect breach, the Imperial columns were again repulsed and the bombardment began anew. However, as the French engineers pushed their excavations forward, news arrived that Blake – supported by a detachment of Murcians – was marching north and, leaving a small force to maintain the siege,[322] Suchet took the balance of his troops and deployed them across the plain to the south of the fortress.

Although he only had some 14,000 men to oppose to the 28,000-strong Valencian army, Suchet was delighted at the prospect of a decisive battle. With his left wing protected by the Mediterranean coast, his principal concern was that the enemy might turn his right, which lay some three miles to the west on the foothills of Sancti Espiritus. Accordingly, he deployed the bulk of his troops here. General Chlopicki, with 3,900 infantry and 450 horse, protected the open flank, while the majority of Harispe's division formed the army's centre. Elements of Habert's brigades constituted the left wing, and the remainder of the army – St Paul's Italian infantry and 1,300 cavalry – were placed in central reserve.

The marshal was perfectly correct in his guess at Blake's intentions: the Spanish general did, indeed, hope to envelop and destroy the western end of the hostile line, while pinning Suchet to his position with a heavy frontal assault. He deployed no less than four divisions – 16,000 bayonets, 1,700 horse and four artillery batteries – to crush the French right wing, whilst the formations of Zayas and

Lardizabal, supported by a division of Valencians and eighteen pieces of ordnance, were to mount the frontal attack.[323]

On the morning of 25 October – three days before Hill surprised Girard's forces at Arroyo dos Molinos – the Spanish army advanced to assail Suchet's line. With a numerical superiority of four to one, the massed Valencian battalions of Villacampa and Miranda rolled inexorably up the slope to fall on Chlopicki's scanty detachment. They had not gone far, however, when, to their horror and surprise, the Imperial general attacked. Charging through their own retreating skirmishers, Robert's five battalions assailed the leading hostile formation, while twelve companies of the 44th Line swept down on the eastern flank of Miranda's startled units. Stunned, Villacampa's formation collapsed before Robert's audacious charge and, pouring back down the hill, uncovered the inner flank of Miranda's faltering battalions. Grasping this golden opportunity, Chlopicki's solitary cavalry unit – the 450 Italian 'Dragoons of Napoleon' – galloped forward from the crest of the ridge and, wheeling sharply, smashed into Miranda's left flank. As the dragoons plunged into their midst and the 44th poured volley after volley into their wavering right, Miranda's entire division fell into terrible disorder and, mingling with Villacampa's fleeing soldiery, fled back down the slope in wild confusion. Hurtling on through the enemy's shattered foot troops, the dragoons now swept into the 1,700 cavalry of General San Juan and dashed them to fragments, driving them into the few battalions of hostile infantry that had not been committed to the assault and plunging the whole bewildered mass into disorder. Seeing the progress his cavalry were making, Chlopicki led his infantry in another determined charge and, quite unable to resist the onslaught, the whole of Blake's left wing disintegrated and was driven from the field.

Shortly before the total collapse of the western flank, the Spanish centre and right had been sent into the attack. Leaving the Valencian battalions in reserve at the bridge over the Picador, the veteran divisions of Zayas and Lardizabal thrust at the middle of Suchet's position. Annoyed by the fire of some Allied gunboats hovering off the shore and assailed by the infantry to his front, General Habert was gradually forced to refuse his flank. Simultaneously, Lardizabal dislodged Harispe from a mound in the French left centre and, dragging his artillery to its summit, proceeded to pound his opponent's units with devastating effect.

Faced by the possibility of a major enemy breakthrough in the very midst of his line, Suchet ordered Harispe to counter-attack and dislodge the hostile cannon. To support him, three squadrons of cavalry were drawn from the reserves and, together, they flung

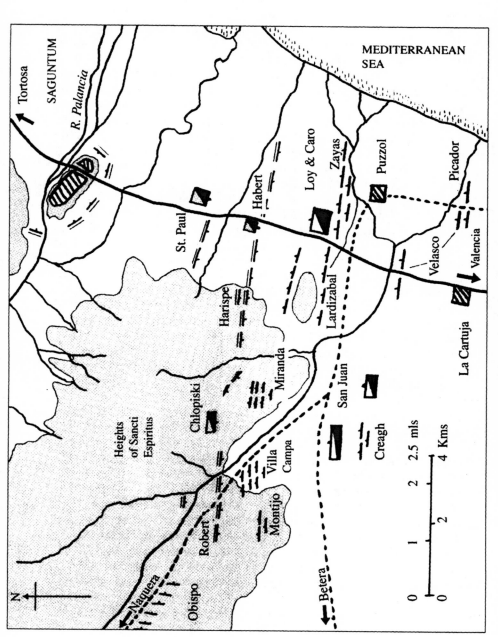

THE BATTLE OF SAGUNTUM, 25 October 1811

themselves against the hillock and retook it. Nevertheless, the triumphant advance of the Imperial troops rapidly came to a halt as Lardizabal brought up the regiments of his second line. In another effort to force him back, Suchet summoned an artillery battery and deployed it so as to enfilade his opponent's right flank. But the massed Spanish cavalry immediately swept up the highway and, catching the French horsemen in the act of reforming, sent them scurrying to the rear.

This withdrawal by the units covering his eastern wing placed Harispe's division in a potentially lethal situation. As the hostile cavalry overran part of Suchet's battery and threatened to wheel into the flank of the startled Imperial infantry, the action entered its most critical phase. The marshal, however, rose to the challenge. Drawing back the left-hand regiment of Harispe's formation, Suchet redeployed it in an oblique line to protect the open flank. Then, summoning two squadrons of the 13th *Cuirassiers* and St Paul's brigade from the fast-dwindling reserves, he set about driving off the enemy horsemen.

The 350 *cuirassiers* led the counter-attack, sweeping back the disordered mass of cavalry with remorseless energy. In moments, the tide had again turned in Suchet's favour as, slaughtering their panic-stricken opponents, his horsemen galloped to the very banks of the Picador and overran one of Lardizabal's batteries. Minutes later, St Paul's battalions also came into action. Crashing through some olive groves, the Italians suddenly ploughed into the left of the ragged Spanish line. Already demoralised by the rout of their cavalry, Lardizabal's foot troops – caught between this new threat and Harispe – finally began to waver and retreat. Withdrawal rapidly degenerated into rout and, pursued by their elated adversaries, the Spanish centre collapsed and headed for the Picador bridge.

This heralded the retreat of all of Blake's army that was still in action. Zayas' division quickly curtailed its attacks on the French left wing and made off via Puzzol. Seeking to annihilate his opponents as they filtered through this bottle-neck, Habert assailed the village. Only a heroic covering action by the Walloon Guards saved Zayas from complete destruction and, followed by what few Guardsmen survived, his division escaped over the Picador.

Suchet, meanwhile, had kept up the pressure on Lardizabal. Flinging in the 24th Dragoons – his last remaining unit – he struck across the Picador at the reeling Spanish division and completed its discomfiture. His horsemen then turned on the Valencian reserve formation and, pushing it into precipitant retreat, embarked on a pursuit that lasted for seven miles. By the end of this action, the Spanish had lost 6,000 killed and wounded, hundreds of prisoners, several cannon and four standards. Moreover, having witnessed the rout of Blake's attempt to relieve them, the beleaguered garrison of Saguntum also surrendered; giving Suchet, whose own casualties totalled 1,000 men, a further 2,500 prisoners.

Such a defeat put further offensive action beyond the capability of Blake's ragged and despondent army, and they duly fell back on Valencia. Nor was Suchet willing to advance. Though his army's morale was currently excellent, his force had always been relatively small and, after Saguntum had been garrisoned and escorts provided for the vast convoys of prisoners, he was reluctant to move against Valencia which he knew had been heavily fortified. Confronting a Spanish contingent in the field could be a very different proposition from dislodging one from a city – as Saragossa and Gerona had demonstrated – and the marshal decided to wait for reinforcements before resuming his offensive. Thus, there was a delay of several weeks before the next round of operations and both sides spent the time in consolidating their respective positions.[324]

II The Fall of Valencia

Gradually, Suchet's forward units attained sufficient strength to resume the offensive. Napoleon sent him Reille and Severoli's divisions, and Musnier gave General Caffarelli responsibility for holding Aragon and moved his own division down to the Mediterranean. By 24 December – four days after Leval besieged Tarifa – the marshal had 33,000 men poised for action, and the following day advanced on Valencia.

After weeks of hectic building by Blake, the city had acquired an impressive series of earthworks extending for eight miles along the northern front. However, this seemingly formidable belt of defences was to prove of little use in stopping Suchet. He simply massed nearly all his army on the western tip of the lines, while pinning down the centre and right wing with a flurry of feint attacks. Completely taken in, Blake was convinced that the real threat lay against his centre and, having deployed the bulk of his 20,000 men there, was horrified to discover that 25,000 Imperial troops were assailing General Mahy's solitary division on the left. The French emerged triumphant. Although Mahy's men had a strong position, they were outnumbered by more than five to one and demoralised by their recent defeats. They took off to the west at the outset of the fighting and, pursued by the Imperial cavalry, abandoned Valencia to her fate.

Meanwhile, General Habert had flung his division across the

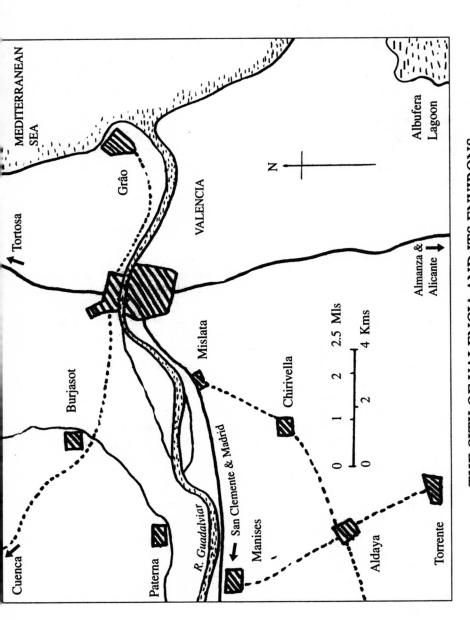

THE CITY OF VALENCIA AND ITS ENVIRONS

Guadalviar at the Mediterranean end of the lines. The Spanish right wing, under General Obispo, was soon in difficulties and, like Mahy's dispirited troops, crumbled at the first onslaught. With both his flanks turned, Blake had no choice but to abandon the central stretch of redoubts and, as the remains of the disconsolate Spanish army retreated into Valencia, Suchet's mass of troops swung round the southern suburbs and linked up with Habert, sealing off the city.

Apart from the fugitive columns of Mahy and Obispo, Blake's entire army of some 17,000 men was now bottled up in Valencia, along with 100,000 civilians. The state of affairs in the city was appalling. Blake was shunned and despised by his own troops, and indiscipline and demoralisation reached a remarkably bad level. Furthermore, there were no food stocks and it was clear that the city must soon surrender or starve. The Spanish commander made a feeble effort to cut his way out through the besiegers' lines, but the escape bid failed miserably and, after a sharp skirmish with French pickets around the village of Burjasot, Blake's army poured back into Valencia.

The end was not long in coming. The French rapidly brought their siege train up from Saguntum and, on New Year's Day 1812, work on the first trenches and batteries was begun. The disheartened Spaniards made little effort to cling to the few outposts still in their possession and, abandoning the last of the earthworks, retired into the city. This lack of resistance had a twofold significance for Suchet: firstly it enabled him to advance his excavations swiftly and, secondly, it gave him a reliable indication of the condition of Spanish morale. Judging Blake's men to be on the verge of collapse, he began a remorseless bombardment.

His surmise proved to be completely correct. As a hail of shells poured into the crowded streets, Blake's long-suffering army finally disintegrated and, on 8 January, surrendered. The spoils of Suchet's victory were immense. As well as Valencia itself, he secured the capture of over 16,000 enemy troops, more than 370 pieces of ordnance, twenty-one colours and standards, and a colossal store of military equipment. Furthermore, he levied a huge indemnity on the city and extracted 53,000,000 Francs from the unfortunate population.[325]

Valencia secured, Suchet now felt that he could safely forego the services of Montbrun's column which, after skirmishing with a small corps of Murcians about Cuenca, was approaching from the northwest. However, instead of returning to Marmont immediately,[326] Montbrun turned off in pursuit of Mahy towards Alicante. Having found the Spaniard too strongly entrenched to tangle with, he subsequently retraced his steps; arriving at Toledo on 31 January.

Here he received tidings of an opportune attack by Wellington on Ciudad Rodrigo and, seriously disturbed, completed the remaining 200 miles of his journey with an astounding series of forced marches. Nevertheless, all was in vain. As we shall see, the fortress had already fallen and the northern gateway into Spain was under the Allies' control.

Suchet, meanwhile, had continued his southward march, extending his run of victories with the capture of Denia and the capitulation of the long-beleaguered stronghold of Peñiscola. His emperor was suitably grateful and awarded him an Imperial peerage – the dukedom of Albufera. Thus, this ex-division commander became the only one of the marshals to hold a Spanish title. He had, indeed, come a long way since the days of Belchite and Maria.

The advance of his triumphant divisions was, however, soon to be halted. Providing escorts for his numerous prisoners and garrisons for his growing territories sapped the strength of his field force and, when Napoleon withdrew still more troops for the Russian campaign, further offensive operations became impossible. Moreover, Suchet contracted fever and, bedridden for weeks, was unable to lead his men. Accordingly, the advance on Alicante was postponed and the Imperial troops took a well-earned rest. The Spanish, meanwhile, made the most of this unexpected lull, rebuilding the 'Army of Valencia' around Mahy's tattered division. By the time hostilities resumed in this quarter they had assembled over 20,000 soldiers and, as we shall see, this Anglo-Spanish force was to play a significant part in Wellington's grand offensive of 1812.

Chapter XXI

FORCING SPAIN'S GATES

I The Siege of Ciudad Rodrigo, January 1812

As we have seen, the closing weeks of 1811 witnessed some ferocious fighting in the south of the Peninsula: Suchet crushed Blake at Saguntum and took Valencia; Leval besieged Tarifa; and d'Erlon's forces clashed with Hill at Arroyo dos Molinos and Merida. Throughout this period, however, the main Allied army remained largely inactive. Since narrowly escaping destruction by Marmont at Fuenteguinaldo in September, Wellington, his forces paralysed by deteriorating weather and disease, had retired to the Beira frontier. He had wanted to take the offensive in support of Blake and, above all, to secure Ciudad Rodrigo which guarded the route into northern Spain. But for much of the time the opposing French forces were dauntingly strong and, as Wellington confessed, 'Even if an opportunity had been offered . . . for undertaking anything on this side, the unfortunate state of . . . [our] army would have prevented it.'[327] Thus, apart from the Light Division who aided the insurgents in cutting off the fortress, the Anglo-Portuguese forces were unable to molest Ciudad Rodrigo.

Nevertheless, while his units recuperated, Wellington's battering train was slowly brought forward from the Douro Valley and siege material was assembled at Almeida, whose repair was also taken in hand. In late December, as his army regained its strength, he received the tidings of Montbrun's march to the east and this – coupled with the knowledge that Napoleon was withdrawing vast numbers of troops for his impending war with Russia – convinced him that the time was ripe for an offensive: the depleted French divisions would prove incapable of simultaneously containing him and continuing to make progress in Valencia. In early January 1812, the seven divisions of the Anglo-Portuguese army concentrated for action on the Agueda. The heavy ordnance, engineers and stores trundled forward in their wake and, on 8 January, the siege of Ciudad Rodrigo was able to begin.

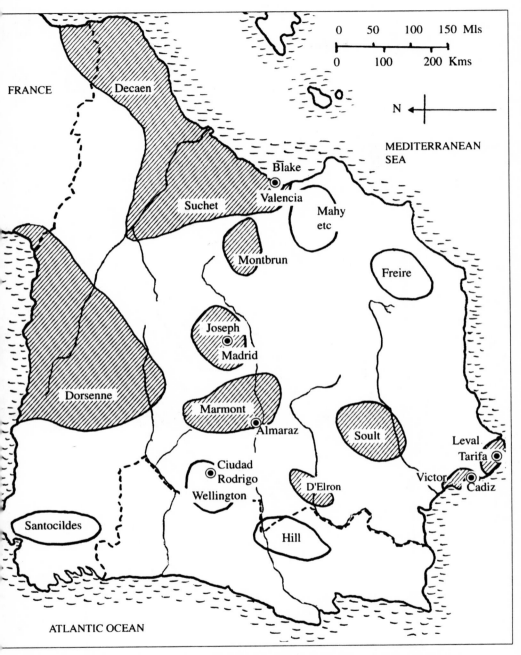

THE GENERAL STRATEGIC SITUATION, Winter 1811–12

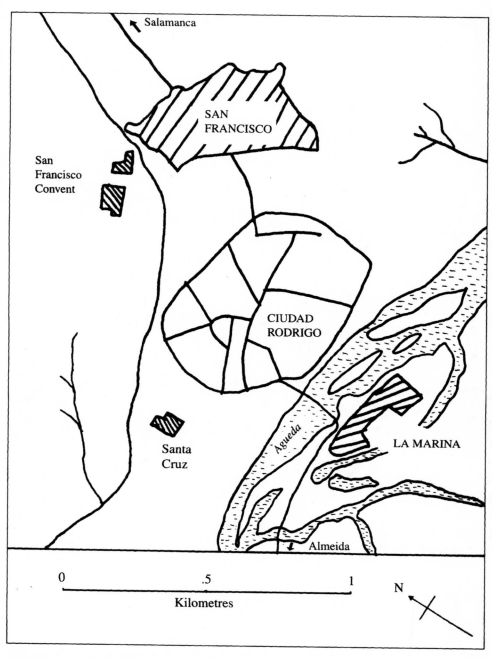

CIUDAD RODRIGO AT THE TIME OF THE PENINSULAR WAR

Apart from repairs to the breached walls, the fortress had barely changed since Marshal Ney had besieged it in 1810. To prevent any hostile forces from utilising his old line of approach a number of earthworks, notably the Renaud Redoubt, had been constructed but, otherwise, the defences remained unaltered. The garrison, under General Barrié, numbered only 2,000 – and, although there were huge stocks of cannon and ammunition, there were insufficient gunners. Nevertheless, Ciudad Rodrigo was a powerful fortress and, despite the Allies' strength, the governor was confident that he could hold out until help arrived.

However, that was precisely what Wellington feared might happen and was equally determined to seize the stronghold before Marmont could even begin to respond. Accordingly, he pushed the siege operations forward at a staggering rate. On the first night, a detachment from the Light Division was sent to remove the obstacle posed by the Renaud Redoubt. The riflemen crept to within a few paces of its walls and, opening fire, kept the defenders' heads down while their colleagues rushed the perimeter. In minutes, the redoubt was under Allied control.[328] The French in the main fortress bombarded it remorselessly, but Wellington, who had merely wished to neutralise the position, now began the excavation of his first trenches. Using entire divisions as work-parties and digging night and day, he had completed a parallel and seven batteries by 11 January. Although the French shelled the earthworks at every opportunity and the Allies' tactics proved costly in both men and equipment, the excavations continued and Wellington was soon considering launching an assault.

After much deliberation, however, he and his chief engineer, Colonel Fletcher, decided that a second parallel would have to be constructed first. 13 January saw the commencement of a new series of excavations and, that night, another raiding party cleared the French from the outlying Convent of Santa Cruz. With this obstacle neutralised, work could begin in earnest and the second parallel was soon within 200 yards of the fortress walls.

Barrié, meanwhile, was preparing a foray to slow down the alarming rate of Wellington's advance. Having noticed that the Allied work-parties were relieved each day at 11 am, he resolved to strike then: in the brief period when the enemy's earthworks were devoid of troops. Accordingly, on 14 January, when the night shift limped off to their camps and the next relay approached, a mass of French soldiers suddenly swept out of the fortress. Before anybody realised what was happening, they had retaken Santa Cruz and inflicted considerable damage on the second parallel. Then, having suffered no appreciable losses, they headed back to the city, leaving

the Allies' encampment in uproar. Furious at this reverse, Wellington pushed his men even harder and, by late afternoon, most of the
damage had been repaired. Opening fire with twenty-seven siege
guns, the Allies now bombarded the San Francisco Convent and
those areas of the walls that bore the scars of Ney's breaches. By
evening, the convent had been taken and, during the night, the
hard-pressed French abandoned their remaining outposts, concentrating all their scanty infantry for a final defence of the city
proper.

It was soon evident, however, that the repairs to Ney's breaches
had not been particularly effective: the mortar was weak due to a
shortage of lime and rapidly crumbled. Despite heavy casualties
amongst their work-parties and gunners the Allies advanced at a
disturbing rate and, on 18 January, the artillery of the second parallel
burst into action; inflicting tremendous damage on the tottering
masonry and tearing another rupture in the walls. Unable to clear the
debris from the base of these gaping holes, Barrié's men realised that
an assault was imminent and began to construct internal defences.
Wellington had been itching to storm the fortress at the earliest
possible opportunity and had already decreed that the attack would
be at 7 pm on 19 January. While the Third Division was to assail the
principal breach, the task of storming the lesser one fell to Craufurd
and his light regiments. Simultaneously, two minor columns, under
O'Toole and Pack, were to escalade the south wall to distract the
exiguous garrison.

At the appointed hour, the Allied troops hurled themselves at their
respective targets. That the attack succeeded at all was almost
entirely due to the numerical weakness of the garrison. Barrié simply
did not have sufficient soldiers to protect adequately all the points at
which he was threatened, and had deployed nearly all of his men at
the principal breach. Finding few French troops to oppose them, the
columns of O'Toole and Pack penetrated into the city with ease and
the Light Division, too, had a relatively simple task. At the main
rupture, however, the story was to prove very different and, without
the success of the supporting attacks, Wellington's hastily-mounted
assault would have ended in catastrophe.

Braving a tremendous fire from the defenders' artillery and
muskets, Picton's men scrambled up the debris to the main breach to
find a tangle of *chevaux de frise* and barricades, and a terrifying,
twenty-five-foot drop into the city streets. Unable to go forward,
they were crowding onto the lip of the rupture when a discharge of
canister from two twenty-four pounder guns blew the head of the
column to shreds and sent the rear cascading back. With conspicuous gallantry, the besiegers pressed forward again and, in

spite of horrendous losses, regained the crest of the breach. But this magnificent effort was completely futile. The French fired into the struggling redcoats as fast as they could load and, apart from a few who managed to clamber up the masonry on either side of the gap, the besiegers made no progress. Nevertheless, the action was going in Wellington's favour, for, although Picton had been effectively contained, the other Allied attacks had broken through the thin French defences and, shrugging off substantial casualties, were now converging to assist the Third Division.

With enemy troops on their flanks and rear, Barrié's men on the western wall began to falter. A few brave souls from Picton's battalions scrambled up to the parapets on either side of the great breach and, falling on the crews with their bayonets, silenced the last of the defenders' artillery. At this, the French retreated into the town, where they fired a huge mine which demolished the area around the principal breach and cut down scores more of the attackers, including General Mackinnon. Nevertheless, the battle was won and, as the garrison laid down their weapons, the British troops embarked on an orgy of drunken looting, violence and vandalism. Only after several hours was discipline restored and then, in the words of one witness, the storm-parties marched out of the city 'dressed in all varieties imaginable. Some with jack-boots on, others with white French trousers, others with frock-coats with epaulettes, some even with monkeys on their shoulders . . .' The Fifth Division cheered and presented arms to this bizarre procession, while a bemused Wellington muttered to his equally stuporous staff 'Who the devil *are* those fellows?'[329]

The seizure of Ciudad Rodrigo was a triumph for the Anglo-Portuguese army. In addition to the fortress itself, a colossal amount of ordnance and 1,300 wounded prisoners were taken. Barrié also had 500 men slain or wounded in the twelve-day siege. However, it had been a costly business for Wellington's courageous soldiery who had sustained 1,300 casualties including two major-generals: Mackinnon and the dashing 'Black Bob' Craufurd, mortally wounded at the head of his Light Division.[330] Nevertheless, that the stronghold fell in under a fortnight surprised even Wellington,[331] who had expected it to take at least three weeks.

Marmont and Dorsenne were horrified. Having discounted rumours that the Allies were astir, they had consistently refused to believe that a siege would be attempted until spring brought an improvement in the weather. Craufurd's blockade had proved so effective that it was not until 13 January that Marmont knew that the fortress was even under attack, by which time it was too late for the marshal and his colleague to be of any help to Barrié.

II   Marmont in Portugal

After his skirmish with Wellington at Aldea da Ponte in September, Marmont had retired on his base at Almaraz for the winter. Here, he received new orders from Paris: henceforth, Dorsenne was to administer only north-eastern Spain, and the divisions of Bonnet and Souham – in the Asturias and Leon respectively – were to transfer to Marmont's command which would assume responsibility for defending the north-west frontier.

Although the 'Army of Portugal' was thus increased by 16,000 men, it was in effect weakened for its commitments were, in turn, considerably enlarged. Marmont had to maintain the garrisons in Leon while keeping a large force permanently based about Almaraz to secure his communications with Soult's 'Army of the South'. When these detachments had been made and Montbrun's column dispatched to Valencia, the marshal found that only four of his eight divisions were available for action against Wellington and those were scattered over enormous distances. Thus, when news of the attack on Ciudad Rodrigo finally arrived, Marmont took several days to muster three divisions. Hurrying to Salamanca, he heard of the fall of the fortress on 21 January and was still debating his next move when new orders arrived from Paris.

Napoleon, arguing that even a minor offensive by the 'Army of Portugal' was bound to 'contain' Wellington, urged Marmont to advance into Beira.[332] On the emperor's maps this doubtlessly looked feasible, but his calculations were, as usual, badly out of date: Wellington had already entrusted the Beira frontier to the Portuguese militia and was in full march for Estremadura to strike at Badajoz. Moreover, as Marmont was aware, an offensive into Portugal posed no real threat to his adversary and, given the weak logistical system of their army and the barren countryside, was likely to end in calamity for the French. Convinced that with Ciudad Rodrigo in their hands the Allies would now try to capture Badajoz, he set his master's directive aside and proposed to concentrate his army at Almaraz.

Accordingly, he ordered Montbrun – belatedly returned from Valencia – to wait for him in the Tagus Valley, and was preparing to shift the bulk of his other troops there when another Imperial missive plunged his arrangements into confusion. This time, Napoleon decreed that Bonnet's division was to be transferred from the 'Army of Portugal' to the 'Army of the North', for Dorsenne – deprived of thousands of men by the impending Russian expedition – was gradually being overwhelmed by insurgents. However, appreciating Marmont's difficulties, the emperor also ruled that, if attacked by the British, he could call on Dorsenne for reinforcements of up to 10,000 men. With this compromise, Napoleon reasoned, the north-east could be pacified and Wellington simultaneously kept in check.

This infuriated Marmont, and virulent correspondence was soon plying between his headquarters and Paris. 'I am informed', he wrote indignantly,

> that . . . the Army of the North will be in a position to help me with two divisions if I am attacked. I doubt whether His Majesty's intentions on this point will be carried out, and in no wise expect it. I believe that I am justified in fearing that any troops sent me will have to be long waited for, and will be an insignificant force when they do appear. Not to speak of the inevitable slowness in all joint operations, it takes so long in Spain to get dispatches through, and to collect troops, that I doubt whether I shall obtain any help at the critical moment.[333]

However, news of the fall of Ciudad Rodrigo soon provoked another change of course by the emperor: he returned Bonnet's division to Marmont and urged the marshal to assume an offensive posture to pin down Wellington – whose army he underestimated by 20,000 men – on the northern frontier of Portugal. This was precisely what he had ordered in January, and Marmont's reasons for oppos-ing it then were still valid. On 2 March he wrote to Imperial headquarters that

> If the emperor relies with confidence on the effect which demon-strations in the North will produce on . . . Wellington, I must dare to express my contrary opinion. Lord Wellington is quite aware that I have no magazines, and is acquainted with the immensely difficult physical character of the country, and its complete lack of food resources . . . He knows that my army is not in a position to cross the Coa, even if no-one opposes me, and that if we did so we should have to turn back at the end of four days, unable to carry on the campaign, and with our horses all starved to death.[334]

Napoleon remained unimpressed. Dismissing as 'mad' the sugges-tion that Wellington would move against Badajoz with a French army threatening the Coa – even though that is precisely what he had done in May 1811 – he ordered Marmont to march west immedi-ately.[335] Concentrating four divisions, the marshal reluctantly com-plied and, by 30 March, was in the vicinity of Ciudad Rodrigo. The situation there was as he had expected. Before departing for the south, Wellington had effected makeshift repairs to the damaged defences and had left a garrison of over 3,000 Spanish troops. As his own battering train had been stored in the city and had thus fallen into Allied hands, there was little Marmont could do to incommode seriously the defenders and so, leaving a division to blockade the place, he moved west to probe at Almeida, the insurgents cutting his communications as he advanced.

That stronghold proved no more vulnerable than Ciudad Rodrigo had and, after some petty skirmishing with the local levies, Marmont struck down the Coa to Sabugal, where he lingered for several days. Arriving at Guarda on 14 April, he surprised and routed the Portuguese militia of Generals Trant and Wilson. However, although he had penetrated deep into enemy territory and had taken over 1,500 prisoners, he was painfully aware of the strategic futility of his operations. As one Allied officer observed: 'He can do no more than drive off some cattle, burn some cottages and ruin a few wretched peasants.' Indeed, Wellington was later to report to Lord Liverpool that

> The partial success over the Portuguese militia on their retreat from Guarda, and the murder and plunder of the inhabitants of a few villages in lower Beira – already suffering from the enemy's former depredations – are the only fruits of Marshal Marmont's expedition . . . to divert our attention from the siege of Badajoz.[336]

Having lost over 1,500 horses through disease and starvation, Marmont – as he had predicted – was obliged to retreat.[337] Ironically, Paris had come to accept his strategic analysis and, alarmed by Wellington's attack on Badajoz, now sent him orders to hurry south. But the matter was already decided: the fortress had been stormed on 6 April and Marmont's army, floundering in the Portuguese wilderness, might as well have been on the moon.

III   The Third Allied Siege of Badajoz

Quite unmoved at the prospect of an offensive by Marmont's impotent divisions, Wellington had marched south in late January. Having taken Ciudad Rodrigo, he was now anxious to secure Badajoz and thus enjoy control over both the northern and southern gateways into Spain. Preparations for another siege were begun and, by the middle of March, 60,000 troops – including 1,000 artillery men and engineers, with fifty-eight heavy calibre guns – were assembled between Elvas and the frontier. This vast force consisted of all eight of the regular Anglo-Portuguese divisions, four independent infantry brigades and virtually all the disposable cavalry – including two new formations of heavy dragoons, recently arrived from Britain. With an army of this size, Wellington was confident that he could invest the fortress and still have sufficient troops to beat off any relief column that the hard-pressed Soult could muster. The only threat to these calculations was the possibility that Marmont might come to his colleague's aid – just as he had done the previous June. However, as yet, he evinced no sign of doing so and, as we have seen, was to be prevented from making the move by inept directives from Paris. But Wellington was, of course, not to know this and, in an effort to reduce the chances of a successful intervention by the 'Army of Portugal', resolved to take Badajoz as quickly as was practicable.

As an opening move, a large pontoon was laid across the Guadiana and, on 14 March, the Allied army began to cross. Two days later Wellington divided his forces into three groups; the first – under himself – was to prosecute the siege, while the other two – commanded by Hill and Graham – marched off to contain d'Erlon's troops who promptly retreated eastwards. In addition, a contingent of 5,000 Spaniards, under General Villemur, set out to threaten Seville. Having given Soult more than enough to think about, the Allied commander was free to concentrate on Badajoz.

The diligent Phillipon had been anything but idle since Wellington last assailed him. The breaches from the second siege had not only been repaired but had also been revetted with huge stone blocks, while the defences of San Cristobal in particular had undergone considerable improvement. Furthermore, the garrison had striven to deter assaults on the more exposed areas of the perimeter: the western front had been honeycombed with tunnels packed with explosives, and approach to the south-eastern corner had been made difficult by the damming and flooding of the Rivallas Brook. The mines, an extremely ingenious line of defence and quite undetectable, were primed for detonation at the first hint of trouble. Indeed, the Allies were planning to launch their attack against the western wall and would doubtlessly have sustained a catastrophe had a French deserter not alerted them to the danger.

After a lengthy reconnaissance, Wellington decided to strike at the south-eastern quarter and preliminary operations against the Picurina Fort were begun on the night of 17 March. Opening their parallel at 200 yards, some 2,000 Allied troops toiled, in heavy rain, in a desperate effort to establish themselves before daylight. The next morning was foggy and wet, and the French gunners and snipers could only manage an occasional effective shot. Thus, the besiegers worked on unretarded and were making considerable progress when the weather suddenly changed sides. For four days, there was a tremendous downpour. The Guadiana burst its banks and swept away the pontoon, and the trenches to the east of the city were inundated with mud and water. Unable to move their cannon across the quagmire, the Allies could not build new batteries until the weather improved on 24 March when they redoubled their efforts and, by the next day, had twenty-eight guns in action against the Picurina and the eastern defences.

Although the outpost was damaged, its garrison was in good spirits when the Allies attacked. The storming-parties moved forward during the night of 25 March and, in a vicious scrimmage, sustained casualties of over sixty per cent. Nevertheless, the position was eventually carried and the besiegers advanced their artillery to within 400 yards of the city wall. The French commenced a relentless shelling of the area around the Picurina, and it took four days of labour and many killed and wounded before a solitary Anglo-Portuguese battery was installed in the stronghold. However, covered by the fire of these pieces, more heavy ordnance was dragged forward and, by 31 March, three companies of guns were in action here. Such concentrated fire inflicted considerable damage and Wellington was soon making preparations for an assault. However, as Phillipon had hoped, the flooded Rivallas proved a major obstacle and, after an attempt to take the San Roque Lunette had been beaten off, the Allies realised that their columns would have to assail the breaches from the western bank of the stream.

The siege rapidly moved towards its climax. Three more Allied batteries came into action, enlarging the existing two ruptures and creating another. The French worked constantly to repair the damage and, although suffering heavily from the besiegers' fire, succeeded in constructing some elaborate, internal defences. However, time was running out. Advised that d'Erlon and Soult were on the move, Wellington had elected to storm Badajoz at the earliest possible moment and was preparing to attack on 6 April.

That he was moving too quickly cannot be doubted. He was proposing to hurl troops at imperfect breaches, defended by men who were far from dispirited. This is what he had done at Ciudad Rodrigo and, as happened there, the assault on Badajoz only succeeded because of the defenders' numerical weakness. For want of a few companies of infantry Phillipon could not adequately protect all of the city's perimeter and, while – like Barrié – he repulsed his adversary's main effort, a series of minor incursions brought about his defeat.

Wellington's plan called for an assault on the main breaches by the Light and Fourth Divisions while the Third staged a diversionary attack against the castle on the eastern side. In a further effort to

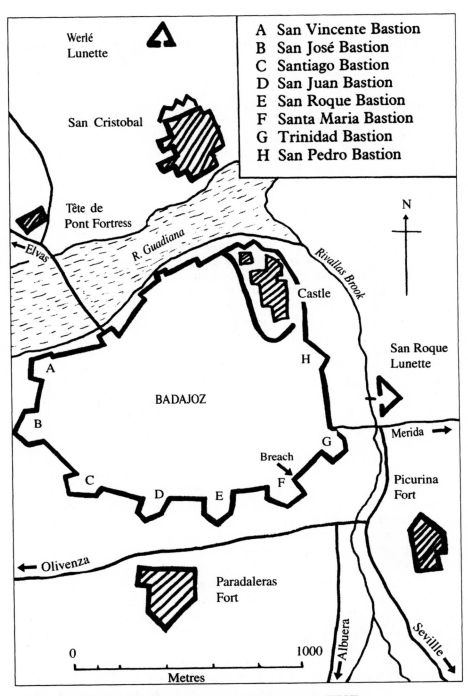

Werlé
Lunette

A   San Vincente Bastion
B   San José Bastion
C   Santiago Bastion
D   San Juan Bastion
E   San Roque Bastion
F   Santa Maria Bastion
G   Trinidad Bastion
H   San Pedro Bastion

San Cristobal

Tête de
Pont Fortress

← Elvas

R. Guadiana

Rivallas Brook

N

Castle

San Roque
Lunette

H

A

BADAJOZ

Merida →

B

G

Breach

Picurina
Fort

C

D   E   F

← Olivenza

Paradaleras
Fort

Albuera

Seville →

0   1000

Metres

THE FORTRESS OF BADAJOZ DURING THE
PENINSULAR WAR

distract the garrison the Fifth Division was to assail the western wall and other troops were to descend on the San Roque Lunette. From the outset, things went badly for the besiegers. The assault had been set for 10 pm but, fifteen minutes before, Picton's division was spotted in the trenches and, heavily shelled by the French, immediately surged into the attack. The Fifth Division, too, failed to engage on time: the marshalling of the 4,000 troops took longer than anticipated and the battalions were not ready until after 11 pm. Thus, only the main assault was delivered on schedule.

Advancing down the west bank of the Rivallas, the Light and Fourth Divisions immediately came under heavy fire. They were still some distance from the city when the latter unit encountered a water-filled ditch – around twelve feet deep – which claimed several men before the whole formation veered off to the left to find a clear path. They soon came across a dry moat barring the approaches to the Santa Maria Bastion. This looked innocent, but was dotted with mines and heaps of combustible material which, when the trench was packed with British troops, the French ignited. The two leading parties – each about 500 men strong – were obliterated in an instant. Almost every single soldier was killed or wounded, and virtually all the engineers and officers directing the assault were cut down. Minutes later, the main wave arrived and, steadily losing their order, poured into the trench to support their faltering colleagues. The Fourth Division, as it swerved over from the right, collided with the battalions of light troops and, in seconds, the whole force was reduced to a chaotic mass into which the French poured a hail of shot and musketry.

The carnage was appalling. Hardly any of the Allied troops set foot on the breach, for most were shot down when still struggling in the moat. Tiny groups of gallant soldiers did push forward, only to be exterminated when they finally reached the wall. Their bravery was remarkable. Around forty of these desperate little bands hurled themselves on the defenders in the space of two hours but, after more than 2,200 casualties had been sustained, Wellington acknowledged defeat and ordered the stricken divisions to withdraw.

Meanwhile, Picton's battalions had been assailing the castle walls. The overstretched French could spare only 300 men for this sector, but they put up a determined fight. Scores of the attackers were shot down while struggling to erect their scaling ladders – many of which proved too short[338] – and the first two assaults were beaten off with grave losses. Only when Picton sent in his last brigade did the tide turn in his favour. Outnumbered by thirteen to one and with pockets of enemy soldiers establishing themselves on the ramparts, the exhausted defenders finally turned and fled.

During this gory escalade, around 700 Allied troops were killed or wounded – including Picton himself, who was seriously injured. Nevertheless, it ultimately proved successful and, by midnight, the castle was overrun. Elsewhere, too, the besiegers emerged triumphant. Attacking the bastion of San Vincente, the Fifth Division overwhelmed their handful of opponents and joined Picton's men in a relentless advance through the streets. Taken in the rear, the defenders of the main breach began to falter and, as the depleted Light and Fourth Divisions returned to the attack, most of the garrison laid down their arms.[339] A few determined cavalrymen, however, cut their way through the Allied lines and carried the news to Soult. Meanwhile, the civilian population of Badajoz – French and Spanish alike – were subjected to appalling acts of savagery as, for twenty-nine hours, 10,000 frenzied British troops rampaged through the city.[340]

IV   The Disconsolate Duke of Dalmatia

Soult was not surprised by the fall of the fortress. Like Marmont he had concluded that, after storming Ciudad Rodrigo, the Allies would turn against Badajoz and, in early February, had formulated a joint strategy with the 'Army of Portugal' for its defence.[341] Promised that Marmont would, as he had in spring 1811, come to his support should Badajoz be threatened,[342] Soult had continued with the tedious task of pacifying his insurgent ridden domain and was supervising the investment of Cadiz when Wellington was reported at Elvas.

A familiar chain of events ensued. Alerted to the enemy's offensive, Soult struggled to assemble a field army and, having mustered 13,000 troops, marched to the assistance of d'Erlon's small corps. Arriving at Llerena on 4 April, he concentrated 25,000 men, but, outnumbered by more than two to one, was unwilling to try conclusions with the Allies until Marmont had come to his aid. That, however, had been overruled by Paris and, thus, when they were both needed and expected on the Guadiana, Marmont's divisions were engaged in their futile invasion of Portugal.

The tidings of this disastrous development only reached Soult on the morning of 7 April and, shortly after, he also heard of the fall of Badajoz.[343] With the enemy before him in overwhelming strength, and the attacks of Villemur and Ballesteros wreaking havoc to his rear, the exasperated marshal turned his columns about and hastened to protect Seville. A few days later, d'Erlon's containing force was edged back across the Estremadurian frontier and, satisfied that Soult would now remain on the defensive, Wellington left Hill to observe the 'Army of the South' and retraced his steps to Ciudad Rodrigo.

V The Raid on Almaraz, May 1812

With both the northern and southern routes into Spain under his control, Wellington now possessed the initiative and, hoping that the strategic repercussions of a blow against Marmont would jeopardise Soult's position as well, he resolved to mount an all-out offensive against the overstretched 'Army of Portugal'. Given a clear insight into the dispositions of Marmont's forces by a wealth of captured dispatches, Wellington decided that he would first isolate his target from the 'Army of the South'. Accordingly, Hill's corps was ordered to destroy the weakly guarded pontoon bridge at Almaraz.

Hill gathered 7,000 troops and, leaving the rest of his forces to contain d'Erlon, marched for the Tagus. Wellington, meanwhile, dispatched General Graham with two divisions to ensure that Hill had adequate cover should Soult bring an army to d'Erlon's aid. Arriving at Trujillo on 15 May, Hill struck across the mountains with remarkable speed and, only two days later, emerged at the Pass of Miravete, one and a half miles to the south of the bridge. Here he encountered the most outlying of Marmont's defensive works and, after a lengthy reconnaissance, concluded that a serious attack on this formidable position could only end in disaster. Accordingly, he decided to distract the defenders of Miravete with a feint assault, while a large detachment – under Brigadier Howard – approached the bridge by another route. With the help of a peasant, Howard located a mountain track through the Pass of Cueva and, by sunrise on 18 May, was well in the rear of the enemy's outposts and approaching the crossing itself.

The French, however, had glimpsed Howard's troops descending from the hills and the garrison of Fort Napoleon inflicted heavy casualties on the advancing formations. Nevertheless, the attackers persevered and, when a few of Howard's men were established on the ramparts of the fortress, the infantry company defending that sector inexplicably panicked and broke into retreat. The rest of the garrison followed suit and, apart from the commandant, Colonel Aubert, who refused to surrender, gave up their weapons or fled. In minutes, the outpost was in Allied hands and Howard's men surged forward to tackle the next obstacle; a large redoubt dominating the approach road to the crossing. It was defended by 360 Prussians from the 4th *Étranger* who, at the sight of Fort Napoleon's capture, took off across

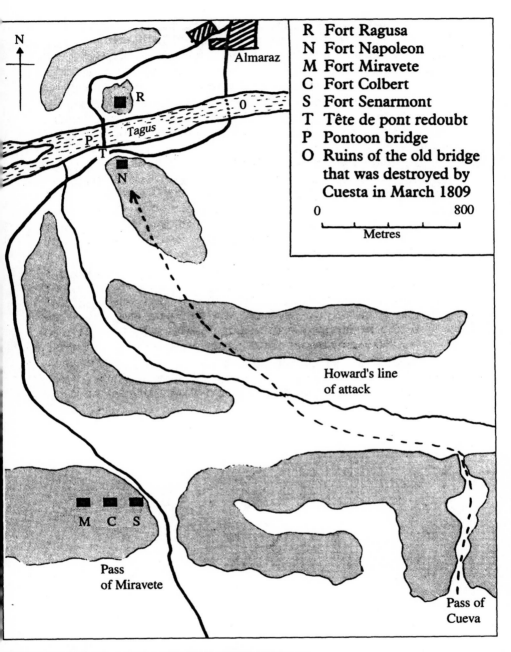

R Fort Ragusa
N Fort Napoleon
M Fort Miravete
C Fort Colbert
S Fort Senarmont
T Tête de pont redoubt
P Pontoon bridge
O Ruins of the old bridge that was destroyed by Cuesta in March 1809

0   800

Metres

Almaraz

Tagus

Howard's line of attack

M C S

Pass of Miravete

Pass of Cueva

THE ALLIED ATTACK ON THE FORTS
AT ALMARAZ, 18 May 1812

the bridge without firing a shot. This disgraceful rout was a calamity for the French; for the Allies – intermixed with their fleeing adversaries – now rushed across the Tagus towards Fort Ragusa whose defenders, unable to fire for fear of hitting their own comrades, were only saved from the embarrassing dilemma by the fortuitous collapse of the central pontoon. However, when the Allies began shelling Ragusa with the captured guns of Fort Napoleon, the demoralised garrison succumbed to panic and joined the rest of their forces in headlong retreat.

Thus, there was nothing to prevent Howard's elated men from repairing the crossing and completing their mission. After taking the stores from the captured strongholds, they demolished both the forts and the bridge and retired to Trujillo. Shortly after, General Foy's division hastened across from Talavera but, apart from the intact garrison of Fort Miravete, nothing could be salvaged and Hill's column had long since gone.[344]

As intended, this daring raid effectively separated the armies of Soult and Marmont. Furthermore, Hill's sudden lurch forward, coupled with the arrival of Graham's two divisions, convinced Soult that a fresh Allied onslaught was imminent and it was some time before he stopped bombarding Madrid with alarmist reports of '40,000 enemy troops marching against Andalusia'.[345] But he was in no immediate danger: having isolated the 'Army of Portugal', Wellington was preparing to strike in the north[346] and, within four months, had liberated Madrid and was hammering on the gates of Burgos.

Chapter XXII

THE SALAMANCA CAMPAIGN

I Wellington's Offensive

Having separated Soult from Marmont, Wellington now outlined his intentions to Lord Liverpool: 'I propose', he wrote on 26 May,

> as soon as the [army's] magazines are brought forward, . . . to move forward into Castille, and to endeavour . . . to bring Marmont to a general action. . . . I am of the opinion . . . that I shall have advantage in the action, and that this is the period . . . in which such a measure should be tried.

After listing the various improvements in his own forces, he concluded:

> Strong as the enemy are at present, . . . they are weaker than they have ever been during the war. . . . We have a better chance of success now, therefore, than we have ever had; and success obtained now would produce results not to be expected from any success over any single French army in the Peninsula upon any other occasion.[347]

To reduce the odds against him in this crucial offensive, Wellington did his utmost to complete Marmont's isolation by mounting diversions against the other Imperial forces. Santocildes' 16,000-strong 'Army of Galicia' was again urged to take the offensive, while Hill and Ballesteros were ordered to pin down Soult. To ensure that the 'Army of the North' could spare no troops, Wellington incited the guerillas to redouble their efforts in Castille and Navarre, and arranged for a large naval contingent, under Admiral Popham, to support them with a vigorous campaign along the Biscay coast. Naval might was also to occupy Suchet: a mixed force of British, Sicilians and Spanish was to be assembled in Majorca under General Maitland and landed in Catalonia.

His preparations complete, Wellington crossed the Agueda on 13 June with eight infantry divisions, four cavalry brigades and fifty-four guns. His vanguard soon neared Salamanca but, although some *chasseurs* came out to observe them, encountered no resistance.

In fact, Marmont was endeavouring to avoid a clash. As usual, his forces were short of rations and concentration would only aggravate the problem. Accordingly, he delayed assembling his divisions until the last moment and, leaving a small contingent to defend Salamanca's strongholds, withdrew to the north. His scattered detachments gradually converged and, by 19 June, he had 36,000 infantry, 2,800 rather poor cavalry and eighty guns. Nevertheless, he was still significantly outnumbered, particularly in mounted troops, so he played for time and sent urgent appeals for help to Madrid. However, King Joseph was in a quandary. Soult had reported that *he* was under attack from '60,000 of the Allies',[348] and now Marmont was insisting that an enormous army was threatening Salamanca. Convinced that one or the other must be mistaken, and reluctant to act in the absence of conclusive evidence, the monarch demanded irrefutable proof that the 'Army of Portugal' was genuinely under pressure. Thus, it was some time before the French high command even knew which quarter they were threatened from and, by then, Wellington's offensive had made appreciable progress.

Indeed, the French were fortunate that Wellington had not exploited his advantage more conclusively. 'I have adopted every measure in my power to prevent the enemy from collecting their forces against us,' he told Lord Liverpool.[349] Yet, having gained his concentrated army a central position, he declined to attack his scattered foes and destroy them piecemeal. This peculiar decision is explained by his determination to fight a *defensive* battle on a selected site east of Salamanca[350] and, having posted most of his army here, he relinquished the initiative and turned on the city's French-held forts.

These three strongholds dominated the main bridge over the Tormes and were actually fortified convents – the San Vincente, the San Cayetano and La Merced. Reinforced with stone provided by the demolition of parts of Salamanca's university, although incomplete, they were remarkably strong and held 800 men and thirty-six small pieces of ordnance. Wellington decided to siege rather than blockade them. However, he had neglected to provide an effective battering train for his army, and had only four heavy guns with 100 rounds apiece and two engineering officers.

On the night of 17 June, the Sixth Division began the attack on San Vincente by excavating a trench from the town hospital towards the stronghold. Although the work-parties were given additional

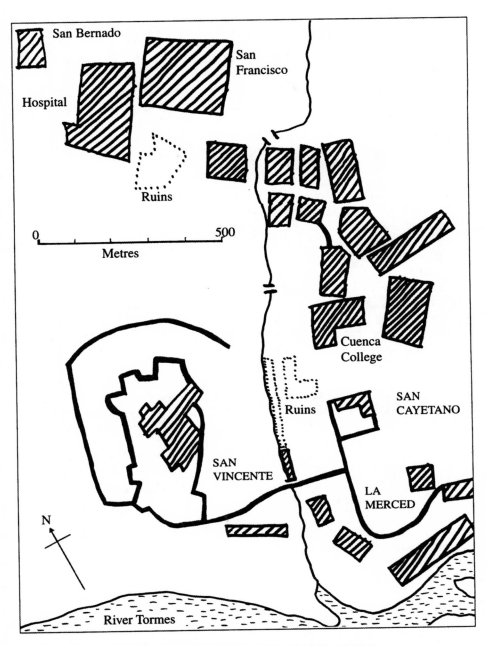

THE FORTIFIED CONVENTS OF SALAMANCA

cover by the ruins of some college buildings, the accurate French artillery soon halted the digging. The besiegers hoisted two cannons onto the roof of the San Bernado Convent in an attempt to reply to the remorseless shelling, but the French were barely incommoded by this distant cannonade and it was only when 300 snipers added to the fire that the intensity of the defenders' salvoes diminished. In the next few days, another two batteries were brought into action, the French retaliatory fire began to slacken and areas of San Vincente's defences started to show traces of appreciable damage. However, just when the Allies seemed to be on the verge of a breakthrough their paltry stocks of heavy ammunition ran out; obliging them to halt and mark time.

Marmont, meanwhile, was on the move and, during the afternoon of 20 June, came dangerously close to the main Allied forces on the Heights of San Cristobal. A mild artillery exchange ensued and the French launched a probing attack on the village of Morisco, but, daunted by Wellington's strong position, declined to attempt anything further. Wellington hoped for a general action on the morrow and began making preparations. However, Marmont had no intention of being lured into such a trap. He had only 30,000 troops, his cavalry was weak and the Allies were strongly entrenched. In spite of efforts to provoke him he remained on the defensive all day and, by the evening of 22 June, had withdrawn to a defensive position some six miles to the north-east.

This cautious behaviour by his adversaries moved Wellington to indignation. 'It appears to me', he complained to a colleague, 'that they are determined as I am not to fight ... in a disadvantageous situation.'[351] Again, in a letter to Graham on 3 July, he grumbled:

> It appears certain that Marmont will not risk an action unless he should have an advantage; and I shall certainly not risk one unless I should have an advantage; and matters therefore do not appear likely to be brought to that criterion very soon.[352]

But this stalemate was largely of Wellington's making and exclusively to his detriment. He had declined to exploit his central position early in the campaign and, consequently, his opponent had slipped away to await reinforcements. Time was on Marmont's side and with every day he threatened to grow stronger – perhaps too strong. As he told Joseph he had no intention of fighting until his army was 'at least equal to that of the Allies' and would, meanwhile, 'manoeuvre around Salamanca, so as to try to get the enemy to divide his army, or to move it out of its position, which will be to my advantage.'[353]

As the two armies drifted apart, Wellington returned to the siege of the Salamanca forts. Although it was virtually undamaged and, indeed, had barely been attacked, he directed that San Cayetano was to be stormed immediately. Dutifully, 400 light infantry from the Sixth Division assailed it on 23 June but, unable to make any impression, were cut down by the score. 120 men – including General Bowes, the commander – failed to return and, coming soon after the bloody attacks on Ciudad Rodrigo and Badajoz, the episode further undermined confidence in Wellington as a siege commander.

While the fighting around San Cayetano had been under way, Marmont had slipped a contingent across the Tormes at Huerta, and next morning these troops launched a heavy attack on the isolated dragoons of General Bock. Wellington, however, had anticipated such a move, and quickly shifted Le Marchant's horsemen and the First and Seventh Divisions to Bock's support. At this, the French called a halt and, sustaining trifling losses, retired beyond the Tormes once more.

Events elsewhere, however, were nearing a climax. Fresh ammunition having arrived on 26 June, the bombardment of the forts was begun again and, by firing red-hot shot into its wooden roof, the besiegers soon set San Cayetano ablaze. Coupled with a growing breach in the northern wall, this convinced the weary garrison that further resistance was pointless and, as the assault columns advanced, the commandant surrendered. Demoralised, the other strongholds joined in the capitulation and, after stripping the buildings of all supplies, the Allied engineers demolished them.

Coming as it did after increasingly despondent signals from the beleaguered forts, the abrupt termination of the cannonade at Salamanca indicated to Marmont that the strongholds had fallen and he promptly retired to the Douro. He was still awaiting Bonnet's division from the Asturias and a column from the 'Army of the North', promised by its new commander – General Caffarelli – in a letter of 14 June.[354] However, Caffarelli had since been subjected to such relentless pressure by the guerillas and Admiral Popham that he could spare no men – irrespective of Marmont's plight. Desperate for tidings of Bonnet, Marmont now sent Foy's division on reconnaissance down the river to Toro. He reported that Santocildes was besieging Benavente and Astorga, while a Portuguese contingent – under Silveira – had beleaguered Zamora. The Allied vice seemed to be gradually tightening on the isolated 'Army of Portugal'.

However, if matters seemed gloomy to the French commander, Wellington was gloomier still. Regretting not having attacked on 21 June when the opportunity had existed, he sought to regain the initiative by hurrying after the French. Hoping that Santocildes would likewise close in on the enemy, he was dismayed to learn that the Spanish general had commenced a full siege of Astorga, which, as he had no heavy cannon, was unlikely to incommode the garrison or do anything of much benefit for the Allied cause. Moreover, news had arrived that Maitland's expedition to Catalonia was behind schedule and, consequently, there was a danger that Suchet might dispatch troops to assist his colleagues on the Douro, further disrupting Wellington's calculations.

Indeed, while he dallied about Salamanca, the French high command was feverishly seeking to respond to his offensive. Having established that Soult was not under pressure, Joseph demanded that he send troops to assist against Wellington. But the marshal was as recalcitrant as ever and, repeatedly ignoring his superior's commands, prevaricated for weeks.[355]

Marmont, meanwhile, found matters turning more in his favour. His forces had taken up a strong position to the north of the Douro between its confluence with the Pisuerga and Pollos. On 7 July, Bonnet finally arrived, having taken an eccentric route to avoid Santocildes. With his division the French army rose to 43,000 bayonets, 2,200 sabres and seventy-eight cannon, but the cavalry remained poor and many of the troopers were mounted on requisitioned, untrained horses that were incapable of performing the sophisticated manoeuvres of the drill-book. Indeed, this largely explains why they gave such bad service throughout the Salamanca campaign.

Wellington, too, had moved to the Douro but, although the Imperial armies were now threatening to concentrate against him, he still refused to attack and merely urged Santocildes and Maitland into action. 'It is obvious', he wrote to Lord Bathurst on 14 July, 'that we could not cross the Douro . . . without sustaining great loss, and could not fight a general action under circumstances of greater disadvantage than those which would attend the attack of the enemy's position . . .'[356] The deadlock continued until Marmont – advised that no help was available and having raised his army to a size similar to that of Wellington's – resolved to wait no longer and, with Joseph's permission,[357] suddenly took the initiative.

The first problem, to cross the Douro under Wellington's very nose, was overcome with remarkably little difficulty. On 15 July, the marshal sent two divisions across the river at Toro in what seemed to be an all-out attack and Wellington rushed the bulk of his army to meet them. However, this movement was only partially complete when, to his horror, the Allied general discovered that the French were retracing their steps and that the whole of their army was pouring over the undefended crossing at Tordesillas. Having massed his forces on the south bank, Marmont swung westwards and, urging

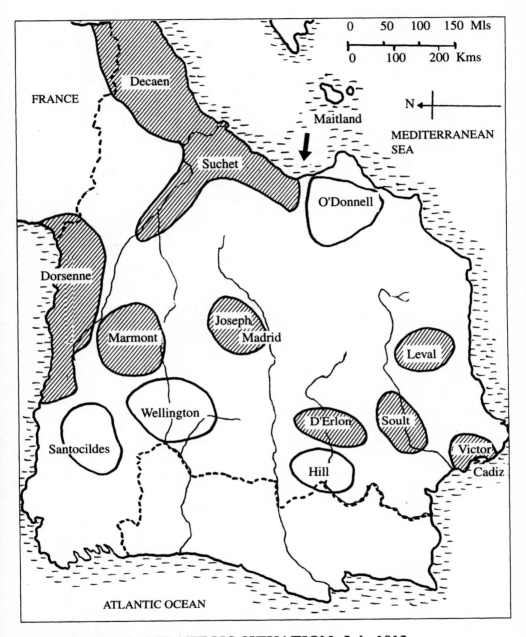

FRANCE

Decaen

Maitland

MEDITERRANEAN
SEA

N

Suchet

O'Donnell

Dorsenne

Joseph

Madrid

Leval

Marmont

Wellington

D'Erlon

Soult

Santocildes

Hill

Victor

Cadiz

ATLANTIC OCEAN

0   50   100   150 Mls

0   100   200 Kms

THE GENERAL STRATEGIC SITUATION, July 1812

his men through the village of Nava, established contact with the rear of Wellington's army.

The Eighteenth saw the Allies in headlong retreat with Marmont's cavalry close behind. Indeed, on one occasion, they cut their way into the midst of Wellington's rearguard and, overrunning a horse artillery battery, came face to face with him and his entire staff. Fortunately for the Allied commanders, their reserve cavalry hurried to the rescue and drove the French off. But Wellington had escaped death or capture by a whisker and, thoroughly shaken, hurried his forces towards the Guarena river. The Imperial cavalry raced after them and the Allies were taking up positions along the western bank when General Clausel directed the French vanguard to assail the village of Castrillo. After a bitter fight, Brennier's infantry dislodged their opponents from the settlement but, as the French sought to advance up the slopes beyond, they were met by the lines of Anson and Stubbs and, after an unequal musketry exchange, Brennier's columns reeled back.[358] Meanwhile, further south, a brigade of French dragoons had also crossed the river, but were charged by Anson's light horse while deploying. Although forced to retreat, they fought back skilfully and their 160 casualties only slightly exceeded Anson's losses. Nevertheless, in the fighting between the two infantry arms the Allies had emerged as clear winners and Clausel's forces retired.

Marmont was disappointed by the poor results of his strategic manoeuvre. His troops were tired after their long march and their gains were negligible. Instead of being caught dispersed, Wellington's units were entrenched in a compact position behind the Guarena and their recent losses amounted to only a few hundred men. As another frontal assault was not to his taste, the marshal turned his columns southwards in an endeavour to outflank his adversary. However, Wellington also moved his forces upstream. The armies found themselves marching parallel to one another for several miles and, as they converged on the village of Cantalpino, Marmont sought to bring on a major engagement. But Wellington, again declining such a clash, wheeled westwards towards Salamanca. In an effort to maintain their turning movement, the French edged more to the south and, finding Huerta unoccupied, crossed the Tormes during the evening of 21 July. Nearer Salamanca, the Allies, too, had passed to the south bank and, doused by a tremendous thunderstorm, spent the night deploying on the terrain where General Bock had fought the indecisive action of 24 June. Though neither side appreciated it, the scene was set for one of the most decisive and controversial battles of the war, and few could have imagined that before the sun would set again Marmont's mighty army would be dashed to pieces.

II   The Battle of Salamanca

It is evident from their correspondence that neither commander expected a major battle to develop on 22 July.[359] Wellington planned to continue his retreat and Marmont his turning movements. Indeed, due to the wooded and undulating terrain, the armies were largely obscured from one another and it was only when he spotted the Allied Seventh Division that Marmont ordered a limited engagement to molest his opponent's expected retreat. A heavy skirmish erupted as Foy's *voltigeurs* tried to dislodge the 2nd *Cacadores* and the 68th Foot from their positions around Nuestra Senora de la Peña. Bonnet's division, meanwhile, worked its way south and secured the hills of the Southern Arapiles which Marmont had selected as the 'pivot on which the flanking movement should be made'.[360] The rest of the marshal's units now passed behind these troops and gradually began to edge their way westwards.

Wellington, meanwhile, was bringing the last of his units onto the south bank of the Tormes and, seeing the French manoeuvres, drew his army up in an L-shape, with Cole's division – opposite Bonnet – forming the angle and the arms extending north and west. As the bulk of the Allied reserves shifted to the right of the new line, Marmont, watching from the Southern Arapiles, became convinced that his opponent was retreating and strengthened his forces on the left ready to molest the withdrawal.[361] Maucune's division deployed in front of the village of Arapiles and, at 2 pm, attacked it with artillery and skirmishers. A vigorous exchange was soon under way and, as Maucune pushed forward, the battalions of Thomières slipped behind the fighting line and moved off towards Miranda. Clausel, meanwhile, marched up from behind Bonnet's men and deployed on Maucune's right.

While all this manoeuvring was still going on, Wellington was busy making the final adjustments to his own dispositions and snatching a bite of lunch. Anticipating a serious assault against the Arapiles village, he disengaged the Seventh Division from its bickering with Foy and, leaving the Light Division in its stead, moved it across to support the right wing. This section of his line now consisted of most of his army: in addition to Alten's light brigades, only the First Division had been left on the northern part of the L-shaped front. However, having massed some five infantry divisions and five cavalry brigades, Wellington was still awaiting the expected French onslaught when the growing gap between the formations of Maucune and Thomières was brought to his attention. Casting a cursory glance through his telescope, he immediately came

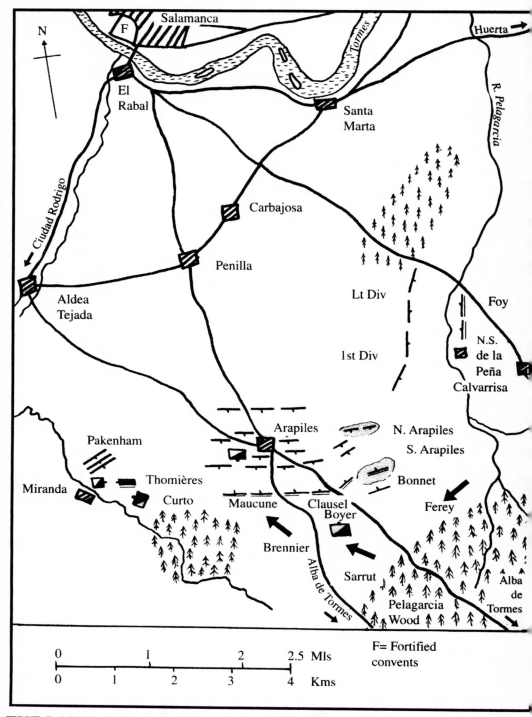

THE BATTLE OF SALAMANCA – THE BEGINNING OF MARMONT'S MANOEUVRE

to a momentous decision and, with the words 'This will do at last, I think', galloped off to launch an all-out attack.[362]

Wellington's sudden resolve to switch to the offensive had been brought about by a reckless oversight on the part of his adversary. As Jourdan later observed: 'It is evident that the Marshal, in order to menace the Allies' retreat, extended his left much too far.'[363] From Thomières' units – who were *still* moving west – to the fighting between Foy and Alten, there was a distance of six miles, and much of the front was totally undefended. Wellington's forces, by way of contrast, lay in a compact block, perfectly poised to launch a sudden blow against the dispersed enemy divisions. As a result of this tragic misjudgement by their usually cautious commander, the 'Army of Portugal' was about to be assailed and subsequently destroyed almost piecemeal.

The attack was opened by D'Urban's Portuguese cavalry, who, screened by the broken terrain, suddenly intercepted Thomières' line of march. The leading regiment of the French division – the 101st Line – was caught patently unprepared for action and, struggling to deploy into battle order, opened an ineffective fire. At that moment, Pakenham's Third Division arrived to support D'Urban's horse and, ploughing into Thomières' right flank, routed his whole formation. Curto's cavalry hastened to stem this collapse, but their untrained horses proved incapable of effective manoeuvre and, after a couple of feeble assaults on the infantry of Pakenham's right, the horsemen turned their unwieldly mounts about and vanished as quickly as they had appeared.

With nothing before them now but Thomières' disorientated infantry, D'Urban and Pakenham ruthlessly pursued their adversaries and, in minutes, Thomières was dead, his artillery was taken and half his men were killed, wounded or captured. At about this time, Marmont – trying to regroup his army from his post on the Southern Arapiles – was seriously wounded by an exploding shell. His successor, General Bonnet, was likewise cut down moments later and dozens of aides were dispatched to advise the unfortunate Clausel that he was now in charge. While this break in command must have aggravated the army's disorder, Marmont's later insistence that it was *the* decisive factor does not, however, stand up to examination. As Foy observed in his recollection of the battle:

The Duke of Ragusa committed us to the action – he brought it on contrary to Clausel's advice. The left was already checked when he received his wound, by which time it was impossible either to refuse to fight or to give the fight a good direction. All that could be done was to attenuate the disaster – that Clausel did. There was no

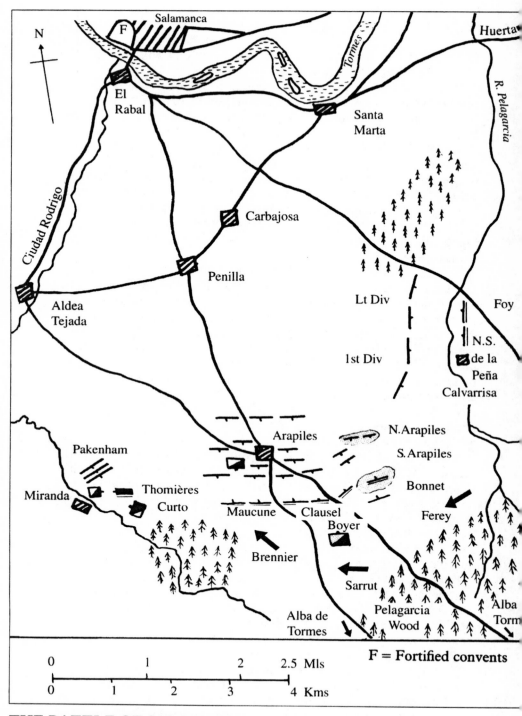

THE BATTLE OF SALAMANCA –
WELLINGTON'S COUNTER-ATTACK

gap in the command – we should have been no better off if the marshal had never been hurt.[364]

While Pakenham was crushing the French left wing, the Fourth and Fifth Divisions had moved against the enemy's centre, and bitter fighting had broken out south of Arapiles. Screened by a swarm of Allied skirmishers, Cole's division engaged Clausel's men while Leith's brigades rolled forward to try conclusions with Maucune. As the massed light troops swarmed onto the plateau, the French *voltigeurs* and artillery withdrew and, expecting to be assailed by the advancing Allied cavalry, Maucune pulled his regiments back and redeployed them into squares. Minutes later the British line loomed over the horizon and was greeted by a series of blistering volleys. Down crashed Leith and 300 men, but the retaliatory fire of the Anglo-Portuguese units broke up the squares and caused them to waver. Catching the enemy at this opportune moment, General Le Marchant's 1,000 horsemen charged onto the plateau and crashed into the left flank of Maucune's retreating division.

Although desperately resisted by the 66th Line, the 4th and 5th Dragoon Guards carried all that lay before them. Soon, half of Maucune's battalions were scattered and, bringing up the 3rd Dragoons, Le Marchant searched for fresh prey. He quickly found Brennier's vanguard, who, hurrying forward to support their comrades, were caught in columns of march. Bursting from the hordes of fugitives, the British troopers were only ten yards away when the startled Frenchmen opened fire and sent a quarter of them plunging from their saddles. Grievous though these losses were, the cavalry proved undaunted and waded into the enemy's midst. The plight of the courageous foot troops was hopeless from the outset and, after offering stubborn resistance for some minutes, they yielded and fled to the east, losing scores of prisoners. Nevertheless, elements of the shattered battalions refused to acknowledge defeat and, rallying on the edge of the woods, reformed and advanced. This provoked the cavalry into charging again and though, this time, the French were irretrievably broken, several more dragoons were slain, including Le Marchant.

As the Third and Fifth Divisions gathered in their prisoners, the broken French formations streamed eastwards. However, conspicuous among them were four regiments that maintained their order and, executing a fighting withdrawal, united with Curto's cavalry. His troopers now urged their unwieldy mounts to advance a second time and, falling on the disordered Allied horsemen, scored their first successes of the day. Having checked their adversaries – if only temporarily – the determined Frenchmen continued their withdrawal and retired to the rear of Clausel's embattled units.

Unlike his colleagues to the west, that general was in the ascendancy: while the Allies had emerged triumphant from their combat with the French left, he and Bonnet had redeemed the situation in the centre and were now mounting a counter-attack to sweep the Fourth Division from the field. The rot had begun to the east of Arapiles, where Pack's Portuguese had assailed Bonnet's battalions. Advancing through the rye fields towards the French position, the leading regiment – the 4th *Cacadores* – was devastated by a volley and hurled back with the bayonet. Soon, Pack's grenadiers and line regiments had also been overthrown, allowing Bonnet's troops to turn to their left and attack the startled Cole. Already locked in a gruesome fire-fight with the determined troops of Clausel, this proved too much for the wavering Fourth Division. An extemporised flank guard of the 7th *Cacadores* was swept away and, as Bonnet's regiments hurtled into contact, Cole's men faltered. Grasping his chance, Clausel, too, ordered the charge and, as the Imperial attacks converged on their line, the redcoats fled.

Clausel could now either retire his battalions and cover the withdrawal of the army, or he could press his advantage and thrust into the midst of Wellington's line. For better or worse, he chose the latter option and, calling up Boyer's dragoon division, urged his men after Cole. Initially, the attack enjoyed considerable success and, with Cole badly wounded and his units in headlong retreat, Clausel and Bonnet rolled forward, quashing intermittent pockets of resistance. However, as Wellington committed his massive reserves, the tide turned. The Third and Seventh Divisions came up on Clausel's left, and the Sixth Division moved to bar Bonnet's path. Simultaneously, Campbell led his First Division in a counter-attack on the Southern Arapiles and, as the outnumbered defenders retired, captured the artillery battery there. After a heated musketry exchange, Bonnet was halted and, as his colleague's battalions retired in confusion, Clausel, too, went to the rear. His bid to break the Allied line had failed and, now, with his forces on the verge of being destroyed, his one hope lay in retreat.

The situation facing the 'Army of Portugal' was parlous. All the formations of the left and centre were in retreat, and the only intact unit left covering them was the hard-pressed division of Sarrut. However, as these men neared collapse, the regiments of Ferey arrived to save the day. Deploying seven of his nine battalions into three-deep lines, Ferey posted his remaining troops in squares to cover his wings. Then, from his position on the edge of the Pelagarcia Wood, he poured a volley into the advancing Sixth Division, laying low some 800 men and sending the rest reeling back.

Suspending their pursuit of the broken 'Army of Portugal', the massed Allied divisions turned on Ferey and the edge of the forest was soon a sheet of flame. 'The cruel fire cost us many lives', recalled one French officer,

> and, at last, slowly, and after having given nearly an hour's respite to the remainder of the army, Ferey gave back, still protected by his flanking squares, to the very edge of the forest where he halted our half-destroyed division. Formed in line, it still presented a respectable front, and stood – despite the English batteries which enfiladed us with a thundering fire.[365]

Desperate to end this obstinate resistance, Wellington ordered forward Rezende's Portuguese, supported by the rest of Clinton's division and, as our diarist recalls, another bitter struggle ensued:

> Formed right up against the trees, no longer with any artillery to help, we saw the enemy marching against us in two lines, the first of which was composed of Portuguese. . . . We fired first, the moment that they got within range, and the volleys that we delivered from our first two ranks were so heavy and continuous that, although they tried to give us back fire for fire, the whole melted away. The second line was coming up behind – this was English. We should have tried to receive it in the same way, still holding our ground though enfiladed by artillery, but suddenly the left of our line ceased firing and fell back into the wood in complete disorder.[366]

Ferey's brave resistance had been curtailed by the pressure on his flank from the Fifth Division. For losses of 1,000 men – including Ferey himself – the French battalions had secured their colleagues' retreat and had all but wrecked the brigades of Clinton. The remnants of the Imperial rearguard executed a fighting withdrawal through the rambling woods and, uniting with Foy who had marched down swiftly from the north, followed the rest of the army towards the bridge at Alba.

The final phase of the battle at Salamanca is shrouded in controversy. Believing Alba to be occupied by a Spanish garrison, Wellington thought the French were trapped and, as he later told Graham, 'When I lost sight of them in the dark, I marched upon Huerta . . . and they went by Alba. If I had known there had been no garrison in Alba, I should have marched there, and should probably have had the whole.'[367]

Superficially, this is reasonable. There had been part of a Spanish division in Alba, but they had retired on 20 July at Marmont's approach and had apparently neglected to advise Wellington of their move: they realised no more than he did that a major battle was imminent and could not foresee the town's subsequent strategic value. There are, however, other points to be made regarding Wellington's claim. Firstly, the scale of the pursuit that he mounted appears to have been remarkably small. Tomkinson confirms that the cavalry was hardly involved[368] and Wellington himself states 'I pursued them with the First and Light Divisions . . . and Anson's brigade of the Fourth Division, and some squadrons of cavalry . . .'[369] As Cole's battalions had suffered badly and the Light Division had been fighting nearly all day, it is difficult to see how this force could have been either strong or fresh enough to stage an effective pursuit. Moreover, this last remark by Wellington only complicates the issue further; for Foy reveals that he was followed by the Light Division towards *Alba* for several miles[370] and so why Huerta should have been seen as the enemy's objective is baffling. Everything suggested that the French were retreating to Alba and a vigorous drive in that direction would have incommoded them – whether the town was occupied by the Spanish or not. The truth, one suspects, is that Wellington mishandled the pursuit and attempted to blame his error on his Spanish allies.

Nevertheless, Salamanca was his greatest victory yet. For losses of around 4,800 men, he had inflicted 13,000 casualties. The 'Army of Portugal' had lost 6,000 in slain and wounded; the latter group including Marmont, Clausel and Bonnet, whilst Ferey and Thomières were both killed. In addition to 7,000 prisoners, the Allies captured twenty pieces of ordnance, eight standards and a vast amount of equipment. As a magnanimous General Foy was later to confess: 'This battle is the most cleverly fought, the largest in scale, the most important in results, of any that the English have won in recent times. It brings up Lord Wellington's reputation almost to the level of that of Marlborough.'[371]

III   The March to Madrid

Dawn on 23 July revealed that the French had, indeed, retreated through Alba and the Allies set out in pursuit, Bock and Anson's cavalry leading the way. On nearing Garcia Hernandez, Wellington spotted a brigade of Curto's *chasseurs* and, failing to notice Foy's infantry division in a dip in the ground, launched his cavalry at the retiring horsemen. As Bock's 770 KGL dragoons spurred after them they encountered an enemy infantry regiment, deploying in square, on their left. A volley from the Imperial troops shattered the leading squadron and the rest of the startled German cavalry had to wheel sharply to face this new threat. Two further salvoes peppered their ranks and, for a time, it seemed that, as usual, the square would triumph. However, on this occasion the cavalry proved to be in luck. As one of their number crashed to the ground his mount rolled into the infantry and, crushing the Frenchmen in its path, bulldozed a hole through their ranks. The rest of the dragoons promptly converged on this gap and, pouring into the square, completed its discomfiture; scores of the foot troops surrendering at once.

However, this remarkable action was not yet over. Having witnessed the demise of the 76th Line, the next regiment of Foy's division – the 6th *Léger* – moved off, in column, onto higher ground to the east. The dragoons gave chase and, as their adversaries galloped up the hill, the infantry struggled to form square, letting off a few wild volleys. The rear companies of the column had not finished redeploying when the cavalry waded into them and, after a confused *mêlée*, the foot troops scattered. The front of the column had, meantime, succeeded in forming an imperfect square but, disordered by fugitives from the scrimmage on the lower slopes, melted away as the cavalry approached; dozens more prisoners were taken.

Intoxicated by their own success, the cavalry now wheeled against Foy's two remaining regimental squares. But the outcome of this clash was a more familiar story. Unable to break the hedge of bayonets, the frustrated dragoons were blasted with musketry and, after losing dozens of men, fled in confusion. Nevertheless, the action had been a triumph for the Allied cavalry who, for losses of around 130 men, had inflicted nearly 1,000 casualties on Foy, exterminating half of his dispirited division. Thankful to have escaped at last, the French general set out after the main army and, after a few miles, united with the long-awaited reinforcements from the 'Army of the North'. This cavalry brigade – all Caffarelli could spare – covered the retreat of the French through Penaranda and, moving at an extraordinary pace, soon left the pursuing Allies far behind.[372]

Caffarelli's column was, however, not the only force moving to succour Marmont: King Joseph, too, was on the march with almost all of his 'Army of the Centre' and Palombini's division of the 'Army of Aragon'. Realising that Soult, Suchet and Caffarelli were unable or unwilling to assist the 'Army of Portugal' on any appreciable scale, he had scraped together 14,000 troops and set out from Madrid to do the job himself. The disruption of the French communications by the guerillas had, however, been so effective of late that Marmont had no idea that the king was on his way, and when the 'Army of the Centre' arrived at Espinar on 23 July its commander received his first reliable report of the battle at Salamanca.

It was evident that the 'Army of Portugal' had been crushingly defeated and that the Allies were now in full march for the heart of the Peninsula. Deciding that to join Clausel would be pointless, Joseph retreated to bar the enemy's approach to his capital and left the 'Army of Portugal' to complete its withdrawal towards Burgos. On hearing that the king had retired to Madrid, Wellington resolved to pursue Clausel and, urging Santocildes and Silveira to close in along the Douro, set his forces in motion for Valladolid, which the French hastily evacuated on the afternoon of 30 July. Having garrisoned it with a large Spanish contingent, however, Wellington now decided that the advantages offered by marching on Madrid outweighed those of any other course of action. Accordingly, leaving General Clinton with 18,000 men to hold the line of the Douro and observe Clausel's army, he took his remaining 36,000 effectives and, by 10 August, had reached the Guadarrama.

Joseph, meanwhile, was trying to get his subordinates to release enough men to rescue Clausel and save Madrid. He had been urging Soult to send troops for days and, on 6 July, had ordered him to dispatch a powerful contingent to join the 'Army of the Centre' at Toledo.[373] But Soult had flagrantly disobeyed, and replied with a suggestion that the king should abandon northern Spain and join in a campaign against Hill in Estremadura. This took the monarch's strained relations with the marshal to breaking point and, indeed, in the acrimonious correspondence that followed, he suggested that Soult resign.[374] He refused, however, and, disregarding further orders to evacuate Andalusia and support the forces reeling before Wellington, clung to his position until the end of August.

But by then Madrid was lost. As Wellington approached, the French struggled to evacuate the trappings of their four-year occupation: the Royal household, innumerable officials, masses of paperwork, the treasury, art collections, tons of *matériel* and dozens of *Afrancesados*. It was slow work and, in a forlorn attempt to retard the Allies' advance, Joseph dispatched Treillard's cavalry division.

The vanguard of Wellington's army – D'Urban's seven Portuguese squadrons, the KGL heavy dragoons, a horse artillery battery and a battalion of light infantry – was camped at Majalahonda when the massed French cavalry suddenly attacked. The line formed by D'Urban's Portuguese was cut to pieces and, capturing the Allied cannon, the Imperial horsemen surged into the village of Las Rosas and fell on the KGL dragoons as they deployed. In the ensuing scrimmage the French got the upper hand. However, as the KGL light infantry commenced a galling fire from the safety of the buildings and Wellington's main force came hurrying down the highway, the Imperial troopers retreated, abandoning the captured guns. Their losses in this short, sharp action were not particularly severe. The Allied casualties, on the other hand, were over 200 men.

This small success, however, could not save Madrid. With the enemy at hand in overwhelming strength, the king fled to Ocaña, leaving 2,000 men in the Retiro arsenal and a large number of immovable sick. The Allies entered the city on 12 August and received a tumultuous welcome from the inhabitants. Totally isolated, with no fresh water and inadequate food stocks, the garrison on the Retiro soon found themselves in dire straits and, when Wellington made preparations for an assault, meekly surrendered. Thus, the colossal military stores passed into Allied hands and the liberation of Madrid came to a bloodless conclusion.

IV A Dozen Diversions

Meanwhile, the other Allied forces had been implementing Wellington's diversions. We left Hill facing d'Erlon's corps in Estremadura. Hill had some 19,000 Anglo-Portuguese troops, plus 4,000 Spaniards, deployed south of Merida and west of the Matachel. Beyond the river – keeping well to the east in the wake of the raid on Almaraz – lay d'Erlon and Daricau's divisions, supported by Lallemand's dragoons. With only 12,000 troops, d'Erlon was content to stay on the defensive and only when Hill received Wellington's directive to press Soult did the period of relative tranquillity end.

The new bout of Allied operations was actually opened by Ballesteros. Slipping out of Gibraltar early in May, the wily Spaniard marched his 9,000 men over the mountains to Bornos where Conroux's French division was based. Screened by mist, the Spanish surprised the hostile outpost, gaining some initial success. However, although outnumbered by two to one, the French general rallied his men and drove the enemy from the field with a series of spirited counter-attacks. Ballesteros lost four cannon and 1,500 men; French casualties totalled 500.

The latest incursion by this persistent nuisance provoked Soult into making preparations for a second attempt to capture Tarifa and crush the raiders. However, the preliminary operations had barely begun when Hill – seeking to distract the marshal – again advanced on d'Erlon and compelled Soult to hurry westwards.

On 11 June – two days before Wellington opened his offensive –
Hill's vanguard, passing through Llerena, encountered elements of
Lallemand's division whom Slade's heavy cavalry promptly overthrew and pursued for several miles. Suddenly, however, the British
regiments – the 1st 'Royal' Dragoons and the 3rd Dragoon Guards –
were assailed by Lallemand's reserve squadron. This audacious little
band hurled themselves against the enemy's flank and, routing
Slade's exhausted troopers, bought their main force time to rally. As
the whole of Lallemand's division joined the *mêlée* Slade's troopers
became the hunted party and, chased for four miles, suffered
appalling losses. Wellington was infuriated by the incident which, he
told Hill, was due to

> The trick our . . . cavalry have acquired of galloping at every thing,
> and . . . galloping back as fast. . . . They never consider their
> situation, never think of manoeuvring before an enemy – so little
> that one would think they cannot manoeuvre excepting on
> Wimbledon Common. . . . The Royals and the 3rd dragoon guards
> were the best regiments in this country, and it annoys me par-
> ticularly that the misfortune has happened to them. I do not
> wonder at the French boasting of it . . . [375]

This humiliating episode was the last major clash between d'Erlon
and Hill. The latter, having distracted Soult, retraced his steps and
the two armies encamped on the very ground they had held in May.
Ballesteros, meanwhile, raided Malaga. But, pursued by Generals
Leval and Villatte, he was unable to regain Gibraltar and so he turned
into central Andalusia, attacking Osuna before slipping away once
more.

The war in this region was, however, rapidly drawing to an end. In
mid-August Soult received news of Salamanca and, faced with
Joseph's increasingly uncompromising directives, realised he could
not delay forsaking Andalusia any longer. Accordingly, the
province's evacuation was immediately begun and, by the twenty-
sixth, an enormous convoy of troops, booty and *Afrancesados* was
streaming from Seville. The demolition of the Cadiz lines was started
forthwith and d'Erlon was ordered to retire. Soon, all 50,000 men of
Soult's army were trekking east and, advancing in their wake, Hill
and Ballesteros finally liberated the south.

In northern Spain, Admiral Popham and the guerilla bands had,
meanwhile, mounted a vigorous offensive to prevent Caffarelli from
sending any significant aid to the 'Army of Portugal'. Caffarelli had
some 35,000 troops scattered in garrisons and little contingents
across the north-east provinces. To oppose them, Popham had two

battleships, five frigates and a flotilla of transport vessels onto which he loaded some 11,000 Anglo-Spanish marines. As Wellington advanced from the Agueda and Marmont began the concentration of his army, Popham set sail from Corunna, while the guerillas of the Asturias – now unhindered by the French – moved into Old Castile and Navarre to unite with the other insurgents.

On 21 June, Popham began his raids on the scattered detachments of the 'Army of the North'. Using his warships to support his marines and the guerillas who came down to the coast, he attacked a series of French installations including the garrisons of Lequeitio, Guetaria and Portugalette. Not all these raids were successful, but they did prevent Caffarelli from sending assistance to the 'Army of Portugal'. Having drawn the attention of his adversary to his interests in the east, the admiral now took advantage of the flexibility of maritime transport to shift his forces west to Santander. Unable to match this ease of movement, Caffarelli marched reinforcements to the threatened sector, only to find that, after a lengthy struggle, the garrison had relinquished the city to the enemy. Over the next few weeks, Popham turned this port into a major base for Allied operations and Santander replaced Lisbon as the corner-stone of Wellington's logistical system, giving Allied forces operating in the north the advantages of much shorter communications and closer logistical support.

Popham's raids, however, did not conclude with the seizure of Santander. On 13 August, his forces descended on Bilbao in overwhelming strength and obliged the French to evacuate that, too. Shortly after, a second attempt was made to capture Guetaria, but the Imperial garrison again held firm. Caffarelli, meanwhile, had marched on Bilbao with 7,000 men and regained it after a grim, two-day battle. But Popham had achieved his objective: the 'Army of the North' sent only a brigade of cavalry to the 'Army of Portugal' and even that arrived too late for the battle at Salamanca.[376]

The remaining major diversion arranged by Wellington was the landing of Maitland's Anglo-Sicilian forces in Catalonia. As we have seen, Suchet had been relatively inactive since he had taken Valencia in January. His army was overstretched by its commitments and, faced by the remnants of Mahy's forces (12,000 troops under José O'Donnell, supported by 4,000 more at Alicante and over 4,000 British and Spanish at Cartagena), he was already unwilling to advance his feeble field force beyond the River Xucar when he received warning of Maitland's approach from Majorca. Thus, when King Joseph asked him to send a column to Marmont's assistance he bluntly refused.

Indeed, Suchet's position was generally deteriorating. Aragon remained as rebellious as ever, and General Lacy's 8,000-strong division mounted increasingly daring raids on Decaen's vulnerable garrisons in Catalonia; one attack, on 16 July, nearly cost the French control of Lerida. Within two weeks, Maitland's 11,000 men landed at Palamos and Decaen's position became still more precarious.

But Maitland's stay was short-lived, for disaster had befallen O'Donnell's Murcian army. Anxious to provide Wellington with the diversion he sought and doubting that Mailand would arrive in time, O'Donnell had taken the offensive alone, attacking Harispe's division at Castalla on 21 July – the eve of Salamanca. With just his own infantry and Delort's cavalry, Harispe could pit only 5,000 men against the 11,000 Spaniards, but O'Donnell had divided his corps into three widely separated bodies and when the armies first clashed his flanking units were still some distance away. Thus, Harispe was able to concentrate against O'Donnell's central column alone. Nevertheless, the Spanish still enjoyed a considerable numerical advantage and Delort was soon dislodged from the town. However, as Harispe's regiments came up, the Imperial cavalry led a ferocious counter-attack and swept O'Donnell's men out of the settlement and onto the plain beyond, where they broke into retreat. Witnessing this, O'Donnell's approaching wings also turned and, pursued by their exuberant foes, fled to Alicante.[377]

The Spanish losses in this disaster exceeded 3,000 men; Harispe's were under 200. Moreover, the Murcians' morale was so badly shaken that it was clear to Maitland that they would be *hors de combat* for weeks. Without their support an offensive would be unwise, so he re-embarked and sailed for Alicante. Assimilating the Anglo-Spanish garrison, he assembled 15,000 troops,[378] but still declined to advance for his army lacked proper logistical support. Furthermore, Maitland had heard the news of Salamanca and Joseph's retreat southwards. With rumours that Soult was retiring eastwards, it seemed that 80,000 Imperial troops were about to concentrate before him. Daunted he resolved to remain at Alicante until Wellington could send fresh orders.

Chapter XXIII

MADRID AND MOSCOW

I Temporary Triumph

We left Wellington and the main Allied army occupying Madrid. Following the surrender of the Retiro on 14 August, the British commander spent several days in deliberating his opponents' next move. Great difficulty was encountered in establishing exactly what the French were about: it was rumoured that Soult was evacuating Andalusia, but no confirmation of this was available until the end of the month; Clausel's movements were also shrouded in doubt. Although it seemed more than probable that the enemy were amassing a colossal army to oust the Allies from the capital, Wellington judged that several weeks would pass before any French offensive could materialise and, directing Hill to bring his contingent up to Madrid, he resolved to pursue Clausel in an effort to inflict further damage on the battered 'Army of Portugal'.

Marching north with 21,000 men, Wellington joined Clinton at Arevalo on 3 September. To his astonishment, he discovered that Clausel had been anything but inactive. The French general – anxious to relieve the pressure on King Joseph and determined to rescue the beleaguered garrisons of Zamora, Toro and Astorga – had rallied his army with lightning speed and had re-equipped it with *matériel* drawn from the enormous depots at Burgos. He had then given his reorganised regiments a rest and endeavoured to rebuild their morale. As he explained to the Minister of War on 6 August: 'It is usual to see an army disheartened after a defeat, but it would be hard to find one whose discouragement is greater than that of these troops.'[379] Nevertheless, Clausel persevered and, leaving behind the worst of his units, he set out on 13 August with 25,000 men.

This sudden counter-offensive by their supposedly beaten adversaries caught Clinton and Santocildes off their guard and, while the Galician general forsook Valladolid, Clinton's 7,000 men retreated from Cuellar to Arevalo. The French moved with remarkable speed to consolidate their advantage: Foy thrust down the Douro to Toro and rescued the garrison and, after demolishing the fortifications, headed for Astorga, intending to relieve its defenders, too. Finding it had fallen on 18 August, he turned on the fleeing Santocildes and cut up his rearguard in a relentless march on Zamora; relieving its beleaguered garrison on 26 August. Reducing the fortifications there to rubble, Foy, rejecting the temptation of a raid on the Allied depots at Salamanca, then retraced his steps, reuniting with Clausel at Valladolid on 4 September.

Staggered by this whirlwind of operations, Wellington called on Santocildes to return to Valladolid while he set out in pursuit of Clausel who had begun to retire. But the chase was conducted with anything but vigour: the Allied army moved at an average speed of only six miles per day and Clausel soon outstripped them. Leaving the garrison of Burgos to fend for itself, he withdrew to await reinforcements.

II Blunders at Burgos

Abandoning the chase, Wellington invested Burgos on the morning of 19 September. The castle, which lay on a towering hill dominating the city, had been ruined by fire in 1736, but had been reconstructed on Napoleon's orders. Although lack of money had prevented the completion of the work, the fortress was in reasonable order and defended by 2,000 bayonets under General Dubreton. As it doubled as a depot for the 'Army of the North', it was exceptionally well stocked with rations and ammunition, and was perfectly capable of resisting the Allies until Clausel could come to its relief. While, in view of the developing strategic situation, it is not clear what Wellington hoped to gain by its seizure, he had resolved to take the fortress – a task which he evidently believed could be easily accomplished; for, notwithstanding the sanguinary lessons that virtually all his sieges had given him and the availability of scores of heavy cannon captured at Ciudad Rodrigo and Madrid, he brought up only eight heavy guns to breach the defences. This force was to prove lamentably inadequate and, in this and other aspects of the operation, Wellington's complacency and ineptitude were to cost his troops dear.

Before they could attack Burgos itself, the Allies had to capture an outlying hornwork that commanded the only viable approach to the fortress. Wellington recklessly neglected to bother with any preliminary bombardment and simply sent forward Pack's Portuguese brigade and elements of the First Division. Advancing under a full

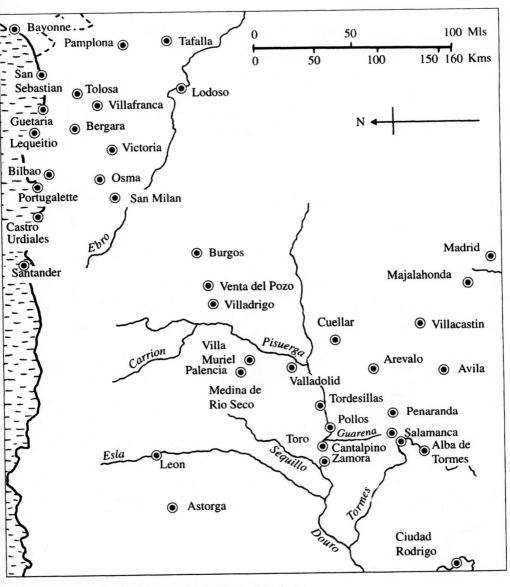

WELLINGTON'S OFFENSIVES, 1812–13:
THEATRE OF OPERATIONS

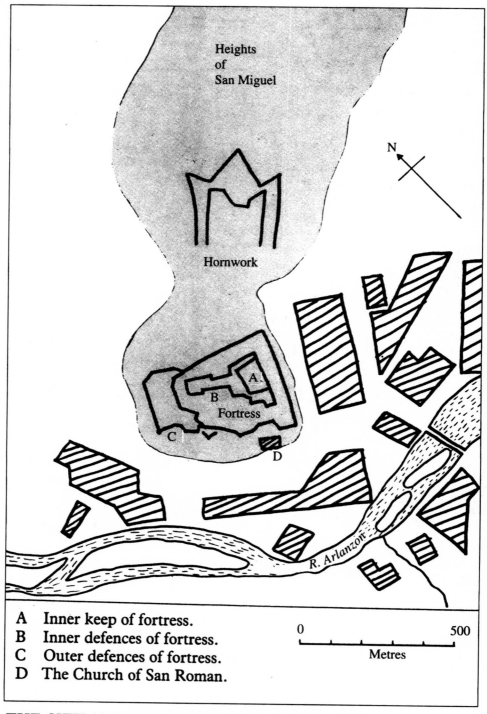

A Inner keep of fortress.
B Inner defences of fortress.
C Outer defences of fortress.
D The Church of San Roman.

0   500
Metres

THE CITY AND FORTRESS OF BURGOS AT THE
TIME OF WELLINGTON'S SIEGE

moon, they were immediately spotted by the French and subjected to heavy fire which, in moments, cost the 42nd Foot alone over 200 men, while Pack's exposed formations sustained another 100 casualties. Fortunately for Wellington, as the principal assault wave recoiled in disorder some light troops from the First Division managed to scramble into the back of the hornwork. Opening fire on the rear of the defenders, they plunged them into panic and, as they fled into Burgos, the Allies overran the position. This gave Wellington early control of the outpost; but he had again been saved by the lucky success of a minor attack and the casualty list – over 400 men – was an enormous price to pay.

The fortress itself was now open to attack and, under heavy fire, the Allies began erecting their first batteries. However, before these cannons had come into action, Wellington, encouraged by his success at the hornwork, launched his infantry in an attack on the castle's outer walls. This was beaten off with the contempt it deserved: without any bombardment to pave their way, the First and Sixth Divisions were hurled at the defences and, unable to penetrate the stronghold's perimeter, sustained nearly 200 casualties. As the broken battalions poured back, Wellington finally realised that a full siege operation would be required. Accordingly, on 23 September, he reluctantly comenced a parallel against the castle's western front and, pushing a sap towards the enemy's positions, placed a thousand-pound mine beneath the foundations of the wall. On 29 September this was detonated and a storm-party rushed forward to assail the expected breach. To their dismay, they found the walls intact and, scattered by the defenders' fire, fled back to their parallel with loss. Apparently, in constructing the sap, the Allied engineers had encountered the remnants of part of the ruined, ancient fortress and, taking this derelict stonework to be the *existing* wall, had buried their mine beneath it. Consequently, on exploding, it demolished the buried ruins, but left the current perimeter of the Burgos castle quite undamaged.

Infuriated by this humiliating reverse, Wellington directed his engineers to construct a new sap; insisting, this time, that they get their mathematics right. To help create what, he hoped, would be a major breach, he shifted his diminutive force of heavy ordnance about and erected a three-gun battery directly before the intended point of assault. Dawn on 1 October revealed this to the French and, pouring a concentrated fire onto the unfinished redoubt, they soon destroyed two of the cannons and wiped out most of the crews. By the following day, after tremendous exertions, the besiegers had dragged forward replacement ordnance but, replied to by the skilful French gunners, that too was destroyed in minutes.

Sending to Santander for more guns, Wellington persevered. By 4 October the new mine was ready and, supported by the fire of the remaining heavy ordnance, blew a considerable gap in the north-west wall. Storming-parties advanced and, after bitter fighting in which they sustained over 220 casualties, established a foothold within the outer defences. However, no sooner had the digging towards the inner wall begun than Dubreton launched a sudden foray against the toiling Allied troops. Before anybody realised what was happening, the French were in the trenches and, in the confused *mêlée* that followed, nearly 150 of the besiegers were hacked down, their equipment was destroyed or carried off and the excavations seriously damaged. Shaken by this bloody check, the Allies plodded forward. But they had barely made good the damage from the first French attack when Dubreton struck back with another sortie. Again, the Imperial troops took their opponents unawares and, as well as inflicting 184 casualties, did enormous damage to the besiegers' excavations before retreating with minimal losses.

Wellington's position was looking decidedly bad. His few pieces of heavy ordnance were proving inadequate to their task and their numbers were diminishing on an almost daily basis. Moreover, the stocks of powder and ammunition were now so low that the besiegers were reduced to firing back any French shot that fell in their positions. Rain began to fall in torrents – flooding the excavations – and, with the news that Souham (who had replaced the ailing Clausel) was astir, Wellington resolved that an assault must be attempted.

Accordingly, on 18 October, the British engineers fired a mine they had planted in the outlying Chapel of San Roman and, in the wake of this distraction, foot troops hurried forward to assail the western and northern walls. On the latter front, the tiny rupture that the cannon had created was easily defended and the attacking columns soon melted away before the constant fusillade that poured from the ramparts. The assault on the western wall, too, was equally ineffective and, leaving 170 killed and wounded, the beaten Allied infantry fled back to their sodden trenches.

His final stroke easily repulsed, and with Souham and Caffarelli bearing down from the north, Wellington ordered withdrawal. However, even the winding up of the siege proved calamitous: the removal of many of the heavy guns was impossible in the time available and they had to be abandoned; moreover, when the engineers attempted to demolish the captured hornwork – the sole tangible gain of the entire operation – their mines failed to explode and the position had to be left, intact, to the French.

On the morning of 22 October, Dubreton was relieved and the

scale of the Allied disaster became apparent. The garrison's casualties totalled 300 dead, and a few seriously wounded; Wellington had lost more than seven times this number, plus a good deal of equipment. The whole operation had been a tragic farce and had served no useful purpose.[380] Now, as an immense Imperial army advanced to regain Madrid, the scattered Allied forces were pressed into headlong retreat.

III Return of the King

While Wellington had been dallying at Burgos, the French had been mustering their might. Caffarelli, having contained Popham's forces with 20,000 men, brought 12,000 bayonets and sabres to unite with the 'Army of Portugal' and, when these were joined by a column from Bayonne, enabled Souham to concentrate 53,000 troops. The king, meanwhile, had united with Soult and was moving on Madrid with over 60,000 men, giving a total disposable field force in excess of 110,000.

To oppose to them, Wellington had around 73,000 men: his own force of 24,000 Anglo-Portuguese; Santocildes' 11,000 Spaniards; Hill, at Toledo, with 20,000 men; and Alten, at Madrid, with a further 18,000. Not only was the Allied army significantly outnumbered, but Wellington's move on Burgos and his erratic dispositions had also scattered it across two lengthy fronts on each of which the enemy had a marked, local superiority. Desperately worried lest Hill should be overwhelmed by Soult, Wellington frantically organised a couple of diversions to distract the marshal: Maitland's detachment was urged to press onwards to Valencia, while Ballesteros and the forces from Cadiz were to advance into La Mancha and place themselves on the flank of any westward movement that Soult might make.

However, neither manoeuvre fulfilled Wellington's hopes. Firstly, he totally overlooked Suchet's army, which was perfectly capable of containing Maitland – at least for a while. Secondly, Ballesteros' advance was delayed until November, and by that time the French had regained Madrid. On 2 October, the *Cortes* had officially made Wellington Commander-in-Chief of the Spanish armies. This infuriated Ballesteros, who, as an arch-jingoist and veteran of innumerable fights, saw the appointment of a foreigner as an insult to Spain, her generals and her Army. He bluntly refused to implement his orders, and it was only when the *Cortes* had him arrested and replaced by Del Parque that his forces moved to threaten the flank of Soult's advance. By that time, however, the marshal had passed beyond Madrid and the manoeuvre was entirely obsolete.

The day after Burgos was relieved, Souham led his divisions in pursuit of Wellington, his impressive force of 6,000 cavalry spearheading the chase. The Imperial horse were short of a talented leader and they showed an untypical lack of skill, but there were some serious clashes as the Allied rearguard – the cavalry of Anson and Bock, the Spanish lancers of Julian Sanchez, several horse artillery batteries and two battalions of KGL light infantry – were hustled out of one position after another.

The first major action took place at Venta del Pozo, where the 16th Light Dragoons were badly mauled while covering the withdrawal and were thrust back on the main body of the Allied rearguard at Villadrigo. When the bulk of their cavalry arrived, the French sent detachments – under Boyer and Faverot – to turn the enemy's flanks, while their principal force prepared to attack the Allied centre. As Faverot's troopers slipped across the stream in their front, General Cotton issued some ambiguous orders to the waiting British soldiers. His directives misunderstood, his units subsequently became intermixed and confused and, as the Imperial cavalry advanced, Cotton frantically called on his artillery to open fire. But the gunners misjudged the elevation and sent their shot flying harmlessly over the enemy. In desperation, Cotton ordered his men to meet charge with charge and the opposing blocks of cavalry – each of around 1,000 men – promptly waded into one another. After a tremendous *mêlée*, the British were put to flight. While they struggled to rally, Boyer's men appeared on their flank and completed the rout; scattering the troopers of Anson and Bock before turning to attack the KGL foot troops. This force, however, deployed in square, succeeded in stemming the collapse and, beating off their assailants, covered the withdrawal of the broken Allied detachment. Cotton's losses totalled 200 men, the French somewhat less.

Wellington's main force, meanwhile, was approaching the River Carrion whose line the British commander was planning to defend. However, the French were determined that he should be given no respite and, on 25 October, Foy attacked the Spanish division that formed the enemy's left, while Maucune's battalions crossed the river at Villa Muriel. Dislodging his opponents from Palencia, Foy inflicted heavy casualties as he drove them south. With Maucune pushing west, the Allied left was soon in danger of being encircled, and Wellington was obliged to launch a counter-attack to push Maucune back across the Carrion. Flinging four brigades into the assault, Wellington retook Villa Muriel after a period of hectic fighting. Nevertheless, he had sustained over 800 casualties –

compared with a French loss of 350 – and, more importantly, Foy's remorseless advance had completely turned the line of the river. Unable to cling to his position, the Allied commander withdrew the next day, using his left as an improvised rearguard and ingeniously swinging his army *eastwards* to place the Pisuerga between himself and the French. Taken aback, Souham spent the next couple of days in a reconnaissance of Wellington's new line. However, on 29 October, the diligent Foy managed to get a party of troops across the Douro at Tordesillas and, turning the Allied left, was rapidly reinforced by the rest of the army.

Ousted from yet another position, Wellington destroyed the bridges over the Douro behind him, forsook Valladolid and withdrew to unite with Hill. Souham, however, had abandoned the chase, for his army was dwindling. As the bulk of the occupation forces had marched west to confront Wellington, the north-east had exploded into rebellion once more and Caffarelli was obliged to retrace his steps. Deprived of his 12,000 men, Souham was unwilling to continue and, deploying the 'Army of Portugal' along the valley of the Douro, impatiently awaited Joseph's arrival.

IV Eclipse

While Wellington was retreating to Valladolid, Hill was preparing to try conclusions with Soult. The lateness of the autumn rains had kept the level of the Tagus unusually low so, as it would clearly prove no real obstacle to the advancing foe, Hill shifted his forces from Toledo to defend the Jarama river. He had not been there long when disquieting reports arrived from the north, followed, on 29 October, by a peremptory order from Wellington to abandon Madrid and retreat with all speed to the west. Hill began the withdrawal early and the following day, leaving 4,000 men, under Skerrett and Cole, to hold the Puente Larga, near Aranjuez, which had defied demolition and would give the French easy access to the west bank of the Jarama. Arriving at this bridge on the wet and gloomy morning of 30 October, Soult was unable to discern the size of the defence force but, after a couple of probing columns had been driven back, he concluded that the bridge was held in strength and contented himself with a bombardment. Dawn revealed that Cole had retreated and, followed by the 'Army of the Centre', Soult resumed his march on Madrid.

Hill, in headlong retreat, abandoned the capital by noon of 31 October. Demolishing the Retiro and burning vast quantities of food, his troops poured towards Villacastin, followed by a convoy of despondent refugees. Receiving fresh orders to proceed to Alba de Tormes, he struck west to unite with the main Allied army and, after some days, joined Wellington south of Salamanca. The French, in the meantime, had reoccupied the capital and the leading elements of the king's straggling army set off in pursuit of Hill. Uniting with Souham on 8 November, the monarch now had the troops of three entire armies at his disposal and proposed to crush Wellington. Giving Soult command of the 'Army of the Centre' as well as the 'Army of the South', Joseph also substituted d'Erlon for Souham before marching on Salamanca in search of a decisive battle. An Allied attempt to prevent him crossing the Tormes, at Alba, was thwarted by a large southward turning movement and, as his 80,000 soldiers advanced, Wellington abandoned his plans for a defensive engagement and went into precipitant retreat.

The retreat from Salamanca did untold damage to the Allied army. Already sick and weary, Wellington's men tramped along appalling roads, in the worst of the autumn weather. The hasty evacuation of the depots at Salamanca had led to a complete breakdown of the logistical system and both men and horses began to fall by the score. Wellington, only months after the triumphs of Salamanca and Madrid, faced a major calamity. However, Joseph had forsaken all ideas of a pitched battle and, to the disgust of his enthusiastic men, stopped all but Soult's cavalry from continuing the chase. Foy angrily recalled:

> We had an army stronger by a third than Wellington's and infinitely superior in cavalry and artillery. Confident expectation of victory was in every man's head. The chance had come of beating the English – perhaps of driving them from the Peninsula. This grand opportunity, so splendid, so decisive, with so few adverse chances, was allowed to slip.[381]

Foy spoke for many senior officers and the truth of his comments cannot be denied. Had Wellington been forced to fight, it is difficult to see how he could have avoided sustaining considerable losses, if not a catastrophic defeat. About 8,000 of his men had already abandoned their colours, thousands more were sick or exhausted, everybody was cold and hungry, the cavalry and artillery were virtually paralysed and, with the collapse of the logistics network, munitions were in desperately short supply. As it was, Soult's cavalry did a remarkable amount of damage, taking 600 prisoners on 16 November alone. The next day this number was doubled and included General Edward Paget – recently appointed as Wellington's second-in-command. By the end of the retreat, the Anglo-

Portuguese army had over 5,000 men missing. Many had been captured, but most had perished from exposure and hunger.

On 17 November, the Allies were finally hustled across the Huebra and, bombarding the dense columns with twenty-four guns, the French concluded their pursuit.[382] Again, the Anglo-Portuguese were fortunate to escape with relatively light losses; for the sodden ground swallowed up the shells, greatly reducing their effectiveness. Wellington wasted little time in bringing out convoys from the supply depots at Ciudad Rodrigo to feed his famished divisions, and, as his exhausted forces crawled into their winter quarters, searched for a scapegoat to blame for their recent misfortunes. Subsequently, in a disgraceful memorandum to his senior officers, he heaped unjustified criticism on everybody in the army – except himself.[383]

V The Victors and the Vanquished: The Tidings from Moscow

The condition of Wellington's army was deplorable: over 18,000 of his remaining men were on the sick-list and a tremendous amount of equipment had been lost. The state of the Spanish divisions, too, was little better and it was evident that a considerable period must elapse before fresh operations could be undertaken. In the meantime, 5,000 drafts from Britain had to be absorbed into the ranks, and Wellington – now Commander-in-Chief of the Spanish armies – also had to take in hand the reorganisation and administration of the 160,000 Spanish regular troops. Given the lamentable state of many of the Iberian units, this proved enormously difficult and was further complicated by resistance from many Spanish officers who, like Ballesteros, resented Wellington's appointment and opposed his reforms.

Clearly there were very considerable problems for the Allies to overcome. But, generally, matters were turning in their favour. The gains of the 1812 campaign far exceeded anything achieved in earlier years: in addition to the triumph of Salamanca and the temporary liberation of Madrid, the enemy had been cleared from Andalusia, Estremadura and the Asturias. Furthermore, a host of important fortresses and cities had been captured or destroyed, including Ciudad Rodrigo, Badajoz, Astorga and Seville. Although the financial difficulties of the Allied Powers – particularly Portugal – remained, the importation of Indian gold relaxed the pressure on British specie and enabled Whitehall to guarantee Wellington a monthly subsidy of at least £100,000.

After four years at the helm of the Peninsular conflict, that general enjoyed the total confidence of the Allied governments and, by the beginning of 1813, was being regularly consulted – rather than ordered – on military policy. As the tidings of Napoleon's disaster in Russia percolated through, it became clear that fresh wars in Poland and Germany were likely; a development that could have major implications for the struggle in the Peninsula. As Lord Liverpool wrote to Wellington on 22 December:

> The most formidable army ever collected by Bonaparte has been substantially destroyed ... Under these circumstances the question naturally occurs whether he will leave the French army in Spain? ... The only efficient French army at the present moment in existence is that under Soult: and whatever it may cost Bonaparte to abandon Spain, I think he will prefer that alternative to the loss of Germany.[384]

Faced with the possibility of a final confrontation with the 'Corsican Ogre' in Central Europe, the British cabinet now sought to withdraw forces from Spain to mount expeditions in Italy, Holland and Germany. This policy – limited interventionism on the fringes of Napoleon's empire – was a relic from the years preceding the Peninsular War and had invariably led to catastrophe. Adamant that its effect would be very limited and determined to maintain the pressure on the French through the vigorous second front of the Peninsula, Wellington systematically quashed most of the proposals for expeditions. Nevertheless, for all his influence, he proved unable to thwart the politicians entirely and, brushing aside his protests, the cabinet ordered 2,000 men to sail from Alicante.

As Napoleon had but a few thousand frost-bitten men to oppose to the hordes of Swedes, Russians, Prussians and, later, Austrians that threatened to overrun the heart of his empire, the British were confident that he must abandon the Peninsula and concentrate his armies for the defence of France. However, although he summoned Soult to his side and extracted a sizeable contingent from Spain, a complete withdrawal never entered his head and 200,000 French troops remained in the Peninsula. That Napoleon could afford to leave so many men on what was now regarded as a secondary front completely staggered the Allies. Totally underestimating the resilience, will-power and resourcefulness of the genius they had fought for so long, they looked on in horror as he undertook the creation of a new *Grand Armée*. Setting himself the ambitious target of having 656,000 troops in the field by mid-1813, the emperor recovered from his reverses in Russia with astonishing speed. Within a few weeks of his return to Paris, he had mustered over a third of this total and, leaving the remainder to assemble in his rear, was marching eastwards, over the Saale, by the beginning of May.

Meanwhile, having driven Wellington back to the Portuguese frontier, Joseph's forces were reoccupying central and northern Spain; the latter proving especially recalcitrant. The recent Allied offensive, coupled with Popham's raids and the incessant guerilla attacks, had turned it into a hotbed of rebellion that defied subjugation. His problems compounded by the winter weather, Caffarelli struggled to bring order to the region, but the guerilla leaders Mina and Duran alone had 14,000 men in Navarre and, within weeks, the situation was hopelessly out of control. His garrisons besieged, his troops unable to forage and the collection of taxes at a virtual standstill, Caffarelli's occupation of the north was more apparent than real. Communications between France and Madrid were effectively cut, and the passage of vital orders and information – slow at the best of times – was now reduced to a crawl. As a direct result of this, it was as late as 6 January before Joseph first heard of the retreat from Moscow and it was not until the middle of the following month that sufficient information had arrived to give a good indication of the enormity of the *débâcle*.

Among his brother's melancholy missives, Joseph received directions on the strategy to be adopted in the Peninsula. Napoleon suggested that the king should establish his headquarters at Valladolid and keep no more than a small garrison in Madrid. Attaching great importance to communications between Paris and the armies in northern Spain, the emperor was infuriated by the breakdown of order in Biscay and, directing that Caffarelli should be replaced by Clausel, who had just returned from sick-leave, ordered Joseph to detach the 'Army of Portugal' to assist in quelling the insurrection. While Clausel and the generals of the 'Army of the North' were thus employed, Gazan, who had superseded Soult, was to deploy the remaining divisions in defensive positions between Salamanca and Valladolid and contain any advance that Wellington might make.[385]

Despite the massive influx of troops, the situation in Biscay remained grim. Equipped with siege cannon by the British, Mina assaulted and captured Tafalla in February, repulsing a relief column of 3,000 men. Incensed, Clausel now drew on the 'Army of Portugal' and, sending Barbot's division in search of the guerilla, attempted to trap and destroy him. However, Barbot advanced with remarkable carelessness and, surprising his vanguard at Lodosa on 30 March, Mina inflicted nearly 1,000 casualties before bolting for the Pyrenees. Constantly harassed by their elusive foes, Clausel's battalions followed. Striking at Mina's camp in the Roncal Valley, they brought him to a general action on 12 May and, capturing his hospitals and destroying his stores, inflicted over 1,000 casualties. On the same day Foy, with another three divisions, ousted the Anglo-Spanish garrison from Castro-Urdiales and, shelling the enemy as they took to their ships, did considerable damage before they sailed out of range. Nevertheless, these two small successes were the only gains that six entire divisions secured in several weeks. Biscay remained as unruly as ever and continued to absorb a vast number of French soldiers. This, as we shall see, was to have the most appalling consequences for Joseph.

PART SIX

Nemesis by Degrees

Overleaf: Joseph Bonaparte's flight from the Battle of Vitoria
(*Photo:* BBC Hulton Picture Library)

Chapter XXIV

THE ADVANCE TO THE PYRENEES, 1813

I   The Liberation of the North

While Clausel and the guerillas were locked in their struggle for control of Biscay, Wellington was preparing an offensive to drive the French out of northern Spain altogether. 'I am certain', he wrote to Lord Bathurst on 11 May,

> that I shall never be stronger ... or more efficient than I am now; and the enemy will not be weaker. I cannot have a better opportunity for trying the fate of a battle, which, if the enemy should be unsuccessful, must oblige him to withdraw entirely.[386]

Massing every available unit, he prepared to commence this operation 'by turning the enemy's position on the Douro – by passing the left of our army over that river within the Portuguese frontier.'[387]

In addition to his scattered garrisons and detachments, the Allied commander had 81,000 Anglo-Portuguese and 21,000 Spaniards at his immediate disposal. A further 12,000 Allied troops were active in the north against Clausel's garrisons, while a corps of 14,000 more, under Henri O'Donnell, were moving to join Wellington from Cadiz. On top of this were 50,000 men opposing Suchet and, of course, the innumerable insurgents who were harassing the French in every quarter.

Calling on the Allies in Catalonia to prevent Suchet from assisting the king, Wellington divided his main army into two columns and opened his offensive at the end of May. The southern column – 30,000 men under General Hill – was set in motion some days before the northern contingent – General Graham's – and, occupying Salamanca on 26 May, seemed to the French to be the only hostile force in the region. However, having drawn the enemy's attention to the south side of the Douro, Wellington shifted the emphasis to its far bank and, ordering Graham to march, brought a further 64,000 men into play.

Anxiously plotting Hill's progress, General Daricau – whose division was encamped at Zamora – was unaware of the danger that lurked to the north-west. His cavalry had executed a sweep beyond the Esla river as recently as 20 May and, arriving only hours before Graham began to concentrate, had retired to report that all was well. Consequently, the news that a vast army was bearing down on his rear came as a complete surprise to the horrified Daricau and, abandoning Zamora, he fled east to alert the king. Graham took the town on the morning of 2 June and, thrusting down the Douro, united with Hill's vanguard at Toro the following day. By that evening the French were frantically regrouping; Wellington, having concentrated 90,000 men on the north bank of the river, was ready to implement his next move.

King Joseph hastily mustered 51,000 men in the triangle bounded by Valladolid, Medina and Tordesillas but, on realising that Wellington outnumbered him by nearly two to one, abandoned his plans for a battle and, pleading with Clausel to send reinforcements, retired towards Burgos on 3 June. Wellington had no intention of following. Predicting that his adversary would take up a defensive position along the Pisuerga, he sent little more than his cavalry after the French and, wheeling his army onto a north-easterly course, swung his divisions around the enemy's flank. Unimpressed by the feeble diversions to their front, the Imperial forces became suspicious and, anticipating the turning manoeuvre, evacuated Burgos on 13 June. Convinced that Wellington could not possibly move his army over the barren, difficult countryside to the north, Joseph now took up a fresh defensive line behind the Ebro and impatiently awaited Clausel. However, the luckless monarch was not to know that the Allies had established a logistical network on Popham's depots at Santander and were perfectly capable of advancing over the mountains. By means of hard marching and the efforts of his commissariat officers, Wellington was able to thrust forward at a staggering rate. In less than three weeks, despite the rough terrain, he traversed half of northern Spain and, by the middle of June, his main force was descending on Vitoria while his left wing was threatening Bilbao.

On 17 June, Joseph's patrols finally located the advancing Allies and, after some sharp skirmishes around Osma and San Milan,[388] the monarch realised that his position was lost and resolved to retreat once again. Although Jourdan insisted that they should unite with Suchet, the king was adamant that the Bayonne highway should be

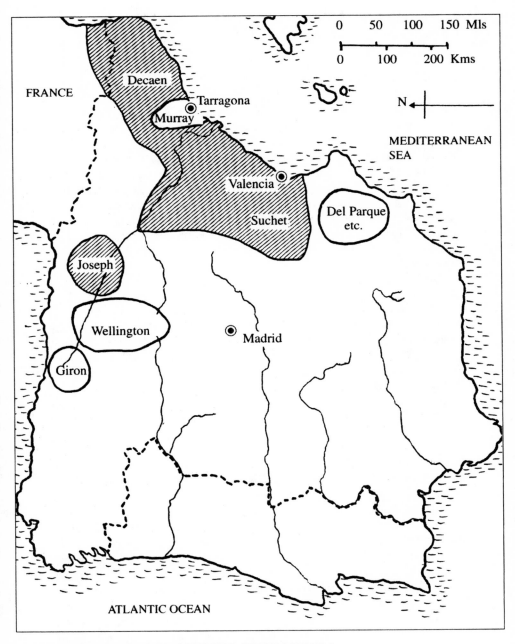

THE GENERAL STRATEGIC SITUATION,
Early June 1813

held at all costs and, selecting Vitoria as his position, began the reconcentration of his army on 19 June.

II   The Battle of Vitoria

Nevertheless, it would seem that Joseph had doubts about this course of action and was only toying with the idea of standing when attacked and compelled to fight. Certainly, his position was anything but formidable: an undulating plain – dissected by the valley of the meandering River Zadorra – with Vitoria at its eastern end. It was overlooked by hills to the north and west and, though his units had the Zadorra to protect their front, such basic precautions as the destruction of the various bridges over the river had not been taken.[389] Furthermore, the battle front – extending for nearly twelve miles – was far too long for the available forces and large sectors were very weakly defended.

Impatiently waiting for Clausel, Joseph frittered away both men and time. While vast convoys of booty, *matériel*, *Afrancesados* and other refugees were provided with generous escorts and dispatched along the highway to Bayonne, the Allied masses converged on the unsuspecting French and, by the evening of 20 June, Wellington had 80,000 men poised for the assault – over 20,000 more than Joseph had at hand. Realising that the king's forces were hopelessly overstretched, the Allied commander resolved to launch four huge columns simultaneously at his position. The first, 20,000 men under Hill, was to cross the Zadorra to the west of the hostile army and assail their left flank via the Heights of Puebla. Further north, two columns – totalling 30,000 men – were to descend on the French between Mendoza and Nanclares, while General Graham led a further 20,000 troops against Joseph's rear and flank about Yurre.

At 8 am on 21 June, Hill opened the attack on the startled foe and a bitter struggle was soon under way for the Puebla Heights. Driving Maransin's outnumbered brigade before them, the Allies made rapid progress and, when reinforcements – in the form of Conroux and Daricau's divisions – had failed to stem the collapse, Jourdan was obliged to commit elements of Villatte's formation. However, while the French staff were striving to contain the enemy on their left, the roar of cannon, further east, announced the beginning of Graham's drive on Yurre. Unable to hold back the great masses of enemy troops, Sarrut's division of Reille's 'Army of Portugal' withdrew from its forward position, at Aranguiz, and fell back to the Zadorra. Heavy fighting promptly erupted at Durana, Abechuco and Gamarra

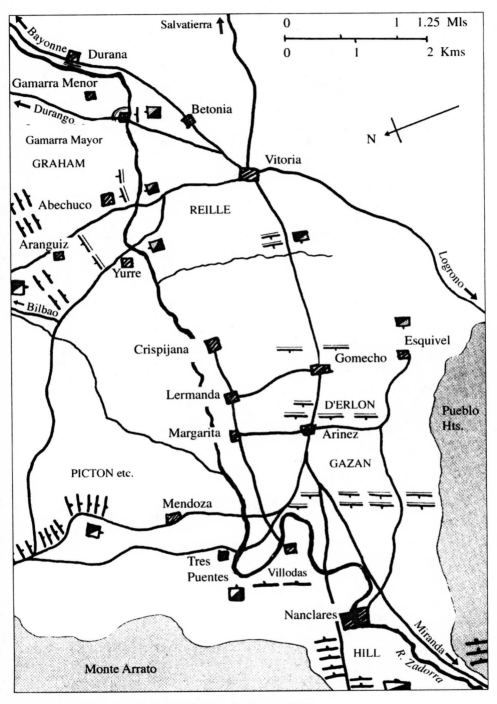

THE BATTLE OF VITORIA, 21 June 1813

as Graham's formations struggled to dislodge Reille's units from these vital bridge-heads.

Meanwhile, Kempt's brigade of the Light Division, finding Tres Puentes undefended, slipped across the Zadorra unopposed. Likewise, Sir Thomas Picton led his Third Division across the unprotected bridge at Mendoza and a powerful Allied bridge-head had soon been established in the very midst of the enemy's line. As Colville's brigade began to thrust east – towards Margarita – and other Anglo-Portuguese units debouched from Villodas and Tres Puentes, the lone French formation of General Leval found itself in a parlous situation and was obliged to fall back on Darmagnac's battalions. This retrograde movement by his centre prompted King Joseph to order the whole of the 'Army of the South' to retire and adopt a new line from Margarita, through Arinez. This called for the extrication of the troops fighting on the Puebla Heights where, ironically, things were finally turning in Villatte's favour. He had just routed the 71st Foot with appalling losses, and was engaging the rest of Cadogan's brigade and Morillo's Spaniards when the orders arrived for him to retreat. Although protesting that this would uncover the army's left flank, he duly retired northwards.

Elsewhere, too, the Allies made headway. Though Darmagnac repulsed an attack on Margarita with heavy losses, masses of Anglo-Portuguese troops poured over the Zadorra at Nanclares to harry Leval's retreating battalions. Simultaneously, Picton's division, supported by Kempt's light infantry, intercepted the blue-clad columns about Arinez and, despite desperate resistance, swept them from the settlement. The loss of this key position compromised Joseph's plan for a new battle line and, already much disordered by the earlier fighting and changes of front, the units of Maransin, Daricau and Conroux retreated further east, while Darmagnac was obliged to abandon Margarita.

Having secured the northern flank of their advance, the Allies rolled onwards to Lermanda. By stubbornly clinging to the settlement, Darmagnac sought to provide an anchor for the other Imperial divisions who were rallying to the south. However, remorselessly attacked by the Seventh Division and Vandeleur's light infantry, the French and German battalions gradually faltered and, despite inflicting fearsome casualties, were eventually driven from the village.

While the remnants of the 'Army of the South' and the 'Army of the Centre' struggled to form a new line on Esquivel and Crispijana, the fighting between Reille and Graham continued. Although the British general failed to press home his attacks, there were furious clashes around the bridges over the Zadorra. At Gamma Mayor, for example, the Fifth Division encountered the staunchest resistance from Lamartinière's units and, even after all three Anglo-Portuguese brigades had been committed, the bridge remained firmly under French control. Similarly, Longa's Spanish division hurled themselves against the defenders of Durana and, after a period of heated confrontation, succeeded in prising Reille's grip from much of the settlement, only to be brought to a halt at the bridge itself. However, although the Allies had failed to force a passage over the Zadorra, the proximity of their guns, at Durana, rendered the Bayonne highway virtually impassable for Imperial forces and thus secured Graham's wider strategic aims. Joseph's communications with France were now effectively cut.

The disastrous tidings had barely sunk in at the king's headquarters when, at around 4 pm, Wellington renewed the assault on Joseph's left and centre. By this time, the monarch had the remnants of six infantry divisions in a ragged line between Crispijana and Esquivel, supported by 4,500 cavalry and seventy-five guns. Opposing them were 30,000 Allied troops, backed by thirteen batteries of artillery. Badly shaken and disorientated by the earlier fighting and ceaseless regrouping, the French were already unlikely to mount an effective defence when General Gazan extinguished their last hopes. Threatened on his left flank by Hill's relentless advance along the Heights of Puebla, the commander of the 'Army of the South' disregarded Joseph's instructions and withdrew his divisions,[390] leaving only the units of d'Erlon's 'Army of the Centre' to face the Allied onslaught. While he did his utmost to save the situation, the outlook was hopeless from the start. Pouring into the gap left by Gazan, Anglo-Portuguese skirmishers quickly captured Gomecho and turned the French left, while, simultaneously, Darmagnac's formations were ousted from Crispijana. His line in tatters, Joseph was left with no option but to order an all-out retreat and the remnants of the beaten Imperial armies duly set off up the Salvatierra road.

The battle irretrievably lost, it only remained to be seen how many of the French formations could escape. The 'Army of Portugal' was still locked in its struggle with Graham when d'Erlon's line collapsed and the Allies began to converge on Reille's divisions. Threatened on his rear and left flank, he ordered an immediate withdrawal and, posting some infantry and cavalry in Betonia to act as a rearguard, abandoned his cannon and hurried over the fields to join the rest of Joseph's beaten forces.

As Graham's powder-stained columns raced over the Zadorra to unite with their victorious colleagues, the remnants of the three French armies poured up the secondary road to Salvatierra. Choked with panic-stricken soldiers – intermingled with over 3,000 vehicles and dozens of artillery pieces – it rapidly became a scene of wild disorder and, as they scrambled to safety over increasingly difficult terrain, the Imperial divisions steadily lost all semblance of order.

Fortunately for Joseph, however, the Allied pursuit lacked thoroughness. Although some of Wellington's infantry chased their opponents for several miles, the Anglo-Portuguese cavalry – as at Salamanca – seems to have been conspicuous by their absence; seven of the nine brigades taking no part in the operation. Furthermore, many of the Allied troops lost all interest in the fighting when they came across the mounds of forsaken French booty. There was a fortune quite literally lying around for anyone who cared to gather it up: several million pounds in gold and silver coin; plate; art treasures; and tons of military equipment ranging from wagons and horses to fire-arms and pieces of ordnance. Indeed, most of Wellington's men set to looting and marauding, leaving only a handful to maintain the pursuit. Nevertheless, by the end of the day the Imperial forces had lost some 5,000 killed and injured, 3,000 prisoners, 150 cannon and masses of other *matériel*. The Allies sustained total casualties of some 5,000 slain and wounded.[391]

III   The Flight of Foy and Clausel

Leaving a powerful garrison in Vitoria, Wellington belatedly set his forces in motion at 10 am on 22 June. As all contact with the enemy had been lost the previous day and Joseph had left Salvatierra at dawn, the Allies were unable to catch them and the advance soon lost any sense of urgency. Although it became clear that the king's main army had successfully evaded any further appreciable damage and, indeed, would soon be crossing the Pyrenees, Wellington did entertain hopes of intercepting Clausel – reported to be moving up the Ebro from the south-east – and Foy, whose detachments were hastily evacuating Biscay. Accordingly, having invested Pamplona on 25 June, he dispatched a contingent under Graham to molest Foy, while the bulk of the Anglo-Portuguese divisions headed for the Ebro.

Already threatened by the advance of Giron's 'Army of Galicia', Foy learnt of the Vitoria disaster late on 22 June. Uniting part of his division with various small garrisons that were retiring before Graham up the Bayonne Road, he halted the progress of Longa's Spaniards at Bergara. However, with the rest of Graham's columns marching round one of his flanks and Giron approaching the other, Foy soon realised that his situation was untenable and, having secured the remaining northern garrisons sufficient time in which to extricate themselves, retired to Villafranca.[392] Graham headed in the same direction and, for a time, it looked as though Foy would be encircled. However, Villafranca turned out to be occupied by an entire French division – that of Maucune, who, having escorted one of Joseph's convoys to the French frontier, had been returning to Vitoria when the battle was fought. Realising that Foy's salvation rested with him, Maucune clung to Villafranca and, beating off Graham's attacks, enabled his colleague to pass safely before retiring himself.

Concentrating at Tolosa, the Imperial generals now had some 16,000 troops and, on 27 June, offered battle to Graham. He readily accepted and, joining with Giron's Galicians, put nearly 26,000 men into an assault, large numbers being told off to envelop the enemy's line. However, grossly underestimating both the strength of the French position and Foy's martial ability, Graham – not the best general in the Anglo-Portuguese forces, as Aitchison records[393] – lost all patience with the sluggishly moving action and, declining to wait until the turning movements developed properly, launched a premature frontal assault. The Allies soon found themselves in serious difficulty and were repulsed with heavy losses. Only when the flank attacks finally threatened to encircle him did Foy quit Tolosa and, their opponents too battered and exhausted to pursue, the French retired the following day.[394] Strengthening the garrison of San Sebastian, they withdrew across the Bidassoa; destroying the bridges behind them. Here, Foy united with Reille's divisions – who had marched up to reinforce him – while Graham invested San Sebastian and posted pickets to observe the hostile army beyond the frontier.

IV Collapse of a Kingdom

In response to Joseph's summons, Clausel had forsaken his futile operations against Mina's guerillas and, withdrawing his divisions from the Pyrenees, had started to move up the Ebro Valley towards Vitoria when he learnt of the battle. Wellington had already set off to engage him when Clausel – realising the extent of the Vitoria disaster – turned about[395] and, marching by way of Saragossa, ventured back into the Pyrenees, uniting with the rest of Joseph's forces at St Jean-Pied-de-Port on 15 July.

By then, however, Wellington had halted the pursuit. His army depleted by sickness and desertion and his supply convoys having been left far behind, he was unwilling to advance further towards France until he could verify what was happening in Central Europe. His latest information was that Napoleon, having won a series of victories, had concluded an armistice and peace negotiations were under way. Should these prove fruitful, the emperor would be free to devote all his resources to the Peninsula and would be likely to repel any attempted invasion of France. Accordingly, Wellington decided to consolidate his position and, having directed his leading units to evict Joseph's outposts from the mountain passes along the Bidassoa, issued orders for the reduction of Pamplona and San Sebastian.

Meanwhile, relieved to discover that their adversary had no intention of penetrating beyond the Bidassoa, the French were frantically reorganising their battered divisions. The emperor, locked in negotiations with Russia and Prussia, received the tidings of Vitoria at Dresden on 1 July and was utterly dismayed by the magnitude of his brother's defeat. Already faced with a difficult situation in Central Europe and struggling to persuade the Austrians not to join the coalition against him, he now learnt that Joseph's army, although 100,000 strong, had been driven back and that half of the Peninsula had been lost in a few weeks. This had a profound effect on the vacillating Austrians and it soon became evident that Vitoria had cost Napoleon not only Spain, but also all hope of a political settlement in Germany. Such incompetence could not go unpunished and, directing Soult to return to the Peninsula to try to redeem the situation, the emperor banished Joseph to his estate in France and recalled the luckless Jourdan.

V The Siege of San Sebastian (Part One)

Judging San Sebastian of greater strategic importance than Pamplona, Wellington resolved to starve out the latter and devote the bulk of his resources to a full siege operation against the former. A small but formidable fortress, San Sebastian had first been sealed off by Spanish troops when Foy had retreated beyond the Bidassoa at the end of June. A weak British naval squadron had also blockaded the harbour, but this flimsy maritime cordon proved far from impenetrable and, throughout the siege, the governor, General Rey, was able to move both men and *matériel* in and out by boat.

Throughout the first week of July the Allies, immeasurably assisted by their naval forces, assembled troops and equipment: ammunition and forty heavy artillery pieces were landed at Passajes, while Graham brought up the siege corps – the Fifth Division and Bradford's Portuguese. Deciding that a straightforward thrust along the isthmus was too dangerous, Wellington directed Graham to establish just a lodgement there prior to opening the principal assault which was to be made against the city's eastern boundary. Although

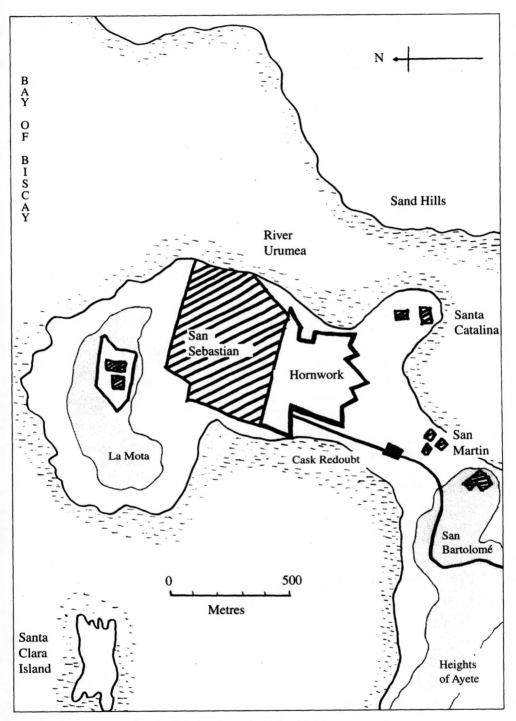

THE CITY OF SAN SEBASTIAN AT THE TIME OF THE PENINSULAR WAR

the walls here were washed by the River Urumea, it was noticed that at low tide the sea-level fell dramatically, leaving the estuary almost dry. It would then be feasible for troops to cross the sands and assail the eastern defences.

This imaginative plan was put into operation on 14 July. As soon as their heavy ordnance was in place, the besiegers began to bombard the Monastery of San Bartolomé which guarded the approach to the promontory. But the defenders resisted stubbornly and an attempt to storm it on 15 July was repelled with loss. After two further days of shelling, a second attack effected an entry and the garrison retreated through San Martin to the hornwork which protected the city's southern front. Pursuing them too far, the Allied columns came under intense artillery fire and recoiled with over 200 casualties.

With the Heights of Ayete and the monastery under their control, the besiegers set about the construction of batteries to enfilade the eastern wall of San Sebastian. During the evening of 19 July the French evacuated the outlying Cork Redoubt and, the following morning, a spirited artillery exchange began, both parties suffering serious losses. Although heavy rain made digging difficult, the Allies commenced an approach trench from San Martin and, stumbling across a large sewer that ran southwards from the city, were able to place a mine beneath the western end of the hornwork. Meanwhile, their guns maintained a relentless bombardment of San Sebastian's south-eastern defences and, by 26 July, what seemed to be a viable breach had appeared.

Rey, however, like Phillipon at Badajoz, was a commander of the first order. Inspiring his men to ever greater efforts, he employed every ruse his fertile mind could think of to render the breach impracticable: already separated from the street level by a drop of twenty-two feet, the rupture was sealed off internally with barricades and access to the ramparts on either side was barred by specially constructed walls. Placing reserve artillery pieces in dominating positions, Rey also had all the overlooking buildings loopholed and occupied by infantry, while companies of marksmen were concealed along the fortress walls to harry the Allies' advance.

Failing to discern these preparations, Wellington and Graham ordered their infantry forward. At around 5 am on 25 July, the mine beneath the hornwork was detonated and elements of the Allied army sallied out of San Martin. The explosion did appreciable damage, but the attack here was nothing more than a diversion which the French beat off with ease. Over on the eastern wall, however, there was to be a far more serious contest.

Filing out of their approach trench, the main storming party, led by the 'Royal Scots', hurried over the sands of the estuary between the castle walls and the receding tide. Dawn not yet having broken, the whole operation had to be undertaken in poor light, and the troops soon lost their alignments as they stumbled and slipped over seaweed-encrusted rocks. Breathless and disordered, the leading company arrived at the foot of the breach and, clambering up to the lip, had just glimpsed the staggering drop into the town when the defenders opened fire.

The effect was horrendous. Pulverised by the rain of shot and shell, the head of the column ceased to exist as 600 men fell in minutes. Unable to make the slightest progress, the assailants eventually fled in utter disarray, sweeping away their supporting battalions – the 1/9th Foot and the 1/38th Foot. The French – having sustained only sixty casualties and having retained every inch of their positions – emerged as the clear victors and, much to their credit, magnanimously rescued the scores of Allied wounded who, littering the base of the breach, had been left to the mercy of the now advancing tide.

The long-suffering British troops felt bitter over the latest example of their generals' incompetence in siege operations and, when Wellington suggested that the Fifth Division – who had lost so many men in the assault – were alone responsible for its failure,[396] the soldiers' anger bubbled violently to the surface. 'I am afraid', wrote William Gomm,

> our success at Ciudad Rodrigo and Badajoz, owing to the most miraculous efforts of the troops, has stopped the progress of science among our engineers, and perhaps done more; for it seems to have inspired them with a contempt for so much of it as they had attained before. Our soldiers have on all occasion stood fire so well that our artillery have become as summary in their proceedings as our engineers; and, provided they can make a hole in the wall by which we can claw up, they care not about destroying its defences, or facilitating in any degree what is . . . the most desperate of all military enterprises. In fact we have been so called upon hitherto to ensure the success of our sieges by the sacrifice of lives, that our chief engineers and commandants of artillery remind us of what Burke says of the Revolutionary philosophers: ' . . . They seem to consider men as no more than mice in an air pump', and calculate upon the expense we shall incur in carrying such and such a post with as much *sang froid* as they do upon the supply of ammunition necessary to bring down the wall.[397]

Within six hours Wellington had heard of the calamity and, riding over from his headquarters at Lesaca, arranged for more guns and ammunition to be brought up with a view to intensifying the siege.

However, as he returned from Graham's camp, he was met by a series of breathless messengers all bearing ominous tidings from the east: weeks before he would have believed it possible, the French field armies were fully operative again, and heavy fighting had erupted at the Passes of Maya and Roncesvalles. Suspecting that this heralded an attempt to relieve the garrisons in Pamplona and San Sebastian, Wellington immediately directed Graham to suspend his siege and remove the equipment to the safety of the fleet. Assured that this would be done, he then galloped off to organise resistance to the thrust at Pamplona.[398]

Chapter XXV

THE REPERCUSSIONS OF VITORIA: THE COLLAPSE IN THE SOUTH-EAST

I   Suchet's Check at Castalla

Following his seizure of Valencia, Marshal Suchet – ill, and lacking resources – had postponed his advance on Alicante and had placed his divisions in cantonments along the River Xucar. Similarly, the Allies – cowed by O'Donnell's thrashing at Castalla in July 1812, and paralysed by an inadequate logistical network – had remained quiescent about Alicante. To Wellington's annoyance, while his own units struck into the heart of the Peninsula and besieged Burgos the deadlock on the east coast dragged on for months as the leadership of the Allied forces in Valencia devolved upon one British general after another. It was not until early March 1813 that the Anglo-Spanish units, commanded by Sir John Murray, finally lumbered northwards to try conclusions with Suchet's exiguous army.

Even then, the project that was actually mounted was anything but decisive and Murray's unsuitability for independent command rapidly became painfully evident. As well as his own sizeable detachment of Anglo-Sicilian troops, he had 8,000 Iberians – under Roche and Whittingham – who had been trained by British officers and were among the finest Spanish soldiers available. He could also call on the 15,000-strong Murcian army – now commanded by General Elio, who had superseded O'Donnell – at Yecla and the 15,000 men of General Del Parque, *en route* from Andalusia. With this heterogeneous force of 52,000 men, he outnumbered Suchet by more than three to one and should have been able to subject him to very considerable pressure. However, after a token advance, Murray, disturbed by tidings of civil disorder on Sicily, curtailed his plans for an attack on Valencia and lapsed into inactivity, halting near Castalla.

By this time though, Suchet was again astir and had already decided to strike a blow at his vacillating adversaries. Puzzled but

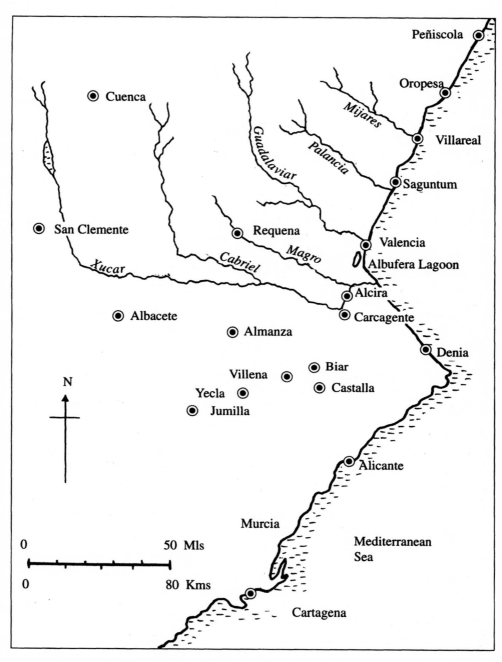

SUCHET'S CAMPAIGNS IN VALENCIA, 1811–13:
THEATRE OF OPERATIONS

relieved by their inaction, he left a thin screen of troops to observe Murray's main body and concentrated most of his units at the western end of the theatre. At dawn on 11 April he fell on Elio's vanguard at Yecla and captured the town, inflicting 1,500 casualties. Leaving the startled Murcians fleeing towards Jumilla, Suchet now swung eastwards to deal with Murray. By evening, his leading units had overwhelmed the Spanish garrison of Villena and, the following morning, established contact with Murray's outposts at Biar.

A heated confrontation ensued, in which both parties lost around 300 men. The Allied detachment holding the village consisted of the 2,200 polyglot troops – mostly light infantry – of Colonel Adam, supported by a battery. As Suchet's vanguard drove them out of the settlement and up the slopes beyond, the Allied soldiers, offering masterful resistance, were forced to abandon two artillery pieces. But an attempt by Suchet's cavalry to turn retreat into rout was foiled by three companies of the 27th Foot, who, skilfully concealed from view, ambushed and repulsed the horsemen. After holding off their adversaries for five hours, Adam's men were finally forced to relinquish their grip on the hills above the village and, retiring in good order, joined Murray's main body at Castalla.

By the morning of 13 April, Suchet had assembled some 11,000 bayonets, 1,250 sabres and twenty-four guns along the north-western edge of Murray's chosen battle-ground. The Allied army numbered 17,000 infantry – supported by nearly 1,000 horsemen and thirty pieces of ordnance – and was mostly deployed along a daunting belt of high ground that ran westwards from Castalla. With their right flank protected by an area of flooded land and their left guarded by extensive vineyards, Sir John's divisions seemed so secure that Suchet hesitated for some time before electing to attack. Judging the Allied right to be virtually inaccessible, he directed part of Boussard's horsemen to keep it under surveillance, while General Robert – temporarily in command of Musnier's division – led his battalions at Whittingham's Spaniards on Murray's left. Habert's units, meanwhile, pinned down the enemy's centre with cannon-fire and skirmisher attacks.

Picking their way towards the summit, a swarm of *voltigeurs* opened a galling fusillade on Whittingham's left as Robert's battalions moved against his front. The Allied division, acting on Murray's orders, simultaneously began marching west in an effort to turn the French right wing, leaving a dangerous gap in the very path of Robert's advancing formations. However, realising the folly of this manoeuvre, Whittingham boldly overruled Murray's directive and returned his division to its original position, detaching one battalion to drive away the *voltigeurs*. His troops got back in line just

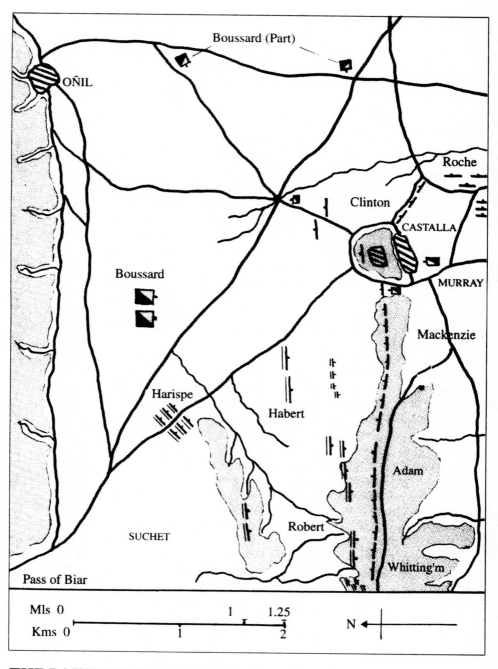

Boussard (Part)

OÑIL

Roche

Clinton

CASTALLA

Boussard

MURRAY

Mackenzie

Harispe

Habert

Adam

SUCHET

Robert

Whitting'm

Pass of Biar

Mls 0   1   1.25

Kms 0   1   2   N

THE BATTLE OF CASTALLA, 13 April 1813

in time to confront Robert's leading units and a fierce musketry exchange promptly ensued; the British-trained Spanish infantry fighting with great professionalism. Meanwhile, the left-hand column of Robert's division – the 121st Regiment – had advanced to try conclusions with Adam's battalions. Raked by volleys from the 27th Foot, the French regiment attempted to redeploy into line to return the fire, but rapidly fell into disarray. Pursued by the triumphant British, the 121st fled back down the slope, precipitating a withdrawal by the whole of Robert's division.

His worst fears realised, Suchet had little option but to retreat. He summoned Boussard's squadrons back to the Biar road, directed Habert to abandon his pinning attack and, using Harispe's battalions and his artillery to cover the withdrawal, extricated Robert's battered units. The marshal had sustained some 1,300 casualties compared with the Allies' 440 and, leaving Murray to unite with Elio's rallied divisions, he sullenly retired on the Xucar.[399]

II   The Tarragona Fiasco

Some four weeks later, Murray was roused into motion again by directions from Wellington, who was finalising the arrangements for the offensive that was to culminate in Vitoria. He was anxious that Suchet be prevented from sending any assistance to Joseph in the north, and urged Murray and his colleagues to press the marshal as relentlessly as possible with a simultaneous offensive in the eastern theatre. For this, Wellington had developed a plan with two principal components. The first was an assault on Tarragona; Murray was to ship a large detachment up the coast, from Alicante, to rendezvous with the Catalan division which, despite the efforts of the occupation forces, was still running amok. Once the French were absorbed in warding off this threat, the Spanish armies of Elio and Del Parque would assail the weakened divisions left about Valencia. Not only would Suchet be kept from aiding Joseph, but, with any luck, both Tarragona and a large chunk of south-eastern Spain would be liberated.

Murray duly assembled his task-force. Much to the interest of Suchet's patrols, Elio's troops replaced Sir John's redcoats about Yecla, while a flurry of Allied naval activity off Alicante also suggested that something substantial was afoot. With reinforcements flooding into the port from England and elsewhere, Murray eventually gathered 15,000 foot, 800 horse and twenty-four field guns – in addition to siege artillery – and set sail on 31 May, disembarking two days later within eight miles of Tarragona. General Copons – who had superseded the unpopular Lacy after an abortive raid on Lerida – came down from Reus with his 7,000 Catalans and, having covered Murray's landing, joined him in advancing on the fortress.

The garrison consisted of 1,600 men under General Bertoletti. The fortifications were in a lamentable condition, having never been fully repaired after Suchet took the place in 1811, and – invested by a well-equipped, 20,000-strong army and menaced from the sea by 180 Anglo-Spanish ships – the French outpost had little cause for optimism. Nevertheless, Bertoletti refused to be intimidated into submission and made it clear that, if the Allies wanted Tarragona, they would have to fight him for it.

The governor's bluster had a profound effect on Murray who, hopelessly lacking in confidence, was thoroughly daunted by his allotted task and, throughout the project, was to see the safety of his expeditionary force as his prime concern. Shaken by Bertoletti's failure to surrender, he gave directions for a full siege operation to be commenced and, although it was obvious that an immediate assault would almost certainly secure the objective, few on the Allied staff dared question the wisdom of the general's policy. Apart from any other considerations nobody except Murray had actually seen Wellington's campaign plans and, indeed, Sir John waited until the operation was over before sharing this vital information with his officers.[400]

Dutifully, the Allied army settled down to beleaguer the fortress. Several parallels were begun near the lower city on 4 June and, covered by a naval bombardment, the besiegers wheeled six heavy guns into position which, by 7 June, had seriously damaged the tottering, outer walls. Although advised by his engineers that an assault was now practicable, Murray rejected calls for an attack and gave directions for the excavation of new trenches, towards the upper city. Accordingly, artillery pieces were hauled up the Olivo Heights and, supported by fire from the flotillas, proceeded to pound the defences of Tarragona's eastern quarter.

Suchet, meanwhile, was on the move. In view of Elio's recent odd manoeuvres and the departure of Murray's transport fleet from Alicante, he had deduced that an amphibious assault – spearheaded by British troops drawn from Valencia – was in the offing and had surmised that Tarragona would be the target. Leaving a strong detachment to contain Elio and Del Parque, he mustered every available soldier and hurried up the coast to succour Bertoletti. Simultaneously, in the north of Catalonia, General Decaen also responded to the Anglo-Spanish attack. Alerted to Murray's landing on 5 June, he immediately dispatched reinforcements to support General Mathieu, the governor of Barcelona. Assimilating these into

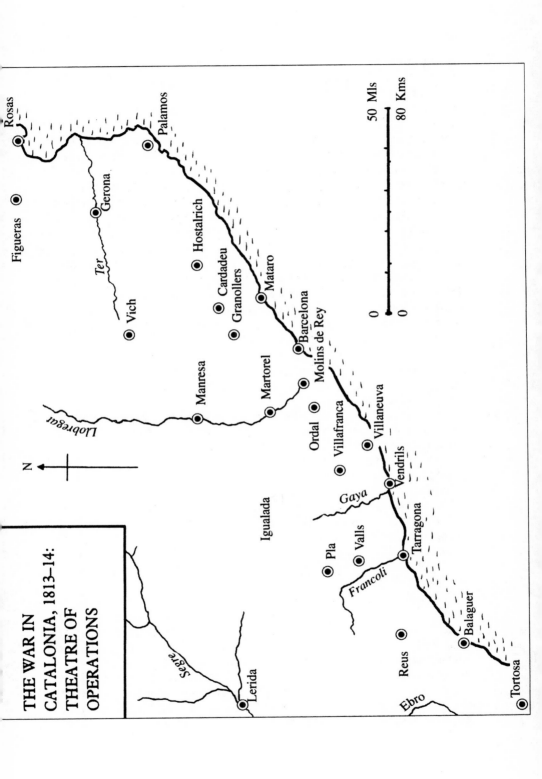

THE WAR IN
CATALONIA, 1813–14:
THEATRE OF
OPERATIONS

N

Segre

Lerida

Ebro

Reus

Tortosa

Balaguer

Pla

Valls

Francoli

Tarragona

Igualada

Gaya

Vendrils

Villaneuva

Villafranca

Ordal

Manresa

Martorel

Molins de Rey

Barcelona

Mataro

Granollers

Cardadeu

Hostalrich

Vich

Ter

Gerona

Figueras

Rosas

Palamos

Llobregat

50 Mls

80 Kms

0

0

his command, Mathieu assembled a *colonne mobile* of 6,000 men and, on 11 June, began to probe towards Tarragona in search of the enemy. However, discovering himself to be outnumbered by at least three to one, he retraced his steps and, sending urgent pleas for more resources to Decaen, loitered in the region of Villaneuva.

Nevertheless, the mere approach of a French field force had plunged Murray into new throes of panic. He discounted intelligence reports which accurately placed Suchet and Mathieu well out of striking range and, grossly overestimating the size of the advancing columns, resolved to challenge Mathieu. However, having urged Copons to assume a defensive stance along the River Gaya and having promised to come to his assistance, Sir John lost all inclination to fight when on 11 June he heard, incorrectly, that the two French detachments were about to unite at Reus. Convinced that 20,000 enemy soldiers were liable to descend on him within a day, he abandoned the attack on Tarragona and directed the siege corps to flee to their ships. While a spate of hasty and often conflicting orders turned the evacuation into a veritable farce, Copons' detachment was totally overlooked and it was not until 12 June that he learnt of the cancellation of the action on the Gaya. Furious at the way he had been forsaken, he shrewdly retired before the advancing foe, while Murray, spiking his artillery, completed the withdrawal of his own bewildered units.

To the dismay of his subordinates, no sooner had Murray got his remaining men and *matériel* aboard the fleet than he changed his mind again and landed a large detachment for a pre-emptive strike at Suchet's vanguard. But this latter force, under General Pannetier, calmly concluded a reconnaissance of the Allied dispositions before scurrying southwards to rejoin their army. His intended victim having escaped, a disgruntled Murray turned his regiments about and marched against Mathieu's position, calling on Copons for support. Once more, however, Sir John swiftly underwent a change of heart and, again neglecting to advise his Spanish colleague, returned his redcoats to their ships, leaving the unwitting Catalans to face the French alone.

Fortunately for Copons, the Imperial forces were distracted at this crucial moment. Suchet, having successfully drawn Murray away from Tarragona, and increasingly worried by the sabre-rattling of Elio and Del Parque, left Pannetier to keep the British under surveillance and marched to rejoin his units on the Xucar. Mathieu, when he heard of the lifting of the siege, cautiously probed towards Tarragona with his 6,000 men, moving off the coastal road to avoid the danger of bombardment by warships. Emerging near Reus on 17 June, he was minutes too late to intercept the Catalans who, realising they had been deserted, fled into the mountains. Hours later, Lord Bentinck arrived to replace the inept Murray and eventually returned the corps to Alicante, concluding one of the greatest Allied fiascos of the war.

Murray was later brought before a court martial for his behaviour, but escaped with the lightest of sentences. Although the whole expedition proved something of a calamity, it did, at least outwardly, fulfil its broader, strategic objectives: Suchet was unable to send a single soldier to Joseph. However, given the relationship between the monarch and the marshal, one could fairly question whether any meaningful assistance would have been forthcoming anyway.[401]

III Valencia Forsaken

While Suchet and Murray were manoeuvring about Tarragona, General Harispe, with 14,000 troops, was holding the line of the Xucar against the forces of Del Parque and Elio. In accordance with Wellington's master-plan, the two Spanish generals set their 33,000 men in motion during the first week of June and were approaching the settlement of Carcagente when Harispe suddenly launched a counter-offensive, destroying Del Parque's scattered columns and inflicting more than 1,500 casualties. With three of his brigades routed, the Spanish commander retreated to Castalla where, totally disconsolate, he impatiently awaited the return of the Anglo-Sicilian corps. However, it was nearly July before Bentinck reached Alicante, and then the utter demoralisation of the supporting Spanish divisions and the chronic lack of transport vehicles deterred him from attempting any forward movement. Moreover, the diligent Suchet was known to have regained the Xucar and the dejected Allies were unwilling to risk a fresh clash with such a wily opponent.

Nevertheless, within a few days the marshal had been obliged to relinquish his territories in Valencia and, indeed, had begun to withdraw from many of the regions he had controlled since 1809. Advised of Joseph's defeat at Vitoria and Clausel's subsequent retreat through Saragossa, he was suddenly confronted with the prospect of losing his traditional base and being cut off in south-eastern Spain. Without Clausel's support the scanty garrisons in Aragon could not hope to keep Wellington – who was reported to be in pursuit of that general – at bay. Thus, Suchet was left with no other option but to evacuate both Aragon and Valencia, and sullenly ordered for a general retreat on Catalonia. Leaving the occasional garrison to disrupt the Allies' advance, he led his disconsolate men back to Tarragona and, as Bentinck was still in no position to move, was able to extricate his personal forces unmolested. Elsewhere, though, the story was different. Severely harassed by Mina's 9,000 guerillas, General Paris abandoned Saragossa on 10 July. Without enough troops to give the great convoys of booty and *Afrancesados* adequate protection, he found himself in dreadful trouble and, leaving many vehicles and collaborators to the enemy, eventually executed an untidy retreat through Jaca to France. Likewise, in Catalonia, Decaen and Mathieu were plunged into panic by the tidings from Suchet and Clausel. Forsaking their latest effort to trap the elusive Catalan regulars, they immediately withdrew on Barcelona; one of their columns being roughly handled by Copons as he chased them from Vich.

During the next few days, the respective armies adopted new positions ready to resume the conflict. Bentinck finally got his formations on the march and, leaving Elio and one of Del Parque's divisions to beleaguer the French garrisons in Valencia and Tortosa, pushed on to Tarragona, intending to unite with Copons. On the Allies' approach, Suchet demolished key areas of the city's fortifications and withdrew further north. Cautiously following him, Bentinck detached Del Parque to secure Saragossa and, joining with the Catalans, concentrated over 28,000 men between Tarragona and Ordal.

Suchet, however, had resolved to launch a counterstroke. Moving swiftly forward from Molins de Rey, he led 12,000 men against the Anglo-Spanish vanguard – under Colonel Adam – at Ordal, while Decaen, with 7,000 troops, descended on Villafranca from Martorel. Arriving before the enemy's encampment at 11 pm on 13 September, the marshal was surprised to discover that the Allied commander – doubtlessly complacent in his immensely strong position – had failed to post any pickets. Seizing his opportunity, Suchet hurried his leading battalions across the great ravine that protected his adversary's front. Filing off the solitary, narrow bridge, these troops rapidly deployed and proceeded to advance over the mile of rising ground that separated them from the dozing Allied soldiers. They were bound to disturb some light sleeper and, their suspicions aroused by noises emanating from near the ravine, a party of Spanish horse trotted down to investigate. Running headlong into the foe, these troopers were decimated by a blast of musketry before they turned and fled. Seconds later complete pandemonium broke out as Adam's astonished soldiers awoke to find the French 7th Line Regiment bearing down on them.

The fighting was over in minutes. The bulk of his men swept from their positions with dreadful losses, Adam stubbornly pitched his reserves into a counter-attack, only to see them collapse in utter rout.

As a second French battalion, further to the south, picked its way across the ravine, the Allies found themselves caught in a cross-fire and, abandoning four pieces of ordnance, fled into the night pursued by Suchet's cavalry. Adam's command was torn limb from limb as the triumphant French horsemen exacted revenge for Castalla. The entire formation was scattered across the hills and, by the end of the action, had sustained over 600 casualties, including Adam himself. The 2/27th alone lost over 360 men, and the two rifle companies were diminished by half. The French suffered a loss of 270, all ranks.

While Suchet's exuberant infantry rested, the cavalry pushed on to Villafranca to join Decaen's turning force. Bentinck's main body was entrenched here but, on learning of the French advance, he prescribed an immediate retreat to Tarragona. Decaen having been delayed by the atrocious condition of the track he was using, the Imperial horsemen set out alone to impede the Allies' withdrawal as best they could. A number of fierce cavalry clashes ensued, both sides losing about 100 men. But nothing decisive was achieved by either party and, having given his opponent a sanguinary lesson, Suchet halted his offensive.[402]

Chapter XXVI

THE 'BATTLE OF THE PYRENEES'

I Soult Takes Command

On July 1813, Marshal Soult took control of the battered French forces on the Bidassoa and immediately began their reconstruction: *matériel* was hurried down from Bayonne; all invalids were evacuated and, in compliance with Napoleon's orders, many of the cavalry were dispatched to Germany. The marshal also abolished the command structure he had inherited by forming the four armies that had fought in the Vitoria campaign into a single 'Army of Spain', consisting of nine infantry divisions, two cavalry divisions and a large reserve, supported by 140 cannon. Although transport shortages remained a problem and the mounted units – weakened by Napoleon's deductions – were grossly under-strength, the new army fielded no less than 73,000 bayonets, 7,000 sabres and some 4,000 train troops. Morale, too, improved dramatically and, while food was still short, Soult had his new command fully operative as early as 20 July.

After Vitoria, Joseph and Jourdan had been expecting Wellington to continue his advance and cross the frontier into France. Indeed, the Allies' sudden halt at the Bidassoa had come as a welcome surprise to the French commanders, who were frantically struggling to prepare their defences. As Wellington's forces settled down to beleaguer San Sebastian and Pamplona, his relieved adversaries continued to take steps to resist the offensive they believed must eventually come. However, the arrival of Soult saw a drastic departure from this defensive mentality. Convinced that the best means of defence lay in attack, he boldly resolved to thrust the 'Army of Spain' into the midst of the scattered Allied divisions and relieve Pamplona. The precarious nature of his logistical support dictated that the campaign be concluded as swiftly as possible, and thus he proposed to strike with the utmost celerity.

For his part, Wellington firmly believed that Soult would attempt

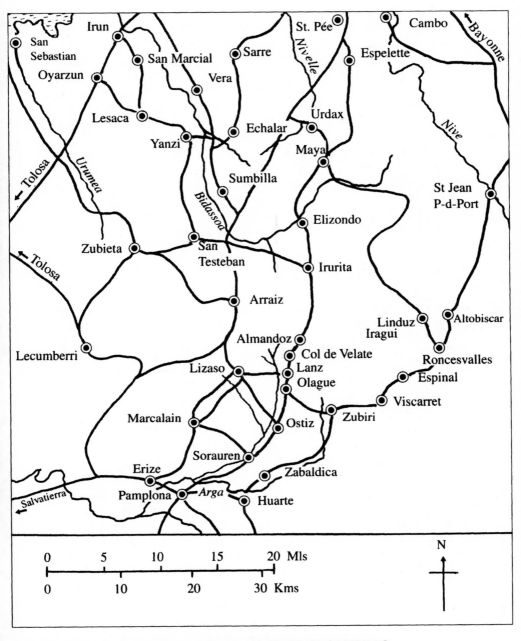

THE AREA OF OPERATIONS IN THE FIGHTING
FOR PAMPLONA, Summer 1813

to relieve San Sebastian and, consequently, dismissed reports of French troop movements beyond Maya and Roncesvalles as mere feints. At 11 am on 25 July, he learnt of the failure of Graham's assault on the fortress and, having spent some time giving him fresh orders, was horrified to hear that heavy fighting had erupted in the region of the upper Bidassoa. The prospect of a major enemy thrust down the mountain passes dismayed him. The bulk of his forces were deployed to cover the lower Bidassoa and the siege at San Sebastian: his headquarters were at Lesaca, the Light Division was at Vera, the Seventh was at Echalar, the Sixth at San Testeban and the major part of Stewart's Second Division was encamped about Maya. Other than O'Donnell's rather unreliable Spanish corps, the only units in any position to bar the enemy's route to Pamplona were Picton's at Olague, Cole's at Viscarret, and Morillo's Spaniards and Byng's brigade of the Second Division at Altobiscar.

II Roncesvalles and Maya

Bitter fighting had indeed occurred in the high passes north-east of Pamplona. At dawn on 25 July – as Graham's assault was being repelled at San Sebastian – Soult, leaving Villatte with 20,000 men on the lower Bidassoa, had launched the bulk of his army against the Allied outposts. Each entrusted with three infantry divisions, d'Erlon marched on Maya, while Clausel and Reille advanced from St Jean-Pied-du-Port.[403] This last general, however, in an effort to outflank Byng, turned off the main road and led his troops up a mountain track, intending to emerge at Linduz. Similarly, small parties of French National Guards wended their way into the valleys on either side of the Roncesvalles Pass and mounted noisy diversions.

At around 6 am, Clausel's leading division – that of Vander-maesen – made contact with Byng's foremost units. Finding the Allied infantry well entrenched, the French made slow progress, and only after three battalions had picked their way over the mountain tops and turned Byng's right did his skirmishers retire on his main body. Their position at Altobiscar was so formidable that Clausel declined to assail it, and was preparing to mount another turning manoeuvre when thick fog descended and curtailed the action.

Meanwhile, to the west, Reille's column had begun to trickle onto the Linduz Plateau when they encountered the vanguard of Cole's Fourth Division, under General Ross, who had moved his units up to support Byng's defence. A bloody scrimmage was soon under way as the British struggled to prevent the enemy from debouching onto the plateau. The cramped defile prevented Reille's men from deploying on all but the narrowest of frontages and, the head of their column repeatedly shot away by the long lines of opposing troops, the French proved unable to establish a lodgement. As at Altobiscar their advance came to a halt and, as fog enveloped the embattled divisions, the fighting here, too, ground to a stop.

Some time after the actions at Altobiscar and Linduz began, d'Erlon's columns fell on the Second Division about Maya. The British commander, General Stewart, had, like General Sir Rowland Hill – the officer with overall responsibility for this wing of Wellington's army – ridden eastwards to investigate the activities of the French National Guards, and leadership of his division had devolved upon the inexperienced Brigadier Pringle. To make matters worse, Stewart had neglected to have his battalions take adequate precautions against any sudden French attack and, thus, the redcoats were largely unprepared to face the impending onslaught.

Expecting the advance of Reille and Clausel to have turned Hill's right flank, d'Erlon was somewhat taken aback to find the Allies still holding a position as far forward as Maya. Nevertheless, after carefully reconnoitring the enemy's dispositions, he skilfully advanced his troops through dead ground and arrived within half a mile of Pringle's outposts before being spotted. His leading division – Darmagnac's – promptly sent a swarm of *voltigeurs* into the attack and the startled Allied pickets, caught off balance, had both their flanks turned. In a trice, they were virtually exterminated; 400 men being killed, wounded or taken. Advancing in the wake of their skirmishers, the rest of Darmagnac's troops swiftly established themselves on the Maya Plateau and prepared to resist the inevitable counter-attack.

It was not long in coming. Anxious to dislodge his opponents from their dominating position, Pringle sent to the Seventh Division for help and directed his own battalions forward in a series of desperate charges. Falling on the French from the south and west, the British were met with extraordinary resolution. Hurrying up the road from Maya, the 34th Foot were mowed down by a devastating volley and recoiled in disorder. Further west, the 39th were dealt with in the same peremptory fashion, while, attacking over the plateau, the 50th were repulsed by Darmagnac's right wing. In a final bid, Pringle dutifully placed himself at the head of elements of the 92nd and 28th and led them forward. But after exchanging volleys with their adversaries for several minutes sixty per cent of his men had fallen and, as the French launched a bayonet charge, the rest crumbled into flight.

Barely had this calamity occurred than Cameron's brigade –

further west, on the Elizondo road – suddenly came under attack from Maransin's division as it debouched from the Urdax defile. The British were driven from one position to another and, soon, virtually all of Pringle's battalions were in retreat. However, Stewart, alerted by the gunfire, now came galloping onto the scene and, directing his shattered division to regroup towards Elizondo, took advantage of a lull in the French attacks to disengage his battered units. Destroying two artillery pieces and losing two more to the enemy, he led his men in an untidy withdrawal to the south and eventually established them in a new position on the slopes of Mount Alcorsunz.

Having reformed his regiments, Maransin resumed the assault supported by Abbé's fresh battalions. The British gradually yielded, but rallied as the leading units of the Seventh Division began to arrive from Echalar. Spearheading an audacious counter-attack, the 82nd, 6th and Brunswickers regained some of the lost ground. The French, however, swiftly reformed on their own ample reserves and were preparing to renew the struggle when d'Erlon – believing himself to be faced by two entire divisions and reluctant to press on in the rapidly fading light – called an end to the fighting. Thus, the battle gradually died out, much to the relief of Stewart. While he had inflicted some 2,000 casualties, his own force had been very roughly handled and had lost 1,500 men – a quarter of all those engaged.

III   The Retreat of Hill and Cole

Although they had managed to contain Soult's offensive, the Allies were in a dangerous predicament. Returning from his reconnaissance, 'Daddy' Hill found Stewart's division in an appalling state and, shortly after, news arrived that the friendly forces about Roncesvalles – deciding not to risk a fresh clash with Clausel and Reille – had retreated towards Zubiri. With his right flank uncovered, Hill had little option but to prescribe an immediate withdrawal and, accordingly, Stewart's weary command set off down the road to Irurita, leaving their badly wounded to the French. After their earlier ordeal the Allied regiments were unfit for fresh exertions, and the retreat was accompanied by a good deal of straggling and disorder. Fortunately for Hill, however, d'Erlon remained quiescent and he was able to withdraw unmolested.

Nevertheless, overall, the Allied army was in an unfavourable position. Wellington – having nothing other than a few vague reports to go off – had only a superficial impression of what was afoot and, floundering in the fog of war, was unable to co-ordinate an effective response to Soult's apparent manoeuvres. Having hoped to retain the forward passes while his army concentrated behind them, he was dismayed to learn – at 3 am on 26 July – of Stewart's retreat from Maya. Acting on this news, he directed the bulk of the Sixth Division to move to Irurita, followed by any of Dalhousie's troops still about Echalar. Similarly, the Light Division was summoned from Vera, while Graham was ordered to accelerate the evacuation of his siege equipment from San Sebastian. Having taken these precautionary measures, Wellington rode north in an effort to gain intelligence of the happenings at Roncesvalles.

On his arrival at Irurita, he found Hill peacefully awaiting d'Erlon's next move. The Imperial general, however, evinced little desire to stir from his position at Maya. Worried about Dalhousie and the other Anglo-Portuguese units to his right, he was reluctant to march further south without detailed reports of the enemy's dispositions. Having dispatched patrols in every direction, he was still awaiting this vital intelligence when he received the tidings of the fall of Roncesvalles. Confident that this development must oblige Hill to retire or risk being outflanked, d'Erlon decided to remain, inactive, at Maya – a resolve that was reinforced by the news that Sir Rowland was strongly entrenched at Irurita and would only be dislodged with great difficulty.

In the Allied camp, too, more accurate details of the strategic situation had begun to arrive. Having seen Dalhousie's vanguard safely united with Hill, Wellington had taken the Sixth Division to secure the Col de Velate and had established his headquarters in Almandoz. Here, more by luck than design, he received the long-awaited report from Cole. The courier – travelling by a circuitous route to avoid French patrols and believing Wellington still to be at Lesaca – had happened to encounter Long's cavalry near Lanz. Long prudently made a copy of the report for General Hill's information and forwarded it to Irurita. Sir Rowland immediately appreciated its importance and promptly sent it on to Wellington, who, receiving it at 8 pm on 26 July, finally had a clearer picture of the situation: Cole was in retreat before a large army and was planning to unite with Picton's units at Zubiri.[404] Directing the Third and Fourth Divisions to hold that place at all costs, Wellington moved every available formation to their support: Hill and the Sixth Division were hurried southwards, while O'Donnell was asked to detach a division from the Pamplona blockade.

Unfortunately for Wellington, however, this concentration was based on information that was already obsolete. Severely threatened by Clausel, Cole had united with Picton, but had retreated beyond Zubiri to Sorauren where he was later joined by O'Donnell. While the Allies took up a defensive position here, the French had struggled after them: Clausel had followed the narrow track south-wards, while Reille – trying to cut across the mountains from Linduz to seize the Col de Velate – lost his way in swirling mists and eventually emerged at Espinal, *behind* his colleague's column. The solitary road jam-packed with men and equipment, the Imperial divisions crawled painfully onward until, at 9 am on 27 July, they finally encountered the enemy's line.

IV   Sorauren (I)

Wellington, meanwhile, was racing to join Cole. On his arrival at Ostiz, however, he learnt of the evacuation of Zubiri and the imminent action at Sorauren. Leaving staff officers to direct the Sixth Division and Hill's column to the new front, he galloped ahead to take control. As he spurred onto the field, the despondent Anglo-Portuguese soldiers began to cheer and chant his title – a development that thoroughly alarmed the French on the hills beyond. Indeed, the incident had a particularly profound psycho-logical effect on Soult; he seemed to lose much of his self-confidence and declined to start the battle until all his troops were at hand. As his divisions were still largely strung out along the Zubiri road, this necessitated an inordinate delay when prompt action could well have secured victory. Nevertheless, rejecting the entreaties of General Clausel, the marshal refused to budge and, after a bite of lunch, settled down for a nap, further exasperating the general who was later observed 'leaning against an oak tree . . . beating his forehead with rage, muttering "who could go to sleep at such a moment?" '[405]

Having spent much of the afternoon slumbering, Soult eventually agreed to mount a limited attack. The objective – to establish the dimensions of the Allied line – was rapidly accomplished and, as a violent storm erupted, the French probing columns scurried back to their positions. Much of 27 July having been wasted, Soult prepared for an assault on the morrow. Orders were finally sent to d'Erlon to rouse him into action, while the troops of Clausel and Reille con-tinued to file out of the Arga Valley and onto the rugged plateau. The difficult terrain made deployment a nightmare: obliged to wait for daylight, only a few squadrons of cavalry could be got into position and no more than four pieces of ordnance were utilised out of the mass of available artillery. The French took hours to complete their preparations and it was not until nearly noon on 28 July that the action could be opened.

By this time, however, the initiative was rapidly slipping from Soult's grasp and he was acutely aware of the fact. Wellington had clearly ordered a general concentration and, indeed, the Sixth Division – preceding Hill's columns, who were preparing to advance via Lizaso and Marcalain – was already coming onto the field. Realising he could delay no longer, the marshal issued his orders: General Foy was to pin down the enemy about Huarte, while Clausel and Reille would assail Wellington's centre with the majority of the army. Conroux, meanwhile, was to intercept and contain the Sixth Division as it approached Sorauren.

The French generals set to their respective tasks. While Foy engaged in petty bickering with Picton's division, Conroux's men were drawn into an escalating struggle with Pack's battalions. Eventually, concerned lest he should be enveloped, Conroux bade his men fall back into Sorauren itself and an arduous struggle was soon raging as the Anglo-Portuguese troops attempted to enter the village. However, the Allied soldiery rapidly found the undertaking too hot to handle. Encountering pertinacious resistance, Madden's brigade alone lost 300 men and Pack himself was severely wounded. Command of the division subsequently passed to General Pakenham, who called off his units and had them regroup.

Meanwhile, Clausel and Reille were locked in confrontation with Wellington's centre, and many a veteran of Bussaco was reminded of that battle by the scene now before him. As solid columns of French infantry slowly panted up the towering, 1,000-feet high hills of the Allied position, the long, thin lines of Anglo-Portuguese troops made ready to receive them. Wellington had deployed his units with his customary skill and the Allies were to enjoy every advantage in the coming clash. Nevertheless, the Imperial soldiery put up an impressive struggle and, at several points along the front, were to make appreciable headway.

With a dense screen of skirmishers – consisting of *voltigeurs* and grenadiers – protecting his columns, Taupin led his division against Ross's brigade. The 16 French *élite* companies swiftly overthrew the opposing light troops and, followed by their serried colleagues, crested the ridge and opened a galling fire on the main enemy position. Simultaneously, Vandermaesen's division – again, sheathed by an unusually strong skirmisher cordon – came up the slopes further to the east and assailed Campbell's men. They gradually began to waver and Stubb's battalions had to be committed on their left to give them support. Nevertheless, the rot continued to spread and, after exchanging volleys with the foe for some minutes, Stubb's troops broke and ran to the rear, leaving the inner flanks of both Campbell's and Ross's formations unprotected.

Still further east, however, the French were not faring so well. One of Maucune's brigades – having deployed insufficient

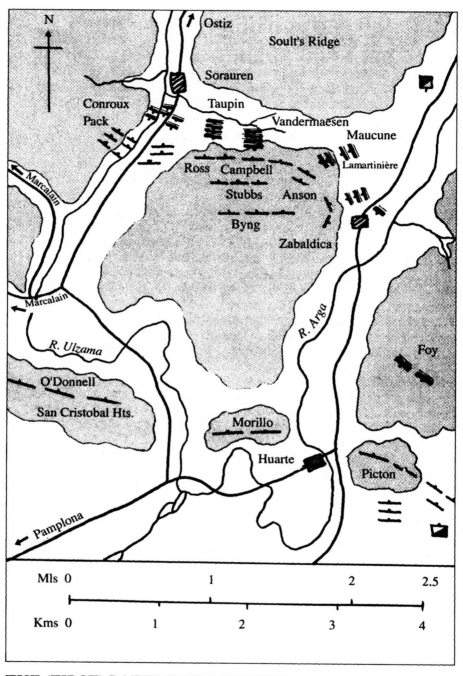

THE (FIRST) BATTLE OF SORAUREN, 28 July 1813

skirmishers to explore ahead and pave their way – staggered up the slope to be greeted by a crushing salvo from Anson's battalions. Recoiling in disorder, they careered back down the hill, while their adversaries, supported by Byng's troops, swept diagonally across the slopes to assail the flank of the next division. Thus, just as his men were concluding the discomfiture of Ross and Campbell, Vandermaesen found himself under attack from his left and was obliged to fall back, initiating a withdrawal by Taupin's disappointed troops.

Above Zabaldica, too, the fighting was bitter and prolonged. Advancing against the 40th Foot and its supporting Spanish units, elements of Lamartinière's division had, like Taupin's battalions, thrown out a powerful skirmisher screen. Exhausted and disordered by the steepness of the slope, the French were initially held at bay by heavy fire, but a second assault succeeded in cresting the ridge and, as the Spaniards were put to flight, the full weight of the attack fell on the 40th. Although they lost 130 men in a few moments, the 'Somersets' clung tenaciously to their position and eventually repelled the onslaught. Another effort by Lamartinière to seize the hill was, likewise, defeated – his men being too weary after their climb – and, as his battalions joined the rest of the French in retiring down the ridge, the battle petered out. The Allies had sustained some 2,650 casualties, the French rather more – probably over 3,000.

V The Strategy Recast: Sorauren (II) and Lizaso

While the battle at Sorauren was under way, the contingents of Hill and d'Erlon had been endeavouring to unite with their respective main armies. The violent storm that had raged during the night of 27 July had, however, caused immeasurable damage to the region's little roads; rendering movement even more difficult than before. As vehicles crashed and men slipped in the mud, the advance of both parties was reduced to a crawl. Indeed, so bad had things become by 28 July that Hill deemed his corps incapable of making further headway and duly halted at Lizaso.

For his part, d'Erlon had lost all real contact with his immediate opponent. Probing from Maya towards Uririta on 27 July, he had halted before Hill's position and had camped for the night. Dawn, though, revealed that the redcoats had slipped away, covered by the storm. Setting out in pursuit he eventually reached Lanz but, apart from the stragglers his troopers raked in, there was no sign of the Allied column. Undaunted, his cavalry continued to explore ahead and, during the early hours of 29 July, a relieved d'Erlon heard the welcome news that Soult was at Sorauren, while Hill was motionless at Lizaso.

Although heartened by the tidings that d'Erlon had arrived within supporting range, Soult had abandoned all hope of realising his prime objective. Having penetrated to within eight miles of Pamplona, the marshal – his intended final blow successfully parried by Wellington, whose forces seemed to grow stronger by the hour – had forsaken his aspirations for the relief of the fortress and, his precious supplies nearly exhausted, had already decided on retreat. Accordingly, he had dispatched all his artillery, baggage and virtually the whole of his cavalry back to Roncesvalles, planning to follow with the infantry the next day. However, the morning of 29 July saw him formulating a new course of action. Wellington having now been joined by another division – the Seventh, who, unlike Hill's column, had pushed on beyond Lizaso and had marched throughout the night – it became evident to Soult that, from the sheer size of his opponent's force, the bulk of the Allied army must now be at Sorauren. This presented the marshal with a chance to implement an imaginative manoeuvre that might, if successful, change the whole face of the campaign and bring about a major French triumph. Realising that there could now only be a relative handful of hostile units between him and San Sebastian, Soult boldly resolved to swing his divisions northwards. Using d'Erlon's corps as a vanguard, he would carve a path through Lizaso and thrust towards the Biscay coast. With luck Hill would be mauled if not badly defeated, and Graham's diminutive wing – pinned to the lower Bidassoa by Villatte's 20,000 men – would be encompassed and destroyed, allowing the Imperial columns to relieve San Sebastian. Unwilling to pass up the opportunity of dealing his adversaries such a devastating blow, the marshal duly issued new orders to his waiting foot troops and, after dark, moved north to join d'Erlon.

Wellington, in the meantime, had grown concerned that Soult might attempt to manoeuvre round his position as a prelude to renewing the drive on Pamplona. Directing Hill to remain at Lizaso, he bade the Seventh Division cover Sir Rowland's right flank and urged the Light Division – far to the north at Zubieta – to march on Lecumberri. While these precautions were being taken, the rest of Wellington's disposable forces continued digging in about Sorauren. Most significantly, General Cole's men dragged forward a number of artillery pieces and, by dint of almost superhuman exertions, several batteries were eventually established on the precipitous escarpment.

These cannon were to play a decisive role in the events of 30 July. The passage of his army, by night, over the mountainous countryside presented Soult with considerable problems and, when the sun rose,

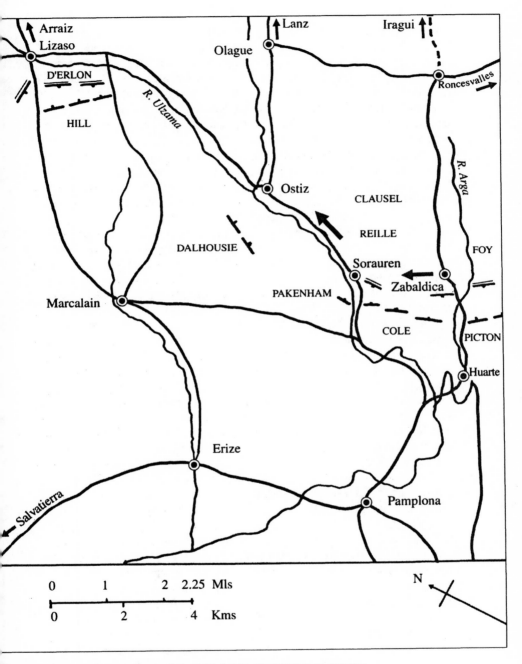

THE (SECOND) BATTLE OF SORAUREN & THE
ACTION AT LIZASO, 30 July 1813

only Clausel's divisions had safely cleared the Allies' front. The rest of the French army were still picking their way over the rugged slopes before Wellington's position, presenting him with a ridiculously easy target. Seizing the initiative, he attacked at once; his artillery wreaking havoc amongst the straggling columns. The French could only respond with the greatest difficulty and, already in some disarray, rapidly fell into confusion. Desperate to secure the escape of the army's centre and rear, Clausel hastily countermarched the regiments of Maucune and Conroux and established them in Sorauren. No sooner had this been accomplished, however, than Wellington's leading units opened a fierce assault on the settlement; elements of the Second Division wheeling in from the west while Pakenham's battalions attacked from the south. Although they resisted the enemy foot troops with the utmost tenacity, the Imperial infantry had no reply to the Allies' artillery fire and, as the village collapsed in ruins under the barrage, Conroux began to withdraw. Raked by cannons at close range and repeatedly assailed by infantry, the blue-clad columns sustained fearsome losses and nearly 3,000 men were ultimately slain, wounded or taken.

The situation irretrievably lost, the dislocated French formations now took their shortest respective routes to Olague. Clausel, coming under pressure from the Seventh Division, edged back from about Sorauren, while Reille, the Allies snapping at his heels, scampered over the foothills to join him. General Foy, however, swiftly lost his bearings on the mountain tracks and, becoming separated from Reille's principal column, eventually emerged at Iragui, well to the east. Once here, threatened by the advance of Picton's contingent, he decided against trying to rejoin the main army and ultimately made his own way back to France.

Whilst his entire strategy was being undermined at Sorauren, Soult was at Lizaso supervising d'Erlon's crucial assault on Hill. Disturbed by the rumble of artillery fire to the south and alerted to the approach of Dalhousie's division, he had quickly surveyed Hill's position – a wooded ridge, to the south of the village – and had ordered d'Erlon to attack without further delay. The count promptly sent his brigades forward: Abbé and Maransin manoeuvring to envelop the Allied left, while Darmagnac's regiments mounted a containing operation against their front. However, things soon began to go awry as this last officer, instead of merely pinning the enemy to their positions, threw his battalions into an all-out assault. Battling against Hill's entrenched troops, his units sustained needless heavy losses and were just being compelled to retreat when *l'attaque débordante* suddenly made its presence felt. Forced to recoil by this fresh onslaught, Sir Rowland was edged off his ridge and, having failed to prevent the northward eruption of Soult's army, sullenly retired to lick his wounds. In this latest clash with d'Erlon, he had lost in excess of 1,000 troops. The French casualties neared 800 – mostly in Darmagnac's formations.

There can be little doubt that the French had gained a significant victory at Lizaso. With the capture of this settlement and its vital road junction, the way was now open for Soult to implement his drive to the north: Hill's shaken units were in no position to interfere effectively and the principal Allied body was still far to the south. However, the tidings from Sorauren soon put paid to Soult's aspirations. With most of his army crippled, the marshal had no option but to retreat directly to France and, ordering d'Erlon to hold his positions, he began to withdraw the remnants of his other columns through Lizaso.[406]

The French retreat was a qualified success. Passing behind d'Erlon, the troops of Reille and Clausel steadily filed through the Arraiz Pass and headed for Echalar. Hill, meanwhile, roused his weary men into activity again and, at 10 am on 31 July, fell on the enemy's rearguard. However, these troops, under General Abbé, offered masterful resistance and, after beating off three attacks with heavy losses, retired on the approach of Dalhousie's division. Plodding after the foe, the Anglo-Portuguese columns soon lost contact and, summoned by Wellington to Almandoz, Hill's command eventually wended their way over the hills to the east; leaving the Seventh Division in sole pursuit of the French.

This peculiar manoeuvre was a direct consequence of Wellington's erroneous view of the strategic situation. Distracted by the perambulations of Foy's small column, he was convinced, mistakenly, that Soult was withdrawing through Maya and, consequently, concentrated his own troops along routes that were actually well to the east of the fleeing French army. It was not until 1 August – when he was joined by Hill – that he finally realised his error, by which time the pursuit had been irretrievably fumbled. Hoping to achieve something with the Light Division, Wellington ordered it to move to Sumbilla, via Zubita, and Alten – who had spent the entire campaign in fruitless marches – set his tired men in motion once more.[407]

By this time, though, Soult's vanguard – Reille's units – had reached the bridge over the Bidassoa at the crossroads between Yanzi and Echalar. Encountering a small party of Spanish troops, the French cleared the lane and, lumbering off in considerable disorder, continued their march towards France. The overwhelming majority of their army was able to proceed unmolested. However, as the rearmost unit – Darmagnac's division – filed past the Yanzi road, Alten's footsore troops began to appear on the scene. From beyond the Bidassoa, the British poured a series of volleys into the startled masses, plunging them into chaos. Hemmed in by a steep cliff, the French were unable to deploy on the cramped track by the river's edge and, abandoning 1,000 sick and lame, eventually scurried off up the road.[408]

This incident effectively concluded the campaign. The next day Wellington arrived with the Fourth Division and, joining with Alten and Dalhousie, pushed the dispirited French back to Sarre.[409] Then, having successfully thwarted Soult's once dangerous offensive, the Allied commander returned his own exhausted units to the positions they had held on 25 July. His total losses in this arduous contest had come to 7,000 men. The French sustained nearly 13,000 casualties.[410] Nevertheless, Soult was determined to make at least one more attempt to relieve San Sebastian and, after tending his ragged divisions for a month, was to return again to the attack.

VI   The Siege of San Sebastian (Part Two)

While Wellington and Soult were doing battle in the Pyrenees, Graham had dutifully maintained his position before San Sebastian. Without their heavy guns and other siege equipment – temporarily removed to safer quarters – the besiegers were unable to incommode seriously the garrison and were obliged to adopt a policy of simple blockade. Similarly, Rey's troops were generally content to remain quietly within the city's walls, busying themselves with preparations for any renewal of the conflict: fresh personnel and supplies were ferried in by boat; wounded and sick soldiers were evacuated; the damage inflicted by Graham's mine on the hornwork was repaired; and, most significantly, a wall – fifteen feet in height and loopholed – was erected to block off the breaches internally. By the time his adversaries were able to recommence the siege proper, Rey had completed these projects and was able to put some 3,000 troops, backed by sixty guns, into the fighting line.

Matters, meanwhile, had not proceeded quite so smoothly for the besiegers. While withdrawing his cannon – as directed by Wellington – on 26 July, Graham was caught off guard by a sudden foray and lost 200 men and a substantial amount of valuable equipment. Already badly shaken by their disastrous repulse of the previous day, the besiegers were thoroughly demoralised by this second reverse and, indeed, over the next few weeks, desertion became a significant problem. In other respects, too, Graham's operations were dogged with complications and delays. As the threat posed by Soult's offensive receded, the general gave orders for the return of his siege

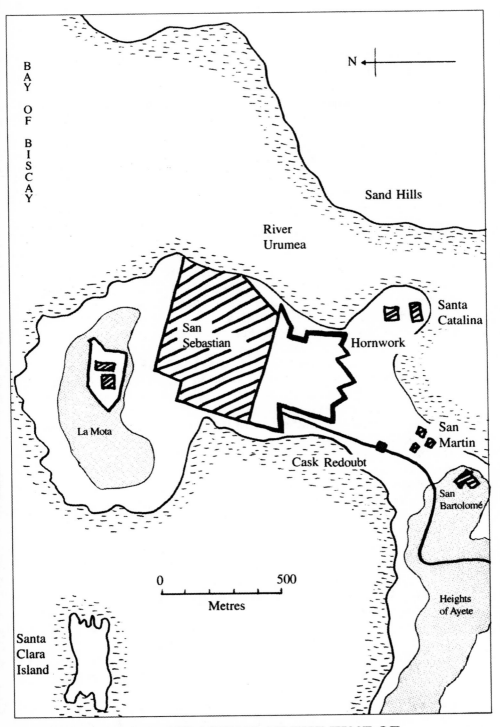

N

BAY OF BISCAY

Sand Hills

River Urumea

San Sebastian

Santa Catalina

Hornwork

La Mota

San Martin

Cask Redoubt

San Bartolomé

0   500

Metres

Heights of Ayete

Santa Clara Island

THE CITY OF SAN SEBASTIAN AT THE TIME OF
THE PENINSULAR WAR

matériel to San Sebastian. However, the undertaking progressed inordinately slowly and, for example, it was as late as 18 August before the sixty-three heavy guns of the besieging corps were back in position. Even then they could not be activated at once, for no ammunition arrived for a further five days. Moreover, the numbers of miners and sappers remained lamentably low until new units belatedly arrived from England.

By 26 August all was finally ready and Graham's batteries burst into action once more. The Allies' projected assault was to be a duplicate of that tried before but, this time, the preparation was to be more intense. For five days, the ordnance pounded the areas around the existing ruptures in the city walls. One by one, the defenders' cannon were silenced and, by 30 August, a 300 yard gap had been torn in San Sebastian's south-eastern boundary, plus a lesser breach further north. Elsewhere, too, the besiegers made headway: a battery was pushed forward to cannonade the hornwork, while another was established on the island of Santa Clara. Nevertheless, the French refused to be cowed and, shrugging off mounting casualties, worked feverishly to keep their inner defences in good repair.

The city's fortifications seemingly devastated, Wellington and his engineers judged the time to be ripe for an assault. Low tide being expected at around noon on 31 August, the start of the attack was fixed for 11 am. Insisting that the failure of the attempt made on 25 July had essentially been the fault of the storming-parties, Wellington, adding insult to injury, proposed to support those battle-scarred stalwarts with units who would 'show the Fifth Division that they have not been called upon to perform what is impracticable.'[411] Accordingly, for the assault on the principal breach, several volunteer companies from the Light and First Divisions were brought up,[412] while Bradford's Portuguese were allotted to assail the lesser rupture.

The wily Rey, meanwhile, had been finalising his arrangements for the impending struggle. With most of his cannon out of action, he had no option but to rely on the skilful utilisation of small-arms and explosives to repel the assault. Accordingly, each of his remaining 2,500 soldiers was given three muskets, plus assorted projectiles, while a number of mines – including a 1,400-pounder, buried in the midst of the great breach – were concealed along the city's eastern boundary. The construction of walls to seal off the ramparts to either side of the damaged defences and the clearance of the rubble from the inner base of the breaches concluded his preparations.

At 10.55 am on 31 August, the remorseless Allied artillery fire suddenly ceased and, led by General Leith, the Fifth Division, followed by 750 volunteers, hurried forward to mount the principal breach. On the far bank of the Urumea, Bradford's Portuguese began to splash into the receding tide while, circling about in boats, other units threatened to land on the northern side of the castle. Emerging from their improvised shelters, the garrison took up their battle stations and, simultaneously detonating the small mines along the city's eastern boundary, proceeded to riddle the flank of Leith's column with bullets.

Clambering over fallen masonry, the already decimated Fifth Division groped their way to the foot of the breach. Scrambling up the face, the head of the column reached the lip of the rupture, only to encounter the precipitous drop into the streets. Unable to get forward, the brave troops clung to their position for nearly half an hour, but all was in vain. Ravaged by concentrated fire, the column eventually recoiled, leaving hundreds of dead and dying men littering the breach. Likewise, at the lesser gap further north, Bradford's Portuguese fared no better and, after suffering heavy losses, also retreated to the base of the wall.

What Wellington had asserted was practicable was rapidly degenerating into a catastrophe. Huddled at the foot of the breaches, the Anglo-Portuguese infantry continued to sustain terrible casualties – including Leith – and steadily fell into appalling disarray. With defeat staring them in the face, the Allies resorted to desperate measures and, firing over the heads of their crouching storming-parties, Graham's artillery endeavoured to bombard the French inner defences. At a range of 600 yards this was a potentially lethal undertaking. However, the British gunners managed to bring down a deadly fire on the enemy's positions without inflicting serious losses on their own men. Subjected to this murderous cannonade, many of the Imperial soldiers lining the walls beyond the breach were literally pulverised and, as their opponents' fire slackened, the Allied infantry returned to the attack.

The material obstacles in their path having been greatly reduced, they soon established a lodgement on the southern tip of the walls and, threatening to cut the Imperial troops in the hornwork off, compelled them to retreat. Moving to their right, Leith's men had just begun to percolate behind the fortifications that closed off the main breach when fate dealt the French here a crippling blow: some mishap led to the accidental detonation of their stock of bombs and cartridges, and a chain of explosions devastated the position, slaying sixty of the garrison and injuring many more. In the ensuing chaos, elements of the second brigade of the Fifth Division managed to penetrate along the ramparts towards the lesser breach, only to be hurled back at bayonet-point by a handful of determined

Frenchmen. Although astounded by the resilience of their adversaries, the British flung company upon company into the *mêlée* until, overwhelmed by weight of numbers, the French were edged back. Their right flank threatened, Rey's men at the second rupture were, in turn, obliged to give way and, as Bradford's troops joined Leith's in pouring into the city, the defence of San Sebastian finally broke.

Nevertheless, Rey still refused to give in. Contesting every inch of the blazing streets, he led his remaining 1,300 bayonets back through San Sebastian to the sanctuary of the Castle of La Mota. Here, he intended to make his last stand, but the Allied soldiery evinced little interest in further fighting and, as the city burned around them, embarked on a three-day orgy of looting and atrocities.[413] Wellington declined to intervene and virtually all of the great port was destroyed – deliberately, many Spanish believed; for it had always been a rival to Britain's own commercial centres. The issue soured Anglo-Spanish relations for months to come.[414]

Secure from immediate attack by the rampaging Allied troops, Rey settled into his mountain-top refuge and maintained fanatical resistance until 8 September when, his position having been pounded by over sixty heavy guns for days on end, he finally agreed to submit. His incredible stubbornness had cost his adversaries dear. Some 3,500 Allied soldiers had been killed or wounded in the second round of operations against the fortress, over 2,200 in the actual assault. This latter figure alone was three times that incurred in the disastrous repulse of 25 July. Whilst Wellington had gained another castle and a valuable port, once more he, as Gomm remarked, had considered men as 'no more than mice in an air pump'. The large degree of good fortune the besiegers enjoyed in the operation – apart from any other considerations, the huge French mine in the great breach failed to explode – leads one to conclude that the affair could very easily have ended in an unmitigated catastrophe for the Allies. That it did not was hardly the responsibility of their commanders.[415]

VII   San Marcial

As the assault of 31 August was taking place, serious fighting had broken out to the east of San Sebastian. Wellington – increasingly perturbed by the delays to Graham's preparations, and fearing a second relief attempt by Soult – had taken the precaution of constructing a series of defensive earthworks between the fortress and the Bidassoa. Moreover, he had substantially increased the number of troops in this quarter, supporting Alten's men and the 16,000 Spaniards of the 'Army of Galicia' – the existing cordon along the frontier – with units of the First and Fourth Divisions, plus Lord Aylmer's strong brigade which had recently landed from Britain. The commands of Pakenham and Dalhousie were also kept close at hand, should they be needed.

These safety measures had been taken none too soon; for Soult had, indeed, opted to make one more bid to relieve Rey's garrison. Having re-equipped and rested his tattered formations for some four weeks, the marshal planned to strike a sudden blow at the Allies around Irun and Vera, sweep across the Bidassoa and cut a path through to San Sebastian. Seven divisions, under the command of Reille and Clausel, would implement the principal assault, while d'Erlon, advancing from Ainhoue with a further four brigades, would protect the main army's flank and rear. There was little time to spare if the offensive was to achieve its objective: San Sebastian would succumb if not relieved soon and the chances of a successful penetration diminished with every moment the relatively dispersed Allied forces were given to concentrate.

Accordingly, towards the end of the month, Soult concentrated all nine divisions of his army between Ainhoue and St Jean de Luz. At daybreak on 31 August, screened by the morning mists, this enormous host rolled forward and, covering their crossing with vast batteries of guns, proceeded to ford the Bidassoa. The Allied pickets were taken by surprise, and the French had established substantial bridge-heads at both Vera and Irun before the alarm was raised. However, it was some time before the 'Duke of Damnation' had got sufficient forces across the narrow fords to mount an attack and it was not until 9 am that the action commenced; by which time his opponents had managed to form a reasonably solid line.

Supported by the fire of their massed artillery, the three leading brigades of Reille's corps slowly moved up the ridge towards San Marcial, where 16,000 men of the 'Army of Galicia' – now under General Freire – were waiting. Struggling through the thickets that dotted the hillside, the Imperial formations rapidly lost all semblance of order and, by the time they neared the crest, had degenerated into a confused mass of men. The Spanish, as Hennell – not usually their warmest admirer – testifies, behaved in an exemplary manner and, after greeting their adversaries with a blistering volley, charged them and swept them back down the slope.[416] While Freire's soldiers returned to their positions, Soult rallied the broken battalions and, supporting them with Villatte's fresh troops, launched a second attack at noon. Again, the French – clearly in very poor spirits after their drubbings of the previous months – put in an untypically feeble performance and, after making a few momentary gains, were beaten off much as before. This time, however, there was nothing their commanders could do or say to persuade the unenthusiastic rank and file to return to the fray. Many began to wander back across the Bidassoa, and it took Soult no less than three hours to restore cohesion and order to his disconsolate regiments.

Eventually, his whole offensive crashing in ruins about him, the disheartened marshal ordered a general withdrawal and sullenly led Reille's corps back through Irun. He had been thwarted solely by the steadfastness of the Iberian troops and when, towards the conclusion of the engagement, Freire had requested British reinforcements Wellington had gently refused, commenting: 'As he has already won his victory, he should keep the honour of it for his countrymen alone.'[417]

Around Vera, too, the French offensive had failed to go according to plan. Having forded the Bidassoa without much difficulty, Clausel, with four divisions, had endeavoured to sweep round the right flank of Freire's position at San Marcial. Driving the Allied outposts from Vera itself, Taupin and Darmagnac had become involved in an escalating engagement as more and more Anglo-Portuguese formations hurried over from the south-east. Meanwhile, d'Erlon, having moved forward from Ainhoue to protect Clausel's flank, also found himself coming under rapidly mounting pressure about Urdax.

Clearly matters were already going awry and the two French commanders were on the verge of pulling back when orders to retreat arrived from Soult at Irun. The Imperial generals quickly implemented this directive, but Clausel soon discovered that heavy rain – which had been falling since 4 pm – had swollen the Bidassoa into an impassable torrent. With the fords under several feet of water, the only line of retreat for the 10,000 French troops stranded on the left bank was over the tiny bridge at Vera. However, at the eastern end of the crossing were some fortified houses which were subsequently found to be occupied by a company of the British 95th Rifles. Obliged to take these buildings, the Imperial infantry had no option but to mount a series of costly frontal attacks over the narrow bridge. General Vandermaesen – the senior officer present – was killed, and some 200 men were slain or wounded before the last house was stormed.

The bridge finally under their control, the French were able to withdraw in safety, bringing Soult's abortive offensive to an end. Some 4,000 casualties had been sustained, compared with Allied losses of 2,500; mostly Spaniards cut down at San Marcial.[418]

The reverse could not have come at a worse time for the marshal's troops. Already badly shaken by their recent beatings, they were soon to learn of the storming of San Sebastian. These tidings arrived fast on the heels of the news that Austria had finally come off the fence and had joined the Allies. In Central Europe, the emperor was fighting for survival and Wellington was now almost certain to invade France from the south. War-weary and despondent, Soult's divisions had lost all heart and, except in a few inspired flashes, were never again to fight with their once customary skill and zeal.

Goya's famous portrait of
Wellington (National Gallery,
London)

Jourdan (The Mansell
Collection)

Vitoria (The Mansell Collection)

A view of San Sebastian from the British batteries on the dunes east of the fortress
(National Army Museum, London)

The principal Peninsular War generals. *Top row, left to right:* Sir Thomas Picton, General Craufurd, Sir Thomas Graham, Sir Henry Clinton, Sir Rowland Hill, Sir John Moore, Marshal Lord Beresford. *Third row:* Napoleon, Wellington. *Fourth row:* Marshal Soult, Marshal Massena, Marshal Ney. *Fifth row:* Marshal Marmont, General Junot, Marshal Victor, Marshal Suchet (From *The War in The Peninsula* by H. R. Clinton, London)

Goya's *No se puede mirar* (Fotomas)

Chapter XXVII

TWILIGHT

I The Crossing of the Bidassoa

After the fall of San Sebastian and the repulse of Soult at San Marcial, the Allied high command urged Wellington to advance immediately into France. However, until he should have reliable information regarding the likely trend of events in Germany he was unwilling to do so and, even then, had reservations: 'I shall put myself in a situation to menace a serious attack,' he told Bathurst,

> and to make one immediately if I should see a fair opportunity, or if I should hear that the Allies have been really successful, or when Pamplona shall be in our possession. I see that, as usual, the newspapers ... are raising the public expectation, and that the Allies are very anxious that we should enter France, and that our Government have promised that we should *as soon as the enemy should be finally expelled from Spain*; and I think I ought, and will bend a little to the views of the Allies, if it can be done with safety ... notwithstanding that ... I should prefer to turn my attention to Catalonia, as soon as I shall have secured this frontier.[419]

Soult was pleasantly surprised when Wellington failed to launch a major offensive in the wake of the San Marcial calamity. Grateful for this stay of execution, he set to constructing a series of fortified positions along the Bidassoa, ready to receive the inevitable enemy onslaught. While he did not discount the possibility that the offensive might come through the highland passes via St Jean-Pied-du-Port, the onset of the Pyrenean winter[420] made such an eventuality relatively unlikely. The extreme right of the French army – posted behind the broad waters of the lower Bidassoa – also seemed to be in a virtually impregnable position. Thus, the marshal identified the areas at greatest risk as the centre and middle-left of his entrenched line: the sector running for some ten miles eastwards from Vera to Ainhoue and beyond.

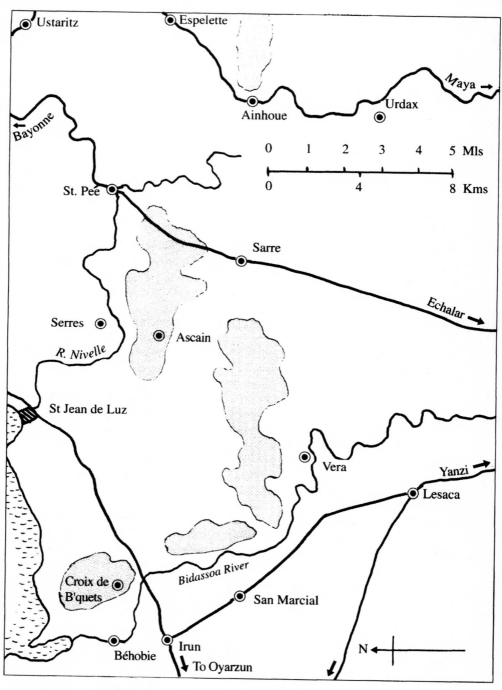

THE BIDASSOA AND NIVELLE:
AREA OF OPERATIONS

Accordingly, leaving Foy's command at St Jean-Pied-du-Port to cover the southern flank while Reille, with two divisions, guarded the lower Bidassoa, Soult concentrated most of his units in the central sector east of Vera: six divisions, under Clausel and d'Erlon, firmly ensconced in formidable positions along a series of mountainous uplands. Dug in behind earthworks, walls and redoubts, and with the terrain in their favour, this force, he reasoned, should contain any Allied thrust. However, this purely static defence – which, incidentally, bears a striking resemblance to those methods adopted during some First World War battles – suffered from one fatal flaw. Any chain is only as strong as its weakest link, and Soult's chain – stretching for nearly twenty-three miles – was too long for the available forces to protect every potential danger point adequately. If enough pressure was brought to bear on the cordon, something was almost bound to break and then the units that did maintain their ground would also have to retreat, lest they be cut off and exterminated.

Wellington was aware of this weakness in the French position and intended to make full use of it. As he later explained to General Colborne, who, daunted by the formidable nature of the opposition's defences, doubted that the lines could be carried without grave losses:

> These fellows think themselves invulnerable, but I will beat them out and with great ease.... It appears difficult, but the enemy have not men to man the works and lines they occupy ... I can pour a greater force on certain points than they can concentrate to resist me.[421]

This was to be the basis of his strategy. While demonstrations were staged to convince Soult that the assault would, indeed, fall on his centre and left, Wellington gathered men and equipment for an attack over the lower Bidassoa. Greatly assisted by local fishermen, he had, unlike the French, discovered that much of the estuary was dry at low tide and, even in areas where substantial amounts of water continued to flow, there were a number of fords. As far as his unsuspecting adversaries were concerned, Béhobie was the lowest crossing-point and the shallows here were suitably protected by elements of Reille's command. The estuary then widened to over half a mile and the weak division of Maucune was deemed sufficient to keep an eye on it. By 7 October, the day selected for the assault, Wellington had massed 24,000 bayonets here.

Although numerous deserters and intelligence reports had warned him of the enemy's preparations – notably the assembly of troops and, above all, a vast pontoon train at Oyarzun – Soult remained persuaded that the Allies would assail the eastern reaches of his line and his dispositions were left unchanged. During the night of 6 October, Wellington's columns moved forward and took up positions along the western bank of the Bidassoa. This generated a good deal of noise and several of Maucune's men dutifully reported what they had heard to their chief. Nevertheless, he remained convinced that with the river between him and any foe he was secure, and cheerfully retired to bed.

However, at dawn Maucune's camp was plunged into uproar. The far bank of the Bidassoa was alive with great masses of hostile soldiers, the first of whom were already advancing over the dry mud flats. Hopelessly outnumbered, Maucune's men barely had time to deploy before the leading Anglo-Portuguese battalions were across the river and, after a petty scuffle, took to their heels.

At Béhobie, too, the matter was speedily concluded. Faced by four entire brigades, the solitary Imperial battalion here fought a brief skirmish before relinquishing the village. Retreating on Croix de Boquets, elements of Maucune's fleeing battalions reformed and joined with the 105th Regiment which had been brought up by Reille in person. In spite of his determined efforts, however, the badly outnumbered Imperial troops were again swiftly overwhelmed and compelled to continue their retreat. Within a couple of hours of the start of the crossing, Wellington's forces had secured all their objectives along this part of the front and Soult's defensive cordon had been irreparably broken.

Meanwhile, Soult's forces at Vera had also come under serious pressure. Here though, the Allies had little hope of surprising the French in their dominating position on the heights beyond the village and Alten's Light Division, backed by several of Giron's Spanish regiments, were obliged to make a frontal assault on the formidable enemy entrenchments. Furthermore, this section of Soult's line was relatively strongly held and the Allies, with only 6,500 troops themselves, were faced by some 4,700 opponents drawn from the divisions of Conroux and Taupin. However, the Imperial troops were in poor spirits after their recent beatings and most only offered token resistance. 'Had they fought as French troops *have* fought, and as they *ought* to have fought,' one British officer confessed, 'we should have lost a great number if not have been repulsed.'[422]

When the French forces along the Bidassoa had first come under attack, Soult was far to the east at Ainhoue, inspecting d'Erlon's formations and seeking some hint of the expected onslaught. Alerted to the developments along the river by a breathless messenger from

Reille, he promptly spurred away to the endangered sector but arrived to find the situation irretrievably lost. Many of Reille's troops had been scattered, with over 1,000 more cut down or captured, while the Allies, who had lost only a few hundred men, had established several powerful bridge-heads and were getting stronger by the minute. From the western end of Clausel's sector the news was also grim: although Anglo-Spanish forces had suffered heavily in an advance through Vera, the soldiers of Taupin and Conroux had been ousted from all but a handful of their positions along the heights, and those remaining under French control would clearly soon become untenable.

With his defences irreparably holed in several places, Soult ordered a general withdrawal. His forces duly fell back to the River Nivelle, where, despite the lessons of the past hours which had cost him 1,700 casualties, he set his tired soldiers to the construction of yet another line of entrenchments.[423] Although Wellington, whose losses totalled 1,600 men, was confident that he could punch a gap in this new French wall, his strategy was still being dictated by events in Central Europe and the tidings from Germany continued to be mixed. While the Imperial armies had suffered reverses at Dennewitz and on the River Katzbach, the emperor had just thrashed the Austrians in a huge battle at Dresden. The outcome of the war in the east was still very much in the balance and, until he could be sure that Soult would not be reinforced by a triumphant Napoleon, Wellington was unprepared to push deep into France. Leaving Soult unmolested, he turned his attention to Pamplona, which was still under the enemy's control.

II The Siege of Pamplona

Pamplona had been blockaded since 25 June, when Joseph's vanquished army had been hustled over the Pyrenees. The original garrison – a 3,000-strong detachment from Clausel's forces – had, before the siege commenced, been joined by dozens of stragglers and sick. With adequate men and eighty heavy guns, the commandant, General Cassan, had deterred the Allies from attempting to breach and storm the stronghold, and they were reduced to trying to starve out the garrison. Weeks had ticked by, punctuated only by the defenders' forays to secure more food.

Towards the end of July, however, Cassan's hopes for an end to this deadlock received a significant boost: on 25 July, distant firing was heard from the direction of Roncesvalles and, coupled with the sudden northward movement of elements of the blockading forces, the appearance of scores of camp-fires about Sorauren, on 27 July, announced the imminent arrival of Soult's relieving army. To Cassan's bitter disappointment, however, the marshal was, as we have seen, repulsed in the fighting that occurred over the next few days and, as the sound of the gunfire gradually retreated, the garrison of the beleaguered city lost all hope of relief.

Nevertheless, Cassan, realising that while the French held Pamplona Wellington would have to detach precious forces both to invest the city and prevent Soult from again attempting its relief via the high Pyrenean defiles, resolved to hold out to the last. When the defenders had exhausted every source of food – including rats and dogs – he prepared to demolish key areas of the fortifications and submit. However, informed that Wellington would, after any capitulation, have him, all his officers and one-tenth of the rank and file shot should the castle be damaged,[424] he reluctantly abandoned this plan and, on 31 October, after having resisted for four months, led his famished troops out to surrender.[425]

III   The Battle of the Nivelle

With this irritating thorn removed from his side at last, Wellington was prepared to mount another limited drive against Soult; who had taken up a defensive posture along the Nivelle river on a twenty-mile front running from St Jean-de-Luz to beyond Ainhoue. Although most of the terrain in the area afforded many advantages to a defending army and even the naturally weaker points had been strengthened with redoubts, Soult's new position – and his plans for holding it – suffered from the same basic flaw that had led to the breaching of his first barrier of entrenchments on the Bidassoa only weeks before. Again, the available forces were simply not powerful enough to hold every sector of such a lengthy position in adequate strength: Reille's shaken troops were entrusted with the protection of the whole of the lower Nivelle; Clausel, with only three divisions, was expected to hold most of the central area – including a network of outposts and earthworks around Sarre – while d'Erlon's two divisions guarded the front beyond Ainhoue. As the weather had rendered the high Pyrenean valleys virtually impassable, Foy, pulling his units out of the passes and drawing nearer to d'Erlon's left, was also able to play a more active role in the defence of the main French position. Nevertheless, this modest addition to Soult's disposable army was more than balanced by the corresponding release of Hill's contingent who, having kept Foy under surveillance over the past weeks, were, likewise, now able to quit the mountain defiles and move across to join their principal army.

By the beginning of November, having massed 82,000 bayonets backed by substantial numbers of cannon, Wellington was poised to hurl a blow at some point along Soult's over-extended line. By this same period, the marshal – even after having absorbed several drafts of raw conscripts to replace the recent losses in his divisions – disposed of only 62,000 bedraggled men. This numerical advantage was, in Wellington's opinion, quite sufficient to compensate for any benefits Soult might derive from his position, and a sudden, massive assault against a narrow region of the front, supported by widespread feints and pinning attacks, was confidently expected to succeed.

After a careful reconnaissance, Wellington decided to make his principal effort against the middle of the hostile line, while powerful demonstrations were undertaken against both wings. This second task fell to Generals Hope and Hill. The latter officer, in his usual position on the right, was given 22,000 men to contain d'Erlon and Foy; Hope had 25,000 to keep Reille's units in play; and Marshal Beresford, with 33,000 men, was to be responsible for the major attack.

The battle opened on 10 November. Hope, moving against the lower Nivelle, drew the bulk of Reille's units into insignificant sparring, pinning down the whole of Soult's right wing. Similarly, Hill conducted his attack with the utmost economy and, after resisting limply for some hours, d'Erlon – subjected to mounting pressure from Beresford's columns who, as the day progressed, broke through Clausel's sector and wheeled to support Sir Rowland – eventually retired with minimal losses. Foy, too, saw a limited amount of fighting. In an effort to draw attention from his colleagues, he executed a sudden thrust towards Maya but was checked by some Spanish battalions left there by Hill and, realising that his manoeuvres were to no avail, retraced his steps.[426]

While the troops of Hope and Hill were thus engaged in menacing the French wings, Beresford had directed his 33,000-strong central column against Clausel's three divisions. Outnumbered by more than two to one and already demoralised after their defeats of the past months, the majority of the Imperial soldiers made only half-hearted efforts to restrain the enemy's progress. Those few battalions that did resist were soon compelled to retire as fickle units to their right and left abandoned their positions.

The weaker links of Soult's defensive chain having given way, Beresford's formations made alarming headway and, after a lengthy struggle across the hills around Sarre and Ascain, Clausel's regiments finally deserted their redoubts and retreated in growing disorder towards the north and east, initiating a general withdrawal by the marshal's entire army. Soult had lost some 4,300 men – nearly all in Clausel's badly mauled battalions – plus a large number of positional artillery pieces. Allied casualties neared 3,400, again mostly incurred in the central area of the front.[427]

Having been ousted from yet another network of seemingly formidable defensive lines, Soult now led his demoralised army across the River Nive towards his principal depot at Bayonne. Expecting Wellington to follow, he was mystified but thankful to find that the Allies quickly halted their pursuit and, indeed, subsequently placed their divisions in encampments between St Jean-de-Luz and Espelette. Wellington's strategy was still being largely determined by political and military developments in Germany and, having heard of the defeat of Napoleon at Leipzig, he was waiting to see the broader trend of events before committing himself to a serious incursion into France. His colleagues in the Allied high command were, at this time, increasingly concerned about the shape of post-war Europe. The British and Austrians, in particular, were anxious to maintain a balance of power, and were reluctant to see Napoleonic France eclipsed by a potentially more dangerous combination of Russia and Prussia. In the wake of Leipzig, it was possible that the triumphant eastern members of the coalition might secure satisfactory peace terms from the emperor; especially if, as the Hapsburgs hoped, he could be induced to surrender all his possessions beyond France's 'natural boundaries' – the Alps, Pyrenees and Rhine – in return for his throne being guaranteed. Alternatively, the Allies might be compelled to cross the Rhine and march on Paris to bring France to the negotiating table. If that should prove necessary, would they subsequently elect to keep Napoleon as head of the French state, or would the Bourbons be restored to power? Furthermore, if an invasion of France was undertaken, would it provoke a popular backlash of the kind Napoleon himself had encountered in Spain?

It was the beginning of December before Wellington began to receive some satisfactory answers to these complicated questions. The Allies having finally decided on an invasion of France to topple Napoleon from power, Wellington was urged to press forward on the western front. However, the danger of provoking a popular rising still worried him and he resolved to counter the possibility by issuing strict orders against plundering and by sending his Spanish units to the rear. By this time, the army's logistical arrangements were in complete turmoil and the Iberian contingents especially were starving to death. This, coupled with their natural desire for revenge, made them potentially more of a liability than an asset. As Wellington explained to Lord Bathurst:

Our success and everything, depends upon our moderation and justice, and upon the good conduct and discipline of our troops. . . . Hitherto, these have behaved well, and there appears a new spirit among the officers . . . to keep the troops in order. But I despair of the Spaniards. They are in so miserable a state, that it is really hardly fair to expect that they will refrain from plundering a beautiful country, into which they enter as conquerors; particularly adverting to the miseries which their own country has suffered from its invaders. I cannot, therefore, venture to bring them . . . into France, unless I can feed and pay them . . . Without pay and food, they must plunder; and if they plunder, they will ruin us all.[428]

But strict ordinances and even better food and pay were not enough to keep the Spanish from seeking to avenge the atrocities and humiliations of the past years:[429] many had sworn to burn every settlement and put every Frenchman to the sword.[430] Desperate to avoid such damaging indulgences, Wellington decided to leave the greater part of his Spanish troops behind. Although this slashed his numerical advantage over Soult, it did help in securing the vital tacit – if not active – support of the majority of the French civilian population and thus avoided the terrible danger of a national rising.

IV The Nive and St Pierre

Despite this reduction in his army's strength, Wellington still found that he could muster 64,000 bayonets and sabres. This was an impressive force of seasoned soldiers and promised to be more than a match for Soult's battered divisions which, in spite of the absorption of still more green conscripts and reservists, now totalled only 63,000 men. The new campaign opened on 9 December. For the advance on Bayonne, Wellington had divided his forces into three masses. The first, the equivalent of four divisions under Hope, was to implement a straightforward drive along the coastal road from St Jean-de-Luz towards the objective. Simultaneously, the second – the Third and Sixth Divisions under Beresford, followed by the Seventh and Fourth – was to march on Ustartiz and construct bridges or find fords to pass over the Nive. They were then to turn towards Bayonne. Still further along the river, Hill, with three infantry divisions and two cavalry brigades, would execute a similar manoeuvre through Cambo. The maintenance of communications between the widely separated contingents of Hope and Beresford was entrusted to the Light Division.

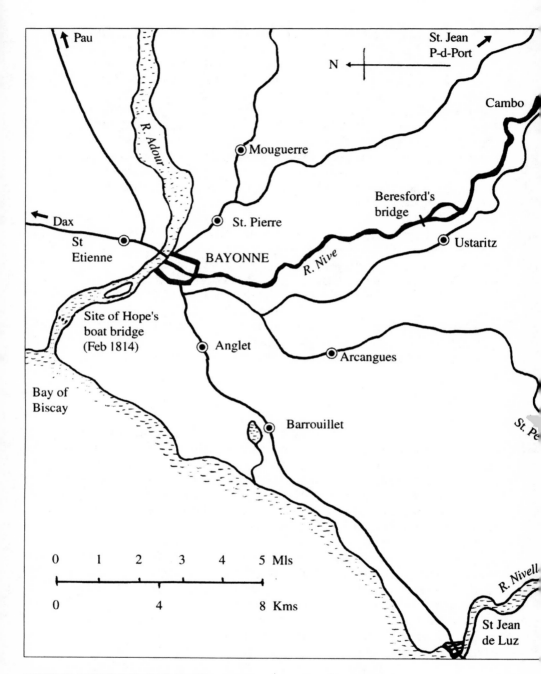

THE BATTLES ON THE NIVE, 9–13 December 1813: AREA OF OPERATIONS

The offensive began at first light. Hope, moving up the coast with the First and Fifth Divisions, plus the independent brigades of Aylmer, Bradford and Campbell, penetrated as far as Anglet before encountering any resistance. After a sharp fight, the Imperial troops deployed here withdrew into the formidable defences about Bayonne itself, while Hope, in compliance with his orders, posted pickets and retired to make camp for the night.

Meanwhile, further south, Beresford, quite unopposed, had erected a pontoon bridge near Ustaritz and had begun to pass his leading formations over the Nive. By evening, the greater part of the Third and Sixth Divisions were on the eastern bank, and the Fourth and Seventh were coming up in their wake. Similarly, Hill, at Cambo, found his crossing virtually uncontested and, advancing along the right bank, fought a trifling skirmish with elements of d'Erlon's two divisions before halting to the south of Bayonne.

Having successfully penetrated to within a few miles of Bayonne for absolutely minimal losses, the Allied commanders were delighted with the day's work. For Wellington himself, it appeared to be just one more triumph in a long line of operations, beginning at Oporto, during which he had repeatedly outwitted Soult. However, the situation was not as comfortable as he believed: his adversary's army had taken some serious knocks in the past months, but it was, nonetheless, still a potent force and Soult was a skilled commander, capable of imaginative stratagems. Indeed he was preparing one. Encouraging Wellington to scatter his divisions across a broad front dissected by the Nive, he had allowed him to complete an undisputed crossing. With his own forces concentrated in their central position at Bayonne, Soult, acting on interior lines, could now mass superior numbers against either part of the Anglo-Portuguese army before Wellington could respond. '[He] has lost his numerical advantage by extending himself in this manner', the marshal explained to a subordinate, 'and I intend to attack him in the false position he has adopted.'[431]

During the night, Soult's divisions began to concentrate against Hope's unsuspecting command. Leaving their camp-fires burning so as not to betray their departure to Hill, d'Erlon's troops slipped away in heavy rain and began filing through Bayonne to unite with their colleagues on the west bank. The atrocious weather and the inherent difficulties of marching in darkness severely hampered the implementation of Soult's plan, but by dawn on 10 December he had sufficient forces up to open his assault and the Battle of the Nive erupted.

Expertly concealed behind woods and in dips, Clausel's three divisions suddenly burst from their cover and fell on the outposts of the Light Division to the north of Arcangues. Initially surprised, the Allied troops hastily fell back to strong defensive positions in and around the settlement which the French, bringing up twelve artillery pieces, proceeded to cannonade.

Before this rather desultory skirmish even got under way, however, decidedly more intense fighting had broken out nearer the sea where Hope's astonished troops came under determined attack from Reille's two infantry divisions and a brigade of dragoons. The Anglo-Portuguese forces were badly scattered in camps stretching back towards the Nivelle and relatively few soldiers were immediately available to confront the advancing foe. Engulfed by Reille's formations, the pickets of the Fifth Division were overwhelmed; scores of men being taken captive. Minutes later, the leading French units swooped on Campbell's brigade, who, opening an erratic fire, bravely endeavoured to buy time for the other Allied regiments to deploy in to their rear. However, barely had this desperate resistance commenced than a charge by Sparre's dragoons swept away the 1st Portuguese Line with horrendous losses and hustled the remnants of Campbell's other battalions back into Barrouillet.

At this juncture, the shattered Portuguese were joined by their compatriots under General Bradford and by Robinson's brigade of the Fifth Division. However, the French, too, received timely, substantial reinforcements in the form of Villatte's command and the battalions of Foy's division. The latter quickly united with Boyer's regiments, who, ploughing through the thickets to the east of Barrouillet, succeeded in turning the Allied right flank while Leval's troops maintained the pressure on their front.

The action was rapidly escalating in size and ferocity when Greville's brigade of the Fifth Division came hurrying onto the scene. Hurled against Foy's units in a bid to beat back the enemy's turning movement, these panting battalions failed to stem the collapse and, after an arduous struggle, were pressed back in disorder. As the French vice steadily tightened on Barrouillet, it seemed as though much of Hope's command must be encircled and destroyed, when, in the nick of time, the brigades of Lord Aylmer and the First Division finally arrived. Spearheading a counter-attack, these relatively fresh troops fell on Reille's tiring forces. Nevertheless, the Imperial soldiery disputed every inch of territory and it was only after several hours of hectic fighting that they sullenly retired.

The Allies' losses in this grim struggle came to 1,500 men; those of the French several hundreds fewer. However, during the night, affected by the tidings of Leipzig, three of Soult's German battalions deserted to the enemy and, to prevent the others following suit, he disarmed them and sent them to the rear. Having already lost many veteran troops through casualties and Napoleon's constant requisitions for the eastern front, he found his forces markedly enfeebled. It seemed doubtful whether he could maintain the war of attrition against Wellington for much longer.

Nevertheless, the afternoon of 11 December saw the French renewing their assault on Hope. Joined by one of Clausel's divisions, Reille again attacked Barrouillet in strength. The apparent quiescence of his adversaries throughout the first hours of daylight had lulled Hope into a false sense of security and his brigades were once more caught unprepared, losing over 400 men in minutes. This time, however, the Allies had masses of troops at hand: Wellington had directed the Fourth and Seventh Divisions to remain on the west bank of the Nive and had also moved Beresford's contingent back across the river. When Clausel reported from Arcangues that great columns of enemy soldiers were hurrying across to Barrouillet, Soult realised that his opportunity to crush Hope had passed and he halted Reille's attack. His casualties in this abortive action neared 200; Allied losses were more than double this number.

Having lured most of Wellington's forces to the west of the Nive, Soult now made full use of his central position to turn on Hill's isolated detachment. After spending another day in petty bickering with Hope's command, he detached three divisions to hold Bayonne and, as soon as darkness fell on 12 December, began shifting the remainder of his army to the right bank. Left alone when Beresford was ordered back to the western sector, Hill's disposable forces came to just 14,000 men with twelve pieces of ordnance. Deployed on a narrow front across broken and hilly terrain, his corps was in a strong defensive position south of St Pierre, its flanks resting securely on the Rivers Adour and Nive. Hill had been warned to expect an attack and when, on 13 December, the morning mists lifted to reveal masses of French troops debouching from Bayonne, he was not surprised. Nevertheless, as column upon column of hostile soldiers crowded onto the cramped plateau before him, the veteran general began to doubt whether his own scanty command could possibly contain them until Wellington arrived with assistance.

However, in the coming battle, the terrain was to work very much in favour of the Anglo-Portuguese. Hill's forces were deployed along a chain of three heights; the middle hill being separated from its neighbours by deep, water-filled chasms. While this hindered communication between the various component parts of the Allied corps, it also restricted Soult's choice of strategy. Already unable – because of the rivers guarding Hill's wings – to outflank their opponents, the French found the field effectively broken up into three distinct, narrow sections, assailable only from the fore. Moreover, although

Soult had some 40,000 bayonets, the cramped battle front could only accommodate a portion of them at any one moment. Severely irritated by these tiresome drawbacks that threatened to rob him of a spectacular victory, the marshal had to resign himself to mounting a series of simple, head-on blows in the hope that Hill's defence-in-depth would, at some point, cave in.

A little after 8 am, Abbé's division, supported by twenty-two guns, advanced to try conclusions with Hill's centre, while Daricau's battalions opened a probing attack on the Allied left. Confronted by the troops of Barnes' brigade of the Second Division and Ashworth's Portuguese, Abbé's infantry pushed up through numerous enclosures towards the crest of the enemy position. As they neared the summit, they came under heavy fire from a ten-piece battery but, shrugging off mounting losses, continued to press forward; their *voltigeurs* picking off the Anglo-Portuguese officers and gunners with horrifying accuracy.

Having secured more room for his second-line units to manoeuvre in, Soult was now able to unleash an attack against his adversary's right. Chassé's brigade of Darmagnac's division, backed by Foy's command, promptly dislodged Byng's battalions from Mouguerre and threatened to sweep into Ashworth's rear. The situation was beginning to look gloomy for the Allies, and Hill repeatedly scoured the horizon for some glimpse of reinforcements from Wellington.

Meanwhile, over in the centre, events were fast nearing their climax. The Allied reserves were now reduced to nothing other than the weak Portuguese brigade of General Buchan, and Soult was bringing up horse artillery and Gruardet's battalions to clinch the victory. With defeat staring him in the face, Hill decided on a desperate counter-stroke. Placing himself at the head of his remaining formed units, he led the battered centre in a spirited charge. Abbé's smoke-blackened troops began to give ground and their commander urgently appealed to Gruardet for support. For reasons which are not clear, however, that general failed to come to his colleague's assistance – as did the intact divisions of Maransin and Taupin – and stood watching as his compatriots were thrust back down the hill. Justifiably furious at the way his men were, seemingly, being left to their fate and their hard-won gains tossed aside, Abbé bid his troops retire to the bottom of the ridge. This they slowly did, firing all the way, while, likewise, Daricau's battalions, disheartened by the retreat of their comrades, gradually pulled back from the Allied left.

As much through French mismanagement as anything else, Hill had snatched victory from the jaws of defeat. In the next few minutes Wellington finally appeared from beyond the Nive and, as the footsore Third and Sixth Divisions poured onto the field, the vanquished Imperial army fell back to Bayonne.

By 3 pm, the Battle of St Pierre was over. Some 1,800 Allied soldiers had been cut down, including Generals Barnes, Ashworth and Lecor. The French casualties cannot be stated with any certainty, but they were probably considerably higher, perhaps as many as 2,400. Although the numbers of troops that had actually taken part in the fighting were relatively small, the action had been particularly bloody and Abbé's battalions alone had sustained very appreciable losses.[432] Soult's failure to quash Hill effectively marked the end of military operations in 1813. The deteriorating weather compelled both parties to seek winter quarters and the French subsequently withdrew into Bayonne and beyond the Adour, while Wellington's forces made camp in the Franco-Spanish borderlands. Here they were to remain until February, when large-scale hostilities were resumed once more.

Chapter XXVIII

THE LAST DAYS

I Talks and Treaties

Having failed to secure a military victory to save his tottering empire, Napoleon found himself increasingly compelled to resort to diplomatic negotiations to achieve his aim. During the closing weeks of 1813, he opened talks with the eastern members of the Allied coalition and, taking up a suggestion made by them, subsequently offered to withdraw his troops to France's 'natural frontiers' – the Rhine and Alps – in return for peace and his position on the throne being guaranteed. To the Spanish, too, he extended appetising terms. If Prince Ferdinand – held captive on French soil since 1808 – would agree to marry an Imperial nominee, end hostilities and terminate the alliance with Britain, Napoleon would restore him to the Spanish throne and withdraw Suchet's army from Catalonia.[433] The final phases of the deal would consist of the repatriation of the thousands of Spanish troops held in French prisoner-of-war camps and, for Ferdinand's part, an amnesty for all *Afrancesados*.

Negotiations duly opened on the basis of these suggestions. It is questionable whether either side was completely sincere in its proposals, but, overall, it was the Allies that emerged as the intransigent party. When, after some hard bargaining, Napoleon agreed to the 'natural frontiers' proposal, the eastern Allies promptly withdrew the suggestion altogether and, instead, offered him nothing more than France's 1792 boundaries instead. This did little to strengthen his faith in the negotiations and, furthermore, he found the proposed new basis for continuing the talks to be wholly unacceptable. As he told his Foreign Minister in a letter of 4 January:

> I think it is doubtful whether the Allies are in good faith, or that England wants peace; for myself, I certainly desire it, but it must be solid and honourable. France without her natural frontiers,

without Ostend or Antwerp, would no longer be able to take her place amongst the States of Europe.[434]

Barely had Caulaincourt received this letter, however, than Napoleon learnt that the Allied armies had commenced crossing the Rhine. The possibility of a diplomatic settlement – at least on this front – was at an end and the final shape of France's eastern boundaries was to be decided by force of arms.

The outcome of Napoleon's negotiations with the Spanish, however, promised to be more successful. While some historians have dismissed the emperor's attempts at securing peace with such inveterate opponents as naïve, he had nothing to lose by trying and, if successful, stood to gain a great deal. Sooner or later, a French government – with or without Napoleon's leadership – would have to set aside the years of warfare and come to terms with the Spanish. The emperor realised this and, with Ferdinand, Catalonia and thousands of prisoners as bargaining chips, was in a strong position to exact the concessions he sought. Certainly, Wellington believed it very likely that the Spanish authorities would sign the agreement and, thus, at the stroke of a pen, destroy the political and logistical foundations of his army's existence.[435]

Furthermore, Napoleon appreciated that peace with the Iberians and the subsequent withdrawal of British forces from Spanish soil could lead to a radical change in the gloomy strategic situation facing him on the Rhine. The release of the great majority of Soult and Suchet's divisions could enable him to fling back the Austrians, Prussians and Russians, and thus retain both his throne and France's 'natural frontiers'. The series of brilliant victories which, with a relative handful of troops, he secured in the east during February 1814 made such expectations seem far from fantastic. Certainly, the central European Allies were beginning to panic[436] and, if Spain could be induced to sign a settlement, Napoleon's fortunes could ascend once more.

Indeed, for some time, the so-called Treaty of Valençay seemed to have come to fruition. Ferdinand signed the document in the name of the Spanish government and was repatriated, while Napoleon began the withdrawal of elements of his armies on the Pyrenees: Soult was required to detach another 14,000 seasoned troops to the eastern front and Suchet's force was diminished by 11,000.[437] However, it gradually became clear that the treaty lacked real foundations. Ferdinand had seen it purely as a means to escape back to Spain, while the *Cortes* and its executive – the Council of Regency – bluntly refused to ratify it. Indeed, even if Ferdinand had been genuine in his negotiations with Napoleon, he was in a poor position to enforce any pact. The *Cortes*, riddled with liberals, was determined to remain in government and sought to control the monarch's powers through constitutional laws. The Treaty of Valençay, they argued, had been signed by a figure who lacked the legal authority to do so and was, therefore, void.

But the French – perhaps relying too much on Ferdinand's word or, alternatively, consciously deciding to strengthen their forces on the Rhine at the expense of those on the secondary Pyrenean front – seemingly had great faith in the agreement's validity and continued to act accordingly until as late as the end of March when its worthlessness became apparent. Consequently, as we shall see, some Imperial units in Catalonia were duped into believing that the war was over before hostilities had actually ceased, and several fell victim to such Machiavellian machinations before the abortive treaty was finally discarded.

II Bayonne Besieged

When hostilities resumed about Bayonne in mid-February 1814, Soult's army – badly enfeebled by detachments leaving for the eastern front, the disbandment of most of the German and *Juremen-tado* units, and the desertion of the rest – had shrunk to only seven divisions of infantry, one of cavalry and a few garrisons: a total of some 60,000 troops with seventy-seven guns. Against these, Wellington, even without the great majority of the available Spanish formations, could bring over 70,000 men. Anticipating that his opponent would try to cross the Adour on the eastern side of the city, Soult had deployed the bulk of his army along the River Bidouse, but Wellington, as so often before, was planning to strike where least expected and intended to establish a bridge-head on the seaward side of the city.

Nevertheless, the opening moves of the campaign seemed to support Soult's hypothesis. Resolving to drive the French covering divisions further east before commencing any operations against Bayonne, Wellington dispatched three large bodies of troops to oust them from their position on the Bidouse. After a stiff fight at St Palais, Hill's column effected a lodgement on the right bank and, his left flank turned, Soult withdrew to the valley of the Saison. The Anglo-Portuguese, however, continued to press forward. On 17 February Hill's contingent appeared before the French position at Arriverayte and, crossing the Saison via a number of fords, compelled their adversaries to withdraw once more. Having pushed the enemy's main force as far east as the River Gave D'Oloron,

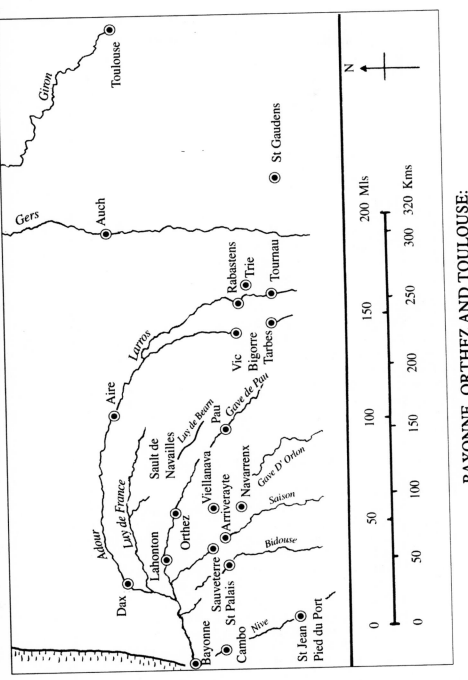

**BAYONNE, ORTHEZ AND TOULOUSE:
THE THEATRE OF OPERATIONS**

Wellington was now able to open his attack on Bayonne. Accordingly, General Hope's 31,000 troops were directed to close in on the city and begin crossing the Adour.

On 23 February, covered by a feint attack to distract the garrison, Hope ferried a small party over the estuary on rafts and began to establish a bridge-head to the west of Bayonne. The operation continued without interruption; for the French were more interested in the mock assault on the city. Indeed, much to Hope's relief, they did no more than send a diminutive column of infantry to observe his activities and even they retired when fired upon.

The following morning, an Allied naval flotilla arrived and, supplementing Hope's rafts with larger vessels, enabled the number of soldiers on the north bank to be dramatically increased. The construction of a huge pontoon bridge was also begun and, completed with remarkable celerity, this new crossing was opened to traffic on 26 February. By that evening 15,000 men had passed over the Adour and, to complete his encirclement of Bayonne, Hope moved to seize the outlying suburb of St Etienne.

However, in stark contrast to the peculiarly indifferent manner in which they had allowed the Allies to cross the estuary, the French tenaciously defended every inch of the settlement and its capture proved expensive. Obliged to fight for every lane and building, Hope's infantry spent much of 27 February locked in a gory struggle and sustained nearly 400 casualties – double those of their adversaries. Nevertheless, they eventually emerged triumphant and, as the French withdrew into Bayonne, the Allied pincers closed around the city. The last great siege of the Peninsular War had begun.

III   Orthez and the Final Crisis in Catalonia

Meanwhile, Wellington had maintained the pressure on Soult's field army. Resolving to evict the French from the Gave D'Oloron, he embarked on another eastward drive. Continuing the practice he had used throughout the campaign, he planned to turn the enemy's left flank with Hill's contingent while other columns mounted feint frontal assaults to both distract Soult and pin him to his position.

The new offensive opened early on 24 February. As Beresford and Picton menaced the French outposts between Sauveterre and Navarrenx, Hill, unopposed, constructed a boat bridge to supplement the ford at Viellanave and began moving his columns across the river. Although Picton suffered a costly repulse at Sauveterre, the plan worked overall. By dusk, there were some 20,000 Anglo-Portuguese troops on the eastern bank and Soult, having been manoeuvred out of yet another position, was in full retreat for Orthez.

The French army reached its destination on 25 February and paused to await Wellington's next move. Reluctant to risk a pitched battle, he had already decided to try to manoeuvre them out of their position. Thus, while Hill was advancing directly on Orthez, Beresford was executing a circuitous march through Lahonton to turn the enemy's right flank.

On this occasion, however, Soult was determined to make a stand. Although his casualties had been minimal over the previous two weeks, he had been manoeuvred out of three successive positions at trifling cost to his adversaries. A great deal of territory had been relinquished and all contact with Bayonne had been lost. Accordingly, he deployed his army in a naturally strong position on the ridge overlooking Orthez. He had 33,000 bayonets, 3,000 sabres and forty-eight pieces of cannon at his immediate disposal. Against these, Wellington was advancing with 40,000 infantry, over 3,000 horse and fifty-four guns. The Allies' strategy was relatively complex: while Hill launched a frontal assault on Orthez itself and then swung round the French left flank, Beresford would attempt to envelop Soult's right wing. In the meantime, Picton's three divisions would occupy his centre. If all went well, both flanks of the Imperial army would crumble away, Beresford and Hill would wheel inwards and, on uniting, would sever Soult's line of retreat.

The battle commenced at 8.30 am on 27 February. Advancing up one of the three parallel spurs that branched off the French ridge, Cole's Fourth Division fell upon Taupin's battalions about St Boes. After some initial success, however, the attackers were repelled and their supporting artillery was put out of action by the rapid and accurate Imperial cannon-fire. The Anglo-Portuguese columns eventually returned to the attack, but, encountering stubborn resistance, were, once again, repulsed with serious losses; the French recovering another part of the settlement. With Brigadier Ross wounded and two-thirds of the division now badly mauled, Cole appealed for reinforcements. The 1st *Cacadores*, were duly sent over from the Light Division, but proved incapable of stemming the collapse and, after a few more minutes of hectic fighting, most of Cole's regiments finally took to their heels, leaving the whole of St Boes under French control.

While the shaken Allied left, fearful of a counter-attack, feverishly struggled to restore cohesion to their depleted ranks, the Third and Sixth Divisions were, likewise, having a hard time in the centre. Unable to press forward any distance until Cole should have mastered St Boes, Picton could only look on while the French

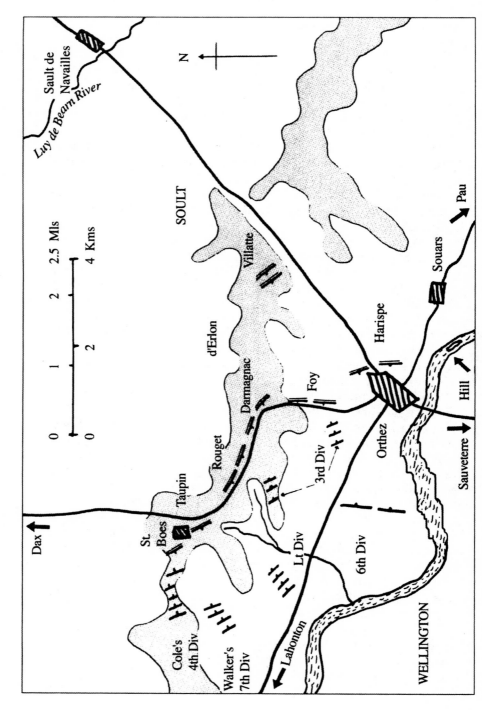

THE BATTLE OF ORTHEZ, 27 February 1814

artillery pounded his command. With even his skirmishers pinned down by the accurate fire, Sir Thomas soon found his position untenable and, by 10.45, d'Erlon's battalions were edging him back along the spur.

His flank attack having failed, Wellington now committed his reserves and hurled the bulk of his army against the enemy's right and centre. Reinforcing Cole with Walker's troops plus more elements of the Light Division, he urged his rapidly tiring men forward once more. Another grim struggle erupted around St Boes, while Picton again advanced to try conclusions with d'Erlon. Eventually, subjected to remorseless infantry attacks and stricken by the escalating Allied cannonade, Foy's division, their commander wounded, began to give ground. At this, Harispe – who had been containing Hill around Orthez itself – also fell back to avoid being cut off and, thus, permitted Sir Rowland's 12,000-strong column to cross the Gave de Pau and threaten the French left flank.

By noon, the tide had turned in the Allies' favour. As Foy retreated, the full weight of Picton's assault fell on Darmagnac's troops and, followed by Rouget's division, they, too, began to withdraw. This retrograde movement by the French centre created a gap between Taupin's men – still battling on in St Boes – and the rest of Soult's army. As the 52nd Foot advanced into this, Taupin, realising he must retire or be encircled, extricated his smoke-blackened soldiers from the village and, grouping them around him, carried out a disorderly retreat.

Covering the flight of his broken formations with the divisions of Villatte and Harispe, Soult executed a fighting withdrawal towards Sault de Navailles. The battle had cost him some 4,000 casualties and, moreover, demoralised by their defeat, significant numbers of the raw conscripts who had been drafted into his army proceeded to desert their colours. By the time they had shaken off their pursuers and crossed the River Luy de Bearn, Soult's divisions were in a lamentable condition.

Nevertheless, Orthez had been a hard-won victory. The French had resisted with determination and, at times, came close to winning themselves. The Allies' losses neared 2,200 and Wellington himself was hit by a musket shot. The bullet, however, struck his scabbard and he suffered nothing more than a seriously bruised hip.[438]

Following his defeat, Soult headed for Aire on the upper Adour and, on 2 March, his rearguard fought a brief skirmish there with Hill's pursuing columns. After grappling with Le Cor's Portuguese and the Second Division for some time, Harispe withdrew, leaving the town to Hill. The Allies, however, declined to follow further and, judging Soult's forces to be *hors de combat* for the time being,

Wellington now elected to focus his attention elsewhere and arrangements for the seizure of Bordeaux were taken in hand.

That great port lay at the heart of a traditionally royalist region and, for some time, Bourbon sympathisers there had been urging the Allies to 'liberate' the city. The idea of gaining popular support for the presence of his forces had significant appeal for Wellington. So far, his men had been actively welcomed into France only by the merchant classes, who, putting money above all other considerations, saw the invading army as a lucrative market. If the occupation of Bordeaux could spark off a popular rising against Napoleon's regime, then it could prove very advantageous. Furthermore, the city's major port facilities gave it great potential as a logistical base.

Accordingly, on 7 March, Beresford marched on the city with a large force.[439] At his approach, the Prefect had all the military warehouses evacuated and, followed by the town's Bonapartists, took his few soldiers and withdrew. On 12 March, Beresford entered France's second city in triumph, and the Bourbon flag was raised in the central square. Here at least, Napoleon's reign was officially over.

Elsewhere, too, the First French Empire was drawing to its end. Paris was threatened by enormous Allied armies and what remained of the possessions in the Peninsula were in jeopardy. When last we examined Suchet's position in Catalonia he had just routed Adam's column at Ordal in September 1813. In the wake of that disaster, Lord Bentinck had been replaced as head of the Anglo-Spanish forces in this theatre and his successor, General Clinton, had declined to attempt an advance beyond Tarragona again. Indeed, by the new year the war on the east coast had effectively died out. With neither party undertaking any fresh offensive movements, the Allied high command gradually broke up Clinton's army; several battalions were transferred to the Adour front and others to Sicily.

Despite this apparent deadlock, however, Suchet was gradually forced to relinquish his grip on upper Catalonia. With nearly half his units bottled up in besieged fortresses, his disposable army dwindled away, reducing the amount of territory he could safely occupy. Like Soult, he had to disband his German regiments as they became unreliable and, as thousands more troops were called to the Rhine, Suchet found himself with only 17,000 men. Such a meagre force was quite insufficient to guard every potential trouble spot and, by the middle of March, he had been compelled to abandon most of Catalonia; other than Figueras, only Barcelona – and the beleaguered fortresses beyond the Llobregat – remained under French control.

However, even many of these last vestiges of Napoleon's Peninsular empire were soon to be erased. Forging Suchet's signature, a treacherous staff officer called Van Halen sent dispatches to the governors of Tortosa, Lerida, Mequinenza and Monzon. These counterfeit directives advised the beleaguered defenders that the Treaty of Valençay had been formally approved by the *Cortes* and ordered the commandants to evacuate their respective fortresses. Only General Robert, at Tortosa, saw through the ruse; the other three garrisons – some 1,900 men – dutifully marched out and were taken prisoner.

Shortly after this humiliating episode, Prince Ferdinand – having been released by Napoleon following the signing of the Treaty of Valençay – arrived at Perpignan. Suchet could have detained him but, in return for a written pledge that the tricked Imperial detachments would be released, let him continue. Needless to say, Ferdinand had no more intention of keeping this agreement than he had of honouring his pact with Napoleon and the marshal was never to see the unscrupulous prince – or the captive garrisons – again.

This incident effectively marked the end of the long French occupation of Catalonia. Although General Habert clung to Barcelona until well after Napoleon's first abdication (and then only surrendered with great reluctance), Suchet's depleted divisions continued their slow retreat, finally halting on the Pyrenees. The other few pockets of Imperial troops left in the province – totally isolated, without hope of relief or fresh rations – gradually succumbed to the inevitable and capitulated. Napoleon's empire in the Peninsula was at an end.

IV Toulouse

Having secured Bordeaux, Wellington quickly began the preparation for a new drive against Soult. Bringing another 10,000 Spanish troops into play and recalling most of Beresford's column to the front, he concentrated over 50,000 men around Aire and, on 18 March, began to move south-eastwards.

Unable to penetrate the dense screen of 8,000 cavalry that sheathed the Allied columns, Soult's patrols experienced great difficulty in gathering information about the enemy's strength and movements. By this time, the marshal's field force totalled only 35,000 men – many of them raw conscripts and National Guards – and he was unwilling to risk another pitched battle. Accordingly, he withdrew towards Tarbes where, on the evening of 20 March, his rearguard fought a brief but fierce action, holding off the Allied Light and Sixth Divisions to enable the rest of the French army to make good their escape. Having successfully shaken off his pursuers,

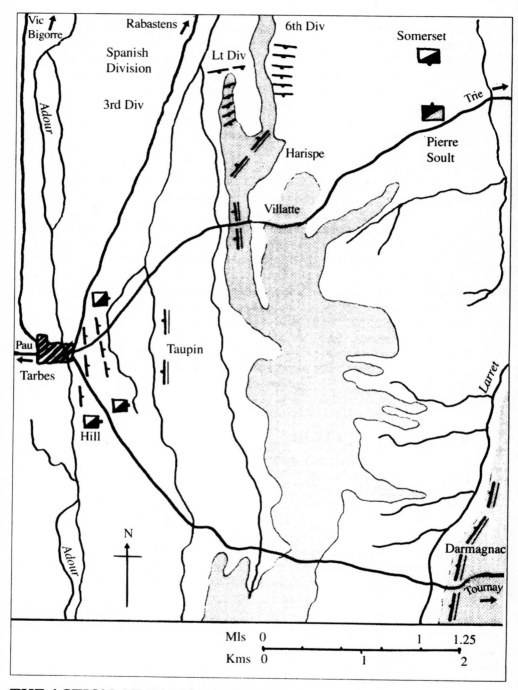

THE ACTION AT TARBES, 20 March 1814

Soult continued his retreat towards Toulouse. The Allies set out after him again on the morning of 21 March, Hill marching via St Gaudens with 13,000 men, while Wellington and the main force took the rather poor road through Trie. Slowed by its bad condition, the hunters proved unable to intercept their quarry and Soult reached his destination on 24 March.

Toulouse was a major depot for the French Army. Packed with supplies, it was also the assembly point for a number of new conscript formations and, thus, on entering the town, Soult's ragged divisions received a timely input of both men and equipment. Of long-standing strategic importance, the city was protected by ancient fortifications which, some weeks beforehand, the marshal had directed were to be strengthened with a network of redoubts and other earthworks. Moreover, a number of broad waterways – notably the River Garonne and the Royal Canal – almost encircled the city, leaving only the south wall relatively accessible to an attacker.

Nevertheless, Wellington was not destined to strike here. The final approach to the city proved complex and dangerous. Having managed, with great difficulty, to construct a pontoon bridge over the mighty Garonne below Toulouse, the Allied commander began to move his army onto the far bank on 3 April. However, when only 19,000 men had crossed, the rain-swollen river swept away the bridge, leaving this vanguard stranded. Had the French elected to attack Beresford's isolated contingent, it is difficult to see how Wellington could have avoided a disaster. It took four days to re-establish communications with the forces on the east bank, during which time they remained exposed to the full strength of Soult's army. He, however, remained within the city and made no effort to molest the stranded divisions.

Even so, the incident discouraged Wellington from relying further on makeshift crossings and, securing a proper bridge at Croix d'Aurade, eventually brought most of his force onto the east bank and sealed off Toulouse on three sides; the vulnerable southern boundary, lying between the Garonne and the Royal Canal, had to be ignored.

The scene was set for an epic struggle. Wellington's army – some 49,000 bayonets and sabres, backed by over fifty cannon – was poised to assail a fortified city defended by 42,000 Imperial troops. The civilian population – like that of Bordeaux – was predominantly composed of Bourbon sympathisers and rendered Soult little active support. But for this the Allies could well have found themselves up against the kind of fanatical resistance that had proved so costly to the French at Gerona and Saragossa. Nevertheless, the battle for the city was to prove murderous and in this – the last great engagement of

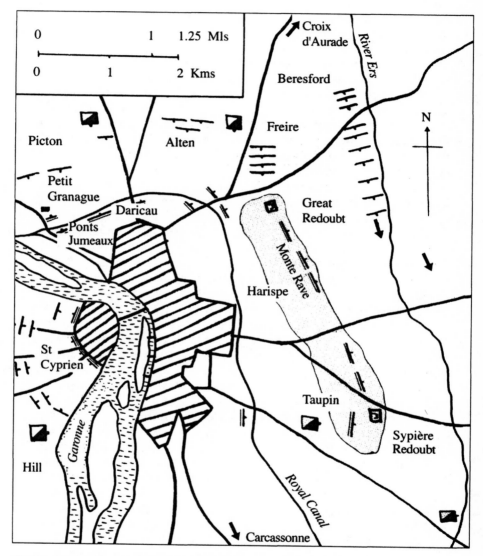

THE BATTLE OF TOULOUSE, 10 April 1814
(Initial dispositions)

the Peninsular War – several thousand men were to be killed or maimed.

Wellington's plan for the reduction of Toulouse called for the staging of pinning attacks at selected points all around the perimeter, while a major assault was launched against the eastern wall. Hill, with 14,000 men, was directed to assail the transpontine suburb of St Cyprien, while the Third and Light Divisions mounted feint attacks along the northern boundary. Supervision of the principal assault was given to Beresford, who, with the Fourth, Sixth and Spanish Divisions, was to assail the Monte Rave. This ridge dominated Toulouse's eastern quarter and, if secured, would provide the Allies with a perfect site for siege cannon. Soult was well aware of this and had covered the hill with earthworks, liberally furnished with infantry and heavy guns.

The battle opened at 5 am on 10 April – Easter Sunday. In accordance with his orders, Hill began a diversionary attack on St Cyprien, which was defended by the 3,700 bayonets of Maransin's division. The operation was conducted with consummate skill and, although the fighting here was frequently intense, the assailants managed to keep the garrison fully occupied throughout the day without incurring more than a few dozen casualties.

Elsewhere, however, matters did not go so favourably for the Allies. On the northern side of the city, Picton, forgetting he was mounting only a distraction, launched his brigades into an impetuous assault on Daricau's nigh impregnable position. Unable to penetrate beyond the Royal Canal, the Third Division became embroiled in heavy fighting around the Petit Granague Farm and the Ponts Jumeaux bridge-head. His troops repelled at every point with dreadful losses, Picton's rashness was severely punished and he eventually retired.

Further east, while the Light Division – following Wellington's plan to the letter – pinned down their opponents with an imposing feint attack, the main assault force rapidly got into difficulties. Unable to approach their objective directly because of the marshes of the River Ers, Beresford's troops had to march south for two miles before wheeling into line to assail the Monte Rave. So muddy was their path, however, that the infantry columns were reduced to a crawl and the artillery could not keep up at all. As the beginning of the attack slipped further and further behind schedule, Beresford ordered his gunners to deploy their cannon where they were and, as the foot troops toiled on, the batteries prematurely turned to face the hostile line and opened fire.

The commencement of this cannonade, however, had tragic repercussions. The formation allotted for the assault on the north-east tip of the Monte Rave was General Freire's Spanish corps. Directed not to attack until Beresford's men were in position, they had impatiently waited for the Fourth and Sixth Divisions to complete their southward trek but, taking the sudden gunfire as an indication that the manoeuvring was finally over and the main assault had begun, the unsupported Galicians surged forward to assail the enemy position. Charging up the hill with great enthusiasm, they succeeded in pushing back the French *voltigeurs*. However, coming under an intense bombardment from the cannons in the Great Redoubt, they hurriedly took shelter in a sunken lane, refusing to advance further. The French gunners pounded the area with devastating accuracy, while parties of snipers worked their way forward to enfilade the wavering hostile battalions with musketry. After being ravaged by this pitiless fire for several minutes, nearly all the dispirited Iberian regiments poured back down the slope in headlong rout. The Cantabrian *Tiradores*, however, bravely stood their ground, only withdrawing when ordered to do so.

As this tragic episode came to its gory conclusion, Beresford finally got his forces into position and attacked the southern end of Monte Rave. As the troops of Anson and Lambert mounted the slopes near the Sypière Redoubt, however, they came under vigorous attack from elements of Taupin's division. At first, it seemed as though the Imperial columns would carry all before them, but – as one French officer recalled – Taupin – overlooking the painful lessons of the past six years – had committed an old, tactical blunder that was to lead to disaster:

> By one of those deplorable errors of which our late campaigns gave too many examples, Taupin, carried away by his ardour and the hope of a brilliant success, . . . instead of deploying his brigade . . . advanced with his whole force still in column, the 12th *Léger* leading. . . . The English . . . instead of giving the French time to deploy, took up a brusque offensive and commenced a vigorous fire. . . . Amongst our massed ranks no shot could fail to find a mark, and we could reply with only the insufficient fire of the first battalion of the 12th *Léger*. The men in the rear ranks, seeing comrades fall on every side without being able to retaliate, became discouraged. General Taupin, trying to keep up his soldiers' confidence, and to animate them by his personal example, was seen in the forefront of his leading brigade. Soon, expiatory victim of his own error, he fell mortally wounded, . . . the brigade recoiled and the English advanced.[440]

Once again, the line had triumphed over the column and, as

Taupin's formation retreated in chaos, neighbouring French units were infected by the panic and also took to their heels. Nevertheless, after streaming down the back slope of the Monte Rave, the Imperial regiments quickly rallied. Occupying a second belt of earthworks, they hurriedly brought up their reserves and, filled with fresh determination, prepared to meet the expected onslaught. However, after several suspense filled minutes, the Allied formations had still not appeared and a peculiar silence descended. Having occupied the abandoned Sypière Redoubt, Beresford – still trying to get his guns further forward and anxious to be supported by Freire in any new attack – had ceased firing and was marking time.

This sudden lull led to a further error by Picton who, after his earlier ill-considered attack on the Ponts Jumeaux district, had been keeping his men at a respectful distance from the enemy. However, when, from his position to the north of the city, he witnessed the collapse of Freire's attack, Sir Thomas had his own troops prepare to advance once more. Unable to see the Fourth and Sixth Divisions beyond the Monte Rave and noting the abrupt termination of Beresford's cannonade, he concluded that the whole of the main assault force had been repulsed. Seeking to distract the enemy and relieve the pressure on Beresford at what he believed to be a critical moment, the well-meaning but headstrong general launched Brisbane's battalions into a fresh attack on the Ponts Jumeaux. Once again, however, the Anglo-Portuguese were roughly handled and, after Brisbane himself and 350 others had been cut down, the brigade recoiled in confusion.

Two hours after he had first seized the Sypière position, Beresford had finally got his artillery onto the Monte Rave and was ready to turn against Harispe's division. Likewise, Freire, having restored order to his tattered regiments, began to advance up the hill a second time and, moving round to its eastern face, assailed the Great Redoubt once more. Again, however, the heavy French fire was to prove too much. Led by Freire himself and a cluster of other senior officers, the two Spanish divisions penetrated to the very outworks of the redoubt, where they were met by devastating blasts of canister and musketry. Struggling to effect an entry, the Iberians lost four generals and over 1,000 other ranks in moments. Unable to withstand this pernicious fire, the attacking columns rapidly disintegrated and, in utter confusion, poured down the slope, never to return.

Beresford, meanwhile, was locked in a bitter contest further south. Moving along the Monte Rave towards the Great Redoubt, the Sixth Division had taken the hill's defenders in the flank and had begun to thrust them back. At this Harispe had sent in his reserves and, pouncing on the 42nd and 79th Highlanders, had checked the advancing Allies and stabilised the situation. Nevertheless, feeding in fresh troops, Beresford persevered and, despite suffering 1,600 casualties, edged the French back. Having lost nearly 1,000 men himself, Harispe retreated to the Great Redoubt. Joining with elements of Darmagnac's command, he subsequently kept the enemy at bay while the guns were evacuated and, eventually, retired across the Royal Canal.

With his forward units badly ravaged and his artillery ammunition nearing exhaustion, Wellington was not prepared to mount an assault across the waterway and by 6 pm the battle had petered out. The casualties were appalling: the Allies had lost 4,600 slain and wounded, while Soult found his force diminished by 3,200. Indeed, so badly battered were the majority of Wellington's divisions that the whole of the next day had to be devoted to their recuperation.

The battle, however, was not to be renewed. Unwilling to risk a second day of fighting or to remain bottled up in a pro-Bourbon city, Soult withdrew during the night of 11 April. Evacuating what remained of the huge military stores, but leaving his seriously wounded, he slipped away, unmolested, through the unblockaded southern gate and made his way to Carcassonne. The population of Toulouse wasted no time in inviting the Allies into the city and their senior officers were entertained to dinner by the civil authorities on the evening of 12 April. For many, however, this glittering event was marred by tidings from the north: following the fall of Paris on 31 March, Napoleon had abdicated at Fontainebleau. The Battle of Toulouse had been fought several days after peace had officially been declared and thousands of men had perished needlessly. After six gory years, the Peninsular War was at an end.[441]

The killing, unfortunately, was not. In addition to Toulouse, one more significant action was fought after peace had been concluded. This occurred at Bayonne, where General Thouvenot's 14,000-strong garrison – well supplied with food – had continued to defy Sir John Hope's besieging army. From the outset, Hope had proceeded lethargically. Undertaking only to starve the garrison out, he had made no tangible gains and, as late as mid-April, the situation was much as it had been when the siege commenced.

The Fourteenth of that month, however, saw a dramatic end to the deadlock. Deciding to mount a major foray, Thouvenot poured 6,000 infantry into a sudden pre-dawn attack on the outlying suburb of St Etienne. The besiegers – lulled into a false sense of security by days of relative inactivity – were caught unawares and, in a trice, their pickets were annihilated; General Hay of the Fifth Division being amongst those killed. Overrunning the settlement with light-ning speed, the French proceeded to take scores of prisoners, including Hope himself – who was wounded – and two of his aides. Only after some considerable time did the Allied reserves come to the rescue and, even then, a good deal of hard fighting took place before the French were finally driven back into Bayonne. By the end of this fierce action, over 800 Allied troops, and a similar number of French, had been killed, injured or captured. These were, more or less, the tragic, last victims of the Peninsular War. After this sudden sortie, Thouvenot remained comparatively quiet within the walls of Bayonne until, having received a direct order to do so from Soult, he finally surrendered on 26 April.[442]

V Postscript

Within a few days of the sortie from Bayonne, Napoleon bid an emotional farewell to his Old Guard and, accompanied by 1,000 volunteers, departed for his gilded cage on Elba. Hours later, on 30 April, the triumphant Allied Powers concluded the Treaty of Paris with the newly-restored Bourbon monarchy and, thus, crowned their total military victory by formally reducing France to her 1792 boundaries.

After twenty years of virtually uninterrupted warfare against Revolutionary and then Imperial France, Europe was utterly exhausted. Millions had perished in the conflict, whilst its economic costs – aggravated by the Continental System and Britain's retaliatory maritime blockade – were incalculable. France was particularly hard hit: having fought for two decades without respite, she had lost hundreds of thousands of men and had been carried to the verge of bankruptcy. While – as the Bayonne sortie demonstrated – the Army had remained fiercely loyal to the emperor to the bitter end, much of the civilian population had become indifferent. Certainly, by 1814 he was sustaining the struggle almost entirely with his own incredible will-power, and his brief campaign of that year – although quite brilliant from a tactical and strategic point of view – was, many have argued, never likely to achieve more than a postponement of his inevitable military defeat. Napoleon's star had finally run its course; only he would not accept that fact.

Indeed, there was to be yet another bout of bloody warfare before Europe was released from Napoleon Bonaparte's disruptive ambitions once and for all. Having observed growing popular discontent with the restored Bourbons, he resolved to put in a last desperate bid for power. Slipping through the cordon of patrolling British warships, he and his minute army sailed to France and landed on 1 March 1815. Much of the country quickly rallied to his cause and, within three weeks, Napoleon was again the ruler of France. His peace overtures firmly rejected, he elected to strike before the Allied governments could remobilise the whole of their colossal military forces. Accordingly, in June *La Grande Armée* marched again. However, after some initial successes, Napoleon was finally defeated by the combined forces of Blucher and Wellington in the 'near run thing' of Waterloo. Four days later, he signed his second abdication and, within a month, was on his way to exile on St Helena in the South Atlantic. Here, constantly guarded, he was destined to remain until his death in 1821.

An analysis of the factors that led to his downfall reveals that the Peninsular conflict – the 'Spanish Ulcer' as he dubbed it – played a major role. What began as an opportunist gamble rapidly turned into a ruinous war of attrition that dragged on for six years. Napoleon's war in the Peninsula eventually came to mean for him what Vietnam was later to mean for the Americans, or, indeed, what Afghanistan currently represents for the Russians. Disregarding the age-old maxim that a simple military conquest does not in itself secure one's political aims, he made a fatal error by sending his troops into Spain, destroying any hope of winning popular backing for the government he sought to establish and, simultaneously, committing himself to a costly second front.

Once this blunder became apparent, however, Napoleon, too concerned for his pride and prestige, declined to write off his losses and order his forces to retire to the Ebro or Pyrenees. Instead, encouraged by intermittent successes, he allowed the futile conflict to drag on, and his army was subsequently bled white and demoralised in its constant search for the decisive military victory. Prior to 1808 his forces had only been pitted against the professional armies of other monarchs, and wars against such opponents had easily been presented as a crusade to spread the gospel of the Revolution. In the Peninsula, however, the emperor's troops found themselves encountering mass resistance from the very people they sought to 'liberate' and this, as we have seen, entailed both a dramatic change from the *Blitzkrieg* to which they had become so accustomed and the loss of any sense of moral justification they might once have had. The conflict eventually appeared all too clearly as naked Imperialist aggression against a seemingly weak neighbour who, convinced that she was waging a just war, turned into the most implacable of foes. Thus, the few *Afrancesados* that did appear were constantly attacked by their fellow Spaniards as traitors and collaborators, while the French themselves regarded them with more than a degree of suspicion. In such an atmosphere, King Joseph's regime could never succeed in creating firm foundations on which to build support.

Not only did this lead to disaster in the Peninsula itself, it also had appalling repercussions for Napoleon's empire as a whole. Calamities like Baylen and Vitoria, coupled with the day to day failure to subdue the Iberians, did untold damage to the myth of French invincibility. Furthermore, the dozens of regiments that were squandered in the unpromising operations in Spain could, on two occasions, have been much more usefully employed elsewhere: firstly, in 1809 when Austria suddenly turned on France; and, more significantly, in 1813 when Napoleon – fighting for the very survival of his empire in Central Europe in the wake of the Moscow disaster – was denied the services of the 200,000 veteran troops then bogged down in the Peninsula. Almost certainly, these could have secured a French victory in the conflict for Germany. Indeed, had they been available, it is doubtful whether the Russians would have felt sufficiently strong to risk an advance beyond Poland, or that the Prussian authorities would have dared to sanction the rebellion against French rule. The Allies' decision to carry the war into the heart of Napoleon's empire was largely inspired by the knowledge that he was already heavily committed on the Iberian front and, thus, the 'Spanish Ulcer' played a major role in his ultimate downfall.

But for Spain and Portugal the price of this victory was enormous: ravaged by years of warfare they had lost hundreds of thousands of people, their territories had been occupied and their resources drained, many cities had been reduced to rubble and both states' economies brought to the brink of collapse. Furthermore, the complex political and social problems that the war had either generated or aggravated also grew in intensity and, for years to come, Spain in particular was to be plagued by violent political upheaval.

This state of affairs contrasted markedly with the repercussions the Peninsular War had for Britain. In addition to earning him great wealth and innumerable honours, Wellington's masterful handling of the conflict gained Britain tremendous political and military prestige and, when taken in conjunction with her spiralling economic and naval might, secured her a leading role in establishing the post-war order. The provisions of the Congress of Vienna contained the seeds of future conflicts. But one hundred years were to elapse before the European powers aligned themselves in another war on the scale of that against Napoleon.

CHRONOLOGY

(F denotes a French, and A an Allied, victory)

1807

27 Oct.	Treaty of Fontainebleau.
30 Nov.	Junot occupies Lisbon. F

1808

2 May	The Madrid rising.
25 May	The Asturias lead the provinces in declaring war on France.
8 June	Action at the bridge of Alcolea (Andalusia). F
8 June	Action at Tudela (Navarre). F
10 June	Action on the Llobregat (Catalonia). F
12 June	Action at the bridge of Cabezon (Leon). F
12 June	Engagement at Mallen (Aragon). F
15 June	First siege of Saragossa begins (Aragon).
18 June	French open first attack on Gerona (Catalonia). A
21 June	Action at River Cabriel (Valencia). F
23 June	Merle takes Santander (Old Castile). F
24 June	Action at the Cabrillas defile (Valencia). F
26 June	Moncey attacks Valencia, but retires after two days (Valencia). A
14 July	Battle of Medina de Rio Seco (Leon). F
14 July	Castaños opens the Baylen offensive (Andalusia).
19 July	Battle of Baylen (Andalusia). A
24 July	French open second attempt to take Gerona (Catalonia).
29 July	Action at Evora (Portugal). F
1 Aug.	British expeditionary force lands (Portugal).
13 Aug.	First siege of Saragossa abandoned (Aragon). A
15 Aug.	Action at Obidos (Portugal). A
16 Aug.	French abandon second siege of Gerona (Catalonia). A
17 Aug.	Battle of Roliça (Portugal). A
20 Aug.	Duhesme besieged in Barcelona (Catalonia).
21 Aug.	Battle of Vimiero (Portugal). A.
30 Aug.	Convention of Cintra (Portugal).
13 Sept.	French begin evacuation of Portugal.
25 Oct.	Actions at Logrono and Lodosa (Navarre). F
30 Oct.	French evacuation of Portugal completed.
31 Oct.	Action at Zornoza (Biscay). F
7 Nov.	St-Cyr invests Rosas (Catalonia).
10 Nov.	Battle of Gamonal (Old Castile). F
11 Nov.	Battle of Espinosa (Old Castile). F
23 Nov.	Battle of Tudela (Navarre). F
28 Nov.	Rosas falls (Catalonia). F
30 Nov.	Action at the Somossierra (Old Castile). F
4 Dec.	Napoleon takes Madrid (New Castile). F

16 Dec.	Battle of Cardadeu (Catalonia). F
17 Dec.	The relief of Barcelona (Catalonia). F
20 Dec.	Second siege of Saragossa begins (Aragon).
21 Dec.	Battle of Molins de Rey (Catalonia). F
21 Dec.	Cavalry action at Sahagun (Leon). A
26 Dec.	Action at Benavente (Leon). A
30 Dec.	Engagement at Mansilla (Leon). F

1809

3 Jan.	Action at the Cacabellos defile (near Villafranca, Galicia). A
13 Jan.	Battle of Uclés (New Castile). F
16 Jan.	Battle of Corunna (Galicia). A
21 Jan.	Soult takes Ferrol (Galicia). F
20 Feb.	Second siege of Saragossa ends (Aragon). F
25 Feb.	Battle of Valls (Catalonia). F
5 March	Action at Monterey (Galicia). F
12 March	Chaves taken by Soult (Portugal). F
20 March	Engagement at Braga (Portugal). F
26 March	Battle of Ciudad Real (New Castile). F
28 March	Battle of Medellin (Estremadura). F
29 March	Battle for Oporto (Portugal). F
2 May	Engagement at Amarante (Portugal). F
10 May	Action at Grijon (Portugal). A
12 May	Second battle for Oporto (Portugal). A
14 May	Action at Alcantara (Estremadura). F
19 May	Oviedo falls to the French (Asturias). F
23 May	Battle of Alcaniz (Aragon). A
24 May	Third siege of Gerona begins (Catalonia).
15 June	Battle of Maria (Aragon). F
18 June	Engagement at Belchite (Aragon). F
28 July	Battle of Talavera (New Castile). A
8 Aug.	Action at Arzobispo (Estremadura). F
11 Aug.	Battle of Almonacid (New Castile). F
12 Aug.	Action at Baños; Ney collides with Wilson (Estremadura). F
18 Oct.	Battle of Tamames (Leon). A
11 Nov.	Action at Ocaña (New Castile). F
19 Nov.	Battle of Ocaña (New Castile). F
28 Nov.	Battle of Alba de Tormes (Leon). F
11 Dec.	Third siege of Gerona concludes (Catalonia). F

1810

12 Jan.	Victor takes Almaden (New Castile). F
19 Jan.	Action at La Carolina (Andalusia). F
23 Jan.	Engagement at Jaen (Andalusia). F
24 Jan.	Augereau relieves Barcelona (Catalonia). F
31 Jan.	Bonnet takes Oviedo (Asturias). F
1 Feb.	Seville falls to King Joseph (Andalusia). F
5 Feb.	Victor begins the two-year investment of Cadiz (Andalusia).
20 Feb.	Action at Vich (Catalonia). F
6 March	Suchet blockades Valencia (Valencia).
10 March	Suchet retires from Valencia (Valencia). A
21 March	Action at Villafranca (Catalonia). A
15 April	Suchet besieges Lerida (Catalonia).

21 April	Junot takes Astorga (Galicia). F
23 April	Battle of Lerida-Margaleff (Catalonia). F
12 May	Capture of Hostalrich by Severoli (Catalonia). F
14 May	Lerida falls (Catalonia). F
15 May	Suchet invests Mequinenza (Catalonia).
30 May	Ney invests Ciudad Rodrigo (Leon).
18 June	Mequinenza falls (Catalonia). F
9 July	Fall of Ciudad Rodrigo (Leon). F
24 July	Action on the River Coa (Portugal). F
24 July	Ney invests Almeida (Portugal).
28 July	Almeida falls (Portugal). F
14 Sept.	O'Donnell's raids about Gerona (Catalonia). A
27 Sept.	Battle of Bussaco (Portugal). A
11 Oct.	Massena halts before the Lines of Torres Vedras (Portugal).
4 Nov.	Milhaud routs Blake near Baza (Granada). F
19 Dec.	Suchet besieges Tortosa (Catalonia).

1811

2 Jan.	Suchet takes Tortosa (Catalonia). F
21 Jan.	Soult captures Olivenza (Estremadura). F
27 Jan.	Soult besieges Badajoz (Estremadura).
19 Feb.	Battle of the Gebora (Estremadura). F
4 March	Massena begins the retreat from Santarem (Portugal).
5 March	Battle of Barrosa (Andalusia). A
10 March	Soult captures Badajoz (Estremadura). F
12 March	Action at Redinha (Portugal). A
14 March	Action at Cassal Nova (Portugal). A
15 March	Action at Foz d'Aronce (Portugal). A
15 March	Latour-Maubourg takes Albuquerque (Estremadura). F
25 March	Action at Campo Mayor (Portugal). F
3 April	Macdonald invests Figueras (Catalonia).
3 April	Battle of Sabugal (Portugal). A
11 April	Massena concludes his retreat at Salamanca (Leon).
3 May	(First) Battle of Fuentes de Oñoro (Border of Leon and Portugal). A
5 May	(Second) Battle of Fuentes de Oñoro. A
6 May	Beresford invests Badajoz (Estremadura).
8 May	Suchet invests Tarragona (Catalonia).
10 May	The French abandon Almeida (Portugal).
16 May	Battle of Albuera (Estremadura). A
10 June	The Allies abandon the second siege of Badajoz (Estremadura). F
18 June	Santocildes opens summer campaign in Leon.
28 June	Suchet takes Tarragona (Catalonia). F
2 July	Soult relieves Niebla (Andalusia). F
– Aug.	Santocildes concludes northern campaign (Galicia).
9 Aug.	Soult repulses Freire's offensive (Granada). F
19 Aug.	Macdonald retakes Figueras (Catalonia). F
23 Sept.	Suchet besieges Saguntum (Valencia).
25 Sept.	Action at El Boden (Leon). F
25 Oct.	Battle of Saguntum (Valencia). F
28 Oct.	Action at Arrayo dos Molinos (Estremadura). A
20 Dec.	Leval besieges Tarifa (Andalusia).
25 Dec.	Suchet encircles Valencia (Valencia). F
29 Dec.	Action near Merida (Estremadura). F

1812

8 Jan.	Wellington besieges Ciudad Rodrigo (Leon). Valencia falls. F
19 Jan.	Wellington captures Ciudad Rodrigo (Leon). A
16 March	Wellington besieges Badajoz (Estremadura).
7 April	Wellington captures Badajoz (Estremadura). A
19 May	Action at Almaraz (Estremadura). A
14 June	The Salamanca forts are invested (Leon).
22 June	Admiral Popham takes Lequeitio (Biscay). A
27 June	The Salamanca forts surrender (Leon). A
8 July	Popham takes Castro Urdiales (Biscay). A
19 July	Popham is repulsed at Guetaria (Biscay). F
21 July	O'Donnell defeated at Castalla (Valencia). F
22 July	Battle of Salamanca (Leon). A
3 Aug.	Popham captures Santander (Old Castile). A
11 Aug.	Action at Majalahonda (New Castile). F
12 Aug.	Madrid taken by the Allies (New Castile). A
19 Sept.	Burgos besieged by Wellington (Old Castile).
21 Oct.	Siege of Burgos raised (Old Castile). F
23 Oct.	Action at Venta Del Pozo (Old Castile). F
25 Oct.	Action at Villa Muriel (Old Castile). A
2 Nov.	French retake Madrid (New Castile). F
17 Nov.	Wellington regains the Huerba (Leon).

1813

12 April	Action at the Pass of Biar (Valencia). A
13 April	Battle of Castalla (Valencia). A
3 June	Tarragona besieged by Murray (Catalonia).
12 June	Murray abandons siege of Tarragona (Catalonia). F
21 June	Battle of Vitoria (Navarre). A
25 June	Pamplona blockaded (Navarre).
27 June	Action at Tolosa (Navarre). A
28 June	San Sebastian invested (Biscay).
10 July	General Paris evacuates Saragossa (Aragon). A
25 July	Actions at Maya and Roncesvalles (French-Spanish frontier). A
28 July	First Battle of Sorauren (Navarre). A
30 July	Second Battle of Sorauren (Navarre). A
30 July	Action at Lizaso (Navarre). F
31 Aug.	San Sebastian stormed (Biscay). A
31 Aug.	Battle of San Marcial (Biscay). A
8 Sept.	Citadel of San Sebastian surrenders (Biscay). A
13 Sept.	Action at Ordal (Catalonia). F
7 Oct.	Allies cross Bidassoa (French-Spanish frontier). A
31 Oct.	Pamplona surrenders (Navarre). A
10 Nov.	Battle of the River Nivelle (Franco-Spanish frontier). A
9 Dec.	Battle of the Nive (Gascony, France). A
10 Dec.	Battle of the Nive, conclusion. A
13 Dec.	Battle of St Pierre (Gascony, France). A

1814

27 Feb.	Siege of Bayonne begins (Southern France).
27 Feb.	Battle of Orthez (Southern France). A
20 March	Action at Tarbes (Southern France). A

6 April	Napoleon abdicates.
10 April	Battle of Toulouse (Southern France). F
14 April	Sortie from Bayonne (Southern France). A
27 April	Bayonne surrenders (Southern France). A

APPENDIX 1

Select list and biographical details of important individuals appearing in text

FRENCH PERSONALITIES

Augereau, Marshal Pierre Francois Charles, Duke of Castiglione (1757–1816): Enlisted 1747; divisional general 1793; marshal 1804; 1805–7, distinguished service in Austria, Prussia and Poland. Replaced St Cyr as VII Corps' commander in 1809, capturing Gerona. Military Governor of Catalonia until April 1810.

Bessières, Marshal Jean-Baptiste, Duke of Istria (1768–1813): Distinguished commander of Napoleon's Guard cavalry. Corps commander (1st) 'Army of Spain'; victorious at Medina de Rio Seco (July 1808). Initially II Corps' commander, (2nd) 'Army of Spain', but transferred to cavalry and replaced by Soult. After Wagram (1809), commander of new 'Army of North'. In Russia, 1812; killed in action, 1813.

Bonaparte, Joseph (1768–1844): King of Naples 1806; King of Spain 1808; Lieutenant General of France 1814.

Bonaparte, Napoleon (1769–1821): First Consul 1799; First Consul for Life 1802; Emperor of the French 1804; King of Elba 1814; Emperor of the French March–June 1815; defeated at Waterloo and exiled to St Helena.

Caffarelli Du Falga, General Marie Francois Auguste, Count (1766–1849): Divisional general 1805; sent to Spain 1809. Replaced Dorsenne as commander of 'Army of the North' during May 1812; recalled January 1813.

Clarke, Henri Jacques Guillame, Duke of Feltre (1776–1818): Napoleon's Minister of War.

Clausel, General Bertrand, Count (1772–1842): Brigade general 1799; took command of 'Army of Portugal' during Salamanca; commander of 'Army of the North' under Soult after Vitoria; marshal 1831.

Decaen, Charles Mathieu Isidore (1769–1832): Governor of Catalonia 1811–14.

D'Erlon, General Jean-Baptiste, Count (1765–1844): Commissioned 1782; brigade general 1799; divisional general 1803; marshal 1843. A distinguished officer, d'Erlon was posted to Spain in 1810 as commander of the improvised IX Corps. After service with Massena, he moved to Andalusia where he remained until mid 1812. He then led the 'Army of the Centre' in the recapture of Madrid before replacing Souham as commander of the 'Army of Portugal'. Restored to the 'Army of the Centre', he fought at Vitoria and, for the rest of the war, played a major role in Soult's campaigns as a corps commander – a part he again fulfilled at Waterloo.

Dorsenne, General Jean Marie (?–1812): A lieutenant-colonel in the Imperial Guard, he became Governor of Burgos (1810–11) and commander of the 'Army of the North' (1811–12).

Dupont De L'Etang, General Pierre, Count (1765–1840): Commissioned 1784; brigadier 1795; divisional general 1797; distinguished service in Austria, Prussia and Russia, 1805–7; count, 4 July 1808. Defeated and captured at Baylen; repatriated and disgraced.

Gazan, General Honoré Theodore Maxime, Count de la Peyriène (1765–1845): Brigadier 1799; wounded leading division at Albuera, 1811; commander, 'Army of South', 1813; Soult's Chief-of-Staff 1813–14.

Jourdan, Marshal Jean Baptiste, Count (1762–1833): Celebrated general of Revolutionary Wars (victor of Fleurus, 1794); marshal 1804; Chief-of-Staff to King Joseph 1809 and 1812–13.

Junot, General Jean Andoche, Duke of Abrantes (1771–1813): A distinguished general, Junot was entrusted with the first invasion of Portugal. Defeated at Vimiero, he signed the Cintra Convention; leaving Portugal to the British. Returned to the Peninsula as commander of VIII Corps and then III Corps, fighting at Saragossa. Commanded VIII Corps in Massena's invasion of Portugal, but left the Peninsula after Fuentes de Oñoro (May 1811). Served in Russia and Germany; went insane and committed suicide.

Kellermann, General Francois Etienne, Count, later Duke, of Valmy (1770–1835): Son of Marshal Kellermann; commissioned 1785; brigadier 1797; divisional general 1800. Commander of Junot's cavalry in Portugal; negotiated Cintra Convention; Governor of Leon 1809–11; recalled, May 1811; served in Russia, Germany, France and at Waterloo.

Macdonald, Marshal Jacques Etienne, Duke of Tarentum (1765–1840): Brigadier 1793; divisional general 1794; duke and marshal 1809; commanded VII Corps in Catalonia 1810–11; served in Russia, Germany and France 1812–14.

Marmont, Marshal Auguste Frederic Louis Viesse de, Duke of Ragusa (1774–1852): Commissioned 1792; brigadier 1798; divisional general 1800; marshal 1809. Replaced Massena as commander 'Army of Portugal', May 1811. Defeated at Salamanca (July 1812). Served in Germany and France 1813–14.

Massena, Marshal André, Duke of Rivoli, Prince of Essling (1758–1817): One of Napoleon's most talented subordinates. Divisional general 1793; marshal 1804; prominent in 1809 war with Austria. Commander of 'Army of Portugal' 1810–11.

Mortier, Marshal Edouard Adolphe, Duke of Treviso (1768–1835): Brigadier and divisional general 1799; marshal 1804; duke 1808; commanded V Corps in Spain 1808–11 (victor on the Gebora, February 1811). Served in Russia, Germany and France 1812–14.

Moncey, Marshal Bon Adrien Jannot de, Duke of Conegliano (1754–1852): Enlisted 1769; brigadier 1794; divisional commander 1794; marshal 1804; commanded III Corps, 'Army of Spain', 1808; duke, July 1808; recalled 1809.

Murat, Marshal Joachim, Prince and King of Naples (1767–1815): Enlisted 1787; brigadier 1796; divisional general 1799; marshal 1804; prince 1805; Duke of Berg and Cleves, 1806; outstanding cavalry commander. Appointed Napoleon's Lieutenant in Spain (February 1808), he suppressed the Madrid Rising before retiring on health grounds. Replaced Joseph Bonaparte as King of Naples.

Ney, Marshal Michel, Prince of the Moskwa, Duke of Elchingen (1769–1815): Enlisted 1787; brigadier 1796; divisional general 1799; marshal 1804; VI Corps commander 1805–11. An exceptionally famous officer, Ney – 'Bravest of the Brave' – commanded the VI Corps throughout the campaigns in Spain and Portugal until being dismissed by Massena for insubordination. Served in Russia, Germany, France and at Waterloo.

Reille, General Honoré Charles, Count (1775–1860): Volunteer 1791; brigadier 1803; division commander 1806; count 1808; Spain 1808 (took Rosas); Wagram 1809; commanded 'Army of Portugal' October 1812–Vitoria; corps commander in Soult's 'Army of Spain' 1813–14 and at Waterloo; marshal 1847.

Reynier, General Jean Louis Ebénézer, Count (1771–1814): Volunteered 1792;

brigadier 1795; division commander 1796; served in Italy and Austria, 1807–9. Commanded II Corps in Spain from 1810, serving with Massena in Portugal and at Fuentes de Oñoro. Count, 1811. Russia and Germany 1812–13; captured at Leipzig.

Sebastiani, General Horace Francois Bastien de la Porta, Count (1772–1851): Commissioned 1789; brigadier 1803; *général de division* 1805. Replaced Marshal Lefebvre as IV Corps' commander in February 1809, fighting at Talavera. Count, December 1809. Served in Granada 1810–11; Russia, Germany and France 1812–14. Prominent politician after 1819; marshal 1840.

Souham, General Joseph, Count (1760–1837): A distinguished general of the Revolutionary Wars, Souham did lengthy service as a division commander in the VII Corps in Catalonia. Wounded at Vich (1810), he returned to Spain the following year and, as commander of the 'Army of Portugal' in 1812, drove Wellington from Burgos. Thereafter he served in the east, fighting at Leipzig and Paris.

Soult, Marshal Nicolas Jean de Dieu, Duke of Dalmatia (1769–1851): An immensely distinguished officer by 1807, this vain and ambitious son of a Gascon noble was given command of the II Corps (2nd) 'Army of Spain', with which he completed the pursuit of Moore to Corunna. His (1809) invasion of Portugal was thwarted by Wellesley at Oporto, but, given control of three corps, he subsequently swept into the Allies' rear during the Talavera campaign and drove them south of the Tagus. A period as King Joseph's Chief-of-Staff followed, culminating in Ocaña and the invasion of southern Spain; the theatre in which Soult was to remain for 2½ years. Badajoz's fall and Salamanca eventually compelled him to evacuate his domain, but, joining with Joseph, he retook Madrid and hustled Wellington back into Portugal.

Recalled to France in early 1813, Soult fought in Germany. However, Vitoria led to his return as Commander-in-Chief. Although eventually pushed back into France, he maintained the western front against awesome odds and, in 1815, served as Napoleon's Chief-of-Staff. Banished by the Bourbons, he returned to France in 1820. He subsequently became a peer (1827); Minister of War (1830–34); Foreign Minister (1839); President of the Council of Ministers (1832–34 and 1840–47) and Marshal General of France (1847). His brother, General Pierre Benoit (1770–1843), also saw extensive service in the Peninsula as a cavalry commander, often fighting under his distinguished sibling.

Suchet, Marshal Louis Gabriel, Duke of Albufera (1770–1826): Probably Napoleon's most able Peninsular commander. Commissioned 1791; brigadier 1798; divisional general 1799; division commander, V Corps, 1805–9, serving in Austria, Prussia, Poland and Spain; count, 1808. Replaced Junot as III Corps' commander in April 1809. His series of victories in Aragon, Catalonia and Valencia led to him being made a marshal (1811) and duke (1812), but he was repulsed at Castalla (1813) by Murray and subsequently evacuated Catalonia.

Victor, Marshal Claude Victor-Perrin, Duke of Bellune (1764–1841): Enlisted 1781; brigadier 1795; divisional general 1797; marshal 1807; duke 1808. Commanded I Corps in Spain, 1808–December 1811. Victorious at Espinosa and Medellin, but repulsed at Talavera and Barrosa. Served in Russia, Germany and France, 1812–14.

ALLIED PERSONALITIES

Alten, General Sir Charles, Count von (1764–1840): This Hanoverian officer first served in the Peninsula with the KGL and took control of the Light Division on Craufurd's death (1812).

Areizaga, General Carlos (?–1816): Served as a division commander in Blake's 'Army of the Right' (1809). After Belchite he was given command of the new 'Army of La Mancha', but was decisively defeated at Ocaña. Ousted from the passes about Baylen, he failed to prevent the French overrunning Andalusia and most of his remaining forces were dispersed at Jaen (January, 1810). His command then passed to General Freire.

Ballesteros, General Francisco (1770–1832): Asturian general. After being routed at Bilbao in 1809, he became pre-eminent in the war in southern Spain. However, he rebelled over Wellington's selection as Generalissimo (1812) and was dismissed by the *Cortes*.

Bathurst, Henry, 3rd Earl (1762–1834): Liverpool's Secretary for War and the Colonies.

Beresford, General William Carr, Viscount (1764–1854): After serving at Corunna, Beresford was entrusted with the training of the Portuguese Army; being created a Portuguese marshal in March 1809. A brief period of independent command ended with his hard won victory at Albuera, but Wellington regularly entrusted him with important strategic roles during the campaigns of 1813–14.

Blake, General Joachim (1759–1827): Of Irish extraction, Blake commanded the 'Army of Galicia' in 1808. After Espinosa he was replaced by La Romana and made commander of the forces of the Coronilla. He fought throughout the years 1809–11 in the south and east of the Peninsula; conducting several major campaigns and battles. He was eventually captured at Valencia (January 1812).

Canning, George (1770–1827): Foreign Secretary 1807–9; wounded in duel with Castlereagh, 1809.

Castaños, General Francisco Xavier, Duke of Baylen (1756–1852): Victor at Baylen; defeated at Tudela. Held various administrative posts – served on Council of Regency – and minor field commands, 1809–13. Dismissed by *Cortes* in command reshuffle of 1813, but remained prominent in politics.

Castlereagh, Robert Stewart, Viscount (1760–1822): Secretary for War and Colonies from 1805; consistently supported Wellington in Peninsula. Foreign Secretary 1812–22; Marquis Londonderry 1821; committed suicide.

Clinton, Lieutenant-General Sir Henry (1771–1829): Clinton served at Corunna and, in 1811, assumed command of the Sixth Division – a post he retained until 1814. His brother, William, succeeded Bentinck as Allied commander in Catalonia (1813).

Cole, General Sir Galbraith Lowry (1772–1842): Posted to the Peninsula in 1808, Cole served as the Fourth Division's commander for most of the period 1810–14. Wounded at Albuera and Salamanca.

Craufurd, Major-General Sir Robert (1764–1812): The martinet 'Black Bob' Craufurd served in the Corunna campaign and was given command of the Light Division on its formation in 1810. Probably Wellington's best divisional commander, he was mortally wounded at Ciudad Rodrigo (1812).

Cuesta, General Gregorio Garcia de la (1740–1812): Obstinate and cantankerous. Captain General of Old Castile, 1808; defeated at Medina. Commanded 'Army of Estremadura', 1809; defeated at Medellin. Joined Wellesley in Talavera campaign; paralysed by a stroke shortly after.

Dalhousie, General Sir George Ramsay, 9th Earl (1770–1838): Commissioned 1788; joined Peninsular army in 1812 as the commander of Seventh Division. Prominent in 'Battle of Pyrenees'.

Del Parque, General Don Lorenzo Fernandez de Villavincencio, Duke of Del Parque and San Lorenzo (1778–1859): Colonel 1801; brigadier 1808; commander 'Army of Left', 1809; defeated at Alba; replaced Ballesteros in 1812.

Freire, General Manuel (1765–1834): Active in Murcia and Granada, 1810–12. Replaced Giron as commander of 'Army of Galicia' in 1813; victor of San Marcial.

Giron, General Pedro Augustin, Duke of Ahumada (1788–1842): Nephew of Castaños. Commander of 'Army of Galicia' in Vitoria campaign; replaced H. O'Donnell as commander of 'Army of Reserve of Andalusia' after the Nivelle; fought at Bayonne.

Graham, General Sir Thomas, Lord Lynedoch (1748–1843): Moore's ADC at Corunna; Walcheren, 1809; Peninsula from 1810; Commander of British garrison of Cadiz, defeating Victor at Barrosa (March 1811). Thereafter served with Wellington's main army as commander of First Division and, often, of the whole left wing. Besieged San Sebastian (1813). Increasingly troubled by an eye complaint, he retired after the Bidassoa.

Hill, General Sir Rowland, Viscount (1772–1842): The immensely popular 'Daddy' Hill took part in all the campaigns of 1808–9, but fell ill during 1810. He returned as commander of the army's southern wing and operated in an independent capacity for much of 1811–12. After Salamanca he assumed command of Wellington's right wing, playing crucial roles in every ensuing campaign. Baron 1814; viscount 1842; Commander-in-Chief 1825–39.

Hope, Lieutenant-General Sir John, 4th Earl of Hopetoun (1765–1823): A division commander at Corunna, Hope returned to the Peninsula in 1813; replacing the ailing Graham as head of the army's left wing. Captured at Bayonne.

La Romana, General Pedro Caro y Sureda, Marquis of (1761–1811): Commanded Baltic 'hostage' corps, 1807–8. Replaced Blake as head of the Galician forces. Assisted Moore in the Corunna campaign and remained active in the north until November 1809 when he replaced Del Parque as head of the 'Army of the Left'. Failed to save Seville in January 1810, but operated effectively in Portugal and Estremadura until his death, from a heart condition, whilst attempting to relieve Badajoz.

Liverpool, Robert Banks Jenkinson, 2nd Earl of (1770–1828): Foreign Secretary 1801–3; Home Secretary 1804–6 and 1807–9; Secretary for War and Colonies 1809–12; Prime Minister 1812–27.

Longa, General Francisco (1770–1831): Initially a highly successful guerilla leader, his forces steadily grew and he was given commands in the regular army, fighting with distinction at San Marcial.

Mina, General Francisco Espoz y (1781–1836): Celebrated Navarrese guerilla leader, made a general in 1813. His nephew, Xavier (1789–1817), was also a prominent guerilla commander, but was captured in 1810 by Suchet's troops.

Moore, Lieutenant-General Sir John (1761–1809): Commissioned 1776; major-general 1798; knighted 1804; lieutenant-general 1805. An extremely distinguished soldier, he replaced Burrard as commander of the British forces in Portugal (1808). Mortally wounded at Corunna.

O'Donnell, General Henry Joseph, Count of La Bispal (1769–1834): Of Irish descent, O'Donnell played a leading role fighting the French in Catalonia. From 1812 he commanded the 'Reserve Army of Andalusia', serving at Pamplona and Sorauren. His brother, José, briefly commanded the 'Army of Murcia', but was dismissed after his disastrous defeat at Castalla (July 1812).

Pakenham, Edward (1778–1815): Deputy Adjutant-General in the Peninsula 1810–12; Third Division commander 1812; Sixth Division commander 1813. Killed in action, New Orleans.

Palafox Y Melzi, General José, Duke of Saragossa (1780–1847): Commanded the defenders of Saragossa 1808–9; prisoner until 1814. His brother, Francisco, was a minor guerilla leader.

Picton, Lieutenant-General Sir Thomas (1758–1815): Coarse, moody and impetuous, Picton took command of the Third Division in 1810. Badly wounded at Badajoz, he next served at Vitoria. His headstrong nature often got him into difficulties, but he was undoubtedly one of Wellington's ablest subordinates. Killed at Waterloo.

Sanchez, General Don Julian (?): Retired soldier whose mounted guerillas fought throughout Leon and Old Castile, becoming regular cavalry in 1813.

Stewart, Lieutenant-General Sir William (1774–1827): Commissioned 1786; commanded Second Division 1811–14.

Venegas, General Francisco Xavier (?–1838): Brigadier 1808; defeated at Uclés and Almonacid. Served in Latin America until 1811, when he returned to Spain and took up a post in the Galician corps.

Wellesley, Field Marshal Sir Arthur, Duke of Wellington, Viscount Douro (1769–1852): Commissioned 1787; Lieutenant-colonel 1793; India 1797–1805; Copenhagen 1807; Lieutenant-general and commander of the forces in Portugal 1808; 'Commander of the Forces' in the Peninsula 1809–14; victor at Waterloo; Prime Minister 1828–30.

Wellesley, Richard Colley, Marquis (1760–1842): Wellington's brother; marquis 1799; Ambassador to Spain 1809; Foreign Secretary 1809–12.

APPENDIX 2

Select list of Peninsular War Armies and their strengths

THE FIRST FRENCH 'ARMY OF SPAIN'

GENERAL JUNOT'S ARMY CORPS (*Later 'Army of Portugal'*)

1st Div. (Delaborde)	7 Batts.	7,850
2nd Div. (Loison)	7 Batts.	8,480
3rd Div. (Travot)	8 Batts.	5,540
Cavalry (Kellermann)	7 Sqds.	1,750
Artillery etc.		1,300
Total:		24,920

GENERAL DUPONT'S ARMY CORPS

1st Div. (Barbou)	9 Batts.	7,840
2nd Div. (Vedel)	7 Batts.	6,890
3rd Div. (Frere)	5 Batts.	5,200
Cavalry (Fresia)	15 Sqds.	3,300
Artillery etc.		1,200
Total:		24,430

MARSHAL MONCEY'S ARMY CORPS

1st Div. (Musnier)	17 Batts.	9,700
2nd Div. (Gobert)	17 Batts.	8,400
3rd Div. (Morlot)	13 Batts.	7,150
Cavalry (Grouchy)	12 Sqds.	2,850
Artillery etc.		1,250
Total:		29,350

MARSHAL BESSIÈRES' ARMY CORPS

1st Div. (Merle)	6 Batts.	5,250
2nd Div. (Verdier)	16 Batts.	8,520
Cavalry (Lasalle)	7 Sqds.	1,100
Artillery etc.		400
Garrisons	5 Batts.	
	2 Sqds.	3,820
Total:		19,090

GENERAL DUHESME'S ARMY CORPS

1st Div. (Chabran)	8 Batts.	6,050
2nd Div. (Lecchi)	6 Batts.	4,600
Cavalry (Schwartz and Bessières)	9 Sqds.	1,700
Artillery etc.		360
Total:		12,710

GENERAL DORSENNE'S IMPERIAL GUARD CONTINGENT

Infantry	3,070
Cavalry	1,770
Artillery etc.	1,580
Total:	6,420

TROOPS JOINING ARMY DURING SUMMER, 1808

Commands of General Mouton, Reille, Chabot, Bazancourt and Chlopiski:	23,190
Cavalry of the Guard:	3,900
Misc. battalions, companies, drafts etc.	21,110
Total:	48,200
GRAND TOTAL:	165,120

THE SPANISH ARMIES, AUTUMN 1808

'ARMY OF ARAGON' (*Palafox*)

1st Div. (O'Neille)	13 Batts.	9,760
	1 Sqd.	170
	3 Guns	80
Total:		10,010
2nd Div. (St March)	13 Batts.	8,440
	4 Sqds.	620
Total:		9,060
3rd Div. (Lazan)	6 Batts.	4,600
	1 Cav. Troop	24
	3 Guns	64
Total:		4,688
GRAND TOTAL:		23,758

'ARMY OF GALICIA' (*Blake*)

Vanguard (Mendizabal)	5 Batts.	2,880
1st Div. (Figueroa)	7 Batts.	4,018
2nd Div. (Martinengo)	7 Batts. 4 Sqds.	4,764 302
		5,066
3rd Div. (Riquelme)	7 Batts.	4,800
4th Div. (Carbajol)	10 Batts.	3,530
5th Div. (San Roman)	8 Batts.	5,294
6th Div. (Acevedo)	11 Batts.	7,630
Reserve Div. (Mahy)	5 Batts.	3,000
Artillery etc.	38 Guns	1,000
GRAND TOTAL:		37,218

'ARMY OF ESTREMADURA' (*Belvedere*)

1st Div. (Belvedere)	5 Batts. 3 Sqds. 12 Guns	4,160 360 408
Total:		4,928
2nd Div. (Henestrosa)	5 Batts. 2 Sqds. 12 Guns	3,300 300 440
Total:		4,040
3rd Div. (Trias)	4 Batts. 2 Sqds.	3,580 300
Total:		3,880
GRAND TOTAL:		12,848

'ARMY OF CATALONIA' (*Vives*)

Vanguard Div. (Alvarez)	10 Batts.	5,500
	1 Sqd.	100
Total:		5,600
1st Div. (Caldagues)	7 Batts.	4,528
	4 Sqds.	400
	6 Guns	70
Total:		4,998
2nd Div. (Laguna)	5 Batts.	2,076
	2 Sqds.	200
	7 Guns	84
Total:		2,360
3rd Div. (La Serna)	5 Batts.	2,458
4th Div. (Milans)	4 Batts.	3,710
Reserve Div.	Infantry	777
	Cavalry	80
	4 Guns	48
Total:		905
GRAND TOTAL:		20,031

'ARMY OF THE CENTRE' (*Castaños and Pignatelli*)

1st Div. (Villariezo)	5 Batts.	3,548
2nd Div. (Grimarest)	13 Batts.	6,000
3rd Div. (Rengel)	8 Batts.	6,500
4th Div. (La Pena)	13 Batts.	7,500
5th Div. (Roca)	15 Batts.	7,000
6th Div. (Pignatelli)	15 Batts.	11,000
Cavalry	12 Regts.	3,500
GRAND TOTAL:		45,048

'ARMY OF GRANADA' (*Reding*)

1st Div.	7 Batts.	8,200
2nd Div.	5 Batts.	6,000
Cavalry	4 Sqds.	670

Artillery etc.	6 Guns	130

GRAND TOTAL: 11,550

THE ARMY AT SOMOSIERRA (*San Juan*)

Detached from 'Army of Centre'	14 Batts.	7,650
Misc. detachments, levies, etc.	6 Batts.	3,000
Cavalry	6 Sqds.	600
Artillery etc.	22 Guns	300

GRAND TOTAL: 11,550

RESERVES

Asturias	5,300
Estremadura	7,000
Murcia and Valencia	6,000
Andalusia	11,000
Balearic Is.	3,400
Aragon	12,000
Galicia	6,660

Total: 51,360

THE SECOND FRENCH 'ARMY OF SPAIN'

MARSHAL VICTOR'S I CORPS

1st Div. (Ruffin)	10 Batts.
2nd Div. (Lapisse)	12 Batts.
3rd Div. (Villatte)	12 Batts.
Cavalry (Beaumont)	2 Lt Regts.

Total: 33,940

MARSHAL BESSIÈRES' II CORPS (*Later Soult*)

1st Div. (Mouton, later Merle)	13 Batts.
2nd Div. (Merle, later Mermet)	17 Batts.
3rd Div. (Bonnet)	8 Batts.
Cavalry (Lasalle)	2 Lt, 1 Med. Regts.

Total: 33,050

MARSHAL MONCEY'S III CORPS

1st Div. (Mathieu later Grandjean)	12 Batts.
2nd Div. (Musnier)	9 Batts.

3rd Div. (Morlot)	8 Batts.
4th Div. (Grandjean)	9 Batts.
Cavalry (Wathier)	1 Heavy, 2 Lt Regts.

Total: 37,690

MARSHAL LEFEBVRE'S IV CORPS

1st Div. (Sebastiani)	12 Batts.
2nd Div. (Leval)	9 Batts.
3rd Div. (Valence)	6 Batts.
Cavalry (Maupetit)	1 Med., 2 Lt Regts.

Total: 22,900

MARSHAL MORTIER'S V CORPS

1st Div. (Suchet)	16 Batts.
2nd Div. (Gazan)	12 Batts.
Cavalry (De Laage)	2 Lt Regts.

Total: 24,550

MARSHAL NEY'S VI CORPS

1st Div. (Marchand)	12 Batts.
2nd Div. (Lagrange, later Mathieu)	14 Batts.
Cavalry (Colbert)	2 Lt Regts.

Total: 20,000

GENERAL GOUVION ST-CYR'S VII CORPS

1st Div. (Chabran)	8 Batts.
2nd Div. (Lecchi)	6 Batts.
3rd Div. (Reille)	12 Batts.
4th Div. (Souham)	10 Batts.
5th Div. (Pino)	13 Batts.
6th Div. (Chabot)	3 Batts.
Cavalry (Bessières)	1 Heavy, 1 Lt Regt.
Cavalry (Schwartz)	2 Lt Regts.
Cavalry (Fontane)	1 Med., 1 Lt Regt.
Cavalry (?)	1 Med. Regt.

Total: 42,380

GENERAL JUNOT'S VIII CORPS

1st Div. (Delaborde)	9 Batts.
2nd Div. (Loison)	7 Batts.
3rd Div. (Heudelet)	9 Batts.

Total: 25,000

THE RESERVE

1st Div. (Dessolles)	12 Batts.	
2nd Div. (Saligny)	4 Batts.	
Total:		10,000

IMPERIAL GUARDS

Six Infantry Regiments:	14 Batts.	8,000
Five Cavalry Regiments:		3,500
Artillery etc.	36 Cannon	600
Total:		12,100

CAVALRY RESERVE

1st Div. (Latour-Maubourg)	6 Dragoon Regts.	3,700
2nd Div. (Lahoussaye)	4 Dragoon Regts.	2,020
3rd Div. (Lorges)	4 Dragoon Regts.	3,100
4th Div. (Millet)	4 Dragoon Regts.	2,900
5th Div. (Milhaud)	3 Dragoon Regts.	2,940
6th Div. (Franceschi)	3 Lt, 1 Med. Regt.	2,400
Total:		17,060
GRAND TOTAL:		278,670

INFANTADO'S 'ARMY OF THE CENTRE', JANUARY 1809

VANGUARD DIV. (*Albuquerque*)	9 Batts.	3,929
1st Div. (Coupigny)	16 Batts.	5,121
2nd Div. (Orgaz)	14 Batts.	5,288
Reserve (La Peña)	9 Batts.	4,295
Cavalry	14 Regts.	2,800
Artillery etc.	14 Guns	769
Total:		22,200

VENEGAS' FORCE AT UCLÉS

Infantry:	9,500
Cavalry:	2,000
Artillery etc.	480
Total:	11,980

THE FRENCH ARMY IN SPAIN, 1 FEBRUARY 1809

(The following figures are effectives only. Add 56,000 sick and 36,000 detached.)

VICTOR'S I CORPS

1st Div. (Ruffin)	9 Batts.	5,430
2nd Div. (Lapisse)	12 Batts.	7,700
3rd Div. (Villatte)	12 Batts.	6,380
Cavalry (Beaumont)	3 Lt Regts.	1,870
Artillery etc.	48 Guns	1,556
Total:		22,936

SOULT'S II CORPS

1st Div. (Merle)	15 Batts.	6,150
2nd Div. (Mermet)	15 Batts.	5,120
3rd Div. (Delaborde)	9 Batts.	4,610
4th Div. (Heudelet)	10 Batts.	2,820
Cavalry (Franceschi)	3 Lt, 5 Med. Regts.	3,000
Artillery etc.	54 Guns	1,740
Total:		23,440

JUNOT'S III CORPS

1st Div. (Grandjean)	10 Batts.	5,566
2nd Div. (Musnier)	9 Batts.	3,244
3rd Div. (Morlot)	13 Batts.	2,340
Cavalry (Wathier)	1 Heavy, 3 Lt Regts.	1,350
Artillery etc.	40 Guns	1,240
Engineer corps for Saragossa		2,340
Total:		16,080

SEBASTIANI'S IV CORPS

1st Div. (Sebastiani)	12 Batts.	5,660
2nd Div. (Leval)	9 Batts.	3,130
3rd Div. (Valence)	6 Batts.	3,910
Cavalry (?)	1 Med., 2 Lt Regts.	1,780
Artillery etc.	30 Guns	910
Total:		15,390

MORTIER'S V CORPS

1st Div. (Suchet)	16 Batts.	8,480
2nd Div. (Gazan)	12 Batts.	7,100
Cavalry (De Laage)	2 Lt Regts.	930
Artillery etc.	30 Guns	1,450
Total:		17,960

NEY'S VI CORPS

1st Div. (Marchand)	12 Batts.	6,860
2nd Div. (Mathieu)	12 Batts.	6,910
Cavalry (Lorcet)	2 Med., 2 Lt Regts.	1,440
Artillery etc.	30 Guns	1,570
Total:		16,780

GOUVION ST-CYR'S VII CORPS

1st Div. (Souham)	10 Batts.	6,220
2nd Div. (Chabran)	6 Batts.	4,040
3rd Div. (Chabot)	3 Batts.	1,640
4th Div. (Reille)	7 Batts.	3,980
5th Div. (Pino)	13 Batts.	8,000
6th Div. (Lecchi)	6 Batts.	3,940
Westphalians (Morio)	7 Batts.	5,320
Cavalry	1 Heavy, 2 Med., 4 Lt	3,600
Artillery etc.	54 Guns	2,680
Total:		39,420

CAVALRY RESERVE

1st Div. (Latour-Maubourg)	6 Dragoon Regts.	2,530
2nd Div. (Milhaud)	4 Dragoon Regts.	2,125
3rd Div. (Millet)	4 Dragoon Regts.	1,480
4th Div. (Lasalle)	1 Med., 3 Lt Regts.	1,500
Artillery etc.	24 Guns	700
Total:		8,335

RESERVE AT MADRID

1st Div. (Desolles)	12 Batts.	8,500
Royal Guards	8 Batts.	2,200
Cavalry	1 Lt Regt.	500
Total:		11,200

NORTHERN GARRISONS (*Bessières*)
Total: 19,900

ARTILLERY PARK
Total: 2,580

GRAND TOTAL: 194,021

ELEMENTS OF VICTOR'S ARMY PRESENT AT MEDELLIN

Villatte's Division	12 Batts.	6,000

Ruffin's Division	9 Batts.	5,000
Leval's Division	5 Batts.	2,000
Latour-Maubourg's Division	5 Dragoon Regts.	2,000
Lasalle's Division	3 Lt Regts.	800
Artillery etc.	50 Cannon	1,000
Corps cavalry	2 Lt Regts.	1,000
Total:		17,800

ELEMENTS OF CUESTA'S ARMY PRESENT AT MEDELLIN

Trias' Division	4 Regts.	3,750
Henestrosa's Division	4 Regts.	3,750
Del Parque's Division	4 Regts.	3,750
Albuquerque's Division	6 Regts.	5,000
Portago's Division	4 Regts.	3,750
Cavalry	8 Regts.	3,100
Artillery etc.	30 Cannon	800
Total:		23,900

(There was also a garrison of five battalions in Badajoz.)

WELLESLEY'S ARMY AT TALAVERA (EFFECTIVES)

FIRST DIVISION (*Sherbrooke*)

Campbell's Brigade	2+ Batts.	2,045
Cameron's Brigade	2+ Batts.	1,364
Langwerth's Brigade	2+ Batts.	1,388
Low's Brigade	2 Batts.	1,167
Total:		5,964

SECOND DIVISION (*Hill*)

Tilson's Brigade	3+ Batts.	1,891
Stewart's Brigade	3 Batts	2,014
Total:		3,905

THIRD DIVISION (*Mackenzie*)

Mackenzie's Brigade	3 Batts.	2,276
Donkin's Brigade	2+ Batts.	1,471
Total:		3,747

FOURTH DIVISION (*Campbell*)

Campbell's Brigade	2+ Batts.	1,032
Kemmis' Brigade	3+ Batts.	1,928
Total:		2,960

CAVALRY DIVISION (*Payne*)

Fane's Brigade	2 Regts.	1,070
Cotton's Brigade	2 Regts.	989
Anson's Brigade	2 Regts.	910
Total:		2,969

ARTILLERY

Three British Batteries	18 Guns	681
Two German Batteries	12 Guns	330
Total:		1,011

MISCELLANEOUS

Staff Corps	63
Engineers etc.	22
Total:	85
GRAND TOTAL:	20,641

CUESTA'S ARMY AT TALAVERA (EFFECTIVES)

Vanguard	(Zayas)	5 Batts.	3,685
1st Div.	(de Zayas)	7 Batts.	5,159
2nd Div.	(Iglesias)	7 Batts.	5,200
3rd Div.	(Portago)	6 Batts.	4,422
4th Div.	(Manglano)	7 Batts.	5,100
5th Div.	(Bassecourt)	6 Batts.	4,500
Cav. Div. 1	(Henestrosa)	8 Regts.	3,440
Cav. Div. 2	(Albuquerque)	6 Regts.	2,687
Artillery		30 Guns	800
Total:			34,993

KING JOSEPH'S ARMY AT TALAVERA (EFFECTIVES)

FIRST CORPS
(Victor)

1st Div.	(Ruffin)	9 Batts.	5,086

2nd Div.	(Lapisse)	12 Batts.	6,662
3rd Div.	(Villatte)	12 Batts.	5,935
Cavalry	(Beaumont)	2 Regts.	880
Artillery		28 Guns	700

Total: 19,263

FOURTH CORPS
(Sebastiani)

1st Div.	(Sebastiani)	12 Batts.	7,918
2nd Div.	(Valence)	2 Batts.	1,400
3rd Div.	(Leval)	9 Batts.	4,337
Cavalry	(Merlin)	4 Regts.	1,088
Artillery		28 Guns	700

Total: 15,443

RESERVE CAVALRY

1st Div.	(Latour-Maubourg)	6 Regts.	3,179
2nd Div.	(Milhaud)	6 Regts.	2,256
Artillery		8 Guns	200

Total: 5,635

FROM MADRID

1st Brigade	(Dessolles)	6 Batts.	3,137
Guard Inf.			1,600
Guard Cav.			350
Line Cav.		2 Sqds.	250
Artillery		16 Guns	400
Misc.			60

Total: 5,797

GRAND TOTAL: 46,138

SUCHET'S 'ARMY OF ARAGON', MAY 1809

1st Div.	(Laval)	8 Batts.	4,000
2nd Div.	(Musnier)	8 Batts.	4,400
3rd Div.	(Morlot)	2 Batts.	900
Misc.		5 Co.	450
Cavalry	(Wathier)	2 Lt Regts., 1 Heavy	800
Artillery etc.			450

Total: 11,000

Note: Three regiments – nine battalions – of Morlot's division were in Castile and Navarre. Six of these battalions (3,000 men) joined Suchet at Maria on 15 June.

BLAKE'S 'ARMY OF ARAGON', MAY–JUNE 1809

Vanguard:	(Creagh)	3 Batts.	2,300
1st Div.	(Roca)	7 Batts.	4,890
2nd Div.	(Lazan)	7 Batts.	5,840
Cavalry	(O'Donnell)	5 Sqds.	700
Artillery etc.			500
Total:			14,230

AREIZAGA'S DIVISION AT BOTORRITA

(3rd Division)	8½ Batts.	5,840
Cavalry	2 Sqds.	370
Artillery etc.		220
Total:		6,430

AREIZAGA'S ARMY IN THE OCAÑA CAMPAIGN

Vanguard Division:	(Zayas)	7 Batts.	7,000
1st Div.	(Lacy)	9 Batts.	7,800
2nd Div.	(Vigodet)	9 Batts.	7,085
3rd Div.	(Giron)	8 Batts.	5,240
4th Div.	(Castejon)	8 Batts.	6,390
5th Div.	(Zerain)	7 Batts.	5,880
6th Div.	(Jacomé)	9 Batts.	7,630
7th Div.	(Copons)	6 Batts.	5,120
1st Cav. Div.	(Bernuy)	5 Regts.	1,440
2nd Cav. Div.	(Rivas)	4 Regts.	1,152
3rd Cav. Div.	(March)	6 Regts.	1,728
4th Cav. Div.	(Osorio)	5 Regts.	1,440
Artillery, Misc., etc.		60 Guns	2,870
Total:			60,775

KING JOSEPH'S ARMY AT OCAÑA

Division Werlé	6 Batts.	4,000
Division Leval	9 Batts.	4,000
Division Gazan	12 Batts.	6,000

Division Girard	12 Batts.	6,000
Brigade Rey	6 Batts.	3,500
King's Guards etc.	8 Batts.	3,500
Division Milhaud	5 Regts.	1,800
Division Paris	3 Regts.	1,000
Division Beauregard	4 Regts.	1,500
Reserve cavalry	1 Regts.	700
Artillery etc.		1,500
Total:		**33,500**

DEL PARQUE'S 'ARMY OF THE LEFT', AUTUMN 1809

Vanguard Division	(La Carrera)	14 Batts.	7,413
1st Div.	(Losada)	14 Batts.	8,336
2nd Div.	(De Belveder)	14 Batts.	6,759
3rd Div.	(Ballesteros)	15 Batts.	9,991
4th Div.	(Mahy)	14 Batts.	7,100
5th Div.	(De Castrofuerte)	7 Batts.	6,157
Cav. Div.	(Anglona)	6 Regts.	1,682
Misc.		1 Batt.	937
Garrison of Ciudad Rodrigo			3,817
Total:			**52,192**

THE FRENCH ARMY IN SPAIN, JANUARY 1810
(Effectives only. Add 27,862 sick.)

I CORPS *(Marshal Victor)*

1st Div.	(Ruffin)	9 Batts.	4,426
2nd Div.	(Darricau)	8 Batts.	5,901
3rd Div.	(Villatte)	12 Batts.	6,339
Cavalry	(Beaumont)	2 Lt Regts.	823
Dragoon Div.	(Latour-Maubourg)	6 Regts.	2,260
Artillery etc.			2,915
Total:			**22,664**

II CORPS *(General Heudelet)*

1st Div.	(Merle)	12 Batts.	5,949
2nd Div.	(Heudelet)	13 Batts.	7,325
Cavalry	(Soult)	4 Lt Regts.	866
Dragoon Div.	(Lahoussaye)	4 Regts.	1,229
Artillery etc.			758
Total:			**16,127**

III CORPS *(General Suchet)*

1st Div.	(Laval)	6 Batts.	4,290
2nd Div.	(Musnier)	11 Batts.	7,173
3rd Div.	(Habert)	7 Batts.	4,329
Cavalry	(Boussard)	1 Heavy and 1 Lt Regt.	1,899
Artillery etc.			1,287
Garrisons			4,162
Total:			23,140

IV CORPS *(General Sebastiani)*

1st Div.	(Sebastiani)	3 Batts.	1,630
2nd Div.	(Werlé)	6 Batts.	4,809
Cavalry	(Perreymond)	3 Lt Regts.	1,351
Dragoon Div.	(Milhaud)	5 Regts.	1,721
Artillery etc.			614
Total:			10,125

V CORPS *(Marshal Mortier)*

1st Div.	(Girard)	12 Batts.	7,040
2nd Div.	(Gazan)	12 Batts.	6,633
Cavalry	(Marisy)	2 Lt, 3 Med. Regts.	2,127
Artillery etc.			812
Total:			16,612

VI CORPS *(Marshal Ney)*

1st Div.	(Marchand)	11 Batts.	6,071
2nd Div.	(Mermet)	10 Batts.	6,857
3rd Div.	(Loison)	19 Batts.	12,250
Cavalry	(Lorges)	2 Lt, 2 Med. Regts.	2,422
Artillery etc.			1,223
Total:			28,823

VII CORPS *(Marshal Augereau)*

1st Div.	(Souham)	10 Batts.	
Cavalry		2 Regts.	
Total:			5,382
2nd Div.	(Pino)	11 Batts.	
Cavalry		1 Regt.	
Total:			6,584
3rd Div.	(Verdier)	23 Batts.	
Cavalry		1 Regt.	
Total:			6,343
4th Div.	(Duhesme)	9 Batts.	
Cavalry		1 Regt.	
Total:			6,211
Artillery, garrisons, etc.			9,963
Total:			34,483

VIII CORPS (*General Junot*)

1st Div.	(Clausel)	12 Batts.	9,346
2nd Div.	(Lagrange)	13 Batts.	8,883
3rd Div.	(Solignac)	12 Batts.	7,060
Cavalry	(St Croix)	16 Provisional Regts.	5,448
Artillery, garrisons, etc.			2,458

Total: **33,195**

GARRISONS ETC.

Valladolid	(Kellermann)	4,978
Biscay	(Valentin)	15,272
Navarre	(Dufour)	8,512
Segovia	(Laval)	4,407
Santander	(Bonnet)	7,064
Madrid		11,474

Total: **51,707**

TROOPS ON MARCH

To Ney	5,792
To Andalusia	8,354
At Bayonne	13,296
IX Corps	16,415
Imperial (Young) Guard	16,401

Total: **60,258**

GRAND TOTAL: **297,134**

WELLINGTON'S ARMY AT BUSSACO, 27 SEPTEMBER 1810

FIRST DIVISION (*Spencer*)

1st Brigade	(Stopford)	2 Batts. + Lt Inf.	1,684
2nd Brigade	(Blantyre)	3 Batts. + Lt Inf.	1,516
3rd Brigade	(Lowe)	4 Batts. + Lt Inf.	2,061
4th Brigade	(Pakenham)	2 Batts.	1,792

Total: **7,053**

SECOND DIVISION (*Hill*)

1st Brigade	(Stewart)	4 Batts. + Lt Inf.	2,247
2nd Brigade	(Inglis)	3 Batts. + Lt Inf.	1,818
3rd Brigade	(Crawfurd)	3 Batts. + Lt Inf.	1,672

Total: **4,743**

THIRD DIVISION *(Picton)*

1st Brigade	(Mackinnon)	3 Batts.	1,808
2nd Brigade	(Lightburne)	3 Batts.	1,160
Portuguese	(Chaplemond)	3 Batts.	1,775
Total:			4,743

FOURTH DIVISION *(Cole)*

1st Brigade	(Campbell)	3 Batts. + Lt Inf.	2,109
2nd Brigade	(Kemmis)	3 Batts. + Lt Inf.	2,448
Portuguese	(Collins)	3 Batts.	2,843
Total:			7,400

FIFTH DIVISION *(Leith)*

1st Brigade	(Barnes)	3 Batts.	1,879
Portuguese	(Spry)	10 Batts.	5,426
Total:			7,305

LIGHT DIVISION *(Craufurd)*

1st Brigade	(Beckwith)	3 Batts.	1,896
2nd Brigade	(Barclay)	3 Batts.	1,891
Total:			3,787

PORTUGUESE DIVISION *(Hamilton)*

1st Brigade	(Campbell)	4 Batts.	2,250
2nd Brigade	(Fonseca)	4 Batts.	2,690
Total:			4,940

INDEPENDENT BRIGADES

1st (Portug.) Brigade	(Pack)	5 Batts.	2,769
5th (Portug.) Brigade	(Campbell)	5 Batts.	3,249
6th (Portug.) Brigade	(Coleman)	5 Batts.	2,345
Total:			8,363

Cavalry (4th Dragoons)	2 Sqds.	210
Artillery	60 Guns	2,230
Miscellaneous		506
GRAND TOTAL:		52,272

Wellington's field army also included the following units that were not actually present at Bussaco:

BRITISH CAVALRY

1st Brigade	(Grey)	2 Regts.	620
2nd Brigade	(Slade)	2 Regts.	967
3rd Brigade	(Anson)	2 Regts.	902
4th Brigade	(Fane)	1 Regt.	430
Total:			2,919

PORTUGUESE CAV.	4 Regts.	1,450

PORTUGUESE DIV. *(Lecor)*

1st Brigade	(Bradford)	5 Batts.	2,811
2nd Brigade	(?)	3 Batts.	2,000
Total:			4,811

GARRISONS, DETACHED etc.

Garrisons	3,306
Sick	6,565
Total:	9,871
GRAND TOTAL:	19,051

---

(1) MASSENA'S 'ARMY OF PORTUGAL', 15 SEPTEMBER 1810

II CORPS: *(Reynier)*

1st Div.	(Merle)	12 Batts.	6,589
2nd Div.	(Heudelet)	15 Batts.	8,087
Cavalry	(Soult)	4 Regts.	1,397
Artillery etc.			1,645
Total:			17,718

VI CORPS: *(Ney)*

1st Div.	(Marchand)	11 Batts.	6,671
2nd Div.	(Mermet)	11 Batts.	7,616
3rd Div.	(Loison)	12 Batts.	6,826
Cavalry	(Lamotte)	2 Regts.	1,680
Artillery etc.			1,513
Total:			24,306

VIII CORPS: (*Junot*)

1st Div.	(Clausel)	11 Batts.	6,794
2nd Div.	(Solignac)	12 Batts.	7,226
Cavalry	(St Croix)	6 Regts.	1,863
Artillery etc.			1,056

Total: 16,939

CAVALRY RESERVE: (*Montbrun*)

1st Brigade	(Lorcet)	2 Regts.	1,092
2nd Brigade	(Cavrois)	1 Regt.	661
3rd Brigade	(Ornano)	2 Regts.	1,426
Artillery			300

Total: 3,479

Misc. 2,608

GRAND TOTAL: 65,050

(2) THE FRENCH ARMY IN PORTUGAL, 1 JANUARY 1811

II CORPS (*Reynier*)

1st Div.	(Merle)	4,368
2nd Div.	(Heudelet)	5,718
Cavalry	(Soult)	1,146
Detached		1,176
Artillery etc.		1,349
Sick		4,485

Total: 18,242

VI CORPS (*Ney*)

1st Div.	(Marchand)	4,987
2nd Div.	(Mermet)	6,252
3rd Div.	(Loison)	4,589
Cavalry	(Lamotte)	652
Detached		3,019
Artillery etc.		1,846
Sick		5,771

Total: 27,116

VIII CORPS (*Junot*)

1st Div.	(Clausel)	4,007
2nd Div.	(Solignac)	4,997
Cavalry	(St Croix)	981

Detached		3,164
Artillery etc.		1,175
Sick		8,156
Total:		**22,480**

RESERVE CAVALRY (*Montbrun*)

Present		2,869
Detached		1,486
Sick		178
Total:		**4,533**

IX CORPS (*D'Erlon*)

2nd Div.	(Conroux)	7,592
Garrisons, detached		11,173
Sick		1,967
Total:		**20,732**

MISCELLANEOUS

Present		1,851
Detached		219
Sick		283
Total:		**2,353**

GRAND TOTAL: 95,456 men, of whom 54,116 were actually present and under arms.

BERESFORD'S ALLIED ARMY AT ALBUERA, 16 MAY 1811

SECOND DIVISION (*Stewart*)

Colborne's Brigade	4 Batts.	2,066
Hoghton's Brigade	3 Batts.	1,651
Abercrombie's Brigade	3 Batts.	1,597
Lt Inf.	3 Co.	146
Total:		**5,460**

FOURTH DIVISION (*Cole*)

Myer's Brigade (Fusiliers)	3 Batts.	2,015
Kemmis' Brigade (Detach's.)	3 Co.	165
Harvey's Brigade (Portug.)	5 Batts.	2,927
Total:		**5,107**

KGL BRIGADE (*Alten*)	2 Batts.	1,098
PORTUGUESE DIVISION (*Hamilton*)	8 Batts.	4,819
PORTUGUESE BRIGADE (*Collins*)	3 Batts.	1,385
PORTUGUESE CAVALRY (*Otway*)	4 Regts.	849
BRITISH CAVALRY (*Lumley*)	3 Regts.	1,164
ARTILLERY	36 Guns	768

SPANISH TROOPS (*Blake & Castaños*)

Vanguard Div.	(Lardizabal)	4 Batts.	2,398
3rd Div.	(Ballesteros)	7 Batts.	3,525
4th Div.	(Zayas)	8 Batts.	4,882
Misc. Inf.	(Espana)	3 Batts.	1,778
1st Cav.	(Loy)	4 Regts.	1,165
2nd Cav.	(Villemur)	7 Regts.	721
Artillery		14 Guns	165

Total:	14,634
GRAND TOTAL:	35,284

SOULT'S ARMY AT ALBUERA, 16 MAY 1811

V CORPS

1st Div.	(Girard)	9 Batts.	4,254
2nd Div.	(Gazan)	10 Batts.	4,183
Total:			8,437

WERLÉ'S BRIGADE	9 Batts.	5,621
GODINOT'S BRIGADE	6 Batts.	3,924
GRENADIER RESERVE	11 Co.	1,033

CAVALRY (*Latour-Maubourg*)

Briche's Brigade	3 Lt Regts.	823
Bron's Brigade	3 Drag. Regts.	1,093
Eclat's Brigade	3 Drag. Regts.	879
Misc.	3 Lt Regts.	1,217
Total:		4,012

ARTILLERY	48 Guns	1,233
GRAND TOTAL:		24,260

(1) THE ANGLO-PORTUGUESE ARMY AT THE BATTLE
OF FUENTES DE OÑORO, MAY 1811

FIRST DIVISION (*Spencer*)

Stopford's Brigade	2 Batts. + Lt Inf.	1,943
Nightingale's Brigade	3 Batts. + Lt Inf.	1,774
Howard's Brigade	3 Batts. + Lt Inf.	1,934
Lowe's Brigade	4 Batts. + Lt Inf.	1,914
Total:		7,565

THIRD DIVISION (*Picton*)

Mackinnon's Brigade	3 Batts. + Lt Inf.	1,863
Colville's Brigade	4 Batts.	1,967
Power's Brigade (Portuguese)	4 Batts.	1,650
Total:		5,480

FIFTH DIVISION (*Erskine*)

Dunlop's Brigade	3 Batts. + Lt Inf.	1,624
Hay's Brigade	3 Batts. + Lt Inf.	1,770
Spry's Brigade (Portuguese)	5 Batts.	1,764
Total:		5,158

SIXTH DIVISION (*Campbell*)

Burne's Brigade	1 Batt.	514
Hulse's Brigade	3 Batts. + Lt Inf.	2,041
Madden's Brigade (Portuguese)	4 Batts.	2,137
Total:		4,692

SEVENTH DIVISION (*Houston*)

Sontag's Brigade	4 Batts.	2,409
Doyle's Brigade (Portuguese)	5 Batts.	2,181
Total:		4,590

LIGHT DIVISION (*Craufurd*)

Beckwith's Brigade	2½ Batts.	1,634
Drummond's Brigade	3½ Batts.	2,181
Total:		3,815

INDEPENDENT BRIGADE (*Ashworth*)

(Portuguese)	5 Batts.	2,539

CAVALRY

Slade's Brigade	2 Regts.	766
Arentschildt's Brigade	2 Regts.	776
Barbacena's Brigade (Portuguese)	2 Regts.	312
Total:		1,854
Artillery etc.	48 Guns	1,253
GRAND TOTAL:		37,606

(2) THE FRENCH ARMY AT FUENTES DE OÑORO

II CORPS (*Reynier*)

Merle's Division	9 Batts.	4,891
Heudelet's Division	12 Batts.	5,491
Cav. Brigade	3 Regts.	682
Artillery etc.	8 Guns	266
Total:		11,330

VI CORPS (*Loison*)

Marchand's Division	12 Batts.	5,872
Mermet's Division	12 Batts.	6,702
Ferey's Division	10 Batts.	4,232
Cav. Brigade (Lamotte)	2 Regts.	334
Artillery etc.	8 Guns	266
Total:		17,406

VIII CORPS (*Junot*)

Solignac's Division	10 Batts.	4,714
Artillery etc.	8 Guns	266
Total:		4,980

IX CORPS (*D'Erlon*)

Claparede's Division	9 Batts.	4,716
Conroux's Division	9 Batts.	5,588
Cav. Brigade (Fournier)	3 Regts.	794
Artillery etc.	8 Guns	266
Total:		11,364

CAVALRY RESERVE (*Montbrun*)

Ornano's Brigade	3 Regts. (dragoons)	461
Cavrois' Brigade	3 Regts. (dragoons)	726
Artillery etc.	6 Guns	80

Total: 1,267

DETACHED FROM THE ARMY OF THE NORTH

Lepic's Guard Cavalry Brigade	4 Regts.	881
Wathier's Cavalry Brigade	4 Regts.	784
Artillery etc.	6 Guns	73

Total: 1,738

GRAND TOTAL: 48,085

THE FRENCH ARMIES IN SPAIN, 15 JULY 1811

THE ARMY OF THE SOUTH (*Marshal Soult*)

FIRST CORPS (*Marshal Victor*)

1st Div.	(Conroux)	10 Batts.	5,905
2nd Div.	(Godinot)	13 Batts.	8,133
3rd Div.	(Villatte)	12 Batts.	5,802
Lt Cav.	(Perreymond)	2 Regts.	1,015
Dragoons	(Latour-Maubourg)	6 Regts.	2,905
Artillery etc.			1,985
Marines, sailors etc. for Cadiz lines			1,456
Sick and detached			8,739

Total: 35,940

FOURTH CORPS (*Sebastiani*)

1st Div.	(Ligier-Belair)	15 Batts.	10,947
2nd Div.	(Dombrowski)	6 Batts.	4,918
Lt Cav.	(Ormancey)	3 Regts.	1,595
Dragoons	(Milhaud)	5 Regts.	2,484
Artillery etc.			886
Sick and detached			2,059

Total: 22,889

FIFTH CORPS (*D'Erlon*)

1st Div.	(Girard)	10 Batts.	4,253
2nd Div.	(Claparede)	12 Batts.	4,183
Lt Cav.	(Briche)	2 Regts.	515
Artillery etc.			618

Badajoz garrison	5 Batts. + Artillery	2,887
Sick and detached		9,840
Total:		22,296

MISCELLANEOUS

Infantry brigade in Cordova	6 Batts.	5,017
Unattached cavalry	4 Regts.	1,942
Unattached artillery etc.		1,381
Total:		8,340

ARMY TOTAL = 90,186 men (68,827 effectives)

THE ARMY OF THE CENTRE (*King Joseph*)

King's Guard			2,500
Spanish Division	(Hugo)	10 Batts. 3 Cav. Sqds.	5,060
German Division		6 Batts.	4,214
French Brigade	(Dessolles)	6 Batts.	3,208
Lt Cav.		2 Regts.	663
Dragoons	(Lahoussaye)	4 Regts.	2,213
Artillery etc.			1,268
Miscellaneous			4,013
Sick and detached			2,398

ARMY TOTAL = 25,537 men (23,139 effectives)

THE ARMY OF PORTUGAL (*Marshal Marmont*)

Foy's Division	12 Batts.	5,541
Clausel's Division	12 Batts.	6,501
Ferey's Division	11 Batts.	5,072
Sarrut's Division	9 Batts.	4,922
Maucune's Division	12 Batts.	5,049
Brennier's Division	12 Batts.	5,332
Lamotte's Lt Cavalry	4 Regts.	613
Fournier's Lt Cavalry	3 Regts.	701
Wathier's Lt Cavalry	3 Regts.	564
Montbrun's Dragoon Division	7 Regts.	1,463
Artillery etc.		2,875
Sick and detached		19,316

ARMY TOTAL = 57,949 men (38,633 effectives)

THE ARMY OF ARAGON (*Marshal Suchet*)

Musnier's Division	11 Batts.	7,689
Frere's Division	12 Batts.	7,826
Harispe's Division	11 Batts.	6,380
Habert's Division	11 Batts.	4,433
Peyri's Division (Italians)	10 Batts.	4,160
Attached cavalry	2 Regts.	732
Compere's Brigade (Neapolitans)	3 Batts.	1,642
Attached cavalry	2 Sqds.	166
Boussard's Cavalry	3 Regts.	1,876
Artillery etc.		3,645
Misc.		2,990
Garrisons		2,244
Sick and detached		7,305

ARMY TOTAL = 51,088 men (43,783 effectives)

THE ARMY OF THE NORTH (*Dorsenne*)

Dumoustier's Division (Imperial Gds.)	11 Batts.	7,666
Roguet's Division (Imperial Gds.)	10 Batts.	7,500
Lepic's Cavalry (Imperial Gds.)	3 Regts.	2,024
Imperial Gd. Artillery etc.		878
Reille's Division (Navarre)	15 Batts.	8,221
Caffarelli's Division (Biscay)	16 Batts.	7,543
Souham's Division (Burgos)	14 Batts.	7,971
Serras' Division (Valladolid)	6 Batts.	5,063
Bonnet's Division (Asturias)	13 Batts.	7,962
Fixed garrisons (Navarre)		1,623
Fixed garrisons (Biscay)		4,340
Fixed garrisons (Burgos)		8,714
Fixed garrisons (Valladolid area)		8,106
Severoli's Division (On march to Aragon)		8,464
Artillery etc.		2,367
Sick and detached		11,000

ARMY TOTAL = 99,442 men (88,442 effectives)

THE ARMY OF CATALONIA (*Marshal Macdonald*)

Mathieu's Division	8 Batts.	5,411
Quesnel's Division	6 Batts.	3,890
Plauzonne's Division	8 Batts.	4,389
Petit's Brigade	6 Batts.	2,416
Lefebvre's Brigade	8 Batts.	3,725

Fixed garrisons	3,335
Artillery etc.	824
Sick and detached	6,669

ARMY TOTAL = 30,259 men (23,590 effectives)

GRAND TOTAL = 354,461 men (291,414 effectives)

THE SPANISH ARMIES AT THE BEGINNING OF SUMMER 1811 (EFFECTIVES ONLY)

THE ARMY OF CATALONIA (*Campoverde*)

Sarsfield's Division	5,462
Eroles' Division	2,538
Courten's Division	4,791
Garrisons of Trotosa and Tarragona:	13,040
Total:	25,831

THE ARMY OF VALENCIA (*O'Donnell*)

1st Div.	(Miranda)	5,055
2nd Div.	(Romré)	3,000
3rd Div.	(Bassecourt)	2,053
4th Div.	(Obispo)	5,159
5th Div.	(Empecinado)	3,250
6th Div.	(Acuña)	3,699
Cavalry (Five regiments, in detachments)		2,565
Artillery etc.		722
Garrisons of Sagunto, Oropesa and Penniscola:		1,999
Total:		27,502

THE ARMY OF ESTREMADURA (*Castaños*)

1st Div.	(España)	3,476
Cavalry	(Villemur)	697
Artillery etc.		568
Garrisons		2,853
Total:		7,594

THE ARMY OF MURCIA (*Freire*)

1st Div.	(Cuadra)	4,015
2nd Div.	(Creagh)	4,442
3rd Div.	(Sanz)	3,220
1st Cav. Div.	(Ladron)	1,014
2nd Cav. Div.	(Osorio)	709

| Artillery etc. | 1,053 |
| Garrison of Cartagena: | 2,180 |

| Total: | 16,633 |

THE ARMY OF GALICIA *(Santocildes)*

1st Div.	(Losada)	5,459
2nd Div.	(Taboada)	3,994
3rd Div.	(Cabrera)	2,567
Cavalry		631
Garrisons of Ferrol, Lugo, Vigo and Corunna:		8,194

| Total: | 20,845 |

| GRAND TOTAL: | 98,405 |

THE ANGLO-PORTUGUESE FIELD ARMIES, SEPTEMBER 1811

(1) WELLINGTON'S FORCE ON THE BEIRA FRONTIER

FIRST DIVISION *(Graham)*

Campbell's Brigade	2 Batts.	1,763
Attached Light Infantry	1 Co.	48
Stopford's Brigade	4 Batts.	1,580
Lt Inf.	1 Co.	38
Lowe's Brigade	3 Batts.	1,497

| Total: | | 4,926 |

THIRD DIVISION *(Picton)*

Wallace's Brigade	3 Batts.	1,898
Lt Inf.	3 Co.	243
Colville's Brigade	4 Batts.	1,847
Palmeirim's Brigade (Portug.)	4 Batts.	1,289

| Total: | | 5,277 |

FOURTH DIVISION *(Cole)*

Kemmis' Brigade	3 Batts.	1,926
Lt Inf.	1 Co.	37
Pakenham's Brigade	3 Batts.	1,489
Lt Inf.	1 Co.	49
Collin's Brigade (Portug.)	5 Batts.	2,982

| Total: | | 6,483 |

FIFTH DIVISION (*Dunlop/Leith*)		
Hay's Brigade	3 Batts.	1,571
Lt Inf.	1 Co.	63
Dunlop's Brigade	3 Batts.	1,305
Lt Inf.	1 Co.	52
Spry's Brigade (Portug.)	5 Batts.	2,014
Total:		5,005

SIXTH DIVISION (*Campbell*)		
Hulse's Brigade	3 Batts.	1,781
Lt Inf.	1 Co.	40
Burne's Brigade	3 Batts.	1,797
Madden's Brigade (Portug.)	4 Batts.	2,069
Total:		5,687

SEVENTH DIVISION (*Sontag*)		
Alten's Brigade	3 Batts.	1,654
Sontag's Brigade	4 Batts.	1,625
Coleman's Brigade (Portug.)	5 Batts.	1,823
Total:		5,102

LIGHT DIVISION (*Craufurd*)		
1st Brig.	1 Batt.	1,005
Misc. Lt Inf.	9 Co.	700
2nd Brigade	2 Batts.	1,203
Misc. Lt Inf.	4 Co.	339
Portug. Brigade	2 Batts.	953
Total:		4,200

PACK'S PORTUGUESE BRIGADE	5 Batts.	2,206

McMAHON'S BRIGADE	5 Batts.	2,489

BRITISH CAVALRY (*Cotton*)		
Slade's Brigade	2 Regts.	778
Alten's Brigade	2 Regts.	790
Anson's Brigade	2 Regts.	717
Grey's Brigade	2 Regts.	727
Total:		3,012

PORTUGUESE CAVALRY (*Madden*)	4 Regts.	1,014

ARTILLERY etc.	66 Guns	1,330
GRAND TOTAL:		46,731

(2) HILL'S FORCE IN ESTREMADURA

SECOND DIVISION (*Stewart*)

Howard's Brigade	3 Batts.	
Byng's Brigade	4 Batts.	
Wilson's Brigade	3 Batts.	
Total:		5,854

HAMILTON'S PORTUGUESE DIVISION	8 Batts.	5,082
ASHWORTH'S PORTUGUESE BRIGADE	5 Batts.	2,419

CAVALRY (*Erskine*)

Long's Brigade	3 Regts.	853
Le Marchant's Brigade	2 Regts.	965
Portuguese Brigade	2 Regts.	648
Total:		2,466

ARTILLERY etc.	30 Guns	663
GRAND TOTAL:		16,484

SUCHET'S ARMY IN THE INVASION OF VALENCIA, SEPTEMBER 1811

FIRST DIVISION (*Musnier*)

1st Brigade	(Robert)	5 Batts.	2,500
2nd Brigade	(Ficatier)	5 Batts.	2,329
Total:			4,829

SECOND DIVISION (*Harispe*)

1st Brigade	(Paris)	7 Batts.	2,786
2nd Brigade	(Chlopiski)	4 Batts.	1,976
Total:			4,762

THIRD DIVISION (*Habert*)

1st Brigade	(Montmarie)	5 Batts.	2,119
2nd Brigade	(Bronikowski)	3 Batts.	1,340
Total:			3,459

FOURTH DIVISION (*Palombini*)

1st Brigade	(St Paul) (Italians)	6 Batts.	3,860
2nd Brigade	(Balathier) (Italians)	5 Batts.	2,359
Total:			6,219

FIFTH DIVISION (*Compère*)

(Neapolitans)		3 Batts.	1,391
CAVALRY (*Boussard*)		14 Sqds.	2,405
ARTILLERY ETC.			3,068
GRAND TOTAL:			26,133

BLAKE'S ARMY AT THE BATTLE OF SAGUNTUM, 25 OCTOBER 1811

1st Valencian Div.	(Miranda)	7 Batts.	3,964
2nd Valencian Div.	(Villacampa)	7 Batts.	3,352
3rd Valencian Div.	(Obispo)	6 Batts.	3,400
Reserve Valencian Div.	(Velasco)	5 Batts.	3,670
1st Murcian Brigade	(Creagh)	3 Batts.	2,218
2nd Murcian Brigade	(Montijo)	3 Batts.	2,410
1st Div. (from Cadiz)	(Zayas)	8 Batts.	2,550
2nd Div. (from Cadiz)	(Lardizabal)	8 Batts.	2,972
Total infantry:			24,536
Valencian cavalry	(San Juan)	16 Sqds.	1,721
Murcian cavalry	(Caro)	8 Sqds.	826
(Cadiz) cavalry	(Loy)	4 Sqds.	294
Total cavalry:			2,841
Artillery etc.		40 Guns	667
GRAND TOTAL:			28,044

SOULT'S 'ARMY OF THE SOUTH', MARCH 1812 (EFFECTIVES ONLY)

NEAR CADIZ:

Barrois' Division	12 Batts. + artillery	7,776
Villatte's Division	12 Batts. + artillery	7,359
The siege corps	Marines, gunners etc.	5,680

AT BORNOS:		
Conroux's Division	8 Batts. + artillery	5,445
AT GRANADA:		
P Soult's Cavalry Division	4 Regts. (3 drag, 1 lt)	2,338
Leval's Division	15 Batts. + artillery	9,404
AT CORDOVA:		
2nd Cavalry Division	6 Regts. (dragoons)	3,477
AT SEVILLE:		
Gendarmes:		610
Jurementado Infantry:	4 Batts.	2,950
Jurementado Cavalry:	6 Regts.	2,521
IN ESTREMADURA:		
D'Erlon's Division	10 Batts. + artillery	6,119
Daricau's Division	10 Batts. + artillery	5,028
1st Cavalry Division	6 Regts. (5 lt, 1 drag)	2,540
The Badajoz garrison:	7 Batts. + 3 Co.	3,861
	1 troop of cavalry	42
	Artillery etc	546
GRAND TOTAL:		65,696

THE FRENCH AND ALLIED ARMIES AT THE BATTLE OF SALAMANCA, 22 JULY 1812

(1) WELLINGTON'S FORCES:

FIRST DIVISION (*Campbell*)

Fermor's Brigade	2 Batts. + Lt Inf.	1,972
Wheatley's Brigade	3 Batts. + Lt Inf.	2,228
Löwe's Brigade (KGL)	3 Batts.	1,823
Total:		6,023

THIRD DIVISION (*Pakenham*)

Campbell's Brigade	4 Batts.	1,876
Wallace's Brigade	3 Batts. + Lt Inf.	1,802
Power's Brigade (Portuguese)	5 Batts.	2,197
Total:		5,875

FOURTH DIVISION (*Cole*)

Ellis' Brigade	3 Batts. + Lt Inf.	1,421
Anson's Brigade	2 Batts. + Lt Inf.	1,261
Stubb's Brigade (Portuguese)	5 Batts.	2,554
Total:		5,236

FIFTH DIVISION (Leith)

Greville's Brigade	5 Batts. + Lt Inf.	3,006
Pringle's Brigade	4 Batts. + Lt Inf.	1,780
Spry's Brigade (Portuguese)	5 Batts.	2,305
Total:		7,091

SIXTH DIVISION (*Clinton*)

Hulse's Brigade	3 Batts. + Lt Inf.	1,464
Hinde's Brigade	3 Batts.	1,446
Rezende's Brigade (Portuguese)	5 Batts.	2,631
Total:		5,541

SEVENTH DIVISION (*Hope*)

Bernewitz's Brigade	3 Batts.	1,954
Halkett's Brigade (KGL)	2 Batts. + Lt Inf.	1,063
Collins' Brigade (Portuguese)	5 Batts.	2,168
Total:		5,185

LIGHT DIVISION (*Alten*)

Vandeleur's Brigade	2 Batts.	1,341
Barnard's Brigade	2 Batts.	1,140
Attached Portuguese	2 Batts.	1,067
Total:		3,548

1st Ind. Portuguese Brigade (Pack)	5 Batts.	2,605
2nd Ind. Portuguese Brigade (Bradford)	5 Batts.	1,894
Total:		4,499

Spanish Division (España)	5 Batts.	3,360

Le Marchant's Dragoon Brigade	3 Regts.	1,022
Bock's Dragoon Brigade	2 Regts.	771
Alten's Lt Cav. Brigade	2 Regts.	746
Anson's Lt Cav. Brigade	3 Regts.	1,004
D'Urban's Dragoon Brigade (Portuguese)	2 Regts.	482
Total:		4,025

Artillery etc.	10 Batteries	1,566
GRAND TOTAL:		51,949

(2) MARMONT'S FORCES

First Division	(Foy)	8 Batts. + Artillery	5,147
Second Division	(Clausel)	10 Batts. + Artillery	6,562
Third Division	(Ferey)	9 Batts. + Artillery	5,689
Fourth Division	(Sarrut)	9 Batts. + Artillery	5,002
Fifth Division	(Maucune)	9 Batts. + Artillery	5,244
Sixth Division	(Brennier)	8 Batts. + Artillery	4,558
Seventh Division	(Thomières)	8 Batts. + Artillery	4,543
Eighth Division	(Bonnet)	12 Batts. + Artillery	6,521
Lt Cavalry Div.	(Curto)	6 Regts.	1,879
Dragoon Div.	(Boyer)	4 Regts.	1,500
Artillery Reserve etc.			3,002
GRAND TOTAL:			49,647

THE STATE OF THE FRENCH ARMIES IN SPAIN, MID-AUTUMN 1812

THE ARMY OF THE NORTH *(Caffarelli)*

1st Div.	(Abbé)	11 Batts. + Misc.	6,597
2nd Div.	(Vandermaesen)	18 Batts.	12,585
Guards Brig.	(Dumoustier)	6 Batts.	4,076
Lt Cav. Brig.	(Laferrière)	3 Regts.	1,662
Garrisons in Navarre, Biscay and Castile			12,769
Sick			5,217
Total:			42,906

THE ARMY OF THE CENTRE *(Joseph, later d'Erlon)*

1st Div.	(Darmagnac)	11 Batts.	5,238
Italian Div.	(Palombini)	7 Batts. + Misc.	3,192
Spanish Div.	(Casapalacios)	3 Batts. + Misc.	1,430
The King's Guards			2,500
Cav. Div.	(Treillard)	4 Med., 2 Lt Regts.	1,793
Artillery etc.			663
Misc. detachments			1,102
Sick			1,914
Total:			17,832

THE ARMY OF THE SOUTH *(Soult)*

1st Div.	(Conroux)	12 Batts.	5,818
2nd Div.	(Barrois)	12 Batts.	5,002

3rd Div.	(Villatte)	12 Batts.	6,097
4th Div.	(Leval)	14 Batts.	8,053
5th Div.	(D'Erlon)	11 Batts.	5,218
6th Div.	(Daricau)	10 Batts.	4,495
Lt Cav. Div.	(Perreymond)	5 Regts.	2,493
Dragoon Div.	(Digeon)	6 Regts.	3,104
Dragoon Div.	(P Soult)	5 Regts.	1,833
Artillery etc.			5,415
Detached			1,968
Sick			6,353
Total:			55,849

Note: D'Erlon (5th Div.) later replaced by Remond.
Note: Barrois (2nd Div.) later replaced by Cassagne.

THE ARMY OF PORTUGAL (*Souham*)

1st Div.	(Foy)	7 Batts.	3,443
2nd Div.	(Clausel)	8 Batts.	4,436
3rd Div.	(Taupin)	9 Batts.	6,048
4th Div.	(Sarrut)	6 Batts.	3,930
5th Div.	(Maucune)	8 Batts.	5,062
6th Div.	(Pinoteau)	5 Batts.	2,617
7th Div.	(Bonté)	5 Batts.	2,334
8th Div.	(Chauvel)	9 Batts.	4,417
Brigade from Bayonne	(Aussenac)	7 Batts.	3,418
Lt Cav. Div.	(Curto)	6 Regts.	1,963
Dragoon Div.	(Boyer)	4 Regts.	1,273
Lt Cav. Brig.	(Merlin)	2 Regts.	746
Artillery etc.			5,172
Detached			4,724
Sick			11,166
Total:			61,049

Note: Merlin's Brigade was on loan from the Army of the North.

THE ARMY OF ARAGON AND VALENCIA (*Suchet*)

1st Div.	(Musnier)	10 Batts.	5,583
2nd Div.	(Harispe)	6 Batts.	4,115
3rd Div.	(Habert)	7 Batts.	4,975
4th Div.	(Reille)	7 Batts. + Misc.	4,450
Italian Div.	(Severoli)	5 Batts. + Misc.	3,909
Brigade from Catalonia		6 Batts. + Misc.	3,849
Cavalry Div.	(Boussard)	1 Cuirassier, 2 Dragoon & 2 Lt Regts.	1,922
Artillery etc.			1,836

Detached			4,015
Sick			4,311
Total:			39,055

THE ARMY OF CATALONIA *(Decaen)*

1st Div.	(Quesnel)	3 Batts. + Misc.	3,625
2nd Div.	(Lamarque)	8 Batts. + Misc.	3,628
3rd Div.	(Mathieu)	8 Batts. + Misc.	6,365
Ind. Brig.	(Petit)	4 Batts.	1,619
Ind. Brig.	(Espert)	5 Batts.	3,077
Garrison of Figueras		4 Batts. + Misc.	3,806
Garrison of Lerida		3 Batts. + Misc.	1,709
Garrison of Tarragona		2 Batts.	1,514
Artillery etc.			4,356
Detached			395
Sick			6,089
Total:			36,183

THE BAYONNE RESERVE FORCE

Misc. units and detachments	7,244
Detached	134
Sick	600
Total:	7,978

GRAND TOTAL: 260,852 men, including 35,650 sick and 11,236 detached.

THE ARMIES AT THE BATTLE OF CASTALLA, 13 APRIL 1813

SIR JOHN MURRAY'S FORCES

Advanced Guard	(Adam)	3 Batts. + detachments	1,179
1st Div.	(Clinton)	5 Batts.	4,036
2nd Div.	(Mackenzie)	5 Batts.	4,045
1st Spanish Div.	(Whittingham)	6 Batts.	3,901
2nd Spanish Div.	(Roche)	5 Batts.	4,019
Cavalry		9 Sqds.	1,036
Artillery etc.		30 Guns	500
Total:			18,716

MARSHAL SUCHET'S FORCES

| 1st Div. | (Robert, for Musnier) | 8 Batts. | 5,084 |
| 2nd Div. | (Harispe) | 6 Batts. | 4,052 |

3rd Div.	(Habert)	4 Batts.	2,722
Cavalry	(Boussard)	8 Sqds.	1,424
Artillery etc.		24 Guns	282
			13,564

| Total: | | | 13,564 |

SPANISH FORCES EMPLOYED IN MURRAY'S TARRAGONA CAMPAIGN, JUNE 1813

GENERAL ELIO'S ARMY

1st Div.	(Mijares)	6 Batts.	4,355
2nd Div.	(Villacampa)	4 Batts., 2 Sqds.	4,564
3rd Div.	(Sarsfield)	5 Batts., 2 Sqds.	5,384
4th Div.	(Roche)	5 Batts.	4,436
5th Div.	(Duran)	4 Batts., 3 Sqds.	5,463
6th Div.	(Empecinado)	4 Batts., 2 Sqds.	4,248
Unattached cavalry		2 Regts.	1,014
Artillery etc.		22 Guns	1,041

| Total: | | | 30,505 |

GENERAL DEL PARQUE'S ARMY

1st Div.	(Anglona)	8 Batts.	5,142
2nd Div.	(Cuevas)	7 Batts.	3,625
3rd Div.	(Murgeon)	7 Batts.	2,774
Cavalry	(Sisternes)	2 Regts.	706
Artillery etc.		12 Guns	344

| Total: | | | 12,591 |

GENERAL COPON'S ARMY

| Field Div. | (Eroles) | 12 Batts., 4 Sqds. | 9,992 |
| Detached, garrisons etc. | | 6 Batts. | 5,769 |

| Total: | | | 15,761 |

| GRAND TOTAL: | | | 58,857 |

BRITISH FORCES EMPLOYED IN MURRAY'S TARRAGONA CAMPAIGN, JUNE 1813

ADVANCED GUARD (*Adam*)
2nd Batt 27th Foot, 1 company of De Roll's Rifles. Calabrese Free Corps, 1st Anglo-Italian Levy Battalion.

FIRST DIVISION (*Clinton*)
Sicilian 'Estero' Regt, 4th Line Batt KGL, 1/58th Foot, 2/67th Foot.

SECOND DIVISION (*Mackenzie*)
2 companies of De Roll's Rifles, Dillon's Regt, 2nd Anglo-Italian Levy Batt, 1/10th Foot, 1/27th Foot, 1/81st Foot.

SPANISH DIVISION (*Whittingham*)
2nd Murcia Regt, Guadalajara Regt, Cordova Regt, Mallorca Regt, 5th Grenadiers.

CAVALRY
2 squadrons 20th Light Dragoons, 1 squadron of foreign hussars, 2 squadrons of Brunswick Hussars.

ARTILLERY ETC
1 Portuguese battery, 2 British batteries, siege artillery and sappers.
Total: 14,345 infantry, 801 cavalry, 906 artillery etc. (Grand Total = 16,052)

SUCHET'S FORCES AT THE TIME OF THE TARRAGONA CAMPAIGN, JUNE 1813

TROOPS IN VALENCIA:

1st Div.	(Musnier)	7 Batts.	4,163
2nd Div.	(Harispe)	6 Batts.	4,064
3rd Div.	(Habert)	6 Batts.	4,120
Misc. Inf.	(Lamarque)	7 Batts.	3,819
Italian Div.	(Severoli)	4 Batts.	1,900
Cavalry	(Boussard)	14 Sqds.	2,273
Artillery etc.		40 Guns	2,450
Total:			22,789

TROOPS IN CATALONIA:

1st Div.	(Mathieu)	8 Batts.	6,900
2nd Div.	(Quesnel)	6 Batts.	2,900
3rd Div.	(Lamarque)	4 Batts.	2,400
4th Div.	(Nogues)	3 Batts.	2,920
1st Brig.	(Petit)	4 Batts.	2,059
2nd Brig.	(Beurmann)	4 Batts.	2,362
Lerida	(Henriot)	2 Batts.	1,423
Tarragona	(Bertoletti)	2 Batts.	1,516
Cavalry	(In detachments)	5 Sqds.	670
Artillery etc.		40 Guns	2,400
Total:			25,550

TROOPS IN ARAGON:

Infantry		7 Batts.	3,389
Misc. Inf. (Including *Jurementados*)			1,975
Cavalry		3 Sqds.	396
Artillery etc.		12 Guns	251
Total:			6,011

GRAND TOTAL:	With Suchet himself, in Valencia:	22,789
	With Decaen, in Catalonia:	25,550
	With Paris, in Aragon:	6,011
		54,350

THE FRENCH AND ALLIED ARMIES IN THE VITORIA CAMPAIGN

(1) WELLINGTON'S FORCES

FIRST DIVISION (*Howard*)

Stopford's Brigade	2 Batts. + Lt Inf.	1,728
Halkett's Brigade (KGL)	5 Batts.	3,126
Total:		4,854

SECOND DIVISION (*Hill*)

Byng's Brigade	3 Batts. + Lt Inf.	2,465
Cadogan's Brigade	3 Batts. + Lt Inf.	2,777
O'Callaghan's Brigade	3 Batts. + Lt Inf.	2,530
Ashworth's Brigade (Portuguese)	5 Batts.	3,062
Total:		10,834

THIRD DIVISION (*Picton*)

Brisbane's Brigade	3 Batts. + Lt Inf.	2,723
Colville's Brigade	4 Batts.	2,276
Power's Brigade (Portuguese)	5 Batts.	2,460
Total:		7,459

FOURTH DIVISION (*Cole*)

Skerret's Brigade	3 Batts. + Lt Inf.	2,049
Anson's Brigade	4 Batts. + Lt Inf.	2,935
Stubb's Brigade (Portuguese)	5 Batts.	2,842
Total:		7,826

FIFTH DIVISION (*Oswald*)

Robinson's Brigade	3 Batts. + Lt Inf.	2,061
Hay's Brigade	3 Batts. + Lt Inf.	2,292
Spry's Brigade (Portuguese)	5 Batts.	2,372
Total:		6,725

SIXTH DIVISION (*Pakenham*)

Stirling's Brigade	3 Batts. + Lt Inf.	2,454
Hinde's Brigade	4 Batts.	2,418
Madden's Brigade (Portuguese)	5 Batts.	2,475
Total:		7,347

SEVENTH DIVISION (*Dalhousie*)

Grant's Brigade	4 Batts.	2,538
Barne's Brigade	3 Batts.	2,322
Lecor's Brigade (Portuguese)	5 Batts.	2,437
Total:		7,297

LIGHT DIVISION (*Alten*)

Vandeleur's Brigade	2 Batts.	1,462
Kempt's Brigade	3 Batts.	2,077
Attached Portuguese	4 Batts.	1,945
Total:		5,484

PORTUGUESE DIVISION (*Silveira*)

Campbell's Brigade	5 Batts.	2,795
Da Costa's Brigade	4 Batts.	2,492
Total:		5,287

1st IND. PORTUGUESE BRIGADE (*Bradford*)	5 Batts.	2,392
2nd IND. PORTUGUESE BRIGADE (*Pack*)	5 Batts.	2,297

Hill's Heavy Cav. Brigade (Hs. Gds.)	3 Regts.	870
Ponsonby's Dragoon Brigade	3 Regts.	1,238
Fane's Dragoon Brigade	2 Regts.	842
Bock's Dragoon Brigade (KGL)	2 Regts.	632
Grant's Lt Cav. Brigade	3 Regts.	1,624
Alten's Lt Cav. Brigade	2 Regts.	1,005
Anson's Lt Cav. Brigade	2 Regts.	819
Long's Lt Cav. Brigade	1 Regt.	394
D'Urban's Dragoon Brigade (Port.)	3 Regts.	685
Campbell's Dragoon Brigade (Port.)	1 Regt.	208
Total:		8,317

ARTILLERY etc	5,199

THE (SPANISH) ARMY OF GALICIA (*Giron*)

1st Div.	(Morillo)	6 Batts.	4,551
2nd Div.	(España)	5 Batts.	3,342

3rd Div.	(Losada)	6 Batts.	5,855
4th Div.	(Barcena)	7 Batts.	5,143
5th Div.	(Porlier)	3 Batts.	2,408
6th Div.	(Longa)	5 Batts.	3,130
Cav. Div.	(Villemur)	7 Regts.	2,628
Cav. Brig.	(Sanchez)	2 Regts.	1,290
Artillery etc.			420

Total: 25,425

THE (SPANISH) ARMY OF RESERVE OF ANDALUSIA (*O'Donnell*)

Creagh's Division	7 Batts.	6,454
Echevarri's Division	7 Batts.	6,617
Barcena's Cav. Brigade	2 Regts.	828
Artillery etc		284

Total: 14,183

GRAND TOTAL: 120,926

(2) KING JOSEPH'S DISPOSABLE FORCES

FROM THE ARMY OF THE SOUTH

1st Div.	(Leval)	14 Batts. + Artillery	4,844
3rd Div.	(Villatte)	12 Batts. + Artillery	5,874
4th Div.	(Conroux)	12 Batts. + Artillery	6,589
5th Div.	(Maransin's brigade only)	6 Batts.	2,927
6th Div.	(Daricau)	10 Batts. + Artillery	5,935
Lt Cav. Div.	(P Soult)	4 Regts. + Artillery	1,671
1st Dragoon Div.	(Tilly)	6 Regts.	1,929
2nd Dragoon Div.	(Digeon)	4 Regts. + Artillery	1,869
Artillery Reserve etc.			1,998

Total: 33,636

FROM THE ARMY OF PORTUGAL

4th Div.	(Sarrut)	6 Batts. + Artillery	4,802
6th Div.	(Lamartinière)	9 Batts. + Artillery	6,711
Lt Cav. Div.	(Mermet)	5 Regts.	1,801
Dragoon Div.	(Boyer)	4 Regts.	1,471
Artillery Reserve etc.			2,465

Total: 17,250

FROM THE ARMY OF THE CENTRE

1st Div.	(Darmagnac)	11 Batts.	4,472
2nd Div.	(Cassagne, from A. of S.)	12 Batts. + Artillery	5,209
Spanish Div.	(Casalpalacios)	3 Batts. + Artillery	2,167

King's Guards		3 Batts. (?)	2,380
Guard Cavalry		2 Regts.	425
Dragoon Div.	(Treillard)	4 Regts.	1,038
Lt Cav. Brig.	(Avy)	2 Regts.	474
Spanish Lt Cav. Brig.		3 Regts.	670
Artillery Reserve etc.			830

Total: 17,665

GRAND TOTAL: 68,551

Note: These figures are derived from May returns and do not make any allowance for wastage prior to the actual Battle of Vitoria. The forces engaged there would, therefore, be somewhat smaller than shown. Furthermore, the Spanish irregular units and the forces under Popham have, along with the French divisions who opposed them, been discounted from the totals.

SOULT'S ARMY, JULY–AUTUMN 1813

(1) THE FRENCH FORCES AT THE START OF THE 'BATTLE OF THE PYRENEES', LATE JULY

1st Div.	(Foy)	9 Batts.	5,922
2nd Div.	(Darmagnac)	8 Batts.	6,961
3rd Div.	(Abbé)	9 Batts.	8,030
4th Div.	(Conroux)	9 Batts.	7,056
5th Div.	(Vandermaesen)	7 Batts.	4,181
6th Div.	(Maransin)	7 Batts.	5,966
7th Div.	(Maucune)	7 Batts.	4,186
8th Div.	(Taupin)	9 Batts.	5,981
9th Div.	(Lamartinière)	10 Batts.	7,127

RESERVE: (*Villatte*)

Odd battalions from 14 regiments	18 Batts.	9,102
German Brigade	4 Batts.	2,066
Italian Brigade	3 Batts.	1,349
Spanish Brigade	3 Batts.	1,168
King's Guards	3 Batts.	2,019
Misc. National Gds. etc.		1,550

Total: 17,254

Treillard's Dragoon Division	6 Regts.	2,358
P. Soult's Cavalry Division	10 Regts.	3,981
Cav. attached to infantry divisions	3 Regts.	808
Garrison of San Sebastian		3,000
Garrison of Pamplona		3,500
Garrison of Bayonne (New conscripts)		5,595

Artillery etc.	7,900
GRAND TOTAL	99,806

Of this total, the following were employed by Soult in his attempt to relieve Pamplona:

D'Erlon's column:	21,460
Clausel's column:	17,678
Reille's column:	17,695
Soult & Treillard's cavalry (with horse artillery)	6,739
Total:	63,572

(2) THE FRENCH FORCES DEFENDING THE LINE OF THE RIVER BIDASSOA, OCTOBER 1813

1st Div. (Foy)	8 Batts.	4,654	Deployed about St Jean-Pied-du-Port.
2nd Div. (Darmagnac)	9 Batts.	4,447	Deployed about Ainhoue.
3rd Div. (Abbé)	8 Batts.	6,051	Deployed to the west of Ainhoue.
4th Div. (Conroux)	9 Batts.	4,962	To the south of Sarre.
5th Div. (Maransin)	9 Batts.	5,575	To the south of Sarre.
6th Div. (Daricau)	7 Batts.	4,092	Around Ainhoue & Sarre.
7th Div. (Maucune)	8 Batts.	3,996	Along the lower Bidassoa, centred on Béhobie.
8th Div. (Taupin)	10 Batts.	4,778	Deployed around Vera.
9th Div. (Boyer)	12 Batts.	6,515	East of the Bidassoa, to the north of Vera.
Reserve (Villatte)	18 Batts.	8,018	In reserve about Ascain & Serres.
Artillery etc.		2,000	
Total:		55,088	

Note: Virtually all of Soult's cavalry had been withdrawn to the Nive Valley. General Boyer had replaced Lamartinière, Maransin had replaced Vandermaesen and Daricau had taken control of the 6th Division.

(3) THE FRENCH FORCES AT THE BATTLE ON THE NIVELLE, NOVEMBER 1813

1st Div.	(Foy)	9 Batts.	5,136
2nd Div.	(Darmagnac)	8 Batts.	4,705
3rd Div.	(Abbé)	8 Batts.	6,326
4th Div.	(Conroux)	9 Batts.	5,399
5th Div.	(Maransin)	9 Batts.	5,579
6th Div.	(Daricau)	6 Batts.	5,782
7th Div.	(Leval, formerly Maucune)	8 Batts.	4,539

8th Div.	(Taupin)	10 Batts.	4,889
9th Div.	(Boyer)	12 Batts.	6,560
Reserve	(Villatte)	18 Batts.	8,310
Artillery etc.			2,000

Total: **59,225**

(4) THE FRENCH FORCES IN THE BATTLES ON THE RIVER NIVE, DECEMBER 1813

1st Div.	(Foy)	9 Batts.	5,608
2nd Div.	(Darmagnac)	10 Batts.	5,914
3rd Div.	(Abbé)	8 Batts.	6,372
4th Div.	(Taupin, formerly Conroux)	9 Batts.	6,098
5th Div.	(Maransin)	9 Batts.	5,216
6th Div.	(Daricau)	6 Batts.	5,519
7th Div.	(Leval)	8 Batts.	4,704
9th Div.	(Boyer)	14 Batts.	6,423
Reserve	(Villatte)	14 Batts.	5,397
Ind. Brig.	(Paris)	8 Batts.	3,881
Artillery etc			2,000
Cavalry Brig.	(Sparre)	3 Regts.	600
Bayonne garrison			8,801

Total: **66,533**

Note: The 8th Division was disbanded after the Nivelle; its battalions being distributed amongst the other formations and its commander, Taupin, taking the place of Conroux at the head of the 4th Division.

Within days of the actions on the Nive, Soult's forces underwent further change: the divisions of Leval and Boyer were dispatched to the Rhine front; Villatte's Reserve and Paris' brigade were broken up, and a new 8th Division – under Harispe – was created. All of Treillard's dragoons and half of P. Soult's cavalry division (both of which had been kept in the army's rear for some weeks) were also sent east.

WELLINGTON'S FORCES IN AUTUMN 1813

FIRST DIVISION (*Howard*)

Maitland's Brigade (Guards)	2 Batts.	1,680
Stopford's Brigade (Guards)	2 Batts.	2,042
Hinuber's Brigade (KGL)	5 Batts.	3,176

Total: **6,898**

SECOND DIVISION (*Stewart*)

Byng's Brigade	3 Batts.	2,184
Walker's Brigade	3 Batts.	1,646

Pringle's Brigade	3 Batts.	1,937
Ashworth's Brigade (Portuguese)	5 Batts.	2,713
Total:		8,480

THIRD DIVISION (*Colville*)

Keane's Brigade	4 Batts.	2,347
Brisbane's Brigade	4 Batts.	2,684
Power's Brigade (Portuguese)	5 Batts.	2,303
Total:		7,334

FOURTH DIVISION (*Cole*)

Anson's Brigade	4 Batts.	2,367
Ross' Brigade	3 Batts.	1,799
Vasconcello's Brigade (Portuguese)	5 Batts.	2,419
Total:		6,585

FIFTH DIVISION (*Hay*)

Robinson's Brigade	3 Batts.	1,332
Greville's Brigade	3 Batts.	1,456
De Regoa's Brigade (Portuguese)	5 Batts.	1,765
Total:		4,553

SIXTH DIVISION (*Clinton*)

Pack's Brigade	3 Batts.	2,161
Lambert's Brigade	4 Batts.	2,490
Douglas' Brigade (Portuguese)	5 Batts.	2,067
Total:		6,718

SEVENTH DIVISION (*Le Cor*)

Inglis' Brigade	4 Batts.	1,827
Barnes' Brigade	3 Batts.	1,915
Doyle's Brigade (Portuguese)	5 Batts.	2,326
Total:		6,068

LIGHT DIVISION (*Alten*)

Kempt's Brigade	3 Batts.	1,837
Colborne's Brigade	2 Batts.	1,454
Attached Portuguese	4 Batts.	1,679
Total:		4,970

PORTUGUESE DIVISION *(Hamilton)*

Da Costa's Brigade	5 Batts.	2,558
Buchan's Brigade	4 Batts.	2,391
Total:		4,949

British Ind. Brig. (Aylmer)	3 Batts.	1,930
1st Portuguese Ind. Brig. (Wilson)	5 Batts.	2,185
2nd Portuguese Ind. Brig. (Bradford)	5 Batts.	1,614
Total:		5,729

Artillery etc.	9 Batteries	848

(SPANISH) ARMY OF CALICIA *(Freire)*

Morillo's Division	6 Batts.	5,129
España's Division	5 Batts.	4,580
Del Barco's Division	8 Batts.	5,830
Barcena's Division	6 Batts.	4,154
Porlier's Division	3 Batts.	4,544
Longa's Division	5 Batts.	2,607
Artillery etc.		856
Total:		27,700

(SPANISH) RESERVE OF ANDALUSIA *(Giron)*

Virue's Division	6 Batts.	4,123
La Torre's Division	6 Batts.	3,720
Total:		7,843

GRAND TOTAL:		98,675

Note: General Del Barco had replaced Losoda; Barcena was later replaced by General Espeleta.

Of the forces shown, Longa's Spanish Division withdrew to Spain after the Battle of the Nivelle. Similarly, Giron's Reserve of Andalusia was sent back to Spain after the Nivelle, but, along with the Spanish cavalry which had been left on the Ebro after Vitoria, was recalled to the front in February, joining Hope at Bayonne.

Like their Spanish counterparts, the Anglo-Portuguese cavalry (some 8,000 sabres) played little part in the autumn campaigns of 1813 and so are excluded from this list. Also missing is Mina's Spanish Division (8,500 strong) which was totally absorbed in blockading St Jean-Pied-du-Port.

MARSHAL SUCHET'S ARMY IN LATE 1813

FIELD FORCE

1st Div.	(Musnier)	6 Batts.	3,561
2nd Div.	(Pannetier)	6 Batts.	3,073
3rd Div.	(Mathieu)	4 Batts.	2,373

4th Div.	(Habert)	4 Batts.	3,975
5th Div.	(Lamarque)	5 Batts.	4,205
Cavalry	(Boussard)	5 Regts.	2,501
Artillery etc.			3,000
			———
Total:			22,688
			———

GARRISONS

In Lerida, Sagunto and Tortosa:	9,493
In Gerona:	1,605
In Figueras:	1,742
In Barcelona:	5,844
In various smaller fortresses:	4,918
	———
Total:	23,602

GRAND TOTAL:	46,290

MARSHAL SUCHET'S ARMY AT THE END OF THE WAR, APRIL 1814

Lamarque's Division	11 Batts.	8,491
Mesclop's Brigade	7 Batts.	3,990
Cavalry	7 Sqds.	1,449
Artillery etc.	24 Guns	2,180
		———
Total:		16,110

THE FRENCH AND ALLIED ARMIES AT THE BATTLE OF ORTHEZ, 27 FEBRUARY 1814

(1) WELLINGTON'S FORCES

SECOND DIVISION (*Stewart*)

Byng's Brigade	3 Batts.	1,805
Barnes' Brigade	3 Batts.	2,013
O'Callaghan's Brigade	3 Batts.	1,664
Harding's Brigade (Portuguese)	5 Batts.	2,298
		———
Total:		7,780

THIRD DIVISION (*Picton*)

Keane's Brigade	4 Batts.	2,006
Brisbane's Brigade	4 Batts.	2,491
Power's Brigade (Portuguese)	5 Batts.	2,129
		———
Total:		6,626

FOURTH DIVISION (*Cole*)

Anson's Brigade	4 Batts.	1,814
Ross' Brigade	3 Batts.	1,753
Vasconcello's Brigade (Portuguese)	5 Batts.	2,385
Total:		5,952

SIXTH DIVISION (*Clinton*)

Pack's Brigade	3 Batts.	1,415
Lambert's Brigade	4 Batts.	2,300
Douglas' Brigade (Portuguese)	5 Batts.	1,856
Total:		5,571

SEVENTH DIVISION (*Walker*)

Inglis' Brigade	4 Batts.	1,420
Gardiner's Brigade	3 Batts.	1,865
Doyle's Brigade (Portuguese)	5 Batts.	2,358
Total:		5,643

LIGHT DIVISION (*Alten*)

British	3 Batts.	1,777
Portuguese	9 Batts.	1,703
Total:		3,480

PORTUGUESE DIVISION (*Le Cor*)

Da Costa's Brigade	5 Batts.	2,109
Buchan's Brigade	4 Batts.	2,356
Total:		4,465

Fane's Lt Cav. Brigade	2 Regts.	765
Vivian's Lt Cav. Brigade	2 Regts.	989
Somerset's Lt Cav. Brigade	3 Regts.	1,619
Total:		3,373

Artillery etc.	54 Guns	1,512
GRAND TOTAL:		44,402

(2) SOULT'S FORCES

D'ERLON'S SECTOR

Foy's Division	9 Batts.	4,600
Darmagnac's Division	10 Batts.	5,500

REILLE'S SECTOR

Rouget's Division	9 Batts.	5,000
Taupin's Division	9 Batts.	5,600

CLAUSEL'S SECTOR

Villatte's Division	6 Batts.	5,200
Harispe's Division	13 Batts.	6,600
P. Soult's Cav. Division	6 Regts.	3,200
Artillery etc.	48 Guns	1,300

GRAND TOTAL: 37,000

Note: General Harding (Allied Second Division) had replaced Ashworth. Similarly, General Rouget had taken control of Maransin's formation in Soult's army.

THE FRENCH AND ALLIED ARMIES AT THE BATTLE OF TOULOUSE, 10 APRIL 1814

(1) WELLINGTON'S FORCES

Second Division (Stewart)		6,940
Third Division (Picton)		4,566
Fourth Division (Cole)		5,363
Sixth Division (Clinton)		5,693
Light Division (Alten)		4,275
Portuguese Division (Le Cor)		3,952
Morillo's Spanish Division	6 Batts.	2,001
Freire's Spanish Divisions	7 & 6 Batts.	7,916
Manner's Dragoon Brigade	3 Regts.	1,426
Clifton's Dragoon Brigade	3 Regts.	891
Bülow's Dragoon Brigade (KGL)	2 Regts.	701
Somerset's Lt Cav. Brigade	3 Regts.	1,717
Vivian's Lt Cav. Brigade	2 Regts.	939
Fane's Lt Cav. Brigade	2 Regts.	816
Artillery etc.		2,250

GRAND TOTAL: 49,446

Note: The brigade organisation was essentially the same as at Orthez. Freire's Spanish corps consisted of Barcena's old division (under the control of General Espeleta) and 2 brigades formed into a division under Marcilla, one brigade coming from Porlier's formation of the Army of Galicia, the other from Del Barco's division of the same army.

(2) SOULT'S FORCES

Daricau's Division	9 Batts.	3,839
Darmagnac's Division	11 Batts.	5,022
Taupin's Division	10 Batts.	5,455
Maransin's Division	7 Batts.	3,717
Villatte's Division	8 Batts.	4,609
Harispe's Division	13 Batts.	5,084
Travot's Division (conscripts)		7,267
P. Soult's Cavalry Division	7 Regts.	2,700
Artillery etc.		4,350
GRAND TOTAL:		42,043

Note: Maransin had returned to the command of the division led by Rouget at Orthez.

REFERENCES

For brevity, works listed in the select bibliography are cited by author's surname only. The other abbreviations used in the references are as follows:

NC   Napoleon I, *Correspondance de Napoleon 1er*.
WD   Wellington, A. 1st Duke of. *Dispatches*.
WSD   Wellington, A. 1st Duke of. *Supplementary Dispatches*.
WP   Wellington Papers, University Library, Southampton.
CKJ   Bonaparte, King Joseph. *Mémoires et Correspondance*.
CBS   Coleccion de la Biblioteca del Senado, Biblioteca Nacional, Madrid.
CDF   Coleccion del Fraile, Biblioteca Nacional, Madrid.
AG   Archives de Guerre, Vincennes.
AHML Arquivo Historico Militar, Lisbon.
WO   War Office Papers in the Public Records Office, Kew.

1   See *Cambridge History of the British Empire* (Cambridge, 1940), II, 78 and 105–22.
2   Heckscher, p. 120.
3   Kennedy, p. 144.
4   See Ibid., pp. 143–5.
5   NC XV, 553.
6   See Talleyrand, I, 378–9; Jourdan, p. 9.
7   See NC XVI, 149–50.
8   See Lovett, p. 29; NC XXXII, 59.
9   See Lovett, p. 21.
10 NC XV, 433.
11 See *Spain*, p. 152; Lovett, pp. 23–6 and 90.
12 Bourienne, III, 29.
13 See Neves, I, 218–37 and II, 96–105.
14 See Lovett, pp. 122–3.
15 Girod de l'Ain, p. 111.
16 See Lovett, pp. 121 and 124.
17 See Talleyrand, I, 308–29.
18 Toreno, pp. 16–17; and Arteche, I, 218–43.
19 Lovett, pp. 98–100; *Spain*, p. 152.
20 See Charco-Villasenor; and Lovett, 141–9.
21 Details of Spanish forces from CDF and CBS misc. MSS.; Arteche, I, 473–505, and the appendices in vols. I–XIV; Lovett, pp. 36–8.
22 See Pelet, p. 239. Details of Portuguese forces from AHML. misc. MSS., 1809–14; Halliday; Arteche, I; Chaby, IV, and *passim*.
23 Details of British Forces from WP misc. MSS.; W.O. 28; Oman, *Wellington's Army*; Rogers; Ward, *Wellington's Headquarters*; Hennell, p. 50.
24 Details of French forces from CKJ, *passim*; AG. MSS. C8/347–487; Morvan; Picard; Foy; Martinien.
25 See Gates, Ch. V.
26 Girod de l'Ain, p. 107.
27 Bugeaud, I, v.

28 See Vigo-Roussillon, pp. 5–8.
29 See Gates, Ch. VI.
30 Bugeaud, I, v–vi.
31 See Gates, Ch. VI.
32 See Strachan, p. 52.
33 Lapene, *1814*, p. 382.
34 See H. T. Siborne (Ed.), *The Waterloo Letters* (1983 edition), pp. 388 and 401; Hennell, pp. 89–90; Colville, p. 71.
35 See Chandler, p. 807; B. H. Liddell Hart, *History of the First World War* (1973 edition), pp. 314–16.
36 For details of the naval conflict see Codrington; Callender & Hinsley; Clowes; Crouzet; Kennedy; La Roncière; Mahan; Roskill.
37 See Aitchison, pp. 71–2.
38 Sir A. S. Frazer, *Letters of . . . Frazer*, p. 77. Also see WD VI, 568–9.
39 Marmont, IV, 346–7.
40 Ibid., 350.
41 WD VII, 54.
42 F. C. E. von Muffling, *Passages From My Life* (1853), p. 251. Also see WD IV, 436; Aitchison, p. 78; Blakiston, II, 160–1.
43 See Colville, pp. 33–4.
44 See Lovett, pp. 514–16 and 666–721; Arteche, VII, 5–73; Von Brandt.
45 See Von Clausewitz, pp. 479–83.
46 WD VII, 584.
47 *Spain*, p. 153.
48 Ibid., p. 155.
49 See Artola, *Los Afrancesados*, pp. 145 and 256–8; Lovett, pp. 554–609.
50 See Lovett, pp. 329–33; *Spain*, p. 153.
51 See Lovett, pp. 722–37.
52 Melito, II, 351. Also see Lovett, pp. 509–24, 531 and 552–3.
53 See Aitchison, pp. 24–5.
54 See W.O. 37/3: Soult to Berthier, 14 April, 1812; W.O. 37/3/16a: Joseph to Napoleon, 20 Nov., 1812.
55 See W.O. 37/5: Dorsenne to Jourdan, 16 April, 1812; W.O. 37/9: Joseph to Dorsenne, 25 April, 1812; W.O. 37/19: Joseph to Dorsenne, 1 May, 1812.
56 NC XXI, 130.
57 NC XIX, 378–90.
58 WD VII, 269–71. (1844 edition).
59 See Arteche, II, 483–500.
60 Lovett, pp. 224–5.
61 NC XVII, 427.
62 Details of Baylen from AG. MSS. C8/273–5; Vaughan Papers; Clerc; Foy, I; Arteche, I and II; CDF and CBS misc. MSS.; Savary; Jourdan, pp. 46–57; Lovett, pp. 215–16.
63 Toreno, p. 96.
64 Details from Foy, I; Arteche, II; Savary.
65 See Arteche, II, 622.
66 Ibid., 285–8; St Cyr, *Journal*, pp. 17–25.
67 Details from Arteche, II; Toreno; St Cyr.
68 Details from Napier, I; Foy, IV; Arteche, II, IV and V; Toreno; St Cyr, *Memoires* and *Journal*; Martinien; Belmas, II; Marbot, III; Vacani, II and III; CDF and CBS misc. MSS.; AG. MSS. C7/18, 10, 11.
69 Details from Vaughan Papers; Rudirff; Belmas, I; Arteche, II; Jourdan, pp. 43–4; Lovett, p. 249; CBS and CDF misc. MSS.
70 Details from Savary; (Vaughan Papers) 'Journal of the Operations of Gen. Blake'; AG. MSS. C8/238–9; CDF misc. MSS.
71 See Neves, III, 163–86.
72 See Toreno, pp. 56–70.
73 See Lovett, pp. 156–9.
74 See W.O. 1/903: Documents on Army reform by Castlereagh.
75 See Moore Papers, MSS. 57544: Return of Junot's Corps, Sept., 1808.

76 Details of Vimiero campaign from Thiéubault; WSD II; WD IV, especially pp. 93–7; Simmons; Leslie; Leach; Foy; Neves; Martinien; Soriano; Hulot; Arteche, II; Napier, I; Landsheit; Steevens; *Peninsular Sketches*, I; *Soldier of 71st*; Harris; Col Leslie, *Military Journal* (Aberdeen, 1887).
77 See Arteche, III, 107–46.
78 See Jourdan, pp. 79–81; and NC. XVIII, 38.
79 See Jourdan, pp. 74–97.
80 Oman, *Peninsular War*, I, 440.
81 Details from CBS and CDF misc. MSS.; Arteche, III; Jourdan; Toreno, I; (Vaughan Papers) 'Journal of the Operations of Gen. Blake'; Ségur, III; Balagny.
82 See Ségur, III, 281–95.
83 Arteche, III, 400–1.
84 Toreno, p. 149.
85 See Lovett, pp. 310–14 and 517–20.
86 NC XVIII, 88.
87 See W.O. 1/416–18: Details of Cintra Convention and the Court of Enquiry.
88 See Moore Papers, MSS. 57544 for details of expeditionary force.
89 Ibid., MSS. 57542: Letters from La Romana and Castaños, Nov., 1808.
90 Ibid.
91 See Soult's dispatch in Moore Papers, MSS. 57544.
92 See NC XVIII, 609, 611 and 614.
93 See NC XVIII, 157–8.
94 *Soldier of 71st*, p. 25.
95 Ibid., p. 35.
96 Details from Moore Papers; CDF misc. MSS.; AG. MSS. C8/144; Leith Hay, I; Schaumann; Jourdan; Gordon; Wall; Davies; Blakeney; Surtees; Napier, I; Londonderry, I; Arteche, IV; Toreno, I; Steevens; Foy; Le Noble; Lejeune; Ormsby, II; Neale; Davies; Leslie; Hibbert; Parkinson; Martinien; *Soldier of 71st*.
97 *The Diary of Sir John Moore* (Ed. by F. Maurice, 1904), II, 360.
98 See NC XVIII, 237.
99 See NC XVIII, 187.
100 Details from Jourdan; Arteche, IV; Belmas, II; Rocca; CKJ VI.
101 Jourdan, p. 181.
102 See Rocca, p. 80.
103 Ibid., p. 84.
104 Arteche, V, 301–3.
105 Details from CKJ VI; Rocca; Jourdan; Arteche, VI; Napier, II; AG. MSS. C8/264.
106 See Arteche, IV, 305–24.
107 See Lovett, pp. 274–81.
108 Belmas, II, 294.
109 Lejeune, I, 169.
110 Details from Jourdan; Arteche, II; Belmas, II; Napier, I; Lejeune, I; Rudirff.
111 Jourdan, pp. 174–6.
112 Ibid., p. 204.
113 Ibid., p. 205.
114 Ibid., p. 206.
115 Arteche, V, 389–90.
116 Jourdan, pp. 206–10.
117 Arteche, V, 412–15.
118 Jourdan, pp. 211–13.
119 Ibid., pp. 213–15.
120 Details from Foy; Lenoble; Soult; Fantin; AG. MSS. C8/144–5.
121 Jourdan, pp. 197–8. Also see H. Bonnal, *La Vie Militaire du Marechal Ney* (Paris, 1914), III, 135–220.
122 Details of Galician insurrection from P. de Andrade, *Los Guerillos Gallegos de 1809* (Corunna, 1892).
123 Jourdan, p. 196.
124 Ibid., p. 197.
125 Arteche, VI, 113–16.

126 *Spain*, pp. 156–7.
127 Details from AG. MSS. C8/239, 240, 241, 256, 257, 340, 361; CDF and CBS misc. MSS; Jourdan; Andrade, Op. Cit.
128 Jourdan, p. 203.
129 See W.O. 1/240: Cradock to Beresford, 29 March, and to Castlereagh, 26 March, 1809.
130 See Halliday.
131 Aitchison, p. 34.
132 See Glover, *A Very Slippery Fellow*.
133 *Narrative of the Campaigns of the LLL*; Jourdan, p. 189.
134 See WSD VI, 210–12.
135 Moore Papers, MSS. 57544: Memorandum on Defence of Portugal, 25 Nov., 1808.
136 WD V, 261.
137 WD IV, 250–3.
138 Aitchison, p. 39.
139 WD IV, 249. Also see Aitchison, pp. 38–9.
140 See WD IV, 252–4.
141 Compare Tomkinson, pp. 9–11 and Fantin, p. 231.
142 Aitchison, p. 41.
143 Jourdan, p. 228.
144 Burgoyne, I, 40–1.
145 Girod de l'Ain, p. 81.
146 W.O. 1/238: Wellesley to Castlereagh, 12 May, 1809. For other details of Oporto see: AG. MSS. C8/144–5; Lenoble; Ormsby; Fantin; Fane; Knight; Foy.
147 Aitchison, p. 42.
148 See Jourdan, pp. 225–9.
149 See Arteche, VI, 10.
150 See Suchet, I, 23.
151 Arteche, VI, 75.
152 Details from Suchet, I; CKJ VII; CDF and CBS misc. MSS.; AG. MSS. C8/357–8.
153 See Arteche, VII, 458.
154 See Ibid., 150–3; Vacani, III, 245–55.
155 Belmas, II, 693–4.
156 Arteche, VII, 411–13.
157 Ibid., 428–9.
158 Ibid., 407.
159 CKJ VII, 76–7.
160 Details from: AG. MSS. C8/362; St Cyr, *Journal* and *Memoirs*; Belmas, II.
161 WD IV, 250.
162 WSD IV, 288–9.
163 CKJ VI, 281.
164 Arteche, VI, 353–7.
165 WD V, 341–2.
166 WD V, 80 and 85.
167 Tomkinson, p. 57.
168 Jourdan, pp. 256–9.
169 See Leach, pp. 81–2.
170 Aitchison, p. 53.
171 Details from: AG. MSS. C8/353–4; WD IV, especially 504–10; Tomkinson; Martinien; Jourdan; Ormsby; Moore; Lenoble; *Narrative of the Campaigns of the LLL*.
172 WD IV, 523.
173 Lenoble, p. 320.
174 Jourdan, p. 265.
175 Arteche, VI, 342.
176 Jourdan, pp. 267–8; CKJ VI, 327–33.
177 See Aitchison, pp. 55–8; Schaumann, pp. 193–4; Simmons, p. 32; Leith, I, 166–7; WD V, 71–2.
178 Jourdan, pp. 274–8.
179 CKJ VI, 284–6 and 380–2.
180 Arteche, VI, 370.

181 Jourdan, pp. 270–2; CKJ VI, 334–43 and 354–63.
182 See Arteche, VI, 353–70.
183 WD V, 15.
184 Aitchison, p. 62. Also see WD V, 71–2.
185 WD V, 108.
186 Ibid., 258.
187 See Cookson, *passim*.
188 WSD VI, 350–3. Also see WD V, 274.
189 WD V, 268–77.
190 Ibid., 294.
191 NC XX, 168.
192 See WD V, 230–5 and 268–75.
193 See WSD VI, 372 and 394; Arteche, VII, Ch. 6; Lovett, pp. 336–45.
194 See Lovett, pp. 369–74.
195 See Toreno, pp. 240–5 and 286–8.
196 See WD V, 289–91.
197 Lovett, p. 355.
198 Details from Jourdan; Marchand; CKJ VII, especially 7–11 and 61–2; WD V, 261–2;
     W.O. 1/237: Reports by Cox, 19 and 22 Nov., 1810.
199 See CKJ VII, 12.
200 Ibid., 5–7 and 67–9.
201 WD V, 312–15.
202 See CKJ VII, 79–84.
203 See F. L. Petre, *Napoleon's Campaign in Poland* (1901), pp. 316–17.
204 Details from Jourdan, especially pp. 282–4; Martinien; CKJ VII, especially 13–16 and
     62–4; Arteche, VII; CBS and CDF misc. MSS.
205 See Toreno, p. 232; Arteche, VII, 323.
206 Details from CKJ VII, 17–19; Jourdan, pp. 284–6; AG. MSS. C8/241–2, 250, 255.
207 WD V, 413. Also see Toreno, pp. 240–5 and 286–8.
208 Jourdan, p. 294.
209 CKJ VII, 99–104.
210 NC XX, 146.
211 See Artola, *Los Afrancesados*, pp. 145 and 256–8; Melito, p. 137.
212 Details of Cadiz's defences in Toreno, pp. 245–6.
213 See Melito, II, 385; CKJ VII, 142–3.
214 Details from Jourdan; Lapene; Martinien; Toreno.
215 See NC XIX, 263–4 and 554–5; Thiébault, IV, 448.
216 WD VI, 290.
217 See Stanhope, p. 20.
218 See Hulot, p. 303; Girod de l'Ain, p. 101.
219 See Fririon, p. 157.
220 NC XX, 291.
221 Ibid., 114–21 and 271.
222 See Jones, *Memoranda*.
223 Details from CBS and CDF misc. MSS.; WD V, especially 498–500; Belmas, III.
224 Croker, I, 42. Also see WD VI, 282; Aitchison, p. 101.
225 See p. 217.
226 WD VI, 5–9. Also see Kincaid, (1981 edition), pp. 27–8.
227 See Gates, Ch. VI, Part I.
228 Details from Aitchison; Simmons; Belmas, III; Hulot; Koch; Herrasti.
229 Napier, II, 413–14.
230 Leach, p. 121. Also see Simmons, pp. 77–8.
231 See WD VI, 563–4.
232 See WD VI, 290.
233 Details from Belmas, III; Soriano, III; Koch, VI and VII.
234 WD VI, 428 and 433.
235 Ibid., 351.
236 Ibid., 441.
237 Oman, III, 352–3. Also see Aitchison, p. 111.

238 Girod de l'Ain, p. 107.
239 See Ibid., p. 108; Koch, VII, 192.
240 NC XIX, 379–80.
241 Details of Bussaco from WSD VI, 636–9; Lemonnier-Delafosse; Grattan; Leith Hay, I; Foy; Marbot; Koch, VI; Horward; Sherer; Simmons; Eliot; Hale; Hawker; Martinien; Pelet; Picton; WP MSS. 9/1/2/3.
242 *Victoires . . . des Français*, XXI, 323. Also see Sarrazin, p. 150.
243 Girod de l'Ain, p. 343.
244 WD VI, 518.
245 See Leach, p. 178; Kincaid (1981 edition), p. 15; *Soldier of 71st*, p. 58.
246 WD VII, 54.
247 See Belmas, I, 137; WD VII, 20 and 36.
248 WD VII, 347.
249 See *Soldier of 71st*, pp. 56–9; Kincaid (1981 edition), pp. 19–20; Leach, p. 179; Simmons, pp. 121–37; Lemonnier-Delafosse, pp. 95–103.
250 Details from Koch, VI and VII; Martinien; Kincaid; Simmons.
251 Details of campaign from AG. MSS. C8/257–9, 241–4, 251–2, 345, 19–20, 23–4; WP MSS. 9/1/2/2 and 9/1/2/3; WD V, especially 461–3; WD VI, especially 605–18; Koch, VI and VII; Pelet; Gomm; Aitchison; Beamish; Tomkinson; Eliot; Fririon; Hulot; Livermore; Neves; Anstice; Jones, *Memoranda*.
252 NC XXI, 158–9.
253 See Belmas, I, 472.
254 Chaby, IV, 200–1.
255 Details from WSD VII, 63–7; CBS misc. MSS.
256 See WD VII, 360. Details of siege from AG. MSS. C8/147, 367; Martinien; CBS and CDF misc. MSS.
257 Details of Barrosa from Graham Papers, misc. MSS.; AG. MSS. C8/256; CBS misc. MSS.; WSD VII, 126–33; Blakeney, pp. 188–95;Lapene, pp. 110–21; Surtees, 118–20; Vigo Rousillion, pp. 8–18.
258 See F. L. Petre, *Napoleon's Conquest of Prussia* (1972 edition), pp. 252–3.
259 See WD VII, 360–1.
260 See C. E. Long, *Vindication of the Military Reputation of the Late General Long* (1832).
261 See WD VII, 414 and 432.
262 Lapene, p. 146.
263 See Dickson MSS., pp. 448 and 405.
264 See WD VII, 491–2.
265 Details from C. E. Long, Op. Cit.; D'Urban; Lapene; *Strictures* (1833); WD VII, especially 573–8; Du Casse, *Girard*; E. Fraser, *The Soldiers Whom Wellington Led* (1913).
266 WSD XIII, 654–6; Picard, II, 315–16.
267 WSD VII, 177.
268 Details from *Soldier of 71st*; Tomkinson; Grattan; Fririon; Leach; Wheeler, *Letters*; Hamilton; Koch, VII; WD VII, 514–20; WP MSS. 9/1/2/4; AG. MSS. C8/259.
269 See WSD VII, 123.
270 See WD VII, 567 and 602.
271 Stanhope, p. 90.
272 See WD VII, 586–7 and 604–5.
273 See Dickson MSS., p. 394.
274 See WD VII, 638.
275 See Marmont, IV, 93–5.
276 Details of siege from Jones, I; Lapene; Dickson MSS.; AG. MSS. C8/147, 364.
277 See WD VIII, 58; Farmer, I, 92–7.
278 Details from AG. MSS. C8/147; CBS misc. MSS.
279 Belmas, IV, 15–17.
280 Details from Anon., *Defence of Tarifa* (1812); Napier, IV; Jones, II; Belmas, IV; AG. MSS. C8/356.
281 Details from *Soldier of 71st*; Teffeteller; Sherer; Burgoyne, I; Blakeney; Coste; Du Casse, *Girard*; AG. MSS. C8/147.
282 Details from Cadell; *Soldier of 71st*; Teffeteller.

283 Details from CBS misc. MSS.; AG. MSS. C8/197, 201, 259, 260, 265, 365, 366, 392, 395; D. J. M. Santocildes, *Relacion Historico* (Madrid, 1815).
284 Marmont, IV, 63.
285 Ibid., 163.
286 See Tomkinson, p. 115.
287 Marmont, IV, 64.
288 Details from WSD VII, especially 222–3; Grattan; Larpent; Colville; Donaldson; Schwertfeger; Marmont, IV; Thièbault, IV; WP MSS. 9/1/2/4.
289 See Thièbault, IV, 522–5.
290 See Marmont, IV, 256–8.
291 WD VIII, 495.
292 See NC XX, 308–9.
293 Details from AG. MSS. C7/18 (Part 10), C8/276–7; CBS misc. MSS.
294 Details from Suchet, I; Arteche, III; Martinien; AG. MSS. C8/257–8; CBS misc. MSS.
295 See NC XX, 388; Suchet, I, 196–7.
296 See Arteche, IX, 264–7.
297 Details from Barkhausen; Martinien; CBS misc. MSS.; AG. MSS. C8/278–80.
298 Details from Suchet, I; Vacani, IV; Arteche, IX; Belmas, I; Macdonald; AG. MSS. C8/281; CBS misc. MSS; Martinien.
299 See Codrington, I, 225 and Arteche, IX, 544–5.
300 Suchet was eventually made Duke of Albufera – a region to the south of Valencia. He was the only marshal to gain a Spanish title.
301 Vacani, V, 313.
302 Details from Vacani; Macdonald; CBS misc. MSS; AG. MSS. C7/18 (Part 11).
303 Miscellaneous details of the war in Catalonia during this period from Belmas, III and IV; Arteche, X; Martinien; Codrington; J. M. Riba, *Barcelona durante la occupación francesa, 1808–14* (Madrid, 1949); P. Conrad, *Napoleon et la Catalogne* (Paris, 1909); L. M. Puig, *Girona francesa, 1812–14* (Gerona, 1976); AG. MSS. C8/276–81, 129–30, 133–6; CBS and CDF misc. MSS.
304 See WD V, 518–19.
305 WD V, 411–14.
306 WSD VII, 69.
307 WD V, 434.
308 WD V, 536. Also see WD V, 434.
309 WSD VII, 318.
310 WSD IX, 266.
311 See Colville, pp. 36–7.
312 See WSD VII, 257–88.
313 See Forester; Horsman; Mackay; Perkins.
314 See Lovett, pp. 376–7 and 413.
315 Lovett, p. 154. Also see Ibid., pp. 607–9; *Spain*, p. 155; Artola, *Los Afrancesados* and *La Burguesia Revolucionaria*.
316 See WD VI, 559; *Spain*, pp. 156–7.
317 See Jourdan, p. 302.
318 Ibid., p. 384.
319 Ibid., p. 392.
320 Ibid., pp. 386–94.
321 Ibid., p. 395.
322 Details of siege from Belmas, IV, 1–143.
323 Arteche, XI, 157–9.
324 Details from Suchet, II; Arteche, XI; Vacani, V; Decaen.
325 Details from Suchet, IV; Arteche, XI; Vacani, V; Decaen; Martinien; CBS and CDF misc. MSS.
326 See Marmont, IV, 256–8.
327 WD VIII, 495. Compare Oman, V, 158.
328 Belmas, IV, 265–6.
329 Costello, pp. 151–2.
330 Details from Dickson MSS, II; Jones, *Sieges*, I; Grattan; Simmons; Leach; Belmas, IV; Martinien; WSD XIV.

331   See WD VIII, 536.
332   See W.O. 37/1: Berthier to Marmont, 6 March, 1812.
333   Quoted in Oman, V, 204.
334   Marmont, IV, 350.
335   See NC XXIII, 220.
336   WD IX, 176–7.
337   See W.O. 37/4, 7: Marmont to Berthier, 16 April and 22 April, 1812.
338   See 'Assistant Engineer' (J. E. C. McCarthy), *The Storm of Badajoz* (1836), pp. 4–6.
339   Details of siege from Donaldson; Hennell; Jones, I; Kincaid; WSD XIV; Surtees; Martinien.
340   See Hennell, pp. 17–18.
341   See Marmont, IV, 304–5.
342   CKJ VIII, 355.
343   See W.O. 37/3: Soult to Berthier, 14 April, 1812.
344   Details from Teffeteller; D'Erlon; Sidney; Jones; Dickson MSS., IV; Long; Grattan; *Soldier of the 71st*; Foy.
345   See Marmont, IV, 411; W.O. 37/3/15: Soult to Joseph, Aug., 1812.
346   See W.O. 37/28: Marmont to Jourdan, 1 June, 1812.
347   WD IX, 176–7.
348   Marmont, IV, 411.
349   WD IX, 241.
350   See WD IX, 254–5; Aitchison, 165.
351   WD IX, 269.
352   Ibid., 270.
353   CKJ IX, 38–9.
354   See Marmont, IV, 410.
355   See W.O. 37/35: Joseph to Soult, 7 July, 1812; and W.O. 37/3/4: Jourdan to Soult, 28 May, 1812.
356   WD IX, 286.
357   CKJ IX, 38–9.
358   See Hennell, p. 28.
359   See WD IX, 295–9; Marmont, IV, 237 and 443; Dickson MSS., IV, 679.
360   Marmont, IV, 255.
361   Ibid., 257.
362   Grattan, pp. 239–40.
363   Jourdan, p. 418.
364   Girod de l'Ain, p. 177.
365   Lemonnier-Delafosse, p. 159.
366   Ibid., pp. 161–2.
367   WD IX, 310.
368   Tomkinson, p. 187.
369   WD IX, 304.
370   Girod de l'Ain, pp. 176–7.
371   Ibid., p. 178.
372   Details of Salamanca from WSD XIV; CKJ IX; Hennell; Kincaid; Tomkinson; Lemonnier-Delafosse; Donaldson; Jones; Foy; Cooke; Wheeler, *Letters*; Napier, IV; Leith Hay, II; Grattan; Aitchison; Schwetferger.
373   W.O. 37/35: Joseph to Soult, 7 July, 1812.
374   See Ibid., f. 49: Joseph to Napoleon, 8 Jan., 1812.
375   WD IX, 240.
376   Miscellaneous details of Salamanca campaign from WP MSS. 9/1/2/5; W.O. 37; AG. MSS. C8/188–9, 191, 196, 204–11, 261, 368–9, 387–95; Santocildes.
377   See W.O. 37/37: Suchet to Joseph, 22 July, 1812.
378   See W.O. 37/3/14: Suchet to Joseph, 17 Aug., 1812.
379   CKJ IX, 64.
380   See Aitchison, pp. 208–10; WD IX, 573.
381   Girod de l'Ain, p. 189.
382   Details of Burgos and Wellington's retreat from AG. MSS. C8/205–7; WP MSS. 9/1/2/5–6; WD IX; WSD XIV; Hennell; Foy; Jones; Jourdan; Belmas, IV; Burgoyne, I; Vacani, IV; Arteche, XI; Grattan; Aitchison; Kincaid; *Soldier of 71st*; Tomkinson.

383 See WD IX, 574–7.
384 WSD VII, 502.
385 NC XXIV, 506–7.
386 WD X, 372.
387 Ibid.
388 See Tomkinson, p. 242; *Peninsular Sketches*, II, 39–40; Hennell, pp. 80–2; Kincaid (1981 edition), p. 104.
389 See Hennell, p. 91.
390 Jourdan, p. 479.
391 Details of Vitoria from WP. MSS. 9/1/2/6; CBS misc. MSS.; AG. MSS. C8/212–19, 368–9, 245–9; Vidal de la Blache, I; Kincaid; Hennell; Wheeler, *Letters*; *Soldier of 71st*; Aitchison; Simmons; Ross; Surtees; Tomkinson; Blakiston; Gavin; Cooke in *Peninsular Sketches*, II; Hale; Smith; Fée; Jourdan; Burgoyne, I; Picton, II; L'Estrange; WD X, especially 449; WSD VIII, 4–9 and XIV, 236–40.
392 Girod de l'Ain, pp. 393–4.
393 See Aitchison, pp. 250 and 254.
394 Details from WSD VIII, 44; Aitchison; Foy; Girod de l'Ain.
395 See Croker, II, 233.
396 WD XI, 46.
397 Gomm, pp. 311–12.
398 Details of San Sebastian (Part I) from Aitchison; Gomm; Jones, II; Belmas, IV; Dickson MSS.; Frazer, *Letters from Peninsula*; Burgoyne; WD X; WSD XIV.
399 Details of campaign from WSD XIV; Suchet, II; Landsheit; Whittingham; CBS misc. MSS.; AG. MSS. C7/21, C8/295, 316–29.
400 See *The Trial of Sir John Murray . . . . Recorded by Guerney* (1815), pp. 183 and 186–7; WSD XIV, 274–6.
401 Details of Tarragona from *Trial of Murray*; Vacani, IV; Suchet, II; Vidal de la Blache, I; WSD VIII; Decaen.
402 Details from Suchet, II; WSD VIII and XIV; Vidal de la Blache, I and II; Toreno, III; Decaen; WD X; CBS misc. MSS.
403 Vidal de la Blache, I, 153.
404 See Cole and Picton's reports in WSD VIII.
405 Lemonnier-Delafosse, p. 219.
406 Details of campaign from *Soldier of 71st*; Pellot; Picton; Beatson, *Pyrenees*; Dumas; Clerc, *Pyrenees*; Surtees; Vidal de la Blache, I; Lemonnier-Delafosse; Smith, I; Cooke, I; Colville; Long; Bell, I; Cadell; Hale; Sherer; Hope; Robertson; Batty; Foy; Green; Martinien; *Peninsular Sketches*; D. Horward, *Journal of A. Colomb*, JSAHR, 46, (1968), 20–1.
407 See Hennell, pp. 112–16.
408 Kincaid (1981 edition), p. 120.
409 See Hennell, 116–17.
410 See WD X, 585–99; Vidal de la Blache, I, 280.
411 WD XI, 46.
412 See Hennell, pp. 123–4.
413 See Hennell, p. 130; Harley, II, 83–93; Gomm, p. 319.
414 See Aitchison, p. 267.
415 Details from WSD VIII and XIV; WD X and XI; Aitchison; Jones, II; Burgoyne; Belmas, IV; Cooke, II; Gomm; Hennell; Harley; Leith, II; Frazer; Larpent; Martinien.
416 See Hennell, p. 127.
417 Stanhope, p. 107.
418 Details from Vidal de la Blache, II; Lemonnier-Delafosse; Surtees; Wheeler, *Letters*; Leach; Kincaid; Smith, I; Hennell; CDF misc. MSS.
419 WD XI, 124.
420 See Aitchison, p. 276.
421 Smith, I, 142.
422 Hennell, p. 135.
423 Details from Beatson; Foy; Batty; Smith, I; Costello; Vidal de la Blache, I; Clerc, *Pyrenees*; Dumas; Kincaid; Surtees; Martinien.
424 WD XI, 211.
425 Details from WD XI; Martinien; Belmas, IV; Larpent; Jones, II; Gomm; Gleig.

426 See Girod de l'Ain, p. 406.
427 Details from Hennell; Beatson; Vidal de la Blache, I; Kincaid; Pellot; Dumas; Foy; Smith, I; Clerc; WD XI; WSD VIII; AG. MSS. C8/149.
428 WD XI, 306–7.
429 See Hennell, p. 110.
430 Ibid., p. 108.
431 Vidal de la Blache, II, 163.
432 Details of Nive and St Pierre from WSD VIII, especially 436–41; WD XI; Hennell; Batty; Dumas; Vidal de la Blache, II; Cooke, II; Burgoyne; Gleig; Gavin; Pellot; Lapene; L'Estrange; Larpent.
433 Vidal de la Blache, II, 142–3.
434 NC XXVII, 10.
435 See WD XI, 433–4.
436 See C. J. Bartlett, *Castlereagh* (1966), pp. 127–9.
437 See NC XXVI, 535.
438 Details of Orthez and related operations from Vidal de la Blache, II; Lemonnier-Delafosse; Castello; Cooper; Gleig; Martinien; Dumas; Foy; Blakiston, II; Chaby, III; AG. MSS. C8/150.
439 See WSD XIV, 404–5.
440 Lapene, *1814*, pp. 382–4.
441 Details from WSD XIV, VIII and IX; WD XI; Toreno, III; Cadell; Bell, I; Robertson; Lapene; Martinien; *Soldier of 71st*; Cooke, II; Larpent; Smith, I; Cooper; Surtees; Lemonnier-Delafosse; AG. MSS. C8/150; CDF misc. MSS.
442 Details from Jones, II; Batty; Foy; AG. MSS. C8/229, 222–5.

SELECT BIBLIOGRAPHY

MANUSCRIPT SOURCES

British Library, London
Addit. MSS. 57320–57332 Sir John Moore Papers.
Addit. MSS. 35059–35067 Sir Rowland Hill Papers.
Addit. MSS. 27544 Reports of *Armée du Midi.*

Public Record Office, Kew
W.O. 1 War Office in Letters.
W.O. 2 Indexes of Correspondence.
W.O. 3 Out Letters, Commander-in-Chief.
W.O. 4 Out Letters, Secretary at War.
W.O. 6 Out Letters, Secretary at State, War Office.
W.O. 28 Headquarters Records.
W.O. 30 War Office Miscellanea.
W.O. 40 Selected Unnumbered Papers.
W.O. 133 Papers of General Sir Robert Brownrigg.
W.O. 37 Papers of General Sir George Scovell.
W.O. 135 Papers of General Sir Harry Smith.
P.R.O. 30/43 Papers of General Sir Galbraith Lowry Cole.

National Library of Scotland, Edinburgh
MSS. 3590–3645 Papers of Thomas Graham, Lord Lynedoch.
MSS. 16001–16434 Addit. Papers of Thomas Graham, Lord Lynedoch.

University Library, Southampton
Wellington Papers.

Codrington Library, Oxford
Papers of Sir Charles Vaughan.

Archives de Guerre, Vincennes
MSS. C7/18– C8/486 Correspondence du Roi Joseph, etc.

Biblioteca Nacional, Madrid
Coleccion del Fraile.
Coleccion de la Biblioteca del Senado.
Coleccion Gomez Imaz.

Archivo del Palacio Real, Madrid
Documentos de Farnando VII.

Arquivo Historico Militar, Lisbon
Misc. MSS., 1809–14.

PRINTED PRIMARY SOURCES

Aitchison, J. *An Ensign in the Peninsular War* (ed. W. F. K. Thompson, 1981).

Allen, J. *Journal of an Officer of the Royals* (1811).

Anderson, J. *Recollections of a Peninsular Veteran* (1911).

Azana, M. J. de. *Mémoire de Azana et O'Farrill, 1808–14* (Paris, 1815).

B. . . . , C. *Mémoires sur la dernière Guerre entre la France et l'Espagne* (Paris, undated).

Bapst, G. *Souvenirs d'un Canonier, 1808–14* (Paris, 1892).

Barkhausen, G. H. *Tägebuch eines Rheinbund-Offiziers aus dem Feldzüge gegen Spanien, und wahrend Spanischer und Englischer Kriegsgefangenschaft 1808 bis 1814* (Wiesbaden, 1900).

Batty, R. *Campaign of the Left Wing of the Allied Army, in the Western Pyrenees and the South of France* (1823).

Beatson, F. C. *With Wellington in the Pyrenees* (1914).

Bell, G. *Soldier's Glory: Rough Notes by an Old Soldier During Fifty Years Service* (2 vols, 1867).

Belmas, J. *Journaux des Sièges faits ou soutenus par les Français dans la Péninsule de 1807 à 1814* (4 vols, Paris, 1836–7).

Bigarre, A. *Mémoires du . . . aide de camp du Roi Joseph* (Paris, undated).

Bingham, D. A. *A Selection from the Letters and Dispatches of the First Napoleon* (1884).

Blakeney, S. J. *A Boy in the Peninsular War* (1899).

Blakiston, J. *Twelve Years Military Adventure* (2 vols, 1840).

Bonaparte, King Joseph. *Mémoires et Correspondance du Roi Joseph* (10 vols, ed. A. Ducasse, Paris, 1854).

Bourienne, M. de. *Memoirs of Napoleon Bonaparte* (3 vols, 1836).

Boutflower, C. *Journal of an Army Surgeon During the Peninsular War* (Manchester, 1912).

Bragge, W. *Peninsular Portrait, 1811–14: The Letters of Captain William Bragge, Third (King's Own) Dragoons* (ed. S. A. C. Cassels, 1963).

Broughton, S. D. *Letters from Portugal, Spain and France* (1815).

Buckham, P. W. *Narrative of Adventures in the Peninsula* (1827).

Burgoyne, Sir J. *Life and Correspondence of Field-Marshal Sir John Burgoyne* (ed. G. Wrottesley, 1873).

Burroughs, G. F. *A Narrative of the Retreat from Burgos* (Bristol, 1814).

Cadell, C. *Narrative of Campaigns of the 28th Regiment* (1835).

Casse, A. du. *Mémoires du Roi Joseph* (2 vols, Paris, 1854).

Clausewitz, C. von. *On War* (ed. M. Howard and P. Paret, Princeton University Press, 1976).

Codrington, E. *Memoir of the Life of Admiral Sir Edward Codrington* (2 vols, 1873).

Cole, J. W. *Memoirs of British Generals Distinguished During the Peninsular War* (2 vols, 1856).

Cole, Sir L. *Memoirs of Sir Lowry Cole* (ed. M. L. Cole, 1934).

The Confidential Correspondence of Napoleon Bonaparte with his Brother Joseph, Sometime King of Spain (2 vols, New York, 1856).

Cooke, Capt. J. *Memoirs of the Late War* (2 vols, 1831).

Cooper, J. S. *Rough Notes of Seven Campaigns, 1809–15* (1896).

Costello, K. S. F. *Adventures of a Soldier* (1841).

Croker, C. *The Croker Papers* (ed. L. J. Jennings, 3 vols, 1884).

Daniel, F. *Journal of an Officer in the Commissariat, 1811–15* (1820).

Decaen, C. M. *Mémoires et Journeaux* (2 vols, Paris, 1910–11).

Dickson, A. *The Dickson Manuscripts* (ed. J. H. Leslie, Woolwich, 1907).

Donaldson, J. *Recollections of the Eventful Life of a Soldier* (1841 edition).

Drouet, Comte d'Erlon. *Mémoires* (Paris, 1884).

Dumas, J. B. *Neuf Mois de Campagnes à la Suite du Maréchal Soult* (Paris, 1907).

D'Urban, Sir B. *Peninsular Journal, 1807–17* (ed. J. Rousseau, 1930).

Egglestone, W. M. *Letters of Lt. John Brumwell* (Durham, 1912).

Eliot, W. G. *Treatise on the Defence of Portugal* . . . (1811).

Fane, J. *Memoir of the Early Campaigns of the Duke of Wellington in Portugal and Spain* (1912).

Fantin des Odoards, Gen. *Journal* (Paris, 1895).

Farmer, G. *The Memoirs of G. Farmer, 11th Light Dragoons, 1808–35* (2 vols, 1844).

Fée, A. L. A. *Souvenirs de la Guerre d'Espagne* (Paris, 1861).

Foy, M. S. *Histoire de la Guerre de la Péninsule sous Napoleon* (4 vols, Paris, 1827).

Frazer, Sir A. S. *Letters of Sir Augustus Simon Frazer* (ed. E. Sabine, 1859).

Frazer, Sir A. S. *Letters Written During the Peninsular* . . . *Campaigns* (ed. E. Sabine, 1859).

Fririon, F. N. *Journal Historique de la Campagne de Portugal* (Paris, 1841).

Gavin, W. *The Diary of William Gavin, Ensign and Quartermaster, 71st Regiment* (ed. C. Oman, Oxford, 1921).

Gleig, G. R. *The Subaltern* (1900).

Godoy, M. *Memoirs of Don Manuel Godoy* (1836).

Gomm, W. M. *Letters and Journals of Field-Marshal Sir William Gomm, 1799–1815* (ed. F. Carr-Gomm, 1881).

Gordon, A. *A Cavalry Officer in the Corunna Campaign* (1913).

Grattan, W. *Adventures with the Connaught Rangers, 1809–14* (1902).

Green, J. *The Vicissitudes of a Soldier's Life, 1806–15* (Louth, 1827).

Halliday, A. *Observations on the Present State of the Portuguese Army as Organized by Lt.-Gen. Sir William Carr Beresford* (1811).

Hale, J. *Journal of James Hale, late Sergeant in the 9th Regiment of Foot* (Cirencester, 1826).

Hamilton, Capt. T. *Annals of the Peninsular Campaign* (1829).

Harris, Rifleman. *Recollections of Rifleman Harris* (1848).

Harley, Capt. J. *The Veteran or Forty Years in the British Service* (2 vols, 1838).

Hawker, P. *Journal of a Regimental Officer in Portugal and Spain* (1810).

Hay, W. *Reminiscences, 1808–15, under Wellington* (1901).

Henegan, Sir R. D. *Seven Years Campaigning in the Peninsula* (2 vols, 1846).

Hennell, Lt. G. *A Gentleman Volunteer: The Letters of George Hennell from the Peninsular War, 1812–13* (ed. R. Glover, 1979).

Herrasti, A. P. De. *Relacion Historica* (Madrid, 1814).

Holzing, K. F. von. *Unter Napoleon in Spanien* (Berlin, 1937).

Hope, J. *Military Memoirs of an Infantry Officer* (1834).

Hough, Lt. H. 'The Journal of Lt. H. Hough, R.A. 1812–13' (ed. J. H. Leslie) *Journal of Royal United Services Institute*, No. 444, LXI (1916).

Hulot, J. L. *Souvenirs Militaires, 1773–1843* (Paris, 1886).

Jones, Col. J. *Journal of the Sieges in Spain, 1811–14* (3 vols, 1846).

Jones, Col. J. *Account of the War in Spain, Portugal and the South of France from 1808 to 1814 Inclusive* (2 vols, 1821).

Jones, Col. J. *Memoranda Relative to the Lines Thrown Up to Cover Lisbon in 1810* (1839).

Jourdan, J. B. *Mémoires Militaires, Guerre d'Espagne* (Paris, 1899).

Kincaid, J. *Adventures in the Rifle Brigade* (1852).

Kincaid, J. *Adventures in the Rifle Brigade and Random Shots from a Rifleman* (Abridged edition, 1981).

Knight, Corporal. *The British Battalions at Oporto* (1834).

Knowles, Lt. R. *The War in the Peninsula: Some Letters of Lieutenant Robert Knowles* (1913).

Koch, J. B. F. *Mémoires de Massena, redigés d'après les Documents qu'il a laissés* . . . (7 vols, Paris, 1848–50).

Landsheit, N. *Memoirs, 1793–1815* (2 vols, 1837).

Lapene, E. *Evénements Militaires devant Toulouse, en 1814* (Paris, 1834).

Lapene, E. *Conquête de l'Andalousie: Campagne de 1810 et 1811 dans le Midi de l'Espagne* (Paris, 1823).

Lapene, E. *Campagnes de 1813 et de 1814 sur l'Ebre, les Pyrénées et la Garonne* (Paris, 1823).

Larpent, F. S. *Private Journal of F. S. Larpent* (ed. G. Larpent, 3 vols, 1853).

Leach, J. *Rough Sketches of the Life of an Old Soldier* (1831).

Leith-Hay, A. *A Narrative of the Peninsular War* (2 vols, Edinburgh, 1831).

Leith-Hay, A. *Memoirs of the Late General Sir James Leith* (1919).

Lejeune, L. F. *Mémoires* (2 vols, Paris, 1895).

Lenoble, P. M. *Mémoires sur les Operations Militaires des Francais en Galice, en Portugal, et dans la Vallée du Tage en 1809* (Paris, 1821).

Lemonnier-Delafosse, J. B. *Campagnes de 1810–15* (Havre, 1850).

L'Estrange, Sir G. B. *Recollections: The Peninsular War* (1874).

Londonderry, C. W. V. *Narrative of the Peninsular War* (2 vols, 1829).

Long, R. B. *Peninsular Cavalry General: The Correspondence of General R. B. Long* (ed. T. N. McGuffie, 1951).

Macdonald, Maréchal J. E. J. A. *Souvenirs* (Paris, 1892).

Mackinnon, H. *Journal of the Campaigns in Portugal and Spain* (1812).

Marbot, J. *The Memoirs of Baron de Marbot* (2 vols, 1892).

Marchand, L. *Mémoires de Marchand* (2 vols, Paris, 1952).

Marmont, Maréchal A. F. *Mémoires, 1792–1841* (9 vols, Paris, 1857).

Martin, J. F. *Souvenirs d'un Ex-Officier, 1812–15* (Paris, 1867).

Martinien, A. *Tableaux par Corps et par Batailles* (Paris, 1899).

Melito, M. de. *Mémoires du Comte Miot de Melito, 1788–1815* (Paris, 1880).

'Memorials of the Late War' *Constable's Miscellany*, XXVII & XXVIII (1828).

Military Memoirs of an Infantry Officer, 1809–16 (1833).

Mina, F. E. y. *Short Extract From the Life of Mina by Himself* (1825).

Mina, F. E.y. *Memorias del General Don Francisco Espoz y Mina* (ed. M. A. Gallego, Madrid, 1962).

Mockler-Ferryman, Lt.-Col. A. F. *Life of a Regimental Officer during the Great War, 1793–1815* (1913).

Moore, J. *Narrative of the Campaigns of the British Army in Spain* (1809).

Morley, S. *Memoirs of a Sergeant* (undated).

Napier, Sir W. F. P. *History of the War in the Peninsula and the South of France* (6 vols, 1852 edition).

Napoleon I of France. *Correspondance de Napoleon 1er* (32 vols, Paris, 1858–70).

Napoleon I of France. *Lettres Inédites de Napoleon 1er* (ed F. Lecestre, 2 vols, Paris, 1897).

Narrative of the Campaigns of the Loyal Lusitania Legion under Brigadier General Sir Robert Wilson, with some Account of the Military Operations in Spain and Portugal during the Years 1809, 1810 and 1811 (1812).

Neale, A. *Letters from Portugal and Spain* (1809).

Neves, J. A. *Historia Geral da Invasao dos Francezes em Portugal* (5 vols, Lisbon, 1811).

Ney, Maréchal M. *Documents Inédits du duc d'Elchingen* (Paris, 1833).

Ney, Maréchal M. *Mémoires* (2 vols, Paris, 1833).

Ormsby, J. W. *Operations of the British Army in Spain and Portugal* (2 vols, 1809).

Paget, E. *Letters and Memorials of General Sir Edward Paget* (1898).

Pelet, J. J. *The French Campaign in Portugal, 1810–11* (ed. D. Horward, Minnesota, 1973).

Pellot, J. *Mémoire sur la Campagne . . . dite des Pyrénées en 1813 et 1814* (Bayonne, 1818).

Peninsula Sketches by Actors on the Scene (2 vols, ed. W. H. Maxwell, 1845).

Picton, Sir T. *Memoirs* (ed. H. B. Robinson, 2 vols, 1835).

Picton, Sir T. *Some Unpublished Letters of Sir Thomas Picton* (ed. E. Edwards, 1931).

Porter, Sir R. K. *Letters from Portugal and Spain* (1809).

'Private Soldier' *Narrative of a Private Soldier in the 42nd* (1821).

Robertson, D. *The Journal of Sergeant D. Robertson, late 92nd Foot, 1797–1818* (Perth, 1842).

Rocca, A. J. M. de. *Mémoires sur la Guerre des Français en Espagne* (Paris, 1814).

Ross-Lewin, H. *With the 32nd in the Peninsular and Other Campaigns* (Dublin, 1904).

Rousset, C. *Recollections of Marshal Macdonald, Duke of Tarentum* (1893).

Sarrazin, J. *Histoire de la Guerre d'Espagne et de Portugal de 1807 à 1814* (Paris, 1814).

Savary, Gen. A. J. *Mémoire sur l'Empire* (8 vols, Paris, 1828).

Schaumann, A. L. F. *On the Road with Wellington* (1924).

Ségur, P. P. de. *Histoire et Mémoires* (7 vols, Paris, 1877).

Sherer, M. *Recollections of the Peninsula* (1824).

Simmons, G. *A British Rifleman During the Peninsular War* (1899).

Smith, Lt.-Gen. Sir H. *The Autobiography of Sir Harry Smith* (ed G. C. Moore Smith, 2 vols, 1902).

A Soldier of the 71st (ed. C. Hibbert, 1976).

Soult, Maréchal N. *Mémoires* (Paris, 1851).

Southey, R. *History of the Peninsular War* (3 vols, 1827).

Sperling, J. *Letters of an Officer of the Corps of Royal Engineers* (1872).

St-Cyr, Maréchal L. de G. *Mémoires* (Paris, 1829).

St-Cyr, Maréchal L. de G. *Journal des Operations de l'Armée de Catalogne* (Paris, 1821).

Stanhope, P. H. *Conversations with the Duke of Wellington* (1899).

Steevens, N. *Reminiscences of my Military Life, 1795–1818* (1878).

Suchet, Maréchal L. G. *Mémoires du Maréchal Suchet, Duc d'Albufera, sur ses Campagnes en Espagne* (2 vols, Paris, 1834).

Surtees, W. *Twenty-five Years in the Rifle Brigade* (1833).

Swabey, W. *Diary of Campaigns in the Peninsula* (Woolwich, 1895).

Thiébault, Baron D. A. *Mémoires* (ed. F. Calmettes, 5 vols, Paris, 1893–95).

Thiébault, Baron, D. A. *Relation de l'Expedition du Portugal fait en 1807* (Paris, 1817).

Tomkinson, W. *The Diary of a Cavalry Officer in the Peninsular and Waterloo Campaigns, 1809–15* (1894).

Vacani, C. *Storia delle Campagne e degli Assedj in Spagna, 1808–13* (6 vols, Florence, 1827).

Vaughan, Sir C. R. *Narrative of the Siege of Zaragoza* (1809).

Vigo-Roussillon, Col. *La Guerre d'Espagne: Fragmens des Mémoires Militaires du Colonel Vigo-Roussillon* (Paris, 1891)

Wall, A. *Diary of the Operations in Spain Under Sir John Moore* (Woolwich, 1896).

Warre, Sir W. *Letters from the Peninsula, 1808–12* (1909).

Wellesley, H. *Diary and Correspondence of Henry Wellesley, 1790–1846* (1930).

Wellington, A. 1st Duke of. *Dispatches of Field-Marshal the Duke of Wellington* (ed. Col. Gurwood, 12 vols, 1834–39), and 8 vols (1844).

Wellington, A. 1st Duke of. *Supplementary Dispatches and Memoranda, 1797–1815* (ed. by his son, 15 vols, 1858–72).
Wellington, A. 1st Duke of. *General Orders* (1837).
Wheeler, W. *A Journal, 1809–16* (Corfu, 1824).
Wheeler, W. *The Letters of Private Wheeler, 1809–28* (ed. B. Liddell-Hart, 1951).
Whittingham, Sir S. F. *A Memoir of the Services of Lt.-Gen. Sir S. F. Whittingham* (1868).
Woodberry, G. *The Journal of Lt. Woodberry, 1813–15* (Paris, 1896).

SECONDARY SOURCES

Anderson, J. H. *The Peninsular War* (1906).
Anstice, R. H. *The Decisive Campaign of Torres Vedras* (Aberdeen, 1905).
Arteche y Moro, J. G. de. *Guerra de la Independencia Historia Militar de España de 1808 a 1814* (14 vols, Madrid, 1868–1903).
Artola, M. *Los Afrancesados* (Madrid, 1953).
Artola, M. *La Burguesia Revolucionaria, 1808–69* (Madrid, 1973).
Artola, M. *Los Origenes de la España Contemporanea* (2 vols, Madrid, 1959).
Balagny, D. E. P. *Campagne de l'Empereur Napoleon en Espagne* (7 vols, Paris, 1902).
Beatson, F. C. *Wellington: The Bidassoa and the Nivelle* (1931).
Brandt, H. von. *The Two Minas and the Spanish Guerillas* (1825).
Brett-James, A. *Wellington at War, 1794–1815* (1961).
Brett-James, A. *Life in Wellington's Army* (1972).
Butler, L. *Wellington's Operations in the Peninsula* (2 vols, 1904).
Callender, G. & Hinsley, F. L. *The Naval Side of British History 1486–1945* (1945).
Caulaincourt, A. A. L. *No Peace With Napoleon* (New York, 1936).
Chaby, C. de. *Excerptos Historicos . . . Guerra da Peninsula* (4 vols, Lisbon, 1865–82).
Chandler, D. *The Campaigns of Napoleon* (New York, 1966).
Charco-Villasenor, A. R. 'El Dos de Mayo de 1808' *Revista de Historia Militar*, II (1958).
Clerc, J. C. A. *Guerre d'Espagne: Capitulation de Baylen, Causes et Consequences* (Paris, 1903).
Clerc, J. C. A. *Campagne du Maréchal Soult dans les Pyrénées . . .* (Paris, 1894).
Clowes, Sir L. W. *The Royal Navy* (7 vols, 1897–1903).
Colville, J. *The Portrait of a General* (Salisbury, 1980).
Cookson, J. E. *Friends of Peace: Anti-War Liberalism in England, 1793–1815* (Cambridge, 1982).
Coste, E. *Historique de 40e Régiment de Ligne* (Paris, 1887).
Cronin, V. *Napoleon* (1971).
Crouzet, E. *Blockade and Economic Change in Europe, 1792–1815* (1964).
Crouzet, E. *L'Economie Brittanique et le Blocus Continental* (2 vols, Paris, 1958).
Davies, D. W. *Sir John Moore's Peninsular Campaign* (The Hague, 1974).
Diccionario Bibliografico de la Guerra de la Independencia (3 vols, Madrid, 1944).
Du Casse, R. *Le Volontaire de 1793: Général du Premier Empire Jean Baptiste Girard* (Paris, undated).
Fitchett, W. H. *Wellington's Men* (1912).
Forester, C. S. *The Naval War of 1812* (1952).
Fortescue, Sir J. W. *History of the British Army* (13 vols, 1899–1930).
Fugier, A. *Napoleon et l'Espagne, 1799–1808* (Paris, 1930).
Gates, D. E. *The Creation and Training of the British Light Infantry Arm, c.1790–1815* (Oxford Univ. D. Phil. thesis, 1984).

Girod de l'Ain, M. *Vie Militaire du Général Foy* (Paris, 1900).

Glover, M. *Wellington's Peninsular Victories* (1965).

Glover, M. *The Peninsular War, 1807–14* (1974).

Glover, M. *A Very Slippery Fellow: . . . Sir Robert Wilson* (1977).

Grandmaison, G. de. *L'Espagne et Napoleon, 1804–9* (Paris, 1908).

Grasset, A. *La Guerre d'Espagne, 1807–13* (3 vols, Paris, 1914–32).

Guerra de la Independencia, 1808–14 (Published by the Servicio Historico Militar, 7 vols, Madrid, 1966).

Hales, E. E. Y. *Napoleon and the Pope* (1962).

Hecksher, E. F. *The Continental System* (Oxford, 1922).

Hernandez, M. I. *Antecedentes y Comienzos del Reinado de Fernando VII* (Madrid, 1963).

Herr, R. *The 18th-Century Revolution in Spain* (Princeton, 1958).

Herring, H. *A History of Latin America* (1968).

Hibbert, C. *Corunna* (1961).

Hill, J. W. *Battles Round Biarritz . . . in 1814* (Edinburgh, 1897).

Horsman, R. *The Causes of the War of 1812* (New York, 1962).

Horward, D. *The Battle of Bussaco* (Florida State Univ. Press, 1965).

Humble, R. *Napoleon's Peninsular Marshals* (1973).

Kennedy, P. M. *The Rise and Fall of British Naval Mastery* (1976).

Lachouque, H. *Napoleon's War in Spain* (1982).

Lafvente, M. *Historia General de España* (Barcelona, 1889).

La Roncière, C. de. *Histoire de la Marine Française* (6 vols, Paris, 1930–32).

Lawford, J. C. & Young, P. *Wellington's Masterpiece: Salamanca* (1974).

Leslie, J. H. *The Services of the Royal Regiment of Artillery in the Peninsular War, 1808–14* (1912).

Livermore, H. V. *A History of Portugal* (Cambridge, 1947).

Lovett, G. H. *Napoleon and the Birth of Modern Spain* (2 vols, New York, 1965).

Mackay, E. S. *History of American Privateering* (New York, 1899).

Mahan, A. T. *The Influence of Sea-Power on the French Revolution and Empire* (2 vols, 1892).

Marindin, A. H. *The Salamanca Campaign* (1906).

Markham, F. *Napoleon* (1963).

Marshal-Cornwall, Sir J. *Marshal Massena* (1965).

Mathias, P. *The First Industrial Nation: An Economic History of Britain, 1700–1914* (1969).

Morvan, J. *Le Soldat Impérial* (2 vols, Paris, 1904).

Oman, Sir C. W. C. *History of the Peninsular War* (7 vols, Oxford, 1902–1930).

Oman, Sir C. W. C. *Column and Line in the Peninsular War* (Oxford, 1910).

Oman, Sir C. W. C. *Wellington's Army, 1809–14* (1913).

Parkinson, R. *The Peninsular War* (1974).

Parkinson, R. *Moore of Corunna* (1975).

Perkins, B. *Prologue to War: England and the United States, 1805–12* (New York, 1961).

Picard, L. *La Cavalerie dans les Guerres de la Révolution et de l'Empire* (2 vols, Saumur, 1895).

Quimby, R. S. *The Background of Napoleonic Warfare: The Theory of Military Tactics in 18th-Century France* (New York, 1957).

Rogers, H. C. B. *Wellington's Army* (1979).

Roskill, S. W. *The Strategy of Sea Power* (1962).

Roy, J. J. E. *Les Français en Espagne* (Paris, 1884).

Rudirff, R. *'War to the Death': The Two Sieges of Saragossa* (1974).

Schwartz, B. *The Code Napoleon and the Common Law World* (New York, 1956).

Schwertfeger, B. *Geschichte der Koniglich Deutschen Legion, 1803–16* (2 vols, Hanover, 1907).

Sidney, E. *The Life of Lord Hill G.C.B.* (1845).

Smyth, B. *History of the 20th Regiment, 1688–1888* (1889).

Soriano, S. J. L. da. *Historia da Guerra Civil . . . 1777–1834* (19 vols, Lisbon, 1866–90).

Spain: A Companion to Spanish Studies (Edited by P. E. Russull, 1976).

Teffeteller, G. L. *The Surpriser: The Life of Rowland, Lord Hill* (1983).

Toreno, Comte de J. M. *Historia del Levantamiento Guerra y Revolucion de España* (4 vols, Madrid, 1848).

Victoires et Conquêtes des Français (Paris, 1820).

Vidal de la Blache, H. J. M. C. *L'Evacuation de l'Espagne et l'Invasion dans le Midi, 1813–14* (2 vols, Paris, 1914).

Ward, S. G. P. *Wellington's Headquarters* (Oxford, 1957).

Ward, S. G. P. *Wellington* (1963).

Weller, J. *Wellington in the Peninsula* (1962).

White, A. S. *Bibliography of Regimental Histories of the British Army* (1965).

Williams, G. T. *Historical Records of the 11th Hussars* (1908).

(All printed sources published in London unless otherwise indicated.)

INDEX